RECLAIMING INDIGENOUS PLANNING

McGILL-QUEEN'S NATIVE AND NORTHERN SERIES
(IN MEMORY OF BRUCE G. TRIGGER)
SARAH CARTER AND ARTHUR J. RAY, EDITORS

Reclaiming Indigenous Planning

Edited by

RYAN WALKER, TED JOJOLA, AND
DAVID NATCHER

McGill-Queen's University Press
Montreal & Kingston · London · Ithaca

© McGill-Queen's University Press 2013

ISBN 978-0-7735-4193-1 (cloth)
ISBN 978-0-7735-4194-8 (paper)
ISBN 978-0-7735-8993-3 (ePDF)
ISBN 978-0-7735-8994-0 (ePUB)

Legal deposit third quarter 2013
Bibliothèque nationale du Québec

Printed in Canada on acid-free paper that is 100% ancient forest free (100% post-consumer recycled), processed chlorine free

This book has been published with the help of a grant from the Canadian Federation for the Humanities and Social Sciences, through the Awards to Scholarly Publications Program, using funds provided by the Social Sciences and Humanities Research Council of Canada. Funding has also been received from the Publications Fund at the University of Saskatchewan and from the Canadian Pacific Partnership Program in Aboriginal Community Planning.

McGill-Queen's University Press acknowledges the support of the Canada Council for the Arts for our publishing program. We also acknowledge the financial support of the Government of Canada through the Canada Book Fund for our publishing activities.

Library and Archives Canada Cataloguing in Publication

Reclaiming Indigenous planning / edited by Ryan Walker, Ted Jojola, and David Natcher.

(McGill-Queen's Native and northern series ; 70)
Includes bibliographical references and index.
Issued in print and electronic formats.
ISBN 978-0-7735-4193-1 (bound). – ISBN 978-0-7735-4194-8 (pbk.). –
ISBN 978-0-7735-8993-3 (ePDF). – ISBN 978-0-7735-8994-0 (ePUB)

1. Indians of North America – Land tenure – Canada – Planning. 2. Indigenous peoples – Land tenure – Planning. 3. Community development – Canada – Planning. 4. Community development – Planning. 5. Land use – Canada – Planning. 6. Land use – Planning. 7. Traditional ecological knowledge – Canada. 8. Traditional ecological knowledge. I. Natcher, David C., 1967–, editor of compilation II. Walker, Ryan Christopher, 1975–, editor of compilation III. Jojola, Theodore S. (Theodore Sylvester), editor of compilation IV. Series: McGill-Queen's native and northern series ; 70

HN110.Z9C6 2013   307.1'208997071   C2013-902452-2
                                      C2013-902453-0

Typeset by Jay Tee Graphics Ltd. in 10.5/13 Sabon

Contents

Tables and Figures

Foreword

On 7–9 June 2010, the University of Saskatchewan hosted the three-day International Roundtable on Indigenous Community Planning and Land Use Management, held at Wanuskewin Heritage Park outside of Saskatoon, Saskatchewan, Canada. Leading experts from Canada, New Zealand, Australia, and the United States of America presented on topics ranging from tribal lands planning on reserves and in rural and remote areas, to natural resources, mining, and land title agreements, all with the goal of examining the opportunities and barriers facing Indigenous peoples in applying their own cultural foundations and normative principles to community planning and land-use management.

Building on the international roundtable, editors Ryan Walker, Ted Jojola, and David Natcher have captured some of the most important work, bringing refreshing and insightful perspectives, experiences, teachings, lessons, and awareness to the topic of Indigenous planning and land management.

The three editors of this book have dedicated their careers to the pursuit of higher quality Indigenous planning through curriculum development, teaching, publishing, networking, practicing, and advocacy. Over the last decade, the editors have reached around the world and collaborated with some of the most prominent planners and scholars to bring together examples of how Indigenous communities are asserting their self-governance and self-determination.

Amongst modern society's ever-growing need to consume and dispose and grow beyond available land and resources, the world's Indigenous peoples have been neglected, relegated to reservations, and buried in governmental programs, policies, and legislation. Today, Indigenous communities have to fight to remain relevant on the environmental, social, political, and economic local, national, and international agendas or they will find themselves planned out of existence.

However, there is a movement afoot where Indigenous communities, planning practitioners, universities, governments, and leading experts are collaborating and developing new policies, protocols, and agreements, and sharing best practices from around the world. Through the national and international conferences and roundtables, publications, and the use of technology, great work is being shared and built upon.

This book serves as a catalyst for change. Change in the way we engage Indigenous communities, the way we think and work within Indigenous communities, the way we develop governmental policies, the way we develop curriculum for our universities and colleges, and the way we think as individuals and as a society about Indigenous peoples. There are approximately 350 million Indigenous people in the world; the need for change will be upon us until Indigenous people enjoy the same rights and freedoms as non-Indigenous people.

Aaron Aubin, BES, ACP, MCIP
Member of Da'naxda'xw/Awaetlala First Nation, British Columbia, Canada
Past-Chair of the Canadian Institute of Planners Indigenous Peoples Planning Committee (2004–11)

Preface

RYAN WALKER, TED JOJOLA, AND DAVID NATCHER

This edited volume derives from the proceedings of the International Roundtable on Indigenous Community Planning and Land Use Management that was held 7–9 June 2010 in Saskatoon, Saskatchewan, Canada. Hosted by the University of Saskatchewan's Indigenous Land Management Institute and Regional and Urban Planning program, the roundtable brought together leading Indigenous and non-Indigenous scholars and practitioners from Canada, New Zealand, Australia, and the United States of America. Participants examined the opportunities and obstacles facing Indigenous peoples in these four western countries as they work to enact positive change in their home communities and territorial lands. The majority of chapter contributors to this book were participants at the roundtable. Additional scholars and practitioners who were not at the roundtable in Saskatoon were subsequently invited to contribute a chapter to the book in order to represent the best breadth and depth of wisdom in the field that we could gather in a single volume.

The roundtable was held in the territory of the Treaty Six First Nations and the Métis Nation. The venue was Wanuskewin Heritage Park, a place that has held great cultural and spiritual significance for Northern Plains First Nations for over six thousand years, a significance that was perceived by and provided guidance to our Indigenous and non-Indigenous guests from around the world during the deliberations. We would like to thank the staff at Wanuskewin Heritage Park for being gracious hosts in this unique setting, providing us with the cultural space needed for sharing the knowledge that we now present in this volume for a wider audience.

For extending hospitality through field trips, dinner, and entertainment for our roundtable participants we thank the Saskatoon Indian and Métis Friendship Centre, the Muskeg Lake Cree Nation, Central Urban Métis Federation, City of Saskatoon, and White Buffalo Youth Lodge. For financial support we are grateful to the Canadian Pacific Partnership Program in Aboriginal Community Planning, the Canadian Institute of Planners, Dillon Consulting, Aboriginal Affairs and Northern Development Canada, and the University of Saskatchewan. Without the support of our financial sponsors, neither the roundtable nor the present volume would have proceeded. We are especially grateful to Jacqueline Mason, our editor at McGill-Queen's University Press, and Jennifer Charlton, our copy editor, for their intellectual and managerial contributions to the book.

Planning has been defined in similar ways by professional institutes of planners internationally. The Canadian Institute of Planners (2012), for example, defines planning as "the scientific, aesthetic, and orderly disposition of land, resources, facilities and services with a view to securing the physical, economic and social efficiency, health and well-being of urban and rural communities."

Ted Jojola (2008) provides contours to the emergent paradigm of Indigenous planning as follows:

> Indigenous planning represents both an approach to community planning and an ideological movement. What distinguishes indigenous planning from mainstream practice is its reformulation of planning approaches in a manner that incorporates "traditional" knowledge and cultural identity. Key to the process is the acknowledgement of an indigenous world-view, which not only serves to unite it philosophically, but also to distinguish it from neighbouring, non land-based communities (Jojola 2000). A world-view is rooted in distinct community traditions that have evolved over a successive history of shared experiences.

Jojola points out that the paradigm is emergent in the context of modern planning, yet has existed and been practiced by Indigenous communities for hundreds, if not thousands, of years. The title of this book, *Reclaiming Indigenous Planning*, reflects the goal set by its editors and contributors at the International Roundtable on Indigenous Community Planning and Land Use Management, namely to continue to reconnect past practice with present circumstances, all in the context of planning for the future. Because Indigenous planning is an evolving paradigm in modern scholarship and practice, the contributors include both practitioners and academics. Yet when we engaged one another around the experiences of planning theory and practice with Indigenous communities, we discovered that the collective embodiment of knowledge and skill sets are precisely what we required to add new depth to this emergent field of study and practice.

The contributors to this book are from among the most well-versed and experienced in working for and with Indigenous communities. Their work spans four countries – Canada, the USA, New Zealand, and Australia. Their efforts are premised on informing solutions in a culturally appropriate manner, as well as empowering Indigenous communities to make their own planning decisions. This approach has been characterized among Māori people as "walking backwards into the future" (Kingi 2010). In other words, to plan meaningfully for the future, one must respect and build upon the past. To reclaim and assert Indigenous planning as a necessary field of scholarship and planning practice is the goal of this publication.

Effective planning by and for Indigenous peoples is important for many reasons, including but not limited to the protection of community cultural, social, political, and economic rights and interests; securing self-determined goals related to those rights and interests; and developing and maintaining supportive and productive relations with non-Indigenous communities. It became clear from the presentations and discussions over three days at the roundtable that the efforts of Indigenous peoples to gain equitable access to the institutions that now influence community planning is far from assured. As a result, the rights and interests of Indigenous peoples have too often failed to be reflected in planning outcomes. For this reason, attempts to reclaim planning remains a priority for many Indigenous Nations throughout the world.

We believe that part of this reclaiming process involves a more critical understanding of what "planning" actually entails and how the ideas and visions of Indigenous communities can best be reflected in future planning processes. We further believe that by sharing international experiences we can advance the practice of Indigenous planning in ways that begin to reflect the rights and interests of Indigenous peoples. We hope that this volume gives expression to those rights and to the aspirations and efforts of Indigenous peoples as they work to reclaim their planning processes.

The chapters in this volume are diverse, both geographically and thematically. Geographically, this volume covers the Canadian Arctic to the deserts of Australia. Thematically, the chapters explore a range of topics, including: Indigenous mobilization and various forms of resistance, awareness raising, and visioning taking place in Indigenous communities; Indigenous participation in community planning processes, as well as engagement in state planning processes; forms of governance, whether internal to Indigenous communities, across affiliated communities, or at the state-community interface; and the practice of Indigenous planning presented through case studies, personal narratives, and critiques of "state" planning practices (Lane 2010). Finally, many of the chapters emphasize the critical need for focusing on regaining control of land by Indigenous communities. As the table of contents reveals, the chapters relate to three broad areas relevant to conceptualizing and reclaiming Indigenous planning: 1) Indigenous communities; 2) the urban experience; and 3) lands and resources.

In chapter 1, Hirini Matunga sets the stage for the book by tracing a conceptual framework for Indigenous planning and explaining how the past, present, and future of this field are linked to the ongoing active participation of Indigenous communities in their own planning. He draws on the experience of Māori communities in New Zealand to conceptualize Indigenous planning in colonial-settler states that are the subject of this book. A basis of understanding in Indigenous communities and worldviews provided in Matunga's chapter is necessary to proceed with the book's focus upon planning practice as a professional and scholarly discipline.

Chapters in the first section of the book convey the central importance of Indigenous community values, traditions, and their exercise of self-determination in the conceptualization of planning as a set of future-seeking processes. The chapters travel conceptual terrain, as well as through specific examples from communities across several countries and nations, all focused on the role of planning in Indigenous communities.

Chapter 2 by Stephen Cornell examines the spatial, cognitive, and political boundary shifts that are accompanying Indigenous community self-determination in Australia, Canada, and the USA. He discusses how recasting the boundaries of identification among Indigenous communities themselves, and where colonial powers have tried to fit Indigenous peoples throughout history, can affect the reconstitution of Indigenous Nations.

The use of film is explored in chapter 3 by Leonie Sandercock and Giovanni Attili as a tool for planning and dialogue between settler and First Nation communities in British Columbia, Canada. The authors argue the communicative and transformative value of this planning technique for Indigenous and non-Indigenous communities together in place.

Chapter 4 by Michael Hibbard and Robert Adkins points out how the political changes over past decades resulting from the achievement of greater self-determination and sovereignty by Indigenous peoples has not been met by parallel gains in socio-economic standing. They explore the "cruel choice" that persists between culture and economy through work done in Kake, a Tlingit community in Alaska, USA.

In chapter 5, Laura Mannell, Frank Palermo, and Crispin Smith apply a reflective practice approach to present principles and elements of an evolving model of community-based comprehensive planning. They do this by drawing on lessons from their extensive experience as practitioners in First Nation communities across Canada.

Lisa Hardess, with Kerri Jo Fortier, uses the four-year partnership between the Simpcw First Nation in western Canada and the Centre for Indigenous Environmental Resources to create a comprehensive community plan as a basis for chapter 6. In it they reflect upon the elements of successful planning with First Nation communities and draw out important lessons both for practitioners, and for students and educators engaged in planning education.

Chapter 7, the final chapter in the first section of the book, is written by Sharon Hausam. In it she examines how four tribes in northwest New Mexico, USA engaged in regional planning processes, articulating clear water rights and how the state-driven process was carried out. The chapter draws out lessons about the importance of government-to-government relationships in regional processes, and how there is still work to be done to improve planning between Indigenous and non-Indigenous communities at scales of shared interest.

Chapters in the second section of the book address a key dimension of modern life: urbanization and urbanism. In all four countries of analysis the majority of Indigenous peoples live in urban areas, with growing proportions of urban residents that were born in cities and have never lived on reserves or in remote communities. At the same time, western cities are becoming more cosmopolitan and diverse, and the current and potential role of Indigeneity in the processes of contemporary urban planning are as yet hardly understood. The chapters in this section of the book address this critical area of planning practice and research.

Chapter 8 by Ryan Walker and Yale Belanger engages with the topic of how municipal governments in large cities from the Canadian Prairie region might improve their civic processes of planning and policy-making with Aboriginal communities. They provide ideas for improving planning, grouped in five specific areas of practice, and offer advice for transformative planning practice and the co-production of a planning framework that encompasses Aboriginality in cities.

In chapter 9, Kurt Peters examines the ways in which the cultural identities of Laguna people were preserved in some ways, and transformed in others, by their movement between their home pueblo in New Mexico and their urban settlement at Richmond, California. This all occurs against the backdrop of a hundred-year-old verbal agreement around labour between the Laguna Pueblo and the Atlantic & Pacific and Atchison, Topeka and Santa Fe railroad companies, with lessons for urban and rural planners.

Chapter 10 by Shaun Awatere, Garth Harmsworth, Shadrach Rolleston, and Craig Pauling shares a case study of a major subdivision development, Wigram Skies, undertaken by Ngāi Tahu Property Ltd. This property company is owned by the Ngāi Tahu tribe on New Zealand's South Island, and the case study draws lessons concerning the role of Māori-based approaches and knowledge that can be incorporated into planning processes at the local government level.

Chapter 11 by Chris Andersen advances an argument for the role of statistics in an interventionist agenda for recasting the urban policy relationship between Aboriginals and Canadian governments. He develops a key shift in our understanding of urban Aboriginal self-determination and culture by focusing on its "density," rather than the more common preoccupation with "difference." Lessons for urban planning practice are conveyed in this chapter that connects transformative statistics with Aboriginal density in urban areas.

The second section of the book ends with chapter 12 by Libby Porter. In it she examines how changes that are reconstituting the relationships of coexistence between Indigenous peoples and the state in Australia and Canada are affecting the urban experience. She investigates why it is that Indigenous rights and interests in urban planning are less prominent than in environmental and natural resources planning outside the city, providing a fitting transition to the third and final section of the book.

Chapters in the third section of the book engage the realm of stewardship over lands and resources that has been a cultural imperative of Indigenous communities for centuries or millennia. It is an imperative that persists, though in dynamic tension with modern economic pressures towards land and resource development.

Chapter 13 by Richie Howitt, Kim Doohan, Sandie Suchet-Pearson, Gaim Lunkapis, Samantha Muller, Rebecca Lawrence, Sarah Prout, Siri Veland, and Sherrie Cross challenges the widespread perception in settler countries, drawing on the Australian experience, that capacity deficits in natural resource management systems reside with Indigenous peoples. The authors argue that it may well be the other way around, and advocate for governance systems that prioritize decolonization, social and environmental justice, and secure and sustainable livelihoods for Indigenous peoples.

Chapter 14 by Tanira Kingi, Liz Wedderburn, and Oscar Montes de Oca uses case studies to introduce the Integrated Decision Support Framework "Iwi Futures," which addresses shortfalls in current approaches to land and rural community planning in New Zealand. The framework connects planning practice with Māori world views towards land and environment.

Bethany Haalboom and David Natcher, in chapter 15, critically examine the concept of "vulnerability" as it has been applied to Indigenous communities in the Arctic. They explore the power and peril of community labelling in the North, and point out how it may be at cross-purposes to Indigenous community futures and aspirations in Alaska, USA and the Canadian North.

Chapter 16 by Robert Patrick develops important conceptual and practical links between traditional First Nations knowledge and stewardship over land and water, treaty rights established between First Nations and the Canadian state, and the practice of source water protection planning. He provides a compelling argument for how and why to Indigenize the process of source water protection planning.

Cathy Robinson and Marcus Lane, in chapter 17, examine how the decentralization of natural resource management planning in Australia has interacted with Indigenous community approaches. They focus particularly on the use of Indigenous facilitators, funded by the Australian government, to act as a two-way communication link between Indigenous and non-Indigenous landholders and stakeholders in natural resource management governance processes.

In chapter 18, Deborah McGregor discusses how traditional knowledge has intersected with environmental and resource management. In particular she focuses on forest management planning in Ontario, Canada, and how the provincial government there has worked to formalize Aboriginal involvement through a process called "Aboriginal values mapping."

Andrea Procter and Keith Chaulk close the third section of the book in chapter 19 with their exploration of the practical and structural challenges of planning in an Inuit territory, the region of Nunatsiavut in northern Labrador, Canada. They examine the political context of land-use planning and Inuit-state relations, and offer their views on the strengths and weaknesses of the planning process underway to create the Nunatsiavut Land Use Plan.

Ted Jojola concludes the book in chapter 20 by discussing the ethical, methodological, and epistemological approaches to community design and planning by Indigenous communities. He conceptualizes Indigenous planning by exploring the manner in which Indigenous populations have used a seven generations model to plan for meaningful community development.

REFERENCES

Canadian Institute of Planners. 2012. *Planning Is... Planning Defined*. www.cip-icu.ca. Ottawa: Canadian Institute of Planners.

Jojola, Ted. 2008. "Indigenous Planning – An Emerging Context." *Canadian Journal of Urban Research* 17, 1 Supplement: 37–47

Kingi, Tanira. 2010. *Personal Communication*. International Roundtable on Indigenous Community Planning and Land Use Management. Wanuskewin Heritage Park, Saskatoon. 9 June.

Lane, Marcus. 2010. *Personal Communication*. International Roundtable on Indigenous Community Planning and Land Use Management. Wanuskewin Heritage Park, Saskatoon. 9 June.

RECLAIMING INDIGENOUS PLANNING

I

Theorizing Indigenous Planning

HIRINI MATUNGA

INTRODUCTION

In this chapter I explore various ideas and themes around the concept of
what is now being termed "Indigenous planning." Theorizing Indigenous
planning is potentially risky business. Any attempt to map out conceptual territory must be firmly hitched to analyses of it as a continually
evolving practice by Indigenous peoples and communities around the
world – in other words, planning by, rather than for these communities. As a "distinct" form of planning or indeed scholarly discipline, it
might be deemed to be nascent in method and approach, however, it
has been practiced since time immemorial. Its latest iteration is clearly
a response to the violence of colonialism and a virulent racist discourse
intent on exploiting, devaluing, oppressing, if not exterminating Indigenous peoples. Up ahead, it must weather attempts to destabilize and
unsettle it, particularly as the colonial state and its apparatus continues
to reinvent and redefine itself. Its ultimate aim must be to improve the
lives and conditions of Indigenous people and "refuse" ongoing exploitation, oppression, and, in some cases, extinction. That said, the trick
for Indigenous planning is to frame itself against the backdrop of a still
virulent racist discourse but not get consumed by it. To do this requires
a high degree of creativity, innovation, and reflexivity.

I begin by sketching out a tentative conceptual framework for
Indigenous planning, its characteristics and what it might look like. I
then establish a broader context for its evolution through chronological
sequences. These are the various evolutionary phases that Indigenous
peoples have continued to move in, through, and around as they negotiate their present(s) and futures across diverse cultural, temporal, and

spatial contexts. I then suggest an arrangement for its critical traditions.
Indigenous planning must comprehend its history, its origins, where it
might now be, and how its future as a legitimate, distinct form of planning could evolve. My objective is to show unashamedly that rather
than "passive bystanders," Indigenous peoples have always been "active
participants" in "their" planning. The problem has been the inability of
the colonial-settler state and its progeny to accommodate it. Generally it
ha_____. The latter part of this chapter loops back to a theoretical discus-
si_____ outcome. The concep-
tu_____ f Indigenous planning
ar_____ aches and methods. I
c_____ and challenges for the
fu_____

_____ ENOUS PLANNING

P_____ cholarly discipline and
c_____ vhich much theoretical
p_____ s an activity, "planning"
i_____ ners. It just happens to
b_____ l human function with
a_____
_____ ave always been: Whose
_____ r could look like? Who
is doing the analysis and making the decisions? Who has the authority, the control, the final decision-making power? Whose values, ethics,
concepts, and knowledge? Whose methods and approaches? What
frameworks, institutions, and organizations are being used to guide
the planning processes that most affect Indigenous peoples? Where are
Indigenous peoples positioned in the construction of that future?

Until recently the locus of power and ultimate right to determine this
future rested almost exclusively with colonizing non-Indigenous settler
governments, either through the power of the musket or the power of
law, policy, planning, and technology. Western/metropolitan planning
has generally been complicit in the colonial project, a weapon bran-
dished to erase/eradicate Indigenous peoples or at least contain them in
rural enclaves or urban ghettos.

Already this points to key characteristics of Indigenous planning,
including:

- A strong tradition of resistance, therefore commitment, to political change. Indigenous planning isn't just an armchair theoretical approach or set of methods and practices, but a political strategy aimed at improving the lives and environments of Indigenous peoples. To do Indigenous planning requires a commitment to political, social, economic, and environmental change.
- Indigenous planning has always existed. Indigenous communities predate colonialism and were planned according to their own traditions and sets of practices.
- Recognition that the central tenets of Indigenous planning are essentially community/kinship and place-based. It is a form of planning whose roots and traditions are grounded in specific Indigenous peoples' experiences linked to specific places, lands, and resources. In other words, planning within, for, and by the particular Indigenous community for the place they call theirs. Importantly, it isn't just spatial planning by Indigenous peoples, but has a much broader scope, focusing on the lives and environments of Indigenous peoples. To do Indigenous planning requires that it be done in/at the place *with* the people of that place.

Rather than get caught in the crossfire about whose or what planning theories count, planning "in human terms" is ultimately about the future – whether land-use planning; environmental planning; resource planning; or its recent, more enlightened descendants, collaborative, decentralised, community-based, feminist planning et al. While it has a future orientation that looks at where "we" are now and where "we" might want to be in the future, it must fully be informed by "our" past and critically how that past has constructed the present.

Indigenous people have had to respond/react to the systematic and institutionalized application of colonial practices whose primary aim has been to eradicate them. These were as varied as they were violent across different Indigenous communities. They ranged from the active/aggressive – warfare, death, disease, cultural genocide, territorial conquest, geographic displacement, and population "swamping" through settler occupation – to the more passive/aggressive eradication through imposed law, policy, planning, regulation, top-down authority, dependency, and imposition of private property.

All human communities plan, and as I have signalled already it is critical that Indigenous peoples define the word "plan" for themselves.

might differ from tribe to tribe

Therefore, for planning to be Indigenous, Māori, Aboriginal, or First Nations, it is reasonable to assume it will be done according to Indigenous analyses, frameworks, values, and processes. Indigenous planning implies a claiming and "naming" of the word by Indigenous people. It embraces the adoption/recovery of an Indigenous vernacular or idiom to describe it, give it form and to reflect a local Indigenous community history, reality, and experience. The "naming" of Indigenous planning needs to include, identify, and be contextualized to:

· the people or community (i.e., tribe, mob, clan, nation, iwi, or hapu);
· their space, place, environment, and resources (i.e., their traditional/ custodial territories and resources, including foreshore and seabed);
· their knowledge, values, concepts, and worldviews;
· their practices, approaches, methods, and institutions.

Expanded out, four of the essential components of Indigenous planning include:

· The existence of a group of people, such as a tribe, mob, clan, or nation, linked by ancestry and kinship connections.
· The notion of an inextricable link and association with traditionally prescribed custodial territory that the group claims as theirs, i.e., lands, waters, resources, and environments, irrespective of current title.
· The concept of an accumulated knowledge system about the place, environment, resources, and its history, including values or ethics for managing interactions with the place, environment, or land.
· The existence of a culturally distinct set of practices and approaches, including approaches to making decisions and applying these to actions and activity agreed by the kinship group or community through various institutional arrangements.

To better understand its contemporary shape both as a planning tradition with its own form and focus, and a planning approach with its own sets of methodologies, I will now discuss a chronology or periodicity of Indigenous planning.

A CHRONOLOGY OF (MĀORI) INDIGENOUS PLANNING

Any attempt to construct a chronology of Indigenous planning as a tradition must acknowledge a number of major epochs in the history of

Indigenous peoples and the impact of colonialism. Indigenous responses to colonialism through the colonial era and across different geographic contexts and communities have been temporally and spatially varied. However, a number of themes continue to dominate.

I will illustrate the nature of these colonizing practices/tendencies via reference to specific examples from the New Zealand context. Clearly my experience of Indigenous planning is grounded in local Māori experience. While the local or national might form part of an international Indigenous context with similar themes, global experiences are essentially an aggregate of local encounters. Ultimately, it's the local context that counts.

First among these was a rapacious desire on the part of settler governments that continues to this day for the traditional lands, waters, and resources of Indigenous peoples.

The most recent example in the New Zealand context is ongoing contestation over ownership of the coastal foreshore and seabed. Māori have always claimed ownership of New Zealand's foreshore and seabed based on customary title, historical rights of occupation, and guarantees provided by the Treaty of Waitangi signed in 1840. In 2004 the New Zealand Parliament enacted the Foreshore and Seabed Act, deeming its title to be held by the Crown. While the Act was subsequently repealed by the 2011 Marine and Coastal Area (*Takutai Moana*) Act, the coastline was not confirmed to Māori but rather put into the "public domain," meaning no one owns it. Māori now have to prove customary title through the courts via a series of stringent legal tests. The majority of *iwi* (Māori tribes) are of the view that the 2011 Act makes no tangible difference to the earlier confiscation of their coastal foreshore and seabed. The right to express *mana* over these areas remains their fundamental objective.

Secondly, the industrial-scale seizure of resources was further buttressed by the rapid introduction of colonial technologies, i.e., private property rights, surveying, land-use planning, mapping, and rural and urban planning aimed at consolidating and legitimating the land/resource grab.

In the New Zealand context the original, still lingering example is the Native (now Māori) Land Court established by the settler government in 1865. The unambiguous aim of the court was to convert Māori customary land from communal to individual title. The court required no more than ten owners to be nominated per block, irrespective of the size of the block or numbers of beneficial owners. This completely undermined Māori approaches to land ownership and succession, making it easier to sell to the new settlers. In the 1860s, approximately 80 per cent of the North Island was owned/held by Māori. By 1865, the Crown and NZ Company had "purchased" all but 1 per cent of the South Island. By the early 1900s Māori held only 27 per cent of the North Island and by 2000, as little as 4 per cent of land in New Zealand remained in Māori ownership. The Native Land Court continues to this day.

Thirdly, the colonial enterprise systematically excluded Indigenous peoples from the various decision, planning, and management processes over their lands and resources.

Again, in the New Zealand context, the most recent example is conflict and debate over Māori representation on the new Auckland City Council, the country's largest city. Auckland was originally built on land gifted in the 1800s by the local tribe, Ngati Whatua, and is now home to the largest population of Māori in New Zealand. In 2009 and recognizing treaty rights, a Royal Commission recommended the creation of three electoral seats for Māori on a council of twenty-three. The Auckland "super" city was eventually created in 2010 by amalgamating seven of the region's city/district authorities. However, legislation that created the super city effectively rejected the creation of Māori electorates and specific Māori representation. Finally, colonialism as a project then successfully eradicated and erased the "materiality and memory" of Indigenous communities through a combination of if not extermination, then at least absorption, assimilation, community vaporization leading to invisibility, and the progressive marginalization of the remnants of these communities to a peripheral assemblage of enclaves, reserves, and ghettos.

Ironically, the recent Christchurch/Canterbury earthquakes of September 2010 and February 2011, now sees a colonial city coping with ruptures to its own materiality and memory. Christchurch has always prided itself on its Englishness but is now confronting its own tragedy, loss of lives, buildings, monuments, cathedrals, street patterns, urban landscape, and the familiar. The local tribe, Ngai Tahu, is not only taking a leadership role in the recovery of Christchurch but also negotiating its own re-inclusion in the city.

In New Zealand, as in most countries colonized by settler governments such as Australia, Canada, and the USA, the materiality (i.e., physical quality, presence, and structure) and memory (i.e., recall of experience, even existence) of Indigenous communities has generally been erased. In the cities it was replaced with imperial monuments, colonial buildings, colonial cathedrals, colonial gardens, and colonial city patterns modelled

Resistance Traditions of Indigenous Planning (Post-Contact to the 1970s)

The resistance traditions of Indigenous planning were a reaction to the ravages of colonization, the assertion of private (over tribal collective) property rights, and introduction of colonial technologies, i.e., surveying, mapping, and urban and regional planning to remove Indigenous communities from their lands and environment.

During this phase the aim of colonial governments was to look after settler interests and remove evidence of Indigenous peoples. If they weren't exterminated, they were marginalized to rural enclaves, contained on reserves, or transported to and engulfed in "new" urban ghettos. Generally, "white was right." Urban design and city form through colonial buildings, monuments, and parks became a visual buttress for colonial power. In the countryside, rural form reflected the dominance of settler development, particularly farming interests.

Misappropriation of Indigenous lands and resources was further entrenched through exclusion from the machinery of local, regional, and generally central government. During this phase, Indigenous communities were not only removed from their lands and resources, but had their lifeline to colonial decision-making processes, governance, management, and planning severed. In short, Indigenous peoples were either structured out of existence or, if they survived, herded to rural or urban wastelands away from the gaze of the settler state and its beneficiaries.

Post-contact approaches to planning and managing Indigenous communities and environments retained as much of the characteristics of classical Indigenous planning as the politics of resistance and political advocacy allowed. The planning was often covert and subversive. Generally it was carried out in the enclaves or on the reserves to which Indigenous communities had been marginalized, but with a constant vigil over custodial/traditional lands and resources long ago or more recently alienated.

In the New Zealand context the end of this era coincided with a series of significant actions by Māori that irrevocably altered the dynamics of Māori–government relations, and with that the political landscape of the country. They included the creation in 1975 of the Waitangi Tribunal (to hear Māori tribal claims about Crown/government breaches of the Treaty of Waitangi), the Māori Land March of 1975 (protesting over the continued loss and alienation of Māori lands and natural resources), and the occupation of Bastion Point in 1977–78. These "actions" symbolized the genesis of the modern Māori renaissance movement.

The Waitangi Tribunal, established under the Treaty of Waitangi Act 1975, was a direct result of ongoing Māori protest about Crown/government breaches of the Treaty of Waitangi 1840, which promised Māori protection of their lands, resources, and decision-making authority. The tribunal's responsibility was to investigate actions or omissions of the Crown since 1975 and recommend to the government redress for any grievances. In 1985 the tribunal's jurisdiction was extended back to 1840. By March 2009 the tribunal had produced over one hundred tribunal reports (Waitangi Tribunal 2011).

In the same year, the Māori Land March became a potent symbol for the struggle by Māori to hold on to whatever land remained in Māori ownership. While the focus of the Waitangi Tribunal was on regaining what had been lost, the emphasis of the Māori Land March was holding onto what little of the original resource base remained in Māori ownership. The march of 1975 saw hundreds of Māori protestors and their supporters trek the more than one thousand kilometres from the top of the North Island to the bottom, ending at parliament buildings in Wellington.

The Bastion Point occupation was another seminal event in the history of the modern Māori protest movement. The thirteen acres of land situated on a promontory overlooking the Waitemata Harbour in central Auckland was taken by the Crown for defence purposes in the 1880s. In the 1940s the land was no longer required for defence and rather than being returned to the original Māori owners, the Ngati Whatua tribe was "gifted" to the Auckland City Council for reserve purposes. By the 1970s Bastion Point was prime real estate close to the Auckland city business district. Rather than offering it back to Ngati Whatua, the Crown announced that it would now be selling it on the open market to the highest bidder for high-cost housing. This precipitated a peaceful 507-day occupation of the site by the tribe and its supporters. The occupation was eventually terminated in May 1978, with their forcible removal from the site by the New Zealand police and army (Waitangi Tribunal 1987).

Importantly, this phase also coincided in New Zealand with the passage of the Town and Country Planning Act in 1977. For the first time in any New Zealand planning statute the relationship between Māori people, their culture, and traditions with their ancestral lands was deemed a matter of national planning importance.

Importantly during the latter part of this phase the notion of Indigenous planning as a political strategy requiring both active and passive resistance and a commitment to political change took hold. It created the space for more overt displays of Indigenous planning as an approach quite distinct and separate from the national planning system. The notion that colonized countries had a duality in their planning that needed to be recognized and provided for also gained fledgling currency. In other words, Indigenous communities had been doing their planning all along – "mainstream" planning had just not "seen it" let alone provide for it. That said, the concept of a dual planning heritage – one grounded in Indigenous communities and the other in the colonial settler state – entered the planning equation.

Resurgent Traditions of Indigenous Planning (Beginning in the 1980s)

What I term the resurgent traditions of Indigenous planning coincided in the 1980s with increasing levels of Indigenous peoples' protest at a local and national, but increasingly international, level. Principally it was over the historic theft, ongoing misappropriation, and environmental degradation of traditional resources, i.e., lands, estates, forests, fisheries. Increasingly though, it centred on exclusionary practices in decision and planning processes for these resources. Critically, the resurgent tradition highlighted the causal nexus between alienation from the material resource and exclusion from settler state planning processes about the resource.

Across the globe a plethora of local and national cases was being taken to various tribunals, judicial fora, courts, and national governments, generally protesting land and resource grievances but also settler state abdication of Indigenous rights.

For instance, Māori grievances in the 1985 Manukau Harbour Claim centred on a number of major themes, such as environmental degradation of the harbour and surrounding environs, and loss of lands, estates, and other resources, such as fisheries. Importantly, it also highlighted the ongoing exclusion of iwi/Māori participation from planning for these resources. The claim eventually precipitated a comprehensive review of New Zealand's environmental legislation leading to the passage of the Resource Management Act in 1991 and improved recognition of Indigenous rights and values (Waitangi Tribunal 1987).

Local and national advocacy by/for Indigenous communities expanded rapidly to the international context. In 1982 the United Nations officially acknowledged Indigenous peoples with the establishment of the Working Group on Indigenous Populations to develop international standards concerning Indigenous rights. This was quickly followed by the UN Voluntary Fund for Indigenous Populations in 1985, adoption of the ILO Convention No. 169 on Indigenous and Tribal Peoples in Independent Countries in 1989, International Year of the World's Indigenous People in 1993 and two separate International Decades of the World's Indigenous People (1995–2004 and 2005–2014)(United Nations 2009, 2–3).

Critically for Indigenous peoples locally and internationally also came the recognition that expressions of Indigenous self-determination and its attendant social, economic, cultural, political, and environmental aspirations needed to be more explicitly codified. This has meant the need to "uncover," prescribe, even create a range of iterative Indigenous planning processes, approaches, practices, and tools to underpin the dual process of internal self-definition and expression, and external advocacy with the settler state and its planning systems.

Local New Zealand Māori examples of these include tribal (*iwi*) management plans – as written expressions of tribal authority (*rangatiratanga*) and tribal stewardship and guardianship (*kaitakitanga*), and increasing use of cultural impact assessments to gauge impacts of policies, plans, and development proposals on Indigenous communities.

Crucially, the resurgent tradition highlights the importance of retaining its own distinct tradition, history, contemporary identity, and practice as Indigenous planning, while at the same time developing the capability and indeed tools to advocate, negotiate, and mediate across the planning divide with "mainstream" Western planning.

INDIGENOUS PLANNING AS A PROCESS

Indigenous planning is in one sense a process, approach, or indeed activity that links specific Indigenous communities to defined ancestral places, environments, and resources. While this connection provides both the biological and spatial foundation for Indigenous planning, all attendant cultural, social, economic, even political threats and opportunities arising from this connection come firmly within its purview. It uses Indigenous (and other) knowledge, both traditional and contemporary, to make decisions highly contextual to that community, located within its worldview, set of beliefs and values system, how it sees itself and its future. Clarity of logic or rationale between decisions and specific actions and activities is critical. Ultimately the test is whether the action or activity

Figure 1.2   Indigenous planning as a process

leads to an enhanced state of well-being of/for the Indigenous community concerned, or indeed undermines pursuit of that goal. ✳

The People

Although the prevailing view seems to mitigate against singular, universal definitions as too open or closed, "Indigenous peoples" is generally taken to mean communities, groups, and individuals descended from the original populations resident in a country. Other descriptors include tribal peoples, Aboriginals, Natives, First Nations, or fourth world communities.

For Indigenous planning, the "people" are the first peoples of "that place," in other words, the present-day descendants of ancestors who have lived in that place prior to colonization/invasion by a foreign power since time immemorial.

In some respects it is more helpful to outline "elements" of Indigeneity, including pre-existence, non-dominance, cultural difference, self-

identification as Indigenous, close attachment to ancestral territories and
natural resources, an Indigenous language distinct from a "national"
language, and customary social or political institutions (Hitchcock
1994, 4).

That said, the most universally accepted definition seems to be:

> Indigenous communities, peoples and nations are those which have a
> historical continuity with pre-invasion and pre-colonial societies that
> developed on their territories, consider themselves distinct from other
> sectors of the societies now prevailing on those territories, or parts
> of them. They form at present non dominant sectors of society and
> are determined to preserve, develop and transmit to future genera-
> tions their ancestral territories, and their ethnic identity, as the basis
> of their continued existence as peoples, in accordance with their own
> cultural patterns, social institutions and legal system (United Nations
> 2009, 4).

What this definition infers rather than states explicitly is that Indigenous peoples also continue to be among the most marginalized, oppressed,
discriminated against, poverty-stricken, dispossessed, and exploited
communities in the world today. That this oppression is in/on the lands,
territories, and countries that were once theirs adds an ironic urgency to
the task of rebuilding and strengthening Indigenous communities across
all indices of human development.

In this context Indigenous planning must have as its fundamental aim,
the construction of theory, practice, and methodologies to "plan" these
communities out of this state and in so doing refuse/reject their continued oppression.

Their Place

Indigenous planning is "place-based," therefore identifying which
Indigenous community has the right or responsibility to do the planning will be geographically varied and depend on the issue, its scope,
scale, spatial boundaries, and potential to negatively or positively affect
the community. In one context the "community" might be a national
Indigenous entity. More likely it will be a regional, local, site-specific
community, or indeed various combinations of all. Across a national
context it could extend to aggregations of Indigenous communities (e.g.,

tribes, clans, mobs, or nations), be based around a singular community (e.g., tribe), or indeed sector within a community (e.g., subtribe).

The notion of "place" must also be conceptualized against the colonial backdrop of misappropriation. "Their place" applies not just to what little might remain in the communities' legal title but also contested territory, lands, waters, and resources stolen or excised during the colonial era. Therefore the spatial parameters of Indigenous planning go potentially as far out as the boundaries of traditional pre-contact territory.

In this context, the notion of an affected, relevant, or appropriate Indigenous "community of interest" will often be the subject of protracted inter- and intra-Indigenous discussion and negotiation. In many cases though, it will be generally accepted that a particular Indigenous community "owns" the right/responsibility to plan the space because it is indisputably theirs, if not legally then at least morally.

Their Knowledge

Access to relevant knowledge that is deemed appropriate for the particular purpose and "accepted" as legitimate by that Indigenous community forms the bedrock of "good" Indigenous planning. A significant corpus of literature is now available on Indigenous knowledge as a distinct and legitimate epistemology with its own form, coherence, and justification. That said, Indigenous traditional knowledge can be defined as

> the complex bodies and systems of knowledge, know-how and practices and representations maintained and managed by Indigenous peoples around the world, drawing on a wealth of experiences and interaction with the natural environment and transmitted orally from one generation to the next. It tends to be collectively owned whether taking the form of stories, songs, beliefs customary laws and artwork or scientific agricultural technical and ecological knowledge and the skills to implement these knowledges (United Nations 2009, 64).

Indigenous languages and idiom are also critical conductors of Indigenous-centric knowledge encompassing worldviews, concepts, values, and beliefs, even institutional frameworks and practices. They provide an essential buttress for self-definition and self-expression – defining what is important to that community, why, and how it should/could be expressed in their planning. While much has been retained in the oral archive, much has also been lost during colonialism and is now in the process of being recovered. As critical identity markers and repositories of traditional knowledge about events, people, history, and relationships, Indigenous place names also have a central role in this recovery.

Importantly, this knowledge is also subject to new and evolving interpretation as Indigenous communities continue the very human process of contextualizing traditional knowledge across a range of diverse and previously unpredicted settings. Increasingly, "other" knowledge systems including science, social science, and technology are being co-opted by Indigenous communities. That said, Indigenous planning must equip itself with the best knowledge to hand – whether Indigenous knowledge, traditional ecological knowledge, Western science, or technology. The aim should be knowledge collaboration rather than competition, and alliance rather than combat. Equally, oppositional, binary distinctions between tradition and modernity are unnecessary and should be removed. Indigenous knowledge exists on a temporal continuum of ongoing contextualizing and adaptation by the community. The community alone has the right to determine relevance and epistemic coherence.

Unhelpful knowledge hierarchies should also be rejected. Ultimately it's the Indigenous community's right and responsibility to reconcile the traditional with the modern, determine the appropriate blend of traditional knowledge and its descendants "fit for purpose," and indeed the place/relevance of other knowledges, from across the universal pantheon of knowledge systems.

Their Values and Worldviews

Indigenous worldviews and values are based on a deep and abiding physical and spiritual connection as kinfolk with their place, land, territories, environment, and resources since time immemorial. These worldviews and underlying values reinforce the inextricable link that exists between the community and, via the medium of ancestral land, their ancestors. Of that there is no doubt. Therefore, maintaining and/or re-establishing these links lies at the core of Indigeneity and therefore Indigenous planning.

That said, a wide range of factors from introduced colonial religions and technologies to social contact and miscegenation have had significant impacts on Indigenous communities, resulting in various degrees of syncretization of beliefs. These have had to be negotiated, mediated, and more often than not, fought over to protect the essence of Indigeneity.

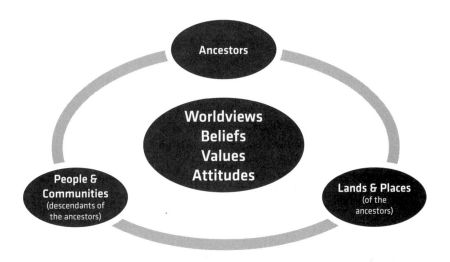

Figure 1.3   Core connections in Indigenous planning

Today, despite continual challenges to their veracity, the deep structure of Indigenous worldviews remains remarkably intact, still predicated on the fundamental causal link between people/communities and the places/spaces of *their* ancestors. These worldviews continue to be articulated, revised, and even reinterpreted through a combination of extant Indigenous practice and custom, fused with community values and attitudes to each other, their lands, and natural environment.

The theft and desecration of. these lands and places has had a profoundly devastating effect on Indigenous communities. These continue to ripple out across all other indices of social, economic, and even cultural deprivation. Poverty, racism, marginalization, material and psychological dislocation are now critical signifiers in the Indigenous planning vernacular. While at its core, Indigenous planning must retain its place-based, spatial orientation, ancestral land is "merely" the fulcrum around which all other aspects of social, economic, and cultural development pivot.

Their Decisions

Indigenous approaches to decision making cannot be separated from the social structure of these communities or their political and administrative institutions. Neither can they be divorced from the lands, environ-

decision-making is wrapped up in many aspects!

ments, even relationships and experiences that define these communities. However, the critical question is, which institutional arrangement has the responsibility/burden/right to make "the" decision and on what basis do they claim that right.

The principle context for Indigenous decision making is still largely the local community (i.e., tribe, subtribe, extended family). Specific issues, opportunities, and threats to Indigenous places, resources, and people are most immediately prevalent at the local level. That said, "local" Indigenous planning – hence decision making – should also position itself within the broader context of Indigenous coalition building at the regional and, where needed, the national level as a hedge against the hegemony of the settler state.

A number of common themes permeate Indigenous decision making, including:

- A determination to strive for general consensus/agreement within the affected group. This takes time and depending on the complexity of the issue often requires extensive discussion and debate to build trust within the group.
- Critical references to core traditional values to guide the decision process and assess the veracity of outcomes, including protecting future generations; protecting the land and environment from harmful, irreversible effects; enhancing the well-being of the community and strengthening community cohesion through reciprocity. These values often need to be mediated, reconciled, even reinterpreted, but never abandoned.
- Access to traditional knowledge unique to the group to underpin decisions, but also drawing on other knowledge systems to enhance the viability of any decision.
- Leadership from within the group. Leaders are generally chosen through a combination of skill, experience, knowledge, proven effectiveness, and ancestry. The ability to unite the group to a common purpose is a critical quality of sustained, effective leadership.
- The importance of the wisdom of Elders. Elders are generally the repositories of group knowledge, values, practices, and history. Importantly, through their assent, consent, or indeed dissent they provide a cultural and ethical check for decision processes and outcomes.
- The importance of being a good host. Hospitality, reciprocity, and conducting decision processes and meetings according to accepted

cultural protocols are essential precursors to quality decision making and sustainable decisions.

Their Practice

Clearly, once decisions are made they need to be acted on. Community leaders, including Elders, specialists, and/or delegates are generally "guardians" of the decisions, manage them on behalf of the community, and activate them through practices and approaches adjudged to be culturally valid and appropriate. There are countless examples today of Indigenous practices that have their basis in tradition but continue to be used as mechanisms for implementing community decisions. These practices are most readily reflected in various approaches to land and resource management that are quite unique. In many respects, they could only ever have arisen from a worldview and value system that continually reaffirms the deep physical and spiritual connection the community has with "its" place and environments.

In the New Zealand Māori context, one such example is the practice of *rahui*. Rahui can be used to regulate specific natural resources (e.g., stretch of land, bush, waterway) that might be under threat from pollution or overuse. Rahui "withdraws" the specific resource from everyday usage for a defined period of time until it is no longer polluted or has been replenished.

Again, the colonial context has created a "tricky" situation where internally derived decisions cannot simply be activated but must be shepherded to appropriate action through a parallel and often highly convoluted and complex dual planning system. In this context, Indigenous communities must be well versed in the political art/act of facilitating implementation of their planning decisions through to agreed practice. The community might have "control" over its internal planning processes and be able to use both customary and contemporary Indigenous practice to implement its decisions. However mainstream planning is ultimately controlled by the settler state and therefore able to wield its hegemonic influence as it wishes.

In this dual context, Indigenous decisions must have an internal coherence that is consistent with Indigenous values, worldviews, and processes. They must also be externalized to the settler state and its planning apparatus through political influence, mediation, negotiation, and advocacy. The ability to use Western legal processes adeptly and skilfully, often against the state and "its" national, regional, and district planning

systems, is critical to affirming Indigenous decisions and facilitating the
pursuit of any desired outcome.

INDIGENOUS PLANNING AS AN OUTCOME

Indigenous planning is not just a rudderless or directionless process
meandering aimlessly through a set of processes, protocols, and rituals,
however. Even "good" processes can potentially lead to "bad" decisions.
Indigenous planning must therefore drive towards a series of environmental, social, economic, cultural, even political outcomes aimed at
improving the present(s) and futures of Indigenous communities and
their environments.

Under the broader rubric of self-determination this brings me to what
I consider to be the five critical aims or indeed preferred outcomes of/for
Indigenous planning. These are:

· improved environmental quality and quantity;
· political autonomy and advocacy;
· social cohesion and well-being;
· economic growth and distribution;
· cultural protection and enhancement.

Indigenous planning as a process needs to strive for balance across
the five dimensions. In pursuit of these aims, it also needs to negotiate, discuss, debate, and mediate "internally" (i.e., within the group) the
difficult terrain between tradition and modernity. Critically this is an
"internal" discussion for Indigenous peoples and communities to have in
specific places, in their own way and own time. It is their discourse and
importantly not a canvas on which to post outdated Rousseauvian fan-
tasies about Indigenous peoples and the land. Indigenous peoples cannot
risk "their" planning being misappropriated into someone else's meta-
phor about Indigeneity and being Native. That said, Western planning
needs to create the space within "its" planning for internalized Indigenous dialogue to occur.

Environmental Quality and Quantity

There is an ethic or duty of care to the land, its resource, and environments, particularly those located within the traditional territories of the
group. By definition, Indigenous planning is placed-based and implies a

Figure 1.4   Indigenous planning as an outcome

long and close association, therefore knowledge of the specific environment and what it can sustain. Resources tend to be communally-owned and relationships (since time immemorial) exist with specific places. Indigenous planning should strengthen, nurture, and consolidate these relationships, protect the resource for future generations, and be symbiotic rather than parasitic (i.e., use not abuse). Critical questions arise, such as: How is this relationship being expressed in planning, resource use, development, and even design? Is the relationship with the resource constructive or destructive? How can Indigenous communities balance important social and economic priorities with environmental objectives?

As suggested, there are also perils in "defaulting" to the position of environmental conscience of the nation, but otherwise still landless and destitute. Indigenous communities must define what "a duty of care" means appropriate to their specific context, rather than risk it being imposed externally by others, usually more economically privileged. Therefore the notion of "environmental quality" also has its context. And, the community, with considerable wisdom and caution must weight these against other social and economic priorities that it, and not others, set.

Indigenous planning should also strive for the return back to its traditional owners of lands and resources, historically or more recently alienated through the colonial process. While this should be a key operating principle, it might also open up other opportunities for co-management and collaboration with the settler government around agreed sets of management principles, approaches, and environmental outcomes. After all, the contemporary resource base is generally only a minute fraction of what it once was. Therefore the emphasis on environmental quality should also be matched with processes to secure re-appropriation of lands and resources "stolen" from the community.

Social Cohesion and Well-Being

Commitment to the group and improving the well-being of the kinship community are paramount. Consensus-based decision making upholds the sovereignty of the group rather than the individual. Therefore, decisions about appropriate resource use and allocation to enhance social well-being need, where possible, to be determined by community consensus. Importantly, the kinship group must be empowered to define the nature of "their" well-being and any associated social priorities.

Indigenous planning should strive for social cohesion within the group; aim to improve well-being across all social indices, including housing, health, welfare, and education; and (as a benchmark) social equity with non-Indigenous communities. The notion of social cohesion and well-being must be measured against the communities' own derivation of priorities and aspirations. Social indicators and preferred outcomes also need to be set by that community, rather than externally prescribed and applied.

Political Autonomy and Advocacy

The pursuit of political autonomy and power-sharing with the state – including planning agencies – are also critical aims of Indigenous planning. So too is the right to be self-determining, self-defining, and to have collective agency. Across specific social and economic settings this notion extends to the right of Indigenous communities always to determine what is most appropriate for their situation and their context. The ability to utilize both endogenous (i.e., Indigenous) approaches and models, and exogenous (i.e., Western and other models), and adapt traditional models to a modern context is itself an expression of self-determination but also resilience of these communities.

Indigenous planning strives for improved, more equitable participation by Indigenous peoples in local, regional, and national politics and planning. It should also seek out reciprocal two-way relationships to realize the potential for Indigenous communities to manage not only their own affairs, but increasingly those of their mainstream neighbours. Indigenous planning isn't therefore just a theoretical position or approach but also a political strategy for invoking change.

Economic Growth and Distribution

Reclamation of traditional lands and resources coupled with the capacity to develop those resources is a critical plank in the pursuit of economic growth. The historic theft of natural and cultural assets during the colonial era has had a profoundly negative impact on Indigenous economies. During the period from first contact, these economies were either destroyed or severely arrested. Most are still in recovery. A critical part of that recovery is the return of what amounts to a minute fraction of the original resource, coupled, where possible, with financial compensation to rebuild the economy. An asset base on which to re-grow the economy, leading to improved social well-being and enhanced future economic viability, is critical.

Consistent with a philosophy which is highly redistributive, the benefits of economic growth should accrue back to the traditional owners of that resource. Therefore, Indigenous planning aims to redistribute the benefits of resource use and allocation equitably across the group, but also acknowledge and reward individual effort and enterprise. Again, definitions of sustainable development, economic growth, and sustainable management of the resource base need to be determined internally rather than externally imposed. Processes for fine-tuning the balance between economic development, social well-being, and indeed environmental protection are also an essential part of the armoury of Indigenous planning.

Cultural Protection and Enhancement

A multitude of concepts, ideas, and definitions about culture, its characteristics, and what it might mean now exist. One of the unifying characteristics is expressed in the tautology that culture applies to the collective
identity of a group, and the characteristics and qualities that make a
group distinctive. At one level of abstraction culture implies the norms,
characteristics, and qualities that make Indigenous people – Indigenous
as distinct from the "mainstream" majority, exotic, or immigrant populations. This distinction arises out of a shared national (and even international) history and experience of colonization – the attendant loss of
life, lands, and resources, but also social and psychological effects of
these experiences through subsequent generations.

At the level most relevant to Indigenous planning, culture connotes the
unseen, unique world views, beliefs, and values that underpin Indigenous thinking and behaviour, attitudes to each other and the environment, and at its essence, what it means to be human. These qualities
achieve visibility through Indigenous practices, institutions, ceremony,
customs, languages, and distinctive idiom – even dress and bodily adorn-
ment that they portray, represent and even re-present. Implicit in this is
the notion that the "unseen" can be re-interpreted and the "seen" re-
expressed across a variety of spatial and temporal contexts while keeping their inherent structure and overall coherence intact. Clearly cultural
protection and enhancement of Indigenous communities, and the very
qualities that make them unique, must be a critical goal of Indigenous
planning.

Support from Within the Community of Planners

In addition to broad goals for Indigenous self-determination, Indigenous
planning should also expressly advocate and seek support from the local
and national planning community for:

· Greater control over local, regional, and national planning processes,
  particularly those that continue to exert legal and regulatory influence
  over Indigenous communities.
· Improved utilization of Indigenous knowledge, concepts, approaches,
  and practices in "mainstream" planning and management. This does
  not mean redefining these concepts but rather accommodating and
  providing a place for them in planning.

gain support to bring planning to the communities' lead, not outside lead

- Improved socio-economic status for the Indigenous community. "Refusing" intergenerational poverty, dispossession, and displacement, and redressing the ravages of colonization should be a priority item on any mainstream planning agenda.
- Reclamation of traditional lands and resources. As already discussed, without their lands and natural resources, Indigenous communities do not have a "place to stand" and be Indigenous. Indigenous peoples are inextricably bound to their ancestral lands and environments. While reclamation is generally the preferred option, there are other forms of reclamation or association, such as co-management, collaborative management, or management by objective.

INDIGENOUS PLANNING AS A TRADITION AND METHODOLOGY

In its contemporary context, the primary aim of Indigenous planning is to improve the lives and environments of Indigenous peoples. Taking account of discussion so far, suitable working definitions could include Indigenous peoples analyzing their situation, making choices, and implementing decisions about their resources, their land, environments, and places – using their knowledge, values, practices, and approaches to enhance their collective social, economic, and cultural well-being. Or in rather more basic/fundamental terms: Indigenous peoples making decisions about their lives, their environments, and their futures.

Indigenous planning is principally concerned with transforming the lives and environments of Indigenous communities. That said, colonialism has created a socio-political context that requires internal navigation within these communities and external advocacy across the plethora of state planning structures that have retained hegemonic dominance. Therefore, Indigenous planning has to function within two critical contexts: its own internal community setting that it can largely control, circumscribe, and define, and an external political and planning environment over which it has very little control, except for its ability to influence.

While the focus of this chapter has been the internal context of Indigenous planning or planning by and for Indigenous communities, its broader context is the national state planning system within which, due to historical necessity and ongoing state hegemony, it must sit. Consequently, the "sequence" of Indigenous planning is critical. Its first priority must be self-defining with the community continually mapping out its preferred future and creating planning approaches and tools to consolidate this future. Its second priority must be to advocate this future and influence the external political and planning environment through professional planning and political alliances, which nevertheless continue ultimately to dominate it.

Therefore Indigenous planning must position itself both as a theory and practice of internalized self-definition and externalized advocacy. Clearly, planning processes within and across the two contexts must be iterative, but also function in a highly reflexive, self-definition-advocacy loop. Furthermore, Indigenous planning can be conveniently defined according to two key characteristics (adapted from Moser's gender planning framework, 1993, 90):

· The notion of a planning tradition (i.e., a form of planning that has its own particular focus, knowledge base, objectives, agenda, organisation).
· Planning methods or methodologies (i.e., ways of organizing material, knowledge, etc. to guide actions).

While it is beyond the scope of this chapter to delve into this in any significant detail, applying these characteristics to Indigenous planning leads to a range of schema or organizing set of concepts, including those in table 1.1.

Taking this particular schema, the focus, goals, and objectives for Indigenous planning to a large extent have remained constant throughout history. What has varied are the political and social contexts that Indigenous communities have had to move through to survive. As a response, knowledge systems and planning frameworks have also had to evolve to cope with the constantly changing colonial setting. That said, Indigenous planning has to retain its transformative intent and have the freedom to co-opt, even create, new knowledges, planning tools, and approaches in pursuit of its ultimate goal.

However, any transformative process is by definition very political, creates high levels of anxiety, and always has potential for conflict both within the Indigenous community of interest and through its engagement with external agencies. Consequently, approaches and methods that acknowledge the importance of planning as a process that requires discussion, debate, mediation, and negotiation in order to seek "resolution," if not consensus, are essential. Given the political and often volatile climate within which it must function, Indigenous planning must use and consciously create "new" tools and methods to improve its

Table 1.1   Indigenous planning as a tradition and methodology

Focus	Indigenous peoples and their environments (i.e., lands, resources etc.)
Knowledge	Indigenous theories and knowledge including: • Traditional ecological knowledge • New indigenous knowledge, using indigenous epistemologies • Community-based knowledge • Other co-opted/adapted knowledge, e.g., science
Goals	Indigenous peoples' autonomy over themselves and their environments
Objectives	Achievement for indigenous communities of the following: • Improved environmental quality and quantity • Political autonomy and advocacy • Social cohesion and well-being • Economic growth and distribution • Cultural protection and enhancement
Planning Framework	Iterative Indigenous planning processes using: • Indigenous planning tools, e.g., tribal management plans, cultural impact assessments • Indigenous planning procedures, e.g., meetings, gatherings • Indigenous planning practice, e.g., traditional and adapted approaches to planning, policy analysis, resource management

internal strength and external bargaining or negotiating power. These processes are never "neat," "rational," or "comprehensive" – culturally constructed as these terms might be, but often "piecemeal," tentative, and exploratory.

CONCLUSION

Indigenous planning has always been a "work in progress." That, in many respects, is its key strength – an ability to move and adapt as the context changes and evolves, but at its essence fixed to the unchanging goal of Indigenous peoples self-determination.

Classifying its various traditions from the classic to resistance then resurgence as I have, is a way of writing Indigenous planning back into history. Until relatively recently it had been excluded. Colonialism didn't bring planning to the non-planning Natives. The Natives already had their institutions, practices, and planning systems. However, the colonial rhetoric of racial superiority simply could not comprehend Natives

planning, let alone planning with any degree of sophistication or complexity. The rhetoric needed to be buttressed by a conceptualization
of Natives as capable, only of the savage things that Natives do – rituals, ceremonies, cannibalism, warring et al. Colonialism didn't create
order from chaos. Order already existed. And despite the proselytizing
ideology, the Natives weren't waiting to be missioned or planned into
civil society. However, the colonial "othering" of Indigenous peoples as
savage and uncivilized catapulted the rhetoric of superiority from the
ideological to the hegemonic, effectively closing the door on Indigenous
planning and excluding it from the national planning grid.

This is not to say that Indigenous communities did not embrace
change, adapt to new circumstances, or co-opt new technologies. Far
from it, even during early-stage colonialism the adaptive ability and
resilience of these communities was highly evident. In some contexts
adaptation took place over hundreds of years, while in others colonialism was grotesquely compressed, leading to cataclysmic consequences
for these communities.

While colonial discourses fixated on planning Indigenous communities out of existence, Indigenous planning continued, as a unique
form of resistance away from the gaze of the colonial enterprise, on
rural Native reserves, remnant homelands, wastelands, and even urban
enclaves. The door had been closed, but a window to the colonial world
had been opened. Indigenous communities became highly adept at traversing these alternate worlds, navigating – as they still do today – the
twin orbits of colonialism and Indigeneity.

Conservative estimates currently put the number of Indigenous peoples
today in excess of 370 million, residing in over ninety of the world's 190
or so countries (United Nations 2009, 1). In other words, just under half
of the world's countries have Indigenous communities. Far from dying
out through war, extermination, disease, or government decree, these
communities and their descendants have tenaciously refused extinction.
However, they remain among the most marginalized, oppressed, and
poverty-stricken of communities – still largely positioned materially and
ideologically on the periphery of these nations. This situation is not an
accident, nor just an unfortunate by-product of history. These communities were "planned" into this state.

It would be remiss to conclude this chapter without unsettling the
dominant discourse of planning that still pervades contemporary nation
states, or indeed failing to nudge Indigenous planning along the road to
its next possible iteration.

If Indigenous peoples were planned into oppression, equally they can be planned out of it. In the distant and recent past, as well as continuing present, colonial planning and the planning profession has been a willing subaltern; its complicity with the colonial project has contributed significantly to Indigenous people's oppression and their continued material and ideological marginalization. Therefore, it has a critical role and ethical responsibility to support the recovery of Indigenous communities and to facilitate the restitution of Indigenous materiality and memory across spaces and places that once were theirs. The asymmetric impact of colonization justifies an equally asymmetric and differentiated colonial planning response to plan these communities out of this predicament. It requires more than simply "grafting" Indigeneity to "mainstream" planning as another "tricky" yet worthy agenda item. Fundamentally, mainstream/colonial planning must create a conceptual space for Indigenous planning through the acceptance of its legitimacy as a parallel tradition with its own history, focus, goals, and approach. It must then facilitate planning frameworks and tools to connect the two traditions, thereby altering the trajectory of its own future. This could have happened during an earlier period of colonial contact, but it didn't and there is now a lot of catching up to do.

Does Indigenous planning have a place for non-Indigenous planners? In my view it definitely does. Indigenous planning is as much an ethic and philosophy as it is a planning framework with a set of approaches and methods. It is highly collaborative but with an unambiguous focus on Indigenous peoples' self-determination. Being "grounded" in the Indigenous community of interest and a commitment to historical redress and recovery of these communities is critical. Therefore, Indigenous and non-Indigenous planners equipped with the ethical fortitude, desire, and skill to navigate the parallel planning worlds of Indigeneity and colonialism are an essential part of Indigenous planning as an ongoing project.

That Indigenous planning has always existed is the central thesis of this chapter. As a "work in progress" it must continue to be investigative, and develop new ways and not be fixed to a closed set of methods and approaches. While its frameworks over time might evolve, the focus, goals, and objectives of Indigenous planning will, for the most part, likely remain unchanged. Having said that, its adaptive, exploratory nature mean it is well positioned to actively embrace its own criticality, be self-exploratory, self-examining, and quite analytical in its self-questioning around many of the critical internal issues confronting Indigenous communities today, including the gendered nature of Indigenous power relations, the blend between tradition and modernity, balancing cultural imperatives with the exigencies of social and economic advancement, even new ways of constituting tradition, traditional values, and approaches. Against significant odds, Indigenous peoples have survived. Perhaps now is the time to look beyond resurgence to a new critical tradition for Indigenous planning that has its focus on evolving notions of Indigeneity that still has Indigenous peoples' autonomy over themselves and their environments as its goal, but which moves beyond the gaze and strictures of colonialism.

This chapter, like all narratives, is incomplete, and there remains ample opportunity for further work, discussion, dialogic debate, even dissension within and across the twin orbits of colonial/mainstream planning and Indigenous planning, given the two are now inextricably linked by history.

REFERENCES

Hitchcock, R. 1994. "International Human Rights, the Environment and Indigenous Peoples." In *Endangered Peoples – Indigenous Rights and the Environment, Colorado Journal of International Environmental Law and Policy*. Colorado: University Press of Colorado.

Moser, C. 1993. *Gender Planning and Development – Theory Practice and Training*. New York: Routledge.

United Nations, Department of Economic and Social Affairs. 2009. *State of the Worlds Indigenous Peoples*. New York: United Nations.

Waitangi Tribunal. 1985. *Report of the Waitangi Tribunal on the Manukau Claim* (WAI 8). Wellington: Waitangi Tribunal.

Waitangi Tribunal. 1987. *Report of the Waitangi Tribunal on the Orakei Claim* (WAI 9). Wellington: Waitangi Tribunal.

Waitangi Tribunal. 2011. www.waitangi-tribunal.govt.govt.nz/reports/longintro.asp.

PART ONE

Indigenous Communities

2

Reconstituting Native Nations: Colonial Boundaries and Institutional Innovation in Canada, Australia, and the United States

STEPHEN CORNELL[1]

What happens to the boundary legacies of colonialism when Indigenous nations begin to assert self-governing powers?

By "the boundary legacies of colonialism," I refer to the boundaries into which colonial powers fit Indigenous peoples over time: spatial or geographical, political/administrative, and even cognitive – the boundaries of identification that separate "us" from "them" in the minds of Indigenous peoples themselves. The "lines," so to speak – spatial, political, mental – that today demarcate Indigenous peoples in Canada, the United States, and Australia (and in a number of other countries as well) are to a significant degree colonial constructions, products in part of European invasion, colonization, and imposed control. What happens to those boundaries when external controls are reduced? What happens to them under conditions of substantive, Indigenous self-determination?

Such questions are particularly topical now in view of recent developments in, among other places, Canada, the US, and Australia. Over the last several decades, Indigenous peoples in all three countries have been trying to reassert self-governing powers, reclaiming the right to shape their own futures in their own ways. In the process, some of these peoples also have challenged these colonial legacies, proposing or enacting new spatial, political, or cognitive boundaries. Some of these newly asserted boundaries have very old roots; their newness lies in their deliberate defiance of an intervening set of imposed constructions. Some are Indigenous responses to changing requirements set by outside governments. Others are new creations. But all are to some degree Indigenous solutions to boundary problems, part of what Lane and Hibbard (2005, 174) call "an effort to reconfigure the terms of indigenous-state relations."

This chapter examines Indigenous boundary challenges, in particular political and cognitive ones – those having to do with identity and the organization of collective political power. It views these challenges as institutional innovations in the field of governance. It organizes a sample of cases from Canada, the US, and Australia in terms of the scope of institutional innovation and the extent of boundary crossing that these cases involve. My argument is that those Indigenous nations that are currently reconstituting themselves as political actors and as bases of collective identity are challenging, to varying degrees, the assumptions and preferred organizational templates of central governments. They also are affecting community planning at a fundamental level. As Ted Jojola (2008) has pointed out for the US, Indigenous communities have long been subjects of planning by others. In recent decades, in both North America and Australia, growing numbers of those communities have struggled to seize the planning initiative for themselves (Lane and Hibbard 2005). Some – the subjects of this chapter – go further still. They are not only reclaiming power in planning and other processes, they are rethinking the boundaries – the units – by which power itself is organized.

Before turning to the nature of institutional innovation in Indigenous boundary challenges in North America and Australia, I explore the nature of boundaries and the historical process of boundary-making on both continents.

MAKING BOUNDARIES: MARKERS AND MEANINGS

Social boundaries are human constructions that involve both markers and meanings in the classification of groups (Cornell and Hartmann 2007). Markers are characteristics such as place of origin, shared ancestry, a distinctive history, skin color, language, cultural practices, behaviours, and so forth, chosen as a classificatory means of distinguishing populations. In their simplest declarative form, they may consist of little more than, "that group is composed of people from over there," or "those are the people who are tall and dark." But markers can be more complex as well, as in "they are the people who did all those terrible things to our ancestors," or "what distinguishes us is our belief in a messiah who is coming to save us."

Meanings are the values assigned to such classifications. They can range from the simple – good, evil, superior, inferior – to the complex, for example: "Those people" – the ones marked by their dark skin, or their place of origin, or their beliefs, or something else – "are too temperamental or ignorant to govern themselves," or "we" – those of us who share this history or ancestry or culture – "are better than you because we have a richer, more sophisticated understanding of life and the natural world." Meanings establish, argue for, or justify relationships between groups, typically including relationships of unequal power.

Combinations of markers and meanings become the bases of boundaries of various kinds: spatial (for example, "you/we belong there, not here"), political/administrative/jurisdictional ("you/we have the following rights or must do things the following way"), and cognitive ("those of us who share this culture, or this history, or this ancestry, are a people," or "those of you who look like that or came from over there are a people").

As this suggests, markers and meanings can be chosen by either insiders or outsiders. One of the critical questions about boundaries is: Who has the power to make their own choices of markers and meanings prevail – that is, to create sustainable boundaries that apply to others or to themselves? More important for this chapter is a subsequent question: When the distribution of power changes, what happens to the boundaries involved?

THE BOUNDARY LEGACIES OF COLONIALISM

Colonialism had at least two sequentially related impacts on Indigenous boundaries: disruption and rigidification. Colonialism disrupted the boundaries by which many Indigenous peoples had organized their lives under conditions of freedom, replacing them with impositions of its own. It then cemented those imposed boundaries into rigid political and administrative structures.

This statement suggests that prior to colonialism, Indigenous boundaries were unambiguous, and that Indigenous peoples thought and acted with widely recognized spatial, political, or cognitive boundaries in mind. On this the evidence is mixed. In some cases this appears to have been so; in others, it clearly was not; and in most cases, it was true only up to a point. Some Indigenous peoples in North America and Australia seem to have had or recognized more clearly defined spatial, political, or cognitive boundaries than others.[2] Where boundary lines were relatively clear, most were mutable and often porous, allowing for considerable spatial and social transboundary movement. The specificity, exclusivity, and certainty that form the backbone of most Western conceptions of social, political, and spatial boundaries were often missing from Indigenous conceptions, which were themselves often illegible to Europeans who were accustomed to simpler boundary schemes and found the nuances and complexities of Indigenous relationships difficult to understand (Helm 2000; Howitt 2001; Sletto 2009; Ross et al. 2011, chapter 3). Even in cognitive terms – in terms of the conceptual boundary or line of identity that separated "us" from "them" – boundaries could be complex and changeable as individuals moved through distinct but related social circles and networks (for example, Anderson 1999; Myers 1991). Such lines tended to overlap, intersect, or diverge depending on events, the activity at issue, and the persons involved. Bright lines were few.

But regardless of the pre-invasion situation, the European arrival in North America and Australia set in motion processes that in many cases directly challenged Indigenous notions of the "whos" and "wheres" of social life: Who is part of the group and who is not? Whose land or country is this? Who can speak for or make decisions for whom in this or that sphere of action or in this or that place? As outsiders imposed their preferred boundaries of various kinds on Indigenous peoples, those peoples' own boundary constructions were suppressed or erased (Sletto 2009), or joined other pieces of Indigenous culture in that set of more or less hidden understandings kept in memory, perhaps still organizing life beneath the surface but invisible to outside power.

Having set such disruptions in motion, colonialism then tried to shape and stabilize the results, assigning Indigenous groups to bounded pieces of land, naming those groups, binding them into more or less permanent administrative or political structures, forcing them to organize in prescribed units, dictating who was and who was not a member of the group, and treating as fixed a host of identities that once had been more fluid – a process of rigidification that continues to the present day. Some of these new boundaries, once embedded in imposed administrative or legal architectures and the policies attached to them, then became the organizational bases of Indigenous action, eventually influencing how Indigenous peoples saw themselves, creating an overlay on older identities or generating new ones and outlasting the pressures that created them. As Charles Tilly (2005, 139) notes, "once an imposed boundary falls into place, it leaves traces of its existence in the relevant social relations and representations even after it loses authoritative backing."

These two processes developed within a context of at least implicit and often explicit value or meaning. Colonial boundary-making reflected in part the assumed inferiority of Indigenous peoples held to be culturally handicapped and incapable of self-government in a civilized world. They needed to be managed. It thus accomplished two mutually reinforcing goals: it facilitated the expropriation of Indigenous lands, and it organized the management of Indigenous peoples.

These processes and their outcomes varied across and within the three countries of concern here, making generalization problematic.[3] Nonetheless – and at the risk of massively simplifying some complex histories – broad patterns are apparent.

In Canada, much of the process of change, proceeding under the Indian Act of 1876, was fragmentational. In effect, Canada pulled Indigenous peoples apart, turning localized or temporary separations into essentially permanent political, administrative, and geographical divides. This kind of dismemberment often involved treating local gatherings – summer fishing villages, for example – as distinct entities, confining these fragments on postage-stamp-sized lands called reserves, expropriating the bulk of the land, and then stabilizing the remnant Indigenous lands and populations as permanent administrative units and calling each a First Nation. Reserves for the Wet'suwet'en in British Columbia, for example, were established around village settlements, fragmenting those who, while residing in separate places, saw themselves as a single people (Mills 1994). As a result, the Wet'suwet'en are divided today into four First Nations. Says Satsan (Herb George), hereditary chief of the frog clan of the Wet'suwet'en, "They shredded us."[4] Historical Wet'suwet'en understandings and historical Canadian conceptions of what and where the "nation" is are radically at odds with each other.

The reverse happened in some parts of the US, particularly the Northwest, where coercive treaty-making forced sometimes unrelated and even antagonistic peoples to settle on single tracts of land called reservations, which then became the administrative units of federal Indian policy. For example, in the 1855 Hellgate Treaty, the US placed three tribes – the Bitterroot Salish, the Upper Pend d'Oreille, and the Kootenai – on a single reservation under a unitary administrative structure (Trosper 1976). In other cases, politically autonomous subgroups of a people sometimes lost their autonomy as they were forced together under single administrative umbrellas, a process that made sense to the colonizers as both conception and convenience but favoured comprehensive and static boundaries over the more complex and fluid boundaries that had organized these peoples' lives.[5]

The Australian case is both different from these and considerably more complex (Sutton 1995). In much of Australia prior to European invasion, social organization was highly localized and flexible, and group boundaries were thin, with individuals often carrying multiple identities based on variable connections to kin and place or country. Social and ritual ties to places and to people were diverse and often overlapping, while individual autonomy and mobility were not only common but highly valued. Large-scale political organization within language or cultural groupings was rare. Arid environments discouraged large aggregations of people for more than brief periods, and extensive kinship relations and a shared dependency on scarce resources encouraged wide-ranging resource use (see, for example, Sutton 1995; Holcombe 2004). Particularly in desert regions, "Aboriginal relationship to country is expressed not through absolute control of a distinct area, but rather through responsibility for sections of Dreaming tracks representing the travels of the ancestral beings" (Young 1995, 88). Even a sense of shared identity – of links to "countrymen" – could vary and change across persons sharing the same language (see Myers 1991 on the Pintupi, and Doohan 2008 on parts of the Kimberly region).

As in North America, European invasion and domination brought numerous attempts to establish clear spatial and social boundaries around Indigenous persons. Writes Elspeth Young (1995, 88), "Creating boundaries which would constrain the wandering habits of 'the first people,' carried out principally through the alienation of their land and the relocation of Aboriginal groups to government and mission administered reserve communities, was a feature of the non-Aboriginal settlement period," and "it remains dominant." This sort of boundary reorganization is not only spatial. The concentration of Aboriginal people in mission or social service centres – some of it imposed, some of it by choice – often brought together multiple kinship, language, or cultural groups, now co-resident many miles from the territories they previously occupied and treated by outside administrators as single populations. Over time, such settlements could become the basis of new collective identities (Tonkinson 1974, 139–41; Holcombe 2004; Taylor 2005; Ivory 2009).

These processes are not only historical; contemporary Australian government policy – ricocheting around from encouraging regional bodies to discouraging any Indigenous political organization to imposing its own changing regulations on how Indigenous people organize – constantly recreates them. Referring to such Australian processes and to James Scott's (1998) work on generic state efforts to make "legible" to itself the "illegible" organization of non-sedentary populations, Diane Smith (2008, 79) comments that, "There are now legal categories of people – such as 'traditional owners,' 'authorised claimants' and 'native title holders' – who have to be registered and certified, and 'councillors,' 'chairpersons,' 'bodies corporate' and 'governing boards' who are required to operate under legal and constitutional guidelines." Colonial boundary-making is both multi-layered and continuous – an ongoing construction project.

Not all Native nations had the same experience. Particularly in the US, thanks in part to a long history of nation-by-nation treaty-making, imposed administrative boundaries were more likely to coincide with cognitive boundaries – with Indigenous concepts of peoplehood – although even there, some nations were broken up, others were forced together, and many were removed from their homelands. But most avoided the extreme fragmentations and consolidations more common in Canada and Australia.

In recent decades, the terrain of Indigenous-non-Indigenous relations has shifted in all three countries. This is a product of Indigenous political demands, of state responses to those demands, and – particularly in Canada and Australia – of court decisions that bolstered certain Indigenous rights. One result – more in Canada and the US than in Australia – has been the gradual opening of space in which the enactment and expansion of a genuinely Indigenous practice of governance has become more possible (Cornell 1988a; Jorgensen 2007; Smith 2004). In all three countries, this, in turn, has fed a movement by Indigenous nations to reclaim governance as an Indigenous right and tradition. While it seems unlikely that states intended any such outcome (see, for example, the critique in Alfred 2005), what is most interesting about these developments is not state intentions but Indigenous action as a growing number of Native nations have moved to enact their own conceptions of self-determination and self-governance. In the late twentieth century, the boundary legacies of colonialism provided the organizational templates for much of that action, even when it was subversive in nature and intent. But as the new century got underway, it became evident that in some cases, those boundary legacies had themselves become targets of new Indigenous designs.

WHO IS THE "SELF" IN SELF-DETERMINATION AND SELF-GOVERNANCE?

The ideas of collective self-determination or self-government assume the existence of a recognizable "self": a community that aspires to control its own future and in which rights to self-determine or self-govern may be vested. But who identifies that community? To be true to the spirit of self-determination, identification of the relevant community should be left to the people whose future is at stake. Self-determination should mean, among other things, the right to determine the self. But even when that logic prevails, the process typically begins from colonial starting points. It begins with Indigenous entities that are themselves products, to at least some degree, of colonial processes. It is not surprising that central governments – inevitably implicated in these situations – tend to assume that those who are trying to self-determine or self-govern will do so within the structures that colonial processes have produced.

And this is what often happens. As Indigenous nations assert self-governing powers and reclaim the right to determine their own futures, many are acting on the basis of these boundary legacies, imposed or not. For many of them – probably for most – acting within contemporary spatial, political, and cognitive boundaries makes sense. They are convenient, providing an existing organizational basis for action; some are continuous with Indigenous self-concepts and homelands; some may not be continuous but have become part of how Indigenous peoples view themselves; and they are recognized by other governments. Furthermore, it is challenging enough simply to reclaim practical power in daily affairs. Doing so while at the same time rejecting boundary legacies can be a tall order indeed.

Nonetheless, some nations are reconsidering these legacies, challenging the boundaries (and their attendant meanings) that outside governments have assumed or imposed. They are reconsidering the appropriate social bases of collective action, what Hunt and Smith (2006, 22) call "the cultural geography of governance." The result is institutional innovation: either the revitalization of older political or cognitive boundaries or the creation of entirely new political units. In either case, these then become vehicles for assertions of governing power. In essence, these nations are developing innovative structures of governance – innovative in their departures from received structures and in their propositions of new governing units. Given – or seizing – the freedom to act collectively on their own terms, they are providing new answers to the question of who the "self" will be in self-determination and self-governance (Hunt and Smith 2006; also Peters 1999; Taylor 2004; Cornell 2007). In effect, these nations are asking themselves: For our own political purposes, what – or who – constitutes the nation, or the people, or the relevant community?

This is a significant departure. Policy-makers, experts, and the public for a long time have ignored such questions, or have assumed the answers. The fact that largely taken-for-granted boundaries have become, in some cases, matters of dispute is itself an indicator of a shifting power dynamic.

These boundary challenges have diverse origins. Some are attempts to revitalize or reclaim older bases of collective action. Some are attempts to gain political clout or economies of scale through consolidation, or are shaped by specific problems a nation is trying to address. Others are responses to requirements set by outside governments, such as the Northern Territory's regionalization policy in Australia that precipitated institutional innovation by some Indigenous populations (for example, Smith 2008). And some may reflect combinations of these factors.

The results are various. Not all boundary-related institutional innovations look the same. How might we think about the boundary-challenging, institutional steps that some Indigenous peoples are taking in these three countries?

TWO ASPECTS OF INDIGENOUS BOUNDARY-MAKING

At least two aspects of Indigenous boundary-making appear to be important. Each can be captured with a question and illustrated with a sample of ten cases drawn from all three countries.

Question 1: To what extent does each institutional innovation create new governmental structures that reorganize the lives of citizens?

In one way or another, all are rejecting, subordinating, superseding, or reimagining units that the colonial power created or recognizes, but not all such assertions or innovations are equally comprehensive or have comparable effects. Some are Indigenous governmental actions that may organize only limited portions of people's lives or create opportunities for new kinds of behaviour or activity within limited policy domains, but do not significantly reorganize Indigenous government itself. Others involve the comprehensive reorganization of Indigenous government with the potential to alter allegiances and compel new behaviours or activities. We can think of this as a matter of institutional scope – an imprecise metric, but a proxy of sorts, for the impact that these innovations have on communities.

At the more institutionally modest end of a continuum is the Gwich'in Steering Committee and the biennial Gwich'in Gathering, both originating in 1988 as part of a response by the Gwich'in peoples of Alaska, and the Yukon Territory and Northwest Territories of Canada to proposed oil drilling in the breeding grounds and range of the Porcupine Caribou Herd, long a primary economic and cultural resource to the Gwich'in (Gwich'in Steering Committee 2005; Bass 2004). Every two years, Gwich'in from both countries gather for a week to exchange ideas, celebrate Gwich'in culture, and discuss issues that in 2010 ranged from health care to climate change, from the current condition of the caribou to the challenges that Gwich'in relationships face as a result of tightened security along the international border.[6] As its origins suggest, there is a clear political dimension to the Gathering, an effort to facilitate coordinated Gwich'in action on critical policy issues, most importantly on the protection of the caribou and of the land on which both caribou and the Gwich'in depend. Ignoring the international boundary that cuts through their territory, both the Gathering and the Steering Committee – a non-profit entity that is the formal organizational expression of the Gwich'in Nation, itself a work-in-progress – represent a challenge to the imposed political and spatial separations that currently organize much of Gwich'in life (Starks, McCormack, and Cornell 2011).

A somewhat more robust institutional development is the Great Bear Initiative of the Coastal First Nations, a coalition of eleven First Nations along the central and northern coasts of British Columbia and the islands of Haida Gwaii. The Initiative is a multi-pronged effort to combine local economic development with natural resource stewardship in the Great Bear Rainforest. Its goal is to preserve resources and culture while supporting economic sustainability and assuring that these First Nations are full participants in all decisions affecting not only their lands but the entire rainforest. Over the last ten years, working through the Initiative, these nations have negotiated agreements with provincial and other governments to protect the land and support Indigenous self-determination and development. While the institutional structure (the Great Bear Initiative is the organizational arm of the Coastal First Nations' joint efforts) is focused on development and stewardship, it involves mutual commitments by participating nations and represents a form of joint governance across a limited set of issues, a venture in collaborative decision making with potentially significant effects on participating First Nation communities and their citizens.[7]

A comparable effort to build sustained, coordinated action across imposed boundaries is the Meadow Lake Tribal Council (MLTC). Founded in the 1980s, the council links nine Canadian First Nations in Saskatchewan in an assortment of economic and social service activities. MLTC manages a number of companies that are jointly owned by the participating First Nations and, in some cases, outside partners, and operates social service programs for all nine nations. Through these activities, MLTC provides the citizens of those nations with significant opportunities and services, and links the nine participating First Nations in a formal, structured collaboration. While it does not supersede its participating governments, MLTC is involved in assisting those governments not only in development and social services, but in strengthening their own governance capacities, and has become a prominent voice for its associated nations in dialogue with other governments and entities.[8]

These first few examples are cases of collaborations that transcend imposed boundaries, but they stop short (so far) of a formal reorganization of extensive governmental authority. The Noongar Nation in Australia begins to approach such a reorganization. The Noongar people are dispersed across the southwestern corner of Australia but share links of language, culture, and identity. While there appears to be no Indigenous history of comprehensive Noongar political organization, the 1992 Mabo decision by the Australian High Court and the Native Title Act of 1993 led to a succession of Noongar efforts to pursue land claims in the region. These claims were diverse, sometimes overlapping and even competing. In 2003, working through a new Noongar organization called the Southwest Aboriginal Land and Sea Council (SWALSC), the Noongar managed to consolidate most of these claims. Both SWALSC, which is the Native title representative body of the Noongar, and the comprehensive claim it has pursued are expressions of a Noongar identity that is taking cognitive and nascent political form in the concept, gradually gaining currency, of a Noongar Nation.[9] While SWALSC's focus remains land claims, it represents a move towards regional Noongar governance and, along with the Nation, provides a foundation for additional governance functions on a comprehensive, Noongar scale, something never envisioned in federal or state policy.

More substantial transfers of governing authority can be found in the inter-tribal courts of the US. Many American Indian nations have established their own tribal court systems. Charged with enforcing tribal law and, in some cases, with constitutional review, these courts have substantial civil and some criminal adjudicatory powers. However, it has been difficult for some nations to develop appeals processes that escape the small-community pressures of tribal politics. In response, a number of tribes have developed intertribal court systems that hear appeals and sometimes provide other services to tribal courts. Examples include the Southwest Intertribal Court of Appeals, the Intertribal Court of Southern California, and the Northwest Intertribal Court System.[10] These are institutions of considerable power that typically cross political, administrative, and sometimes cultural boundaries as they link separate nations in a single justice process. They represent a vesting – through formal resolutions adopted by the participating nations themselves – of significant governmental authority in new entities that have no precedent in the colonial boundary system.

The Tohono O'odham Nation in the southwestern US is engaged in a different kind of institutional innovation, but one that crosses a critical boundary. In 1853, the so-called Gadsden Purchase established the current southwestern border between the US and Mexico. Ignoring Indigenous peoples, the border cut through the lands of the Tohono O'odham, leaving a majority of the tribe in Arizona (US) and a minority in Sonora (Mexico). Today, the Tohono O'odham Nation located in Arizona argues that citizenship in the Nation should be sufficient for citizenship in the US, regardless of residence. But it not only makes the argument; despite US insistence that O'odham south of the border are Mexican citizens with no rights north of the boundary, the Nation treats them as citizens, attempts to extend its services and protection to them, and complicates US efforts to fortify a boundary that the O'odham consider an unjust imposition upon their lands and people. In doing so, it challenges, within the domain of citizenship, a destructive boundary legacy of colonialism (Castillo and Cowan 2001; Meeks 2007, 246–47; Starks, McCormack, and Cornell 2011).

Finally, there are a number of examples in Canada and Australia of efforts to construct entirely new governments that transcend imposed boundaries of various kinds or their meanings, either restoring older sets of relationships or imagining new ones as the organizational and conceptual bases of governmental authority. Two examples in Australia are the West Central Arnhem Regional Authority and the Thamarrurr Regional Council. Notable cases in Canada include, among others, the Grand Council of the Crees and the Ktunaxa Nation.

Beginning in 2003 in response to a federal policy of regionalization, a number of Aboriginal communities in West Arnhem Land in the
Northern Territory of Australia set out to create an Indigenous regional
authority that would allow them "to say what we want in our communities" and "have a much stronger voice speaking as one to government" (quoted in Smith 2008, 86). The West Central Arnhem Regional
Authority was to embrace twenty-five thousand square kilometres of
Aboriginal freehold land, including "several inter-related language and
landowning groups, three large discrete landowning communities (two
of which were on islands) and numerous small dispersed outstations."
Over a period of three years representatives of these diverse communities worked to design a viable governing system that would displace
existing local government organizations and would respect Indigenous
cultural geographies and conceptions of how collective authority should
most appropriately be organized and exercised on such a scale. Within
the imposed policy of regionalization, it was to establish an Indigenous
governance structure. This effort, while receiving critical assistance from
community development officers of the Northern Territory government,
came to be plagued eventually by that government's repeated and erratic
policy reversals, imposed criteria for governmental organization, and
refusal to recognize Indigenous governance solutions as valid. While the
future of this venture is unclear, it nonetheless represents an effort by
Indigenous peoples to build governing authority on new boundaries and
to infuse that authority with Indigenous understandings and practices
(Smith 2008).

The Port Keats region of the Northern Territory of Australia is an
isolated area approximately 320 kilometres southwest of Darwin. Its
population – almost entirely Aboriginal – speaks a number of related
languages and is divided into numerous clans. While originally dispersed
through much of the region, that population is concentrated today in
the township of Wadeye. In the mid-1990s, conflicts over governance
issues led the leadership of the primary land-owning clan in the township, the Kardu Diminin, along with leaders of other clans residing on
Diminin lands in Wadeye, to begin a search for a more inclusive and
effective governance structure. This led in 2003 to the development
of the Thamarrurr Regional Council, a structure that recognized and
brought together in a single governing body the various clan groups of
the region, now mostly resident in Wadeye. The council echoed, both in
its name ("Thamarrurr," which refers in the Murrinh-patha language
to balance and conflict resolution) and in its function, a pre-colonial

structure through which clan leaders from the surrounding region met periodically to address matters of common interest or concern such as inter-clan disputes, resource use, and ceremony. The contemporary version of this structure – the Thamarrurr Regional Council – is an Indigenous creation designed to address both governance issues internal to the community and larger economic and political relationships with territorial and federal governments (Ivory 2008; Taylor 2004).

The vast homeland of the James Bay Crees occupies much of northern Quebec east of Hudson Bay. In the 1970s, threatened by a massive hydroelectric scheme that would have flooded a huge portion of their lands – a scheme in which the Crees were neither considered nor consulted – the Crees of the James Bay region decided that resistance would require an unprecedented scale of organization. The result was the Grand Council of the Crees, the governing body of the James Bay Crees today, born out of crisis and with no precedent in their history. It binds together in a single government widely dispersed·Cree settlements that, while sharing language and culture, had no prior mechanism for coordinated, sustained, political action. In forming the council, the Crees not only found a mechanism for organizing resistance to an energy project; they also directly challenged the political and administrative structure of the Indian Act that had long linked individual villages directly to federal and provincial bureaucracies. They also challenged the embedded assumptions in that structure about who the Crees were and how they should be organized. In effect, the Crees reconstituted themselves as a nation, putting in place a structure of governance that reflects their own ideas about who they are and how they can best survive as a people (Awashish 2005; Papillon 2008; also Salisbury 1986; Niezen 1998).

At the other end of Canada in British Columbia, colonial processes and the US-Canada boundary fragmented the Ktunaxa people who occupied lands near the Kootenay and Columbia Rivers. Four Ktunaxa bands located in different parts of their traditional territory eventually were assigned tiny reserves in British Columbia and designated First Nations; they were later joined by a Shuswap group. Two other Ktunaxa bands ended up in the US. Today, using the British Columbia Treaty Process as a vehicle for rethinking how they govern, the five First Nations in Canada have made a conscious decision to reorganize themselves. In defiance of their colonial history, they have joined together to form the Ktunaxa Nation: an explicit rejection of historical fragmentation and its boundary legacy and an effort to give contemporary institutional form to an older identity that, while undermined by the imposed band structure, was never lost. Fundamentally, it is an attempt to reconstitute the nation. As one Ktunaxa leader said, "I don't know if we'll get a treaty out of this BC Treaty Process, but we'll get a government out of it, and it will be a Ktunaxa government."[11] According to the Nation's website, "The Elders of the Ktunaxa Nation often refer to the past hundred and fifty or so years as a time when the Nation 'went to sleep' ... The process of building a modern Ktunaxa government is likened to 'waking up.'"[12] In 2010, the Nation held its annual general meeting of citizens in Bonners Ferry, Idaho in the US, with citizens of the US groups in attendance, underlining the idea that the Ktunaxa remain, even today, a single people.

Question 2: How much boundary-crossing does each institutional innovation involve?

Institutional scope is not the only thing that varies in these examples. So do the boundaries being crossed. Multiple boundaries are in play. They include more or less obvious ones, such as the political boundaries established by recognition by an external government, the administrative boundaries that reflect that government's convenience, the boundaries of citizenship, the geographical boundaries demarcating reserved space or title, and the international boundaries that sometimes divide Indigenous nations. But they also include less tangible or easily specified boundaries, such as those embedded in language, culture, identity, and more.

Some innovations cross more boundaries than others. At the more modest end of the scale, few boundaries are involved – perhaps only one – while at the other end an innovation may involve multiple boundaries of various kinds. So, for example, the Grand Council of the Crees crosses few boundaries. It disregards the locally based administrative boundaries operating under the Indian Act but, in asserting a more comprehensive Cree boundary, operates within a shared identity, language, and culture. On the other hand, the inter-tribal courts of the US involve, in some cases, significant boundary crossing as distinct peoples and multiple tribal governments agree to defer to a common judicial structure. While the Gwich'in Gathering and Gwich'in Steering Committee cross boundaries between different Gwich'in groups and locales, both remain within the reach of shared Gwich'in language, culture, and identity. But they also straddle the US-Canada international boundary. The Coastal First Nations, with their Great Bear Initiative, and the Meadow Lake Tribal Council do not deal directly with international boundaries, but both cases involve crossing linguistic, cultural, and cognitive boundaries, as well as the administrative ones that all Canadian First Nations face. The Noongar Nation crosses clan and locational boundaries but asserts a common Noongar identity, and the Thamarrurr Regional Council links distinct but related peoples. On the other hand, the West Central Arnhem Regional Authority, in its most recent manifestation, is working across not only clan but linguistic, cultural, and geographical divides as well.

As this suggests, however, there is more than multiplicity involved. Some boundaries are more difficult to cross than others. For example, the Ktunaxa Nation links four Ktunaxa and one Shuswap group – all within British Columbia – in an emerging governmental structure. It is already an ambitious effort. But should the Nation try to extend that structure across the US-Canada boundary to include the two Ktunaxa groups who ended up on the US side of the line, it will find itself with an even more difficult challenge, as the Tohono O'odham Nation knows only too well.

COMPARING INSTITUTIONAL INNOVATIONS

Institutional scope and extent of boundary crossing are two different dimensions of innovation in these emergent governmental institutions. Treating institutional scope as an x-axis and boundary-crossing as a y-axis yields a two-dimensional space into which we can sort the examples from the previous section (Figure 2.1). Scope broadens to the right along the x-axis; boundary-crossing rises along the y-axis.

One thing that is missing from this picture is change. The figure is a snapshot of dynamic processes. Each case has a history and a future and we should expect change in some of these positions over time. Looking ahead, we might predict at least some movement to the right – that is, expansions of institutional scope. Some innovations may become more comprehensive over time as new relationships are built, new connections begin to pay off, new horizons for self-governance open up, or nations become more comfortable with new institutional arrangements and attempt to expand them.

Movement up, on the other hand – crossing additional boundaries – may be more difficult to accomplish, particularly when encountering well-established cultural or cognitive boundaries or de jure political ones, such as international borders. It clearly can be done, but it may take longer to accomplish.

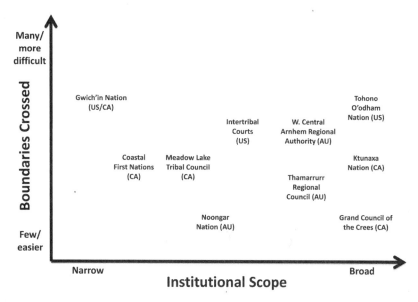

Figure 2.1   Scope and boundary-crossing in ten examples of Indigenous institutional innovation

All of the cases summarized here are notably consolidational: they either enact or envision larger units of self-determination and self-governance. While some are limited to narrow policy or institutional domains – US inter-tribal courts, for example, or the Meadow Lake Tribal Council – all represent a reach towards more comprehensive units of action. This may be simply an artifact of the sample and of the particular histories involved, and there are counter-examples out there. The Māori situation in Aotearoa/New Zealand offers one. Policies that encourage *iwi* – often translated as tribes – as the primary bases of Indigenous economic and political organization have sometimes encountered opposition from *hapu* – often translated as subtribes. Māori self-determination may be as likely to disaggregate some units as to consolidate them (see Durie 1998, chapter 8, and O'Sullivan 2007). But the consolidational pattern may also reflect the fact, learned by Indigenous nations through hard experience, that politics often rewards larger scale. Of course, consolidation may fit some colonial interests as well; at the very least, it simplifies administrative tasks. But in the cases touched on here, this offers small consolation to the colonizer, for in each one we see Indigenous peoples moving to expand their political power.

TURNING THE TABLES

For more than two centuries, non-Indigenous forces reshaped Indigenous boundaries and attached their own meanings to the entities that
resulted. Now, in the ten cases briefly summarized here and in others
like them, Indigenous peoples are turning the tables, asserting power
via units or structures that either depart from externally established and
supported models or were not conceived as vehicles for the range of
power now being claimed.

I have called all of these boundary challenges, but some are more challenging than others. As Indigenous innovations move up and to the right
within the two-dimensional space in Figure 2.1, they animate boundaries or claim governing powers that are increasingly at odds with external assumptions about who constitutes the nation or people, how the
nation should organize, or what powers it can exercise. They may also
be at odds, in many cases, with their own recent histories and the learned
assumptions within them. On both counts, as they move up and to the
right, these institutional strategies become more challenging to the status
quo and more difficult to implement.

There is considerable practical force behind them. Reconstitution –
at least in the examples presented here – is not only about asserting
Indigenous identities or rejecting colonial boundaries. It is about practical problem solving. What boundaries make sense to the people whose
futures are at stake? What organizational structures provide adequate
governance tools for pursuing a people's objectives? How can small
nations increase their political power? What scale of organization
is likely to be most effective at enlisting citizen allegiance, mobilizing
resources, making decisions, or resolving disputes? How do you effectively manage fragmented lands? What kinds of institutions are required
for resource management on ecosystem scales? What kinds of relationships make sense with central governments? And so forth. In short, these
institutional innovations are Indigenous efforts to address practical governance challenges.

They also can be conceived as both bases and examples of what Lane
and Hibbard (2005, 182) call "transformative planning," planning that
alters the nature of Indigenous relationships with surrounding states.
They provide *bases* for such planning in that they launch planning processes from a new and largely Indigenously determined starting point.
The message to central government in effect is this: "We'll start planning
not from the point, organizationally and conceptually, where you put us

but from the point where we want and imagine ourselves to be." In this conception, Indigenous nations will build their own boundaries, choosing the markers and meanings that make sense to them, not the markers and meanings that make sense to someone else. And their planning will reflect the boundaries they create. Even in Australia, where government still imposes its own detailed ideas of how Indigenous peoples should organize and for what purposes, the people of Thamarrurr and of the West Central Arnhem Regional Authority chose for themselves how to operate within those imposed constraints. Their organizations may have been a response to external impositions, but the peoples involved chose how to respond and how to work within the spaces that those impositions left open to them.

At the same time, in their practical manifestations, these boundary challenges also provide examples of "transformative planning": here are Indigenous Nations that are building new organizational foundations for action. It is a fundamental kind of planning going on here, a necessary precursor to what development or land-use planning conventionally involves. It is an exploration of such questions as "who are we, and who do we want to be, and who should we choose to be in the circumstances we face?" For far too long, other entities, other powers, insisted on answering such questions for Indigenous peoples. Now, in a move towards substantive self-determination, they are answering those questions for themselves.

NOTES

1 I have benefitted greatly from conversations on this and related topics with Miriam Jorgensen, Joseph P. Kalt, and Diane Smith, and from comments on earlier versions of this paper from Randy Akee, members of the Native Nations Institute's research group at the University of Arizona, and participants in the International Roundtable on Indigenous Community Planning and Land Use Management, University of Saskatchewan, June 2010. I would like especially to thank Kim Doohan for her insights during the roundtable and Ryan Walker and Dave Natcher for their subsequent suggestions.

2 See, for numerous examples, Driver 1969 on North America generally; Cornell 1988b on the US; Sterritt et al. 1998 and Helm 2000 on different parts of western Canada; Sutton 1995 on Australia generally, and Ivory 2008, referring to Stanner 1964, on the Port Keats region.

3 This work is part of a larger comparative project examining changing patterns of Indigenous governance in Australia, Canada, the US, and Aotearoa/New Zealand. Time and resource constraints have limited the present discussion to the first three of these countries, but on Aotearoa/ New Zealand, see, for example, Ballara (1998), Van Meijl (1997), and O'Sullivan (2007).

4 In a presentation at the University of Arizona's James E. Rogers College of Law, November 2005. See also Royal Commission on Aboriginal Peoples (1996).

5 See, for example, Spicer 1962 on the San Carlos Apaches, Meyer 1967 on the Santee Sioux, and Walker 1968 on the Nez Perce, all discussing the gradual replacement, through the reservation system, of localized ties by more comprehensive political and administrative organization and, eventually, identity; and more generally, Cornell 1988b.

6 See http://www.fortyukon.org/gathering_schedule.pdf, accessed 28 September 2010.

7 See http://coastalfirstnations.ca/ and http://www.moore.org/init-newsitem.aspx?id=3180, both accessed 28 September 2010.

8 See http://mltc.sasktelwebhosting.com/index.htm, accessed 22 September 2010.

9 See Barcham (2008); also http://www.noongar.org.au/images/pdf/newsletters/swALSC_NewsletterFeb2010.pdf, accessed 3 June 2010, especially p. 2. The Noongar effort has not been entirely successful; see Maddison (2009, 137–38).

10 On the Southwest Intertribal Court of Appeals, see http://www.ailc-inc.org/swITCA.htm, accessed 21 September 2010 ; on the Intertribal Court of Southern California, see http://www.icsc.us/Welcome.html, accessed 21 September 2010; on the Northwest Intertribal Court System, see http://www.nics.ws/, accessed 21 September 2010, as well as Harvard Project on American Indian Economic Development (2003).

11 Personal communication.

12 "Ktunaxa History Timeline," http://www.ktunaxa.org/downloads/4pillars/language/timeline.pdf, accessed 3 June 2010, 25–6; also Dolan (2009).

REFERENCES

Alfred, Taiaiake. 2005. *Wasáse: Indigenous Pathways of Action and Freedom.* Toronto: University of Toronto Press.

Anderson, Gary Clayton. 1999. *The Indian Southwest, 1580–1830: Ethnogenesis and Reinvention.* Norman: University of Oklahoma Press.

Awashish, Philip. 2005. "From Board to Nation Governance: The Evolution of Eeyou Tapay-Tah-Jeh-Souwin (Eeyou Governance) in Eeyou Istchee." In *Canada: The State of the Federation 2003: Reconfiguring Aboriginal-State Relations*, edited by Michael Murphy. Montreal and Kingston: McGill-Queen's University Press, for the Institute of Intergovernmental Relations.

Ballara, Angela. 1998. *Iwi: The Dynamics of Māori Tribal Organization from c. 1769 to c. 1945*. Wellington: Victoria University Press.

Barcham, Manuhuia. 2008. "Noongar Nation." In *Contested Governance: Culture, Power, and Institutions in Indigenous Australia*, edited by Janet Hunt, Diane Smith, Stephanie Garling, and Will Sanders. CAEPR research monograph no. 29. Canberra: The Australian National University E Press, 265–82.

Bass, Rick. 2004. *Caribou Rising: Defending the Porcupine Herd, Gwich-'in Culture, and the Arctic National Wildlife Refuge*. San Francisco: Sierra Club Books.

Castillo, Guadalupe, and Margo Cowan, eds. 2001. *It Is not Our Fault: The Case for Amending Present Nationality Law to Make all Members of the Tohono O'odham Nation United States Citizens, Now and Forever*. Sells, Arizona: Executive Branch, Tohono O'odham Nation.

Cornell, Stephen. 1988a. *The Return of the Native: American Indian Political Resurgence*. New York: Oxford University Press.

– 1988b. "The Transformations of Tribe: Organization and Self-Concept in Native American Ethnicities." *Ethnic and Racial Studies* 11, no. 1 (January):27–47.

– 2007. "Organizing Indigenous Governance in Canada, Australia, and the United States." In *Aboriginal Policy Research, Vol. 4: Moving Forward, Making a Difference*, edited by Jerry P. White, Susan Wingert, Dan Beavon, and Paul Maxim. Toronto: Thompson Educational Publishing.

Cornell, Stephen, and Douglas Hartmann. 2007. *Ethnicity and Race: Making Identities in a Changing World*, second edition. Thousand Oaks: Pine Forge Press.

Dolan, Jamie. 2009. "The Ktunaxa Nation: Reclaiming Self-Governance, Rebuilding a Nation." Unpublished field report. Native Nations Institute for Leadership, Management, and Policy, University of Arizona.

Doohan, Kim. 2008. *Making Things Come Good: Relations between Aborigines and Miners at Argyle*. Broome: Backroom Press.

Driver, Harold E. 1969. *Indians of North America*, second edition. Chicago: University of Chicago Press.

Durie, Mason. 1998. *Te Mana, Te Kāwanatanga: The Politics of Māori Self-Determination*. Auckland: Oxford University Press.

Gwich'in Steering Committee. 2005. *A Moral Choice for the United States: The Human Rights Implications for the Gwich'in of Drilling in the Arctic National Wildlife Refuge.* Fairbanks: Gwich'in Steering Committee.

Hämäläinen, Pekka. 2008. *The Comanche Empire.* New Haven: Yale University Press.

Harvard Project on American Indian Economic Development. 2003. *Honoring Nations: Celebrating Excellence in Tribal Government.* Cambridge: Harvard Project on American Indian Economic Development.

Helm, June. 2000. *The People of Denendeh: Ethnohistory of the Indians of Canada's Northwest Territories.* Iowa City: University of Iowa Press.

Holcombe, Sarah. 2004. "Socio-Political Perspectives on Localism and Regionalism in the Pintupi Luritja Region of Central Australia: Implications for Service Delivery and Governance." Working paper no. 25. Canberra: Centre for Aboriginal Economic Policy Research, The Australian National University.

Howitt, Richie. 2001. "Frontiers, Borders, Edges: Liminal Challenges to the Hegemony of Exclusion." *Australian Geographical Studies* 39, no. 2 (July):233–45.

Hunt, J., and D.E. Smith. 2006. "Building Indigenous Community Governance in Australia: Preliminary Research Findings." Working paper no. 31/2006. Canberra: Centre for Aboriginal Economic Policy Research, The Australian National University.

Ivory, Bill. 2008. "Indigenous Leaders and Leadership: Agents of Networked Governance." In *Contested Governance: Culture, Power, and Institutions in Indigenous Australia*, edited by Janet Hunt, Diane Smith, Stephanie Garling, and Will Sanders, 233–62. CAEPR research monograph no. 29. Canberra: The Australian National University E Press.

– 2009. "*Kunmanggur*, Legend and Leadership: A Study of Indigenous Leadership and Success Focusing on the Northwest Region of the Northern Territory of Australia." Doctoral dissertation in progress. Charles Darwin University.

Jojola, Ted. 2008. "Indigenous Planning – An Emerging Context." *Canadian Journal of Urban Research* 17, no. 1 (Summer).

Jorgensen, Miriam, ed. 2007. *Rebuilding Native Nations: Strategies for Governance and Development.* Tucson: University of Arizona Press.

Lane, Marcus B., and Michael Hibbard. 2005. "Doing It for Themselves: Transformative Planning by Indigenous Peoples." *Journal of Planning Education and Research* 25:172–84.

Maddison, Sarah. 2009. *Black Politics: Inside the Complexity of Aboriginal Political Culture.* Sydney: Allen & Unwin.

Meeks, Eric V. 2007. *Border Citizens: The Making of Indians, Mexicans, and Anglos in Arizona.* Austin: University of Texas Press.

Meyer, Roy W. 1967. *History of the Santee Sioux: United States Indian Policy on Trial.* Lincoln: University of Nebraska Press.

Mills, Antonia. 1994. *Eagle Down Is Our Law: Witsuwit'en Law, Feasts, and Land Claims.* Vancouver: UBC Press.

Myers, Fred R. 1991. *Pintupi Country, Pintupi Self: Sentiment, Place, and Politics among Western Desert Aborigines.* Berkeley: University of California Press.

Niezen, Ronald. 1998. *Defending the Land: Sovereignty and Forest Life in James Bay Cree Society.* Boston: Allyn and Bacon.

O'Sullivan, Dominic. 2007. *Beyond Biculturalism: The Politics of an Indigenous Minority.* Wellington: Huia Books.

Papillon, Martin. 2008. "Federalism from Below: The Emergence of Multilevel Governance in Canada: A Comparison of the James Bay Crees and the Kahnawá:ke Mohawks." Unpublished doctoral dissertation. University of Toronto.

Peters, Evelyn J. 1999. "Geographies of Aboriginal Self-Government." In *Aboriginal Self-Government in Canada*, edited by John H. Hylton, 411–30. Saskatoon: Purich Publishing.

Ross, Anne, Kathleen Pickering Sherman, Jeffrey G. Snodgrass, Henry D. Delcore, and Richard Sherman. 2011. *Indigenous Peoples and the Collaborative Stewardship of Nature: Knowledge Binds and Institutional Conflicts.* Walnut Creek: Left Coast Press.

Royal Commission on Aboriginal Peoples. 1996. *People to People, Nation to Nation: Highlights from the Report of the Royal Commission on Aboriginal Peoples.* Ottawa: Royal Commission on Aboriginal Peoples.

Salisbury, Richard F. 1986. *A Homeland for the Cree: Regional Development in James Bay 1971–1981.* Montreal and Kingston: McGill-Queen's University Press.

Scott, James C. 1998. *Seeing Like a State: How Certain Schemes to Improve the Human Condition Have Failed.* New Haven: Yale University Press.

Sletto, Bjørn. 2009. "'Indigenous people don't have boundaries': Reborderings, Fire Management, and Production of Authenticities in Indigenous Landscapes." *Cultural Geographies* 16 (April):253–77.

Smith, Diane. 2004. "From Gove to Governance: Reshaping Indigenous Governance in the Northern Territory." Discussion paper 265. Canberra: Centre for Aboriginal Economic Policy Research, The Australian National University.

– 2008. "Cultures of Governance and the Governance of Culture: Trans-
forming and Containing Indigenous Institutions in West Arnhem Land."
In *Contested Governance: Culture, Power, and institutions in Indigenous
Australia*, edited by Janet Hunt, Diane Smith, Stephanie Garling, and Will
Sanders, 75–111. CAEPR research monograph no. 29. Canberra: The Austral-
ian National University E Press.

Spicer, Edward H. 1962. *Cycles of Conquest: The Impact of Spain, Mexico,
and the United States on the Indians of the Southwest, 1533–1960.* Tucson:
University of Arizona Press.

Stanner, W.E.H. 1964. *On Aboriginal Religion.* Oceania monograph no. 11.
Sydney: University of Sydney Press.

Starks, Rachel Rose, Jen McCormack, and Stephen Cornell. 2011. *Native
Nations and U.S. Borders: Challenges to Culture, Citizenship, and Security.*
Tucson: Udall Center for Studies in Public Policy, The University of
Arizona.

Sterritt, Neil J., Susan Marsden, Robert Galois, Peter R. Grant, and Richard
Overstall. 1998. *Tribal Boundaries in the Nass Watershed.* Vancouver: UBC
Press.

Sutton, Peter. 1995. "Country: Aboriginal Boundaries and Land Ownership in
Australia." *Aboriginal History Monograph Series*, no. 3. Canberra: Aboriginal History Inc.

Taylor, John. 2004. *Social Indicators for Aboriginal Governance: Insights from
the Thamarrurr Region, Northern Territory.* Research monograph no. 24.
Canberra: Centre for Aboriginal Economic Policy Research, The Australian
National University.

– 2005. "Population and Patterns of Residence." In *Macquarie Atlas of
Indigenous Australia: Culture and Society through Space and Time*, edited
by Bill Arthur and Frances Morphy, 66–77. North Ryde, New South Wales:
Macquarie Library Pty Ltd.

Tilly, Charles. 2005. *Identities, Boundaries, and Social Ties.* Boulder: Paradigm
Publishers.

Tonkinson, Robert. 1974. *The Jigalong Mob: Aboriginal Victors of the Desert
Crusade.* Menlo Park: Cummings Publishing.

Trosper, Ronald L. 1976. "Native American Boundary Maintenance: The
Flathead Indian Reservation, Montana, 1860–1970." *Ethnicity* 3, no. 3
(September).

Van Meijl, Toon. 1997. "The Reemergence of Māori Chiefs: 'Devolution' as a
Strategy to Maintain Tribal Authority." In *Chiefs Today: Traditional Pacific
Leadership and the Postcolonial State*, edited by Geoffrey M. White and
Lamont Lindstrom, 84–107. Stanford: Stanford University Press.

Walker, Deward E., Jr. 1968. *Conflict and Schism in Nez Perce Acculturation: A Study of Religion and Politics*. Pullman: Washington State University Press.

Young, Elspeth. 1995. "Aboriginal Frontiers and Boundaries." In appendix 1 of "Country: Aboriginal Boundaries and Land Ownership in Australia" by Peter Sutton, 88–92. *Aboriginal History Monograph Series*, no 3. Canberra: Aboriginal History Inc.

3

The Past as Present: Film as a Community Planning Intervention in Native/Non-Native Relations in British Columbia, Canada

LEONIE SANDERCOCK AND GIOVANNI ATTILI[1]

Volume one, part one of the *Royal Commission on Aboriginal Peoples* (1996) posed the following question: "How do participants move away from a relationship characterized by disparity in power, violations of trust, and lingering unresolved disputes? How do they move toward a relationship of power sharing, mutual respect, and joint problem solving?"

This question poses many challenges for planners working with/in Indigenous communities in Canada. For much of the past century, it has been argued that planners have been part of the problem rather than part of the solution (Jojola 1998, 2008; Porter 2010; Sandercock 2004; Hibbard and Lane 2004; Lane and Hibbard 2005). Western planning has been deeply implicated in the colonization process and still operates for the most part as a form of colonialism, imposing an alien worldview that ignores traditional knowledge and cultural identity and refuses to recognize Indigenous claims to land and sovereignty (Jojola 2008). The spatial technologies of power that planners wield, such as the laws of private property, the practices of surveying, naming, mapping, as well as the processes of urban and regional planning, continue to reinforce patterns of domination and segregation established in the colonization process (Jacobs 1996; Jackson 1998; Sandercock 2004; Stanger-Ross 2008).

Is there a way forward? Can planning practices be decolonized and move towards a relationship of power sharing, mutual respect, and joint problem solving, thereby addressing the vexed question raised by the

Royal Commission? Can planning work in a transformative way to confront the history of toxic relationships between Native and non-Native Canadians, relationships that are inscribed in the ordering of space, in the lines drawn on maps (Harris 1997, 2002)?

For the past five years the authors have been working with and documenting the struggles of two First Nations in north-central British Columbia (BC), subtribes of the Carrier Nation, tracing their journey from colonization to revitalization, and to partnerships in economic and social development with non-Native neighbours. This project has involved the making of a documentary, *Finding Our Way* (Attili and Sandercock 2010), in collaboration with the Cheslatta Carrier Nation and the Ts'il Kaz Koh First Nation, followed by screenings and community dialogues that used the film as a catalyst for difficult conversations in a historically deeply divided community. As planners, we have been exploring the use of film as a tool for encouraging healing and reconciliation, as well as a way of engaging deeply divided communities in a joint visioning process. This chapter tells the why and how of that story and reflects on outcomes thus far.[2]

We begin with a brief overview of First Nations in BC, pre-contact and post-contact. That is followed by an outline of our conceptual lenses, grounded in two complementary literatures: one addresses the prospects of decolonizing and transformative planning with/in/by Indigenous communities, the other explores digital ethnography (Attili 2007; Sandercock and Attili 2010a, 2010b, 2011) as a form of phronetic social science (Flyvbjerg 2001; Flyvbjerg et al. 2012) that is designed to expose injustice and to ask "what might be done?" We then proceed to describe how and why we worked collaboratively with these two First Nations communities to document their stories of dispossession and struggles for revitalization; how we collaboratively designed a process for returning the film to the deeply divided community of Burns Lake, using it as a catalyst for dialogue about the past, present, and future, and the kinds of community planning work that are now proceeding, in part at least as an outcome of the film. Finally, we reflect on the role of film as a dialogical tool in the process of communicative and transformative planning based on our work over the past five years.

THE "RESETTLEMENT" OF BRITISH COLUMBIA

Long before the appearance of European explorers, fur traders, then settlers in the northwest part of the North American continent now known as British Columbia, this land was home to between 250,000 and 400,000 Native people (Harris 1997; Muckle 2007; Tobey 1981). Nations identified by six or seven language families occupied traditional homelands across the extent of BC, from more densely settled coastal areas to the more sparsely settled interior (McMillan and Yellowhorn 2004, 6–7). They lived off the land, had extensive trade networks, and highly organized systems of governance characterized by hereditary chiefs, and elaborate ceremonies such as the potlatch, which had political, economic, and social purposes (McMillan and Yellowhorn 2004, chapter 8).

By 1835, after forty years of limited contact, the Native population had declined to 100,000, and by 1885 after extensive settlement of Vancouver Island and the lower mainland by Europeans, there was an even more drastic decline to 28,000, a 90–95 per cent reduction from pre-European times (Muckle 2007). By 1891, Natives were little more than a quarter of the BC population. In 1921, they were 4 per cent. In half a century, a largely immigrant society had been put in place, systematically displacing Native people from their traditional territories.

The settlers brought with them not only infectious diseases but, even more devastating to Native life, the desire and the tools to colonize the land and its original inhabitants. What is now BC became a colony of the British Crown in 1858 and a member of the Dominion of Canada in 1871. Depopulation as a result of contagious diseases like smallpox was quickly followed by deterritorialization as a result of colonial land policies, arguably the first Western planning instruments that set out systematically to destroy the land-based Native economies and ways of life. In the eyes of most British Columbians, "Natives stood in the way of progress and development" (Harris 1997, 271). The reserve system of Indian lands was the solution to the land hunger of immigrants, relegating Natives to tiny patches of marginal land where they were condemned to poverty for lack of a land base. The spatial confinement of Natives began almost as soon as a colony was created. The first reserve was laid out in 1852. Over the next several decades, hundreds of similar reserves were laid out as BC was divided into two vastly unequal parts that came to underlie all its other developments: a tiny fraction of the land set aside for Natives, the rest available, in various tenures, for development. "The lines separating the Indian reserves from the rest became, in a sense, the primal line on the land of BC, the one that facilitated or constrained all others" (Harris 2002, xviii).

The colony, then province, of BC as a settler society, had been adamant from the earliest days of settlement that Native title did not exist, that Natives had no prior claim to the lands they had occupied since time immemorial. With the exception of fourteen early treaties on Vancouver Island and Treaty 8, which spilled over from Alberta into northeastern BC, no treaties were ever negotiated in compensation for the vast territorial dispossession that took place in the second half of the nineteenth century and the early years of the twentieth century. After Confederation in 1871 the new Dominion of Canada began to assert its authority in the western part of the country, seeking to extinguish any Aboriginal claims to land by signing the so-called "numbered treaties" (McMillan and Yellowhorn 2007). Yet BC remained the "anomaly" (Ray 1999), remaining outside the treaty process and refusing to acknowledge or enter into any discussion about Native title, in spite of ongoing Native resistance to colonial land appropriation (Galois 1992; Tennant 1990).

By the time BC joined the Dominion in 1871, there were 140 reserves. By 1898 that number had grown to a thousand, and by the 1930s there were 1,536 small reserves scattered across the province, a reserve geography with no close North American equivalent (Harris 2002, 263). Natives were now confined to 835,000 acres, little more than a third of one percent of the land base of the province (Harris 2002, 261). This was the product of the pervasive settler assumptions, backed by the colonial state, that most of the land they encountered in BC was waste, waiting to be put to productive use, or, where there was some Native use, that these uses were inefficient and should be replaced (Harris 2002, 263).

After 1871 the Native population of Canada was subjected to the federal policy of assimilation, first through the Indian Act of 1876, which took away their sovereignty and made them wards of the state, then through the Indian residential schools, which forcibly removed children from their families, forbade them to speak their language, and, according to official documents, was intended to destroy the culture by killing the Indian in the Native child (Milloy 1999). One hundred and fifty thousand children were taken from their homes by police and priests and placed in these schools. In some decades, as many as forty per cent of those children died there as a result of diseases, physical cruelty, or attempting to run away. Historian John Molloy has described this as a "national crime" and in 2008 the prime minister of Canada formally apologized to Aboriginal people for this policy of assimilation and acknowledged that much of the ongoing dysfunction in Native communities is directly linked to the intergenerational effects of the Indian residential schools.

By the early twenty-first century, 203 First Nations in BC were recorded under the Indian Act, seventeen of them Carrier bands ("band" being the Indian Act terminology for formerly sovereign Nations and their subtribes). Traditional Carrier territory, located in north-central BC, stretches from the Rocky Mountains in the east to the Lakes District in central BC. Nineteenth-century Catholic missionary Father Morice recorded the names and locations of more than twenty Carrier villages between 1893 and 1895 (Tobey 1981) and three distinct dialects. The Carrier had early encounters with Europeans through fur trading posts in their territory but the remoteness of their lands from the Lower Mainland protected them from major colonial impact until the completion of the northern transcontinental railway in 1913. The anticipated land rush following the railway prompted the provincial government to force the Carrier on to reserves between 1913 and 1916. By the 1920s, their children were being taken away to the Lejac Residential School, which operated until the 1970s.

Our work is situated in this Carrier (Dakelh) region, and our story will focus on the struggles of one of the Carrier subtribes, the Ts'il Kaz Koh Nation, more widely known as the Burns Lake Band. This band had been allocated four hundred acres of reserve land in 1914, but lost one third of it the following year when the town site for what is now the village of Burns Lake was laid out. That expropriation marked the beginning of what has been a century-long battle between the band and the village, a battle that culminated in a confrontation in 1999–2000 that ended up in the Supreme Court of BC. What had begun apparently as a municipal water and sewer issue was transformed into an Indigenous rights/human rights issue that exposed the ongoing operations of colonialism at the municipal level (Sandercock and Attili 2012). That was the trigger for our involvement in this community. But before we embark on that story, we present an overview of our conceptual lenses.

CHANGING THE LENS: THEORIES AND METHODS

Soon after the release of our first documentary, *Where Strangers Become Neighbours* (Attili and Sandercock 2007), we were invited to Burns Lake by Pauline Goertzen, a local anti-racism coordinator and community activist. She had seen our film, which tackled racism in an immigrant community in Vancouver, and thought we might be interested in the story that was unfolding in her community about a different kind of race relations. Pauline had been mentored in anti-racism work by Norma-Jean McLaren, with whom Leonie was teaching cross-cultural planning at UBC. Norma-Jean had also been involved in diversity training with the RCMP in Burns Lake and in community healing work following the Supreme Court case. Through Norma-Jean and Pauline we heard about the dispute over land and taxation which had resulted in the Burns Lake Band taking the village to the Supreme Court of BC and winning in 1999, and the village responding by shutting off water, sewer, and fire services to the reserve in the year 2000, in the middle of winter, in a region where temperatures are typically around minus 30 degrees Celsius. How could such an instance of "municipal colonialism" (Stanger-Ross 2008) happen in twenty-first-century Canada, a country with an international reputation as a defender of human rights? Was this an anomaly, or an instance of an ongoing history of colonization?

But we also heard a very different story about this same town. In 2005 some of the local youth had come together, Native and non-Native (along with a non-Native musician and music teacher), and written and performed a song about racism and violence in their town, calling their song "Leave it Behind." This raised another question of whether and how, amidst a history of segregation and conflict, some people were struggling to change things. How well were they faring?

As planners, we had written about the "dark side of planning" (Sandercock 1998a, 1998b) – that is, the operations of power through which planning comes to serve the interests of dominant cultures and classes at the expense and exclusion of the less powerful. We were particularly interested in the role of planning in settler societies in so far as it served to render Indigenous populations invisible, to deny them rights, to exacerbate their geographical and economic marginalization, and to provide them with culturally inappropriate programs and services (Jojola 1998, 2008; Sandercock 1998b, 2004; Jackson 1998). We brought a social justice orientation to our work, grounded in theories of radical planning (Friedmann 1987), insurgent planning (Sandercock 1998a), and empowerment planning (Reardon 2003). And we were interested in the literature on transformative planning with/in Indigenous communities (Hibbard and Lane 2004; Lane and Hibbard 2005) and the fundamental challenge to mainstream planning practice expressed in the concept of decolonizing planning (Jackson 1998; Porter 2004, 2010).

We had also, as a research team, begun to explore the potential of film as a catalyst for social transformation (Sandercock and Attili 2009,

2010a, 2010b, 2012). Our first film had investigated anti-immigrant sentiment in a rapidly changing neighbourhood in Vancouver and how there had been a shift towards building an inclusive community through the work of a community-based organization with whom we had become involved. We used that film in workshops in five cities across Canada as a catalyst for dialogue about the social integration of immigrants through a community development approach, and we had found the film to be a far more powerful tool than those typically used by planners in engagement processes (Sandercock and Attili 2010a; Sarkissian and Hurford 2010).

In the past two decades there has been a dawning recognition in the planning community that planning practices have all too often been used to render Indigenous communities invisible, to exclude them, silence them, and further marginalize them. Indigenous communities, for their part, have long been mobilizing to fight for their rights to land, voice, autonomy, economic opportunity, and more (Galois 1992; Jojola 2008; Lane and Hibbard 2005), and in the process, complex cross-cultural conflicts have unfolded. These conflicts have brought to the surface issues of knowledge and who is deemed to possess it; of power and how it is used (the spatial technologies of power that planners wield); of process (how certain processes exclude certain peoples); and of land and property rights and the incommensurability of Western and Indigenous ways of thinking about these (Smith 1999; Bishop 2005; Wilson 2008; Little Bear 2009).

An even more challenging perspective for non-Indigenous planners is the recognition that planning has been deeply implicated in the colonization process, historically through its spatial technologies of power and still today in its contemporary processes of consultation or inclusion, which fail to acknowledge Aboriginal rights, title, or sovereignty. In other words, as several authors have cogently argued (Matunga 2000; Jojola 2008; Porter 2010), planning itself must be decolonized if it wants to present itself as an ethical practice. Porter (2010) describes the task in the title of her book as "unlearning the colonial cultures of planning." She argues that changing planners' attitudes and values is not enough. What is required is "the ability to focus on moments within institutional rules and parameters where real and lasting change can be achieved," which means using state-based systems to find "strategic moments of opportunity that can result in recognition of Indigenous rights and responsibilities and the material privileges that should ultimately flow" (Porter 2004, 109).

Hibbard and Lane (2004) maintain that the failure of state planning to serve Indigenous peoples, a failure to understand, respect, and give expression to distinct Indigenous needs in the use and management of land, contradicts the ethical potential of planning. But they also describe cases in which Indigenous agency has reshaped state-society relations, using planning as a means to achieve sovereignty and as a means of rebuilding community and culture. Lane and Hibbard (2005, 182) describe such an approach as "transformative planning by Indigenous peoples," a deliberate attempt to transform the institutional bases of Indigenous subjugation and dependence that has resulted in a "rough justice for Indigenous peoples," (but justice nevertheless) involving shared jurisdiction over custodial lands and a degree of autonomy to shape community destiny. Implicit in the work of Porter, Jojola, and Lane and Hibbard is an argument that unless non-Native planners assist Indigenous communities in this struggle they are still part of the problem rather than part of the solution. We would argue with Jojola (2008, 45) that this amounts to no less than a "long-overdue paradigm shift" for mainstream planning, and it is within such a paradigm shift that we aim to work.

Given this conceptual framework, we have also been attracted to the work of Flyvbjerg (2001) and others (Flyvbjerg et al. 2012) who have developed an action-oriented approach to research which Flyvbjerg has called "phronetic social science," or value-rational research. When we screen our films in academic settings we sometimes receive the comment/question: "It's powerful, it's moving, but is it science?" One answer to this question is that we are not doing science, we are doing social change work. Rather than doing academic "fieldwork," we describe what we do as collaborative planning and collaborative film making for social change purposes. But Flyvbjerg has given us an effective language for addressing the question of whether this is "real social science." Value-rational research, as he describes it, is an approach that, by explicitly focusing on values, can effectively deal with public deliberation and praxis. Using this approach, the point of departure is a series of classic value-rational questions: Where are we going? Is it desirable? What should be done? For anyone in the planning and policy fields, researchers, or practitioners, these questions ought to be central to praxis, along with their obvious companions, "Who gains and who loses, through what kinds of power relations? What possibilities are there for changing existing power relations? And is it desirable to do so?" (Flyvbjerg 2001, 130–31).

Working with this approach, we look at what has happened in Burns Lake historically and in the present day. Who has gained and who has lost by the historic and current mechanisms of power operating in this particular socio-cultural landscape? We ask whether this has been fair or desirable according to the espoused values of Canadian society today, values expressed in the Constitution Act of 1982 and the Charter of Rights and Freedoms passed by the national parliament. And we collaboratively explore with key actors in the town whether there is a way forward and what that might look like. What should be done, and how might our research contribute to transformational planning (that is, social change) through our research design?

The final piece of our conceptual framework links digital ethnography with phronetic social science and collaborative (or communicative) planning. We situate ourselves within a postpositivist framework that embraces story, or narrative, as a means of inquiry and a form of meaning-making, associating ourselves thereby with the "story turn" in planning (Sandercock 2004; Sandercock and Attili 2010b, 2012). Attili (2007) has elaborated the idea of digital ethnography to describe a research perspective through which the communicative potentialities of an ethnographic analysis are widened by the use of digital languages. The language of film can give expression to a dense qualitative analysis of social phenomena in a territorial context. It can be used to give thick and complex accounts of a city or community focused on stories, interviews, and narration. Qualitative analysis succeeds in expressing what lies beyond the surface of maps, physical objects, classifications, and aggregate quantitative data. Using film enables us to explore and convey what normally remains invisible in planning, and implicitly questions the way planners typically explore, analyze, and represent space. Our joint work has evolved into an exploration of the potential of film as a mode of inquiry, a form of meaning-making, a way of knowing, and a way of provoking public dialogue and community engagement around planning and policy issues. Our intent is that this is a contribution to transformative planning.

With this conceptual background, we were eager to see whether there was a role for us as researchers/planners/filmmakers in helping to bring about a shift towards more equitable economic, social, and political relations between Native and non-Native peoples in Burns Lake (and possibly beyond). We became involved in a local struggle for both reconciliation and the decolonization of planning at the invitation of one local activist. And we brought with us these conceptual tools along with technology and artistry, specifically film as an expression of the power of story; and our values as planners, our epistemology and ontology, which are grounded in an "unlearning of the colonial cultures of planning."

Thus began a three-stage, five-year (and still continuing) action research project using film as a way of approaching collaborative and transformative planning: as a mode of inquiry, a form of meaning-making, and as a planning intervention. We were invited to the town by one activist (who was known locally as "the anti-racism lady") as potential storytellers, and we set about meeting and talking with as many people as possible, Native and non-Native, to get a sense of the scope and complexity of the story, and eventually to develop a collaboration with both the village and the band. We had close to a hundred conversations over a twelve-month period with Native and non-Native people, Elders and youths, the mayor and four chiefs (from six local First Nations), community activists, business and religious leaders, school teachers, and the staff sergeant of the Royal Canadian Mounted Police (RCMP). By the time we started filming, we had a collaborative relationship with two First Nations (the Burns Lake Band and the Cheslatta Carrier Nation) and the village of Burns Lake. Eventually, we recorded fifty interviews on camera, ranging in length between ten minutes and three hours. All interviews cited in the text that follows are those that appear in the final cut of the film, *Finding Our Way*. For reasons of space and focus, we will not discuss that part of our film that deals with the Cheslatta story.[3]

The rest of this chapter discusses the role of film in a deeply divided community, asking to what extent it can open up a new space for dialogue about the past, present, and future. And, beyond dialogue, to what extent it can lead to action, to different ways of doing things, to alternative imaginings that can reshape the fragile coexistence of two peoples, Native and non-Native Canadians, towards reconciliation and partnership.

We begin with the story of the research, filming, and editing of *Finding Our Way*, explaining the "who, what, and why" of our collaborative filmmaking, our partners and purposes, fears and hopes. We then describe the action piece of the action research: how, with help from colleagues (see Appendix), we took the finished film back to the communities whose stories it tells, organized screenings followed by dialogue circles, evaluated that process, and then engaged in ongoing planning activities with these communities. Finally we discuss how, at the invitation of other communities in BC and beyond, and in partnership with First Nations colleagues, we are using the film as a planning intervention by working with its teaching and inspirational elements, and the ways in which we envisage expanding this work to include capacity-building with Native youth and developing a medium and longer term evaluation framework. In a concluding section of reflections, looking back as well as forward, we ask what has been achieved and in what ways film can be seen as a way of advancing transformative planning and contributing to the decolonization of planning in (post)colonial societies.[4] We also reflect on our own privileged positions as non-Indigenous filmmakers embedded in post-secondary institutions with access to research grants, distributors, and so on, by contrast with several generations of Indigenous filmmakers who preceded us and had some of the same intentions yet fewer opportunities.

FINDING OUR WAY: THE CONTEXT AND PROCESS OF THE
ACTION RESEARCH

Burns Lake, located on Highway 16 more or less midway between Prince Rupert on the coast and Prince George to the east, has a population of almost five thousand people, almost equally divided between First Nations and non-Native Canadians. According to Statistics BC, there are 2,100 non-Native residents, but First Nations are not included in their data. According to First Nations sources, there are close to 2,700 Indigenous residents divided among six Nations, the largest of which is the Lake Babine Nation with over two thousand members. While Native people had been living in this region for thousands of years, the settlers had only begun arriving after the completion of the northern transcontinental railway in 1913. Five hundred Carrier warriors had assembled on horseback on a ridge above the present-day town site in 1912 to express their opposition to the coming of the railway (interview with Burns Lake Band chief, Rob Charlie). Two years later, the Carrier were forced onto reserves by agents of the provincial government. The Burns Lake Band were allocated four hundred acres by the lake, but the following year the Burns Lake town site was laid out, appropriating a third of that allocation.

More land was appropriated for "community purposes" over the next fifty years, including a substantial acreage allocated to the Lake Babine Nation, who were forcibly removed from their traditional territory in the 1950s. As recently as 2005 another conflict erupted when the school district got funds for a new high school. The old high school had been built on band land and they now wanted that land returned to them along with the buildings on it. But while this was being discussed, the school district started to tear down the buildings, prompting the band to occupy the site. Eventually the band was given the land on a ninety-nine-year lease and they wanted to turn it into a Gathering Place for all the clans to replace their Feast House that had been torched by the Indian Agent in the 1950s (interviews with Ryan Tibbetts and Rob Charlie). The conflict had rubbed old wounds and the ongoing planning process of trying to get development permits for the new premises through the village's planning bureaucracy has been a further illustration of the persistence of a colonial planning process and mentality.

As filmmakers and researchers who are also community planners, we entered this northern community in 2006 with a very specific research question: What was the nature of the conflict between the village of Burns Lake and the Burns Lake Band that came to a head with the band taking the village to the Supreme Court of BC and winning its first ever victory in the colonizer's legal system, and the village retaliating by shutting off water and sewer services to the reserve? But we had many broader questions. What was the history of relations between the village and the band? What had changed, if anything, since the Supreme Court case? What opportunities and obstacles were there for First Nations' economic and social development? Why had some of the youth in the town written and performed an anti-racism song? Were they potential change agents? Who were the other change agents? And what might our role be?

The more we learned about the operations of power and privilege in Burns Lake, the more compelling we found the story to be. Our perception was that much of this was grounded in history. On the part of many (perhaps most) non-Native residents, there was a lack of awareness of the consequences of First Nations' lived experience of colonization, and particularly of the dysfunctional and intergenerational effects of Indian residential schools. And on the part of First Nations there was anger and frustration since historic injustices had never been acknowledged, were ongoing, and were not being addressed. In other words, the past was still very much present, distorting what contemporary goodwill existed, and blocking a path forward. This was particularly so because since the Supreme Court case there had been some significant changes in attitudes and social relations, as well as some attempt at a partnership approach to economic development (through a Community Forest joint venture), important changes in the operation of the new high school, and in relations between the band and the RCMP. Yet there were clearly ongoing struggles and frustration in the relationship between the village and the band.

The more we talked with Native people, the more we heard about healing, about the kinds of healing that they had undertaken, as individuals and as a community. What really began to strike us was that there had been very little healing between Native and non-Native folks, although a community healing project had been initiated after the Supreme Court case. We wondered how planning issues could be dealt with without further healing work across the cultural divide.

We began to conceive the film of the Burns Lake story as a way of encouraging a difficult dialogue, of changing the lens on the past. And because we wanted to encourage dialogue but were starting from a different point (a new lens), we envisaged a collaborative filmmaking process in which we were creating the space for new stories to be told, by voices hitherto unheard. The film would begin with an investigation of the causes of the events of 1999–2000, the Supreme Court case and the shutting off of the water and sewer, revealing not only a contemporary quarrel over the taxation of a mill on band land, but also the preceding eighty years of conflict between the village and the band over expropriated land. Then we would excavate even further, to uncover the story of colonization and its technologies of power, which had resulted in First Nations being forced onto reserves and subsequently losing some of that land to expansionist village activities. Finally, we would look at attempts from within the community to begin to shift these toxic relationships and pose the question, Is there a way forward?

We approached both the band and the village seeking their collaboration. We explained our ethical protocol, which was to bring back rough cuts of the film to the community (Native and non-Native) at every step of the editing process to ask for their input; to offer every individual whom we interviewed the opportunity to withdraw from the film if they didn't like how we used their words; and to bring the final cut back to the community for a community-wide dialogue. (At the same time, we were always conscious that there was an asymmetrical power relationship embedded in our presence as outsiders, from the university, and also aware of our ultimate authorial responsibility.)

We asked our collaborators what they would like to see come out of such a process. The mayor, Bernice Magee, somewhat guardedly agreed to co-operate. As she says in the film, "working with First Nations is a challenge." But she also says that "it's a learning process" and that "it's their community as much as it is ours." We had made the case to her that the film could potentially contribute to a shift in understanding within the village, between Native and non-Native residents, a shift that might result in a less confrontational stance and more willingness to collaborate on joint projects for economic and social development. The band was much more enthusiastic. They wanted their story to be heard and they trusted us to tell it. They were not sure what might change, if anything, as a result of the telling. But they recognized, as Chief Rob Charlie explains in the film, that they could not survive alone, and they were willing "to forgive, although not to forget, in order to move forward as a people" (interview with Chief Rob Charlie). They were also concerned that their Elders were passing and more and more stories and teachings were being lost. Capturing some of those stories would be a valuable secondary outcome of the film, so we offered to make a digital archive for them of the interviews we did with all band members.

Another piece of the puzzle that drew us to this story was the demographic reality of Burns Lake. Divided roughly fifty/fifty between Native and non-Native people, this was a deeply divided community, living as "two solitudes," side by side but segregated for most of the twentieth century. "When I was growing up here, Natives walked on one side of the street, non-Natives on the other. We weren't allowed into certain stores. There was no Native employment" (interview with Ryan Tibbetts, Burns Lake Band councillor). Now the demographic balance was about to shift in favour of First Nations and it was clear (although not widely accepted in the town) that the two peoples were in fact interdependent and would have to start figuring out how to do economic and social development planning together. And in this respect, Burns Lake could be seen as a microcosm of many such communities across Canada that share the same demographic reality, in the same national context of shifting rights and claims resulting from court cases mounted by First Nations in pursuit of land and resource rights as well as sovereignty.

This raised a major ethical question for us concerning our responsibility to the wider community (Native and non-Native). Were we going to judge and vilify the settlers as "colonizers," or listen to them, try to hear and empathize with their stories, as well as identify "tension points" (Flyvbjerg 2012) where change might be possible? We committed in our minds to the latter, which meant being committed to something other than making a pure advocacy film with and on behalf of First Nations. Our commitment as planners was to finding a way forward, beyond history's tragic antagonisms, and that meant not vilifying but rather letting each side tell its story in its own words.[5] We needed to understand and appreciate where relationships were already changing, why, how, and how to build on those changes.

During the spring and summer of 2007 as we filmed the interviews and then debriefed late into the night, trying to make sense of what we were hearing, it dawned on us that the story we would tell would have both a timeless theme – a people dispossessed, deep historic wounds, ongoing suffering, still unresolved conflict, and a desire for justice – and a very specific historical and political setting. This is twenty-first-century Canada. It is one small village in conflict with one small First Nation community. And yet events there are unfolding against a much larger political, legal, and constitutional canvas (the struggle for rights and recognition by Native people), as well as a larger attitudinal canvas of guilt, as well as some denial in the wider society regarding the ongoing effects and practices of colonization. So it became a story with a question mark. Is there a way forward? What can and should be done? And what can planning and planners do?

RETURNING THE FILM TO THE COMMUNITY

What did we hope to set in motion with our presence and with our film? The project was always conceived as an intervention into an already highly charged political force field. Initially we discussed two potential contributions with our collaborators. One was that we could provide some fresh eyes through which a polarized community might be able to stand back and see itself in a different light: seeing both its dark past and the potential now being demonstrated by some leaders and in some local institutions to move towards a future based on mutual respect, recognition, and partnership for economic and social development.

A second was that the film could assist other northern communities with similar demographic profiles (substantial Native populations, in some cases likely to become local majorities) and similar politics (histories of the dominance of settler communities, now being unsettled by legal challenges for Indigenous rights and title at the provincial and national levels) to begin to come to terms with the past and develop a different collective vision for the future of their communities. A third possibility emerged as we began to screen versions of the rough cut outside BC and our audiences were telling us that this was not just a BC problem but a national problem, and that our story could make a difference, could open hearts as well as minds. This had been the response from many delegates after our keynote presentation and screening to the Canadian Institute of Planners conference in Winnipeg in 2008.

It took us two-and-a-half years to edit the ninety-minute, three-part film, during which time we returned to Burns Lake eight times for community feedback on different rough cut versions. This involved separate screenings for each First Nation in their band offices on at least three occasions, one-on-one screenings between Leonie and key interviewees, such as the mayor, and a community-wide screening, facilitated by Norma-Jean McLaren, of the first full rough cut in July 2008. Several months before its completion in Spring 2010 we began applying for grants to assist with developing a process for sharing the film with the community in a dialogical way, as opposed to simply screening it and walking away. We partnered with Scott Graham, director of community development with the Social Planning & Research Council of BC (SPARC) for this purpose and were awarded fifteen thousand dollars by the province under its "Embrace BC" program, which was funding intercultural dialogues. We proposed to use the film as a catalyst for such a dialogue. A team of five of us then embarked on three months of careful planning for this dialogical process (see Appendix), as we will now describe.

Designing a Dialogue in a Divided Community

Our first step was to convene an advisory group in the town, comprising the mayor, two new village councillors, the two chiefs whose bands' stories had been told in the film, the senior policy advisor to the Cheslatta First Nation, the high school principal, the drama and dance teacher at the high school (who has a prominent role in the film), the staff sergeant of the RCMP and one of his First Nations officers, alongside our own project team. We convened a full-day meeting with this advisory group, which began with the screening of the just-finished film. Half the people in the room were in the film as interviewees, and had seen its evolution through the various rough cuts, but others were seeing it for the first time, so it was a test of sorts about its likely impact. The question in the mind of everyone on the dialogue project team was, would this film further polarize existing conflicts or could it start to shift the discourse? We were literally holding our breath waiting for their responses.

The first person to speak was one of the new village councillors, Lianne Olson. She was visibly shocked and began to describe how, as a teenager when there were race riots in the main street of the town, her father locked her indoors and told her that "those damn Indians were trying to take over the town." When the water and sewer dispute erupted, she had automatically assumed that "it was those darn Indians expecting something for nothing again," as her father had taught her. But, having just watched the film, she said that she finally understood now why the town had always been so divided, and how people like herself had been misinformed. This confession of ignorance and pre-judgement set the tone for comments that followed. Chief Leween spoke about how, finally, their (Cheslatta) truth had been told, and that this would not be an easy film for the wider community to watch, as it was not "sugar-coated." Here are some other reactions that we recorded, as each person revealed their own fresh insights.

> The leaders gathered here today are demonstrating good will and taking an important step for the future for our communities. We do need to move forward. The old guard is moving out and new leaders are moving in ... I am so glad to have two of our younger councillors with me today so they can be part of this change ... This film is important and sometimes difficult to watch, and I think it will help us address some of the challenges that hold us back. *Mayor Bernice Magee*

> We need to use this film to make a positive change in our community and we need to show that this process is going to move things ahead ... We need to build on our strengths and create a process that involves people in moving forward together. *Chief Rob Charlie*

> This film is very refreshing for me to see as a leader because it connects me and will connect others to the story of our people. There is lots in this film that is not sugar-coated – we need a film like this to make the truth plain to see. The presence of people here today – watching this film together – demonstrates a willingness to move forward together and I am glad to be a part of this. *Chief Corrina Leween*

> I came here in my teens and this film makes sense of many of the divisions that I have seen in this community. It helps me see the truth of what has happened here. It explains the causes for the division and differences at play in our community. *Councillor Lianne Olson*

We are experiencing a lot of changes in our community at the moment. We are in a season of change and this film holds important pieces of information that can help us improve cross-cultural relationships. There are stories in this film that show us what it takes to work together. We need true partnerships. *Councillor Quinten Beach*

The conversation that unfolded surprised us. Instead of resisting the film, the non-Native community leaders were embracing it, yet recognizing that it would be challenging for many in the community to face the account of past injustices and give proper acknowledgement to that, and use it as an occasion to move forward together. So this advisory group then came up with their own idea of how to lead this change process. The mayor and the chiefs first agreed to issue a joint press release urging the community to come and watch and discuss the film. Then, mindful of the strong emotions that could be aroused in an audience – from anger and denial to guilt and shame, as well as hope and inspiration – one member of our dialogue team (Nathan Edelson) suggested that both the chiefs and Mayor Magee should stand up together before the screening started and speak to the community about keeping an open mind and being prepared to learn and to discuss. To our great relief, they all readily agreed.

Attention then turned to the question of designing the dialogue that would follow the screening. We suggested two workshops: one for youth, the other for the community at large. Our emphasis on youth was something we learned from our interviewees. In the film, Chief Rob Charlie talks about the band being involved in a social transformation process, and how their energy is devoted to working with the young people, particularly through the Little Angels intercultural daycare facility located in the Gathering Place/band office. "That's where the diamond is," he says. Mayor Magee talks about change coming about "through the younger generation, who are more open to change than I am and what I've been taught." And the high school drama and dance teacher, Rayanne Charlie (a non-Native woman who is married to the chief), talks about the hope for change residing in the younger generation and describes the work she is doing with them through dance and drama, in allowing them to express themselves, to "remove the hand that has been clapped over their mouths," and opening conversations and performances about previously taboo topics, such as the Indian residential schools.

Regarding the film screening and dialogue, the team proposed breaking the audience into small groups and facilitating dialogue circles with no more than eight people per circle. We were attracted to the idea of dialogue circles in part because they resemble a traditional Native way of talking through difficult issues (the "talking circle" concept, in which everyone gets to speak, uninterrupted) and would therefore be likely to make our First Nations participants more comfortable. As an engagement method in cross-cultural dialogues, our colleague, Scott Graham, had done a lot of work with dialogue circles, adapted from "a guide for training public dialogue facilitators," developed by the group Everyday Democracy. The *Discussion Guide* (Sandercock and Graham 2010) that accompanies our film and that is included in the DVD package elaborates on this as a technique for ensuring that all participants have an equal opportunity to contribute to the discussion. Participants set their own ground rules with a view to fostering a climate of mutual respect and shared responsibility for the quality of the discussion. A facilitator leads the dialogue to ensure that everyone has the space to contribute their feelings and thoughts, and encourages the group to stay true to the guidelines it has set for itself. The main organizing principle is a "round approach," which means that the turn to speak moves around the circle, ensuring that everyone who so desires has the opportunity to speak.

We also proposed training local youth, as well as adults, as facilitators and the advisory group suggested pairs of facilitators, each pair comprising a First Nations person and a non-Native person. The project team felt that this session was a huge success in getting hitherto antagonistic community leaders on board with us. Leonie went directly from this meeting to an interview with the local newspaper, *The Lakes District News*, and at the end of the hour with the new owner of the paper, Laura Blackwell, we had a commitment from her of free advertising for our event and at least two articles covering it.

The team returned to the community a month later to spend two evenings training the facilitators, who had been recruited from the community, thanks to the help of an energetic young First Nations woman, Danielle Ogen. Norma-Jean, Scott, and Pauline conducted this training. We had eight youth and five adult volunteers, of whom six were First Nations. Again, we began by showing them the film and having a dialogue circle to discuss their responses to it, and again we were surprised at the profundity and honesty of the responses. Some of the non-Native youth spoke with heavy hearts and tears about their own ignorance of the town's history of relations between Native and non-Native peoples. There was also anger that this was being kept from them in the silence of the school text books. They wanted to take the film home that night and show their parents and have family discussions. Among the Native youth, some spoke of growing up ashamed of being Native but now, with the existence of this film, they could finally be proud of who they are and they wanted to show the film to all their friends immediately. Others spoke of growing up not wanting to hear their parents' stories of pain, especially the pain of the residential school experience, but now they understood why it was important to hear and discuss those stories and understand the intergenerational impact.

Each person in the circle spoke in these deeply felt ways. At the end of the first evening, everyone was energized to take the film out into the community. By the end of the second evening, we felt that this group had bonded and was galvanized to become a future leadership cadre for the town. After the community screenings, even more energized by their own role as facilitators, these youth formed a Six Nations Youth group in June 2010 and started a Facebook page to inspire other youth to get involved in social change.

In the wake of the advisory group meeting, Leonie had side conversations with the high school principal, Mike Skinner, about the importance of doing a special screening for the teachers before the community screenings so that they could be prepared for the conversations that the high school youth might want to have about the content of the film. That screening took place immediately after our facilitator training. It was "professional development" day at the high school, and teachers had a variety of activities to choose among, but twenty-two of the twenty-nine teachers came to our screening, along with the principal, and stayed for ninety minutes of discussion. We witnessed people again reaching into places of profound honesty, displaying emotions from shame to anger to relief. The relief expressed was that finally, as one teacher put it, "the veil of silence about what's been going on in this town has been lifted." One white male teacher spoke of trying to imagine how he would feel if his children were forcibly removed from his family and taken away for ten months of the year to where they were not allowed to speak their own language or engage in their own cultural practices. Women teachers nodded in agreement. The principal acknowledged that the school had been part of the problem, that it had indeed been "redneck high (school)," that fights between Native and non-Native students had been common, and that the school had in fact lost its accreditation ten years earlier and ever since had been struggling to reinvent itself, as the film in fact depicts. The overall response was captured by one teacher who asked, "How soon can we have this for classroom use?" And seven teachers volunteered to help facilitate the community dialogues as well as to recruit youth for the youth screening.

After three months of this careful planning, we were as ready as we could be for the two community screenings. Each event began with food, accompanied by music played by the local musicians whose anti-racism song had so intrigued us in the first place, Native and non-Native playing together (and who are on the film soundtrack). The music and food were followed by the mayor and two chiefs standing up together and speaking about the importance of the film to the community and asking people to watch with an open mind, emphasizing that the intent of the workshops was to move from a reflection on and hopefully new understanding of the past, to a tough look at the present, culminating in a concrete conversation about how to move forward together. Then we launched into the ninety-minute screening, followed by an intermission (more live music) while we re-arranged chairs into dialogue circles. The facilitated dialogues then ran for ninety minutes and focused on three questions: What was the most significant impact the film had on you? Is the past still present in this town? And, how might this community move forward together now, on what, and what would your role be?

During the dialogue circles, the project team, along with the mayor and two chiefs, moved about the room as witnesses, listening to what was being said but not speaking. Notes were taken by one of the facilitators in each group, and Nathan Edelson, one member of our project team, was responsible for absorbing what was being said in all groups and summarizing at the end. He highlighted the community's enthusiasm for an intercultural Gathering Place and, in particular, the enthusiasm of youth for being engaged in cross-cultural community activities and the possibility of some youth leadership training. Then the mayor and chiefs had the final words. These closing words from the leaders were inspiring. The mayor acknowledged the past mistakes made by the village and Chief Rob Charlie publicly buried his resentment, noting that four years ago he had given up on this town, but now he was filled with hope in seeing the young people energized for change and the spirit of hope for moving forward reflected in the dialogues.

Even more inspiring were the comments made within the dialogue circles, which became the subject of an editorial in *The Lakes District News* the following week (Blackwell 2010). Strikingly, people who attended were so engaged that they stayed fully five hours, including an extra fifteen minutes in the evening to fill out evaluations. Fifty youth attended the youth screening, roughly half of whom were First Nations, and forty remained for the dialogue. Twenty-one stayed and completed the evaluation. Approximately 150 people attended the community-wide screening. Eighty people stayed on for the dialogue circles, and forty-five stayed to complete the evaluation (required by our funders).

In response to the first question, "How well did this screening and dialogue help your community address racism?" seventeen of twenty-one replies among the youths gave the highest possible score for this answer. In response to the second question, "How well did this screening and dialogue help your community identify pathways to working together across cultural differences?" twenty of twenty-one replies circled very good or good. These responses were similar in the community-wide screening. Thirty seven of the community members in attendance noted a significant shift in awareness. Additionally, there were very positive answers to a question inquiring about people's overall awareness of historical and current-day relations between Native and non-Native peoples before and after the workshops with many respondents noting a significant increase in awareness.

Qualitative answers from both youths and adults to the question, "How will you act on what you have learned through the screening and dialogue?" contained many expressions of the desire to volunteer to work on community projects such as the Gathering Place, which was re-imagined during the dialogues as an intercultural facility for the whole community, rather than as a meeting place just for First Nations. And the two most common answers to the question, "What other types of activities or events that bring people together would you recommend for anti-racism projects?" were either "more films or plays like this one" or "take this film on the road."

Perhaps the final word on this event should be drawn from the editorial (entitled "Inspiring") in the local newspaper: "The youth that viewed the documentary were so inspiring ... Some felt ashamed, some felt sad, but the consensus with them all was that they felt that what had happened to the First Nations in our community was not right and they are determined to do what they can now to make it right from here on" (Blackwell 2010, 4).

During the months of organizing the community screenings, Pauline and Nathan had also been working with the band and the village to develop a strategic plan for moving the Gathering Place forward as a venue for the band and for youth, and discussing the possibility of leadership training for some of the youth who had volunteered as facilitators or who had expressed a desire during the workshops to get involved in community development projects. After the dialogues, the mayor and the chief and the community took public responsibility for this as an intercultural community project, an expression of a strong desire that had emerged from the community during the discussions. To us, this affirmed that the film was effective as a catalyst for cross-cultural conversation, and had created the space for that conversation.

This is ongoing work for us, as researchers/filmmakers, now monitoring the momentum that our film catalyzed with the youth, and also with the band and village leadership. It has been an emotionally involving project. We now need ongoing evaluations, medium and long-term, so as not to delude ourselves with the initial wave of energy that the film and dialogue circles generated.

BEYOND THE DIALOGUES

In the three months following the screenings and dialogue circles, some small but significant changes occurred. In August of 2010, the village of Burns Lake adopted a motion of support in principle for one of the ideas that had emerged through the dialogues: the renovation of the Gathering Place as an intercultural facility that will serve the entire community in a meaningful way, and for the development of a youth leadership program. The film has been shown to potential funders in an effort to begin to develop ideas and support for the needed feasibility studies, capital, and operating funds for various aspects of these initiatives. The mayor, who for many years was in an antagonistic relationship with the band, drafted a motion that the village council write to the school district, which still owns the land on which the Gathering Place sits, asking that they return the land to the band so that they can qualify for federal funding for capital improvements. And she urged the chamber of commerce and the regional district to write similar letters.

After a new chief and council were elected in October 2010, Nathan, Norma-Jean, and Pauline met with them in December 2010 to inform them of their community planning work with the previous chief and council and to seek their permission to continue working on the Gathering Place project on behalf of the band. More conversations took place in the spring. The mayor's support for this initiative has been constant and forceful. In July 2011, a meeting of the village, Burns Lake Band, school district, high school principal, and Economic Development Association of Burns Lake affirmed the desire to move ahead with this initiative. Culturally appropriate designs were proposed by the new chief, Al

Gerow, and a timeline for seeking school district co-operation in the transfer of land back to the Burns Lake Band (to enable it to raise capital for the new facility) and getting the necessary planning permits through village council was established.

It is too early to expect to see concrete material differences as a result of the dialogues. All we can say is that things are moving in a direction that reflects the new intercultural spirit of co-operation and coexistence that grew out of the dialogues, and that progress will necessarily be slow. The materialization of the Gathering Place, when it happens, will be a significant symbolic as well as social and economic advance for this community. But there are other smaller changes that we can already see and hear about. Word keeps coming back to us from the folks interviewed in the film that they are often stopped in the supermarket or gas station by community members who saw the film and want to talk about it, expressing compassion for what the First Nations have endured, and who confess that it opened a window for them onto something about which they had no previous inkling. What this tells us is that the film and dialogues have augmented some of the developing relational spaces and prospects for reconciliation already nascent in these two communities. One of the comments that we heard many times from a range of people in the dialogue circles was that it was time to make an effort to get to know "the other" (Native or non-Native). And the high school has embraced the film in its curriculum for grades 11 and 12. The veil of silence is lifting.

But for power-sharing and mutual respect to be realized, both Native and non-Native leaders need to come to common understandings of the strengths and challenges each group faces, the limits to their autonomy, and the reality of their interdependence.

REFLECTIONS: EMPOWERING FIRST NATION COMMUNITIES THROUGH FILM?

Can the film be effective as a planning intervention beyond the communities whose stories it tells? Our Burns Lake dialogues were both an end in themselves, as per our original hopes for the project, and also a pilot for possible workshops in other towns in this region. There were a number of people from these towns who came to the Burns Lake workshop and who then requested similar events in their community.

The Smithers Bridging Society approached Leonie in August 2010 asking for our involvement in running a similar event in their town eighty miles west of Burns Lake, for which they had raised their own funding. This took place in November 2010 and had a very similar impact to what we have described as transpiring in Burns Lake. Sixty invited participants – mostly Native and non-Native community leaders – spent five hours together viewing and discussing the film and its relevance to Smithers. At least a third of them wanted to take the film back to their own community group and work with them on these issues. Joanne Ashworth, an independent evaluator from Simon Fraser University's Dialogues Project, was present and conducted her own evaluation, a modification of our Burns Lake questionnaire, which yielded similar results to those we have described for the Burns Lake dialogues.

The intent, from the earliest stages of planning the film, was that it could be used by the community, history's real actors, as a tool for teaching their own story and their learnings from it. Whenever we use the film in these interventions in divided communities, we work in partnership with community members. In March 2011, Leonie worked with Stacy Barter (BC Healthy Communities) to design dialogues for Gold River on Vancouver Island, where the Mowachat-Muchalat First Nation and the non-Native community are trying to figure out how to do economic development together. Leonie, along with Chief Leween and Mike Robertson from the Cheslatta Carrier Nation travelled there and helped facilitate two community dialogues: one with high school students, the other with the wider community.

Simultaneously we are working to promote screenings of the film in strategic venues. The film was featured on the opening night of the annual conference of the Planning Institute of BC in June 2010 with an audience of planners from all over the province. It was screened for one hundred community development folks from all over BC who were in Vancouver in May 2010 for a conference on creative approaches to community development, organized by our colleague at the Social Planning and Research Council of BC. It was used in a series of provincially funded cross-cultural dialogues in four different cultural centres in Vancouver during the spring of 2010 with the intent of raising awareness among different immigrant cultures of the history and contemporary realities of First Nations in Canada. And the Vancouver School District has bought copies for all the high schools in Vancouver and asked us to run workshops for teachers, staff, youth, and community groups. A screening in Melbourne, Australia in December 2010 resulted in Parks Victoria purchasing copies to use in training their rangers in cross-cultural sensitivity and a letter of support from Patrick Fricker, the Aboriginal state manager of Caring for Country in that same government agency. He wrote that we could substitute any Australian Aboriginal tribe for the two First Nations in our film and we would have the same story. A Māori audience at the New Zealand Planning Institute conference in April 2011 elicited a similar response.

We have witnessed extraordinary heart-openings at all of these dialogues as First Nations share their stories, often stories of great pain relating to the ongoing effects of the residential school experience.

Will the film succeed not only as a catalyst for dialogue but also for mobilizing commitment and resources around future planning projects? Like all good stories, ours must end on a note of suspense. We can say that the first community screenings were definitely successful as a catalyst for apparently transformative dialogue. We do not know yet whether this will result in the mobilization of resources around community development projects, but there is now real community momentum behind the Gathering Place.

No planner can precisely predict whether the tool or approach they are using will be an effective catalyst for social change. The analysis of the outcomes of such a process can only be done retrospectively. The field of social interaction and political action is constantly characterized by uncertainty. In this field we don't have a mechanical algorithm in which we insert some initial inputs and after that we can predict how communities will react, interact, dialogue, and possibly provoke changes. The field of social interaction is full of surprises and unintended effects. We can be a little more certain about what happened in the past, things we can now make sense of. We can affirm from our first experience in using film in this way (*Where Strangers Become Neighbours*) that it was very successful both in provoking dialogue and in instigating policy changes (see Sandercock and Attili 2009; Sandercock and Attili 2010). But there are no general rules. Everything depends on the specificities, including our own attention to detail and to relationship-building, but even more on the communities themselves.

We do know from past experiences that some issues cannot be understood through mechanistic or quantitative languages. We know from our own past experiences and recent community screenings of this film that the languages we are using have the potential to provoke dialogue and interaction. And we know that in order to pursue this goal we must not only create the film but also the space in which this interaction can take place, and that is both relational space as well as workshop space. And that is the process we are building right now, which is linked with the potentialities that such films can trigger in the planning field (Sandercock and Attili 2010).

One important element currently missing from our work is the capacity to do medium and long-term evaluations of the effects of this approach. This is an important next step and one in which we are currently facing major institutional barriers. An application to the Social Sciences and Humanities Research Council in 2010 to continue, develop, and deepen this work was not funded in spite of external assessors' evaluations that ranked the proposal as excellent on all criteria. The Adjudication Committee in Ottawa dismissed those evaluations as "uncritical" and gave the project a 50 per cent score, expressing doubt about its "scientific contribution," noting that the "fieldwork was not academic enough" and not supporting the payment of consultants (our First Nations collaborators). Beyond personal disappointment, this kind of culturally insensitive adjudication raises serious concerns for anyone doing community-based, action-oriented research, and especially for those working with/in First Nations communities. We are not doing "science," at least not in the (positivist) sense implied by the adjudicators. We are doing social change work. And we are not doing "fieldwork" in the sense of collecting data on Indigenous communities. Rather, we are working collaboratively with them in change processes, visioning, and community development planning. A new grant that we contemplated applying for at UBC funds "innovative solutions," demands "results" within one to three years, a very difficult task if we are talking about social innovation rather than technical innovation. These are just some of the ongoing challenges of a transformative planning practice.

The planning intervention that we have designed begins with a healing process in the context of historic trauma, catalyzed by dialogues that the film enables. It then proceeds through recognition of "the past as present," and moves on to a visioning process engaging with how things might be different. That final step can evolve into action projects of a more typical planning nature, from land use to economic development to facilities planning to health planning to addressing governance issues. This is very much a work in progress. Nevertheless, "baby step by baby step" (interview with Rayanne Charlie), this small town that was characterized by "disparity in power, violations of trust and lingering unresolved disputes" (RCAP 1996) is moving towards a relationship of mutual respect and joint problem-solving. And our work there is a step towards that "long-overdue paradigm shift" (Jojola 2008, 25) that will eventually decolonize planning.

EPILOGUE: POSITIONALITY, PRIVILEGE, AND POWER

In closing, we acknowledge that there are several generations of Indigenous filmmakers who came before us who have communicated hidden histories, stories of resistance, films about residential schools, experiences with police and child welfare agencies, accounts of traditional ecological knowledge and practices, and much more, with the same intention of opening eyes, minds, and hearts (Alanis Obomsawin, Loretta Todd, Christine Welsh, Gil Cardinal, to name some who have done outstanding work for decades, not to mention a new generation of young filmmakers). These films and their filmmakers struggle for community access and airtime, for film festival screenings, for funding and distribution opportunities. As with the wider society, Aboriginal filmmakers have not always been valued or included. We recognize that we occupy a privileged position in academia and that Leonie, as a senior academic, is able to apply for research grants that are not available to independent filmmakers (Indigenous or non-Indigenous). On the other hand, we have also experienced innumerable rejections (from funding applications to screening at festivals) and in some cases the precise reason given was because we are *not* Indigenous. This is at least a sign that something is changing, that there are now Indigenous gatekeepers, and that there is a contested politics of voice, including a vigorous debate about who has the right to make films about Indigenous communities.

To be clear, though, we do not position ourselves as making films *about* Indigenous communities. Rather, we have made a film collaboratively *with* two Indigenous communities, and that film is about the past, present, and future of relations *between* Indigenous and non-Indigenous people in Canada. (In an epilogue to the film, our Indigenous partners speak to the issue of why they chose to collaborate with us). And, there is something that we have done differently than our predecessors in documentary filmmaking. We have consciously designed a post-production community dialogue into our project, which went well beyond the making of a film, extending to working with that film as a catalyst for social change processes. And this speaks to our other identity as planners, always reflecting on how to design and be engaged in change processes rather than simply assuming (as is too often the case with documentary filmmakers) that the making of the film is the end of the work. For us, it is just the beginning.

We understand and respect (but do not agree with) the argument of some Indigenous scholars and filmmakers that there is no place for non-

Indigenous voices in speaking about Indigenous issues. We have certainly wrestled with this argument and have taken the advice of our mentor, Elder Gerry Oleman (Statliam Nation) who encourages non-Indigenous people to be allies, to "make noise" about injustice when we see it. That is one thing that our film set out to do.

But there is also another way of framing this apparent dilemma. We have no desire to speak *for* Indigenous peoples, and indeed recognize this act as yet another form of colonization. Rather, inspired by scholars as diverse as Taiaiake Alfred (2005), Anne Bishop (1994), and Paulette Regan (2011), we seek to turn the gaze back upon settler society, to foreground the local histories and ongoing acts of colonization, to break through the massive culture of denial and the veil of ignorance: to name the violence, to face the history. We seek to unsettle this settler society, as a first step towards decolonization. But we also choose to offer some critical hope of a way forward, by telling stories of respectful and humble partnerships between Indigenous and non-Indigenous Canadians, and by seeking to model such partnerships in our own practice. There are "small courageous experiments happening everywhere, based in and on local conditions, but aware of the whole world" (Bishop 1994, 124). And this is how a paradigm shift begins.

APPENDIX: COMMUNITY PLANNING AS A TEAM EFFORT

While the making of *Finding Our Way* was a two-person labour of love on the part of Giovanni and Leonie, there were colleagues along the way who enabled and assisted us in many ways, and who also took on key roles during the community dialogues.

A group of anti-racism activists in Burns Lake, Native and non-Native, had been working for more than a decade to build bridges and as a result, created some level of community readiness for the film's intervention. Pauline Goertzen was and remains one of these pivotal community activists. Norma-Jean McLaren had also been engaged in community dialogues, healing work, and anti-racism training after the Supreme Court case. We brought her into our project as a cultural advisor because of this experience.

During the spring and summer of filming in 2007, we hired a Masters student from UBC, Jess Hallenbeck, as a research assistant and to do some B-roll film footage. Norma-Jean and Jess teamed up and did stellar work with ten high school youth over a two-week period, culminating in a dialogue circle during which the youth displayed and talked about the photos they had taken of their community. This was conceived as an "emotional map" of Burns Lake and it opened a space for the (Native and non-Native) youth to tell poignant stories. They also produced a timeline of occupation of the region. All of this was filmed by Giovanni, with the intention of inclusion in the documentary, but a technical mistake with the audio equipment resulted in us losing all of the sound.

In the summer of 2008 we organized a community-wide screening of the first full rough cut of the film in order to write a progress report for our initial funder, the Vancouver Foundation. Norma-Jean McLaren facilitated this event as a more "neutral" person than either of the filmmakers. One of her key skills is an ability to help people with strongly differing views to feel "safe" in talking about their concerns. This was particularly important since historical antagonists were present on that day.

Most of the work of returning to the community with successive rough cuts, absorbing feedback, and nurturing relationships over time and across the cultural divide was done by Leonie.

During this time we also had a critical support group in Vancouver giving us feedback on rough cuts, in particular, Jess Hallenbeck, Norma-Jean McLaren, Nathan Edelson, Scott Graham, Lyana Patrick, and Gerry Oleman. And Richard Chew and Liv Torgerson gave invaluable advice from Los Angeles as successful film editors.

Once the film was finished and we began to plan the community screening and dialogues, our two-person film team expanded to the "dialogue project team," comprising Scott Graham (Social Planning and Research Council of BC), Norma-Jean McLaren, Pauline Goertzen (Community Futures), and Nathan Edelson (42nd Street Consulting), who had recently retired as senior planner with the City of Vancouver, had a wealth of experience in community planning in the downtown eastside of Vancouver, and an extraordinary skill set in being able to bridge cultural, class, ethnic, and professional differences, and bring people into coalition on the most vexing of social and economic development issues.

Scott, Norma-Jean, and Leonie did the initial conceptual planning of the dialogues. Scott, Norma-Jean, and Pauline trained the facilitators from the community. Norma-Jean had an important role in facilitating discussions of the film with the local advisory group and also with the high school teachers. She also did a debriefing with facilitators after the dialogues.

In subsequent workshops and dialogues using the film in the Lower Mainland for the Vancouver school district, and in Smithers for the Smithers Bridging Society, Leonie has partnered with Gerry Oleman (Elder, Statliam Nation); in dialogues in Gold River (jointly with BC Healthy Communities), Leonie partnered with Chief Corrina Leween and Mike Robertson of the Cheslatta Carrier Nation.

Our intent is always to work in partnership with First Nations colleagues in using the film in teaching and dialogue settings.

NOTES

1   We want to acknowledge our indebtedness to four people who enabled this project in the fullest sense. Norma-Jean McLaren and Pauline Goertzen were our cultural guides and mentors in Burns Lake. Mike Robertson's assistance was invaluable in working with the Cheslatta Carrier Nation. Gerry Oleman was and remains a mentor on colonization and healing processes.

2   This chapter uses "we" frequently. Unless otherwise specified, this refers to the authors. But community planning is always a team effort and others joined us along the way, bringing special skills and gifts. The Appendix outlines the significant contributions of various people at different times throughout the project's life.

3   The Cheslatta people were evicted from their homeland in 1952 (with ten days' notice) when the provincial government, working with the federal government, transferred their lands to the Aluminum Company of Canada (Alcan) for the purpose of building a hydroelectric project to fuel their aluminum smelter. The Cheslatta community was separated onto many small parcels of poor land, and a previously self-sufficient people became dependent on monthly hand-outs from the Department of Indian Affairs. They have struggled for fifty years to "keep their heads above water" but theirs is also a story of remarkable resilience and revitalization. See Chapter 3 of the film *Finding Our Way* (Attili and Sandercock 2010).

4   We use (post)colonial in brackets, following Porter (2010), as an indication that colonial relationships are still embedded in much of contemporary law, governance, and professional practices such as planning.

5   Although, to be fair, the mayor and other municipal officials would argue that the film does not sufficiently explain the pressures the village was under to secure finances for services, as well as some of the ways in which their efforts to reach out to the Burns Lake Band were rebuffed.

REFERENCES

Alfred, Taiaiake. 2005. *Wasase: Indigenous Pathways of Action and Freedom.* Ontario: Broadview Press.

Attili, G. 2007. "Digital Ethnographies in the Planning Field." *Planning Theory and Practice* 8 (1):90–7.

Attili, G., and L. Sandercock. 2007. *Where Strangers Become Neighbours* (DVD). Montreal: National Film Board of Canada.

– 2010. *Finding Our Way* (DVD). Vancouver: Moving Images.

Bishop, A. 1994. *Becoming an Ally: Breaking the Cycle of Oppression.* Halifax: Fernwood.

Bishop, R. 2005. "Freeing Ourselves from Neo-colonial Domination in Research: A Kaupapa Māori Approach to Creating Knowledge." In *The Sage Handbook of Qualitative Research*, third edition, edited by N.K. Denzin and Y.S. Lincoln. London: Sage.

Blackwell, L. 2010. "Inspiring." *Lakes District News*, 9 June 2010, 4.

Flyvbjerg, B. 2001. *Making Social Science Matter.* Chicago: Chicago University Press.

– 2012. "Why Mass Media Matter, and How to Work With Them: The Case of Phronesis, Ethics, and Megaprojects." In *Real Social Science*, edited by B. Flyvbjerg, T. Landman, S. Schram. Oxford: Oxford University Press.

Flyvbjerg, B., T. Landman, and S. Schram, eds. 2012. *Real Social Science.* Oxford: Oxford University Press.

Friedmann, J. 1987. *Planning in the Public Domain: From Knowledge to Action.* Princeton: Princeton University Press.

Galois, R.M. 1992. "The Indian Rights Association, Native Protest Activity and the 'Land Question' in British Columbia, 1903–1916." *Native Studies Review* 8 (2a):1–34.

Jackson, S. 1998. *Geographies of Co-existence: Native Title, Cultural Difference and the Decolonization of Planning in North Australia.* Unpublished PhD dissertation. Sydney: School of Earth Sciences, Macquarie University.

Jacobs, J.M. 1996. *Edge of Empire: Postcolonialism and the City.* London: Routledge.

Jojola, T. 1998. "Indigenous Planning: Clans, Intertribal Confederations and the History of the All Indian Pueblo Council." In *Making the Invisible Visible: A Multicultural History of Planning*, edited by L. Sandercock. Berkeley: University of California Press.

– 2008. "Indigenous Planning: An Emerging Context." *Canadian Journal of Urban Research* 17 (1):37–47.

Harris, C. 1997. *The Resettlement of British Columbia.* Vancouver: UBC Press.

– 2002. *Making Native Space*. Vancouver: UBC Press.

Hibbard, M., and M. Lane. 2004. "By the Seat of Your Pants: Indigenous Action and State Response." *Planning Theory and Practice* 5 (1, March): 97–103.

Lane, M., and M. Hibbard. 2005. "Doing it for Themselves: Transformative Planning by Indigenous Peoples." *Journal of Planning Education and Research* 25 (2):172–84.

Little Bear, L. 2009. "Jagged Worldviews Colliding." In *Reclaiming Indigenous Voice and Vision*, edited by M. Battiste. Vancouver: UBC Press.

Matunga, H. 2000. "Decolonizing Planning: The Treaty of Waitangi, the Environment and a Dual Planning Tradition." In *Environmental Planning and Management in New Zealand*, edited by P.A. Memon and C.H. Perkins. Auckland: Dunmore Press.

McMillan, Alan D., and Eldon Yellowhorn. 2007. *First Peoples in Canada*. Vancouver: Douglas and McIntyre.

Muckle, R. 2007. *The First Nations of British Columbia: An Anthropological Survey*, second edition. Vancouver: UBC Press.

Porter, L. 2004. "Unlearning One's Privilege: Reflections on Cross-cultural Research with Indigenous Peoples in South-East Australia." *Planning Theory and Practice* 5 (1):104–8.

– 2010. *Unlearning the Colonial Cultures of Planning*. Surrey: Ashgate.

Ray, Arthur J. 1999. "Treaty 8: A British Columbian Anomaly." *BC Studies* 123:5–58.

Reardon, K. 2003. "Ceola's Vision, Our Blessing: The Story of an Evolving Community-University Partnership in East St. Louis." In *Story and Sustainability*, edited by B. Eckstein and J. Throgmorton. Cambridge, MA: MIT Press.

Regan, P. 2011. *Unsettling the Settler Within*. Vancouver: UBC Press.

Sandercock, L. 1998a. *Towards Cosmopolis. Planning for Multicultural Cities*. Chichester: Wiley.

– ed. 1998b. *Making the Invisible Visible. Multicultural Histories of Planning*. Berkeley: University of California Press.

– 2004. "Indigenous Planning and the Burden of Colonialism." *Planning Theory and Practice* 5 (1, March):118–26.

Sandercock, L., and G. Attili. 2009. *Where Strangers Become Neighbours: The Integration of Immigrants in Vancouver*. Dordrecht: Springer.

– 2010a. "Digital Ethnography as Planning Praxis: An Experiment with Film as Social Research, Community Engagement and Policy Dialogue." *Planning Theory and Practice* 11, (1, March):23–45.

– 2010b. *Multimedia Explorations in Urban Policy and Planning: Beyond the Flatlands*. Dordrecht: Springer.

– 2012. "Unsettling a Settler Society: Film, Phronesis and Collaborative Planning in Small Town Canada." In *Real Social Science*, edited by B. Flyvbjerg, T. Landman, and S. Schram. Oxford University Press.

Sandercock, L., and S. Graham. 2010. *Finding Our Way: Discussion Guide.* In *Finding Our Way*, (DVD) by Attili and Sandercock. Vancouver: Moving Images.

Sarkissian, W., and D. Hurford. 2010. *Creative Community Engagement.* London: Earthscan.

Smith, L.T. 1999. *Decolonizing Methodologies.* London: Zed Books.

Stanger-Ross, J. 2008. "Municipal Colonialism in Vancouver: City Planning and the Conflict over Indian Reserves, 1928–1950s." *The Canadian Historical Review* 89 (4):541–80.

Tennant, P. 1990. *Aboriginal Peoples and Politics: The Indian Land Question in British Columbia, 1849–1999.* Vancouver: UBC Press.

Tobey, M. 1981. "Carrier." In *Handbook of North American Indians: Subarctic*, vol. 6, edited by J. Helm. Washington, DC: Smithsonian Institute.

Wilson, S. 2008. *Research is Ceremony. Indigenous Research Methods.* Halifax: Fernwood Publishing.

4

Culture and Economy: The Cruel Choice Revisited

MICHAEL HIBBARD AND ROBERT ADKINS

The disparity between Indigenous peoples' advances in political self-determination and their socio-economic development is striking. Politically, Indigenous communities have made significant advances in the early years of the twenty-first century. Thanks to the heroic efforts of two generations of Native leaders, Indigenous communities have begun to overcome the political and cultural oppression under which they lived for centuries. This has been achieved in part by re-establishing self-determination and installing their own sovereign policy-making and administrative structures. They have also been successful at reasserting a voice in managing their lands and the associated water, hunting, and fishing rights while reinstituting their own cultural traditions in their schools, health care, and other human services. These advances are admittedly works in progress, but if the changes are not everything Indigenes might wish for, they are nonetheless real and deep (Wilkinson 2005).

However, the transformation in the governance arena has not been matched by comparable socio-economic progress. Although the profound destitution of past times has mostly been lightened, at least in the US, and a few tribes have made great strides, poverty is still a major issue. A few numbers from the US illustrate the point. In 2008, the overall poverty rate was 13.3 per cent (Bishaw and Macartney 2010), but for American Indians it was 24.2 per cent (Infoplease 2010). The median household income in 2008 was $50,112 (DeNavas-Walt et al. 2010), but for American Indians it was $37,815 (Infoplease 2010). The gap between Indigenous peoples and the population as a whole is similar or even larger in other post-colonial nations (Hibbard et al. 2008).

One way of understanding the disparity between the political and socio-economic realms is to note that the principles of self-determination and sovereignty that have animated political thinking about Indigenes since the 1970s have only limited socio-economic parallels. Politically and culturally, earlier policies of extinction, termination, and assimilation – policies that assumed Indigenous social groupings and cultural identities would disappear – have been discredited and largely reversed in the last thirty years (Hibbard 2006, Wilkinson 1987). The rights of tribes to culturally appropriate self-governance and land and resource management have been generally established (Lane and Hibbard 2005, Pinel 2007). However, the analogous right in the socio-economic realm is still contested territory. The purpose of this chapter is to explore the case of culturally appropriate socio-economic development by Indigenous peoples.

APPROACHES TO SOCIO-ECONOMIC DEVELOPMENT IN INDIAN COUNTRY

Two general explanations are offered for the poverty of Indigenes. The first is based in the elementary economic geography concept of location. Indigenes were typically allocated the most economically unproductive lands, often located in isolated areas far from potential markets (Hibbard and Lane 2004). The second explanation holds that Indigenous cultures present substantial economic disadvantages for their peoples even if locational factors can be overcome – for example, by improvements in transportation, infrastructure, communication, and workforce development. Framed in a positive light, the cultural explanation holds that Indigenes prioritize their relationships with family, friends, and the natural world over an "alarm-clock, balance-sheet ethic" (Wilkinson 2005, 329). Less charitably, many who argue that "culture matters" economically say that the poverty of Indigenes is a product of their insistence on clinging nostalgically to cultural traits that are maladapted to contemporary economic realities (see, for example, Grondona 2000).

The cultural explanation assumes that the only real, viable economy is the neo-classic free market which Indigenous peoples have never had and have no prospects for developing, at least on their own cultural terms. Following from that assumption, development efforts have been directed towards facilitating Indigenous peoples' "progress towards a civilized form of economy" (Brody 1983, 62). There is a long history of development programs, institutions, and activities that begin from the premise that the only solution to the socio-economic problems facing Indigenous communities is to shape their local economy in harmony with the mainstream neo-classic economy. Among the more transparent examples of this in recent decades are the reports of the US Presidential Commission on Indian Reservation Economics (1984) and the US Task Force on Indian Economic Development (1986). The findings of both reports called for reservations to make themselves into more favourable sites for business investment and operation, and to take steps to enhance capital formation in Indian country. As the numbers cited above suggest, approaches such as these have not produced the results envisioned by their proponents: increased jobs and wealth in Indian country.

The neo-classic view of economic development is fundamentally at cross-purposes with Indigenous cultures (Jorgensen 1986). It advances policies and programs to which most Indigenous people are indifferent at best (Houser 1995; Pinel 2007). In response, beginning in the mid-1990s, an alternative view of Indigenous socio-economic development has emerged. It parallels the shift in the political and cultural realms, away from assimilation and towards Indigenous political self-determination and sovereignty. It argues that socio-economic development will not be effective in Indigenous communities if it tries to model the mainstream economy. For Indigenous communities, development "is a means toward the end of sustaining tribal character; as such it is vital to formulate all development plans with an understanding of how they impact the overall societal makeup" (Smith 1994, 178). Duffy and Stubben (1998) argue that effective Indigenous development recognizes the interactions among various important components of life, of which the economy is just one factor. Rather than undermining Indigenous culture, enduring, self-sustaining development is contingent on strengthening it (Cornell and Kalt 1998; Smith 2000; Jorgensen 2007).

The question of whether Indigenous communities and peoples have to give up their own cultures, values, and goals and assimilate in order to create and maintain healthy local economies and communities has significant parallels in an ongoing dispute in international development planning. A review of some of the key features in the latter may be helpful in thinking about how to approach socio-economic development in Indigenous communities. We begin with a discussion of the development of development planning and the emergence of alternative development (AD).[1] We next review some of the implications of AD for socio-economic development planning in Indigenous communities. Then, to ground our analysis, we use the example of the Tlingit community of Kake, Alaska,

AD = alt. development

to illustrate the problems and opportunities of applying AD thought to the situation of Indigenous communities. We conclude by briefly assessing the limits of AD for Indigenous communities as they engage in socio-economic development.

DEVELOPMENT: A CRUEL CHOICE?

As with Indigenous development, international development began with the assumption that the only real economy is the neo-classic free market. The paradigmatic statement of that view is surely Walt Rostow's *The Stages of Economic Growth* (1960).[2] He argued that there is a regular five-stage progression in socio-economic development, from "traditional society" to "the age of high mass consumption," and that all economies go through each of these stages in a fairly linear way as they develop. Drawing on the principles of neo-classical economics, Rostow posited a set of universal principles that undergird high mass-consumption societies: society is best understood as a collection of autonomous individuals; self-regulating markets are the best way to allocate resources; and people's wants are essentially limitless. According to Rostow, "traditional societies" lack the impulse towards economic growth that characterizes "high mass consumption societies" because they lack those principles. In Rostow's view, all the world should aspire to become "high mass consumption" and the purpose of development planning should be to help move traditional societies towards that end.

Although the details have evolved over time, the basic neo-classic economic argument still permeates development planning (Stiglitz et al. 2006). Creating and maintaining high aggregate demand – "high mass consumption" – will produce growth in the number of jobs, followed by wage escalation. Development consists of lots of high-wage jobs producing goods and services to meet people's limitless wants.

The development theorist Denis Goulet (1971) pointed out forty years ago that the neo-classic approach to development presents individuals, communities, and even nations with a "cruel choice" between maintaining their traditional culture and being condemned to a life of material poverty or giving up that culture in order to benefit materially. Embedded in the cruel choice is the assumption that the economy is the constant and that cultures have to adapt to it.

The underlying question implied by Goulet is whether a universal theory of development is either possible or desirable. The development economist Stephen Marglin has observed that his field "privileges the

algorithmic over the experiential" (Marglin 2008, 46). That is, it privileges the search for general laws of development over the attempt to
understand the specific contexts in which development activities occur. In
one sense that should not be surprising; since most people working in the
field think of development planning as a science in which there is one best
answer to any question, they have concentrated on the search for univer-
sals. As Ian Morris (2010, 570–1) points out in his recent *tour de force*
on world development, isolating information and treating it independently of its context is a defining characteristic of modern science.

But Goulet did not think of development planning as a science and
he did not see the cruel choice as the only choice. Rather, he sought
to broaden the concept of development to include both economic and
social objectives and to position them within the values that guide a
given society. This was an early formulation of the AD paradigm that
rose to prominence in the 1980s. In simplest terms, for AD the purpose of
development is improving the quality of life of the least well off (nations,
communities, and peoples) by expanding their control over the things
that matter most to them in their own lives. Nobel Prize-winning economist Amartya Sen (2000) summed up the AD view by defining development as the effort to increase economic, political, and social freedom.
Development as freedom might include economic growth, of course, but
it is a much more extensive concept.

Implicit in the AD paradigm is the notion that the neo-classic free
market economy is not a given, it is a social construct. Karl Polanyi
made the point more than sixty years ago in his classic, *The Great Transformation*: "Free markets could never have come into being merely by
allowing things to take their course. Laissez-faire was planned." (1944,
139–40). There is an extensive literature on the relationship between
culture and economy (see, for example, Porter 1990; Landes 1998; Jones
2006). The evidence is convincing that healthy economies emerge from
and are embedded in their cultural context. The conventional development paradigm mistakes ideology (free market economy) for "truth,"
evidently because of its proponents' fixation on science and consequent
drive for a totalizing explanation of development. In contrast, the AD
paradigm privileges context; it seeks to be institutionally specific, historically informed, and able to incorporate local cultural processes (de
Paula and Dymsky 2005).

While the AD paradigm has not displaced the conventional paradigm
in international development, it has had a powerful influence in two
ways. First, while the cruel choice – the concept of a single definition

AD is growing in interest!

of economic development that all societies ignore at their peril – is still dominant, there is substantial support for the view that economies can and should vary with their cultural context. Second, there is growing appreciation of the AD idea that development is concerned with enhancing quality of life and that improved quality of life is not necessarily synonymous with economic growth, that quality of life – and hence development – has cultural and social dimensions as well.

But what are the implications of this for development planning in Indian country and its equivalents around the world?

DEVELOPMENT PLANNING AND THE QUESTION OF CULTURAL INTEGRITY

Just to be clear, the analogue to conventional approaches in international development is the assimilationist approach to Indigenous peoples. It long preceded the advent of development planning, of course, but such tactics as (in the US and Canada) allotment, termination, and relocation are very much in tune with Rostow's three "universal principles" and the development approach that flowed from them. The AD critique of conventional development planning therefore offers lessons for development in Indian country. We have organized them into three closely associated themes, culture and identity, sustenance, and sovereignty.

Culture and Identity

As discussed above, from an AD perspective, the aim of development is to expand a people's control over the things that matter most to them in their own lives, to increase their economic, political, and social freedom as they understand those things through the lens of their own cultural values. In order to articulate "the things that matter most to them" and create development goals based on them, people need to be clear about their cultural values and have a strong identity grounded in those values. They need a sense of themselves as part of a living culture and of the particular meanings of economic, political, and social freedom within that culture. Identity, culture, and development goals are interactive and mutually reinforcing (Figure 4.1). According to AD, when development actions are functioning properly, these components all receive feedback from and support one another.

Deriving development goals from a specific cultural context rather than from an abstract set of universal principles is more than a technical

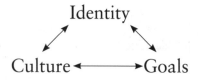

Figure 4.1   Identity, culture, and development goals

process; it requires the active participation of community members. Through their participation they validate the culture, keeping it alive and evolving. By giving voice to their understanding of economic, political, and social freedom and how to advance them, they shape the cultural meaning of those concepts and deepen their commitment to them. They also strengthen their cultural identity, their ties to the culture.

Sustenance

The AD perspective on the cultural basis of economies and of the importance of culture in economic development offers a vital insight to Indigenous development. It admits broader and more complex understandings of sustenance than does the conventional development discourse. In general, it allows for less materialistic definitions of development. From an Indigenous perspective, sustenance might be considered to include spiritual as well as physical aspects, for example. In that case a culturally based economy might be organized to enable people to balance work with other obligations – to family and community, for example. Such an approach might have a different understanding of wealth accumulation, an opportunity for a give-away as in the northwest potlatch, rather than ostentatious accumulation or conspicuous consumption.

Through an AD lens, Indigenous development would encourage and enable people to secure their livelihood through some combination of activities that might include employment, entrepreneurship, and subsistence activities (hunting, fishing, foraging) that is appropriate to their specific culture and circumstances.

Sovereignty

The political sovereignty that Indigenous peoples have been able to secure in recent decades has major implications for an AD approach to Indigenous development. As we have seen, identifying development goals and working out the means of achieving them are technical tasks under the conventional paradigm, since the overall goal – moving towards a high mass-consumption society – is given. But under AD the goals and means of achieving them are worked out through a participatory process. Sovereignty is the key to effective participatory processes in Indian country. It gives the community control over the administrative structures that design and implement the processes through which development goals are conceptualized and over the policy-making apparatus that puts them into effect.

To sum up, AD helps us set out an approach to Indigenous development that is based in cultural integrity.

1 It is a bottom-up, endogenous approach rather than the top-down, exogenous approach of conventional development. It advocates participatory processes to define culturally compatible development goals, processes that also reinforce tribal identity and strengthen culture.
2 It takes a broad view of sustenance, defining it as the ability to secure a livelihood in the ways that are most culturally appropriate.
3 It relies on sovereignty to build and maintain a culturally appropriate institutional framework through which development processes can be carried out.

WHAT DOES KAKE WANT?

We use the critical case of Kake, a Tlingit community located on the northwest shore of Kupreanof Island in southeast Alaska to illustrate the problems and opportunities of the AD approach. A critical case is one that "has strategic importance in relation to the general problem" with which the researcher is concerned (Flyvbjerg 2006, 229). Kake is a critical case because it provides an opportunity to contrast conventional development with AD approaches: What does "development as freedom" mean in one Indigenous community? The experience of Kake is not typical. It has many elements in common with other Indigenous communities, but in an extreme form that makes it a telling example of both conventional development and the emerging AD alternative. This is an "action research" project in that both authors have been actively involved in development planning with Kake for nearly ten years.

The Geography and Early History of Kake

The panhandle of southeast Alaska is an archipelago, a series of mountain chains that are more under the waters of the Northern Pacific than above. The mountains, capped with rocky glaciers, rise steeply above the ocean surface to heights of up to five thousand feet. Its marine ecosystem includes hillsides of western hemlock, Sitka spruce, and red and yellow cedar. Between the tree stands are muskeg, meadows, and (above 2,500 feet) alpine tundra. Medicinal and food vegetation include blueberries, huckleberries, cranberries, devil's club, Hudson Bay tea, and various lichens and mosses. Animals include moose, Sitka black-tailed deer, black bears, wolves, eagles, ravens, and various waterfowl and shorebirds. Sea mammals, fish, and tidal animals are plentiful: whales, orcas, dolphins, and seals; coho, sockeye, chum, and pink salmon; halibut and rockfish; crabs, sea urchins, sea cucumbers, chitons, mussels, cockles, and clams (Fulton 2008).

Eons of geological activity, largely volcanic, left these closely scattered islands accessible by boat via the many straits, fjords, and canals that infiltrate the mountain beaches and fresh water streams. Navigating these waterways for centuries, the Tlingit and other southeast Alaskan tribal peoples adapted autonomously. Historically, the Tlingit have been a very independent people. Relying on the bounty and variety of natural resources available in southeast Alaska, they fashioned their living and societal structure with little outside influence, except through trade with their immediate neighbours. Many of the flora and fauna just mentioned are still important subsistence food sources for the Tlingit.

The Tlingit were largely invisible to global economic and political powers until the 1870s. After the United States purchased Alaska from Russia in 1867, non-Natives began taking possession of land, although the Tlingits never signed treaties, nor did they sell their land (Hinkley 1996). The area around what is now Kake had been a traditional summer gathering site for the Keex' Kwaan (Kake) Tlingits, a base from which they fished, hunted, and smoked their catch. As white settlement encroached on them, Kake gradually became a permanent settlement for the Keex' Kwaan. By 1903 there were at least thirty sawed plank houses in Kake with glass windows and wood stoves, along with a school and a Quaker mission (Campbell 1988).

The Conventional Development Era

In 1906, processors from "outside" (outside Alaska, in Alaskan parlance) opened a commercial salmon saltery in Kake, the beginning of the community's involvement with conventional development (Meinhardt 2011). Another outside company built a salmon cannery on the site of the saltery in 1912, and at about the same time (the exact date is in doubt), Keex' Kwaan tribal Elders established the Kake municipal government (Fulton 2008).

In 1910 the US Congress passed the Organized Village Act, under which Alaska communities could obtain a territorial charter to set up a form of municipal self-government. Native villages were generally excluded from participation because Native people were not US citizens. However, there was a legal provision by which Natives could become citizens. Kake's Elders applied for and received US citizenship and obtained a municipal charter. They made a conscious decision to give up their traditional system of governance and adopt the formal American system. Kake was apparently the first Native community in Alaska to take this assimilative step (Jackson 2003). The Kake city government continues to operate under the laws of the state of Alaska. It provides essential infrastructure services and other typical municipal functions.

The global demand for canned salmon was robust and by 1920, over one hundred canneries were operating in Alaska. However, their financial situation was always precarious. Most of the canneries were undercapitalized and operated on thin margins. The Kake cannery changed hands at least four times – all the owners were outside companies – prior to its acquisition by the Organized Village of Kake (OVK) in 1948 (Meinhardt 2011).

OVK is the federally recognized tribal government of the Keex' Kwaan. It was formed in 1948 under the provisions of the US Indian Reorganization Act (IRA) of 1934. OVK advocates for and protects the resources of the Keex' Kwaan's customary and traditional gathering areas, the lands and surrounding waters for a radius of forty to fifty miles around the current site of Kake that the tribe historically inhabited and utilized. OVK is also responsible for the overall well-being of its tribal citizens. It provides many social services and educational programs for its citizens and the overall community of Kake.

One of the first acts of OVK was to buy the cannery, which at the time had been closed down by its outside owners. The tribe operated the cannery until the late 1970s when, along with many other Alaskan canneries, finances and changing market conditions forced its final closure (Firman and Bosworth 1990). It is important to note that commercial fishing remained a key component of the economy of Alaska, though the market shifted from canned to frozen salmon.

A second resource extraction industry, logging, came to southeast Alaska at about the time the Kake cannery closed. The Alaska Native

Claims Settlement Act (ANCSA) of 1971 transferred 11 per cent of Alaska's lands to Native groups as compensation for lands taken. The land was to be administered through more than two hundred local "village" corporations and thirteen regional corporations. The law established tribal members as shareholders in their village and regional corporations, and required that the Native corporations make a profit from their lands. Thus, the Keex' Kwaan are shareholders in the Kake Tribal Corporation and the Sealaska Tlingit Haida Regional Corporation.

The primary business of Kake Tribal, which was established in 1975, has been forest products. The corporation received title to substantial forest holdings in and around Kake. They created jobs through very large-scale timber operations, clear-cutting large areas of their forest lands, and selling logs and wood pulp on the global market. As Kake's timber allocation was harvested, Kake Tribal was forced to declare bankruptcy in 1999 and by 2004 all logging operations were discontinued; the corporation remains insolvent today.

To sum up, for a century Kake was something of a success story in terms of conventional development. The global demand for their resources, first salmon and then timber, provided a solid economic base for the community. Admittedly, there were problems. Like all natural resource work, it was seasonal and somewhat irregular, depending on market conditions. The cannery was owned by a series of outside firms for the first three decades of its existence. The work itself was gruelling and often dangerous. Nevertheless, these economic opportunities provided the Keex' Kwaan with a substantial material standard of living and brought new technologies to the community, from electricity to the Internet.

With the loss of both the cannery and the timber industries the economy of Kake essentially collapsed. The loss of jobs was so great that between 2002 and 2005 the population of Kake fell from about eight hundred to less than five hundred, as at least 150 working-age residents were forced to leave the community in search of employment. These conditions also brought confusion, distraction, and threats to the way of life of Kake residents. The virtual disappearance of the natural resource economy reinvigorated ongoing local conflicts over social, economic, and environmental change and what it means to be Keex' Kwaan.

A Comprehensive Economic Development Strategy for Kake?

In the winter of 2004 when logging was winding down in Kake, a doctoral student in anthropology at the University of Oregon was doing

field work there. Distressed by the situation, she made it her responsibility to try to find resources for the community. Among other things,
she connected Kake's community leadership with one of the co-authors,
Michael Hibbard. Through discussions, we mutually determined that the
most useful first step in responding to the crisis would be the creation
of a comprehensive economic development strategy (CEDS) plan for the
community. Hibbard invited the other co-author, Robert Adkins, a student with extensive experience in rural community economic development, to participate in the project.[3] As we acquainted ourselves with the
situation it quickly became apparent that the most critical and difficult
immediate issue was an outgrowth of the complex administrative framework in Kake.[4] The three organizations with governance responsibilities
in Kake – the city government, OVK, and Kake Tribal – have different
but overlapping missions and responsibilities. Moreover, they have different orientations towards development. Kake Tribal is by definition
a supporter of conventional development. It is a for-profit corporation
tasked with making money for its shareholders in the market economy.
OVK is the guardian of the Keex' Kwaan's cultural heritage, the people,
and their traditional land and seascape. The city is the provider of basic
services, such as infrastructure and public safety. These organizations
had difficulty communicating with one another and co-operation was
problematic because of a perception that they were engaged in a zero-
sum game in which success for one organization could only come at the
expense of another. As often happens in a crisis, the issues facing the
community were submerged by their rivalry. These divisions had to be
dealt with before any forward motion could occur.

Our approach was to form a CEDS Committee that included leadership from the three groups – the city mayor, the executive director of
OVK, and the vice-president of Kake Tribal Corporation – along with
other community leaders such as the Kake school superintendent and
the head of the newly formed small business association. Adkins worked
with the committee and community on-site in Kake over the summer
of 2004 under Hibbard's direction. The overt purpose was to develop
a CEDS plan for the community – a vision statement and a set of goals
and projects. The tacit aim was to build trust and a sense of common
purpose, with the work of the CEDS Committee as the vehicle.

Following an initial organizing meeting with the CEDS Committee,
Adkins facilitated an open "town hall" meeting to which all Kake residents were invited. They were invited to give input on their perceptions
of the problems and opportunities Kake faced and how the community

could best respond. In the months that followed, the CEDS Committee met several times to go over the information collected at the town hall meeting, to outline the community's vision statement, and to draft a set of goals for the community. At the end of the process all members of the CEDS Committee, acting on behalf of the entire Kake community, signed a Letter of Intent to Co-operate for the combined endeavour of economic development.

While suspicions and rivalries have not completely disappeared, the CEDS process did break down communication barriers among the three governance organizations and enabled the community to come to consensus around a set of community projects. The overall purpose of the CEDS plan, *The Way Forward*, which was promulgated in July 2005, was to identify and prioritize projects that would advance Kake's momentum towards socio-economic health. It called for potential community projects to be evaluated on the basis of four equally weighted priorities. Will the project:

· create local jobs that are a good fit for local workers?
· expand opportunities for local businesses?
· support, protect, and strengthen Tlingit cultural values?
· conserve and restore natural resources?

The Way Forward identified and prioritized fifty-five projects that the community wanted to undertake. Eight of them were accomplished before the plan was finalized in 2005. By 2010, an additional twenty-three projects were completed, were underway, or were funded and ready to implement, for a total of thirty-one project accomplishments. They address all parts of the community, from youth to the elderly; they deal with the environment, with infrastructure, and with personal health and well-being. Some examples of completed or underway projects are: the reconstruction of the dam for the reservoir that supplies water to the community; expansion of the medical clinic; acquisition of certified police personnel; and funding for construction of a multi-use passenger/freight/tourist dock.

CONCLUSION

What do the Kake CEDS process and resulting projects tell us about AD and Indigenous development? Let us return to the three themes of culture and identity, sustenance, and sovereignty.

With respect to culture and identity, it seems unlikely that Kake would have been able to pull itself out of the crisis of 2004 without something like the CEDS process. The community was immobilized by the apparent lack of options for responding to the economic calamity it faced, and the divisions among the competing governing groups seemed insoluble. The bottom-up CEDS process catalyzed the leadership of the three governance organizations and the community as a whole to think together about the substantive future they want for themselves. Intensive fishing and logging provided an economic base for Kake for a century, but it was ultimately unsustainable. The CEDS process allowed the community to think beyond conventional development and the market economy, to refocus on the Tlingit view of social, economic, and political freedom, and in doing so, to strengthen their Keex' Kwaan culture and identity.

Defining *sustenance* as the ability to secure a culturally appropriate livelihood may be the most powerful AD contribution to Kake's development plans. This is immediately apparent in the priorities the community put forward for evaluating possible development projects. The agreed-to priorities balance the environment, culture, and economy, implicitly acknowledging the lack of balance under the former traditional development regime based in commercial fishing and logging. And more explicit evidence is available.

We conducted a survey of the community during summer 2009 in preparation for an update of the CEDS plan. Among other things, we asked open-ended questions to try to assess how residents feel about Kake. In response to a question about "the things we most need to preserve in our community," 49 per cent said that preserving Tlingit culture is important; a further 21 per cent responded that preserving the Tlingit language is important; and 17 per cent mentioned the subsistence lifestyle. When asked what the community should change, 21 per cent stated that improving the town's physical appearance is important, 16 per cent indicated that old and abandoned buildings around town should be demolished, and 15 per cent felt that increasing the amount and availability of employment is important.

These responses directly mirror the priorities established four years previously in *The Way Forward*. Jobs are important but the preservation of Tlingit culture and language are overwhelming priorities. Maintaining opportunities for subsistence or wildlife harvesting also depends on conserving and restoring natural resources. One way to make the question more concrete is to think about the cash versus the subsistence economy in Kake. It is a truism that Keex' Kwaan (and other Native

Alaskan) culture is so bound up with subsistence that it is impossible to have the one without the other (Dombrowski 2001). But however deeply felt its cultural meaning, it is not nostalgia or sentimentality that guides the Keex' Kwaan towards subsistence. On a functional level, everyone who lives in Kake depends in part on subsistence for his or her survival; not everyone engages in subsistence activities but everyone receives the produce of subsistence through trade, gifts, and the like. The reverse is also true. Everyone who lives in Kake depends on the cash economy. However important subsistence is in Kake, there are things it cannot provide. Even though jobs have been scarce since the collapse of Kake Tribal's timber operation, households continue to find ways to generate income – from part-time work, remittances from family members living away from Kake, and from transfer payments. In fact, Kake households rely on what might be called the institutional cash economy to provide the infrastructure that makes the subsistence lifestyle (mixed-economy) possible. Considering "sustenance" in this context, the CEDS plan seems to have done a good job of allowing the community to convey its sense of the appropriate balance between economic growth and the non-economic aspects of Keex' Kwaan culture and lifestyle.

Sovereignty is a delicate and complex theme in the Kake context. In the AD paradigm, a community relies on sovereignty to build and maintain a culturally appropriate institutional framework through which development processes can be carried out. Legally, the only sovereign entity in Kake is OVK. The city is a constituent unit of the state of Alaska. Kake Tribal is a for-profit company. The CEDS Committee is an attempt to establish an institution outside any of the existing organizations through which they can all consult, collaborate, and perhaps reach consensus about issues of importance to the community, without surrendering any of their own autonomy. It is as effective as the members allow it to be, and so far they have given it quite a bit of credence. As such, it has provided the culturally appropriate institutional framework Kake needs to carry out its development planning. But it is not sovereign. To recapitulate, AD privileges cultural context. In the AD paradigm the purpose of development is to expand people's control over the things that matter most to them in their own lives, to increase economic, political, and social freedom as they understand them through their own cultural lens. But that control is not unlimited. There are the political limits we referred to in the introduction to this chapter, limits that are being challenged but are nonetheless still prevalent. But we are thinking of another kind of challenge, one that Indigenous communities have to deal with very carefully. To frame it in the case of Kake, the challenge is to decide collectively what paths and forms of development are appropriate to reach a shared vision of the future. Contrary to making the cruel choice, Kake did not choose one or the other, tradition or modernity, subsistence or cash. Rather they have shown that tradition and modernity are not mutually exclusive and that communities can choose both. Indeed, if Kake is any indication, communities must choose both.

ACKNOWLEDGMENTS

We are grateful to the Keex' Kwaan for allowing us to become involved with their extraordinary community in an especially difficult time for them. We also want to express our respect for the leadership of the members of the Kake CEDS Committee and the OVK Council in providing a vision of the way forward for their community. Finally, it is impossible to adequately put into words our admiration for OVK General Manager Gary Williams; he is a model professional public servant in his dedication to the Keex' Kwaan.

NOTES

1 It is not our purpose here to offer a comprehensive analysis of development planning. Our aim is more limited – to discuss the connections between culture and economy as they are understood in development planning.
2 Rostow considers mostly fairly large (in population and land mass) countries. Although he has little to say directly about smaller entities, his analysis is still important because of its central role in defining the field.
3 Adkins has completed his graduate work at the University of Oregon. He continues to work with Kake as a consultant in planning and economic development.
4 Because of our direct involvement in the process we use the first person to describe the development of the CEDS plan.

REFERENCES

Bishaw, Alemayehu, and Suzanne Macartney. 2010. "Poverty: 2008 and 2009." American Community Survey Briefs ACSBR/09–1. http://www.census.gov/prod/2010pubs/acsbr09-1.pdf. Accessed 1 October 2010.
Brody, Hugh. 1983. *Maps and Dreams*. New York: Penguin Books.

Campbell, Rabich C. 1988. *Raven's Wrinkled Foot: Cultural Resources Overview of Kupreanof Island, Southeast Alaska*. USDA Forest Service Stikine Area, Tongass National Forest.

Cornell, Stephen, and Joseph Kalt. 1998. *Sovereignty and Nation-Building: The Development Challenge in Indian Country Today*. Cambridge: Harvard Project on American Indian Economic Development.

De Paula, Silvana, and Gary A. Dymski. 2005. *Reimagining Growth: Towards a Renewal of Development Theory*. New York: Zed Books.

DeNavas-Walt, Carmen, Bernadette D. Proctor, and Jessica C. Smith. 2010. "Income, Poverty, and Health Insurance Coverage in the United States: 2009." US Census Bureau Current Population Reports P60–238. http://www.census.gov/prod/2010pubs/p60-238.pdf, accessed 1 October 2010.

Dombrowski, Kirk. 2001. *Against Culture: Development, Politics, and Religion in Indian Alaska*. Lincoln: University of Nebraska Press.

Duffy, Diane, and Jerry Stubben. 1998. "An Assessment of Native American Economic Development: Putting Culture and Sovereignty Back in the Models." *Studies in Comparative International Development* 32 (4):52–78.

Firman, Anne S., and Robert G. Bosworth. 1990. "Harvest and Use of Fish and Wildlife by Residents of Kake, Alaska." Technical paper no. 145. Juneau: Alaska Department of Fish and Game.

Flyvbjerg, Bent. 2006. "Five Misunderstandings about Case-Study Research." *Qualitative Inquiry* 12 (2, April):219–45.

Fulton, Kathryn Anne. 2008. *Personhood, Discourse, and Environment in a Tlingit Village*. PhD dissertation, Anthropology Department, University of Oregon.

Goulet, Denis 1971. *The Cruel Choice: A New Concept in the Theory of Development*. New York: Atheneum.

Grondona, Mariano. 2000. "A Cultural Typology of Economic Development." In *Culture Matters: How Values Shape Human Progress*, edited by Lawrence E. Harrison and Samuel P. Huntington. New York: Basic Books.

Hibbard, Michael. 2006. "Tribal Sovereignty, the White Problem, and Reservation Planning." *Journal of Planning History* 5 (2):87–105.

Hibbard, Michael, and Marcus B. Lane. 2004. "By the Seat of Your Pants: Indigenous Action and State Response." *Journal of Planning Theory and Practice* 5 (1):97–104.

Hibbard, Michael, Marcus B. Lane, and Kathleen Rasmussen. 2008. "The Split Personality of Planning: Indigenous Peoples and Planning for Land Use and Resource Management." *Journal of Planning Literature* 23 (2):136–51.

Hinckley, Ted C. 1996. *The Canoe Rocks: Alaska's Tlingit and the Euroamerican Frontier, 1800–1912*. Lanham, MD: University Press of America.

Houser, Schuyler. 1995. "Mending the Circle: Peer Group Lending for Micro-Enterprise Development in Tribal Communities." In *Rural Development Strategies*, edited by David W. Sears and J. Norman Reid. Chicago: Nelson-Hall Publishers.

Infoplease. 2010. "American Indians by the Numbers," from the US Census Bureau. http://www.infoplease.com/spot/aihmcensus1.html, accessed 1 October 2010.

Jackson, Dawn. 2003. *Kake Discourse*. Letter to the Ford Foundation Community Forestry Research Fellowship workshop. Cited in Fulton 2008.

Jones, Eric L. 2006. *Cultures Merging: A Historical and Economic Critique of Culture*. Princeton: Princeton University Press.

Jorgensen, Joseph G. 1986. "Federal Policies, American Indian Polities and the 'New Federalism.'" *American Indian Culture and Research Journal* 10 (2):1–13.

Jorgensen, Miriam, ed. 2007. *Rebuilding Native Nations*. Tucson: University of Arizona Press.

Landes, David S. 1998. *The Wealth and Poverty of Nations*. New York: Norton.

Lane, Marcus B., and Michael Hibbard. 2005. "Doing It for Themselves: Transformative Planning by Indigenous Peoples." *Journal of Planning Education and Research* 25 (2):172–84.

Marglin, Stephen A. 2008. *The Dismal Science: How Thinking Like an Economist Undermines Community*. Cambridge: Harvard University Press.

Meinhardt, Robert L. 2011. *The Keku Cannery National Historic Landmark Preservation Plan*. Juneau: US Bureau of Indian Affairs Alaska Region Branch of Regional Archeology.

Morris, Ian. 2010. *Why the West Rules – For Now: The Patterns of History and What They Reveal About the Future*. New York: Farrar, Straus and Giroux.

Pinel, Sandra Lee. 2007. "Culture and Cash: How Two New Mexico Pueblos Combined Culture and Development." *Alternatives* 32:9–39.

Polanyi, Karl. 1944. *The Great Transformation*. Boston: Beacon Press.

Porter, Michael. 1990. *The Competitive Advantage of Nations*. New York: Free Press.

Presidential Commission on Indian Reservation Economies. 1984. *Report and Recommendations to the President of the United States*. Washington, DC: USGPO.

Rostow, W.W. 1960. *The Stages of Economic Growth: A Non-Communist Manifesto*. Cambridge: Cambridge University Press.

Sen, Amartya. 2000. *Development as Freedom*. New York: Knopf.

Smith, Dean Howard. 1994. "The Issue of Compatibility Between Cultural Integrity and Economic Development among Native American Tribes." *American Indian Culture and Research Journal* 18 (2):177–205.

– 2000. *Modern Tribal Development*. Walnut Creek, CA: AltaMira Press.

Stiglitz, Joseph E., Jose Antonio Ocampo, Shari Spiegel, Ricardo French-Davis, and Deepak Nayyar. 2006. *Stability with Growth: Macroeconomics, Liberalization, and Development*. Oxford: Oxford University Press.

Task Force on Indian Economic Development. 1986. *Report of the Task Force on Indian Economic Development*. Washington, DC: US Department of the Interior.

Wilkinson, Charles. 1987. *American Indians, Time, and the Law: Native Societies in a Modern Constitutional Democracy*. New Haven: Yale University Press.

– 2005. *Blood Struggle: The Rise of Modern Indian Nations*. New York: W.W. Norton.

5

Community-Based and Comprehensive: Reflections on Planning and Action in First Nations

LAURA MANNELL, FRANK PALERMO, AND
CRISPIN SMITH

There is overwhelming evidence of the urgent need for planning in First Nation communities in Canada, planning that is community-based, comprehensive, and ultimately leads to action. This type of planning is not optional, nor should it be seen as an experiment, a distraction, or an imposition on communities, many of which are facing difficult challenges. Thinking ahead, having a direction, taking concerted action, giving communities the tools to shape the future, raising expectations, and providing hope for young and old must be seen as a key priority.

Community-based and comprehensive planning matters. The concepts underlying this approach are important but what is critical are the details and the intention behind this type of planning. Community-based planning is not just about talking to a few people or limited to producing a plan which comes from and is appropriated by the community, it must also raise expectations, challenge the status quo, and serve as a vehicle to build community and local capacity. Comprehensive planning is not just about considering all sectors in a community. More fundamentally it is about seeing the community as a whole, across departments, agencies, budgets, and personalities. It is health, recreation, education, environment, economics, infrastructure – all at the same time. Community-based, comprehensive planning should lead to action that is dynamic, immediate and long-term, and locally empowering. Community-based comprehensive planning is about making a difference.

This chapter describes an evolving planning model and approach to practice emerging from planning efforts in First Nation communities in Canada. The analysis is based on consolidating discoveries arrived at through work in the field using an approach called reflective practice. The approach sees practice, reflection, and learning as a continuous interdependent loop (Schön 1983). Community planning relies on work in the field; ideas, methods, and tools are tested and refined based on experience on the ground. These refinements are then incorporated into practice through plan development and plan implementation. This cyclical approach to practice, reflection, and learning leads to new discoveries. It is that experience of learning from practice which serves as the basis for the evidence and the position taken in this chapter.[1]

In addition to presenting the argument for planning and the need for it to be community-based, comprehensive, and lead to action, this chapter presents a way of measuring whether a plan is truly community-based and comprehensive. It is based on a series of planning elements. Elements are the reasons why planning must be community-based and comprehensive. They describe the benefits that will be achieved through the process of developing and implementing a plan. This chapter also presents a series of planning principles, which are methods about how to conduct good planning in order to achieve the elements; they are specific notions about what needs to be done during plan development and implementation.

THE NEED FOR PLANNING

It is time to put to rest the debate about the need for planning in First Nation communities. It is not a new idea for First Nations or an imported one. As long as people have grouped together into communities, there has been a need for planning. People gathered together to enhance survival and with hopes of prospering. They formed communities to endure in unforgiving environments, protect each other from real or perceived threats, share tasks, form alliances, and build a better future together than they could hope to achieve as individuals. From those very early moments long before planning existed as a profession, the idea of planning has been embedded and fundamental to all communities. Survival, protection, efficiency, and identity were, and are, dependent on it.

It is this collective sense of purpose that holds a community together. What is shared is not just a common history but also more importantly a vision of a brighter collective future. Planning gives individuals a say in how their community is shaped and empowers a community to think beyond individual needs. This perspective requires a clear sense of direction, which provides the basis for a community's organizational structure, as well as a path for all community members to take informed, immediate action.

Planning enables communities to anticipate and direct change, rather than simply react to it. It allows communities to be more self-sufficient, shape their own future and make positive change happen on their own terms. It is a tool for negotiation, decision making, collaboration, coordination, and empowerment. Planning is also a process. It is both significant and transformative; it is a catalyst for change.

George Harrison's (2002) lyric, "If you don't know where you are going, any road will take you there" gets at the heart of the need for a plan. People generally value this need in their personal lives; plans give direction whether practicing an art, training for a competition, or researching an investment. Many First Nations frequently exist in a crisis-driven and reactive mode. Limited resources have to address a bewildering array of pressing daily issues, such as housing shortages, health problems, poverty, and unemployment.

For many years government programs have dictated and shaped development in First Nation communities. Programs and initiatives must fit into the mandates of complicated and limiting bureaucracies to secure funding for even basic and essential projects. Rather than responding to local needs and circumstances, First Nations have to find ways of conforming to program requirements dictated by government programs far removed from the situation on the ground. On top of this, communities must deal with reporting requirements and react to local issues, immediate crises, and global pressures. In many ways, there are too many plans, no single direction, and too much bureaucracy.

Keeping up with basic programs and reacting to current issues can be completely overwhelming and totally consuming for smaller communities. In their attempts to manoeuvre the maze of federal bureaucracy, communities develop structures that mirror federal departments and agencies, in turn creating their own bureaucracies, limiting creativity, and stifling innovation. These issues argue for the need for change. Crises at the local level cannot be dealt with individually nor will they be addressed by the federal government. Change will come from a sense of what the future can and should be, from a sense of hope and empowerment to shape the future.

There is an urgent need for planning in every First Nation community. It must be seen as a priority and invested in accordingly. Planning is

116

an opportunity to build and transform a community. But in order for planning to live up to its potential, in order for it to affect real change, there are two essential ingredients that must be included in the process, the product, and the ensuing action – planning needs to be "community-based" and "comprehensive." The next two sections explain these essential ingredients in greater detail and present a series of elements associated with each.

Community-Based Elements

Historically, planning in First Nation communities has been done by outside agencies, governmental departments, and private consultants. The result is a "community plan" that has little relevance to the local context and is of little use to communities. These plans reflect the needs of outside government organizations and professionals instead of the needs and desires of community members. The opinions of youths, Elders, seniors, off-reserve members, single parents, and many others are often unheard, while the cultural, social, economic, environmental, and spiritual aspects of community life are overlooked.

While the need for planning to involve community members is clear, there is still much debate about what is considered adequate community involvement.[2] There are many "community plans" that are done with little-to-no community engagement. Community engagement is often a token gesture, used to validate work done in isolation of a community. If a plan is going to serve as a collective expression of community aspirations, provide motivation and direction, establish an approach and attitude towards action, and make change happen far into the future, then it must involve a broad cross section of a community.

There are six elements that detail the "what" and the "why" of community-based planning. These elements refer to the benefits of genuine community involvement and provide the basis for measuring whether or not a plan is community-based. A community-based approach will establish awareness, build community, develop capacity, raise expectations, voice opinions, and nurture creativity. Each of these elements implies that a plan is not done for or to a community but by a community. Community in this regard includes everyone and cannot be limited to the chief, councillors, and band staff. The plan is not the chief's direction, or the staff's hopes, or a councillor's pet project; its life, intentions, and scope have to be more inclusive. The community must be involved in every way, from beginning to end: researching, analyzing, discussing, imagining, inventing, mapping, drawing, designing, building, updating, and maintaining. The term "community-based" should only be applied to plans that achieve these elements.

ESTABLISH AWARENESS

As Judy Bear (2010) of the Flying Dust First Nation said, "You don't have to be a Chief or a councillor to make change happen. You don't have to be in leadership to be a leader." But it is common for residents to feel uncertainty about how they can make a difference in their community. Not having a venue for discussion or someone who is willing to listen can lead to apathy, lack of confidence, and disenfranchisement. Planning is a tool for change. Establishing awareness of planning ensures that people understand this tool, how to use it and that there are tangible benefits that come from getting involved in one's community. Awareness of planning and understanding that it will make a difference encourages individuals to actively participate in their community, engage in decisions about their future, and take a role in making positive change happen.

During plan development in Woodstock First Nation (NB), for example, youths were engaged in a planning activity where they were encouraged to draw pictures of what they would like to see in their community. A common theme in many of the pictures was the local school bus driver, illustrating his cruelty and some graphic images of what the kids hoped would happen to him. The session became an opportunity to probe the issue further.

The issue was taken to the chief and council who investigated the situation and discovered that the youths indeed were dealing with an abusive situation and they took action to fire the bus driver. The youths felt greatly empowered and pleased that their involvement in the planning process had led to change. Following this, they created a youth Planning Work Group (PWG) that met regularly to work on the plan and share ideas for what kind of a future they wanted to see in Woodstock.[3] This example illustrates how planning develops awareness of issues, as well as confidence that the process can affect change; the benefits of planning encouraged a group of youths to get involved in their community and make change happen.

BUILD COMMUNITY

The process of bringing people and ideas together is at the core of what builds community. Developing and implementing a community-based plan intrinsically builds a greater sense of community. It builds consensus and encourages co-operation and communication, provides a forum to discuss problems, and overcomes differences to develop common goals for the future. It is also an opportunity to share local knowledge, history and culture. Planning allows a community to come together, work collaboratively, and accomplish more as a group than would be possible as individuals.

During the development of their plan, Cowessess First Nation (SK), for example, held a series of workshops to develop a vision: a bold statement of their community's ambitions and long-term aspirations. These meetings were some of the first instances that participants could remember where representatives from every family sat down at the same table to discuss their community without animosity. In leaving their differences at the door, Cowessess community members were able to work together to create their vision statement: "We respect and honour the diversity of our First Nation; from this strength we will all walk together to flourish as a united, healthy community for generations to come" (Cowessess First Nation and Cities and Environment Unit [CEU] 2009, 63). The vision also includes a postscript stating that the vision is not just the responsibility of the chief and council but the shared duty of the entire community.

Inspired by the vision, Cowessess community members, with support from the chief and council, took it upon themselves to open their own coffee shop. Their goal was to create a place where people young and old could gather to share stories and learn from each other. The coffee shop serves meals, snacks, tea, and coffee. Run by volunteers and supported by donations from band members, it has become a place for the whole community. It is a hub for meetings and informal gatherings and a spot for posting information and community bulletins. The actions taken by Cowessess community members illustrate the power of a community-based process and its ability to build community both socially and physically.

DEVELOP CAPACITY

Community-based planning builds the capacity and confidence of community members. This allows them to play a meaningful and ongoing role in planning, decision making, and in the development of their community. Throughout the development of a plan, skills and knowledge are built in civic engagement and communication, organizing and hosting community meetings and events, and creating newsletters and websites pertaining to community activities. As a plan is implemented and projects are initiated, designed, and built, other skills are developed in fundraising, project management, design, and construction. A community-based approach ensures that the community has the skills, knowledge, and awareness to be a force for action and change.

For example, a local planning team, or Planning Work Group (PWG) in Standing Buffalo Dakota Nation (SK) was established when the planning process began in 2009. The group quickly became involved in many aspects of community life: organizing and running meetings, publishing newsletters, creating blogs, and developing a community calendar to publicize events and promote the Dakota language. These tasks were taken on by the entire group, which provided many individuals an opportunity to gain new experiences and develop skills.

The PWG made a point of visiting other communities from the Saskatchewan pilot project to learn from their planning experiences. They visited Kahkewistahaw First Nation (SK) in 2009 as they were developing their community market, Kinistin Saulteaux Nation (SK) in 2010 as they were constructing their powwow arbour, and kept in regular touch with members of Pasqua First Nation while developing their plan. All were opportunities for the PWG to be inspired, develop skills, and learn from other First Nations about planning, design, and organizing community projects. In 2010 the PWG began work on a community garden, greenhouse, and storage shed. The construction process attracted a number of volunteers. One volunteer, realizing her enjoyment and skill in carpentry, applied to a carpentry apprenticeship program referencing her recent experiences and was accepted. This example demonstrates how capacity-building is a fundamental part of community-based planning and the impact it can have on individual band members and the community alike.

RAISE EXPECTATIONS

For many politicians and community leaders, there exists a fear of raising expectations through the development of a community plan. Broad community engagement leads to many projects and ideas about how a community can create a better future. Occasionally, there is hesitancy by leadership to include these projects in a plan, especially when there is such uncertainty about funding. While some would argue the need to maintain more "realistic" expectations, there is an urgent need to raise expectations. Planning is an opportunity to elevate hope for a brighter future.

Many First Nations face an assortment of difficult issues including poverty, alcoholism, drug addiction, depression, suicide, unemployment, and gambling. These can lead to feelings of hopelessness that will persist without a positive view of the future. Planning is about moving beyond the status quo. It is about being proactive as opposed to constantly reacting to day-to-day crises. It involves thinking about where a community wants to be down the road and taking calculated actions to achieve this future. In this way a plan creates hope. It raises expectations and cultivates a belief that a community can be anything and everything it wants to be.

The Kinistin Saulteaux Nation (SK) provides an example. They published their plan in December 2009, and in the summer of 2010 community members began exploring the idea of constructing a powwow arbour and hosting their first powwow since the 1980s. Using recycled power poles as supports, an innovative tensile roof structure, and the skills and hard work of many band members, the community built its arbour over a two-week period in mid-July. The new structure addresses a number of issues identified in the plan including a lack of opportunities to showcase artistic talent, limited cultural activities, a need for spaces to host celebrations, and the ongoing loss of traditional knowledge and values (Kinistin Saulteaux Nation and CEU 2009). The arbour was seen as an opportunity to fortify traditions and create opportunities for celebration and in this way was much more than a physical structure. As one community member articulated, the powwow arbour was about "building hope and the raising of expectations" (Lumberjack 2010).

The Kinistin arbour inspired many community members to see that anything is possible. It raised expectations by turning a long-standing dream of the community into reality without being limited by funding or programs.

VOICE OPINIONS

Communities are made up of many individuals with diverse needs and different opinions about what they value, what areas need urgent attention, and what is not subject to compromise about the place they call home. As a result there are often competing interests, priorities, and agendas. At the same time, community members frequently share similar opinions but may be hesitant to discuss them publicly for fear of being chastised, especially if touching on a sensitive topic. A community-based approach promotes dialogue and creative solutions to difficult problems

Figure 5.1   Building the Kinistin Saulteaux Nation powwow arbour. Courtesy of Cities and Environment Unit, Dalhousie University

Figure 5.2   Kinistin Saulteaux Nation powwow arbour. Courtesy of Cities and Environment Unit, Dalhousie University

by providing an inclusive forum for discussion, negotiation, compromise, and consensus-building. Community-based planning enables everyone in a community to voice opinions in a supportive environment and to be heard by others. It brings difficult subjects into the open, allowing them to be discussed, debated, and ultimately addressed. This approach builds a plan that has real relevance to the local context and that will be of true value to local residents

Flying Dust First Nation (SK) community members, for example, embrace a number of spiritual beliefs and perspectives on Christianity, traditionalism, and atheism. These differences of opinion came to the forefront during the development of value statements for their community plan. Value statements are meant to "describe what the community believes to be important and enduring truths about the quality of life" (CEU 2003b, 36) in a community. The planning process enabled participants to have an honest and open discussion about their differences and determine together values that were reflective of the whole community; values about love, family, and friendships, the teachings of Elders, commitment, respect, understanding, and tolerance (Flying Dust First Nation and CEU 2007).

The planning process enabled many voices to be heard and opinions to be expressed and eventually consensus was built. Ultimately, band members were surprised to realize that despite their diversity, most community members shared the same dreams, desires, and ambitions for their community.

NURTURE CREATIVITY

First Nation communities are frequently settling for solutions that have been designed for another context: imported prefabricated homes, standard suburban subdivisions, imposed policies, and band governance structures. These solutions are intended to work for all communities, despite the differing physical, social, cultural, and population characteristics of the places where they are applied. Consequently, they are often fraught with problems, as they do not meet the needs of local residents or build on local opportunities.

A plan developed and implemented by community members will reflect the local context as well as the creativity of community members. Residents are encouraged to get involved, share ideas about their community, and highlight what is special. As a result, no project in a community will be "off-the-shelf" – every project will be seen as an opportunity for the community to design for its needs and create something that is unique. This approach ultimately demands more from community members themselves, as well as the consultants, engineers, architects, and government officials with whom they work. It nurtures creativity by encouraging community members to think outside the box, challenge the status quo, and not settle for anything mediocre. In doing so, this approach strives to achieve the most for the least, having far-reaching benefits beyond a single project or individual.

The idea for Shoal Lake Cree Nation's (SK) outdoor classroom, for example, was outlined in the action chapter of their plan and was constructed during the summer of 2008 (Shoal Lake Cree Nation and CEU 2007). In a community where the housing stock is dominated by prefabricated ready-to-move imported homes, the design of the classroom was a refreshing opportunity to draw inspiration from the local landscape, customs, traditions, and technology (Shoal Lake Cree Nation and CEU 2008). The curved trusses of the roof structure are inspired in part by the curved shapes of traditional snow shoes, while the techniques used for curving the timber beams made use of an indigenous technology, a cradleboard jig, to bend and shape wet wood. The circular shape implied by the classroom's decking reflects the importance of the circle in traditional design. The project demonstrates a new attitude towards building not just a classroom but any project in the community.

The community-based approach to developing this project involved many community members and engendered significant support for the project in the community. This support was most apparent in the group of youth who took an active role in building the classroom. The youths were initially sceptical of the project and threatened to burn it down as soon as it was completed, but over the course of the project they became active participants in its construction. By being involved, the kids developed a sense of ownership for their outdoor classroom and even christened it with a nickname, the ODC, an acronym for "outdoor classroom," and a true mark of ownership.

Comprehensive Elements

There are many plans being produced with and for First Nation communities: infrastructure plans, health plans, capital plans, economic development plans, and land-use plans to name a few. Having a community plan that is comprehensive and holistic is a way of aligning all these other plans under a common umbrella, ensuring that they are all working towards a common goal for the future. Comprehensive

Figure 5.3   Building the Shoal Lake Cree Nation outdoor classroom. Courtesy of Cities and
Environment Unit, Dalhousie University

planning means seeing a community as a whole, across departments,
agencies, budgets, and personalities; it considers and connects all aspects
of a community. In this sense, planning is not just another project or
program, it is the glue which holds all projects and programs together. A
comprehensive approach to planning ensures that planning is a priority
and not just one part of a larger strategy.

In order for planning to succeed in First Nation communities it must
be comprehensive; it cannot be seen as a side project or fit neatly into a
single department or "silo." It is not the agenda of one chief and council for one term or election. It is the shared direction that must guide
every policy, project, and action over the long-term. A comprehensive
approach to planning must see a community whole, identify gaps, consider the local and global contexts, and think long-term but lead to

Figure 5.4   Shoal Lake Cree Nation outdoor classroom. Courtesy of Cities and Environment Unit, Dalhousie University

immediate action. The following section outlines these four comprehensive elements in detail.

SEE A COMMUNITY WHOLE

First Nation communities are often organized in ways that stifle creativity and narrow people's perspectives. Band administration and programs are arranged to mirror federal departments and funding structures, limiting the potential for collaboration and coordination. The result is redundancy, repetition, and competition: a school gym that is closed while Elders look for a place to exercise; a health van sitting idle while recreation programs scramble to find transportation; ready-to-move housing that is bought from across the province while skilled community members sit at home jobless.

While there is no shortage of planning activities in First Nation communities, what is often missing is a connection between these initiatives. Comprehensive planning identifies these connections thereby clearing the way for people and departments to coordinate efforts and collaborate across departmental boundaries. It enables leadership, band staff, and all other community members to step back from departmental goals and think about their community as a whole. It reduces competition, strengthens communication, and facilitates the sharing of resources. Projects and programs become the responsibility of not one department, councillor, or individual, but the responsibility of everyone.

Pictou Landing First Nation (NS) provides an example. They completed their community plan in 2002 and shortly after began developing conceptual designs for a community centre, a key project that emerged from their plan (CEU 2002). The health centre was the first component to be built. It was seen as an opportunity to bridge departments within the community and at the federal level. Thinking about local materials became an opportunity to develop the community's managed forest, selectively cutting small-diameter spruce trees and restructuring the community-run sawmill. This provided an opportunity to develop an innovative heating system that could use sawdust and woodcuttings as a fuel source. This centre was designed and constructed to build capacity and training in addition to the economic and employment spinoffs. A variety of federal departments supported the project, including Health Canada, Aboriginal Affairs and Northern Development Canada, Human Resources Canada, and Environment Canada.

Government departments were able to think differently about what a health centre might achieve because the community itself began to fundamentally change its own notion of what a health centre could be. Initially viewed as a place for sick people and carrying a corresponding stigma, over the course of many discussions it evolved into a more comprehensive idea of staying healthy by being active, eating well, and engaging the community. The new health centre was positioned in the middle of the small fishing community, occupying a central place not just in the community, but in the daily routines and lives of band members, providing spaces for health facilities, a community kitchen, administrative offices, a meeting hall, a police office, classrooms, and an outdoor space which included a medicinal herb garden. This example is an illustration of the collaboration, co-operation, and success that is possible when a community is looked at as a whole.

IDENTIFY GAPS

While a comprehensive approach to planning is useful for recognizing overlap and common ground between various aspects of a community, it is also useful in identifying gaps in services and programming, identifying vulnerable segments of the population, and recognizing needs that are going unmet. A comprehensive approach considers projects and ideas that are outside the responsibilities of any individual or department. A comprehensive planning approach ensures program and service voids are identified and addressed.

The Shoal Lake Cree Nation (SK) Community Plan, for example, defines five "action areas," which describe priority areas where the community needs to focus more energy and attention. In developing their action areas, community members were encouraged to think about their community as a whole, and determine if there were outstanding issues in the community that were not being addressed. "Community togetherness" emerged as an important theme, including ideas about reconnecting members to the land and each other, providing a broad range of cultural and recreational activities to bring people together, and opening new avenues of communication (Shoal Lake Cree Nation and CEU 2007). After completing their plan, Shoal Lake re-examined how they were organized, keeping in mind their plan's action areas. They realized that "community togetherness" was no one's responsibility and that there were no existing programs focusing on this area. To address this gap, the community proposed adding a councillor position. This person would be responsible for this portfolio area and would work on this priority on an ongoing basis. This example demonstrates that by thinking about a community comprehensively and looking for opportunities to collaborate and find connections, it is possible to identify and address gaps in services.

CONSIDER THE LOCAL AND GLOBAL CONTEXTS

A comprehensive planning approach considers and respects the local and global contexts of a community. It capitalizes on local knowledge, labour, and materials to develop skills, build capacity for future projects, promote local business, and create employment. The approach requires that every project be considerate of the community scale ensuring that projects fit within the community's physical and social contexts.

But communities do not exist in isolation: once-remote fly-in communities are now connected by roads and highways while mobile phone service, satellite television, and high-speed Internet connect communities to vast sources of knowledge and inspiration. This wealth of information and access to learning provide best practices and cases studies that can be adapted to local circumstances. Communities are also increasingly affected by world events. Global climate change, political and economic instability, and global pressures to increase resource extraction all have direct effects on Canadian First Nations. A comprehensive approach to planning ensures that a plan is a tool to help navigate regional, national, and global contexts by being clear about what action is needed at home.

An example can be found in the Mikisew Cree Nation (AB), which is located 225 kilometres north of Fort McMurray, the centre of the oil sands industry in Canada. A significant portion of oil sands development is situated within the lower Athabasca watershed, affecting the health of the water, air, and land that Mikisew members consider to be their traditional lands and infringing on their ability to hunt and eat wild meat and fish from the area. With increasing development pressure and the associated environmental, cultural, and economic challenges and opportunities, band members and leadership recognized the urgent need to think about their future. The negative impacts of the oil and gas industry influenced the community's vision statement, which recognizes that the community's "traditional culture and connection to the Land are essential to [the community's] future well-being" (Mikisew Cree First Nation and CEU 2010). The statement establishes the important linkage between the people and the land and presents this as the foundation for a "strong, healthy and independent First Nation" (Mikisew Cree First Nation and CEU 2010). It also recognizes the community's wants and needs and in doing so provides the community with a substantial instrument for negotiations with government and industry. The vision statement provides a useful tool that can have substantial effects on both the local and global communities of which Mikisew is a part.

THINK LONG-TERM AND TAKE IMMEDIATE ACTION
While long-term thinking is fundamental to planning, it is equally important to take immediate action. Many plans focus on larger-scale, longer-term projects such as new housing developments, improved community facilities, and expanded infrastructure. While these projects are vital, it is also important for planning to encourage immediate action: rethink daily routines, improve day-to-day operations, and develop small-scale community projects right away. Comprehensive planning is about considering projects of many scales, both short and long-term. This perspective encourages projects that can be accomplished not just by band staff and leadership, but also by community members.

This idea is essential for maintaining momentum for planning and to ensure that planning does not end once a plan document is published. Immediate action builds assurance in community members that their ideas matter and that planning is both necessary and will make a difference. Every project, big or small, is an opportunity to take action and change a community.

During the development of their plan, George Gordon First Nation (SK) identified the need for more opportunities to showcase local talents and focus on cultural events including powwows, round dances, sweats, and musical performances (George Gordon First Nation and CEU 2007). Prompted by this need, band members decided to take immediate action and build a powwow arbour. A site was chosen, funding was secured, and many community members got involved in building the arbour. This project created a sense of pride for all those involved and increased momentum and excitement for planning before the plan document was even complete.

George Gordon held their first powwow in 2008 and it has since become an annual event and highlight on the Saskatchewan powwow trail. The powwow held in the arbour each year enables community members to continually showcase local talent and focus on cultural events. This achievement will be celebrated far into the future.

Planning makes a difference. It leads to action and change. The elements begin with creating awareness about planning's ability to make a difference. They end with taking action both long-term and immediate, actually making that difference a reality, and making significant, noticeable change happen on the ground.

PLANNING PRINCIPLES

Principles are important ideas about how to conduct good planning in order to achieve the elements. They are important notions about how to make the process, the product, and the action community-based and comprehensive. There are six major principles described in this section. They are not specific to the community-based or comprehensive elements of the approach, but rather affect both. Each principle has corresponding best practices that describe an approach and attitude regarding how to incorporate the principle into planning practice.[4]

Engage a Broad Cross-Section of the Community (Build Redundancy)

A plan cannot be championed by a single individual or implemented by one department alone. A fundamental aspect of the community-based planning process is to engage a broad cross-section of a community (not only leadership, or those in powerful positions) to ensure broad awareness of planning. Communities are dynamic places: community members move to and from reserves, band staff come and go, chiefs and councillors are elected to fixed terms. If a plan becomes the responsibility of one department, if it is understood by only a few individuals, or if it is the portfolio of just one councillor, it will not have adequate momentum to keep planning alive. A plan cannot just come from the community; it must be understood, championed, and appropriated by the community. This is a large part of what makes a community plan such an effective tool for change. It is a responsibility shared by many individuals, all departments, and every elected official. This "redundancy" helps maintain and build momentum for planning despite a community's ever-changing nature. Every person in a community has the potential to affect change. If a plan is to be a tool for change, then the more widely and more broadly understood it is, the more powerful a tool it will be.

To ensure broad community involvement in the planning process, the creation of a local PWG is a necessity. This group is intimately involved in developing and implementing a plan. The PWG is meant to be representative of the whole community, therefore it should include band members from different age groups (youths, adults, Elders), genders, educational backgrounds, skill levels, and occupations (band administration, business people, farmers, parents). In many First Nation communities it is also important to ensure that different families are represented. The inclusion of many community members from different "walks of life" ensures a plan will represent many perspectives.

The PWG's job is to increase awareness of planning. It is involved in community outreach, providing information about how individuals can get involved in planning. It gives updates to community members who are unable to attend meetings and prepares articles for newsletters and websites. The PWG also ensures that planning is an open process, discussions are held publicly, and decisions are not made behind closed doors. Its involvement is essential, not just through plan development, but extends into implementation where it takes an active role selecting priority projects, getting them off the ground, applying for funding, and ensuring the continued involvement of community members. Having a PWG builds redundancy that is essential for ongoing momentum and effective action. By having many individuals involved in the development and implementation of a plan, the local team ensures that there is a collective memory of discussions held and lessons learned. As the community changes, the PWG provides continuity and stability to ensure that planning is ongoing.

The PWG also works to make planning exciting and accessible. One of the biggest challenges to planning is attracting people to be involved in the process. Arranging transportation and childcare, connecting planning meetings to other community events, and offering incentives such as door prizes and meals are a few typical, well-tested strategies used to reduce barriers and increase excitement around community planning. In Flying Dust First Nation (SK) planning workshops included "Plan and Scan" photo parties, accompanied by meals, slide shows, and storytelling to add to the excitement of open houses. These events were an opportunity to scan and save old photos, collect historical information, share the band's history with a younger audience, and complete the community timeline. In Muskoday First Nation (SK) live music enticed members to open houses, while charades and playdough sculpting were used to keep them there to develop a community vision (Muskoday First Nation and CEU 2007).

Making planning more accessible can also be done through the use of visible products like large-scale maps, posters, and timelines. These are effective ways to communicate information at workshops and can be left behind in public spaces for people to read and edit before, during, or after a meeting. Posters with empty spaces encourage workshop participants to contribute new information without having to speak up in front of a large audience or if they were unable to attend a meeting. Physical models illustrate ideas that can be difficult to decipher on a map or from a photo. Newsletters, emails, radio announcements, Facebook, home visits, and websites are some ways of engaging band members who are not able to make it to community meetings. School assemblies, Elders' teas, and one-on-one interviews are other ways of engaging specific groups of community members. The PWG in Standing Buffalo Dakota Nation (SK) developed a monthly community newsletter as part of the planning process. The newsletter inspired several departments to contribute articles (Standing Buffalo Dakota Nation and CEU 2010).

Every community is unique and the means of encouraging and attracting community members to planning events is similarly diverse. The PWG will ensure that ideas on how to engage membership are appropriate and effective.

Engage Youths

Young people are the future leaders, trades people, administrators, entrepreneurs, educators, and advisors of the community. Engaging youths in a meaningful way through plan development and implementation enables a community to accurately invest in the needs of their youths. It helps communities focus on how to create a place where youths can grow up healthy, safe, happy, and educated, and take an active role to ensure it becomes a place they want to live, invest in, and be a part of. Involving youths in planning should not be done as a formality, but should be thought of as a critical part of the planning process. If youths become involved in the development of a community plan, they will have a true sense of ownership of the plan and their participation will continue long into the future. It will raise their expectations, inspire hope, and build their capacity as future leaders and responsible community members. It will empower them to affect change in the community.

School visits ensure many youths of varying ages are engaged in the planning process, either through visits to classrooms or school assemblies. These venues provide an opportunity to discuss community, sustainability, civic engagement, and other topics. It gives young people a chance to contribute to the overall plan. Ideas that come from these sessions are extremely valuable and often quite revealing. Many adults are unaware of how young people view their community and what they would like to see in the future. These discoveries can motivate a community to action.

Developing a youth plan can be fundamental in building awareness and interest in planning amongst youths. It ensures that their voice is heard and inspires other community members to get involved. In Big River First Nation (SK), youths were engaged in a day-long condensed version of the planning process. They discussed background information and strengths and issues, developed a vision statement, and thought about ways to improve their community. The vision identified the youths' desire to have a community with "more fun activities, that is clean of drugs, alcohol, pollution and garbage, and whose people are healthy and happy" (Big River First Nation and CEU 2010, 10). In Kahkewistahaw First Nation (SK) a children's version of the plan was identified as a priority project. This plan, written and designed to be accessible to children, would be incorporated into the school curriculum to help explain planning, inspire youths, and motivate action (Kahkewistahaw First Nation and CEU 2007).

Developing a separate youth PWG allows young people to focus on issues that are important to them. Youths may also feel more comfortable sharing ideas with their peers as opposed to adults. A representative from this group should also be on the community-wide PWG to ensure collaboration. The youth PWG in Mikisew Cree First Nation (AB) decided that the destruction of their natural resources as a result of oil exploration and extraction is a serious concern for all youths. This group organized and participated in a rally to protest the actions of oil companies in and around their community. The formation of this group enabled the young people of this community to take action on an issue important to them and let everyone know that they want to grow up in a healthy and safe environment.

Value Local and Traditional Knowledge as Well as Outside Ideas

In order for a plan to be accurate, relevant, and meaningful it must value local and traditional knowledge. A community plan cannot be developed from the outside looking in. It cannot be done *for* a community, it must be done *with* and by a community. The plan must incorporate local ideas, build on local knowledge, and develop local skills to address a community's needs. Community members know their community best. By valuing and building on local knowledge a plan will be appropriated by a community, reflect local needs, and motivate action.

While planning requires the involvement of the community, an outside perspective is also valuable. Professional planners, engineers, and architects; representatives from tribal councils and other communities; academics; and scientists bring with them new ideas, knowledge, and experience. By being open to new ideas and connecting them to what is happening locally, communities are better able to identify and celebrate the special qualities that make them unique as well as recognize new possibilities. As a result communities will have more tools and knowledge to achieve something extraordinary.

During plan development, mapping exercises carried out with community members highlight important and sensitive areas of a community's land base. This is essential in determining what areas should be protected and where future development should occur. Engaging and encouraging community members to map vegetation and wildlife, water and drainage, steep slopes, important soils, and culturally significant areas also enables participants to define what they want to classify as sensitive. Examples include eagle habitat in Flying Dust, nuts and berries in Kahkewistahaw, areas prone to flooding in Shoal Lake, sweet grass in Kinistin, and the "ups and downs" (a lakeside valley trail) in Pasqua. Involving community members not just in mapping these areas but also in deciding what areas to map, adds significantly to their local relevance.

Reflect on the Past and Present

Planning is about the future, but it relies on information from the past and present to understand what a community is about: what it was like many years ago, what it is like today, and how it got to be in its current situation. This information provides a basis for determining where the community should go next. Many First Nations do not have a consolidated written record of their past or complete up-to-date information on key components of their community. Recording history and background information is valuable in terms of ensuring that past events and stories are not forgotten and that there is a baseline of data readily available that communities can use when pursuing projects or measuring the success of future initiatives.

Understanding the current situation also requires reflecting on a community's strengths and issues, and exploring the underlying causes of these strengths and issues. Discussing possibilities and challenges that exist in a community as well as the reasons behind them, works towards determining what can be built on and what needs to be changed. In addition, it brings attitudes and values to the surface that can be used as building blocks for establishing a collective future direction.

Reflecting on the past and present provides a venue within the planning process for people to come together to share and learn from each other. It can be therapeutic as it is often the first time people openly discuss their thoughts, both good and bad, about their community. It is impossible, however, for a plan to capture everything there is to know about a community's past and present. While this information is important, the focus of a plan should be about future action. Therefore, how information is documented and made accessible is essential. Categorizing and gathering information under land, people, settlement, and economics provides a simple method of organizing the work and understanding the community. This information identifies what really stands out and matters to people. Such approaches provide a snapshot and specific products such as maps, statistics, information about language and culture, and historic timelines that enable discussion about the current situation and future potential.

The intent of identifying the strengths, issues, and root causes is to obtain an understanding of what can be built on and what needs to be changed. Compiling, organizing, and synthesizing strengths and issues in a plan are essential, as this information is often scattered and rarely recorded. This data provides a useful reference throughout the planning process reinforcing a particular direction or action. There is not always consensus when discussing strengths and issues, but it is important to record all ideas, including those not recognized or shared by everyone, as this brings the attitudes and perceptions of a community to the surface and identifies areas that require further research. Acknowledging people's perceptions is just as important as knowing the facts because perceptions often influence behaviour. For example, if data suggests that a lake is not polluted but people refuse to swim in the lake because they think it is polluted, then that perception, whether it is correct or not, influences the use of the lake.

Determining the root causes of issues leads to a broader understanding of why issues exist in the first place and reveals the future implications if these issues are not addressed. Root causes also indicate what changes need to happen in a community. As such, these types of discussions provide an opportunity to inform project ideas and how to make positive change happen. Identifying common root causes should also be a priority in order to determine if any issues are the result of the same root cause. Acknowledging these connections ensures that when people consider what projects to undertake, they are thinking broadly of how one project or program can address as many issues as possible.

Connect the Physical and the Social

With limited finances and a finite land base there is an urgent need for First Nations to understand and plan for the physical organization of their community. This undertaking ensures that projects are developed in the right location in a community. It also assures that existing resources and infrastructure are used economically and that public buildings, outdoor spaces, and gathering places are connected and accessible. It addresses the need to protect and maintain sensitive areas such as wetlands, forest, and productive farmland.

But planning cannot isolate a community's physical organization from the social landscape. Doing so can have disastrous, expensive, and harmful consequences. It can destroy a community. The physical and social structures of a community are intrinsically linked; the layout of houses, roads, services, and facilities influence the health, happiness, safety, and well-being of its residents. For instance, the destruction or preservation of the natural environment will greatly impact opportunities for cultural events as well as economic potential. Planning must embrace and connect both the physical and social components of a community.

Settlement and development in First Nation communities generally follows one of two patterns. The lack of planning and the struggle to keep up with the demand for on-reserve housing often leads to a pattern of development where homes and services are scattered haphazardly throughout a reserve. This increases the costs of infrastructure, reduces the size of intact wilderness, causes problems regarding access, and creates a place with no sense of community. There is no central core and community members are far from services and from one another. In the second pattern, housing and services are grouped together into tight-fitting clusters reminiscent of suburban subdivisions. These designs are often provided by developers, government, or lenders, and are meant to minimize the costs of development and maximize the efficiency of infrastructure and land. In many communities, however, this pattern has led to unclear boundaries between homes, non-existent private space, animosity between neighbours, and common areas that are neglected. The positive elements of a healthy neighbourhood are non-existent.

A useful tool for guiding development is a structure map. The structure map shows basic community infrastructure and envisions where future housing will be located in order to minimize the costs of new infrastructure. It lays the foundation for future community development by showing how the physical and social components of a community are connected and should be organized. It also highlights places where people come together for coffee, meetings, sporting events, and informal gatherings. These gathering places are essential hubs encouraging informal meetings between neighbours and fostering a greater sense of community. The structure map also considers a community's connectivity, recognizing the need to ensure that gathering places are accessible to all. In laying out a settlement pattern that considers both the physical and the social aspects of community, the structure map recognizes the elements and qualities that pull a community together.

Establish a United Direction for the Future

Planning is a forward-looking activity. Working towards a brighter, better future must be in the forefront of all planning activities. Establishing a united direction brings community members, families, departments, and all other aspects of a community together for a common purpose. It launches the community towards a single destination. It reduces overlap, improves communication, and encourages co-operation and collaboration. It becomes a mandate for chiefs and councils, a legacy that outlives every administration, providing continuity and cohesion over the long-term. It similarly provides focus for every department and committee who may then set more specific goals and objectives with this common purpose in mind. It allows a community to proactively strive towards a decided future, rather than working towards many different, changing, and sometimes conflicting goals.

Establishing a vision is essential to every plan. While change is constant, communities can determine what important, enduring beliefs they wish to maintain. Value statements embody what community members believe to be fundamental truths about the quality of life. They transcend trends, elections, preferences, and generations. Value statements are the essential components that remain the same; they help to inform the rest of the planning process. Their inclusion in a plan ensures that important decisions coincide with the values of community members. In some communities, the value statements are included in the preamble section of all community acts, policies, codes, and legislation.

These values guide a community vision. The goal is to develop a clear and simple united direction for the community that will inspire focused change. It is a creative, challenging, and exploratory process that involves taking risks, questioning the current state of affairs, and taking the community's eyes away from the past and focusing them on the future. Based on a clear understanding of how things are and how they got to be that way, the vision looks ahead and imagines how things might be; it defines where the community wants to go. Beginning to create the vision is the moment when the community takes an active role in shaping its future. It is the point when the community declares itself willing to shape what will happen according to one shared view.

A vision must be specific enough to guide action but general enough that no one feels left out. The process, as well as the product, must be inclusive and empowering. A strong vision can be used to unite various groups and coordinate actions more effectively.

CONCLUSION: THE NEED TO MAKE A DIFFERENCE

There is an urgent need for change in First Nation communities. There is a need to take action, identify difficult issues, and ultimately address those issues. The most common complaint about planning is that strategies and plans often end up on shelves, collecting dust and having no real impact on a community. If planning is seen as just another project, inevitably it will be shelved once complete. If planning is to make a real difference, if it is to have a positive and lasting impact on communities, it must be community-based and comprehensive; this will lead to action.

Community-based and comprehensive both matter. They are fundamental to the planning process. Community-based planning highlights a community's needs and motivates, inspires, and builds up community members so they have the skills and confidence to participate in addressing those needs. Comprehensive planning is a way of seeing a community whole; it ensures that all agendas are moving forward in the same direction. As demonstrated in this chapter, the community-based and comprehensive elements of planning are not limited to the development of a community's plan. These ideas extend into implementation and become routine aspects of daily operations, project development, and decision making. Planning must not be confined to dreaming about a better future, it must be about taking action to make that future a reality.

Much has been said about the importance of community-based and comprehensive plans, and of their usefulness as instruments for communities to define and shape their own future. Not nearly enough has been done to connect community-based and comprehensive planning to action. Community-based and comprehensive planning creates an attitude that change can happen. It builds action into the process as well as the product to ensure that planning is ongoing. This ensures that a plan does not end up collecting dust on an office shelf; instead it becomes a dynamic and useful tool – a living document and a catalyst for change.

Moving Forward

This chapter has presented two fundamental ideas about planning with Indigenous communities that apply to the process, product, and the ensuing action: planning must be community-based and comprehensive. It has provided definitions of these terms as well as described the elements against which to measure the progress and success of a plan. Principles have been provided to guide the successful delivery of a plan that satisfies the definitions of community-based and comprehensive.

The discoveries presented in this chapter were arrived at through practice and experience on the ground. These ideas have been developed, applied, and adapted through reflective practice in work with many First Nation communities across Canada over the past decade. The position presented by this chapter is that even though there is more to learn and learning should never stop, it is time to proceed with more confidence,

energy, and long-term commitment to community-based and comprehensive planning in First Nation communities. It is necessary. It is time to
move beyond pilot projects, short-term funding, and lukewarm support.
The next steps involve increasing awareness of planning and extending
the benefits of planning to all First Nations; sharing skills, experiences,
and resources across communities; and providing greater support for
communities to ensure that planning is ongoing and continues to make
a difference.

NOTES

1   The findings presented in this chapter have been gathered over many years
    of planning with First Nation communities in Canada, beginning in 1999
    with the Atlantic Region First Nations Community Planning Project. The
    project began with the development of the First Nations Community Plan-
    ning Model, which was then tested in three pilot communities. It expanded
    to eighteen more First Nation communities in Nova Scotia, New Bruns-
    wick, Prince Edward Island, and Newfoundland and Labrador. A second
    version of the First Nations Community Planning Model was published
    in 2003 along with the First Nations Community Planning Workbook.
    The Comprehensive Community-Based Planning Pilot Project began in
    Saskatchewan in 2006. The project began developing plans with four First
    Nations in 2007 and expanded to seven more communities in 2008 and
    2009. The Mikisew Cree First Nation Comprehensive Plan, Alberta began
    in 2008.
2   The Canadian Institute of Planners (CIP) endorses the importance of
    "meaningful public participation" in their Statement of Values. It is part
    of the CIP's Code of Professional Practice and meant to inspire and guide
    planners in Canada (Canadian Institute of Planners 2010).
3   See the planning principles for a detailed explanation of the local planning
    team and the Planning Work Group.
4   The First Nations Community Planning Model (Cities and Environment
    Unit 2003a) and the First Nations Community Planning Workbook (Cities
    and Environment Unit 2003b) both provide more detailed information on
    many of the best practices described in this section.

REFERENCES

Bear, Judy. 2010. Personal communication, 11 September 2010.

Big River First Nation and Cities and Environment Unit. 2010. *Big River First Nation Community Plan*. Unpublished manuscript.

Canadian Institute of Planners. 2010. *Statement of Values and Code of Practice*. Retrieved from Canadian Institute of Planners website: http://www. cip-icu.ca/.

Cities and Environment Unit. 2002. *Pictou Landing First Nation Community Plan*.

– 2003a. *First Nations Community Planning Model*, second edition.

– 2003b. *First Nations Community Planning Workbook*.

Cowessess First Nation and Cities and Environment Unit. 2009. *Cowessess First Nation Community Plan*.

Flying Dust First Nation and Cities and Environment Unit. 2007. *Flying Dust First Nation Community Plan*.

George Gordon First Nation and Cities and Environment Unit. 2007. *George Gordon First Nation Community Plan*.

Harrison, George. 2002. "Any Road." *Brainwashed*. US: Dark Horse/EMI.

Kahkewistahaw First Nation and Cities and Environment Unit. 2007. *Kahkewistahaw First Nation Community Plan*.

Kinistin Saulteaux Nation and Cities and Environment Unit. 2009. *Kinistin Saulteaux Nation Community Plan*.

Lumberjack, Marlene. 2010. Personal communication, 20 July 2010.

Mikisew Cree First Nation and Cities and Environment Unit. 2010. *Mikisew Cree First Nation Community Plan*. Unpublished manuscript.

Muskoday First Nation and Cities and Environment Unit. 2007. *Muskoday First Nation Community Plan*.

Schön, Donald. 1983. *The Reflective Practitioner: How Professionals Think in Action*. New York, NY: Basic Books.

Shoal Lake Cree Nation and Cities and Environment Unit. 2007. *Shoal Lake Cree Nation Community Plan*.

– 2008. *Beyond the Classroom: Shoal Lake Cree Nation*.

Standing Buffalo Dakota Nation and Cities and Environment Unit. 2010. *Standing Buffalo Dakota Nation Community Plan*.

6

Co-creative Planning: Simpcw First Nation and the Centre for Indigenous Environmental Resources

LISA HARDESS, WITH KERRI JO FORTIER

The role of the non-Indigenous planner working with Indigenous communities continues to be discussed, adapted, and refined. The emancipatory and self-determining role of planning for transformative change, and the role of the planner as partner are increasingly discussed in the literature (see Jojola 2008; Lane and Hibbard 2005; Porter 2004, 2006; Forester 1991; Sarkissian 2010). The thoughts and suggestions for practice shared by these experts, however, seem to remain on the periphery for mainstream planners and in the curriculum of planning education.

As discussed by Porter (2006), while we are planning in a (post)-colonial time, the impact of colonization on Indigenous peoples continues. This has an impact on external planners who may not even be aware at the start of work with an Indigenous community of the many layers of history, assumptions, and expectations (on all sides) that are at play. As a result, First Nations in Canada continue to encounter consultants who approach their work with the Indigenous communities as they would any other client, with results that do not serve the Nations in the long-term (or perhaps even it the short-term), and likely do not lead to further work for the planner.

External planners who delve into the issues, ask questions, and engage in self-reflection are becoming more aware of their own cultural lenses and embracing the many ways of knowing and acting that can result in success. This includes unpacking their assumptions and looking into methods for decolonizing their own processes. As Porter (2004) describes, her own shift in awareness and understanding as a practitioner changed from a desire to help Indigenous people participate in the planning processes in order to create more collaborative plans, to supporting Indigenous people in the assertion of their rights through planning. This is a fundamental change in mindset that creates opportunities for planning to be a critical governance tool for self-determination and accelerate transformative change.

Indigenous communities are going through their own process of decolonization as they rebuild capacity and pride in their own cultures and abilities, and regain self-determination (see for example Jojola 2008; Lane and Hibbard 2005). Assertion of land and water-based rights by Indigenous peoples have resulted in legal and political challenges. Resulting legal rulings in Canada have further defined these rights and the need for consultation with Indigenous people. At the same time the courts have challenged the parties involved to find a better way to work together and to see the opportunity in these issues for reconciliation – to come to agreement and avoid legal action. Planning provides an opportunity to work together and through issues, to understand the rights and responsibilities of the actors involved, and create results that embody respect and reciprocity. As Lane and Hibbard note (2005), planning's forward-thinking and solution-oriented focus on organizing to achieve land, resource, and economic development goals, and increasingly also social and cultural goals, make planning an essential tool for Indigenous communities.

Together these many shifts have resulted in Indigenous communities that are more adept at and confident in articulating their own needs, and partners who are ready and able to listen, understand, and work together for solutions. In the case of planning in Canada, these external partners remain key; few First Nations have internal planning staff or access to Indigenous consultants with relevant education and experience. As a non-Indigenous woman working in Indigenous planning, people have said to me in the past that "it is great to see the four worlds working together on these issues" and "we want our people doing this work but we also need people who can be bridges and provide the help we need." In this case study, the "help we need" is key, as opposed to the help an external funder or a consultant believes is needed.

This chapter tells a story in Canada of a nearly four-year partnership between the planning team at the Centre for Indigenous Environmental Resources and the Simpcw First Nation. The resulting comprehensive community plan (CCP) incorporated contributions from both parties to the plannng process and the writing of the final document. I start out by setting the stage for the relationship by introducing the two partners: Simpcw First Nation and the Centre for Indigenous Environmental

Resources (CIER). The next sections provide a brief overview of First Nations' relationship with planning; discuss capacity-building for community planning; community planning in Simpcw; and the co-creative planning process, including work with Elders and youths, on goal-setting and writing the plan document. The final section reflects on opportunities for First Nation community planning in Canada, including the role of planning schools and professional associations.

THE PARTNERS

Centre for Indigenous Environmental Resources

The Centre for Indigenous Environmental Resources is a national, Canadian, First Nation non-profit organization and charity. CIER was created in 1994 by a small group of First Nations leaders from across the country and remains the only national environmental First Nation organization in Canada. CIER is not funded by government and operates as a social enterprise through four program areas: protecting lands and water, conserving biodiversity, taking action on climate change, and building sustainable communities. Partnerships with First Nations are essential for every project as these communities are the true "clients" of the organization and working together to help them build capacity to meet their environmental objectives is the mission of CIER.

In recent years, CIER has offered capacity-building support to First Nations in comprehensive community planning, climate change adaptation planning, land-use planning for species at risk, watershed planning, and community/regional land-use visioning. All of these variations on planning are understood by CIER to directly support its vision of "sustainable First Nations and a healthy environment." While Western society tends to define "environmental" in relatively narrow terms, Indigenous peoples' understanding of environment is far more holistic and includes the "two-legged," or humans. As such, while CIER is an environmentally focused organization, the social, cultural, and economic elements related to a particular planning project are included to the degree that the community partner(s) consider appropriate.

Simpcw First Nation

The Simpcw ("People of the North Thompson River") are a division of the Secwepemc ("Shuswap") who occupied the drainage of the North

Thompson River in British Columbia upstream from McLure to the headwaters of the Fraser River, from McBride to Tête Jaune Cache, over to Jasper (Alberta), and south to the headwaters of the Athabasca River. The Simpcw speak the Secwepemc language (Secwepemctsín), a Salishan language shared among many of the First Nations in the Fraser and Thompson River drainage. During the winter months they assembled at village sites in the valleys close to rivers, occupying semi-underground homes. Archaeological studies have identified winter home sites and underground food cache sites at a variety of locations, including Finn Creek, Vavenby, Birch Island, Chu Chua, Barriere River, Louis Creek, and Tête Jaune Cache.

Today about one third of the over six hundred Simpcw people live on the Simpcw First Nation Indian Reserve at Chu Chua, north of Barrier, and on the Louis Creek Indian Reserve in British Columbia (approximately eighty kilometres north of Kamloops). The administration is governed by the Simpcw Council that oversees the social, educational, and economic development of the community. With other Secwepemc communities, the Simpcw are taking steps to have their Aboriginal rights to their traditional territory recognized by the provincial and federal governments.

Since 1989 the community of Simpcw has come together once a year in the fall or winter to do planning for the upcoming year. As part of the planning activities, participating members prioritize the community needs, develop an action plan, and select individuals to carry out the plans. In November 2002 the planning session resulted in the community vision, which has been revisited and reaffirmed annually. These planning sessions are scheduled away from the community, in order for people to focus on the planning tasks at hand. With each passing year the community priorities change. At the same time, the First Nation leadership wanted to have a higher-level community plan to guide overall community development and link community decisions to Simpcw First Nation's vision: "The Simpcw are a culturally proud community valuing holistic, healthy lifestyles based upon respect, responsibility, and continuous participation in growth and education."

FIRST NATIONS AND PLANNING

Long-term planning is not new to First Nations; people don't survive in an often-harsh country like Canada without the ability to plan ahead. The rich culture seen across the lands and waters is evidence that First

Nations in Canada did in fact thrive and dedicate time to art, music, and dance. And in many instances these "cultural events" were closely tied to both short-term and long-term planning and the overall sustainability of the nation (Knudtson and Suzuki 1992). For example, Simpcw ancestors would gather to determine the sites to be used for the next season for gathering and hunting.

Potlatching, where families celebrated together and re-distributed food, goods, or money to demonstrate respect, reciprocity, and establish status, was and now is again important for many First Nations on the west coast of Canada (after a ban of potlatching by the Canadian government from 1884 to 1951). While differences exist among cultural groups, from a planning perspective, potlatching is an example of a community gathering that strengthens bonds and the likelihood of success into the future – a key element of a Nation's planning process and strategy. Observing and understanding patterns of migration of animals critical to the nation's survival (e.g., caribou, buffalo) and making decisions about where to live, when to move, which animals to hunt, and so on, is an example of how Indigenous knowledge, community sustainability, and planning were inextricably linked.

For many First Nations this connection to the land, to place, has been harmed by restrictions imposed by the Indian reserve system. Despite this, knowing when and how to do things and making decisions based on this reciprocal relationship with the Earth continues at many levels in First Nations across Canada. Indigenous Knowledge (IK) "is knowledge gathered over generations by Indigenous people about their communities, the plants and wildlife and water and landscapes in their territories" (CIER 2011); IK can contribute to the planning process, product, and implementation. First Nations can and are using the planning process as a means of strengthening this source of knowledge, the role of Elders in community decision making, and reconnecting youths and Elders. IK continues to contribute to community planning processes and decisions – sometimes in ways people themselves do not recognize but take for granted because they see it as simply "our way."

Indigenous Knowledge encompasses many things, including ecological knowledge, and also knowledge about community processes, collaboration, and governance (Figure 6.1). Bringing IK into the planning process strengthens it as a whole, community commitment to the outcomes, and likelihood of success. Whether or not this is "labelled" IK as part of the planning work depends largely on the First Nation and its own views, terminology, and comfort level. The interest and abilities of the planning

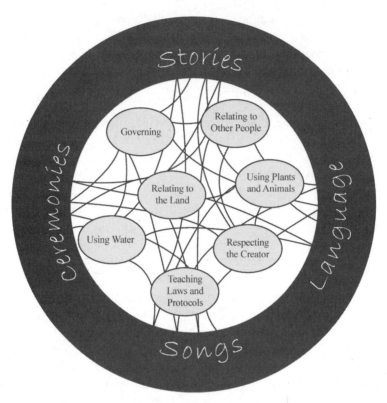

Figure 6.1   Indigenous knowledge relationship diagram

Source: CIER, 2011

team to work together with the community to understand and bring together their way of knowing and doing things into the (typically Western) planning process, in my view, will make or break the long-term success of the initiative.

The presence or strength of IK in each community is different. The impact of the residential school system, Western religions, the passing of Elders, and the desire of many youths for a "modern" lifestyle all contribute to the challenges Indigenous communities face as they work to revitalize and rebuild their Indigenous language, culture, and knowledge. Talking with a First Nation about knowledge holders and IK must be approached with respect for the local views, understanding of recent history, and compassion. Planners can help support a community's efforts to strengthen their IK by asking questions about local knowledge (e.g., of plants, animals, soil conditions, family dynamics), local processes (e.g., of engagement, of approvals), and bringing this into the work. Planners can work with local people as part of the planning team to weave together Indigenous and Western processes, and to decide how all the information can contribute to better processes and outcomes.

Despite a rich history of planning and a present desire to plan for their future, First Nations in Canada have had difficulty engaging in strategic and holistic community planning. Unlike the situation in the United States of America, comprehensive planning has not been a part of federal legislation or an organized move towards self-determination; similarly though, the planning that has taken place in First Nations, as in Indian country, has experienced sporadic government funding (Jojola 2008). Many First Nations do not have access to their own sources of revenues and rely significantly on the federal government to operate and run local programs, and so most First Nations in Canada are still searching for funding opportunities to develop a comprehensive community plan.

In general, community planning in First Nations has not been a priority for Canadian government funding. Federal departments often distribute funds through their regional offices and in the case of community planning there is no national strategy on community planning for the regions to follow. In the past ten years, some regions have provided funding and training support for community planning; other regions have not. As a result, First Nations in some areas of Canada have been able to move ahead with their planning while others continue to wait. This has resulted in inconsistencies and frustration across the county. Recent calls for proposals from First Nations by the federal government in one region resulted in so many requests for funding that many communities were told to try again in the future or given minimal funding for strategic plans that address only a small fraction of what was anticipated. Clearly, the need and desire to engage in community-based and comprehensive planning continues. The majority of planning that *has* been done in First Nations has been at a secondary or sector level (e.g., economic development, housing, health pandemic plans) and is often linked to receiving related government funds. Recently, land-use planning funding has been available in some regions. In the absence of an overarching plan, these specific plans can lack the connections and associated opportunities for synergies, efficiencies, and increased effectiveness that strategic and comprehensive community planning can provide.

CAPACITY-BUILDING FOR COMMUNITY PLANNING

CIER and Simpcw First Nation came together on planning in 2007 as part of a three-year project to develop and deliver group training and community-specific technical planning support to six First Nations in Canada. Simpcw First Nation was one of over forty interested communities and demonstrated the internal capacity and leadership support that was necessary for this project partnership, which philosophically and logistically relied on substantial community-level leadership.

Capacity-building related to planning has been a focus at CIER since its initial days in education. The Environmental Education and Training Program that ran from 1995 to 2002 included courses in land-use planning, environmental assessment, and social-impact assessment. The program was unique in both content and delivery and included team teaching by Western scholars, Indigenous scholars, and Indigenous Elders. This focus on bringing together ways of knowing and methods related to planning information, analysis, and application to help community practitioners develop an approach that uses Western and Indigenous knowledge and process remains a critical focus of project and planning work at CIER.

CIER's own strategic initiative (which included local meetings with over 130 First Nation communities and organizations from 2004 to 2006) showed "comprehensive community planning" as the top governance need, and "tools and actions" as the desired support. Subsequent financial support from Aboriginal Affairs and Northern Development Canada was used to develop four weeks of intensive and interactive Comprehensive Community Plan (CCP) curriculum, identifying First Nation partners, delivering group training to First Nation community planners in Winnipeg, Manitoba, and supporting each community individually, both remotely and locally, over the course of approximately a year and a half. The planning group came together for training for one week every four to six months and stayed connected through monthly conference calls to continue to learn together and share ideas. Funding for the training and technical support was provided to each First Nation as part of CIER project funding; each First Nation had to designate an internal community planner as part of their own budget costs and commitment. To highlight the focus on partnership and co-creation of the plan, CIER used the term "local community planner" (as opposed to a local champion) to signify their significant role.

The CIER planning team connected directly with each local community planner on a more regular basis to support their specific planning activities and to plan community visits. During these visits CIER staff and First Nation staff co-hosted community planning activities with the leadership, with Elders, with students at the local school, and with the membership through public events. These visits were planned to include a lot of time for discussion, for flexibility that allowed for last-minute changes, and to best support the local First Nation planner's needs. The eighteen-month relationship between CIER and each community planner and their First Nation allowed the personal and professional relationships to develop that were necessary as part of the capacity-building. Regular contact and increasing levels of trust made it easier for people to share their planning needs and ideas, receive feedback, and plan together. Over this time, CIER also came to better understand the community dynamics and related activities (e.g., health planning, youth initiatives, defining the age of an Elder) that were often opportunities to build on, or "elephants in the room" to address.

Each community has their own catalyst or driver for the planning work it is doing. In some cases this may be community health and well-being, improving quality of life, economic development opportunities or threats, or cultural renewal. Whatever the driver, making the linkages to all elements of sustainability (i.e., environmental, economic, social, cultural) as part of the community dialogue on planning needs, vision, and priority is an easy conversation in First Nations; people are well equipped to see these connections. Talking about the interconnections that exist in daily activities, in the longer-term projects and programs, and in decisions in general is a good starting point for community discussions on comprehensive community planning. Identifying where a goal or new project idea could be further developed to enhance all areas of sustainability (instead of missing these opportunities, or worse, inadvertently causing harm) is exciting and demonstrates for people the on-the-ground benefits that can come from community planning. With the CCP process – for perhaps the first time in living memory – community members are coming together to talk about the future they want and the process to achieve it.

Similarly, each community is comfortable, and capable, of a different pace of planning. The path from plan initiation to plan completion is not straightforward. At the end of the INAC-funded CCP project, Simpcw First Nation had not finished their CCP and wanted to continue the relationship with CIER. With CIER's help, Simpcw submitted a successful proposal to complete the comprehensive community plan (including salary support for the local planning and updating their website to include

CCP) to the New Relationship Trust in British Columbia. Through this additional funding Simpcw and CIER worked together on planning for an additional year.

COMMUNITY PLANNING AT SIMPCW FIRST NATION

Simpcw First Nation has both historical and recent experience in planning. Annual community meetings beginning in 1989, followed by a formal vision in 2002 and the contributions of several well-educated members (both traditionally and via the Western education system), provided a strong foundation for the CCP work. Simpcw First Nation's annual community meetings had given guidance to ongoing project priorities on a somewhat ad hoc basis but had not resulted in a formal plan. Recognizing this need, Simpcw submitted a letter of intent to participate in CIER's CCP project, was accepted, and in September 2007, Kerri Jo Fortier started her position as the Simpcw community planner. The mandate of the position was to complete a comprehensive community plan with the capacity-building component supplied by CIER. To fund other elements of the CCP process and the planner position, the community planner sought additional funding through proposal submissions to further Simpcw's community planning work.

The community planner staff position was included as part of the sustainable resource development team at Simpcw. This group is responsible for forestry, fisheries, land use, and rights and title initiatives for the nation and meets regularly with other administrative staff, community members, and chief and council. The inclusion of a planning position within this group has been a good fit and information is shared between the staff members who often contribute to each other's project work. The decision to attach the planning position to this group was the decision of the then-council with the intent that the community planner would also work on projects related to the land, water, economic development, and governance issues. Embedding the planning position in the administration and linking it to other community initiatives (to strengthen connections, improve decision making through information sharing, and access various funding opportunities) has been a success that other First Nations can learn from and apply in their own communities.

During the course of Simpcw and CIER's work together, the community planner was on maternity leave. In her absence, the council designated the fisheries coordinator to continue working on the CCP to maintain momentum and participation in the training workshops in Winnipeg.

This decision and the co-operation of the members of the sustainable resource development team demonstrate the commitment of Simpcw to community planning and was instrumental in keeping the process moving forward. The absence of the community planner for a year would have otherwise stalled the process and jeopardized the momentum and ability to complete the CCP. As an added value the participation of another staff member in developing the CCP meant that another person within the First Nation had first-hand knowledge of the planning process. To continue with the project, commitment to the CCP existed at the council and the staff level. This was in contrast to other First Nations where the commitment and/or the ability to continue with CCP were not as strong and as a result the process faltered. Lessons for First Nations moving forward on any type of planning from this experience include the absolute need for support from the chief and council and senior administrators so that when decision and/or changes are needed the staff can continue on with their work. Simpcw First Nation's ability to fund the local position by including salary costs as part of related proposals, could also be applied by others to create the in-house position that is critical to implementation of the plan once the relationship with the external planner comes to an end.

CO-CREATIVE PLANNING

CIER staff visited Simpcw First Nation at Chu Chua three times between 2006 and 2009 and worked closely with the community planner to analyze existing data, engage community members, and plan the next steps for the planning process. The visits were between three and four days and were planned so that both meetings and flexible time were included in each day's schedule. Intentional "blank" timeslots were included in the schedules so that we could respond to necessary meeting changes (e.g., when something of a high priority came up for the staff) while still having time to sit down as a planning team to debrief and strategize. This time, perhaps seen as "downtime" to others was critical to relationship-building and created the time for the team to go together to a nearby town for refreshments or community lunch (and talk and learn from each other during the trip), to play Yahtzee over lunch with the sustainable development team (and get a better understanding of their work, the purpose of the CCP, and the connections), and to spend time in the community hub of the administration building/band office (meeting people who drop in, talking with Elders hosting a bake sale, and learning about upcoming events and priorities from posters on the various notice boards).

The meetings, workshops, and events are important ways of engaging people in the planning process. At the same time, the space *between* the structured meetings and events were critical to relationship-building, information gathering, and gauging community support for elements of the plan. When working with and in First Nations, external Western planners need to adjust to the local timeframes and priorities. Back in the office, deadlines, budgets, and schedules matter; in the community these things still matter but so does taking the time to know each other as people and pausing when local issues arise, often unexpectedly. External planners who learn to switch between the go-go-go of the Western planning world and the go-with-the-flow First Nation world – while continuing to be on time and on budget – will demonstrate competence to their client and earn their respect.

One of the first tasks CIER and Simpcw worked on together was a large summary table that demonstrated Simpcw's achievements to date, organized into categories, and in relation to the many suggestions and planning objectives that had resulted from the annual planning sessions. For example, the Elders home and the main building (housing the band office, health office, gym, and school) were very close to each other but separated by a small creek; to go between them people had to walk up to and along the main road. During one of the annual planning sessions this issue came up along with an idea for a bridge to shorten the walk. Within the next year a small bridge was built! In the absence of a formal connection back to the planning meeting, people had missed the connection.

The summary table helped to demonstrate these connections and the value in the planning process. This helped people see the value of their ongoing participation and illustrated for them that while in some cases similar issues arose each year, many concerns and needs had been addressed along the way. This was critical given the length of time people had been meeting to discuss community planning. An appreciation of the work done to date also helped to counter the sentiments of "why are we talking about this again" and "I already told you my ideas and what became of them anyway?" The community planner shared this table with the community at the 2007 community planning session; people were impressed and pleasantly surprised to see how much had been accomplished. This summary also highlighted areas that need continued attention, helped focus the goals and needs for the CCP, and

renewed enthusiasm among people to continue their community planning efforts. CIER also created a draft of a poster that showed some of
these achievements as a visual summary for the community.

Community engagement was a significant focus of our time together
during the community visits and included the Elders, students at the
local school, administrative staff, key committees, and the general public within the community at Chu Chua. The local community planner
hosted many other community engagement events independently and
presented to committee and council on her own, or with other community staff support. For several of these meetings she and I talked and
planned together ahead of time by phone, email, and Skype. Video chat-
ting was a new form of communication for Simpcw when we first started
our weekly planning chats using this media in 2009. These weekly chats
allowed us to talk about the CCP, and often more importantly created the
time and space for ongoing mentorship and opportunities to talk about
the other related projects. In addition to these chats, we used video con-
ferencing to remotely facilitate a meeting with the education committee to formulate the CCP education goal and objectives to create more
personal communication while saving on travel time and costs. Simpcw
has used Skype subsequently for meetings with other organizations and
during job interviews.

WORKING WITH THE SIMPCW FIRST NATION ELDERS

The Elders play an important role in Simpcw First Nation, as they do in
many Indigenous communities. Elders are the First Nation's connection
to its past, and hold the education of cultural traditions and Secwepemctsín; the Elders' continuous encouragement provides community members with the strength to learn and preserve Simpcw's traditional way of
life. With the help of the community health worker for the Elders, the
planning team hosted a salmon luncheon and a traditional foods luncheon to talk about planning priorities, gather their ideas, and generate
enthusiasm and support for the plan. Rather than talk with them about
"swot" (strengths, weaknesses, opportunities, threats), we framed the
conversation using "park" (see Jones 1990) to understand, from their
perspectives, what they would *preserve* (what is working well now that
we should preserve?), *add* (what positive aspects are missing?), *remove*
(what is not working well or is negative that we should remove?), and
keep out (what negative aspects do we want to keep out, or have worked
hard to remove but must be vigilant to keep out?). Using this as a means

of framing the discussion and then analyzing the relationship of the answers to the community goals and priorities was a good fit for this audience. The Elders talked most about what they would preserve and add, which is often the case during meetings with older people who draw in their experiences and lessons from the past in relation to the present and future.

WORKING WITH THE SIMPCW FIRST NATION YOUTHS

The voices and opinions of the young people in the community are highly valued. Supporting their growth, development, and education is seen to be critically important and the First Nation is fortunate to have a youth coordinator who runs activities for eight to eighteen year olds, and the Neqweyqwelsten school (kindergarten to grade 6). The Neqweyqwelsten school operates through an agreement with the Board of Trustees of the Kamloops/Thompson School District. Youths in the community go to middle school and high school in the nearby town of Barriere. Simpcw invites and hosts cross-cultural awareness days with the town and high school as part of relationship-building with their non-Indigenous neighbours. As part of the CCP process we worked with the students in all of the classes at Neqweyqwelsten school twice, co-hosted sessions with the youth coordinator, and included the students and youths in community luncheons and events that focused on prioritizing project ideas. Youths were also targeted specifically during the annual planning sessions. The creative and colourful banners they created in 2009 were shared with the Elders and at a community luncheon to generate conversations and to demonstrate to other community members the energy and ideas presented by the youths.

At these planning sessions with the school, students learned about the four pillars of sustainability (environment, economy, society, culture), a key foundation for the CCP, and shared their ideas of what each of these areas meant to them (Figure 6.2). They participated in a web-of-life game to talk about the connections between all living things – with a parallel for the adults involved with the CCP and the connections between the decisions and actions taken within the community. Older students made postcards from the future with drawings of what their vision included (e.g., new hiking trails, a bike park, and a community garden), with a message to someone coming home to Simpcw First Nation after many years away. These activities helped the planning team understand the values and priorities of the youths in the community (e.g., pictures of

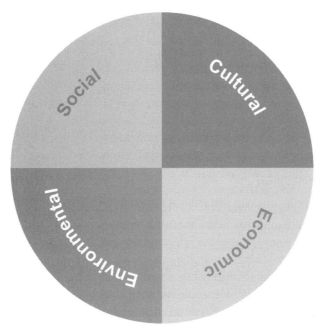

Figure 6.2   Four pillars of sustainability

Source: CIER, 2011

being with their families; of fishing; to represent society and culture, respectively; explanations of economy as being more than what people do for money to include critical other roles in the community, such as grandparents caring for children, women making clothes and jewellery) in order to reflect these voices in the CCP.

Unlike the majority of First Nations in Canada where the populations are young and growing, Simpcw First Nation has relatively few babies born each year. This has been slowly improving, with an average of three new Simpcw members born a year. As this demographic is growing slowly, the other side of the picture is that the aged population has grown at an enormous rate in recent years. Simpcw First Nation has begun to realize the importance of planning for the effects of having a large population of sixty-one-plus years of age. The changes that need to happen concerning health care needs, infrastructure requirements or improvements to buildings or homes, and the supports systems needed for an aging population need to be considered in both long and short-term planning decisions.

DEVELOPING GOALS

Goals are an important part of any plan – they are the glue between the long-term vision and the yearly operational work plan. Goals ground the plan in reality by setting achievable results to create change in the direction of the vision; goals give structure and create transparency for decision making on projects and programs. For years Simpcw had operated with a vision and project ideas and priorities generated through the annual community planning meetings. Why some projects went ahead while other didn't was unclear in the absence of clear goals where project decisions are made to achieve priority goals. People also felt that the process wasn't moving forward because the connection between the completed projects and the vision wasn't articulated; goals help to do this.

Identifying goals in a participatory way can be a challenge, but especially in the case where many goals exist, involving people in setting priority goals helps them to understand and support implementation. In my experience, people like to talk about projects and activities and tend not to talk about strategic priorities or readily identify synergies between on-the-ground ideas to then formulate goals. As it relates to community planning with Indigenous communities, I think that this is likely because many of the people participating in the community engagement events are operations people. These people run the programs, committees, and daily activities for the nation – and in many cases are performing more than one role in order to keep things running. When they do have the time for strategic thinking and planning, oftentimes immediate issues or crises that need their attention interrupt their days. The facilitated sessions that the CCP planning team hosted on goals were not overly successful and so we tried a different approach and drafted preliminary goals based on the planning work and engagement. These were shared with community members and the leadership at events and meetings, still with little feedback.

After more discussion, it seemed that the need for goals and their connecting role between the vision and projects needed more explanation. To do this in a way that was easy for people to understand and relate to we created a flower-type graphic where the centre of the flower stated the vision, the first layer of petals were the goals, and each of these goals had two objectives, which formed the second layer of petals. Plan actions could branch out from these outer petals and could connect in a web-like fashion where one action or project intersected with more than one objective – a desired and value-added approach. This graphic

Figure 6.3   Simpcw flower graphic

Source: CIER, 2011

(Figure 6.3), which started out as pencil and paper, was created digitally with some petals blank. The community planner was able to use this to generate discussion with the leadership at a chief and council meeting to develop the leadership goal, and to eventually approve all the goals and objectives for the CCP. She has shared this graphic with others in the community, as well as First Nations in the area who appreciated the visual representation of these key elements of Simpcw's plan. The relatively longer-term nature of the goals and objectives (as compared to the actions outlined in the details of the plan document) makes this graphic useful for continued community planning meetings and events, and easy to update over the years.

WRITING THE PLAN

The actual writing of the plan document took place over many months and was a collaborative effort. Review of other First Nation CCPs and Simpcw documents provided the team with ideas of what Simpcw First Nation's CCP should include and how it should look. Comprehensive community planning is still relatively new in Canada and there is no standard content or format. While CCP is far from a cookie cutter process, review of other plans to determine content, format, or even look and feel can help a community develop its own document. As it stands, there are not that many documents to refer or compare to. Certainly, CCPs that have been developed and written with the First Nation in partnership are rare. CIER created an initial table of contents for the CCP to guide the writing process. Together we reviewed and agreed on the plan outline and identified writing responsibilities, and began writing up the plan while the final thinking and decisions continued. One year and ten drafts later, our final version of the plan was ready to go to council for final approval. The council's participation in the planning process over the years from annual community sessions, committee involvement, and planning presentations at their regular meetings meant that they were familiar and supportive of the plan when it was ready in its final form. On 20 January 2011, Simpcw First Nation chief and council formally approved their comprehensive community plan.

Information about the past and a current baseline is included both within the CCP itself and as a separate "community profile"-type report by other consultants and communities. CIER and Simpcw decided that this information should be included in a separate report as an accompaniment to the CCP. This "State of the Nation" report was completed using an annotated table of contents that CIER created as a tool for First Nations working on CCP and, to some extent, remains a work in progress because not all sections are completed to the extent that the community may wish. This document can serve as a decision-support tool over time and areas that have missing data can be addressed as needed. Gathering background information for a community plan can seem overwhelming at first and before the critical information needs are identified. Of course, the planning team often would like to have all of the information possible but on closer review, likely does not need all the information immediately to move forward on the CCP. As opportunities arise, Simpcw can fill in more information through specific project activities (e.g., traditional use studies as part of a future territorial land-use planning initiative) and as the baseline data (e.g., population statistics, housing stock) changes. Other planning tools and documents that helped create the plan (e.g., communication surveys and reports, project priority graphs, community gifts surveys, achievements tables) can also be adapted and used as part of the CCP implementation and as part of the monitoring and adaptation process.

In addition to the full planning document, CIER created a mini version of the plan called the "CCP Household Summary." As part of its emergency response planning in 2006, Simpcw created small handbooks for each household on reserve. The CCP planning team decided that a summary version of the CCP would be a good way for community members to understand the vision and goals set out in the current plan and allow Simpcw to share its plan at a high level with others, while keeping the detailed plan for internal decision making. This 17x17 cm book is twenty-two pages long and was created using a free online book-making software, which allows Simpcw to print and order more copies if and as needed. Chief and council and staff members have all received a copy of the mini plan; chief and council and managers have a copy of the full plan for their use and reference. The community celebrated the completion of their CCP and their contribution to implementation at the community planning session in the fall of 2012.

OPPORTUNITIES FOR FIRST NATION COMMUNITY PLANNING IN CANADA

First Nations that have engaged in community planning are using these strategic planning documents as governance tools to bring people, projects, and programs together in ways that contribute to a better quality of life for their members (Cook 2008; Jojola 2008). Planning also provides First Nations with the opportunity to assert rights and raise their interests and concerns early in the decision-making process to work collaboratively with other jurisdictions (Porter 2004, 2006; CIER 2007) and ideally avoid lengthy and expensive litigation. Planning as a tool for self-determination and sovereignty requires a shift in mindset among external non-Indigenous planning consultants and government planners. As Lane and Hibbard (2005) discuss, this challenges the typical planning approach where all citizens are considered to have equal rights, and requires revisiting and even reconfiguring the Indigenous-state relationship. Coming to terms with the roles and rights of actors in multi-party land, resource, and water-planning processes (where the Indigenous people involved have unique rights) will be a step forward in planning. As Indigenous nations gain more control of the resource on their lands and engage in planning as a means to inform their members and others of their future plans, their impact on policy and on the landscape will increase. For planners working on regional, rural, resource-based, or even urban planning, improving their knowledge and skills in Indigenous planning will be critical to success for all parties.

Unfortunately, many First Nations in Canada are without the comprehensive community plans that set the overall vision and direction for the nation, and help create a framework for other planning initiatives. Although most First Nations would likely choose to engage in planning if the funding were available, community planning has been a topic that has not been seen as a priority for funding sources within government. Planning in Canada tends to take place at a provincial level; First Nations in Canada, however, are subject to federal legislation and liaise with federal government departments. As a result, First Nation reserves are "federal lands" that exist like a patchwork quilt among provincial lands where different legislative and policy realities exist. While both the federal and provincial governments in Canada are representatives of the Crown, and the Crown has a fiduciary duty to First Nations, the provincial governments – and the planning departments – are not heavily involved with First Nations. This is one of the main challenges facing First Nation planning and has impacts on funding, plan development, and plan implementation.

Formally, there are provincial/territorial planning ministries – for example, the Ministry of Natural Resources in Ontario drives much of the land-use planning; Manitoba Intergovernmental Affairs is home to the planning department; the Environment Department in British Columbia engages in water-use planning. Saskatchewan has the Community Planning Branch within the Ministry of Municipal Affairs. Planning schools that teach future planners about the legislative and policy contexts use case studies and assignments based on the provincial context where they are located. The Canadian Institute of Planners, the professional organization, while national, has provincial affiliates where the accreditation and most of the support and professional development opportunities take place.

As a result, most planners do not understand the legislative – let alone the cultural, social, and legal – realities in First Nations. A First Nation may also have its own unique policies, bylaws, and service agreements (e.g., custom election codes, certificates of possession of land – or not; agreements with municipalities for waste disposal; with provincial school boards for delivery of curriculum at schools on reserve). Federal legislation that applies directly or uniquely to First Nations (e.g., First Nations Lands Management Act, First Nations Fiscal and Statistical Management Act, and, of course, the antiquated Indian Act) also makes this planning context different from the Canadian norm.

The majority of First Nations in Canada are small in population yet have the administrative responsibilities of a municipality and more (as a result of their status as nations). In many First Nations, a small number of people work hard to meet wide-ranging and varied responsibilities. As discussed, a funded planning position within their government or band office generally does not exist. Given the often overwhelming responsibility and workload of staff, "extra" planning work is hard for people to do. An actual long-term planning position as exists in Simpcw First Nation is rare. Elected First Nation councillors also rarely have planning portfolios within their suite of responsibilities – in part because there is no federal funding directed at planning on a regular basis. As a result, planning initiatives tend to be sporadic. Linked to this is the fact that, in general, First Nation youths do not understand the role of a planner or the value planning can make to their community and so, for the most part, are not pursuing a planning education. External planners working with a First Nation can help on this front by working with youths to expose them to planning's value, build apprenticeship or mentoring into the project, and be a role model so that young people consider a planning education and career among their options.

Many First Nations that do have completed plans have hired – or better yet, partnered – with a planning consultancy. While there may have been a "planning champion" involved at the local level to participate in the work and facilitate community involvement, this is typically a part-time position funded as part of the planning project. A First Nation's ability to continue to fund a planning position as part of implementation of the plan through its own sources of funds is challenging unless it has its own sources of revenue (e.g., through economic development) and could result in "robbing Peter to pay Paul" for other programs. The planning champion's capacity to lead the implementation depends on his or her previous education and experience, and the hired consultant's commitment to mentorship as part of plan development. Community planning is, however, too important to be left to non-statutory or unofficial sources of soft money.

Simpcw First Nation has been able to sustain the position of community planner over the past four years and has involved their planner in a wide range of planning-related projects. While the position is not secure (in that it is not a permanently funded position through government sources or programs), Simpcw has sustained the position through internal sources, grants, and project fees. The more than twenty-year engagement in community visioning and informal planning at Simpcw, in combination with their sustainable and economic development initiatives, has made the need and value of the planning position clear to the leadership. This consistency has been critical to the successful development of Simpcw's CCP and will make the transition to plan implementation and connections with other plans and initiatives much easier.

CIER's planning approach allowed for a long-term relationship, formal group workshops, one-on-one coaching, focused in-community support, and ongoing remote support for the process and to the community planner. This partnership approach provided a platform for the capacity-building and participatory process that resulted in a CCP that Simpcw First Nation has co-created and can internalize as its own. The process was not always easy and went through pace changes through the years as a result of internal community realities and external funding starts and stops. Creativity and innovative thinking, partnerships with other projects, and new funders (including others that Simpcw applied to directly), as well as a commitment to the community, kept the process alive and led to the completed plan.

While a long-term planning process such as the one shared here may not always be possible, lessons from this experience provide many important considerations for planners working with Indigenous people: be a good listener; foster a good relationship with a community member, or members, who are part of your project team; allow the time for unexpected events and meetings while you are in the community; listen to and respect the wishes of the people you are working for; do not be afraid to ask questions and make suggestions; be humble and know how to laugh at yourself; be flexible and adaptable in order to create new or other ways of planning together; be a mentor; inspire young people to strive for a better quality of life and understand how planning can contribute. Simple cross-cultural planning tips are on the surface perhaps not necessarily easy to live by on a daily basis but are part of continuous professional planning and personal development.

In the short-term, more non-Indigenous planners working with Indigenous communities need to expand their planning toolbox to learn about the different planning regulatory and legal frameworks that are the reality for these nations. This should start within the planning schools where students can also be exposed to Indigenous theories and methodologies, and continue as personal professional development for planners who then practice planning with Indigenous communities. National professional planning associations have started to include Indigenous planning by creating committees that, for example, help to educate other members and do community outreach (e.g., CIP, APA). More is needed here. Further education of non-Indigenous planners and other professions (e.g., engineers, architects) is critical because in the foreseeable future, First Nations will continue to look to outside support and expertise to help achieve their goals. Acknowledgment, through some type of accreditation or certification, of the planning responsibilities and accomplishments of First Nation people doing planning locally, who do not have a formal planning education, is also needed and being asked for at the community level.

Planners' on-going learning should also include cultural planning elements (e.g., inclusion of water ceremonies in the watershed plan), learning about and an appreciation of Indigenous worldviews and the ability to listen for ways to be more inclusive (e.g., how to include family dynamics and/or a clan system into the planning process and action responsibilities), and incorporating capacity-building and mentorship of local people into their planning process. Planning institutions that require ongoing professional development to maintain membership (e.g., Canadian Institute of Planners' continuous professional learning units) can support this by allowing these types of workshops, conferences, and readings as acceptable credits or units. Planners need to be patient, to *want* to build relationships with people and communities, and be comfortable switching gears from the deadline-driven office culture to the people-driven community culture. Through these relationships planners will hopefully inspire young Indigenous people to look at planning as a meaningful and rewarding career so that over the long-term, Indigenous communities can work with Indigenous and non-Indigenous planners as they move forward in their hopes, dreams, and plans for a better life.

ACKNOWLEDGMENTS

This work was possible through the dedication and collaboration of Kerri-Jo Fortier and Tina Donald of Simpcw First Nation and the ongoing support and participation of the community members living and working in Chu Chua. Key contributions by staff with the Centre for Indigenous Environmental Resources (CIER) were also provided at various points in the project by Sarah Cooper, Jason Locke, Tracy Ruta Ruchs, and Maria M'Lot and Jeff Cook, Beringia Community Planning. Aboriginal Affairs and Northern Development Canada and the British Columbia New Relationship Trust provided funding for this work. Thank you to everyone who participated in the planning process and helped co-create Simpcw First Nation's Comprehensive Community Plan.

REFERENCES

Centre for Indigenous Environmental Resources. 2007. *Meaningful Involvement of Aboriginal Peoples in Environmental Assessment.*

Centre for Indigenous Environmental Resources. 2011. *First Nations Integrated Watershed Planning. Describing Your Approach: Know Yourself.*

Cook, Jeffrey. 2008. "Building on Traditions of the Past: The Rise and Resurgence of First Nations CCP." *Plan Canada.* Summer.

Forester, John. 1991. *The Deliberative Practitioner Encouraging Participatory Planning Processes.* Cambridge, MA: MIT Press.

Jojola, T. 2008 "Indigenous Planning – An Emerging Context." *Canadian Journal of Urban Research* 17 (1) Supplement:37–47.

Jones, Bernie. 1990. *Neighborhood Planning: A Guide for Citizens and Planners.* Chicago, IL: Planners Press/American Planning Association.

Knudston, Peter, and David Suzuki. 1992. *Wisdom of the Elders.* Toronto, ON: Stoddart Publishing Co. Ltd.

Lane, Marcus B, and Michael Hibbard. 2005. "Doing it for Themselves – Transformative Planning by Indigenous People." *Journal of Planning Education and Research* 25:172–84.

Porter, Libby. 2004. "Unlearning One's Privilege: Reflections on Cross-Cultural Research with Indigenous Peoples in South-East Australia." *Planning Theory & Practice* 5 (1):104–9.

– 2006. "Planning in (Post)Colonial Settings: Challenges for Theory and Practice." *Planning Theory & Practice* 7 (4):383–96.

Sarkissian, Wendy, and Dianna Hurford, with Christine Wenman. 2010. *Creative Community Planning: Transformative Engagement Methods for Working at the Edge*. London, UK: Earthscan.

Tuhiwai Smith, Linda. 1999. *Decolonizing Methodologies: Research and Indigenous People*. London and New York: Zed Books Ltd.

7

Maybe, Maybe Not: Native American Participation in Regional Planning

SHARON HAUSAM

Regional planning processes are sometimes presented as opportunities for Indigenous input into decisions that affect community, land, resources, sacred sites, cultural traditions, and sovereignty. However, Indigenous governments may make decisions about participation in these processes based on a number of factors, not all of which may be immediately apparent to other participants. This chapter considers the nature of these factors and illustrates them with a case study of regional water planning in northwest New Mexico, United States.

REGIONAL PLANNING AND PARTICIPATION

Regional planning is concerned with "a scale greater than a single community and less than a nation" (Perloff 1968, 153). A region may be defined based on ecological characteristics, such as watersheds and mountain ranges, or as a grouping of human settlements, such as rural towns or a central city and surrounding suburbs. Stakeholders in regional planning processes include multiple governments, their constituents, and interest groups.

Stakeholders choose to participate in the planning process. The degree of their participation is affected by the level of interest in the outcome and the likelihood that the process, in comparison with other alternatives, will achieve desired goals.

By definition, a stakeholder is presumed to have an interest in the issue, though not always a very strong one. In some cases, one entity, perhaps another jurisdiction or an organization, may represent the interests of multiple stakeholders, so some of them may choose not to participate directly. If a stakeholder is interested and not otherwise represented, participation in a regional planning process is affected by whether, in comparison to other alternatives, the process will achieve the stakeholder's goals.

If the process seems unfairly weighted towards one perspective it may not achieve those goals. The first indications of fairness occur when stakeholders are recognized and invited to participate. Other clues are apparent in how the process is run: Are meeting locations accessible to all? What languages are used? What forms of knowledge are viewed as legitimate? Is there time for multiple perspectives to be shared? Historical relationships between stakeholders, especially those that involve racial conflict, may also affect perceptions of fairness (Gray 1989; Mier 1994; Wondolleck and Yaffee 2000). If the process is conducted without making an effort to seek out and appreciate a wide range of contributions, stakeholders may sense that their contributions will not be valued and their time and effort would be better spent elsewhere.

Stakeholders weigh participation against other obligations that require time and resources (Abers 2000; Forester 1996; Laurian 2004). Rational planning processes generally require extensive staff time on the part of the organization hosting the process. Politicized processes require dedication from elected and appointed officials. Planning processes that incorporate social movements often use interest groups and committed citizens to mobilize the public. Collaborative planning may engage all these groups, and requires a substantial commitment from all stakeholders for extensive face-to-face dialogue to build relationships and develop goals and objectives.

Minute details of the planning process also factor into commitments to participate. Attendance may be affected, for example, by the personalities of the facilitator or other participants, the room in which a meeting is held, parking availability, a tendency to not stick to the agenda, late-night endings, the type of food and beverages that are provided or whether any are provided at all, and a host of other factors.

Decisions are also affected by the nature of the stakeholders' goals. If the goals are such that there is no room for compromise, processes that result in clear-cut wins and losses may be preferred over consensus-based approaches (Crowfoot and Wondolleck 1990; Dukes and Firehock 2001). Stakeholders may also have objectives that will not be written in a final document or plan for implementation, but that can be achieved through a planning process. Participation can be a way to build relationships and educate others, either to enhance support for goals or for other social and political benefits (Gruber 1993; Innes 1996, 1998, 1999b).

Conversely, it can also result in "getting to know the enemy" (Moote et al. 1997, 883).

Stakeholders consider these factors in the context of their other options, which may include political and legal strategies and social movements. Political and legal strategies work within established governmental and regulatory structures. They include lawsuits or other adjudicative approaches, lobbying for legislative solutions, and efforts to have supporters elected. Social movements may include demonstrations such as rallies, marches, street theatre, and sit-ins; blockades and occupations; petitions and written letters; posters; boycotts and proxy voting on stocks; and other approaches to public education.

Overall, a stakeholder's ability to achieve goals is affected by the stakeholder's power, the capacity to make things happen. Power may come from being a part of the dominant society whose desired goals are already the presumptive outcomes of the planning process. It may also be associated with support from existing structures (legal, bureaucratic, political, epistemological); resources such as money, time, and information; or force or threats of force. Those with a great deal of power may be able to achieve their goals almost regardless of their approach, while those with less power may need to carefully hone their strategies.

Power is also affected by the type of approach used for the planning process. A rational, technical, or bureaucratic planning process begins with assumptions about goals. These assumptions tend to minimize the perspective of, and thus benefits to, non-dominant cultures. Planning processes that are heavily affected by politics generally result in limited benefits for those with less power. Planning processes combined with social movements make an effort to shift parties to a new vision but are often resisted unless they are backed by other types of power. Collaborative planning attempts to develop shared goals and mutually defined objectives where no single entity has all the power and stakeholders are clearly interdependent (Healey 1997; Innes 1999a, 1999b; Innes and Booher 1999; Innes and Gruber 2005).

Stakeholders may opt to fully participate in a planning process, do something entirely outside of it, or some combination. Decisions are made repeatedly as conditions and the planning process change over time.

NATIVE AMERICAN INVOLVEMENT IN REGIONAL PLANNING

Native American stakeholders in regional planning may include tribal governments, traditional tribal leaders, individual tribal members, and organizations at scales ranging from intra-tribal to national organizations. This chapter considers the participation of Native American tribal governments recognized by the United States as representatives of the people of that tribe, although in most communities this is only one form of authority and traditional leaders may have power behind the scenes. Tribal governments (also referred to as "tribes" in this chapter) are likely to be concerned about regional planning processes when the outcomes of those processes may affect community life and the well-being of the people, historic or current lands or resources, culturally significant sites or practices, and their ability to govern their own affairs.

Tribes rarely have the benefit of other entities truly looking out for their best interests and participating in planning processes for them. The Bureau of Indian Affairs (BIA), intended to serve this function, originated as a paternalistic agency antithetical to self-governance, and is mired in inefficient bureaucracy and grossly underfunded. The trust responsibility of other federal agencies to tribes often conflicts with their responsibilities to non-Native constituents. State governments and agencies have historically been in conflict with tribal governments over issues of sovereignty, and although examples of coordination are increasing (Reed and Zelio 1995), support is not reliable. Local (non-tribal) governments tend to be preoccupied with their own concerns and maintain a respectful distance, though they may collaborate very effectively when necessary (Zaferatos 1998). Environmental groups can be powerful allies with tribes, but their interests are not always aligned (Grossman 2002).

Tribes may take a sceptical look at the potential for fairness in planning processes. After centuries of being excluded, ignored, or misunderstood in decision-making processes, it is reasonable to doubt that regional planning might be an improvement. Regional planners often add tribes to a list of stakeholders as an afterthought and hold meetings in large urban areas, in English, with tightly constrained public comment periods. Many tribes have suffered enough at the hands of outside governments that they prefer to minimize their interactions and their risks.

Historically, tribal governments have not had the resources to fully participate in planning processes that last for extended periods of time and require heavy commitment. Initially, the BIA represented tribes. Although this improved with the passage of the Indian Self-Determination and Education Assistance Act (PL 93–638), which allows tribes to contract for federal dollars to run their own programs, tribal staffing levels are often still low. Even if funds are available to hire employees, office space may not be available to house them. Administrative buildings compete for funding with facilities that provide direct services to tribal members such as water and sewer lines, schools, and clinics. Tribes may hire outside consultants or legal counsel, which, at higher costs, may work on a restricted number of projects.

If an issue affects fundamental values, such as the persistence of the people, the relationship with a particular place, the continuation of cultural traditions, or sovereignty, it may not be negotiable. In fact, it may not always be appropriate to talk about these core values to non-Natives. On the other hand, tribes can sometimes benefit from planning processes as a tool for educating others. They may also use the opportunity to learn about their adversaries and define better strategies for meeting their goals.

Tribal power, and thus the likelihood of success in planning and other decision-making processes, is complex. Native American interests, particularly those related to traditional practices and to sovereignty, are not well-recognized or understood within mainstream society. Tribes must make an effort to have their goals understood, much less accepted, placing them at a disadvantage.

Diseases and deception robbed Native communities of the strength they had prior to European contact. They have been impoverished by the theft of lands and resources, abused by the United States educational system, and disenfranchised. Limited funds, poor education, and historical trauma have had long-term effects on their well-being and ability to compete in the dominant society.

Many tribes' power as sovereign nations was initially recognized in treaties made with colonial powers (Churchill 1999; Williams 1990). The rights of the Pueblo tribes of New Mexico were recognized by the Treaty of Guadalupe Hidalgo, signed in 1848 between Mexico and the United States, but the Pueblos were not defined as "Indians" until the US Supreme Court case *United States v. Sandoval* in 1931 (231 US 28). Tribal sovereignty has since been circumscribed by United States Supreme Court cases and federal laws. Tribes now have a "semi-sovereign" status and are defined as "domestic dependent nations," with a relationship to the federal government like "that of a ward to a guardian" (*Cherokee Nation v. Georgia*, 20 US (5 Pet.) 1, 8 L.Ed. 25 (1831)). The federal government maintains a "trust responsibility" over Native American tribes (Deloria and Lytle 1983, 1984). Ultimate control is held by the Secretary of Interior and by Congress (Chambers and Price 1993). The interminable paperwork of the Bureau of Indian Affairs and requirements for signature approval from the Secretary of Interior or the Deputy Secretary of Indian Affairs can be severe constraints on tribal decision-making authority.

However, because of their semi-sovereign status, tribes are generally not constrained by state law (*Worcester v. Georgia*, 31 US (6 Pet.) 515, 8 L.Ed. 483 (1832)). Furthermore, numerous federal laws require consideration of Native American concerns. Tribes have legally defined opportunities to contribute to federal decisions under the National Environmental Policy Act (42 USC, s. 4321–35 and 1979 regulations), the National Historic Preservation Act (15 USC, s. 470a(d)(6)(b) and 470(h), 1992), the Native American Graves and Repatriation Act (25 USC, s. 3002–5 and 3010), the Archaeological Resources Protection Act (16 USC, s. 470cc), and Executive Orders 12875 (1993), 12898 (1994), and 13007 (1996) (NATHPO 2005). The National Historic Preservation Act requires that federal agencies consult directly with Native American entities that attach religious or cultural significance to any properties that may be affected by a federal undertaking (36 CFR 800.2(c)).

In recent years many tribes have capitalized on opportunities available to them as semi-sovereign nations and begun the return to their former strength. The rise of casino gaming has provided some tribes with revenue to improve their members' education, increase tribal government staffing, hire outsiders to lobby in support of their goals, and engage in the political process. Great efforts have been directed at intensifying tribal sovereignty, particularly through management of land and cultural resources, and to reclaiming culture and tradition, especially by speaking original languages.

Enhanced tribal sovereignty and self-governance have benefitted planning on tribal lands. The Indigenous planning model relates to "long and sustained patterns of continuous ownership" and stewardship of the land, rather than to private property rights, capital valuation of the land, and regulation of land use (Jojola 2000, 8). Indigenous planning has been practiced – unrecognized by non-Indigenous peoples – throughout history (Jojola 1998), but re-emerged with Indigenous activism at the American Indian Chicago Conference of 1961, the United Indian Planners Association of the 1970s, and the rise of Indigenous planning principles in the 1990s (Robin 1995). Planning among many Native American tribes has become more strategic and visionary as a result of gaming revenues, and now focuses on goals rather than the deficiencies emphasized in previous comprehensive planning efforts (Jojola 2000). Tribes often plan outside their reservation boundaries, particularly within their historical lands, "exercising ... authority over [their] territorial, social, and political affairs" (Zaferatos 1998, 402).

Sovereignty, self-governance, and increasing tribal populations have also begun to affect non-Native communities. As tribes reacquire lost lands, non-Natives fear losing tax revenue, legal authority over the land, natural resources, and public access, and, in some cases, also becoming subject to additional regulations set by tribal governments. Tribal laws for environmental protection may require neighbouring jurisdictions to meet higher and more expensive standards for water and air quality (Sutton 2001). On the positive side, many tribes have financial resources that can be used to implement regional projects. These interdependencies give tribes some power in negotiations or consensus-based processes.

CASE STUDY: REGIONAL WATER PLANNING IN
NORTHWEST NEW MEXICO

This case study reflects on a regional water planning process that took place in northwest New Mexico, United States. The case is based on participant observation, with most observations occurring between 1997 and 2001, combined with document review. The author was a planner working for the regional planning organization, the Northwest New Mexico Council of Governments, developing the water plan; and later the executive director of the New Mexico Water Dialogue, a non-profit involved with regional water planning. In her current role as planner for the Pueblo of Laguna, she is still modestly involved with water issues in the region. Opinions expressed in this chapter are the personal views of the author in her individual capacity and are not necessarily the views of the Pueblo of Laguna, its staff, or employees.

The Region

The region in this case was defined by political jurisdictions and watersheds. It included all of Cibola County and part of McKinley County, New Mexico, an area which overlaps four federally recognized tribes, the Pueblos of Acoma (Haak'u), Laguna (K'awaik), and Zuni (A:shiwi), and the Navajo (Dineh) Nation, as well as three incorporated cities and various other limited-purpose governments (such as water and sanitation districts in unincorporated areas).

The region includes lands within the Puerco River and Zuni River watersheds, which drain into the Little Colorado River and then to the

Colorado River; the Rio Puerco and Rio San Jose watersheds, which drain into the Rio Grande; the North Plains Closed Basin; and smaller portions of other basins. The Continental Divide passes through the region, separating the watersheds draining into the Colorado River from those draining into the Rio Grande. The region is semi-arid to arid, and typically receives nine to eleven inches (23–28 cm) of rainfall per year, generally inadequate to meet all desired uses.

Overview of the Process

The regional water planning process was initiated and funded by the state of New Mexico. In 1987, a federal court ruled that New Mexico could not deny the use of its ground water by appropriators outside the state without showing that the water was needed in New Mexico. The state funded the first round of water plans in order to quantify the needs and availability of water in each region. In northwest New Mexico the first regional water plan was initiated in 1991 and completed in 1994 (Leedshill-Herkenhoff et al. 1994).

By the early 1990s, in part as a result of citizen activists working together in a group known as the Regional Water Planning Dialogue (later the New Mexico Water Dialogue) (RWP Dialogue 1994), the state realized that its water planning effort needed to consider the unique nature of each region and develop plans that reflected more public involvement. According to the state's *Regional Water Planning Handbook*, published in 1994,

> the diversity of approach in the previous regional water plans confirmed the legislature's intuition that New Mexico communities relate to their water resources in very different ways. Some regions based their plans on traditional custom and culture; others looked at developed needs; still others searched for a balance between the two (NMISC 1994, 2).

Regions also had very different water supplies, using surface water, directly or as recharge to ground water, as well as non-renewing ground water supplies.

The planning process discussed here was managed by the Northwest New Mexico Council of Governments (NWNMCOG), a regional planning organization formed under the authority of the state's Joint Powers Agreement Act (s. 4-22-1 to 4-22-7, New Mexico Statutes Annotated,

1953 compilation). The NWNMCOG felt that substantial improvement could be made to the original plan and received funding from the state to update it through increased public involvement. The process included focus groups starting in 1997, and public meetings starting in 1998. There was substantial community involvement, but little outward public controversy about the plan, and no explicit goal of helping to resolve any differences of opinion between diverse groups in the region, although the state commission at the head of the planning effort "strongly encourage[d] regions to negotiate solutions to local water problems" (NMISC 1994, 5).

The second round of planning incorporated much of the technical information from the first plan. The plans were intended to define alternatives for addressing water needs through conservation, infrastructure, water quality improvements, and other approaches that could be implemented by local, state, or the federal government. However, the second plan document fell short of adopting a detailed plan of implementation. No funds were identified, much less guaranteed, for future projects.

Factors Affecting Tribal Participation

The four Native American tribes with land in the region have cared for its waters since time immemorial. For the Pueblos, water has always been vital for physical sustenance and cultural survival (Robert 1996; RWP meeting, 29 September 1997). The Pueblos have grown crops using irrigation and other methods known as "water-spreader," "runoff," and "nabamu," or "Ak-Chin" irrigation, capitalizing on natural hydrology to direct water to fields. They have also used springs as a source of groundwater (NWNMCOG 1998).

The high value placed on water has necessitated its careful use. According to the Pueblos of Acoma and Laguna, "before the Spanish arrived, before the state of New Mexico even existed, the Pueblo people of the region were regulating water use through a formalized system based upon cultural concepts of what was a valid use of a very scarce, but essential element" (Pueblos of Laguna and Acoma 1998). Pueblo water conservation in the modern era is enforced verbally, without the need for written ordinances (RWP meeting, 29 September 1997), and reinforced through traditional practices, such as constructing homes primarily of cut stone rather than adobe, which requires more water (Pueblos of Laguna and Acoma 1998).

Navajo communities are typically more dispersed than Pueblos, making it difficult to develop efficient shared water systems. In an arid region such as northwest New Mexico, consistent surface water supplies are virtually absent, and groundwater supplies are deep, making domestic wells prohibitively expensive. Thus, many residents of the Navajo Nation do not have a water supply and are required to haul water in tanks, with some limited to one fifty-five gallon tank for two weeks (RWP meeting, 29 September 1997). The Navajo Nation has been working for decades to improve the quality of life for its people by improving access to water (Leeper 2004).

Everyone understands the basic importance of water in an arid region. However, its cultural significance to Pueblos and the Navajo Nation is rarely recognized, and sometimes antithetical to the European way of thinking (RWP meeting, 2 March 1998). Furthermore, the tremendous disparities in access to domestic water are not widely realized. The general American public, in a nation with incredible prosperity and high standards of living, is completely unaware of the disadvantages in many tribal communities. The tribes within the region thus had a weakness in terms of public understanding of their goals and concerns about water.

The planning process did call for incorporating tribal viewpoints along with other perspectives, though it did not suggest approaches to doing this. The legislation enabling the second round of planning specified that the criteria for evaluating proposals for funding water planning would provide for, among other things, "use of an appropriate planning process, including opportunities for participation by those Indian tribes located within the various regions of the state" (NMISC 1994:12; New Mexico Statutes Annotated, s. 72-14-44 2.C(2)). The deputy director and associate planner of the NWNMCOG, among other staff, also had personal commitments to tribal issues.

Tribes were encouraged to participate as members of a technical committee which steered the effort and reviewed all the draft documents; two out of nine technical committee meetings were held on tribal lands. One of four focus group meetings and five of ten public meetings were also held on tribal lands. Public meetings were announced in four newspapers, two of which were tribal, and on two tribal radio stations, along with other stations owned by one (non-tribal) corporation (NWNMCOG 1998). The draft plan was available for review at two tribal and two non-tribal government locations. These ratios do not reflect the percentage of the region's population that is Native American (approximately 66 per cent in 2000), but are higher than is typical for most planning processes.

Regardless of any of these efforts, there is evidence that the tribes did not feel the planning process could truly reflect their perspectives. As the Pueblos of Acoma and Laguna wrote,

> The Pueblos' treatment of water for their public welfare is not always consistent with that of New Mexico. Acoma and Laguna have never been comfortable with the notion that values concerning the use of water resources can be left solely to privately-driven economic trends or their populations at any one time. Their long history in the region and cultural concepts about the importance of physical location of their lands requires that a high value be placed on sustainability long into the future (Pueblos of Laguna and Acoma 1998, 2).

Furthermore, this was a state-driven process focusing largely on watershed-based boundaries, which did not explicitly consider tribal jurisdiction. The Pueblos of Acoma and Laguna, apparently concerned about this, requested that the following language regarding the absence of appropriate intergovernmental agreements be added to the plan: "No joint powers agreement was executed with any of the Indian tribes or Pueblos in the region for them to participate in regional water planning" (Pueblos of Laguna and Acoma 1998, 19). The Northwest New Mexico Council of Governments, as well, was formed under state law. County, municipal, and special purpose governments in the region were members of the NWNMCOG; the tribes were not.

The state's stipulations regarding the methods for projecting future water need conflicted with tribal preferences for data. Future needs for domestic and municipal use were estimated by multiplying the projected population by the expected daily water use per person (per capita water use). The state's regional water planning handbook specified that "population projections shall be based on the Bureau of Business and Economic Research (BBER) model, with any deviations from that model justified. BBER projections and any exceptions shall be reviewed within the public participation program and with Commission staff" (NMISC 1994, 7). The regional water plan commented on this:

> The challenges of estimating water demand based on recent levels of water use and population growth were perhaps underestimated by the original framers of the water planning process. The population growth figures developed by the Bureau of Business and Economic

Research of the University of New Mexico for the Interstate Stream Commission have been hotly disputed throughout the Region 6 planning process. Members of the technical committee and other participants in the process have stated repeatedly that these figures do not accurately represent tribal and Pueblo populations (NWNMCOG 1998, VA-16).[1]

The Pueblos of Acoma and Laguna protested that they

have their own economic and population cycles that do not conform to those of non-Indian communities. For example, the populations of Acoma and Laguna have been steadily increasing despite different population trends for the region as a whole. There are at least two possible explanations for this. The Pueblos are recovering from the significant impacts of epidemics at the beginning of the twentieth century when their populations reached the lowest point in centuries. Also, more Pueblo members are returning to Pueblos to live as economic opportunities become available (Pueblos of Acoma and Laguna 1998, 2).

The Navajo Nation also pointed out that its policy of promoting economic development was intended to decrease the rate of out-migration from the reservation (NWNMCOG 1998, VA-18; also see Leeper 2004). A Navajo participant in the process noted that Native Americans have been playing "catch up" since World War II and struggling to achieve the same standard of living as non-Natives (RWP meeting, 10 March 1998).

Tribal representatives did see some potential benefits from being involved in the planning process to foster future co-operation and collaboration. The notes from a focus group held on tribal lands reflect that "the Navajo Nation spokesperson spoke of the need for co-operation across reservation boundaries. 'We are neighbours, country folks, and city folks, and we can no longer continue to segregate ourselves. We all need to conserve, and Indian people have much to teach in the area of conservation'" (RWP meeting, 29 September 1997, 1). A public meeting participant stated that tribes have more to lose by not participating in the planning process (RWP meeting, 13 January 1998).

The tribes in the region were already taking other approaches to address their water issues. By participating in a process of hydrologic study and legal proceedings known as a general stream adjudication, they were working to determine the precedence and amount of their water rights. The decisions made in an adjudication determine who will obtain water during times of drought or other scarcity. Under strict application of a principle known as "prior appropriation," common in the western United States and incorporated into New Mexico state law, shortages of water are not shared. Water users are known as "senior" and "junior" water rights holders based on the precedence of their water right. When water is scarce, junior water rights holders may not receive any.

In 1983, well before regional water planning began in northwest New Mexico, the Pueblos of Acoma and Laguna and the Navajo Nation became parties to an adjudication of the Rio San Jose stream system. The United States filed a lawsuit on behalf of the Pueblos of Acoma and Laguna to address various issues in an upstream area of the watershed. The Kerr-McGee mining company and city of Grants filed in a state court for an adjudication. The cases were consolidated under the name *State ex rel. Martinez v. Kerr-McGee Corp. et al.*, No. CB-83-190-CV and CB-83-220-CV, commonly called "Kerr-McGee," and are now being addressed in state court. The United States government filed claims for water rights on behalf of the two Pueblos and the Navajo Nation.

An adjudication is a substantial undertaking for the tribal government and tribal members. There are extensive legal procedures and requirements for expert witnesses, along with ethnographic evidence obtained from tribal members. The tribes in this case study have committed to this process for decades in order to assert their water rights. They do not rely entirely on the federal government, believing their trustee may not provide sufficient advocacy on their behalf (Pueblos of Acoma and Laguna 1998, 5).

The legal framework of adjudication treats Indian water rights somewhat differently than those of non-Indian rights. In the classic Indian water rights case, *Winters v. United States* (207 US 564, C.C.A. 9, 1908), the United States sued on behalf of the tribes and bands of the Fort Belknap Reservation in northern Montana to prevent construction of a dam which would have prevented water from the Milk River from flowing to the reservation. Non-Indian irrigators argued that they had put the water to beneficial use first and had senior water rights. The US Supreme Court found in favour of the United States and the tribes, holding that when the United States first reserves land for a tribe, it also reserves for the exclusive use of the tribe the water needed to create a homeland. The priority date for the water use is the date the reservation was established, generally older than the first beneficial use by others, thus giving tribes a senior right.

Many New Mexico Pueblos, including Acoma, Laguna, and Zuni, have lands which were "reserved" for them as reservations or by federal executive order, lands which were granted to them by the Spanish and Mexican governments, and lands which were obtained in other ways. In a decision in another case involving Pueblo rights, *State of New Mexico ex rel. State Engineer v. Aamodt*, the courts determined that the Winters doctrine does not apply to the lands granted to the Pueblos by the Spanish government, since they were not "reserved" for them. The rights are considered "aboriginal," taking precedence over other rights, but the quantity of water is restricted to the amount that would have been sufficient for the lands irrigated up until 1924, when Pueblo land claims were settled through the Pueblo Lands Act (Chestnut et al. 2011).

In addition to the adjudication of the Rio San Jose, the Navajo Nation was also engaged in discussions regarding water rights in other stream basins. In 1976, the state filed an adjudication to resolve Indian water rights in the San Juan River basin (*State of New Mexico ex rel. State Engineer v. United States, et al.*, San Juan County Cause No. D-1116-CV-7500184). In 1996, the Navajo Nation invited the state of New Mexico to engage in discussions that could potentially settle Navajo Nation claims to the San Juan River. The settlement talks would address, among other things, a water supply and infrastructure for what is known as the Navajo Gallup Water Supply Project (NGWSP) (Pollack 2005). Although the San Juan basin was not included in this water plan, the region encompassed a number of Navajo communities that would be served by the NGWSP, making that adjudication relevant to this planning process as well.

The state did not expect adjudication to be affected by planning efforts, but did mention it in the regional water planning handbook's template as a legal issue. The handbook states that "in determining available water supply, planners must consider both hydrological and legal limitations" (NWISC 1994, 11).

Tribal representatives did, however, have concerns about how the water planning process might relate to their water rights (RWP meeting, 13 January 1998). Although the planning process itself would not legally determine tribal water rights (Pueblos of Acoma and Laguna 1998), it could underestimate tribal needs for water, which could place a strain on future tribal water uses (Eriacho 1998). It could calculate a non-Native need that was much higher than what would be available to the non-Natives following a final adjudication, and determination of Pueblo senior right. Tribal participants suggested that quantification of water rights should precede planning, and commented that until water rights are adjudicated, it would be very difficult to address issues such as conservation (RWP meeting, 29 September 1997).

Participation

Tribal participation reflected these circumstances. Early on, technical committee members, primarily water resources staff and executive leadership from tribal governments, requested additional opportunities for tribal involvement, leading the NWNMCOG to hold at least one public meeting on each tribe's lands (NWNMCOG 1998, 1–4). A participant at a meeting in Gallup also requested more meetings, specifically in Zuni (RWP meeting, 13 January 1998).

Technical committee members and community members spoke about the cultural importance of water, including the principles of conservation, and in some cases, provided information on why certain alternatives to increasing water availability, such as cloud seeding, were culturally inappropriate (RWP meeting, 2 March 1998). Some suggested that there was a need to educate non-Indians and help them become "more Indian" (RWP meeting, 29 September 1997).

Technical committee members from the Pueblo of Zuni and Navajo Nation shared data on tribal population counts and projections, based on their own figures rather than those of the state Bureau of Business and Economic Research. The NWNMCOG incorporated this data into the plan as community-derived population projections. Projections for McKinley County were based on the following annual growth rates: 2.48 per cent for the Navajo Nation; 2.2 per cent for Zuni; 1.82 per cent for the city of Gallup; and a range of BBER official growth rates for different time periods, generally lower than the tribal rates, for the remainder of the county (NWNMCOG 1998). Tribally derived populations were not available from the Pueblos of Acoma and Laguna, which are in Cibola County.

Tribal representatives also disputed the figures for average daily water use per person (per capita use). The Navajo Nation and Pueblo of Zuni were actively working to develop water supplies and increase connections to public water systems. With improved water sources, reduced water hauling, and an enhanced quality of life, per capita water use would increase (NWNMCOG 1998, VA-23). The Pueblos of Acoma commented that new community water systems would lead to increased domestic use (Pueblos of Acoma and Laguna 1998). Participants at a public meeting in Acoma stated that a rate of 70 gallons per capita per day (GPCD) was too low; a rate of 130 GPCD would be more accurate (RWP meeting, 9 March 1998). Some tribal members expressed concern during the water planning process that their practices of water conservation, based on both tradition and necessity, could be used against them to subsidize higher consumption off tribal lands (RWP meeting, 29 September 1997).

Finally, all four tribes commented on drafts of the water plan through their representatives on the technical committee, legal review, and other official comment. Near the end of the process, tribal representation in the planning process included legal counsel contracted for the water rights case. The three Pueblos made unambiguous statements that they were not full participants in the regional water planning process but were only observers. The Pueblos of Acoma and Laguna submitted a joint statement through their attorneys, which included the following comments:

When public meetings were being held throughout New Mexico on the potential for regional water planning, Harold Ranquist, the attorney for the Pueblo of Acoma, spoke on behalf of the Pueblo in support of water planning for the Pueblo's non-Indian neighbors, and the idea that the communities surrounding the Pueblo and other Indian lands should consider the existence of tribal water rights in their planning efforts. At that time, however, he was very careful to explicitly state that the Pueblo of Acoma would not be actively joining in the planning process as a means of quantifying its federally recognized and protected water rights. The Pueblos of Acoma and Laguna have participated only as observers in the on-going planning process, consistent with Mr. Ranquist's statement of almost a decade ago (Pueblos of Acoma and Laguna 1998, 1–2).

The Pueblo of Zuni also submitted a letter which stated that

the Pueblo has not actively joined the planning process for Region 6 and has participated only as an observer ... We remind the participants that in addition to the Pueblos that have commented on the legal issues section, the Pueblo of Zuni also has historic, present, and future water uses which need to be protected within the region (Eriacho 1998).

The Navajo Nation Department of Water Resources noted that although the Navajo Nation supports the regional water planning process, as a sovereign nation it reserves the right to approve or disapprove the plan (RWP Technical Committee meeting, 8 January 1997).

The Pueblos of Acoma and Laguna were clear about their reasons for holding to an "observer" status, referring to the different ways in which their people value water and the inaccuracies of non-tribal population and per capita use figures. They were also clear about their reasons for being involved in the process at all:

> In an effort to lessen future conflict, the Pueblos have cooperated with the process, although there was never any intention that it should attempt to apply to, define, or limit their present or future use of water in any way. This is consistent with the original concept of the very limited role of tribes in the regional water planning process, and the position taken by Acoma in support of non-Indian regional water planning. This has been accomplished through the Pueblos' designation of their representatives as "observers" rather than participants in the process (Pueblos of Acoma and Laguna 1998, 3).

And,

> In looking to water use in this region for the next forty years, it is essential that the surrounding non-Pueblo communities understand the constraints placed on their potential uses (Pueblos of Acoma and Laguna 1998, 20).

They also acknowledged that sharing information was an important part of protecting their interests. In their joint statement, they said:

> At the same time, however, the Pueblos of Acoma and Laguna acknowledge that it is in their interest to provide information to regional water planners about their water rights so that the existence of those rights can be taken into consideration when the region looks to possible future water use. If not, conflicts are certain to arise where regional water plans have not taken into account the existence of tribal water rights in addressing future water needs. Planners will assume a much greater supply is available for non-Indian use than actually exists. In an effort to lessen future conflict, the Pueblos have cooperated with the process, although there was never any intention that it should attempt to apply to, define, or limit their present or future use of water in any way. This is consistent with the original

concept of the very limited role of tribes in the regional water planning process, and the position taken by Acoma in support of non-Indian regional water planning (Pueblos of Acoma and Laguna 1998, xx).

Summary

In summary, the four tribes in this case study were clearly interested in protecting their water rights. Participation in the regional planning process was secondary. They would not rely on another entity to express these interests for them. There was no record of difficulties with participation or complaints about the details of the planning process.

The planners managing the process made an effort to incorporate tribal viewpoints. However, the tribes were concerned that their goals could not be fully understood and reflected in the plan. Furthermore, the state-driven process did not consider government-to-government agreements with the tribes and/or recognize tribal knowledge about future water use, indications that it did not respect tribal needs.

The tribes did see that the process could help educate non-Natives on the adjudication process and tribal water rights. They also took this as an opportunity to raise awareness of tribal population growth patterns and projected water use, using the technical nature of the process as a forum, regardless of the state's official acceptance of the data, and were successful in having this information incorporated into the plan.

Ultimately, however, the tribes used their participation in regional planning as a secondary tool. They relied on their options outside the planning process, opportunities available to them under law, such as the federal government's trust responsibility, priority water rights, the Winters doctrine, the Aamodt court case, and sovereignty within their own lands. Three of the tribes stated that they were not official participants, but only observers. They maintained a critical distance and did not commit themselves to the statements in the plan or its implementation.

Outcomes

Regional water planning has had a minimal impact on the tribes in northwest New Mexico. The second version of the plan, completed in 1996, was not officially adopted by the state, largely because it did not fully define a list of alternatives and select priorities for implementation (a task that the NWNMCOG acknowledged was incomplete). Later efforts resulted in a plan that was formally adopted by the state in 2004 (Edwards and Kiely 2004).

The Kerr-McGee adjudication involving the Pueblos of Laguna and Acoma and the Navajo Nation has continued outside the framework of water planning. The city of Grants, which is also part of the adjudication, developed its own municipal water plan effort shortly after the regional water planning process. The city's plan, which was also prepared by the NWNMCOG, noted that the rights of Acoma and Laguna would be the most senior rights in the watershed. In part because of this likely limitation on future supplies, the plan emphasized conservation of existing water (Hausam 1999).

The Pueblo of Zuni has also pursued avenues outside of regional water planning, initiating an adjudication for the Zuni River watershed in federal court in 2001 (US District Court No. 01-CV-0072 BB). Non-Native residents of the watershed felt threatened by the lawsuit, fearing they could lose their domestic water supplies and the value of their homes. The state did not view the Zuni River watershed as a top priority and was frustrated by the Pueblo's efforts to press ahead for its water rights (NM OSE and ISC 2007). By the end of 2006, a contractor working for the United States had completed a hydrographic survey for the area following the state's procedures, and the United States had served legal notice to all water rights claimants and filed claims for Zuni (NM OSE and ISC 2010). By the time the final version of the regional water plan was complete, the Pueblo of Zuni was not able to share information about its future water needs because they could be factors in the adjudication (Edwards and Kiely 2004, 12, citing comments of Zuni Indian Tribe to 18 November 2003 Review Draft, Governor Arlen P. Quetawki, Sr., dated 19 December 2003, 2).

The Navajo Nation continued its negotiations with the state of New Mexico and was successful in not only reaching an agreement but ultimately in obtaining federal funding for the Navajo Gallup Water Supply Project, which will serve various Navajo communities in the region. Navajo water rights in the San Juan basin, though essentially agreed-upon by the Navajo Nation and the state, must still be officially filed in court (Pollack 2005; Widdison and Kelly 2011).

The state has developed a complementary state water plan to address state-wide issues (OSE and ISC 2003). However, the state plan does not integrate the regional water plans. There remain conflicts between regions regarding their assumptions about future water needs and water supplies (Buynak et al. 2011).

CONCLUSIONS

For the governments of Native American tribes and other Indigenous peoples, this case study suggests the integration of Indigenous planning principles into regional planning processes. It may serve as a reminder to carefully assess participation in outside planning processes, basing decisions on how well the process will serve the community's goals. Does it address needs related to land, resources, sacred sites, cultural traditions, sovereignty, or other critical issues? Will the government be represented by another group? Will the process be fair, and is it feasible and palatable to participate? Most important, will it achieve the desired objectives, or are there alternatives which will better serve the community's interests? Is the education of non-Indigenous peoples appropriate and possible through this planning process? Can the process be combined with other options to maximize benefits? How does this change over time? Where does the Indigenous people's power lie, and how can it be best used at this moment?

For planners, the case study demonstrates some of the challenges associated with working with Indigenous peoples in regional planning processes. The field of planning has, for many decades, sought mechanisms to increase participation from people and groups representing a range of perspectives. Planners often attempt, within their ability, to be considerate of meeting locations, languages, and other factors, and to support education within the planning process. They should continue to improve in these areas. Nonetheless, the underpinnings of planning processes, such as funding and frameworks set by state agencies, may present obstacles to Indigenous participation. The status of Indigenous peoples as sovereign entities may provide them with alternative methods for achieving their goals. Encouragement from well-meaning outside planners cannot and should not shift an Indigenous group from determining what is best for its community and its future.

NOTE

1 Bureau of Business and Economic Research projections were based on data from the US Census, which has historically done a poor job of counting Native Americans. Many Natives, in turn, have resisted participating in the Census (National Congress of American Indians 2008).

REFERENCES

Abers, Rebecca Neaera. 2000. *Inventing Local Democracy: Grassroots Politics in Brazil*. Boulder: Lynne Reinner Publishers.

Buynak, Brigette, Susan Kelly, and Joanne Hilton. 2011. "State and Regional Water Planning in New Mexico." Online update of *Water Matters! Background on Selected Water Issues for Members of the 50th New Mexico State Legislature 1st Session 2011*. Albuquerque: Utton Transboundary Resources Center, University of New Mexico School of Law.

Chambers, Reid P., and Monroe E. Price. 1993. "Regulating Sovereignty: Secretarial Discretion and the Leasing of Indian Lands." In *Cases and Materials on Federal Indian Law*, edited by David H. Getches, Charles F. Wilkinson, and Robert A. Williams, 628–32. St Paul: West Publishing Co. Original edition, 26 Stan. L. Rev. 1061, 1061–8.

Chestnut, Peter, Susan Kelly, Jerold Widdison, and Darcy S. Bushnell. 2011. "Aamodt Adjudication." Online update of *Water Matters! Background on Selected Water Issues for Members of the 50th New Mexico State Legislature 1st Session 2011*. Albuquerque: Utton Transboundary Resources Center, University of New Mexico School of Law.

Churchill, Ward. 1999. "The Tragedy and the Travesty: The Subversion of Indigenous Sovereignty in North America." In *Contemporary Native American Political Issues*, edited by Troy R. Johnson, 17–72. Walnut Creek: AltaMira Press.

Crowfoot, James, and Julia M. Wondolleck. 1990. *Environmental Disputes: Community Involvement in Conflict Resolution*. Washington, DC and Covelo, CA: Island Press.

Deloria, Vine, Jr., and Clifford M. Lytle. 1983. *American Indians, American Justice*. Austin: University of Texas Press.

– 1984. *The Nations Within: The Past and Future of American Indian Sovereignty*. New York: Pantheon.

Dukes, E. Franklin, and Karen Firehock. 2001. *Collaboration: A Guide for Environmental Advocates*. Charlottesville, VA: University of Virginia, Institute for Environmental Negotiation; The Wilderness Society; and National Audubon Society.

Edwards, Mark H., and Jeffrey Kiely. 2004. *New Mexico Water Planning Region 6: Cibola/McKinley Regional Water Plan: Executive Summary: Meeting Future Water Resource Needs: Prepared for presentation to the New Mexico Interstate Stream Commission, 21 January*. Gallup, NM: Northwest New Mexico Council of Governments.

Eriacho, Donald F. (Governor, Pueblo of Zuni). 1998. "Letter to Mary Murnane, Regional Planner, Northwest New Mexico Council of Governments, Gallup, New Mexico." 17 March. In Appendix III of NWNMCOG, 1998.

Forester, John. 1996. "Argument, Power, and Passion in Planning Practice." In *Explorations in Planning Theory*, edited by Seymour J. Mandelbaum, Luigi Mazza, and Robert W. Burchell, 241–62. New Brunswick, NJ: Center for Urban Policy Research.

Gray, Barbara. 1989. *Collaborating: Finding Common Ground for Multiparty Problems*. San Francisco: Jossey-Bass Publishers.

Grossman, Zoltan. 2002. "Effects of White Racial Advantages in Environmental Alliances." *Conference of the Association of American Geographers.* Los Angeles.

Gruber, Judith. 1993. *Coordinating Growth Management Through Consensus-Building: Incentives and the Generation of Social, Intellectual, and Political Capital*. Berkeley, CA: University of California at Berkeley, Institute of Urban and Regional Development.

Hausam, Sharon. 1999. *City of Grants, New Mexico, 40-Year Water Plan*. Gallup, NM: Northwest New Mexico Council of Governments.

Healey, Patsy. 1997. *Collaborative Planning: Shaping Places in Fragmented Societies*. Vancouver: University of British Columbia Press.

Innes, Judith E. 1996. "Planning Through Consensus Building: A New View of Comprehensive Planning." *Journal of the American Planning Association* 62 (4):460–72.

Innes, Judith E. 1998. "Information in Communicative Planning." *Journal of the American Planning Association* 64 (1):52–63.

Innes, Judith E. 1999a. "Evaluating Consensus Building." In *The Consensus-Building Handbook*, edited by Lawrence Susskind, Sarah McKearnan, and Jennifer Thomas-Larmer, 631–73. Thousand Oaks: Sage Publications.

– 1999b. "Planning Institutions in the Network Society: Theory for Collaborative Planning." Working paper 99–05. Berkeley, CA: University of California at Berkeley, Institute of Urban and Regional Planning.

Innes, Judith E., and David E. Booher. 1999. "Consensus Building as Role Playing and Bricolage: Toward a Theory of Collaborative Planning." *Journal of the American Planning Association* 65 (1):9–26.

Innes, Judith E., and Judith Gruber. 2005. "Planning Styles in Conflict: The Metropolitan Transportation Commission." *Journal of the American Planning Association* 71 (1):177–88.

Jojola, Theodore S. 1998. "Indigenous Planning: Clans, Intertribal Confederations and the History of the All Indian Pueblo Council." In *Making*

the Invisible Visible: A Multicultural Planning History, edited by Leonie
Sandercock, 100–19. Berkeley, CA: University of California Press.

Jojola, Ted. 2000. "Indigenous Planning and Tribal Community Development."
Planners Network 139 (1):7–9.

Laurian, Lucie. 2004. "Public Participation in Environmental Decision Making." *Journal of the American Planning Association* 70 (1):53–65.

Leedshill-Herkenhoff, Inc., John W. Shomaker, Inc., and Charles T. DuMars.
1994. *40-Year Regional Water Plan, New Mexico State Planning and
Development District 1, San Juan, McKinley, Cibola Counties*. Gallup, NM:
Northwest New Mexico Council of Governments.

Leeper, John. 2004. "Navajo Nation Plans for their Water Future." In *New
Mexico Water Resources Research Institute, 21–30, ed. New Mexico Water
Planning 2003: 48th Annual New Mexico Water Conference, 5–6* Novem-
ber 2003. Las Cruces, NM: New Mexico Water Resources Research Institute,
New Mexico State University.

Mier, Robert. 1994. "Some Observations about Race and Planning." *Journal of
the American Planning Association* 60 (2):235–40.

Moote, Margaret A., Mitchel P. McClaran, and Donna K. Chickering. 1997.
"Theory in Practice: Applying Participatory Democracy Theory to Public
Land Planning." *Environmental Management* 21 (6):877–89.

National Congress of American Indians. 2008. *National Congress of American
Indians Comments and Recommendations on the 2010 Census and Amer-
ican Community Survey*. Washington, DC: National Congress of American
Indians.

NM OSE and ISC (New Mexico Office of the State Engineer and Interstate
Stream Commission). 2007. *New Mexico Office of the State Engineer and
Interstate Stream Commission 2005–2006 Annual Report*. Santa Fe: New
Mexico Office of the State Engineer and Interstate Stream Commission.

– 2010. *New Mexico Office of the State Engineer and Interstate Stream Commission 2008–2009 Annual Report*. Santa Fe: New Mexico Office of the
State Engineer and Interstate Stream Commission.

NMISC (New Mexico Interstate Stream Commission). 1994. *Regional Water
Planning Handbook*. Santa Fe: New Mexico Interstate Stream Commission.

NWNMCOG (Northwest New Mexico Council of Governments) 1998. *Region 6
Water Plan: The Forty-Year Water Plan for Cibola County and the Portion
of McKinley County not in the San Juan Basin*. Santa Fe: Interstate Stream
Commission.

OSE (Office of the State Engineer) and ISC (Interstate Stream Commission).
2003. *New Mexico State Water Plan*. Santa Fe: Office of the State Engineer
and Interstate Stream Commission, State of New Mexico.

Perloff, Harvey S. 1968. "Key Features of Regional Planning." *Journal of the American Planning Association* 34 (3):153–9.

Pollack, Stanley S. 2005. "Indian Water Rights Settlements: Bringing Certainty to Uncertain Water Resources." In *New Mexico Water: Past, Present, and Future* or *Lawyers, Guns and Money*, 141–7, 19–20 October 2005, Corbett Center, New Mexico State University, ed. New Mexico Water Resources Research Institute. Las Cruces: New Mexico Water Resources Research Institute.

Pueblos of Laguna and Acoma. 1998. "Statement of the Pueblos of Acoma and Laguna on the Regional Water Planning Process for Region 6 of the State of New Mexico." In Appendix III of NWNMCOG 1998.

Reed, James B., and Judy A. Zelio. 1995. *States and Tribes: Building New Traditions*. Washington, DC: National Conference of State Legislatures.

Robert, Lisa. 1996. "Zuni's Pledge to its Natural Resources." *Dialogue* 4(2):12–15. Published by the New Mexico Water Dialogue, a joint program of Western Network and the Natural Resources Center at the University of New Mexico.

Robin, Sean. 1995. "The Story of Indigenous Planning with its Basic Principles." *Indigenous Planning Times* 1:3–18.

RWP (Regional Water Planning) Dialogue. 1994. "Where is the Dialogue Project Going?" *Dialogue* 2 (4):2–4. Published by the Regional Water Planning Dialogue, a joint program of Western Network and the Natural Resources Center at the University of New Mexico, funded by The Ford Foundation.

RWP (Regional Water Planning) meeting. 1997. "Focus group meeting held at Acoma Public Administration Building." 29 September. Notes taken by Lucy Moore. In Appendix I of NWNMCOG 1998.

– 1998. "Gallup, New Mexico, Octavia Fellin Public Library." 13 January. Notes taken by NWNMCOG staff. In Appendix I of NWNMCOG 1998.

– 1998. "Public meeting held at Zuni Tribal Assembly Room." 2 March. Notes taken by NWNMCOG staff. In Appendix I of NWNMCOG 1998.

– 1998. "Meeting held at Acoma Tribal Building." 9 March. Notes taken by NWNMCOG staff. In Appendix I of NWNMCOG 1998.

– 1998. "Presentation and discussion with Leadership McKinley class, held at Bluewater Lodge, Bluewater, NM." 10 March. Notes taken by NWNMCOG staff. In Appendix I of NWNMCOG 1998.

RWP (Regional Water Planning) Technical Committee meeting. 1997. 8 January. Notes taken by NWNMCOG staff.

Sutton, Imre. 2001. "Tribes and States: A Political Geography of Indian Environmental Jurisdiction." In *Trusteeship in Change: Toward Tribal*

Autonomy in Resource Management, edited by Richmond L. Clow and Imre Sutton, 239–63. Boulder, CO: University Press of Colorado.

Widdison, Jerold, and Susan Kelly. 2011. "Navajo-Gallup Water Supply Project." Online update of *Water Matters! Background on Selected Water Issues for Members of the 50th New Mexico State Legislature 1st Session 2011*. Albuquerque: Utton Transboundary Resources Center, University of New Mexico School of Law.

Williams, Robert A. Jr. 1990. *The American Indian in Western Legal Thought: The Discourses of Conquest*. New York: Oxford University Press.

Wondolleck, Julia Marie, and Steven L. Yaffee. 2000. *Making Collaboration Work: Lessons from Innovation in Natural Resource Management*. Washington, DC: Island Press.

Zaferatos, Nicholas Christos. 1998. "Planning the Native American Tribal Community: Understanding the Basis of Power Controlling the Reservation Territory." *Journal of the American Planning Association* 64 (4):395–410.

PART TWO

The Urban Experience

8

Aboriginality and Planning in Canada's Large Prairie Cities

RYAN WALKER AND YALE BELANGER

The research on urban Aboriginal peoples of the early twenty-first century
is moving away from the study of lack. It is now starting to focus on urban
communities and the issues related to the development of healthy communities
that can foster and support individual wellness and success, as well as cultural
retention and transformation. While the deficit/Indian problem paradigm
is still dominant, it has started to be complemented by research conducted
using ideas from Indigenous knowledge. This new research paradigm analyzes
urban landscapes using the central notions of relationship and community,
as well as balance and wellness. Indigenous knowledge research requires an
acknowledgement of the positive as well as the negative.

Newhouse and FitzMaurice 2012, xiv–xv

How might city planners facilitate or hinder the creation of Indigenous-
inclusive cities (Walker and Barcham 2010) on the Canadian Prairies?
We argue in this chapter that while many of the interests of Aboriginal
and non-Aboriginal Prairie city residents and their local governments
converge in significant ways, a great deal of work remains to be done to
lodge considerations of Aboriginality firmly and regularly within civic
processes of planning and policy-making.

   Prairie cities situated in First Nation treaty territories, many also
within the traditional lands of the Métis Nation, such as Edmonton
(Treaty Six), Calgary (Treaty Seven), Saskatoon (Treaty Six), Regina
(Treaty Four), and Winnipeg (Treaty One), have large and growing First

Nations, Métis, and urban Aboriginal populations. In the Edmonton census metropolitan area (CMA), for example, 5 per cent of the population in the 2006 Census identified as Aboriginal (i.e., 52,105 people). In the Regina CMA the figure was 9 per cent (17,105 people), and in the Winnipeg CMA, 10 per cent (68,385 people) of the population identified as Aboriginal in 2006 (Statistics Canada 2008). These Aboriginal populations are younger, on average, than the non-Aboriginal population (Townshend and Walker 2010). While still characterized often in terms of socio-economic disparity and "the study in lack" as characterized by Newhouse and FitzMaurice (2012), these populations are highly diverse and have strong Aboriginal cultures and identities, characteristics which represent a tremendous but often underutilized municipal asset (Walker 2008).

After decades of urbanization and the creation in many Prairie cities of a diverse set of Aboriginal-run organizations (Newhouse and Peters 2003a; Peters 2005), there remains a significant social distance between non-Aboriginal and Aboriginal peoples, which varies in degree and character from city to city (Environics Institute 2010). Yet in spite of the persistence of overt and systemic racism, the Urban Aboriginal Peoples Study conducted by Environics Institute (2010) found that the majority of Aboriginal respondents consider the city home and enjoy living in their city. Findings like these have prompted some Indigenous scholars to start shifting discourse from a focus on Aboriginal "urbanization" to Aboriginal "urbanism" (Newhouse and FitzMaurice 2012). Over the last few decades there has been a shift in preferences in a growing segment of the mainstream Canadian population, particularly in large cities, towards participating in and enjoying an urban life – what is often simply called "urbanism" (Grant and Filion 2010). Why would aspirations for participating in and enjoying an urban life be any different for Aboriginal peoples when it is becoming clear that Aboriginal cultural vitality and success in urban life are mutually reinforcing (Environics Institute 2010; Newhouse and FitzMaurice 2012)?

Some Prairie cities (e.g., Edmonton) have developed ambitious policy approaches with Aboriginal communities while others (e.g., Brandon, in Treaty Two territory) have excluded the words "Aboriginal," "First Nation," and "Métis" entirely from the official community plan (Moore, Walker, and Skelton 2011; The Globe and Mail 2011). Still others (e.g., Calgary) are trying to advance ambitious initiatives with Aboriginal communities in the city, but are having trouble adjusting the aperture from last century's preoccupation with fixing what is lacking in the

Aboriginal community (Newhouse and FitzMaurice 2012) to a more vital exploration of Aboriginality as an existing civic strength and a focus for expanded possibility through planning.

Claude Denis (1997) uses the concept of "Aboriginality" to signify a comprehensive cultural project that brings the inherency of Aboriginal ways of life and the basic right of self-determination to bear on how we understand the relationship between Euro-Canadian and Aboriginal peoples. The concept is also becoming relevant in the context of intercultural relations between immigrant newcomers – many from post-colonial countries (e.g., in Africa, Asia) – and Aboriginal peoples in Canadian cities (Gyepi-Garbrah, Walker, and Garcea forthcoming). Reconciliation between non-Aboriginal and Aboriginal peoples and institutions is a central focus of public discourse in Canada and to varying degrees in other settler states like New Zealand, Australia, and the USA. Aboriginal urban identities are in dynamic interplay with evolving concepts of place in our cities (Walker 2013).

We begin by conceptualizing the challenge of urban planning with Aboriginal communities, examining briefly some of the literature on the post-colonial city, the cultural project of urban Aboriginality, critical race theory, and the fundamental principle of Aboriginal self-determining autonomy as it applies in urban areas. We then discuss five idea-sets for improving city planning practice with Aboriginal communities. The conclusion offers some considerations for transformative planning practice and the co-production of a planning framework that encompasses Aboriginality in Prairie cities.

THE POST-COLONIAL CITY, CULTURAL PROJECT OF URBAN ABORIGINALITY, AND CRITICAL RACE THEORY

Cities have historically been critical to the establishment of the colonial state and continue to be the key sites for the reproduction of modern colonial relations. Scholars have grappled with how to give effect to Indigenous-inclusive citizenship in cities where the public sphere is perceived as culturally neutral by the general public and municipal authorities (Shaw 2007; Walker and Barcham 2010). Leonie Sandercock (2003) points out that cities of the twenty-first century will be the sites where we need to rewrite the Canadian modern mytho-poetic story in a way that embraces Aboriginal cultures and viewpoints. Leroy Little Bear, a professor from the Kainai First Nation, emphasizes that our public authorities will need to make Aboriginal people part of the everyday business of Canada, thus "improving Aboriginal political and social visibility" (in Belanger, FitzMaurice, and Newhouse 2008, 50).

Aboriginal arts have been a key feature in the restoration of cultural sovereignty and decolonization in Toronto's Aboriginal communities (Foster 2012). The results of the 2011 Toronto Aboriginal Research Project indicate the Aboriginal arts sector is one area of great promise for rewriting the Canadian story and improving Aboriginal visibility in mainstream culture and shared urbanism:

> The Aboriginal arts are understood to play an important role in raising the overall visibility of Aboriginal people, and establishing and maintaining an Aboriginal community presence in Toronto. Moreover, the Aboriginal arts provide unique perspectives of Aboriginal cultures, contribute to collective community understandings of cultural meaning, and support healing and positive Aboriginal identities (FitzMaurice, McCaskill, and Cidro 2012, 258).

Decolonizing our approaches to urban planning and policy requires that we consciously decentre "Western" authority over procedural and substantive knowledge that dominate and presume cultural neutrality in the physical and aesthetic, social, cultural, economic, and political production of space (Crush 1994; Jacobs 1996; Johnson et al. 2007; Lefebvre 1991; Pualani Louis 2007; Razack 2002; Sandercock 2003; Shaw 2006; Shaw et al. 2006; Wood 2003). Planning as a colonial cultural practice, conceiving the shape and form of modern cities, scarcely engages in relational processes with Aboriginal peoples that might expand its repertoire (Porter 2010; Stanger-Ross 2008). Paracolonial theory builds on criticisms by Indigenous scholars that post-colonial thought is often incongruent with Indigenous concepts, historical narratives, and identities (Barker 2005; Tuhiwai Smith 1999). A paracolonial viewpoint takes Aboriginal and mainstream Canadian cultures as distinct, though not discrete. They exist simultaneously with ebb and flow between them, situated both beside and beyond one another. The civic futures of Prairie cities depend on Aboriginal and non-Aboriginal peoples learning ways of "living together differently without drifting apart" (Maaka and Fleras 2005, 300).

The cultural project of Aboriginality is a basis for decolonization in partnership with settler society. It stands in contrast to the tendency in the Canadian universe of public discourse to engage in what Denis (1997) calls "whitestreaming," or what other race scholars refer to as "whitewishing," a barrier erected by the fantasy of "whiteness" as neutral and objective (Bonnett 1999; Dyson 1999). Linked to this, a series of discourses centred on equality of opportunity, colour blindness, and universal citizenship provides mainstream societal institutions and people with a workable rationale for setting aside Aboriginality (Flanagan 2000; Walker 2006a; Widdowson and Howard 2008). Wendy Shaw (2007) shows how whiteness in Sydney, Australia operates as a set of privilege-making processes and codified practices that are flexible and place-based, suppressing and displacing Aboriginal people and culture. The power of whiteness and whitestreaming, in relation to Aboriginality and within policy and planning processes, is a barrier to realizing the full potential of the Indigenous-inclusive Canadian Prairie city.

Critical race theory was developed in the late 1970s by American scholars driving towards social change and racial equality, in reflecting upon their personal and the communal experience, and to measure the relationship between race, racism, and official power. Critical race theorists revealed the existence of institutional racism and suggested that the social construction of race continued to shape attitudes that legitimized uneven power relations in the name of individual equality (Carbato and Gulati 2003; Dei et al. 2004; Goodman 2001). One important strand of critical race theory was the examination of interest-convergence in civic affairs. Interest-convergence occurs when the interests of the general (mainstream) public converge with those of non-mainstream populations (e.g., Aboriginal), though not necessarily driven by the same rationales. Yale Belanger and Ryan Walker (2009) observe an instance of interest-convergence between the city of Winnipeg and Aboriginal communities in 2002 when the mayor was mandated with "cleaning up" the inner city, dealing with looming retirements in the civic workforce, and hosting the North American Indigenous Games.

At the same time, and for decades prior, Winnipeg's Aboriginal communities had been pursuing self-determination, mutual recognition, and respect between Aboriginal and settler peoples in the territory within and beyond the municipality of Winnipeg, and improvement to socioeconomic circumstances among the growing young Aboriginal population in the city. Interests converged in the approval by city council of a planning document titled *First Steps: Municipal Aboriginal Pathways* (Winnipeg 2003). This did not imply that the city chose at this point to create new space for Aboriginality in Winnipeg's civic identity. The correctives developed to advance Aboriginal interests were a product of mainstream structures, accommodating Aboriginal interests only as they converged with dominant civic interests. Yet when interests converge, as they have in Winnipeg and arguably in other Prairie cities, between Aboriginal and non-Aboriginal citizens and institutions, an important opportunity is presented to build stronger relationships and processes to strengthen the place of Aboriginality in the local civic identity.

ABORIGINAL SELF-DETERMINATION IN CITIES

Central to the decolonization process is an attempt to create meaningful measures of autonomy that give life to the aspirations of Aboriginal peoples in white settler societies (Abele and Prince 2006; Champagne 2007; Maaka and Fleras 2005). Relatively little attention has been paid to how this occurs in urban contexts, and not just on reserves/rural areas (Abele and Graham 2011; Andersen and Denis 2003; Barcham 2000; Maaka 1994; Morgan 2006; Newhouse and Peters 2003b; Shaw 2007; Walker 2006b). Adding substantial gravity to the need to engage the urban context in Aboriginal self-determination is the fact that cities were built on Aboriginal ancestral places, within historic and contemporary Aboriginal territories, some of which themselves were intensely used as places of congregation, trade, and settlement, tantamount in many ways to the functions ascribed to our historic and modern "settler" cities (see Jojola in this volume).

Self-determination encompasses spiritual, territorial, social, cultural, economic, and political dimensions, and refers to the inherent right of Aboriginal peoples to govern their own affairs as original occupants through the reformulation of settler state–Aboriginal society relations (Durie 2003; Green 2005; Henderson 2008; Maaka and Fleras 2005; Mercer 2003). Rather than implying isolation or separation, Aboriginal peoples typically view self-determination as a normative partnership with the settler state that is guided by mutual respect and recognition, the spirit of historic and contemporary treaty relationships, constitutional arrangements, and continuing group rights (Henderson 2006; Macklem 2001). Self-governing Aboriginal urban institutions in sectors like housing, health, education, and child and family services have enriched the complexity of Aboriginal cultures in the city (Peters 2005; Royal Commission 1996; Silver 2006). Positioning self-determination in support of Aboriginal density and complexity in urban areas permits modern cultural hybridity in ways that fixing Aboriginal cultural difference in a static past does not (Andersen 2009; see Andersen in this volume).

Decisions in Canadian courts have clarified some of the terrain around state-Aboriginal society relations in Canadian cities. In the *Misquadis* (2002) decision, the Federal Court ruled that Aboriginal political organizations can represent urban Aboriginal interests, and that Human Resources and Skills Development Canada needed to help fund the infrastructure required for urban service delivery and to establish representative governance. It also defined off-reserve Aboriginal people as a group of self-organized, self-determining, and distinct communities analogous to a reserve community. Further to this, the *Corbiere* (1999) decision by the Supreme Court ruled that First Nation members living off-reserve were entitled to vote in band elections, and the *Esquega* (2007) decision ruled that reserve residence was not required for band councillors. The three cases proclaimed urban Aboriginal communities to be political communities and in the process established a legal framework to guide Aboriginal community leaders; Canadian policy-makers; and federal, provincial, and municipal officials to better determine what an urban Aboriginal community is and what it represents to the various agencies drawn into their orbit. These are not absolute conventions, but rather represent contours that inform an evolutionary process that began several decades ago, and one that continues to offer perspectives that assist in defining "urban Aboriginal community" within complex socio-political and socio-economic matrices.

Juridical steps, like those described above, are important in an emergent public and political dialogue that will, in all likelihood, guide some of the community development strategies of urban Aboriginal leaders and how these are perceived in the urban cultural mainstream. We must remain aware, however, that urban Aboriginal populations have long envisioned acting on their own behalf, something the *Misquadis* decision acknowledged as being an aspect of Indigenous self-determination. The status-blind approach to First Nations and Métis urban community development taken by the Friendship Centre movement in Canadian cities starting in the 1950s, with rapid diffusion through the 1960–70s, is perhaps the most enduring example. Friendship Centres continue to provide a place for service referrals, advocacy, and social, cultural, and recreational programs. The Aboriginal communities of interest created through participation in Friendship Centres were also reproduced and expanded through the development of new organizations run by Aboriginal peoples in cities, a lineage that Evelyn Peters (2005) has examined and interpreted.

Asserted Aboriginal rights (pertaining to customs, practices, and traditions specific to an Aboriginal people in their traditional territory) and specific treaty rights (Aboriginal rights set out in a treaty) are protected under s.35 of the Constitution Act 1982. Fundamental to these is the inherent and continuing right to community self-determining autonomy. This can be respected and fostered through working partnerships between Aboriginal and non-Aboriginal governments, such as in urban planning and policy. Ensuring mechanisms exist for recognizing and implementing self-determination is considered a basis for constructive engagement between a municipal government and Aboriginal communities.

IMPROVING CITY PLANNING AT THE MUNICIPAL-ABORIGINAL INTERFACE

First Nation, Métis, and non-Aboriginal peoples all have rich histories in Prairie cities, providing a basis for a strong shared civic identity. That rich history continues to expand from year to year as newcomers from all over the world migrate to the city to live and work. Steeped in the place histories of many First Nations and the Métis Nation, Prairie cities have a great opportunity to expand the extent to which they reflect their First Nation and Métis communities within their governance, land use, urban design, economic development, culture, and heritage.

There is a growing recognition of the importance of work that improves municipal-Aboriginal urban policy-making and planning (e.g., Belanger and Walker 2009; Hanselmann 2002; Nelles and Alcantara 2011; Peters 2011a, b; Sully et al. 2008; Tomiak 2010; Walker 2003, 2008). Research on Aboriginal policy in Australian local governments found that they were better at symbolic inclusion of Aboriginality in municipal affairs (e.g., festivals, broad inclusionary policy statements) than they were at integrating cultural pluralism into municipal operations (Dunn et al. 2001a,b; see Porter in this volume). The Canadian and Australian experience appear, without conclusive appeal to evidence, to be similar. Despite best intentions the practice of planning and policy-making is not value neutral and privileges the momentum of Western place conceptions and processes over those of Aboriginal peoples (Jojola 2008; Porter 2010; Sandercock 2004). It is not surprising that Aboriginal communities often resist incorporation into mainstream planning processes rather than "play along" (Healey 2004), when resistance might indeed be the better strategy for achieving recognition of the fundamental right to a mutually respectful partnership that would enhance Aboriginality in urban settings. Transformative planning – identifying and implementing strategies that transform structures of Aboriginal political, social, cultural, and economic oppression – can be practiced by Aboriginal and non-Aboriginal practitioners to augment the ability of Aboriginal urban communities to actualize aspirations based on their own assessment of needs and preferences (Friedmann 1987; Lane and Hibbard 2005; Peach 2004; Young 1990).

The following are five areas where Prairie city planners might direct their thinking and application.

1   Relationship-Building Declaration and Accord

Prairie cities should to a greater extent undertake their civic future-seeking in strong partnership with First Nation and Métis peoples. The civic identity should increasingly become one of full partnership, and in order to do this community social capital will need to be strengthened to create bridges between Aboriginal and non-Aboriginal peoples in cities. Community social capital is built on a foundation of strong relationships. Building these bridging relationships will require bold leadership where municipal, First Nations, and Métis leaders take some formal steps together to kick-start relationship-building that will carry through the civic community (e.g., see Peters, and Sandercock and Attili in this volume).

The formal steps taken by municipal, First Nations, and Métis leaders will need to establish a strong standard of mutual recognition and foundation for respectful exchange into the indefinite future. This carries symbolic as well as practical importance. The symbolic importance is related to launching a new era of co-operation between a municipality and the Aboriginal communities. The practical importance is related to the fact that sector-specific and service-specific agreements will be harder to reach and manage in the absence of strong relationship-building. Further, it would be impractical for city councils to expect that either overt racism towards Aboriginal peoples or the discursive fantasy of whiteness as neutral and objective in the city would diminish at a significant pace in the absence of strong council leadership on constructive relationship-building. Best practice in a large Canadian city for doing this kind of work is the city of Edmonton's declaration "Strengthening Relationships between the City of Edmonton and Urban Aboriginal People" and "Edmonton Urban Aboriginal Accord" (Edmonton 2005).[1]

The city of Edmonton's approach offers some lessons for other large Prairie cities. Official community plans in Prairie cities might articulate a clear declaration of intent to strengthen relationships between the municipality and First Nation and Métis communities in and around the city. The declaration may come from city councils and civic administrations in the municipality's official community plan, but the next step – a community accord between the city and Aboriginal communities – would need to be developed collaboratively with First Nation and Métis communities. The declaration, like the city of Edmonton's, is a statement of intent on the part of the city. The accord is a foundational, living document created between the city and Aboriginal communities. The process should be carefully considered and involve elected leaders from the city council, First Nation tribal and band councils, the Métis local council, and those seen to be leaders among Aboriginal community members in the urban civic community who perhaps do not maintain strong ties to reserve communities. For this latter group of community members, the local Friendship Centre, urban Aboriginal councils, or other community organizations (e.g., urban Aboriginal housing corporations) may be appropriate places to seek community-based leadership. Celebrating the development of a community accord between elected leaders of city council, First Nation and Métis communities, and community-based urban Aboriginal leadership is important. Consideration might be given to commissioning a tangible piece of public art, sculpture, or place-naming as the central focal point of a launching event for the new accord. Something symbolic and celebratory that citizens can visit and see and that has a life beyond a press conference or reception (where people come together and then disperse in a short period of time) will help to ensure that citizens of the municipality and surrounding communities can remember the launch of a new era of co-operation and partnership.

2   Protocol Agreements on Areas of Mutual Interest

Official community plans in Prairie cities can set out objectives for the development of protocol agreements between the municipality and First Nation and Métis governments, or urban Aboriginal councils relating to culture, heritage, land use, and infrastructure planning, environment, and economic development. Best practice in a Canadian city for doing this kind of work is the city of Powell River, British Columbia and Sliammon First Nation's "Protocol Agreement on Culture, Heritage and Economic Development" (Sliammon First Nation and City of Powell River 2007).

City administrations would engage with willing First Nation tribal or band councils and urban Aboriginal and Métis local councils on areas of interest where one or both parties can exercise jurisdiction and allocate resources. Each protocol agreement would address areas of mutual interest to both the city and the Aboriginal government signatory.

Attention may be given to developing processes around joint work on items from the municipality's official community plan, zoning bylaw, and future growth planning. In protocol agreements, issues pertaining to how the history of First Nation, Métis, and urban Aboriginal communities is represented in documents like the community plan might be dealt with. Processes for how First Nation tribal or band councils will be involved when planning and infrastructure development issues arise that relate to lands on or adjacent to their land holdings (e.g., urban reserve parcels) in the municipality can be developed. Goals and processes for shared regional strategic growth, land-use compatibility, and infrastructure development planning can be articulated in the protocol agreement between the municipality and each First Nation tribal or band council. This will help to ensure that future growth occurs to maximum mutual benefit and that the acquisition and development, or preservation and protection of lands within or adjacent to current municipal boundaries is planned in a way that maximizes benefits to the First Nation and the city. It will also help to establish trust, partnerships, and good neighbour relationships.

The protocol agreement may also address the concept of Aboriginal local culture as a common asset for the municipal and Aboriginal governments. In other words, mutually acceptable ways of reflecting the full depth of place-history and civic identity in the city might be good for local pride in place, economic development, and for Aboriginal communities within and around the city. The design and naming of public spaces, commemoration of Aboriginal historic and cultural sites and landscapes, street naming, public art, architecture, murals, and signage are all areas that can help reflect in tangible visible ways the presence of First Nation, Métis, and urban Aboriginal cultures in the city. One example from the city of Saskatoon, Saskatchewan is the design of tree grates at River Landing, that city's signature public space in the downtown. The city of Saskatoon won a Premier's Award of Excellence in Design in 2007 for the collaborative design of the tree grates according to secular stories and concepts shared with that city administration's urban design team by an advisory group of Cree and Dakota Elders. St Albert Place, the main civic building in the centre of the city of St

Albert, Alberta (Treaty Six territory), was designed and built by the famous architect Douglas Cardinal of Métis and Blackfoot heritage. St Albert Place houses, among other things, the city's council chambers, main branch of its public library, the city's largest theatre for the arts, a public plaza, the St Albert museum, and many civic offices. The clear presence of Indigenous design principles in the architecture of the building serving as an important civic space in so prominent a location is a good example of the kinds of design decisions that can be made in partnership between Prairie municipalities and First Nation, Métis, and urban Aboriginal communities.

Economic and social development issues may also be considered as items to address in the protocol agreements entered into between urban municipalities and Aboriginal governments. Issues subject to protocol agreements might include decisions regarding mutual economic development interests in casino, hotel, and museum development, joint ventures, economic forums, and place-marketing. Social issues like housing and homelessness, policing, and recreational services may all be subject to protocol agreements.

3   Communication and Joint Governance

There will be a need for communication and joint governance to maintain the community accord and to attend to the business of the protocol agreements. There will also be a need for communication on issues relating to Aboriginal communities generally in the regular and ongoing civic affairs of the city. With respect to the community accord, it may be appropriate for elected members of city councils to meet with the elected members of each tribal or band council, Métis local, or urban Aboriginal council periodically (e.g., once per year). The location of the meeting might alternate between city hall and the places of assembly for the Aboriginal governments, which would likely involve occasional travel to reserves. This would permit all parties to act alternately as guest and as host, both roles being equally important for building mutually respectful recognition as civic partners.

Attending to the business of the protocol agreements can be done by members of civic and Aboriginal government administration staff with direct responsibility for the sectors covered by the agreements. Relationships might be regularized through periodic meetings (e.g., twice per year) and as needed to deal with business arising from the agreements. City administrations may wish, as the city of Edmonton did, to create a new position(s) or office in the administration pertaining specifically to Aboriginal relations. Staff of the office could act as an animator(s) for the whole of the administration and elected officials, matchmaking relevant branch-specific staff or city councillors with their counterparts in Aboriginal communities and work to regularize processes and priorities around Aboriginal engagement within line department operations.

Aboriginal relations/affairs staff might strike and liaise with an advisory committee made up of Aboriginal people who reside in the city, nominated by their peers to serve on the committee. An Aboriginal advisory committee might assist by providing input to a variety of civic affairs not pertaining directly to the creation and maintenance of protocol agreements between the city and Aboriginal governments. Issues dealt with by the advisory committee would relate to a variety of issues important to Aboriginal people in the municipality, regardless of status or national affiliation. Attention might be given to having youth participation on the advisory committee and participation by Elders in the advisory committee processes and proceedings. Apart from dealing with specific municipal-Aboriginal community issues (e.g., preparing the city's role in events of commemorative importance to Aboriginal-settler relations, policing, education, health, public space design), the Aboriginal advisory committee might also work with the city administration and city council on articulating positions on policy areas under the jurisdiction of senior governments (i.e., federal and provincial). In this way, city hall and Aboriginal governments locally and regionally would be able to advocate in a joint manner for improvements to the quality of life of citizens within municipal boundaries, and occasionally on a broader regional basis as "good neighbours" to senior levels of government.

4   *Urban Reserves, Services and Compatibility Agreements, and Regional Relationships*

Urban reserves are satellites to principal reserves located elsewhere and have typically been acquired on a willing buyer-willing seller basis in the real estate marketplace, often with financial resources derived from land claim settlements (Barron and Garcea 1999). The acquisition of urban lands, transferred subsequently to reserve status by application to Aboriginal Affairs and Northern Development Canada, is typically for economic development or other social, cultural, or political goals that serve the interests of the principal reserve community elsewhere or band members in the urban community. Processes for creating urban satellite reserves are outlined in the treaty land entitlement framework agreements in Saskatchewan and Manitoba, and in the federal government's Additions to Reserves Policy, which applies more broadly across the country (Peters 2007). The mechanisms and initiatives taken by First Nations to create satellite urban reserves appear to be unique to Canada within the North American context.

Urban reserves are rare across the country, though not uncommon in Saskatchewan and Manitoba. In total there are 120 urban reserves operating nationally. First Nations in Saskatchewan have taken the lead in this regard: there are currently forty-four urban reserves with an additional forty-nine planned (Belanger 2014). The first urban reserve in Canada was created in Saskatoon in 1988 by the Muskeg Lake Cree Nation in a close working relationship with the city of Saskatoon (Sully et al. 2008). The potential exists for urban reserves to become more commonplace in cities across the country, and indeed, the first one created in Winnipeg by the Long Plain First Nation will house an office building, college, and gas station, among other things. Winnipeg City Council approved a service agreement with Long Plain First Nation for the 1.4 hectare inner city parcel in July 2010.

Agreements between municipalities and First Nations deal typically with four key issues that are important in the urban reserve creation process, namely: (1) compensation paid in lieu of property and school taxes once the land is converted to reserve; (2) the type and financing of municipal services to be extended to the new reserve; (3) bylaw development and compatibility between the First Nation and the municipality, pertaining for example, to land uses considered compatible with neighbouring municipal lands and residents; and (4) a joint consultative process, including a dispute resolution mechanism (Sully et al. 2008). One thing that Prairie municipalities may wish to do is to set a policy direction whereby the city administration actively seeks out First Nation investment in urban lands as urban reserves or in fee-simple, much like an administration might actively seek out corporate investment in the municipality. In 2007–08, the city of Saskatoon's Planning Branch undertook this approach and dedicated some of its staff time to creating a relationship-building and promotional toolkit to use for attracting First Nation land investment and development to the municipality, and attempting to demystify the planning and development processes and personnel in that city.

Given that urban reserves very often meet with community opposition on "not in my backyard" and racist grounds, city councils with a relationship-building declaration and Aboriginal accord in place, and a methodical approach to facilitating the creation of urban reserves as a matter of policy, might find it easier and less politically charged proceeding with urban reserve negotiations. Part of the challenge for planners involves transforming the disposition of citizens and elected officials towards urban reserve creation from a reactive role to a proactive land and economic development role for the municipality. Part of this proactive process will also involve embarking on regional relationships with surrounding First Nations to share the future growth strategy adopted by the municipality with First Nations seeking to invest in urban land holdings. Sequencing of development areas and infrastructure planning can be shared with First Nations and opportunities explored to bring investment from First Nations into the city's land market. Developing a proactive municipal policy framework for dealing with First Nation governments on urban reserve creation, regional growth strategy, and demystifying the city's urban planning and development processes is an important consideration for the future.

5   Aboriginal Citizen Participation and Engagement

General civic processes, including city, regional, and local area planning, would be improved with a stronger set of processes for ensuring Aboriginal citizen participation. Neighbourhood-level engagement techniques can privilege an "area-based" logic over one that is more explicitly "people-centred." Aboriginal mobility, for example, between neighbourhoods and between the city and communities outside of the city places constraints on involvement in civic processes at a single neighbourhood scale. There are other ways of organizing public consultations locally that are more meaningful to some Aboriginal residents than according to neighbourhoods, such as through local cultural, service, or educational organizations that transcend neighbourhood boundaries (e.g., Friendship Centres, elementary and high schools, university Aboriginal student centres). Holding consultations at locations like these and using some of the principles that guide Talking Circles may help to turn Aboriginal citizen engagement into a more open dialogue (Ball, Caldwell and Pranis 2007; see Sandercock and Attili in this volume).

First Nation scholars (e.g., Kovach 2009; Wilson 2008) that have critically examined the fit between Western research methods and Indigenous epistemologies have shared insights which are arguably transferable to community planning techniques. Relational approaches to the process and content of planning techniques, and training in First Nations protocols (e.g., Saskatchewan Indian Cultural Centre 2009) and in basic history relating to the treaty area, municipal settlement, and Aboriginal peoples for each local and regional planning exercise are transferable lessons from work done on decolonizing research. Respecting relational accountability between planners and participants and presenting results from consultative dialogues in a way that balances integrative conclusions with intact contextualized stories in narrative excerpt form will permit a better balance between Western analytic process and Indigenous interpretive approaches (Kovach 2009).

In addition, one direct means of regularizing participation and engagement with Aboriginal citizens in civic processes at the municipal level is through the direct participation of elected Aboriginal city councillors and the local Aboriginal electorate. Few Aboriginal people have been elected as city councillors in large prairie cities. Some city electorates have never elected First Nation members to city council (e.g., Saskatoon). While it is beyond the scope of this chapter to undertake an in-depth assessment of the implications of having our city councils govern municipal affairs without direct peer-to-peer participation by Aboriginal councillors, it is worth noting that at least one comparator settler nation has a system in place that tries to address this issue. Provisions in New Zealand's Local Electoral Act 2001 (s. 24) for local governments to create Māori wards in proportion to the number of local Māori electors are currently being exercised by the city of Nelson (Nelson City Council 2011). A Māori ward (or wards) ensures that Māori who wish to vote for a Māori candidate for city council may do so, and assures that the proportion of Māori citizens is more closely reflected in the number of Māori city councillors elected. Local authorities themselves choose whether or not to exercise the provisions for creating Māori wards, not the central government.

Another example of an innovation in New Zealand local government is the new Māori Statutory Board that advises the Auckland Council (Cheyne 2011). The Māori Statutory Board is independent of the Auckland Council and serves as a mechanism for ensuring that council takes the perspectives of Māori into account when exercising its decision making (Auckland Council 2012). While different, both the creation of Māori wards and the statutory board are means of increasing participation and engagement by Indigenous civic leaders in local (city) government decisions. In general, as argued by Walker (2008), New Zealand is further advanced in its partnership with Māori people at the level of local (city) government than municipalities are in Canada with Aboriginal peoples. In New Zealand, the central government's obligations under the Treaty of Waitangi reach through its levers of control over local government (e.g., Local Government Act; Resource Management Act) to influence city planning (Berke et al. 2002). In Canada, where municipalities take their direction from provincial statute instead of central (federal) government where state-Aboriginal society relations are more clearly articulated, municipalities are left more to their own devices for choosing the extent to which to create new ways of engaging with Aboriginal communities. On this front, Canadian provinces (i.e., enabling municipalities) and municipalities could certainly stand to be more creative and ambitious.

ABORIGINALITY AND CITY PLANNING – FUTURE-SEEKING THROUGH POLICY AND PLAN CO-PRODUCTION

New opportunities exist in Prairie cities with growing young Aboriginal populations, developed communities of interest through self-governing Aboriginal urban organizations, and regional First Nation and Métis community networks between reserves, rural communities, and large cities. This chapter challenges municipalities to improve and regularize relationships with First Nation and Métis governments, and with their Aboriginal citizens and electorate in five specific areas. This can be done with ambitious future-seeking tools like a civic declaration, community accord, sector-specific protocol agreements, a proactive policy framework for urban reserve generation, and more nuanced Aboriginal citizen engagement techniques. It is not so much that municipalities need "an Aboriginal affairs policy" as an end in itself, but rather, they should create a planning framework with Aboriginal communities that adds Aboriginality as a lens through which to approach the municipality's creation of plans addressing community visioning, culture planning, public space design, land use, future growth, urban design, and economic development, among others.

    Civic administrations in Prairie cities should proceed to create a planning framework with Aboriginal communities on the basis of "co-production," where Aboriginal and non-Aboriginal civic interests can converge and First Nation, Métis, and urban Aboriginal peoples can exercise community self-determination in partnership with city hall. The concept of policy and plan co-production (Brudney and England 1982; Casey and Dalton 2006; Nyland 1995) has been examined as a means for transformative urban planning and policy development in urban Aboriginal affairs (Belanger and Walker 2009; Walker et al. 2011). Buttressed by the pursuit of Aboriginal urban self-determination, partnership, and co-production with municipal authorities goes beyond consultation. Co-production requires partners to jointly undertake issue identification, priority setting, implementation, monitoring, and evaluation. A partnership with any chance of longevity requires listening, learning, and doing in the light of mutual respect and recognition. Together they may effectively lodge considerations of Aboriginality within civic processes of planning and policy-making.

NOTE

1 Best practice in a small Canadian city for doing this kind of work is the city of Powell River and Sliammon First Nation "Community Accord" (Gallagher 2008).

REFERENCES

Abele, F., and K. Graham. 2011. "What Now? Future Federal Responsibilities Towards Aboriginal People Living in Cities." *Aboriginal Policy Studies* 1:162–82.

Abele, F,. and M.J. Prince. 2006. "Four Pathways to Aboriginal Self-Government in Canada." *The American Review of Canadian Studies* 36:568–95.

Andersen, C. 2009. "Critical Indigenous Studies: From Difference to Density." *Cultural Studies Review* 15:80–100.

Andersen, C., and C. Denis. 2003. "Urban Natives and the Nation: Before and After the Royal Commission on Aboriginal Peoples." *The Canadian Review of Sociology and Anthropology* 40:373–90.

Auckland Council. 2012. "Māori Statutory Board." www.aucklandcouncil. govt.nz/EN/ABOUTCOUNCIL/HOWCOUNCILWORKS/MAORI_RELATIONS/ Pages/maoristatutoryboard.aspx. Accessed 6 January 2012.

Ball, J., W. Caldwell, and K. Pranis. 2007. "Using Circles to Build Communication in Planning." *Plan Canada* Spring:47–9.

Barcham, M. 2000. "(De)constructing the Politics of Indigeneity." In *Political Theory and the Rights of Indigenous Peoples*, edited by D. Ivison, P. Patton, and W. Sanders. Melbourne: Cambridge University Press.

Barker, J. 2005. *Sovereignty Matters: Locations of Contestation and Possibility in Indigenous Struggles for Self-Determination.* Lincoln: University of Nebraska Press.

Barron, F.L., and J. Garcea, eds. 1999. *Urban Indian Reserves: Forging New Relationships in Saskatchewan.* Saskatoon: Purich Publishing.

Belanger, Y.D. 2014. *Ways of Knowing: An Introduction to Native Studies in Canada,* second edition. Toronto: Nelson Education Ltd.

Belanger, Y.D., K. FitzMaurice, and D. Newhouse. 2008. "Creating a Seat at the Table: A Retrospective Study of Aboriginal Programming at Canadian Heritage." *Canadian Journal of Native Studies* 28:33–70.

Belanger, Y.D., and R.C. Walker. 2009. "Interest Convergence and Co-Production of Plans: An Examination of Winnipeg's 'Aboriginal Pathways'." *Canadian Journal of Urban Research* 18 Supplement:118–39.

Berke, P., N. Ericksen, J. Crawford, and J. Dixon. 2002. "Planning and Indigenous People: Human Rights and Environmental Protection in New Zealand." *Journal of Planning Education and Research* 22:115–34.

Bonnett, A. 1999. "Constructions of Whiteness in European and American Anti-racism." In *Race, Identity, and Citizenship: A Reader,* edited by R.D. Torres, L.F. Miron, and J.X. Inda. Malden: Blackwell.

Brudney, J., and R. England. 1982. "Urban Policy Making and Subjective Service Evaluations: Are they Compatible?" *Public Administration Review* 42:127–35.

Canada (Attorney General) v. Esquega, 2008 FCA 182.

Canada (Attorney General) v. Misquadis, 2003 FCA 370.

Carbato, D.W., and G.M. Gulati. 2003. "The Law and Economics of Critical Race Theory." *Yale Law Journal* 112.

Casey, J., and B. Dalton. 2006. "The Best of Times, the Worst of Times: Community-Sector Advocacy in the Age of 'Compacts'." *Australian Journal of Political Science* 41:23–38.

Champagne, D. 2007. *Social Change and Cultural Continuity among Native Nations.* Toronto: AltaMira Press.

Cheyne, C. 2011. Personal Communication. Associate Professor, Resource and Environmental Planning, Massey University, New Zealand. 21 December.

Corbiere v. Canada (Minister of Indian and Northern Affairs), 1999 2 SCR 203.

Crush, J. 1994. "Post-colonialism, De-colonisation, and Geography." In *Geography and Empire,* edited by A. Godlewska and N. Smith. Oxford: Blackwell.

Dei, G.J.S., L. Karumanchery, and N. Karumanchery-Luik. 2004. "The Banality of Racism: Living 'Within' the Traumatic." In *Playing the Race Card: Exposing White Power and Privilege.* New York: Peter Lang.

Denis, C. 1997. *We Are Not You: First Nations and Canadian Modernity.* Peterborough: Broadview Press.

Dunn, K., B. Hanna, and S. Thompson. 2001a. "The Local Politics of Difference: An Examination of Intercommunal Relations Policy in Australian Local Government." *Environment and Planning A* 33:1577–95.

Dunn, K., S. Thompson, B. Hanna, P. Murphy, and I. Burnley. 2001b. "Multicultural Policy within Local Government in Australia." *Urban Studies* 38:2477–94.

Durie, M.H. 2003. *Ngā Kāhui Pou Launching Māori Futures.* Wellington: Huia Publishers.

Dyson, M.E. 1999. "The Labor of Whiteness, the Whiteness of Labor, and the Perils of Whitewishing." In *Race, Identity, and Citizenship: A Reader,* edited by R.D. Torres, L.F. Miron, and J.X. Inda. Malden: Blackwell.

Edmonton. 2005. "Edmonton Urban Aboriginal Accord Initiative Project (2005–2006)." www.edmonton.ca/city_government/initiatives_innovation/edmonton-urban-aboriginal-accord-initiative.aspx. Accessed 6 January 2012.

Environics Institute. 2010. *Urban Aboriginal Peoples Study: Main Report.* Toronto: Environics Institute.

FitzMaurice, K., D. McCaskill, and J. Cidro. 2012. "Urban Aboriginal People in Toronto: A Summary of the 2011 Toronto Aboriginal Research Project (TARP)." In *Well-Being in the Urban Aboriginal Community: Fostering Biimaadiziwin, a National Research Conference on Urban Aboriginal Peoples,* edited by D. Newhouse, K. FitzMaurice, T. McGuire-Adams, and D. Jette. Toronto: Thompson Educational Publishing.

Flanagan, T. 2000. *First Nations? Second Thoughts.* Montreal and Kingston: McGill-Queen's University Press.

Foster, A. 2012. "Artist-Run Organizations and the Restoration of Indigenous Cultural Sovereignty in Toronto, 1970 to 2010." In *Well-Being in the Urban Aboriginal Community: Fostering Biimaadiziwin, a National Research Conference on Urban Aboriginal Peoples,* edited by D. Newhouse, K. FitzMaurice, T. McGuire-Adams, and D. Jette. Toronto: Thompson Educational Publishing.

Friedmann, J. 1987. *Planning in the Public Domain: From Knowledge to Action.* Princeton: Princeton University Press.

Gallagher, S. 2008. "Intergovernmental Community Planning: The Sliammon First Nation and City of Powell River Experience." *Plan Canada* 48 (Summer):35–8

The Globe and Mail. 2011. "Improving the Urban Aboriginal Experience: Edmonton at Fore of Communities Trying to Help Make Cities Welcoming and Prosperous Homes for Natives." 14 April, A17.

Goodman, D. 2001. "About Privileged Groups." In *Promoting Diversity and Social Justice: Educating People from Privileged Groups*. London: Sage Publications.

Grant, J., and P. Filion. 2010. "Emerging Urban Forms in the Canadian City." In *Canadian Cities in Transition: New Directions in the Twenty-first Century*, fourth edition, edited by T. Bunting, P. Filion, and R. Walker. Toronto: Oxford University Press.

Green, J. 2005. "Self-Determination, Citizenship, and Federalism: Indigenous and Canadian Palimpsest." In *Reconfiguring Aboriginal-State Relations. Canada: The State of the Federation, 2003*, edited by M. Murphy. Montreal and Kingston: McGill-Queen's University Press.

Gyepi-Garbrah, J., R.C. Walker, and J. Garcea. Forthcoming. "Indigeneity, Interculturalism and the Post-colonial City: Aboriginal Peoples and Immigrant Newcomers in Winnipeg, Canada." *Urban Studies*.

Hanselmann, C. 2002. *Uncommon Sense: Promising Practices in Urban Aboriginal Policy-Making and Programming*. Calgary: Canada West Foundation.

Healey, P. 2004. "Editorial." *Planning Theory and Practice* 5:5–8.

Henderson, J.Y. 2006. *First Nations Jurisprudence and Aboriginal Rights: Defining the Just Society*. Saskatoon: Native Law Centre.

– 2008. "Treaty Governance." In *Aboriginal Self-Government in Canada: Current Trends and Issues,* third edition, edited by Y.D. Belanger. Saskatoon: Purich.

Jacobs, J.M. 1996. *Edge of Empire: Postcolonialism and the City*. London: Routledge.

Johnson, J.T., G. Cant, R. Howitt, and E. Peters. 2007. "Creating Anti-colonial Geographies: Embracing Indigenous Peoples' Knowledges and Rights." *Geographical Research* 45: 117–20.

Jojola, T. 2008 "Indigenous Planning – An Emerging Context." *Canadian Journal of Urban Research* 17 Supplement:37–47

Kovach, M. 2009. *Indigenous Methodologies: Characteristics, Conversations, and Contexts*. Toronto: University of Toronto Press.

Lane, M.B., and M. Hibbard. 2005. "Doing It for Themselves: Transformative Planning by Indigenous Peoples." *Journal of Planning Education and Research* 25:172–84.

Lefebvre, H. 1991. *The Production of Space*. Cambridge: Blackwell.

Maaka, R. 1994. "The New Tribe: Conflicts and Continuities in the Social Organisation of Urban Māori." *The Contemporary Pacific* 6:311–36.

Maaka, R., and A. Fleras. 2005. *The Politics of Indigeneity: Challenging the State in Canada and Aotearoa New Zealand*. Dunedin: University of Otago Press.

Macklem, P. 2001. *Indigenous Difference and the Constitution of Canada.* Toronto: University of Toronto Press.

Mercer, D. 2003. "'Citizen Minus'?: Indigenous Australians and the Citizenship Question." *Citizenship Studies* 7:421–45.

Moore, J., R.C. Walker, and I. Skelton. 2011. "Challenging the New Canadian Myth: Colonialism, Post-colonialism and Urban Aboriginal Policy in Thompson and Brandon, Manitoba." *Canadian Journal of Native Studies* 31:17–42.

Morgan, G. 2006. *Unsettled Places: Aboriginal People and Urbanisation in New South Wales.* Kent Town: Wakefield Press.

Nelles, J., and C. Alcantara. 2011. "Strengthening the Ties that Bind? An Analysis of Aboriginal-Municipal Inter-governmental Agreements in British Columbia." *Canadian Public Administration* 54: 315–34.

Nelson City Council. 2011. "Māori Ward." www.nelsoncitycouncil.co.nz/maori-ward/#legislation. Accessed 21 December 2011.

Newhouse, D., and K. FitzMaurice. 2012. "Introduction." In *Well-Being in the Urban Aboriginal Community: Fostering Biimaadiziwin, a National Research Conference on Urban Aboriginal Peoples*, edited by D. Newhouse, K. FitzMaurice, T. McGuire-Adams, and D. Jette. Toronto: Thompson Educational Publishing.

Newhouse, D., and E. Peters. 2003a. "Introduction." In *Not Strangers in These Parts: Urban Aboriginal Peoples*, edited by D. Newhouse and E. Peters. Ottawa: Policy Research Initiative.

– eds. 2003b. *Not Strangers in These Parts: Urban Aboriginal Peoples.* Ottawa: Policy Research Initiative.

Nyland, J. 1995. "Issue Networks and Non-profit Organisations." *Policy Studies Review* 14:195–204.

Peach, I. 2004. *The Charter of Rights and Off-Reserve First Nations People: A Way to Fill the Public Policy Vacuum.* Saskatchewan Institute of Public Policy, paper no. 24. Regina: Saskatchewan Institute of Public Policy.

Peters, E. 2005. "Indigeneity and Marginalisation: Planning for and with Urban Aboriginal Communities in Canada." *Progress in Planning* 63:327–39.

– 2007. *Urban Reserves.* Vancouver: National Centre for First Nations Governance.

– 2011a. "Emerging Themes in Academic Research in Urban Aboriginal Identities in Canada, 1996–2010." *Aboriginal Policy Studies* 1:78–105.

– ed. 2011b. *Urban Aboriginal Policy Making in Canadian Municipalities.* Montreal and Kingston: McGill-Queen's University Press.

Porter, L. 2010. *Unlearning the Colonial Cultures of Planning.* Burlington: Ashgate.

Pualani Louis, R. 2007. "Can You Hear Us Now? Voices from the Margin: Using Indigenous Methodologies in Geographic Research." *Geographical Research* 45:130–9.

Razack, S. 2002. *Race, Space, and the Law: Unmapping a White Settler Society*. Toronto: Between the Lines.

Royal Commission on Aboriginal Peoples. 1996. "Urban Perspectives." In *Report of the Royal Commission on Aboriginal Peoples* volume 4, chapter 7. Ottawa: Minister of Supply and Services.

Sandercock, L. 2003 *Cosmopolis II: Mongrel Cities in the 21st Century*. New York: Continuum.

– 2004. "Interface: Planning and Indigenous Communities." *Planning Theory and Practice* 5:95–7.

Saskatchewan Indian Cultural Centre. 2009. *Cultural Teachings: First Nations Protocols and Methodologies*. Saskatoon: Saskatchewan Indian Cultural Centre.

Shaw, W.S. 2006. "Decolonising Geographies of Whiteness." *Antipode* 38:852–69.

– 2007. *Cities of Whiteness*. Malden: Blackwell.

Shaw, W.S., R.D.K. Herman, and G.R. Dobbs. 2006. "Encountering Indigeneity: Re-imagining and Decolonising Geography." *Geografiska Annaler* 88 B:267–76.

Silver, J. 2006. *In Their Own Voices: Building Urban Aboriginal Communities*. Halifax: Fernwood.

Sliammon First Nation and City of Powell River. 2007. *Sharing "Best Practices" in Intergovernmental Relations and Planning*. Victoria: BC Treaty Commission.

Stanger-Ross, J. 2008. "Municipal Colonialism in Vancouver: City Planning and the Conflict over Indian Reserves, 1928–1950s." *The Canadian Historical Review* 89 (4):541–80.

Statistics Canada. 2008. *Aboriginal Peoples of Canada: A Demographic Profile*. 2006 Census: Analysis Series. Ottawa: Minister of Industry.

Sully, L., L. Kellett, J. Garcea, and R.C. Walker. 2008. "First Nations Urban Reserves in Saskatoon: Partnerships for Positive Development." *Plan Canada* 48 (1):39–42.

Tomiak, J. 2010. "Indigenous Governance in Winnipeg and Ottawa: Making Space for Self-Determination." In *Aboriginal Policy Research: Exploring the Urban Landscape*, edited by J.P. White and J. Bruhn. Toronto: Thompson Educational Publishing.

Townshend, I., and R.C. Walker. 2010. "Life Course and Lifestyle Changes: Urban Change Through the Lens of Demography." In *Canadian Cities in*

Transition: New Directions in the Twenty-First Century, fourth edition, edited by T. Bunting, P. Filion, and R.C. Walker. Toronto: Oxford University Press.

Tuhiwai Smith, L. 1999. *Decolonizing Methodologies: Research and Indigenous Peoples.* London: Zed Books.

Walker, R.C. 2003. "Engaging the Urban Aboriginal Population in Low-Cost Housing Initiatives: Lessons from Winnipeg." *Canadian Journal of Urban Research* 12 Supplement: 99–118.

– 2006a. "Interweaving Aboriginal/Indigenous Rights with Urban Citizenship: A View from the Winnipeg Low-Cost Housing Sector, Canada." *Citizenship Studies* 10:391–411.

– 2006b. "Searching for Aboriginal/Indigenous Self-Determination: Urban Citizenship in the Winnipeg Low-Cost Housing Sector, Canada." *Environment and Planning A* 38:2345–63.

– 2008. "Improving the Interface Between Urban Municipalities and Aboriginal Communities." *Canadian Journal of Urban Research* 17 Supplement:20–36.

– 2013. "Increasing the Depth of Our Civic Identity: Future-Seeking and Place-Making with Aboriginal Communities." In *Indigenous in the City: Contemporary Identities and Cultural Innovation,* edited by E. Peters and C. Andersen. Vancouver: UBC Press.

Walker, R.C., and M. Barcham. 2010. "Indigenous-Inclusive Citizenship: The City and Social Housing in Canada, New Zealand & Australia." *Environment and Planning A* 42:314–31.

Walker, R.C., J. Moore, and M. Linklater. 2011. "More than Stakeholders, Voices and Tables: Towards Co-production of Urban Aboriginal Affairs Policy in Manitoba." In *Urban Aboriginal Policy Making in Canadian Municipalities,* edited by E. Peters. Montreal and Kingston: McGill-Queen's University Press.

Widdowson, F., and A. Howard. 2008. *Disrobing the Aboriginal Industry: The Deception behind Indigenous Cultural Preservation.* Montreal and Kingston: McGill-Queen's University Press.

Wilson, S. 2008. *Research is Ceremony: Indigenous Research Methods.* Winnipeg: Fernwood Publishing.

Winnipeg. 2003. *First Steps: Municipal Aboriginal Pathways.* Winnipeg: City of Winnipeg.

Wood, P. 2003. "Aboriginal/Indigenous Citizenship: An Introduction." *Citizenship Studies* 7:371–8.

Young, I.M. 1990. *Justice and the Politics of Difference.* Princeton: Princeton University Press.

9

Laguna Pueblo Indians in Urban
Labour Camps, 1922–80

KURT PETERS

It is 14 November 1992. Remembrance of the arrival of railroad construction crews, and of the lasting effect of subsequent events on Laguna culture is the object of a sit-down dinner held at the Laguna tribal recreation hall. Nearly a hundred retirees and descendants of labourers for the Atlantic & Pacific Railroad and its successor, the Atchison, Topeka and Santa Fe Railway (AT&SF), are in attendance. The crowd assembles to celebrate the relationship of the Lagunas with the Atlantic & Pacific and AT&SF railroads, a relationship that spans more than a century (Peters 1995).

People cluster together as at any function, some in family groups, some with friends. Others sit in twos and threes, glancing about shyly, now and then acknowledging a friendly face. Several are clearly comfortable at such events and are making the most of the opportunity to catch up on gossip with their friends. Whether anyone has more than a passing acquaintance of all the others at the reunion is not immediately clear. Nearly everyone present is one of the 7,103 enrolled members of the Laguna Tribe of New Mexico, and nearly everyone lives on the reservation or within a fifty-mile radius of it. Most of the people attend the many tribal-based Laguna and Catholic religious events that occur throughout the year, but even those celebrations do not usually occasion a formal sit-down affair (Peters 1995). This group shares something else among the casual, familial, and pious ties that bind them. This night is uniquely Laguna – there is a common denominator here that remains forever a feature of Laguna identity: employment on the AT&SF lines.

Native Americans nearly always play active, rather than singularly passive or restrained roles in events that shape their destinies. In doing so they make complicated and sophisticated decisions that have yet to be fully understood or accounted for by modern scholarship (Edmunds 1989; Spicer 1971). Through historical analysis, this chapter discusses the enduring effect of one such decision made at Laguna Pueblo in 1880. It examines the unique circumstances created by that decision, which have a lasting effect on the lives of the Laguna people, an effect that is extant yet today. The migration of the Laguna people is traceable from their roots as pueblo villagers on the San Jose River in New Mexico into the urban centre of Richmond, California, as well as other centres of off-pueblo railroad labour. This chapter provides an overview of certain aspects of the lived experience of the transplanted Laguna people, and reveals how the Laguna cultural identity was in some ways preserved and in other ways forever changed due to the western expansion of European immigrants (McGerr 1993).

The scholarship regarding westward United States expansion has too often left a view limited to tribal decimation through wars, disease, and theft of land and resources. The argument presented here is one quite different: an informed and sophisticated verbal labour negotiation occurred between the Laguna and the AT&SF in 1880. The resulting "Gentlemen's Agreement of Friendship," coupled with a durable recognition of the Laguna requirements as AT&SF labourers and adherence to that negotiation by the railroad produced a sustainable contract benefitting the needs of both parties. The argument here is that this study is a useful resource for both the urban and rural planner's toolkit, addressing such considerations as negotiating labour and other agreements with groups whose cultural value systems differ substantially from the "mainstream." Finally, it must be noted that loyalty to an agreement is often tethered to the spoken – as well as the written – word among Indigenous communities. Politically, socially, and certainly psychologically, the urban labour camp of Laguna workers served as an inextricable, symbolic linkage to the home pueblo, as proximate to being Laguna while in Richmond as if the workers' labour colony were instead situated along the AT&SF rails at Old Laguna, New Mexico. These points are among the foundations leading the Laguna Pueblo workers and the AT&SF from their 1880 verbal labour agreement into an unbroken one hundred-year employment relationship.

METHODS AND DATA

Compilation of data for this study and direction to the probable sources of corroborative information originated with the retired Laguna AT&SF

employees. This occurred through interviews as a result of the firmly fixed recollection of events and negotiations relating to employment by the AT&SF. Key identifiers assembled from consistencies in Laguna narratives regarding railroad life provide the important cultural markers pointing to corroborative non-Laguna sources.

The anthropological and self-professed origins of the Lagunas and their neighbours from the Acoma Pueblo are virtually the same. Despite this commonality, hundreds of years of animosities over land and water rights, religious foundations, and other ethnocentric divisions complicate Laguna-Acoma contemporary relationships. Such rancour reflects in the attitudes of many Lagunas towards the Acomas who worked for the AT&SF and lived in the village at Richmond. Hiring of the Acomas occurred, according to some Lagunas, when the Shopmen's Strike of 1922 created a severe need for additional labourers to come to Richmond to serve as strike breakers.

Called on by the AT&SF management – under the verbal agreement made in 1880 – the governor of Laguna Pueblo, Charles Kie, faced a need for more workers than his own pueblo could supply. Modern narratives say he called on the neighbouring Acoma Pueblo for additional men. This action created the roots of Acoma participation in AT&SF employment, say informants, and led to the growth of an Acoma section of the village at Richmond. However, the informants stress constantly that the Acomas were never under the umbrella of the 1880 agreement and only received benefits as additional labour invited by the Laguna governor during the 1922 strike (Peters 1995).

During four years of collecting data, the main informants and their contacts often seemed eager to have their history documented. Those for whom English is a second language and those with whom contact initially resulted in avoidance and reticence to discuss any details, are presently almost uniformly in support of this study. Of the hundreds of enrolled tribal members contacted, all have personal or familial employment contact with the AT&SF. As time brought closure to the study, however, hesitancy arose about being "the one" to have his or her attitudes and recollections memorialized as representing the entire group. Phrases and words included in this text represent telescoped results of assembled narratives. This respects the wishes of those who request anonymity while giving a voice to all those participating in the railroading experience. Fortunately, due to the homogeneity of the general experience combined with the richness of individual phrases, the added narrative voice allows depth and breadth of meaning (personal interviews).[1]

After 1880, the Lagunas established themselves in AT&SF labour enclaves all along the railroad lines from Albuquerque, New Mexico to Richmond, California. These groupings occurred not only at urban junctures catering to railroad development, but also at various railway maintenance headquarters along the way. Many Native American "labour camps" significantly populated by Lagunas became mainstays of AT&SF workers. In particular, Gallup, New Mexico; Winslow, Arizona; and Barstow and Richmond, California are important, as they are the only off-reservation groups whose enclaves eventually received recognition from the Laguna governor and tribal council as "colonies" of the Laguna Pueblo in New Mexico (Peters 1996, 1998, 2001). All those interviewed acknowledge the colony at Winslow as having the largest ongoing population of Laguna labourers. However, for the purposes of this study, the former residents at Richmond are the focus. The corroborative data available from the city of Richmond, the National Archives, and other sources, lends itself most readily to a study focused on the village of Richmond. While marginal to this study, the data collected concerning the additional colonies furnishes finely grained text for comparative purposes and sheds light on the overarching question of Native American labour on the AT&SF (Dunning 1985).

LAGUNA ORIGINS

Scholarly and romanticized accounts of how the Pueblo of Old Laguna originated are obscure but consistent on one point: it was founded around 1699 by migrants from other pueblos (Dozier 1961). The pueblo is located on a mass of rock rising above the now intermittent San Jose River, fifty miles due west of Albuquerque, New Mexico. The lifestyle that evolved at Laguna was influenced by continuous contact with Mexican and American settlers, traders, missionaries, and other visitors to the area. Laguna claimed space east to within ten miles of present-day Albuquerque, west to the Pueblo of Acoma, and north and further west to lands guarded by the Navajo (themselves relative newcomers to the area). Although Laguna is among the first pueblos visited by "Americans," the visitors chose to leave little in the way of ethnographic accounts of the Laguna people (DeMallie 1993). A quest for learning the culture and history of the people at Laguna did not drive the steam locomotives across the 35th parallel and through Laguna lands; as now, a desire for wealth drove the engines of the day.

ENCROACHMENT OF THE RAILROAD

By the mid-nineteenth century the United States government began planning to populate exponentially the lands west of the Mississippi, aided by the popularized banner of Manifest Destiny, and abetted by renewed railroad construction in the post-Civil War era. Federal officials, government surveyors, and railroad entrepreneurs alike chose the 35th parallel through New Mexico Territory as a favourable route for railroad lines to connect Chicago, the industrial hub of the United States, with the Pacific seaports. The recently compromised war with Mexico, development of empires based on mineral exploration, and an accelerated flow of European immigrants to the Southwest helped create a need for railroad construction in New Mexico. Added to this were two attractions for investors in railroads: (1) federal grants of huge tracts of land for railroad construction and related town site developments, and (2) an eventual lucrative railroad traffic in freight and passengers. The outcome was US empirical expansion on an unprecedented scale in a relatively short time. The federal government profited from this growth by the addition of new states to the burgeoning national union, with new taxes and lands secured by homesteading. In addition, the government realized substantial income on federally backed railroad construction bonds.

The Southwest did not go unnoticed by either the federal government officials or the expanding group of railroad entrepreneurs. Railroad officials chose the 35th parallel as one primary route due to the temperate climate, availability of water for the steam locomotives, timber for bridges and track supports, local stone for track ballast, and not least, numerous locations for profit-producing town sites. One proposed line would cut directly through the land of the Laguna Pueblo Tribe. After warring with marauding tribes; continually resisting waves of invaders of Spanish, Mexican, and European ancestries; and accommodating squatters of all types, the Laguna Pueblo people came under new pressure regarding their land: railroads would now vie for use of the Laguna living space (Peters 1996, 1998, 2001). In Congress, debates ensued on how to gain clear ownership titles to Native American lands in order to give free land to the railroads as an inducement to quickly build throughout the American West.

A GENTLEMEN'S AGREEMENT

The railroad companies continued to grow and build, entering the Southwest amid significant labour difficulties. Low-skilled white workers, living in remote Southwest labour camps with few amenities presented an ongoing retention problem. To counterbalance the constant attrition of white labourers, railroads began hiring – with better results – local Mexicans, Native Americans, and later, Japanese immigrants, as the companies pushed construction forward into the northern parts of New Mexico Territory and then south to Albuquerque.

Extension of the railroads west in 1880 from Isleta Pueblo near Albuquerque met resistance on entering Laguna Pueblo land. A Laguna representative met the construction crews, forced a meeting with railroad officials, and negotiated an oral, but permanent, agreement. In exchange for building through Laguna lands unmolested, the railroad agreed to forever hire as many of the Laguna as wished to work. Other concessions by the railroad involved free passes for train travel for employees, and other goods and services conferred annually in a meeting reaffirming the original oral agreement, known subsequently by all Laguna as "The Gentlemen's Agreement of Friendship" (Peters 1998, 2001). Pueblo oral history tells that the original notes of the 1880 meeting are in the vest pocket of the man who negotiated that agreement, the late "Jimmy" Hiuwec, who is now interred at Laguna wearing the vest. Copies of later interviews with him record his recollections of that event. Until 1984, annual meetings to reaffirm The Gentlemen's Agreement of Friendship were held at the AT&SF regional office in Los Angeles. Between 1922 and 1980, they took on a near ritual aspect. These meetings are remembered by all tribal members as "watering the flower" of the original agreement, thereby keeping it healthy and productive for the Laguna people.

NEGOTIATING THE RELATIONSHIP

During the forty years between the arrival of the AT&SF in the late 1800s and 1920, hundreds of Laguna sought employment as railroaders and remained on the payroll. By 1900, AT&SF employees, including Laguna, earned an above-average wage of nearly $700 annually, compared with $548 for all railroad employees. By 1915, the annual AT&SF average wage of over $854 remained the nation's highest for railroaders. The onset of the First World War created a dramatic increase in war production and related shipments of military freight and personnel, with a resulting sharp increase in railroad pay due to bonuses and overtime work (Peters 1996). Federal government and railroad management animosities towards labour unions resulted in a series of union-led strikes when management attempted a rollback of the First World War monetary gains. One such strike, the notorious Shopmen's Strike of 1922, strangled the national system of operations. More than three hundred passengers were put off the train by striking workers at Needles, California, and left there stranded in the summer heat (Peters 1998).

The AT&SF responded to the strike by calling on the governor of the Laguna Pueblo, who was traditionally the only administrator with authority to release men for work away from home. The railroad wanted the pueblo governor to honour the contract made in 1880 and quickly send men to replace the strikers (Peters 1996, 2001). The fact that the Laguna men were non-union and technically "scabs" (strike breakers) was not a consideration. Under Kie's direction, the Laguna responded out of strict loyalty to the 1880 agreement.

Present-day Laguna guard carefully the memory of their original agreement with the railroad, and are emphatic that the Acoma have no "legal" recognition under the Gentlemen's Agreement of Friendship. A photograph taken during the late 1940s at a meeting to water the flower amused the former Laguna union representative, Timothy Anallah. He noted that one man in the group was an Acoma, brought there at the invitation of a fellow worker who was a Laguna representing the village at Calwa, California. The presiding governor from the pueblo in New Mexico allowed him to stay, overriding objections from the other Lagunas in attendance. Laguna people often explain more carefully – and with great pride – the relationship between the company, the Lagunas, and the Acomas. While governor of the colony at Richmond, one received a letter from the governor of the Acomas at the AT&SF terminal. A copy of the letter states that the Acomas did not have any agreement, verbal or otherwise with the AT&SF. The then-Acoma governor acknowledges that the agreement of 1880 did not have "anything to do with the Acoma people," and therefore "they weren't entitled to all that we were entitled to." After being transported to Richmond in boxcars, and through the strikers' picket lines at the terminal, the men worked through the strike and were housed and fed in one of the several maintenance buildings at the terminal yards (Peters 1996, 1998, 2001).

By 1923, national labour negotiations resulted in settlement of the strike, with some Laguna employees remaining at the Richmond Terminal or using it as a base from which their track maintenance crews operated. Some returned to the pueblo in New Mexico, while many transferred to maintenance centres along the AT&SF railroad lines, such as Barstow, Calwa, and Needles in California, and Winslow in Arizona. Eventually the railroad unions, called "brotherhoods," opened their ranks to include the Laguna who subsequently remained steadfastly loyal to their 1880 agreement – and now their labour union as well. In a syncretism of loyalties that is an anomaly in labour union history, both agreements remained honoured through the Laguna employment history with the AT&SF. As one Laguna lifetime railroader and staunch defender of the verbal agreement of 1880 remarked of his labour union loyalty, "After the union come in, you join [the union] or you're out."

A former Laguna union representative, the late Timothy Anallah, characterized negotiations between the company and the pueblo as "friendly." Each group, the Lagunas and the AT&SF, accommodated the other during the ritual meetings. The company, he added, was "very conciliatory." During the 1950s and 1960s, Anallah represented the Laguna labourers belonging to the sheet metal workers' union, negotiated tribal matters with the company, and actively participated in other union duties. When asked how the union officials reacted to the annual watering the flower, he responded that the union knew there was a "prior agreement," and felt it was to everyone's benefit to honour it. In turn, the Laguna workers at Richmond honoured the principles of their union membership (Peters 1998, 2001).

A retired man reflected on his union relationship:

Q: They paid well, paid you on time, and took care of your medical?
A: Yeah, after the union came in.
Q: Everybody belonged to the union?
A: After that we belonged to the union. Union really did good for us, went along with us. Our wage goes up when we asked, and medical stuff, and all those things. It was a good union. The union did pretty good.

Laguna railroaders saw no conflict in both accepting the union relationship and at the same time honouring the agreement negotiated by Jimmy Hiuwec in 1880. There was little indication that they felt the company was unfair to them, and yet shortly thereafter they endorsed the union's protection exclusively. It is Laguna Pueblo tradition to accept what advances the common good, and this tradition figured significantly here. To have acted in any other manner would have been uncharacteristic of Laguna attitudes. The maintenance of Laguna identity did not depend on adherence to either the AT&SF or to union role-playing. Labourers cast their status as both union members and company employees, all within a framework of Laguna tradition and custom.

BUILDING A NEW VILLAGE

A "second group" of Laguna moved to the Richmond Terminal to live and work in the late 1930s, as the pressures of the impending Second World War began to mount (Peters 1996). Richmond, the "dull industrial suburb," described by historian James Gregory, soon quadrupled in size to a boom town of more than one hundred thousand people employed by the wartime AT&SF, the nearby Ford Motor Company, and the Kaiser Shipyards (Brown 1973; *The Santa Fe Magazine* 1943, 1951). Many Laguna women report beginning their first employment off-reservation when they moved to the AT&SF labour camps to fill jobs vacated by Laguna men in the military and Japanese-American workers taken away to federal internment camps. "We got the same pay as the men," states one female Laguna Elder. "We wouldn't let them [AT&SF] pay us any less."

During the war years, railroaders bunked in the AT&SF firehouse, but as more families began coming from New Mexico to settle permanently, the Richmond yards began providing converted boxcars as living quarters. The cars were eventually joined in sets of two by a connection for cooking. These "H" shapes evolved in a cluster along unused rail lines in the terminal called sidings, where the boxcar houses had originally been rolled into place on rails, and eventually had their wheels removed. The cluster took on an identity of its own within the terminal, known by residents of Richmond, as well as the US Postal Service, merely as "The Indian Village, Richmond, California." Letters and packages were delivered to the main AT&SF office at the terminal and then given to a designated Laguna "postman" for delivery.

Life for the Laguna families at Richmond took on the aspects of more comfortable labouring people's lives: boxcars were taken off their wheels and made into "permanent" dwellings; white picket fences with flowers and shrubs appeared outdoors; refrigerators and kitchen linoleum became commonplace indoors; the addition of screen doors for summer ventilation and individual house numbers on the boxcars. A local physician in private practice saw the Native Americans and other railroad employees at the Richmond Terminal. His Richmond office was downtown, several blocks away, and the company provided him an office in the train yards for his visits there. "We all went to the railroad company doctor's office," a former villager said. "As for the medical," she said, "the Santa Fe took care of the employees." Like the public outside the train yards, "we went to a family doctor, just like anybody else." In cases involving surgery "or whatever," she said, the Atchison, Topeka and Santa Fe paid for all the medical bills (Peters 1995). All of this was due to the annual watering of the flower in Los Angeles.

One Laguna boxcar was set aside as a general meeting hall, doubling sometimes as a teen club and wedding reception hall, and was shared with the resident workers from the Acoma Pueblo. The latter were required to ask for the use of the hall, reinforcing the Laguna contention that the 1880 agreement did not give the Acoma any of the same benefits; they are seen yet today as mere invitees into the original AT&SF employment contract. Some village residents built traditional beehive-shaped mud brick ovens just outside their boxcars for preparing and serving Native American food to participants at meetings, church confirmations, and myriad community celebrations of Laguna cultural unity.

A testimonial to railroad life at Richmond came at the 1992 reunion of retired Atchison, Topeka and Santa Fe employees:

> I was about five to six years old when my father and four of us children lived in box cars which had about four rooms and were very small. My family all shared the small bedrooms which made us even closer and were happy children. I remember we lived right next to the railroad shop and the tracks. The neighborhood children and I would stand by the fence to watch the trains go by and we would wave at the people. We all shared being together for picnics and celebrations. We were like one big happy family. We had to ride the train to come home to Laguna and we would get off either at Grants or New Laguna train depots. At this time I thought it was something great to ride the trains. On pay days, [father] would treat us to a hamburger dinner or a movie. We looked forward to pay days because we knew it was treat time. I can still remember and cherish those good memories deep down in my heart when I was young and my father worked for the Santa Fe Railroad Company.

Children attended local schools without reported discrimination, and the families received credit in the Richmond shops downtown, courtesies not accorded to the African-American residents of Richmond at that time. These were likely the result of a circumstance understood by everyone in the Richmond area: the Laguna families had status, housing, and use of company facilities as loyal, respected employees of the AT&SF. In addition, each family had a recurring, on-time paycheque for their contribution to the operation and maintenance of the Richmond Terminal and the AT&SF system at large. "We had everything," replied one long-time Indian Village resident, when asked about her early childhood in Richmond.

Growth in the system was bringing changes, however. By the early 1950s, the annual meetings in Los Angeles to water the flower produced indoor showers and commodes, and cozy all-wood interiors with wood-burning stoves for heat and cooking. All of this matched, with similar living conditions, the communal living of the pueblo as close-knit families; boxcar life is remembered fondly yet today. During this time, the AT&SF tried to replace the boxcars with more efficient, newer, modular housing equipped with propane cooking stoves. Most Laguna families refused the new housing, preferring to remain in their comfortable boxcar houses, and the company halted the replacement project. One former resident estimates that at the Richmond Terminal alone there were "about one hundred" families living in the Indian Village.

PRESERVING A CULTURAL IDENTITY

The Lagunas maintained their village as an extension of the home pueblo. Waves of migrant Laguna labourers, augmented with members of the neighbouring Acoma Pueblo, left New Mexico and passed in and out of the terminal at Richmond from 1922 through the mid-1980s when the Indian Village disbanded. They adapted themselves to surrounding non-Native American functions but clung to tradition in the village, returning often to their pueblos for additional nurturing celebrations and rituals (Peters 1995, 1996, 1998, 2001).

During the Laguna workers' sojourn at Richmond, the village functioned as a de facto satellite of the distant pueblo. Sociologically and psychologically, the village remained inextricably a part of the home pueblo as if it were situated along the railroad right-of-way, west of the Rio Grande River in New Mexico. The shared experience of those who intermittently occupied the village is a tribute to the cultural persistence of those who watered the flower of the AT&SF contract. In the process, the participants extended the vitality of the Laguna and Acoma communities and expanded their rich cultural tradition (Peters 1995, 1996, 1998, 2001).

The Laguna labour camps along the AT&SF rail lines were numerous, but varied in size. The Winslow camp housed the largest number of employees, but the Richmond camp was most active in Laguna Pueblo politics. Representatives of the two labour camps, other camp representatives, and officials from both the home pueblo and the AT&SF met annually to water the flower. The camps at Gallup, New Mexico; Winslow, Arizona; and Barstow and Richmond, California all applied to the home pueblo governor during the 1950s for formal social and political recognition as a "colony" of Laguna Pueblo, and the governor formally granted their request. Eventually, the AT&SF adopted the colony identity for the Richmond Indian Village in its official documents. But the Richmond Terminal, despite all the adaptations by the AT&SF and the Laguna to their needs, was only a place of sojourn in an urban labour camp, never a home – the attachment in the heart remained to the home pueblo at Old Laguna, New Mexico.

Reflecting on the "permanence of city residence," the Meriam Report of 1928 reports that many Indians viewed the city as a temporary residence, hoping to return to their homelands as soon as they were economically able (Peters 1995). Likely due to his mandate by the Department of the Interior to measure Indian "acculturative progress," Meriam's study fails to recognize that the homelands of remembrance and that of reality were no longer the same (Meriam 1928). Laguna peoples labouring for the AT&SF in a post–Second World War urban world found themselves caught in a downward spiral of the railroad's need for manual labour. Keeping families clothed and fed both in the cities and at home grew more problematic. Anthropologist Steve Talbot writes of that era, noting, "most Indian workers are poor, unemployed, or underemployed" (Talbot 1985).

The Ramsey study, in the Investigation of Cultural Resources within the Richmond Harbor Development Project, also states that the governor from Laguna Pueblo made annual visits to Richmond in "more recent" years to meet with villagers and railroad officials. "Even now that the village has only four families, these visits are still made." On 12 November 1980, the governor met with "non-village" tribal members, as well as village residents. In former years the meetings included Atchison, Topeka and Santa Fe officials in order for the governor to represent the villagers' interest regarding the 1880 agreement. "Native Americans refer to the Governor's Santa Fe conference as 'watering the flower'," Ramsey says (Ramsey 1981). In 1992 a retired village official said, "The governor never go out there [after 1982] to water the flower ... I don't know why." The annual reaffirmation ritual honouring the principles of the flower was fading away. The dismantling of the village of Richmond would soon follow (Peters 1995).

RAZING THE VILLAGE

In 1970, the AT&SF officially merged with the National Railroad Passenger Corporation's Amtrak, and the company began requiring signed leases for the boxcar houses. A local newspaper reported that the AT&SF had cleaned and repaired the houses in 1964, and then renovated them as part of the lease agreements in 1970, bringing them up to local building and safety codes (*Contra Costa Independent* 1982). Maps attached to the leases identified the boxcar community as "The Richmond, California Colony of the Pueblo of Laguna," and required one dollar per year lease payment for each boxcar house and the land beneath it. One proviso was that at retirement the lessee could elect to move the boxcar elsewhere in Richmond or back to Laguna Pueblo by AT&SF freight (Peters 1995).

Ramsey details the existing village structures as follows: "Newcomers had to live in old boxcars made temporarily by the company ... Partitions were installed, and modifications made to the original boxcars, which became permanent housing, and now have been used for over fifty years." Noting that the company "no longer maintains the buildings as it did in years past," the report characterizes the condition of the ten remaining houses as "deteriorated." "Four boxcars are still being used; families occupy three of them and the fourth is used as a community meeting room,"(Ramsey 1981).

Two of the boxcar houses close to the Richmond Terminal were moved off the AT&SF property in the late 1980s and others were sold off by the company to a local land developer. One retiree talked the AT&SF into shipping a large woodpile and hundreds of bricks back to Laguna Pueblo in lieu of taking his boxcar residence to New Mexico. The bricks and some of the wood remain today, just outside his pueblo home. Some of the boxcar homes remain entombed in the Richmond Terminal, unseen reminders of one of the nation's most lucrative and highly visible railroad systems.

"We hated going over there," said a Richmond Terminal supervisor in 1993. "Those last two boxcars [homes] just wouldn't give up; the wood kept splintering and we broke our hammers." When asked what the wrecking crew did with the last two boxcars, he replied, "We dug a hole and buried them – right over there!" The supervisor pointed to a broad, empty expanse of asphalt in the centre of the terminal parking lot. Later, one of the last boxcar residents at Richmond Terminal, a Laguna woman, speculated about the demise of her boxcar home. "Do you think," she asked, "those scientists [archaeologists] will dig my boxcar up some day? Will they know it was an Indian house?"

KEEPING THE PAST ALIVE

When the Laguna people gathered in 1992 at the community hall in the Catholic Church in Old Laguna, it was the first time in the 112 years since the Atlantic & Pacific originally contracted to employ Lagunas that a real reunion of retirees, wives, children, grandchildren, great-grandchildren, and widows and orphans of deceased AT&SF workers all sat down together. That year marked the 125th anniversary of the founding of the railroad, and connection with railroading affected everyone at the dinner. Many expressed their pleasure, saying, "We thought the company had forgotten us." They were happy their former employer had helped sponsor this reunion, even though there were no AT&SF company representatives present (Peters 1995).

Fading photographs and news clippings only partially recall the alliances, experiences, and memories of working for the AT&SF, and most of the participants awaited the reunion eagerly. A few had tried previously to organize such an event. Guests remembered the Santa Fe All Indian Band, pow wows in Golden Gate Park, children playing at night under the dim security lights of the Winslow train yards, and First Communion dinners in the boxcar meeting hall at the Richmond Terminal. This reunion represented an opportunity, which most attendees hoped would be the first of many, to grasp again threads of experience woven into that seamless cloth of identity, and the persistent sense of being both Laguna and an AT&SF railroader (Peters 1995).

As the catering staff shifted quietly and efficiently between tables and guests, neat white tablecloths, silverware, and crisp salads served on real china plates startled the dinner guests a little. One woman whispered, "I was sure it would be the usual Indian fry bread and a piece of chicken thrown in a paper basket. Wait until my sister hears what she missed." The caterer came from nearby Grants. Once called the "Uranium Capital of the World," Grants is now little more than host to a massive penal colony and weekend shoppers from adjacent reservations and rural non-Native American groups. Lagunas go to town to eat at The Station, a local restaurant. The menu, the décor, and even staff uniforms play up the theme continuous in Laguna life: railroading. Bud Riecke, the owner, is particularly fond of collecting bits of trivia from the heyday of the AT&SF. He is popular among the people who built and maintained that empire; the Lagunas hand-picked him to cater the reunion (Peters 1995).

The colourful dinner settings, the pictures along the walls, and several handmade banners attesting to the continuance of the Laguna-AT&SF relationship gave relief from an otherwise stark atmosphere. Outside, a weathered sign read, "Recreation Hall." Little else in the way of exterior decoration was added to the gray cement block structure. A chain link fence enclosed the hall; some reminisced how "things aren't the same like when we were kids. Now everything has to be locked up." Rolled barbed wire topped the fence to discourage the more persistent intruder (Peters 1995).

Not all Lagunas at the reunion were positive about the Laguna-AT&SF relationship. A thirty-nine-year veteran of railroad life pointed up the slope of the nearby mesa towards the ever-present Catholic Church. The site near the church where the company wished to place railroad cars as a memento of mutual loyalty remained bare. The tribal council voted to refuse the offer. Whether this indicated an act of resistance to further industrial intrusion on tribal lands is unclear. The storyteller was clearly sceptical of the council's wisdom: "Those guys are crazy. If we had let the railroad do that then we could have worked with them on other things. Maybe they would have said, 'Well, those Indians don't have a baseball field or a good recreation hall, so let's put one up for them.'" He appraised the hard, lifeless exterior of the recreation building as he returned to the dinner, exclaiming with a laugh, "Them guys don't know nothing. They're crazy."

A 102-year-old retiree who attended the reunion – the late Santiago Thomas – lived alone in two rooms on the far side of Laguna Pueblo. His single window was on the west side, directly above the buried Atlantic & Pacific track bed. Round cedar beams supported the seven-foot-high ceiling of Thomas's sparsely furnished apartment; fading black and white photographs from his long years with the AT&SF lined the walls of both rooms just below the beams. The 1880 agreement was barely thirty years old when this man began work nearby as a labourer on a section gang, operating from the now-vanished railroad junction called Swanee.

The photographs were visual daily recollections of his railroad employment (Peters 1995).

At the reunion dinner, Thomas was resplendent in a scarlet baseball jacket. The coat was a remnant of days when the company called on Native American railroad workers to display their tribal identity for corporate profit. Native American employees helped the AT&SF market its services using advertising that drew heavily on motifs of southwestern Native American life. The jacket was one of only three that were specially designed by a fellow Laguna for the men to wear as they toured on company business. On the back was a large embroidered profile of a stereotypical war-bonneted Native American; the round blue-and-white AT&SF logo flashed from the left side of the jacket, over his heart, when the old man turned to have his features recorded on film (Peters 1996).

None of the Laguna Tribal Council came to the dinner except one latecomer, the official tribal interpreter. A college-educated Second World War veteran, he made the choice to return home to serve the reservation. Others succumbed to the lures of urban life, appearing only for obligatory meetings and ritual events, but this man remained. He rose proudly and asked through a family member for the opportunity to speak. A few of his opening words were in English, none in Spanish – until two generations ago the second language on the reservation – and the rest of the address in Laguna. Everyone was silent as he spoke. Some younger people may not have fully comprehended his words, but still were silent. His speech was marked with assurance and dignity, and brought the evening to a close.

Later, an older Laguna explained,

> [The interpreter] says that this dinner is a good thing, that we need to remember our past and our responsibility to the agreement we made in the early days with the Santa Fe, when it first come through here. Our women have been reminding us for a long time now, he says, that we should do what we used to, that we should go to the Santa Fe and renew our verbal agreement ... It is the way our people have survived and it is the way we can provide for our children, and for the tribe to continue.

The meaning of this dinner gathering is clear: it was a ritual for renewal, a celebration of the continuity of the tribe. The dinner connected the Laguna people with the event of 1880 as a symbolic marker of Laguna identity (Peters 1995, 1996).

CONCLUSION

Michelene Fixico writes in "The Road to Middle Class America" that "perhaps nothing more illustrates the attachment to their cultural heritage than the Indian's need to be with other Indians where they can just be themselves" (Fixico 1989). Ramsey quotes a 1954 Richmond *Independent* newspaper article which states that the village during that era comprised "the barren strip of land lying northwest of Richmond between the Santa Fe Railroad and Standard Oil Company." By the time of Ramsey's research in the early 1980s, the village covered a "considerably smaller" rectangular area of about two thousand square feet. "What remains of the original site," observes Ramsey, was "nestled between tracks and a swampy marsh along the railroad yard's western edge" (Ramsey 1981).

Waves of migrant Laguna railroad labourers, augmented by members of the neighbouring Acoma Pueblo, passed in and out of the AT&SF Richmond Terminal between 1922 and the mid-1980s. They adapted selectively to the local non-Indian functions but clung to their own traditions, returning often on free rail passes to the home pueblo for family visits, business meetings, and sacred rituals. During the workers' sojourn in California, the Richmond Indian Village functioned as a de facto satellite, indeed a colony, of the distant Laguna pueblo (Peters 1995, 1996, 1998, 2001).

Placing the 1880 verbal agreement at the centre of Laguna identity, as adjunct to shaping and maintaining Laguna being, provides a much larger and more valuable tool for analyzing the effect that American empire-building had on many of the complex groups of Indigenous peoples standing in its path of expansion. The verbal agreement between the Laguna and the AT&SF, rooted in The Gentlemen's Agreement of Friendship of 1880, persists as a historic stabilizing force due to its absorption into the organism of the Laguna cultural continuum. The importance of the Pueblo's railroad experience intensifies when measured for its role in the cultural dynamic of the peoples' persistence as Laguna.

Through the annual reaffirmations to water the flower of the original 1880 agreement, the recognition of the mutual accommodations binding together the Laguna and the AT&SF emerged as markers of identity and self-esteem for Laguna. Subsequent years of affirmations added depth and texture to the value of those markers to specific residents of the labour camps and their descendants. The threads of railroad experience and lifestyle define, in part, the texture of the fabric of Laguna experience. Annually watering the flower enmeshed those threads in the complex weave of Laguna life. Their absence, and thereby the absence of the circumstances created by the 1880 agreement and the urban labour camps, would unquestionably alter the essence of Laguna experience and of the sense of being Laguna today (Peters 1996).

NOTE

1 All original notes, audio, and visual recordings and images, memorabilia, photographs, and miscellaneous ephemera constituting research on this subject are in the author's archives. Interviews in various formats taken by the author span more than two decades, from 1991 to the present. Those interviewed indicated a need for anonymity until the release of the comprehensive volume on this subject. A photocopy of the map attached to the lease agreements is in the author's collection; former residents were reluctant to allow copying of the actual lease provisions, however.

REFERENCES

Brown, Hubert Owen. 1973. *The Impact Of War Worker Migration on the Public School System of Richmond, California, from 1940 To 1945.* PHD dissertation, Stanford University.

Contra Costa Independent. 1982. "The End of Indian Village," 6 August, 1, 4.

DeMallie, Raymond J. 1993. "Narrative and the Ethnohistorical Method." *Ethnohistory* 40 (Fall):525.

Dozier, Edward P. 1961. "Rio Grande Pueblos." In *Perspectives in American Indian Culture Change,* edited by Edward H. Spicer, 165. Chicago: University of Chicago Press.

Dunning, Judith K. 1985. *Harry and Marguerite Williams: Reflections of a Longtime Black Family in Richmond, Regional Oral History Office, The Bancroft Library,* introduction. Berkeley: University of California.

Edmunds, R. David. 1989. "Antelope and Engineers: Challenge and Change in the Indian Communities." In *American Indian Identity: Today's Changing Perspectives,* edited by Clifford E. Trafzer, 10. Sacramento: Sierra Oaks Publishing Co.

Fixico, Michelene. 1989. "The Road to Middle Class America." In *American Indian Identity: Today's Changing Perspectives,* edited by Clifford E. Trafzer, 74. Sacramento: Sierra Oaks Publishing Company.

McGerr, Michael. 1993. "The Persistence of Individualism." *The Chronicle of Higher Education,* 10 February: A48.

McLuhan, T.C. 1985. *Dream Tracks: The Railroad and the American Indian, 1890–1930*. New York: Harry N. Abrams, Inc.

Meriam, Lewis, et al. 1928. *The Problem of Indian Administration: Report of a Survey Made at the Request of the Honorable Hubert Work, Secretary of the Interior, and Submitted to Him, February 21, 1928*. Baltimore: The Johns Hopkins Press.

Peters, Kurt M. 1995. "Santa Fe Indian Camp, House 21, Richmond, California: Persistence of Identity among Laguna Pueblo Railroad Labourers, 1945–1982." *American Indian Culture and Research Journal* 19 (3): 33–70.

– 1996. "Watering the Flower: Laguna Pueblo and the Santa Fe Railroad, 1880–1943." In *Native Americans and Wage Labor: Ethno Historical Perspectives*, edited by Alice Littlefield and Martha C. Knack. Norman: University of Oklahoma Press.

– 1998. "Continuing Identity: Laguna Pueblo Railroaders in Richmond, California." *American Indian Culture and Research Journal* 22 (4): 187-98.

– 2001. "Continuing Identity: Laguna Pueblo Railroaders in Richmond, California." In *American Indians and the Urban Experience*, edited by Susan Lobo and Kurt Peters. Lanham: Altamira Press.

Ramsey, Eleanor M. 1981. "Richmond, California: 1850–1940." In *Investigation of Cultural Resources within the Richmond Harbor Redevelopment Project 11-A, Richmond, Contra Costa County, California*. Courtesy Robert Orlins. California Archaeological Consultants, Inc., Banks & Orlins.

Spicer, Edward H. 1962. *Cycles of Conquest: The Impact of Spain, Mexico, and the United States on the Indians of the Southwest, 1533–1960*. Tucson: University of Arizona Press.

– 1971. "Persistent Cultural Systems: A Comparative Study of Identity Systems that Can Adapt to Contrasting Environments." *Science* 174 (November):798.

Talbott, Steve. 1985. *Roots of Oppression: The American Indian Question*. New York: International Publishers.

The Santa Fe Magazine. June 1943. "Richmond – City that Mushroomed," by H.A. Burroughs, 13. Santa Fe Collection. Topeka: Kansas State Historical Society.

– May 1951. Santa Fe Collection. Topeka: Kansas State Historical Society, 12.

Wilson, Clint C. II, and Felix Gutierrez. 1985. *Minorities and Media: Diversity and the End of Communication*. Beverly Hills: SAGE Publications, Inc.

10

Kaitiakitanga o Ngā Ngahere Pōhatu – Kaitiakitanga of Urban Settlements

SHAUN AWATERE, GARTH HARMSWORTH, SHADRACH
ROLLESTON, AND CRAIG PAULING

Māori and local authorities have made huge strides in developing and fostering positive working relationships, particularly since the passing of the Resource Management Act in 1991. However, despite twenty years of progress there still remains a high degree of frustration over the limited representation of Māori perspectives and knowledge in land-use planning and policy formation. The exclusion of Māori knowledge (*Mātauranga* Māori), values, and representation is particularly evident in urban environments where 85 per cent of Māori now live (Statistics New Zealand 2006).

The low levels of Māori participation generally reflect the dominant mainstream processes of planning and policy and the very low numbers of Māori staff and councillors employed in local authorities. Poor understanding by local authoritiess of Māori values, perspectives and knowledge, and limited *iwi/hapū* (tribe/subtribe) capacity are also significant contributing factors to the poor uptake and incorporation of Mātauranga Māori in urban planning. As a consequence there is a lack of direct Māori input into most planning and decision-making processes. The result is that in areas such as urban design and development Māori contributions are usually scarce and seen as ancillary, or as an afterthought in most planning documents. Mātauranga Māori is generally poorly recognized and understood, but where it is recognized it is often "Europeanized" and co-opted into existing planning processes. Iwi management plans or resource management plans prepared by iwi/hapū are expressions of iwi/hāpu environmental perspectives and are required to be taken into account by local authorities. Most of the first and second-generation iwi resource management plans developed by iwi trust boards and *rūnanga* (councils) for local authorities (Hauraki Māori Trust Board 2003; Huakina Development Trust 1993) have been appendages to main planning documents and are poorly understood or used. This indicates regional/local councils that lack the resources to develop appropriate Mātauranga Māori-based approaches that can be incorporated into planning. All of these issues have led to the current research described here.

This chapter is the result of a three-year Ministry of Science and Innovation-funded research program called "Kaitiakitanga of Urban Settlements," led by Manaaki Whenua Landcare Research. The research program addresses knowledge gaps in the urban planning environment by producing Mātauranga Māori-based frameworks, methods, and tools to facilitate the inclusion of Mātauranga Māori in planning practice and to build Māori and iwi/hapū capacity. It has also established a national network of talented Māori researchers and practitioners that are making significant contributions around Aotearoa-New Zealand in Mātauranga Māori-based planning and urban design. Through this research we have developed a *pātaka* (storehouse of tools and processes) that can be used by planners and iwi/hapū resource managers to increase the use of and evaluate the incorporation of Mātauranga Māori in decision making, policy, and plans. More specifically, we have developed an assessment framework and process that can be used by planners, developers, and iwi/hapū resource managers to plan and evaluate the incorporation of Mātauranga Māori in decision making, policy, planning, and development.

In this chapter we present one case study that has been completed to date. While this case study is context specific, it does provide some key principles and lessons that guide both Māori and the planning fraternity to increase the use of and understanding of Mātauranga Māori. Results demonstrate a wealth of knowledge about how Mātauranga Māori can be incorporated and applied in decision making, policy, planning, and development.

INTEGRATION OF MĀTAURANGA MĀORI INTO MAINSTREAM PLANNING

Māori participation and engagement in the planning process varies throughout New Zealand. The degree of participation has increased, as

Māori have become more politically, economically, socially, and technically involved in resource management and planning issues. The integration of Māori knowledge systems into mainstream planning has been
progressive and is ongoing. The notion of self-determination continues
to shape Māori perceptions of reality and efforts for change. Māori continue to push the political boundaries to effect change.

Formal urban planning law was first introduced in 1926 with the
enactment of the Town and Country Planning Act (TCPA). The regulative
process of the TCPA determined zones for commercial, retail, industrial,
residential, and rural activities. The process of zoning had a significant
detrimental effect on Māori land, both by affecting rights to manage
Māori land and through further alienation of land (Marr 1997, 13).
During this period, local authorities gave little acknowledgment to recognizing and providing for the needs of Māori. Local authorities failed
to take into account the perspectives and needs of Māori and this was
largely the result of poor relationships between iwi/hapū and the Crown,
poor consultation process, and marginalization of Māori from most
planning and policy activity.

Throughout the 1960s, the New Zealand Māori Council (NZMC) via
the bilingual publication, *Te Ao Hou – The New World*, challenged the
prevailing orthodoxy and promoted a more active response to Māori
planning needs. The key issues included removing restrictions and limitations placed on the development of Māori land, poor quality rural
housing, the protection of *urupā* (burial grounds), and the conservation
of *kaimoana* (seafood) (Booth 1963a, 1963b). Māori voices, however,
were virtually non-existent in local authority planning. In the following
decade, there was a groundswell of change. The battle lines had been
declared and at the vanguard of the Māori Renaissance were the Māori
protest movements in the late 1960s and early 1970s. This movement
culminated in the introduction of the Waitangi Tribunal in 1975 and the
launching of a number of environmental/cultural claims. These claims
sought redress from infrastructure projects based on expansionary fiscal policy that impacted on iwi/hapū responsibilities to protect *taonga*,
such as rivers, lakes, harbours, and foreshore (Waitangi Tribunal 1988,
1989a, 1989b, 1992). At the heart of this renaissance were claims such
as Motunui–Waitara, Kaituna River, Manukau Harbour, and Mangonui,
all in response to cultural food source concerns, pollution, water quality,
and increasing scarcity of resources. The tribunal declared the schemes
were contrary to the principles of the Treaty of Waitangi because of
the negative cultural and environmental impacts on natural resources.

The tribunal also found that the Crown had failed to recognize Māori interests guaranteed by the Treaty and that Māori interests (including cultural and environmental aspirations) should have been taken into account. Love (2003) provided evidence to show that the tribunal had a profound effect on how local and central authorities managed New Zealand's natural resources. Waterways, estuaries, and harbours were increasingly seen by local communities less as a sink for sewage disposal and industrial waste and more as a clean environment which provided opportunities to enjoy healthy pursuits, local tourism, and recreational activities such as fishing.

It was not until a legislative review in 1977 that Māori values were finally given formal recognition within planning statutes, particularly the TCPA. In this revised version of the Act, section 3(1)(g) declares that the relationship of Māori and their culture and traditions with their ancestral land is a matter of national importance to be recognized and provided for in the preparation, implementation, and administration of regional, district, and maritime schemes. Soon afterward, Kingi and Asher (1981) developed a Māori planning kit to provide guidance to planners regarding Māori land. Many of the issues highlighted by Kingi and Asher included: *papakāinga* (Māori settlements), ancestral land, protection of *waahi tapu* (sacred lands), and *marae* (meeting places); these and many other issues are continually addressed by Māori today. Also at this time, Anderson (1983) promoted the need for urban planning schemes to recognize and provide for the needs of Māori living in urban areas, especially provision and access to development of urban marae. Anderson's report is one of the earliest calls for greater recognition of Māori voices within an urban setting. While section 3(1)(g) was a significant step towards recognizing Māori values in planning, its initial implementation was found to be quite limited due to the absence of case law (Love 2003).

In 1987, a second consecutive term Labour Government initiated a comprehensive reform of resource management in New Zealand, which was led by the then-Environment Minister Geoffrey Palmer. The intention was to bring together several disparate Acts of environmental legislation under one umbrella. Following major free market reform in NZ, the fourth Labour Government set about merging two seemingly incompatible philosophies: neo-liberal economic ideology and sustainable resource management. Out of the reforms emerged the Resource Management Act (RMA) 1991, a major piece of legislation still in place today and which underpins all urban planning and policy. What was a landmark change was that the RMA included provisions to recognize and take into account iwi and hapū environmental interests under sections 6(e), 7(a), and 8. However, Māori perspectives of the RMA, particularly from iwi/hapū, have commonly differed with interpretations used in local authorities. Tutua-Nathan (2003) stated that before these sections could be effectively implemented, "tikanga Māori has to be understood by local and central authorities, the courts, and the general public" (Tutua-Nathan 2003, 40). A point of contention for Māori is that the RMA uses complex concepts, such as *kaitiakitanga* (sustainable resource management), that are inherently Māori and derived from hundreds of years of close association with the natural environment (Crengle 1993; Kawharu 2000; Love 2003; Matunga 2000; Minhinnick 1989), and redefines and simplifies them from an English common law perspective. Therefore in essence, Māori philosophy and ideology are constrained within the framework of resource management legislation (Michaels and Laituri 1999). According to Tomas (1994, 30), *kaitiaki* (sustainable resource managers) and the exercise of kaitiakitanga as used in the RMA are taken out of context:

> Kaitiakitanga is a concept which has its roots deeply embedded in the complex code of tikanga – the cultural constructs of the Māori world which embody the way Māori perceive the natural world and their position within it. It includes the rules and practices which were the means by which Māori regulated their world. Through its inclusion in the RMA the concept has become divorced from its Māori cultural and spiritual context. It has been redefined in terms of guardianship and stewardship, two terms arising out of feudal England. It has also been reduced from a fundamental principle of Māori society to one factor for consideration among many.

The RMA defines kaitiakitanga as the exercise of guardianship, and includes with it the ethic of stewardship. In effect this fundamental Māori principle has been redefined by the New Zealand authorities to fit into a simplified worldview consistent with English common terms and meanings. Māori lawyer Moana Jackson (1992, 8) comments that

> the process of redefinition continues the attempt by an alien world to impose its will on the beneficiaries of a different world. It captures, redefines and uses Māori concepts to freeze Māori cultural and political expression within parameters acceptable to the state. It no

longer seeks to destroy culture and the word through direct rejection or overt denial, but tries instead to imprison it within a perception of its worth that is determined from the outside ... Those who pursue such goals do not acknowledge the values and validity of that philosophy as understood by Māori in terms of their beginning. Rather they misinterpret it or choose those elements which they believe can be reshaped into a bicultural gloss on the exercise of Pākehā [non-Māori] power.

Tutua-Nathan (2003) notes that while Mātauranga Māori ought to be considered within the RMA process, it must be consistent with the sustainable management priorities as defined by the RMA. Māori planner Hirini Matunga astutely notes that while the RMA acknowledges a Māori planning tradition, it lacks the desire to effectively incorporate and/or integrate a Māori planning approach in any meaningful way. Therefore many Māori perceive their role as kaitiaki as having been diminished under consecutive legislative, their value systems misunderstood and marginalized, and there is much evidence showing ongoing problems in finding ways to effectively integrate Māori perspectives and approaches in decision making and in the management of natural resources (Awatere, Ihaka, and Harrison 2000). Complex issues such as this are being addressed in the Kaitiakitanga of Urban Settlements research program.

OPPORTUNITIES AND BARRIERS TO INTEGRATION

There is a growing realization by local authorities that understanding and implementing Māori perspectives and knowledge can enrich and inform natural resource management decision making. There is also an obligation by local authorities (under the Treaty and RMA) to include Māori in all decision making and take into account Māori values and knowledge in all planning and policy. The degree to which councils recognize and take into account Māori values and knowledge around Aotearoa-New Zealand varies from one place to another. However, much evidence over the last twenty years indicates that there have been very low participation rates by iwi/hapū in local authorities resource management processes (Blackhurst et al. 2003; Whangapirita, Awatere, and Nikora 2003). Also noted is that an understanding of Māori values by resource management agencies in New Zealand is inadequate, and that iwi/hapū capacity to be engaged in council planning and policy, and provide quality cultural information has remained low. These issues of low Māori participation and inadequate understanding of Mātauranga Māori are rooted to a large extent in the differing conceptualizations of sustainable management in New Zealand: i) the neo-liberal approach to sustainability that underpin the RMA (Steenstra 2009), and ii) sustainable management based on Māori ideology (Mead 2003).

The New Zealand planning conundrum is further complicated by the fact that although mainstream planners generally express a willingness to work with an alternative paradigm based on a Māori epistemology, the current legislative framework lacks a meaningful commitment to include Māori perspectives and knowledge. Recent studies have identified several reasons for the lack of implementation by local authorities:

· A lack of understanding of the status that iwi and hapū have through the Treaty of Waitangi and in the RMA 1991 process.
· Local authorities are unclear about the extent to which they should consult with iwi or hapū and also the correct processes they should follow.
· The low capacity of iwi/hapū to participate in local authorities planning and policy.
· A lack of understanding towards the relevance of Māori information/ knowledge to environmental issues and how to use and incorporate that Māori information/knowledge (Blackhurst et al. 2003; Whangapirita et al. 2003).

Whangaparita et al. (2003) found that Environment Waikato's Regional Plan, Annual Reports, Regional Policy Statement and Regional Coastal Plan acknowledged matters of significance to Māori within the region. However, a review of Environment Waikato research reports indicated that there was little acknowledgement of matters specific to *tangata whenua* (local Indigenous people) other than stating Environment Waikato's legal obligation to the Treaty of Waitangi. Blackhurst et al. (2003) found that while many district plans had developed processes for iwi participation, there was little evidence to suggest that these processes had been implemented. This was due in part to the reasons identified above, which included issues of low iwi/hapū capacity and a lack of clarity of the status of iwi/hapū in the resource consent process. Furthermore, a survey conducted by the Ministry for the Environment found that nearly two-thirds (72 per cent) of local authorities staff had inadequate knowledge and understanding of Māori resource management concepts (Ministry for the Environment 1998).

In addition to the well-known implementation issues is the fundamental problem of co-opting Indigenous knowledge into Eurocentric frameworks. Since 1991, Māori philosophy had to be consistent with the sustainable management priorities as defined in the Act (Tutua-Nathan 2003) and therefore Māori philosophy and terminology was tailored to fit within the RMA frameworks and process, often distorting its original meaning. This raises an important issue and challenge as to how to effectively incorporate Māori perspectives and Mātauranga Māori into urban planning and policy without altering the original meaning and conceptual understanding, and to remain true to a Māori worldview, philosophy, and epistemologies. The difference in worldviews from local authorities and iwi/hapū is evident. This power/political interplay is not exclusive to Aotearoa but also occurs in other countries with Indigenous populations. In Canada, for example, the consideration of Indigenous knowledge within environmental decision making has been increasingly promoted and in some cases formalized (see McGregor in this volume). In New Zealand, the strategies to recognize and increase the use and understanding of Indigenous knowledge and integrate it in mainstream systems has faced several barriers, including conflicts with authorities or industry agendas, as well as the co-option of Indigenous knowledge by non-Indigenous researchers and practitioners (Jackson 1992; Tomas 1994; Matunga 2000). In the end, these barriers help maintain a power imbalance that exists between non-Indigenous groups (e.g., industry) controlling power and Indigenous people (Ellis 2005).

Therefore, Māori are very wary of providing their perspectives and knowledge in the wrong forums to the wrong people, and there is often an element of distrust in how Mātauranga Māori will be used and exercized. Agrawal (2002, 204) astutely notes that "once the knowledge systems of indigenous peoples are separated from them and saved, there is little reason to pay much attention to indigenous peoples themselves."

This use of knowledge is a major issue for Māori and one of the main reasons why iwi/hapū groups are so reluctant to share their knowledge and information. For example, in the course of assessing many resource management options and trade-offs as required by the RMA, it is common practice for non-Indigenous groups and economists to seek to convert, quantify, and express human and cultural values as a number, such as a monetary valuation. Placing a financial figure on

Māori values and knowledge is seen typically as insensitive and lacks understanding or acknowledgement of the validity of alternative world views. Māori, and especially iwi/hapū, are more supportive of qualitative approaches that are more consistent with expressing Māori values and knowledge. Again, Agrawal (2002) provides a cautionary note of warning for Indigenous peoples where the pursuit of economic goals is at the expense of other aspirational goals, and insists on the need to be open-minded when trying to rectify power imbalances and inequities. Therefore, understanding the relationships between Indigenous peoples and power structures is essential for improving the lives and imbalances of power for marginalized or Indigenous peoples. Agrawal advocates that Indigenous knowledge can be a pathway and a worthy component to achieve empowerment.

To give effective impetus to kaitiakitanga, the recognition of usage and access rights needs to take place. On the one hand, iwi and hapū can exercise their right as kaitaki based on *mana whenua* (authority over land and resources) status and yet within a bi-cultural context there exist other players, such as businesses, local and central authorities, and other environmental interest groups, each with their own agenda that may or may not conflict with those of iwi and hapū. It is through legislation and policy that rights to act as kaitiakitanga are recognized (Kawharu 2000). Through our experiences as Māori planners, resource managers, and academics, recognition of kaitiaki through local authority policy depends on the actions of those within local authority councils to respond to iwi/hapū taking the opportunity to be involved in resource management at a local authority level. While some local authorities respond favourably and are enthusiastic about the chance to be involved with local kaitiaki groups, other councils are defensive and maintain a distance from iwi/hāpu involvement.

KEY DRIVERS FOR INTEGRATION

There are a number of critical factors or key drivers that enable Mātauranga Māori to be effectively incorporated into urban planning and decision making. These have largely been based on Māori reactions and responses to central and local authorities legislation/policy through many years, and issues of self-determination have always been central to the Māori agenda. In terms of trying to incorporate a Māori voice into planning and policy, Māori have used many means for achieving this and various strategies have been employed: resistance, passive and active, and civil through to hostile. A key driver has been the continuum of Māori activism that commonly exhibits itself as a series of intentional actions to bring about political and social change (Durie 1998; Walker 1990). Petitions to the courts, ongoing submissions, disputes over resource ownership and management, and claims to the Waitangi Tribunal are examples that have challenged the boundaries of planning and policy in New Zealand to include and recognize Mātauranga Māori. Alongside these challenges from Māori has been willingness by some local authorities to understand and effectively engage with Māori. The need for local authorities to engage and recognize Māori values and Mātauranga Māori has been largely driven by the RMA. In response to many relationship and partnership difficulties encountered by local authorities and Māori, the Ministry for the Environment (1998) released a report to help guide local authorities on more effective consultation and engagement techniques. The courts have also given direction on provisions and Māori terms contained in the RMA (Ministry for the Environment 1999) to promote and advance effective engagement and to take into account Māori values. Likewise, rulings by the Waitangi Tribunal with regard to waste-water projects, for example (Waitangi Tribunal 1988, 1989a, 1989b, 1992), have prompted local authorities to consider decision and policy impacts on Māori values, particularly for natural resources such as water.

Guidance for Māori participation in urban planning can be taken from core literature written by Māori authors in response to the RMA (Crengle 1993; Kawharu 2000; Love 2003; Matunga 2000; Minhinnick 1989). We believe that these authors, with an in-depth knowledge of Māori ontology, are best positioned to provide an informed Māori perspective for incorporating Mātauranga Māori into planning and policy. This literature provides iwi/ hapū authorities and local authorities with guidelines for effective engagement with iwi/hapū and also provides a background to understanding how Mātauranga Māori can be incorporated and used in urban planning contexts.

It is important to note that Mātauranga Māori is a dynamic and evolving knowledge system (Mead 2003) and this has implications for the way this knowledge is accessed, understood, and applied. Mātauranga Māori is a blend of Māori knowledge forms, from traditional to contemporary, that are not locked in time or space, but originate from a common traditional source and are expressed as the Māori values we see today, often adapted within a hegemony of Western values. More contemporary forms of Māori knowledge therefore include, for example,

Māori adaptation of low impact urban design features that are more sustainable for papakāinga in an urban context (Rolleston and Awatere 2009). Acknowledgment of these contemporary knowledge forms is an integral part of the process for validating Mātauranga Māori and this process recognizes dynamism and evolution of the knowledge as used in this chapter.

METHODS

The case study approach is an important approach used in this research to collect and document information showing how Mātauranga Māori is used in a real-life and practical context. A multiple-case design was selected for the broader research program. We successfully completed nine case studies showing the incorporation of Mātauranga Māori into urban planning, and the case studies represent a range of scales (from regional spatial plans to landscape design for a greenfields development). They are derived from different geographic locations and respond to different needs and issues in each location. For the purposes of this chapter we present one case study here (Table 10.1).

In using a multiple-case design approach (Yin 2003), we followed a series of steps. The initial step of the design was to develop a grounding or underpinning conceptual theory. The main research question, in line with the original research proposition, was: What are the key elements from Mātauranga Māori that can be incorporated into urban planning that complement and improve existing urban planning practices? This lead to the development of several key research questions:

1 What are the key elements based on Mātauranga Māori that can be incorporated into mainstream urban planning and design?
2 How has the Mātauranga Māori been incorporated in or expressed in mainstream planning? (e.g., what form did it take for a given development/plan/strategy/infrastructure project?)
3 How does the incorporation of Mātauranga Māori vary from place to place around New Zealand? Are there good examples?
4 What are the critical factors that lead to Mātauranga Māori being included in mainstream planning? (e.g., does the degree of Mātauranga Māori expressed in planning depend on the strength of the relationship between local authorities/planners/developers and iwi/hapū/marae, and the Māori individuals involved? What is the level of understanding of Mātauranga Māori by council?)

Table 10.1   Case study: Wigram Skies – *Te Heru o Kahukura*

Name of project	Wigram Skies Subdivision Development, Wigram Aerodrome, South West Christchurch
Location	South West Christchurch, South Island, New Zealand
Developer	Ngāi Tahu Property Ltd (NTP) Property manager: Alan Grove Landscape architect: John Marsh Landscape Architects (JMLA) Engineers: Downer Construction Urban design consultants: Woods Bagot (Sydney) Brand consultants: Harvey Cameron
Mana whenua	Ngāi Tahu (iwi) represented by Te Rūnanga o Ngāi Tahu (Ngāi Tahu Tribal Authority) Ngāi Tūāhuriri (hapū) represented by Te Ngāi Tūāhuriri Rūnanga (Council) Ngāi Te Ruahikihiki ki Taumutu (hapū) represented by Te Taumutu Rūnanga (Council) Ngāi Wheke (hapū) represented by Te Hapū o Ngāi Wheke (Rāpaki) Rūnanga (Council)

5 What are the barriers to uptake and implementation of Mātauranga Māori in urban planning?
6 What strategies and actions are used to ensure uptake and implementation of Mātauranga Māori in urban planning?
7 Can we evaluate (e.g., frameworks and tools; the mauri model, urban sustainability frameworks) and measure the effective incorporation of Mātauranga Māori to meet Māori aspirations and values?

Case studies were therefore selected using the following criteria: their relevance to the research questions; whether they could make an important contribution to the research objectives; on the location of key Māori researchers as part of this program, whether information was currently available; and their ability to present some overall value statements at the micro scale (iwi/hapū) and the macro scale that apply to Māori in general.

Within case studies a series of semi-structured interviews was the primary method of detailed data collection. Interviews were carried out with tangata whenua representatives, property development agents, and local authority staff. These interviews were generally discussion-based. Each case study was supported by key documentation including, for example, relevant plans, technical reports, resource consent material, assessments of environmental impact, cultural impact assessments or advisory reports, branding documentation, landscaping and other design plans, presentations, master plans, and proposals.

Researchers in this program were already actively involved in many urban development projects and had detailed knowledge of engagement processes and uptake of knowledge from a tangata whenua perspective. Therefore, case studies were commonly populated with information from these researchers' own experiences as key members of mana whenua working parties and advisory committees involved in the case study projects. This insider research approach has the benefit of providing a greater level of detail and accuracy in each case study. This detailed insight was added to the information gained from literature reviews and interviews, and has enriched the knowledge base for inclusion in this chapter.

OVERVIEW OF HISTORY AND CONTEXT TO DEVELOPMENT

The Wigram Skies subdivision is a major housing development being undertaken by Ngāi Tahu Property Ltd, a property company owned by the South Island tribe Ngāi Tahu. Ngāi Tahu Property's primary function is to make an economic return for its primary shareholder while adhering to a set of Ngāi Tahu-based values. The subdivision is on the site of the formerly Crown-owned Wigram Aerodrome, which was obtained by Ngāi Tahu in 1995 through the Crown land bank process in lieu of the iwi's 1998 Treaty of Waitangi settlement negotiations and the Right of First Refusal (RFR) provisions provided in their deed of settlement. According to Ngāi Tahu Property (2010, 4): "When complete, Wigram Skies will be home to around 4,000 people and will provide leisure and recreation facilities for Wigram and residents of Christchurch's south west."

Due to its history as an aerodrome and base for the New Zealand Airforce, which still includes the National Airforce Museum, the development planning takes into account both this important element of New Zealand history, as well as the significance of the area to Ngāi Tahu. Historic buildings, including the former observation tower and the Airforce Museum, will remain along with the incorporation of both airforce and Ngāi Tahu history, and values in street and neighbourhood names, landscaping, design, and branding.

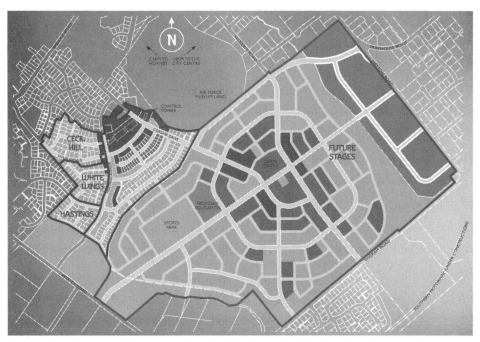

Figure 10.1   Wigram Skies Master Plan
Source: Ngāi Tahu Property Ltd.

Stage one of the development is called Cecil Hills after the first person to make a flight from Wigram and incorporates sixty-two sections
ranging in size from 484 to 780 square metres (Figure 10.1). Sixty of
the sections are zoned "Living One" and will typically be family homes,
while two larger sections are zoned "Living Three" and will likely be
developed as townhouse-style dwellings. Civil works (roads, services,
and drainage) were scheduled to begin in June 2010 and titles became
available in early 2011 (Ngāi Tahu Property 2011). Further stages of
the housing development are subject to a resource consent plan change
(#62) through the Christchurch City Council (CCC) and will be subject
to the CCC South-West Area Plan, which includes policies developed by
mana whenua. The development has also involved the construction of
a major stormwater retention and treatment basin called Awatea, in co-
operation with CCC and Downer Edi Works, to protect and enhance the
values of the Upper Opawaho/Heathcote River.

DEVELOPING POSITIVE RELATIONSHIPS

Developing, building, and maintaining relationships between iwi/hapū, community groups, property developers, and local authorities are essential. While this may even begin as adversarial or conflicting, there is great benefit in achieving a consistent and constant relationship where iwi can be in positions of trust and confidence around key decision making. The Wigram development has provided Ngāi Tahu Property with some valuable lessons for how to work with local iwi/hāpu. From discussions with Ngāi Tahu Property's property manager, Alan Grove, consultation and involvement with local hapū has taken place through a two-pronged process. It seems very little consultation with local hapū was done prior to the original plans being submitted to local authorities for approval at stage one. A change in process at Ngāi Tahu Property in mid-2008 resulted in a desire by the property company to work more closely with local hapū. This positive process helped establish Mahaanui Kurataiao, an iwi/hapū-based organization that helps assist and facilitate mana whenua involvement and consultation with regard to resource management issues.

Discussions were held with Mahaanui Kurataiao in mid-2008 in relation to both the application for a plan change and some discussion around landscape design ideas. This involved a meeting with local mana whenua, as well as a meeting between Mahaanui Kurataiao and John Marsh Landscape Architects to discuss technical aspects of landscaping and appropriate native plant selection. Ngāi Tahu Property also developed a protocol to invite local hapū representatives to sit on a mana whenua advisory committee for the Wigram development. The recognition by local authorities and property developers of the relevance of Mātauranga Māori for contemporary planning is an evolving practice. At the same time, iwi/hapū are allowed the space required to contribute innovative solutions to respond to complex cultural issues in partnership with local authorities/private sector partners.

Relationships are on a number of levels. Local authority relationships are important for macro scale policy and rule-setting (planning). At a micro scale, it is the relationship with the property developer directly that is most critical to what actually ends up on the ground. In response to this critical issue, a new position has been created in partnership between the Office of Te Rūnanga o Ngāi Tahu (the Ngāi Tahu Tribal Authority) and Ngāi Tahu Property to create a position for technical cultural advice on property development. A skilled Ngāi Tahu resource manager has been appointed to this position and started work in June 2010.

Insights from the Wigram case study have highlighted that relationships with property developers are important at a number of critical periods in the development process:

1 pre-lodgement of any application for a permitted activity;
2 post-approved activity, particularly detailed design development, such as landscaping or branding;
3 during construction (blessing ceremony, archaeology, landscaping, waterway protection/enhancement); and
4 opening/implementation (blessing/opening ceremony).

In summary, a positive relationship between local authorities, community groups, developers, and iwi/hapū is more likely to create greater opportunities for Mātauranga Māori to be incorporated into urban planning. Conversely, an adversarial relationship between iwi/hapū and local authorities stymies Mātauranga Māori-based design elements from being implemented.

ACCESS TO QUALITY INFORMATION

All parties, including iwi/hapū, community groups, local authorities, and property developers require quality information in order to make informed and robust decisions. This should be a two-way process of knowledge and information between local authorities and iwi/hapū. Plans, rules, policy, guidelines, and processes play a critical role in influencing outcomes and must be understood by iwi/hapū from the onset. There is a major role for local authorities and property developers to assist iwi/hapū to understand planning information and enable a mutually beneficial outcome.

For the Wigram project, Ngāi Tahu are fortunate to have iwi resource managers with technical expertise in cultural impact assessments. Mahaanui Kurataiao provided a technical review of the cultural impacts of the proposed development on stormwater basins such as the Awatea. The review supported the proposed stormwater design by the developer, as it

has the potential to positively affect Ngāi Tahu cultural values, largely due to the implementation of a ground based stormwater system and the establishment of significant native riparian plants, shrubs and lowland tree species ... [given] that currently there is no such system in place to deal with stormwater coming from surrounding land, which is most likely having a detrimental impact on the river (Pauling 2009, 4).

The technical report also recommended further involvement with stormwater projects adjacent to the Wigram subdivision; provision for cultural use of any materials within the stormwater basins; and that a patch of representative vegetation be established within one of the stormwater basin areas as an alternative to non-native grass.

Mātauranga Māori-based frameworks, methods, and tools can help decision makers actively incorporate, apply, and increase the use of Mātauranga Māori within urban planning contexts. Not all iwi have access to skilled resouce managers so there is a need to better assist iwi resouce managers through the development of a pātaka (or a suite of methods, tools, rules, guidelines, and/or processes. This pātaka could potentially express Mātauranga Māori so that it is easily understood and fits within existing urban planning frameworks. It needs to be flexible and accessible enough to utilize both "quantitative" and "qualitative" tools. This, therefore, reinforces and validates the use of data informed from a Mātauranga Māori perspective, and gives practical application to real-world situations, such as those shown in the Wigram case study.

INNOVATION AND ADAPTABILITY

Mātauranga Māori can offer an important perspective or worldview in the planning process that reflects the dynamism of *tikanga Māori* (Māori processes). Innovation is often sought when an issue is complex and multi-dimensional (e.g., economic, social, cultural, environmental, political) or where there is potential or actual conflict over values and resources. Innovative solutions are required to accommodate the needs and interests of iwi/hapū and help integrate Mātauranga Māori with mainstream planning practice to find win-win outcomes. For example, if there is a shortage of land for accommodating all hapū/iwi members, then medium to high-density housing and papakāinga may provide viable options in cities, as long as it meets certain cultural requirements.

Innovation has also been demonstrated with Ngāi Tahu's response to the branding of the Wigram development. Branding work has been a

Figure 10.2   New logo incorporated into the Master Plan cover
Source: Ngāi Tahu Property Ltd.

key feature of mana whenua involvement, with local Ngāi Tahu artist Priscilla Cowie being involved at the recommendation of Ngāi Tūāhuriri to co-design the logo for the subdivision. Ngāi Tahu involvement in the branding process resulted in a reworking of the original brand logo by Harvey Cameron (Figure 10.2). Input from Priscilla Cowie resulted in a better product from a Ngāi Tahu perspective that for them was more culturally appropriate and grounded with historical references from the area, which drew upon the earlier historical review of southwest Christchurch that was carried out by Ngāi Tahu historian, Te Maire Tau.

To accompany the brand work, Ngāi Tūāhuriri requested that Ngāi Tahu history be incorporated into the development strategy for the Wigram development (Figure 10.3). This resulted in the agreement of mana whenua to the overall Wigram Skies name (Te Heru o Kahukura), neighbourhood names that celebrate the area's history, native birds, butterflies, constellations, and the prevailing winds using Ngāi Tahu names and street names that incorporate and remember aviation history.

Wigram Skies

Wigram Skies has been chosen as the name for the new community being built on the site of the former Wigram Aerodrome. The name reflects the land's history as a flight school, and an air force base, along with the owners' (Ngāi Tahu) vision for the future and the creation of a vibrant community in consultation with the Air Force Museum names have also been short-listed for the neighbourhoods and streets. It is hoped the streets will be named after aircraft, the first 100 students at the Canterbury Flight School, and other air force-related themes. The neighbourhood names will celebrate the area's history, native birds, butterflies, constellations and the prevailing winds using Ngāi Tahu names where possible.

Te Heru o Kahukura

The raukura (feather) depicted in the 'Wigram Skies logo draws reference to the vast Canterbury skyline and the long association Wigram has had with flight. In particular the various forms within the raukura acknowledge the cultural significance of this area to local Māori heritage by referencing a number of local wāhi tapu and wāhi taonga. The heru is a sign of prestige and honour and has been referenced in the Wigram Skies logo as acknowledgement of one of the local waterways known historical as Te Heru o Kahukura.

The heru is suggestive of a traditional comb (heru) used to adorn the topknots of high ranking people. The three koru figures represent three significant wāhi tapu, associated with the Wigram Skies landscape: Ō-Te-Ika-i-te-Ana, Ō-Tū-Matua and Mānuka.

Ō-Te-Ika-i-te-Ana was a large village settlement (pā) occupied by Ngāi Tahu right up until the late 19th century and was used by those hunting and gathering local resources (mahinga kai), including kiore (native rats), koreke NZ quail, tutukiwi (NZ snipe), aruhe (fern root) and tuna (eels).

Ō-Tū-Matua is the spur just above Halswell where an alter (tāahu) was located traditionally and used by the resident tribes to both forecast weather and perform the rituals appropriate to preparing for seasonal mahinga kai activities.

Ō-Tū-Matua is also important as it was used in evidence before the 1868 Native Land Court and the 1879 Smith-Nairn Commission as a boundary marker between the 1848 Canterbury Land Purchase and the 1856 Akaroa Land Purchase.

Mānuka is the name of a large Ngāti Māmoe pā that once stood in a strong defensive position at the foot of the hills not far from Tai Tapu. It was eventually stormed and captured by the Ngāi Tahu chief Te Rakiwhakaputa during his rampage of the Whakaraupō / Lyttelton harbour area.

For further information please refer to **wigramskies.co.nz**

(Cultural information contained in this report is taken from the Cultural Values Report prepared for the South West Area Management plan.)

Cecil Hill – the first neighbourhood

The name of Wigram Skies' first neighbourhood will commemorate the man who made the very first flight at Wigram, on May 7th 1917. Cecil Hill was the chief instructor at what was then the Canterbury Flying School, training airmen for World War One and the Royal Flying Corps. The historic flight was made in a Caudron bi-plane. Sadly, Cecil Hill was killed just two years later when his plane crashed while he was performing aerobatics over Riccarton racecourse. (Image courtesy of Christchurch City Library).

Smooth progress

The earthworks in the Awatea Basins, a cooperative project involving Christchurch City Council, Downer EdI Works and Ngāi Tahu Property, are progressing well, according to Ngāi Tahu Property Development Manager Alan Grove. "We've had a really great run with the weather in April and early May and we're right on target."

"Our Stage 1 site filling project is going well too," Mr Grove says the three organisations have worked together very effectively to achieve a fantastic long term outcome. The basins have been partly hydro-seeded to get a quick, consistent grass-cake before winter and Mr Grove says it's now possible to get an idea of what the area will look like when finished. Planting is to begin shortly.

First sections about to go on sale

The first 62 sections of Wigram Skies, the old Cecil Hill neighbourhood, are due to go on sale shortly.

The sections range in size from around 464 to 780 square metres and will be accessed via extensions to Sioux Avenue and Mustang Ave.

They are adjacent to existing housing at the north-west boundary of the new community. 60 of the sections are zoned Living 1 and will typically be family homes.

Two larger sections are zoned Living 3 and will likely be developed as townhouse style dwellings.

Civil works (roads, services and drainage) are scheduled to begin in June and titles will be available in early 2011.

14th May 2010

What are the Awatea Basins?

Once complete, the Awatea Basins will be a landscaped, park-like area, open to the public at the southern end of the former air base. But they also perform an important function – providing storm water control for the area around Awatea Road and helping reduce flooding in the Heathcote River.

24th February 2010

Figure 10.3   Wigram Skies June 2010 newsletter showing the use of tangata whenua history

Source: Ngāi Tahu Property Ltd.

DEVELOPING IWI/HAPŪ CAPABILITY

There is an opportunity to build technical capacity for iwi/hapū resource managers or planners. Why? Because iwi engagement must be professionally based and seen by local authorities and property developers as providing expert "cultural" advice in the same light as engineers, landscape architects, ecologists, and other experts. There is a need and a challenge to produce high quality cultural assessments that are well researched and mandated by iwi/hapū. The likelihood of high quality feedback is greater if expert "cultural" advice is well resourced and consistently involved in the property development process.

For the Wigram case study, Ngāi Tahu have demonstrated that they have technical capability to provide both culutral and specific technical advice/services and review on particular aspects of the property development. The ability of Ngāi Tahu to provide this technical advice was aided by adequate resourcing from the developer and local authorities to mana whenua throughout the duration of the development process.

Iwi management plans, cultural impact assessments, and other forms of cultural assessment and reporting are critical, particularly prior to the property development process. The elements that are required to smooth the process for mana whenua feedback include being provided with ample time, space, and freedom to research and express opinions in a safe environment, and most critically, at the expense of the property developer or local authorities. This highlights an opportunity to build technical capacity for iwi/hapū resource managers or planners.

CONCLUSION

The key to successful implementation of kaitiakitanga in urban settlements is positive relationships between iwi/hapū, property developers, community groups, and local authorities that have beneficial outcomes for all involved. Establishing meaningful relationships is just the first step in considering the role of tangata whenua in urban planning. Māori participation in the planning process has increased dramatically since the enactment of the RMA. However, Māori continually challenge local authorities and property developers to ensure values such as kaitiakitanga are adequately captured and represented in urban planning development.

Integration of Mātauranga Māori into urban planning and development is more than just window dressing or a superficial display of

Māori art. It runs deeper than this; it includes the aesthetic, such as Māori art, but it also looks at how urban planning and development respond to environmental concerns. Property developers and local authorities ought to consider the environmental aspirations iwi/hapū have for urban environments. These aspirations are diverse and span from water quality, Indigenous biodiversity, cultural heritage, and sustainable energy use, and go beyond the erection of *pouwhenua* (carved posts) and Māori art-stylized buildings. Furthermore, Mātauranga Māori is context-specific and it would be naive to identify generic elements of Mātauranga Māori that can be applied in urban planning throughout Aotearoa. However, what we have found is that there are certain elements and processes that if adhered to can lead to the effective incorporation of Mātauranga Māori into urban planning. A genuine attempt at recognizing kaitiakitanga in urban development will consider the worldview of iwi/hapū together with the sustainability goals of local authorities.

GLOSSARY

hapū	subtribe
iwi	tribe
kaimoana	seafood
kaitiaki	sustainable resource managers
kaitiakitanga	the ethos of sustainable resource management
mana whenua	authority over land and resources
marae	meeting place
Mahaanui Kurataiao	a Ngāi Tahu resource management agency
Mātauranga Māori	Māori knowledge
mauri	life essence
Ngāi Tahu	a principal Māori tribe of the south island of New Zealand
papakāinga	Māori settlements
Papatipu Rūnanga	a Ngāi Tahu Area Council
pātaka	storehouse
pouwhenua	carved posts
tangata whenua	local Indigenous people
taonga	something valued
tikanga Māori	Māori processes
urupā	burial ground
waahi tapu	sacred lands

REFERENCES

Agrawal, A. 2002. "Indigenous Knowledge and the Politics of Classification." *International Social Science Journal* 54 (173):287–97.

Anderson, R. 1983. *Planning for Māori Needs*. Auckland: Town & Country Planning Division, Ministry of Works and Development.

Awatere, S., M. Ihaka, and D. Harrison. 2000. *Tangata Whenua Perspectives of Wastewater. A Report Prepared for the Gisborne District Council*. Gisborne: Gisborne District Council

Blackhurst, M., M. Day, T. Warren, N. Ericksen, J. Crawford, and S. Chapman et al. 2003. *Iwi Interests and the RMA: An Evaluation of Iwi and Hapū Participation in the Resource Consents Processes of Six District Councils*. University of Waikato, Hamilton: The International Global Change Institute (IGCI).

Booth, J. 1963a. "The N.Z. Māori Council Begins its Work." *Te Ao Hou The New World* 43 (June):1.

– 1963b. "The N.Z. Māori Council Some Important Issues." *Te Ao Hou The New World* 44 (September):51.

Crengle, D. 1993. *Taking into Account the Principles of the Treaty of Waitangi: Ideas for the Implementation of Section 8, Resource Management Act 1991*. Wellington: Ministry for the Environment.

Durie, M.H. 1998. *Te Mana, Te Kawanatanga: The Politics of Māori Self-Determination*. Auckland: Oxford University Press.

Ellis, S.C. 2005. "Meaningful Consideration? A Review of Traditional Knowledge in Environmental Decision Making." *Arctic* 58 (1):66–77.

Hauraki Māori Trust Board. 2003. *Whaia Te Mahere Taiao a Hauraki: Hauraki Iwi Environmental Plan*. Paeroa: Hauraki Māori Trust Board.

Huakina Development Trust. 1993. *Waikato Iwi Management Plan: Manuka*. Hamilton: Huakina Development Trust.

Jackson, M., G. Oddie, and R. Perrett. 1992. "The Treaty and the Word: The Colonisation of Māori Philosophy." *Justice, Ethics and New Zealand Society*, 1–10. Auckland: Oxford University Press.

Kawharu, M. 2000. "Kaitiakitanga: A Māori Anthropological Perspective of the Māori Socio-environmental Ethic of Resource Management." *Journal of the Polynesian Society* 109 (4):349–70.

Kingi, P., and G. Asher. 1981. *Māori Planning Kit*. Auckland: Auckland Māori Planning Committee.

Love, M. 2003. "Resource Management, Local Government, and the Treaty of Waitangi." In *Local Government and the Treaty of Waitangi*, edited by J. Hayward, 21–37. Oxford: Oxford University Press.

Matunga, H. 2000. "Decolonising Planning: The Treaty of Waitangi, the Environment and Dual Planning Tradition." In *Environmental Planning and Management in New Zealand*, edited by P.A. Memon and H.C. Perkins, 36–47. Palmerston North: Dunmore Press.

Mead, H.M. 2003. *Tikanga Māori: Living by Māori Values*. Wellington: Huia Publishers.

Michaels, S., and M. Laituri. 1999. "Exogenous and Indigenous Influences on Sustainable Management." *Sustainable Development* 7 (2):77–86.

Minhinnick, N. 1989. *Establishing Kaitiaki: A Paper*. Auckland: Nganeko Kaihau Minhinnick.

Ministry for the Environment. 1998. *He Tohu Whakamārama: A Report on the Interactions Between Local Government and Māori Organisations in Resource Management Act Processes*. Wellington: Ministry for the Environment.

– 1999. *Case Law on Tangata Whenua Consultation*. Wellington: Ministry for the Environment.

Ngāi Tahu Property. 2010. Wigram Skies Newsletter, June. Retrieved from http://www.wigramskies.co.nz/news/27-newsletter-june-2010.

– 2011. White Wings brochure, May. Retrieved from http://www.wigramskies.co.nz/wigram-past-and-future.

Pauling, C. 2009. *Technical Review of Cultural Impacts for the Awatea Stormwater Basin*. Mahaanui Kura Taiao.

Rolleston, S., and S. Awatere. 2009. "Ngā Hua Papakāinga: Habitation Design Principles." *MAI Review* 2:1–13.

Statistics New Zealand. 2006. *Quikstats about Māori*. Wellington: New Zealand.

Steenstra, A. 2009. "A Case Study of Accommodating Indigenous Cultural Values in Water Resource Management: Privatization and Co-management." *Indigenous Policy Journal* XXI (2).

Tomas, N. 1994. "Tangata Whenua Issues: Implementing Kaitiakitanga under the RMA." *New Zealand Environmental Reporter* July:39–42.

Tutua-Nathan, T. 2003. "Kaitiakitanga: A Commentary on the Resource Management Act 1991." In *Local Government and the Treaty of Waitangi*, edited by J. Hayward, 39–42. Auckland: Oxford University Press.

Waitangi Tribunal. 1988. *Report of the Waitangi Tribunal on the Mangonui Sewerage Claim (WAI 17)*. Wellington: The Tribunal.

– 1989a. *Report of the Waitangi Tribunal on the Manukau Claim (WAI 8)*, second edition. Wellington: The Tribunal.

– 1989b. *Report of the Waitangi Tribunal on the Motonui – Waitara Claim (WAI 6)*, second edition. Wellington: The Tribunal.

– 1992. *Report of the Waitangi Tribunal on the Kaituna River Claim (WAI 4)*, second edition. Wellington: The Tribunal.

Walker, R. 1990. *Ka Whawhai Tonu Matou: Struggle Without End*. Auckland: Penguin.

Whangapirita, L., S. Awatere, and L. Nikora. 2003. *Māori Perspectives of the Environment: A Review of Policy Submissions Made by Iwi to Environment Waikato*. Hamilton, New Zealand: Māori Psychology Research Unit, University of Waikato.

Yin, R.K. 2003. *Case Study Research: Design and Methods*, third edition. London: Sage Publications.

11

Urban Aboriginal Planning: Towards a Transformative Statistical Praxis

CHRIS ANDERSEN

Although Aboriginal peoples often present ourselves publicly to non-Aboriginals in terms of our cultural difference, and while Canada positions itself as a paragon and defender of multicultural diversity, our policy relations are marked by a tension between Canada's officially stated multicultural policies on the one hand, and on the other its unwillingness or (more generously) inability to live up to its stated liberal ideals. In this context, separate but related fields of scholarship have explored the normative implications of living in a nation-state faced with the seeming contradiction of positioning itself (and being positioned) within the global community as a beacon of tolerance and understanding while failing to live up to such principles with the Aboriginal peoples who live in territories it has claimed for itself, either in letter or practice (for discussions on the tension between liberalism and Aboriginal issues in Canada, see Coulthard 2008; Tully 1995; Kymlicka 1995; Turner 2006).

While such normatively based discussions are legitimate and have produced important arguments for reframing existing relationships between Aboriginal collectivities and the rest of Canada, they tend to suffer from a common flaw. Namely, they tend to take place at a high level of abstraction with little discussion about the practical contours of such a reframed relationship. In particular, aside from their use as a form of rhetoric in underscoring existing disparities between Aboriginal and non-Aboriginal citizens – usually positioned in terms relating to socio-economic indicators – this literature contains little discussion about the role of statistics in any new relationships. This is puzzling not least because statistics constitute the pre-eminent modality and technology through which Aboriginal social relations are rendered amenable to official social policy intervention and they likewise represent the principle modality through which Aboriginal/social service delivery organizations make claims to government policy-makers.

This chapter will stake out an argument for the role of statistics in the creation of an interventionist (as opposed to simply normative) agenda for reframing the urban policy relationships between Aboriginal people and the Canadian state through a specific consideration of the role of statistics in mediating this relationship. This chapter takes seriously Walker's (2008) argument that urban authorities must engage in "transformative planning" without waiting for such an ethos to trickle down from more authoritative levels of government, and that such transformative planning will, in an Aboriginal context, require identifying and implementing strategies that transform structures of oppression that "[inhibit] people's ability to actualize their aspirations based on their own assessment of needs and feelings, resulting from structural and systemic constraints" (Walker 2008, 23). An argument will be made for what transformative statistics might look like in municipal practice and how they can fit into larger policies of intervention in the lives of urban Aboriginal residents.

The task is undertaken in three major parts. Part one discusses the nearly ubiquitous role of statistics in our everyday lives and in particular, in framing the policy relationship(s) between Aboriginal communities and the Canadian state. Part two will then briefly lay out the notion of and need for a transformative urban agenda rooted in the notion of equitable relations wedded not to an appreciation of Indigenous difference but Indigenous density. This includes a discussion of how many of us understand Aboriginal authenticity, how we might more broadly conceive it in terms relating to a respectful interface of self-determination, and the implications this has for popular and policy-specific understandings of Aboriginality. Part three offers a prescriptive discussion for how statistics might provide for a richer policy understanding of urban Aboriginality, in all its density, by accounting for two contextual elements: (1) the distinctiveness of an urban identity; and (2) the specificity of these collective identities by city. I begin, however, by underscoring the ubiquitous importance of statistics to modern Aboriginal life.

PART I: STATISTICS IN THE MODERN WORLD

As in virtually all nation-states across the globe, statistics hold a place of nearly unquestionable objectivity and power in contemporary Canadian society. Our daily routines are so saturated with and ordered through statistical calculations that we rarely notice their presence. Nonetheless, statistics are crucial to the running of a modern nation-state. A doyen of the governmentality literature initiated by Michel Foucault's (1991 [1979]) musings on the changing nature and exercise of power in modern forms of governance, the work of Nikolas Rose (1999, 196–7) distinguishes between four roles played by statistics in contemporary democratic nation-states, three of which are of particular relevance here. First, statistics' apparent objectivity anchors the fair apportioning of political power in that the number and placement of our parliamentary seats are partly rooted in statistical information about the demographics of election ridings. Second, statistics operate as a form of political and corporate stethoscope: though election seasons in particular are awash in opinion polls, public authorities and private corporations employ statistics on a regular basis to "take the pulse of the nation," whether to sell a product or to elicit information about the general feeling on any number of issues deemed of policy importance.

Third, and more abstractly, Rose (1999, 196–7) argues that statistics are crucial to the efficient and effective governance of modern societies (and liberal societies in particular) in that far from simply recording information that already exists, they actually render arenas of social life "imaginable" and thus amenable to policy intervention and they allow us to judge its success. When we hear government officials making a request for evidence about a particular topic or issue (e.g., homelessness, part-time work, domestic relationships), the evidence called for is almost always statistical in nature and is, at a baseline level, required by government authorities to "look" at a particular public issue in a way that allows for policy intervention. Likewise, since liberal conceptions of governance are based in ensuring that intervention into the "private" or "social" aspects of life is efficient and not too overbearing, statistics render the messiness of complex, local social relations into a form amenable to standardization and thus allow for a scepticism linked to accountability (Rose 1999, 197).

Though seemingly abstract, understanding and positioning statistics in this light has important policy implications. Statistics are not merely tools or forms of rhetorical power used to support debating positions – their contemporary ubiquity plays an integral role in how authorities understand and act upon social relations in a national context. "Numbers, like other 'inscription devices,' actually constitute the domains they appear to represent. They render them representable in a docile form – a form amenable to calculation and deliberation" (Rose 1999, 197).

In an important sense then, statistics render social relations "real" to governmental policy intervention and, moreover, they both presuppose and reproduce the legitimacy of what Curtis (2001) has positioned as "authoritative communities," like those of government. In other words, the authority and technical expertise of such agencies is not natural, but is instead the result of more than a century of labouring to produce "object-subject" agreement between the information sought and the social relations intervened upon. Since authorities generally only intervene into the social world in ways supported by (what is considered) solid evidence, statistics offer a seemingly technical/non-political modality through which such evidence can be collected and acted through and upon.

This is an important problematic in the context of the largely naturalized structures of power that characterize governance in colonial countries like Canada. Despite a virtual vacuum of such Canadian studies, the more general issue of "racial minority" participation in population construction has received much attention elsewhere. Such scholarship has pointed out the relationships between the formulation of statistics (through the census) and the reproduction of colonial orders (see Anderson 1991; Cohn 1996, 1985). And, if standardized, categorization is crucial to modern, synoptic state-building processes, a key category employed in standardization in a colonial context is that of race. In Canada, as elsewhere, historical racial taxonomies were produced without Indigenous input. Perhaps predictably, they tended to reflect the biological "truths" favoured by colonial scientific understandings of human difference (see generally Hall 1997; Said 1993; Young 1997).

Kertzer and Arel (2002) argue that Indigenous involvement in the creation, collection, and interpretation of statistics pertaining to Indigenous issues represents a key political site around which Indigenous collectivities should mobilize and through which they should attempt to legitimize their collective selves in colonial nation-states. Indeed, "bottom up" research (2002, 30) emphasizes the contingent and deeply political character of statistics and thus its positioning by minority interest groups (whether national, ethnic, or linguistic) as a privileged techno-representation of cultural politics and identity formation (see Arel 2002; Urla 1993). Though thoroughly saturated in colonial rationalities, in other words, statistics (whether through the census or similarly authorized instruments) are too important to ignore in the struggles for decolonialism/self-determination and require input from all levels to ensure as representative a statistical configuration as possible.

Although statistics are widely indicted for their central role through which colonial rationalities intervened into the lives of Aboriginal communities and their members, an important question nevertheless arises. Given its colonial genealogy, why does statistical evidence constitute such a key element of Aboriginal relationships with the Canadian state and how might we evaluate the validity of such information/knowledge? Given that most government agencies involved in the creation, collection, and dissemination of statistics gear their intellectual labour towards the technocratic production of robust data, little official documentation or public discussion exists on the innumerable interpretive decisions required to successfully produce a statistics cycle. As such, although statistics are every bit as contingent and arbitrary as competing forms of social power (e.g., media analysis or public commentary, to name but two of many), they retain a privileged place of objectivity in modern society accorded few other forms of power. But how do we know that statistics "work"? Or perhaps more analytically, how can we evaluate their utility in ways that allow us to step outside of conversations about their technocratic sophistication and statistical accuracy, and emphasize instead the conceptual boundaries through which such information is created, counted, analyzed, and disseminated? Curtis (2001, 35) suggests two ways.

First, "the criteria adopted for evaluating census-making should be found in the character of the social relations themselves." In other words, statistics must possess considerable "intersubjective agreement" between those collecting the information and those offering it, both in terms of categories created and the actual conditions of social relations *and* the willingness of enumeratees to offer up such information (which, in Canada, does not currently include all Aboriginal communities). After more than a century of authoritative interpretative labour on the part of Statistics Canada and Aboriginal Affairs and Northern Development Canada (the two governmental agencies most heavily involved in the creation, collection, and dissemination of statistical information on "the Aboriginal population"), the existing categories of Aboriginal "identity" through which virtually all Aboriginal policy is produced – "Indian"/ First Nations, Inuit, and Métis – enjoy nearly the same ubiquity as the statistics that originally created and solidified them in our policy imagination. Although this is addressed further in the chapter's second part, suffice it to say for now that these categories limit the ways we can talk about the complexity of contemporary Aboriginal realities in Canada, a fact particularly salient for the relationship between urban municipal planning and Aboriginal communities.

Second, and closely related to the first point of intersubjective agreement, Curtis (2001, 35) maintains that since not all statistical configurations of social relations are created equal, different configurations offer "different practical possibilities for intervention and administration" and as such, "the worth of census data is related to the projects in whose service they are enlisted." This is a crucial epistemological point because it allows us to solve an apparent paradox; that is, it allows us to think about how existing statistical configurations can be both completely technically accurate and yet completely *in*adequate for measuring the changing social relations of Aboriginality. I will explore this in more depth in part two, but here I want to suggest that it is not a technocratic evaluation of existing statistical configurations that needs to take place but rather, a conceptual one. All research, whether quantitative or qualitative, relies on interpretative labour and decisions at key points throughout its process. Statistics, no less than ethnography or archival research, is only produced in light of such labour and such interpretation. As I discuss in more depth next, modern interpretations of authentic Aboriginality tend to position it in terms relating to both its cultural and its socio-economic difference. This profoundly shapes our ability to discuss issues relating to Aboriginal policy intervention in a manner that does not reproduce the long-toothed statistical categories currently in place.

PART 2: FROM INDIGENOUS DIFFERENCE TO DENSITY
IN URBAN POLICY

In recent years, increasing theoretical attention has been paid to the notion that while often operating on such a premise, urban planning is not, nor has it ever been, value-neutral (Peters 2005; Walker 2008).[1] Rather, steeped in decades (if not centuries) of Western ideals, values, and practices, urban planning has effectively excluded ethnic minorities from the core dynamics and outcomes of such processes. While our prior ownership separates Aboriginal communities from the positioning of these minorities (see Maaka and Fleras 2005; Walker 2008), urban Aboriginal residents and our communities have nevertheless experienced similar marginalization. Indigenous difference, in this sense, has long been positioned as an element to be overcome or eliminated, rather than

something positive deserving of accommodation. More generally, both
Peters (2005) and Walker (2008) point to the value of more respectful relations of urban planning with Indigenous communities, a respect
that must, they suggest, account for this difference, or at least labour to
ensure its accommodation rather than its eradication (Sandercock 1998
in Peters 2005, 328). Peters (2005, 328) suggests that such accommodation produces "a city/region in which there is a genuine connection
with, and respect and space for, the cultural other, and the possibility of
working together on matters of common destiny, a recognition of intertwined fates" (Sandercock 1998, 125 in Peters 2005, 328). That is, as
Walker (2008) states, Aboriginal presence can and should be considered
a municipal asset.

The idea that urban planning must make a more concerted effort to
incorporate or respect difference from a Euro-Canadian norm (a larger
element of a multicultural policy ethos; see Day 2001) is increasingly
reflected in literature pertaining to urban Aboriginal communities and
urban social service delivery in Canada's cities. In Canada, researchers
have increasingly begun to challenge the ways in which existing policies miss the mark for understanding the specificity of urban Aboriginal communities to the extent that they are insufficiently cognizant of
Indigenous difference. Most specifically explored in the context of health
and other social services, research has attempted to examine the extent
to which service providers are able/willing to account for the distinctive
needs of their Aboriginal clientele. DeVerteuil and Wilson (2010, 498)
refer to this as the need for "reconciling Aboriginal special status with
the realities of non-Aboriginal urban welfare states" in the context of the
cultural-appropriateness of these services defined as "services that create a social environment that observes and respects the cultural beliefs
and practices of the individual receiving services" (Trudeau 2008, 682 in
DeVerteuil and Wilson 2010, 498). Likewise, Cardinal (2006, 219–20)
positions urban Aboriginal community distinctiveness in terms of social
sustainability, arguing that future Aboriginal communities will offer key
contributions to urban sustainability in terms of demographics, governance and political involvement, culture, and relations of equity.

Cardinal's (2006) assessment of the current state of research on the
social conditions of urban Aboriginal people in particular potentially
allows for an opportunity to think more broadly about the complexity of these social conditions. However, his own research lapses into
an analysis pegged to a rhetoric of Indigenous difference through his
use of a "traditional medicine wheel" approach to his research: "By

incorporating traditional Aboriginal beliefs, the medicine wheel provides a culturally relevant way to identify indicators, and utilizes a holistic, unifying concept to overcome the fragmenting effect of individual indicators that often segregate singular effects or impacts" (Cardinal 2006, 220). In this context, he purports to explore, in "the four directions," the physical/economic, spiritual/cultural, emotional/social, and mental/environmental balance of the Vancouver urban Aboriginal community. Not surprisingly, his findings indicate that quality of life indicators in all areas/directions were depressed – in some cases significantly – vis-à-vis those of their non-Aboriginal neighbours. While perhaps distinctive for the extent to which his focus targets the messiness of existing policy practices in a specific city (Vancouver), Cardinal's (2006) research none-theless remains rooted in a respect for the distinctive needs (positioned as cultural) of the Vancouver region's Aboriginal community.

A second type of difference also marks relations between Aboriginal and non-Aboriginal planners. While not specific to the urban context, this difference nonetheless marks relations in that context. Here I am referring to difference as articulated in the supposed quality of life gap between Aboriginal and non-Aboriginal citizens. Canadian governing rationalities were anchored in the assumption that Aboriginal society was not evolutionarily equipped to compete with the complexities of civilization (now terminologically evolved into apparently less odious euphemism "modern life"), and as such, Aboriginal policy was predicated either on absorbing "the Indian problem" into the Canadian body politic in the assimilationist era, or to correct the problems that existed in Aboriginal communities to "bring them up to speed," in the integrationist era. Such assumptions were rooted in the similar assertion that contemporaneous Aboriginal ways of life were developmentally delayed – the only difference in policy rationality was related to how to correct it. Such positioning of Aboriginal people was characteristic of urban policy as well – Peters (2005) shows how the urban Aboriginal literature from the 1970s onwards portrayed urban Aboriginals in terms of their developmental gaps, moving only from assumptions of cultural incompatibility to socio-economic gaps.

Walker (2008) and Peters (2005) argue that despite municipal planners' tendency to lump Aboriginal residents and ethnic minorities into a similar policy basket of problems and issues, the problematic of prior occupancy/ownership make such comparisons fraught. Indeed, Walker (2008) argues that relationships between local Aboriginal communities and urban planners must take place in a context of respect, which keys off the recognition of this prior presence as a key normative plank for engaging in policy planning relationships with the local communities. Both Walker (2008) and Peters (2005) clearly mean these relations of respect to offer accommodation for the distinctive needs of the community, as derived from respectful interactions and "fact-finding" engagements with them. Having said that, both argue that urban Aboriginal policy will vary by city such that the practice of self-determination in an urban context cannot be understood in a "one size fits all" paradigm.

Peters (2005) and Walker (2008) are persuasive in their positioning of self-determination in an urban context and their arguments offer important insights for how we can think through the normative implications of municipal-Aboriginal engagement, whether in terms of a respect for cultural difference or developmental gaps. However, we can push the conceptual traces of their argument further to argue that a respect for self-determination should include not simply respect for such differences, but rather, a respect for density (see Andersen 2009). Denis (1997, 83) presents this distinction in terms useful for thinking through the complexity of urban Aboriginality: "It is not so much difference that matters, as separateness – and indeed, wanting to self-govern expresses a will to be separate, autonomous, whether or not you want to do things differently than your neighbour." Denis's notion of "separateness" is a crucial corrective to a focus on difference because it offers a form of conceptual autonomy that allows for the creative position-takings forced upon us by our resistance to and incorporation of colonial rationalities and intervention strategies, and likewise, does not require us to continually demonstrate difference from whitestream normativity as a basis for collective authenticity.

My more general point is that our Indigeneity is far denser than discussion of our difference allows. As such, a policy emphasis rooted in difference potentially carries with it important conceptual truncations. If, as Denis (1997) suggests, the complexity of our historicity is denied through our positioning by whites as "different," this is accomplished practically according to a series of binary oppositions that supposedly (re)affirm a hierarchical relationship of white superiority and Indigenous inferiority (whether through a comparison of governing systems, spirituality, land tenure, or labouring practices, to name but a few). Likewise, a focus on our difference tends, like most stereotypes, to reduce and fix our Indigeneity in both space and time. Such reduction produces a register of authenticity within which historical social relations are positioned at the high watermark while contemporary positionings, such as our increasing location in urban centres, is understood as a partial vestige of that earlier authenticity. A focus on our difference, in other words, not only inhibits a complex recounting of our history and the massive impact of Canadian state intervention into the lives of Aboriginal community members, it reduces the likelihood of public recognition of our modernity and in such cases, casts policy discussions in cultural (i.e., "different") rather than political (i.e., "separate") terms.

At least as a matter of logic, positioning the importance of self-determination in terms of a respect for Indigenous density or complexity rather than difference carries no such baggage. It encourages a proliferation of subject positions and tensions through which Aboriginality is produced and practiced, and it requires no such reliance on demonstrating how our lived experiences differed/differ from those of the non-Aboriginal communities we live/d alongside (though surely they did and do). In the context of offering a "critical africentricity," Gayles (2008, 154–5) argues for a discipline within which "we see the promise of an approach that does not privilege a collective past at the expense of a dynamic understanding of and response to current realities. Such an approach better enables us to actively and organically respond to the world as it is, is becoming, and will be."

In a policy context, while it is naïve to think we can sweep away the conceptual detritus of a focus on difference simply by imagining ourselves more complexly, formally acknowledging the complexity of contemporary Indigeneity has important consequences for how it permits us to imagine Aboriginal policy issues as well as the solutions we deem useful to remedy them. More specifically, it enormously increases the conceptual space of Aboriginality through which we might imagine and practice the "interface" referred to by Walker (2008), and the extent to which Aboriginality may be understood as an asset to the entire city rather than just to Aboriginal peoples who live in a city.

It must be noted, however, that such a conceptual complexity is rendered difficult in practice not only by the fact that non-Aboriginal urban planners have come to position Aboriginality in terms of our difference, but the fact that over the past three decades, social service delivery models, institutions, and practitioners have done so as well. As I pointed out, insofar as a burgeoning literature has tended to critique existing social service delivery models for their lack of "cultural appropriateness," they have tacitly failed to recognize as legitimate the full spectrum of Aboriginal subject positions that dot the lived experiences of urban Aboriginal communities. Ultimately, the overemphasis on Indigenous difference (in academic terms in particular; probably less so in policy practice) does little justice to this larger complexity, and in doing so, runs the very real risk of rendering itself parochial in the face of the existing density of social relations that characterizes urban Aboriginal life. The Ontario Urban Aboriginal Task Force, for example, has demonstrated how the service delivery emphasis of urban Aboriginal communities in Ontario holds the potential to marginalize middle-class Aboriginal residents who fail to use such services (see UATO 2008). In light of my focus on complexity rather than difference, and further, in light of positioning complexity rather than difference as a mark of respect for self-determination, the chapter's third part will address conceptual issues around what a transformative statistical configuration could study, how it differs from configurations currently offered, and how we might work towards its institutional inculcation as a form of praxis.

PART 3: WHAT WE SHOULD BE MEASURING, WHY, AND WHAT IT WOULD LOOK LIKE IN PRACTICE

To put it bluntly, researchers in the field of urban Aboriginal issues still do not know far more than we know about urban Aboriginal policy and the density of nested experiences that comprise urban Aboriginality. Issues about regional variation; program and policy sustainability; needs versus rights-based evaluations; nuanced, geographically distinctive data; long-term evaluations of existing policies, etc.: all of these still possess far more questions than answers. Moreover, in addition to the fact that to date this field has not yet drawn the weight of intellectual labour or the funding characteristic of more long-standing fields of study, Aboriginal communities (urban included) can be among the most challenging of research environs, an attribute that will shape future research relations and ultimately, the forms of knowledge about and characteristics of such community dynamics.

However, as it currently stands most statistical information relating to urban Aboriginal issues – certainly, that which extends across the country and that which is circulated most widely in public forums – is constructed through exactly the same categories as those used for on-reserve Aboriginal policy issues. This seems reasonable at first blush – existing statistics demonstrate that urban Aboriginal communities are beset by the same (if not quite so extreme) quality of life disparities as our non-urban counterparts (see Peters 2005), and insofar as this is accurate, simply cross-tabulating existing data by census metropolitan area location provides access to another level of data through which to imagine Aboriginal social relations from a policy perspective, as well as allowing for comparison across regions. On the other hand, and the Royal Commission on Aboriginal Peoples' (1996) emphasis notwithstanding, urban Aboriginal communities are distinct and growing: certain configurations of power are specific to urban locales that render unlikely the likelihood of understanding this density through categories created in the context of on-reserve colonial administrative policies more than a century old. Existing statistical categories and definitions only *seem* effective or accurate because part of their power lies in the fact that we understand and position them as objective, neutral, and corresponding to an underlying reality, rather than as being rooted in particular assumptions about the social relations being examined and intervened upon, and as such, conjuring up partial elements of their complexity in the very act through which they are positioned as *im*partial and objective accounts of those relations.[2]

What makes urban Aboriginality distinctive that warrants more nuanced statistical configurations than those currently employed? Elsewhere I lay out in detail the elements of urban Aboriginality I think are distinctive and an extended explanation for why (see Andersen 2013). For our current purposes, let me simply list them with the proviso that laundry lists are not a particularly sophisticated way to explore collective identity. Nonetheless, the twelve elements of urban Aboriginal identity I explored included: (1) the specific context of urban economic marginalization; (2) an emerging middle class; (3) racism/social exclusion from whitestream society; (4) cultural diversity; (5) legal diversity; (6) "status blindness"; (7) a policy coordination vacuum; (8) informal networks; (9) distinctive urban Aboriginal institutions; (10) struggles over political representation; (11) attachments to non-urban communities; and (12) the public power of Aboriginal women. While these elements are schematic and certainly not exhaustive, they represent important "nodes" for tracing the relations of power within which distinctive urban Aboriginal identities have emerged.

Beginning with the assumption that existing statistical configurations are insufficient for capturing the density of urban Aboriginality, how might we go about conceptualizing a transformative statistical framework in such a manner that allows us to step outside both the "lesser than"/deficit and "different than"/cultural paradigms that currently hold sway in the Aboriginal policy world? I suggest two statistical configurations with attendant processes of construction rooted in the transformative ethos discussed by Walker (2008): (1) an *Aboriginal Peoples Survey – Urban Supplement*, and (2) city-specific municipal input (whether statistical or not) constructed according to processes produced by its urban Aboriginal community members. Both efforts bear witness to the distinctiveness of urban Aboriginal identity and the more recent findings (i.e., Andersen and Strachan 2011; Peters and Starchenko 2005) that Aboriginal policy relations and communities vary greatly by city, such that interventions successful in one city might, for this reason, fall flat in another.

Urban Aboriginality as a National Object of Governance

Regarding the formation of a national statistical configuration dedicated to respecting the density of urban Aboriginal experiences, policy intervention into urban Aboriginal communities has largely been produced in the absence of government recognition of urban Aboriginals *qua* urban Aboriginals. That is to say, intervention has rarely taken place in the context of positioning urban Aboriginality as a distinct object of governance – it has instead been positioned in the context of provincial residency or a presumed developmental gap shared with a larger object of governance (whether homelessness, job training, domestic violence, or child welfare, to name but a few). This has produced a litany of well-documented effects highlighting the utter lack of policy coordination produced by three generations of jurisdictional "hot potato" (see Graham and Peters 2002). Treating urban Aboriginality as a distinctive form of governance is not without its challenges (not least of which are the numerous points of jurisdictional wrangling around political representation) but it is a worthwhile discussion to have, nonetheless, because status-quo relations simply are not working.

Over the past two decades, Statistics Canada's administrative knowledge of Aboriginality has expanded beyond simple cross-tabulations of socio-economic indicators with main long-form questionnaire indicators of Aboriginality. This has been accomplished in three contexts: through the Aboriginal Peoples Survey (APS), the Aboriginal Children's Survey (ACS), and the First Nations Regional Health Survey (RHS). The APS, conducted in 1991, 2001, 2006, and 2012 on a sample of more than sixty thousand Aboriginal people, provided a wide range of information of policy interest to federal, provincial, and municipal governments. Likewise, the ACS is predicated on the social fact that half of all Aboriginal people in Canada are comprised of children and youth, and was sponsored largely by Human Resources and Social Development Canada and based on a sample of more than eighteen thousand Aboriginal children. The RHS was produced in association with Health Canada and, although predicated rhetorically upon a respect for the essential difference of First Nation communities, has collated data very similar to that collected under the APS and ACS.

Regarding the APS, Statistics Canada delivered the post-censal Aboriginal Peoples Survey for the first time in 1991 as a means of gaining more detailed information on the social and economic conditions of Aboriginal people in Canada. They suggest the data is important for providing a more detailed picture of current conditions, but also to "honour and acknowledge cultural values and diversity."[3] As of the 2006 census, three specific supplements existed which could be delivered in one of at least eighteen different Aboriginal languages: a "Child and Youth Supplement" (youths aged 6–14); a "Métis Supplement"; and an "Arctic Supplement." Currently, StatsCan offers only an Education and Employment Questionnaire. These supplements each asked a variety of in-depth questions relating to education, language, labour activity, income, health, community technology, mobility, and housing. Each survey also asked questions specific to that supplement. The child and youth supplement queried demographics, general health, health care utilization, daily life and medical conditions, injuries, dental care, nutrition, education, social activities and relationships, language use, and household data. The Métis supplement asked questions relating to family background, child welfare, social interaction, and health. The Arctic supplement gathered information on household and harvesting activities, personal wellness and community wellness, and social participation (see APS 2006a, 2006b, 2006c). Finally, the Education and Employment Questionnaire queried off-reserve First Nations, Métis, and Inuit.

The Aboriginal Children's Survey was delivered for the first time in 2006. The ACS focused solely on children between the ages of 0–5 in three different contexts: a general child survey; a "James Bay Cree Supplement"; and a "Northern Children Supplement." The main survey and its supplements offered questions pertaining to child health, food and nutrition, sleep, developmental milestones (0–2 years of age and 3–5 years of age), nurturing, school (for 4–5 years of age), child care, language use, strengths and difficulties, learning and activities, and parent profile. The questionnaires each ran to some sixty pages in length and asked hundreds of questions pertaining to numerous facets of early child development and health. The additional point worth thinking about from a policy context is that both the APS and the ACS asked numerous questions and collect-detailed information on activities, behaviours, feelings, and contexts otherwise unattainable (see ACS 2006a, 2006b, 2006c).

What would an "Urban Supplement" look like? Certainly, while some of the features listed in the previous section either exist in or may be derived from existing data (socio-economic status, an emerging middle class, legal and cultural diversity, and geographical mobility), many are absent. And although I would not presume to present detailed questions to comprise an urban supplement here, we might nonetheless think about its final formulation through one or both of the two consultation processes already utilized by Statistics Canada in the context of formulating the Aboriginal Peoples Survey and the Aboriginal Children's Survey. The APS included extensive consultations and discussions with five of the six national Aboriginal organizations (i.e., Métis National Council, Inuit Tapiriit Kanatami, Native Women's Association of Canada, National Association of Friendship Centres, and Congress of Aboriginal Peoples), as well as with regional partners. The Aboriginal Children's Survey, in contrast, was constructed through a technical advisory group comprised of experts on the various subject matters whose guidance assisted in formulating the eventual questions used to collect policy-relevant information. Aboriginal service providers deemed both surveys largely satisfactory. Given the city-specific character of Aboriginal demographics and community power relations, however, a national statistical instrument is unlikely to capture the density of urban Aboriginality specific to each urban locale.

City-Specific Statistical Configurations

The second prescription for a more transformative statistical configuration is grounded strongly in recent literature that has emphasized the city-specific elements of urban Aboriginal identity. Andersen and Strachan (2011), Peters and Starchenko (2005), and Maxim et al. (2003) have all demonstrated distinct differences not only in demographic characteristics (population size, cultural diversity, proximity of First Nations) but also distinct policy configurations with specific policy histories. Little research has been undertaken to comparatively examine city-distinctive statistical configurations. However, the little research that does exist would seem to validate this line of investigation. For example, in their comparison of Winnipeg with Edmonton, Peters and Starchenko (2005) found marked differences in residential patterns. While the population sizes were relatively equal, Winnipeg's Aboriginal residents were far more residentially segregated than those living in Edmonton. Underscoring their statistical data, Peters and Starchenko interviewed key informants from both cities to understand these surprising differences and found that residential patterns were a result of a combination of provincial and municipal residential policies that either allowed for the clustering of low-cost rental housing (as in Winnipeg) or made a concerted effort to provide "mixed housing" areas (as in Edmonton).

To provide a slightly more recent example, in 2007 and 2008 several academics involved in a SSHRC Major Collaborative Research Initiative undertook research examining the contours of urban Aboriginal policy in several selected provinces.[4] My research team and I were responsible for Alberta, and in this context we examined the policy relations of four cities: Edmonton, Calgary, Fort McMurray, and Cold Lake. Chosen for their mix of size (large and small) and for their differences in Aboriginal demographics, we interviewed various policy delivery informants to explore the distinctiveness of Aboriginal policy relations by city and indeed, found evidence of extremely distinct, city-specific policy making and program planning. Part of this distinctiveness is a function of city size. Small cities like Cold Lake and the municipality of Wood Buffalo (one tenth of the size or smaller of Calgary and Edmonton) are not merely mimicking larger cities on a smaller scale. Existing policy-making and policy delivery infrastructures in smaller cities are simply too small to do much more than act as referral agencies to other, larger cities.

However, we concluded that city-specific policy relations, which I would argue here can be extended to a discussion about the distinctiveness by city of urban Aboriginal communities are, in addition to city size and Aboriginal demographics, a result of the now-intergenerational lack of coordination among urban Aboriginal policy-makers at all levels of government. Over the past four decades, this has fostered a policy climate within which city-distinctiveness rose to the fore more often and more intensely than it might otherwise have. Moreover, depending on a combination of factors, including the diversity and efficiency of policy actors operating in this vacuum, it might enormously impact the "look" of Aboriginal communities and populations over time. How might we capture some of this city-specific distinctiveness in statistical form? Should it even exist in statistical form or is more ethnographic information required at the local level to shape the construction of the statistical configurations at an official national level?

Whatever information-gathering technique decided upon is ultimately less important than the relations involved in its creation. National post-censal surveys like the Aboriginal Peoples Survey or the Aboriginal Children's Survey possess the financial and technical capital to carry out extensive consultations with Aboriginal communities, service providers, and national Aboriginal organizations. Most Aboriginal policy-delivery communities, however, do not possess this kind of "in-house" expertise and statistics can be bewildering to someone not technically equipped to interpret them. Dunning et al. (2008) argue that much can be gained from employing a "mixed-method" approach of both quantitative (i.e., survey-based) and qualitative (interview or ethnographic) methods. It may well be that more ethnographic or interview-based questions at the city level can build in a more reflexive statistical configuration at the national level, though, given the importance of time-series analysis, changing or adding questions to national surveys is both methodologically- and cost-prohibitive. Thus, city-specific grounded research would need to take place prior to the implementation of national surveys.

Taking seriously Graham and Peters' (2002) suggestion that only the federal government has the symbolic and material resources to bring to bear in a way that will exert a meaningful impact on urban Aboriginality as a policy field, perhaps a way exists to dovetail local objectives with existing policy silos. Probably the most focused point of federal intervention into urban Aboriginal communities as a specific object of governance has been through the Urban Aboriginal Strategy (UAS), administered by Aboriginal Affairs and Northern Development Canada (AANDC). The UAS has been in existence for about a decade and most recently was carried out under the auspices of the then-Office of the Federal Interlocutor for Métis and Non-Status Indians (OFI), part of AANDC. The stated basis of the UAS is to improve the social and economic opportunities of urban Aboriginals in targeted cities (which have been expanded over the past decade). Through partnerships with provincial and municipal governments and community and various (though importantly, not all) Aboriginal organizations, the UAS focuses specifically on the improvement of life skills, job and entrepreneurial skills, with a specific emphasis on supporting Aboriginal women, children, and families (Urban Aboriginal Strategy 2005) with an eye for building self-reliance and increasing life choices for urban Aboriginals.[5] The UAS has a five-year, 65-million-dollar funding cycle, and is aimed at thirteen different cities: Vancouver, Prince George, Lethbridge, Calgary, Edmonton, Prince Albert, Regina, Saskatoon, Winnipeg, Thompson, Toronto, Thunder Bay, and Ottawa.

Importantly, the focus of the UAS is not on unilateral implementation of policy, but rather on operating as a leverager of and coordinator for municipal, provincial, and federal efforts. Its main goal, in other words, is to "encourage and utilize existing horizontal funding mechanisms and would be aimed at obtaining increased provincial engagement, not federal program enhancement."[6] Regarding the latter issue of interdepartmental coordination, the UAS suggests that its explicit focus on horizontalization is particularly useful

> where existing terms and conditions limit the ability for departments and agencies to work together in a coordinated fashion. This can result in program duplication or programs being more provider-centric rather than actually responding to community realities and can also result in projects not proceeding or can create overly complicated delivery mechanisms and reporting requirements for recipients.[7]

While the success of the UAS has been uneven across cities, it has worked well in Calgary and, though in a slightly more challenging policy ethos, in Edmonton as well. Part of the process of this horizontalization in Edmonton has been the creation of *Wicihitowin: Circle of Shared Responsibility & Stewardship*, "a community-driven model of an urban governance process that is inclusive of the many Aboriginal peoples and the agencies that serve them in Edmonton."[8] The Wicihitowin process, partnered with the city of Edmonton's Aboriginal Relations Office, the province of Alberta's Aboriginal Relations Ministry, and the then-Indian and Northern Affairs Canada's Office of the Federal Interlocutor for Métis and Non-status Indians, has produced a number of "action circles," one of which is a Research Action Circle. This process might offer an appropriate mechanism through which to produce local knowledge about Aboriginal social relations within a specific city.[9]

Assuming that the urban Aboriginal community in any given city is in favour of a local statistical profile, several options exist for producing robust, reflexive statistical configurations with fidelity to the complexity of local social relations and conditions. One option is to take the route of hiring one of a growing phalanx of consulting agencies (Aboriginal or otherwise) that specialize in such information gathering. *Environics* (2010) recently completed a national, city-specific survey on urban Aboriginal issues and could no doubt fashion something more distinctive to a specific city that might be "slotted" into a larger national configuration (like an Aboriginal Peoples Survey). However, in many cities a second, often less expensive option exists, which is to partner with the local university. Many universities possess both the expertise and the infrastructure to undertake such a task. In Edmonton, for example, the University of Alberta Population Research Centre has undertaken data collection for the Alberta Métis Settlements and could no doubt do so in an Edmonton city survey. Other cities have their own relationships with university-based institutes. In the end, the pursuit of intersubjective agreement and practical utility should guide any efforts to come to terms with the distinctiveness of urban Aboriginal identity and/in its city-specific modalities, whether this takes the form of grounded ethnographic or focus groups or statistical configurations (in the form of city-specific surveys).

CONCLUSION

By way of conclusion, let us return to Walker's (2008) discussion of "transformative planning." Walker asks urban planners to account for and collaborate with Aboriginal community members to produce policy relations more respectful of Aboriginal self-determination (however it might look in any particular city). As Walker states, transformative planning requires the strengthening of respectful relations between Aboriginal citizens and city hall while accounting for the complex sets of dynamics that often characterize the ground between these two locales. The challenges of traversing such territory notwithstanding, he argues that such efforts are crucial to instilling a practical respect of the self-determination of Aboriginal communities, whose presence predates that of other urban residents, often by centuries.

This chapter extends Walker's (2008) insights about valuing Aboriginal self-determination and in particular his emphasis on a respect of Aboriginal difference. More generally modelled by other scholarship as manifesting itself in terms of the cultural appropriateness of Aboriginal social service delivery programs, this constitutes a necessary step in constructing a more equitable relationship between Aboriginal communities and all levels of government (not just that of municipal policy planning). The inevitable translation of respect into respect for difference, however, brings with it conceptual baggage that limits the kinds of policy imaginaries within which the relationship of Aboriginal communities and municipal planning may be conceived and acted upon. I have instead offered a more conceptually autonomous basis of density as the modality through which the relations of self-determination might be constructed and planned within. How existing urban Aboriginal social relations, institutions, and actors, with their (over) emphasis on social service delivery models (themselves rooted in cultural appropriateness), are likely to receive such a positioning is hard to tell. Nevertheless, it is a point worth making.

In the end, normative assessments notwithstanding, more sustained consideration must be accorded to the practical elements of policy intervention. This chapter offered such practical considerations in the central role played by statistics in the construction of Aboriginal "problems," usually wedded to some deficit model, and their solutions, usually wedded to a model of cultural appropriateness. While "statistics" are ubiquitous in modern society, their lack of nuance and current inability to account for the complexity of urban Aboriginality make them ill-suited to serve as a policy basis for respectful relations between urban Aboriginal communities and municipal planners. Any respectful relationship must entail more than a normative awareness of this prior presence (with attempts to incorporate that social fact into contemporary relationships); it should also extend to practical considerations about providing a nuanced basis for evidence at both a national and a more local level. Statistics offer a strong comparative basis for understanding trends across time and place but the little existing scholarship on urban Aboriginal communities demonstrates that they differ greatly by the distinctive characteristics of the city, the demographic size and dynamics of its Aboriginal community and the now-intergenerational history of its policy relations. Thus, city-specific statistics or, failing that, more ethnographic relations constructed to produce a clear picture of an urban Aboriginal community's desires will provide a more complex and comprehensive account of these social relations. If respectful, transformative planning is to take place at a level other than lip service, and if statistical configurations continue, as they surely will, to constitute the primary modality through which municipal planners and urban planners interface in a policy context, better evidence of existing social relations will assist greatly in this transformation. Indeed, it must constitute both the basis and the eventual product of such a transformation.

NOTES

1   I note here that although the reference is to Peters 2005, Ryan Walker co-authored this chapter of the larger monograph.

2 In New Zealand, Māori scholar Mason Durie and others (2005, 2002, 1995) have developed similar lines of analysis in relation to Māori health and well-being indicators.

3 "Aboriginal Peoples Survey (APS)" – retrieved on 17 May 2010 from http://www.statcan.gc.ca/aboriginal/aps/5801794-eng.htm#faq2.

4 This research was conducted under the funding and auspices of a Major Collaborative Research Initiative entitled "Multilevel Governance and Public Policy in Canada," housed at the University of Western Ontario under Dr Robert Young. For more information on this grant, please see http://www.ppm-ppm.ca/.

5 "Terms and Conditions – Urban Aboriginal Strategy Contribution Program" – retrieved on 17 May 2010 from http://www.ainc-inac.gc.ca/ai/ofi/uas/tnc-eng.asp.

6 Ibid.

7 Ibid.

8 Retrieved on 17 May 2010 from *Wicihitown – A Shared Circle of Responsibility and Stewardship* – http://wicihitowin.ca/

9 I say "might" rather than "will" because the process is constructed in the context of short-term funding and is anchored in an emphasis on Aboriginal difference like that critiqued in part one that may complicate the exploration of the density of urban Aboriginality in Edmonton. Still, it offers some promise.

REFERENCES

ACS (Aboriginal Children's Survey). 2006a. *Aboriginal Children's Survey.* Statistics Canada.

– 2006b. *Aboriginal Children's Survey – James Bay Supplement.* Statistics Canada.

– 2006c. *Aboriginal Children's Survey – Northern Children's Supplement.* Statistics Canada.

APS (Aboriginal Peoples Survey). 2006a. *Aboriginal Peoples Survey.* Statistics Canada.

– 2006b. *Aboriginal Peoples Survey – Arctic Supplement.* Statistics Canada.

– 2006c. *Aboriginal Peoples Survey – Métis Supplement.* Statistics Canada.

Andersen, C. 2009. "Critical Indigenous Studies: From Difference to Density." *Cultural Studies Review* 15 (2):80–100.

– 2013. "Urban Aboriginality as Distinctive, in Twelve Parts." In *Indigenizing Modernity: International Perspectives on Urban Indigeneity*, edited by C. Andersen and E. Peters. Vancouver: UBC Press.

Andersen, C., and J. Strachan. 2011. "Urban Aboriginal Programming in a Coordination Vacuum: The Alberta (dis)Advantage." In *Urban Aboriginal Policy Making in Canadian Municipalities*, edited by E.J. Peters, 127–59. Montreal and Kingston: McGill-Queen's University Press.

Cardinal, N. 2006. "The Exclusive City: Identifying, Measuring, and Drawing Attention to Aboriginal and Indigenous Experiences in an Urban Context." *Cities* 23:217–28.

Cohn, B. 1985. *An Anthropologist Among the Historians.* Delhi: Oxford University Press.

– 1996. *Colonialism and Its Forms of Knowledge: The British in India.* Princeton: Princeton University Press.

Curtis, B. 2001. *The Politics of Population: State Formation, Statistics, and the Census of Canada, 1840–1875.* Toronto: University of Toronto Press.

Day, R. 2000. *Multiculturalism and the History of Canadian Diversity.* Toronto: University of Toronto Press.

Denis, C. 1997. *We Are Not You: First Nations and Canadian Modernity.* Peterborough, ON: Broadview Press.

Deverteuil, G., and K. Wilson. 2010. "Reconciling Indigenous Need with the Urban Welfare State? Evidence of Culturally-Appropriate Services and Spaces for Aboriginals in Winnipeg, Canada." *Geoforum* 41 (3):498–507.

Durie, M. 1995. "Te Hoe Nuku Roa Framework: A Māori Identity Measure." *Journal of the Polynesian Society* 104 (4):462–70.

– 2005. *Ngā Kāhui Pou: Launching Māori Futures.* Wellington: Huia Publishers.

Durie, M., B. Stevenson, E. Fitzgerald, T. Kingi, and S. McKinley. 2002. *Māori Specific Outcomes and Indicators: A Report Prepared for Te Puni Kōkiri.* Palmerston North: Massey University.

Dunning, H., A. Williams, S. Abonyi, and V. Crooks. 2008. "A Mixed Method Approach to Quality of Life Research: A Case Study Approach." *Social Indicators Research* 85:145–58.

Foucault, M. 1991 [1979]. "Governmentality." In *The Foucault Effect: Studies in Governmentality*, edited by G. Burchell, C. Gordon, and P. Miller. London: Harvester Wheatsheaf.

Gayles, J. 2008. "Anthropology, Afrocentricity, and African American Studies: Toward a Sincere Discipline." *Transforming Anthropology* 16 (2):147–59.

Graham, K., and E. Peters. 2002. "Aboriginal Communities and Urban Sustainability." Discussion paper F/27: Family Matters. Canadian Policy Research Networks Inc. (CPRN).

Hall, S. 1997. *Representation: Cultural Representations and Signifying Practices.* London: Thousand Oaks/SAGE.

Kertzer, D., and D. Arel. 2002. "Censuses, Identity Formation, and the Struggle for Political Power." In *Census and Identity: The Politics of Race, Ethnicity, and Language in National Censuses*, edited by D. Kertzer and D. Arel, 1–42. Cambridge: Cambridge University Press.

Kymlicka, W. 1995. *Multicultural Citizenship: A Liberal Theory of Minority Rights*. London: Oxford University Press.

Maaka, R., and A. Fleras. 2005. *The Politics of Indigeneity: Challenging the State in Canada and Aotearoa New Zealand*. Dunedin: University of Otago Press.

Peters, E. 2005. "Indigeneity and Marginalisation: Planning for and with Urban Aboriginal Communities in Canada." *Progress in Planning* 63 (1):327–404.

Peters, E., and O. Starchenko. 2005. "Changes in Aboriginal Settlement Patterns in Two Canadian Cities: A Comparison to Immigrant Settlement Models." *Canadian Journal of Urban Research* 14 (2):315–37.

Rose, N. 1999. *Powers of Freedom: Reframing Political Thought*. Cambridge: Cambridge University Press.

Said, E. 1993. *Culture and Imperialism*. New York: Knopf.

Tully, J. 1995. *Strange Multiplicity: Constitutionalism in an Age of Diversity*. Cambridge: Cambridge University Press.

Turner, D. 2006. *This Is Not a Peace Pipe: Towards a Critical Indigenous Philosophy*. Toronto: University of Toronto Press.

Urla, J. 1993. "Cultural Politics in an Age of Statistics: Numbers, Nations, and the Making of a Basque Identity." *American Ethnologist* 20:818–43.

Young, R. 1995. *Colonial Desire: Hybridity in Theory, Culture and Race*. London and New York: Routledge.

Walker, R. 2008. "Improving the Interface Between Urban Municipalities and Aboriginal Communities." *Canadian Journal of Urban Research* 17 (1) Supplement:20–36.

12

Coexistence in Cities: The Challenge of Indigenous Urban Planning in the Twenty-First Century

LIBBY PORTER

It is now well established that Indigenous claims and interests have a profound and potentially transformational effect on planning in post-colonial states. Such challenges are the stuff of restless debate and difficult practical choices in those settings. No longer relegated to the invisibility and silence of marginal colonial space, Indigenous people have struggled their way through to the table and achieved recognition and justice.

Or have they? In many ways, this appears to be so: court decisions, new legislation, and policy guidance are reframing the relationship between states and Indigenous peoples, affording the latter greater power and influence. Australia's Native title regime, for example, puts "coexistence" front and centre in debates about how to reconcile the ongoing processes of land colonization with recognition that pre-existing rights, title, and law continue to thrive in practice. Changes to Canada's Constitution Act 1982 formally recognized Aboriginal rights and title, and court cases such as the Sparrow case (*R. v. Sparrow* [1990] 1 SCR 1075) have affirmed the Canadian state's duty to Aboriginal rights.

Such forms of recognition are also reconstituting the field of planning, defining new stakeholders for planners to consult with, or, in some cases, requiring an entirely different planning approach. The biggest shift has occurred in natural resource management, environmental, and protected area planning. There is a wealth of scholarship in this field either documenting such shifts or taking a critical perspective (see, for example, Jaireth and Smyth 2003; Stevens 1997; Lawrence 2002; Birckhead,

DeLacy and Smith 1992; Lane and Corbett 2005; Lane and McDonald 2005; Lane and Williams 2008; Porter 2007), and a range of more practice-oriented advice and guidance that has enabled quite different forms of land management and governance (see, for example, Beltran 2000; Baker, Davies and Young 2001).

But what to make of this shift to recognition for Indigenous people who live in cities, and for Indigenous people whose traditional territory is now urban? What effect do the kinds of changes that are reconstituting the relationship between states and Indigenous peoples have in cities? In this chapter, I argue that they have rather less impact and have not been able to sufficiently shake colonial assumptions about where Indigeneity is seen as legitimate: the "impossible contradiction" of urban Aboriginality that Evelyn Peters (1996) noticed years ago remains. We have not yet fully come to grips with what coexistence might look like or mean in urban settings.

This point was rather starkly made for me when I was recently undertaking some research fieldwork in my home of Melbourne, Australia, as part of a larger comparative research project looking at the "contact zone" (Pratt 1991) between planning and Indigenous peoples in both urban and environmental planning settings in Canada and Australia. Trying to understand that contact zone involved me conducting in-depth interviews with both traditional owners of the territory that is now Melbourne, and urban planners in both state and local government. It quickly became apparent that the very substantial shifts that had taken place over the past ten years in environmental planning in Australia had not yet filtered into the urban planning system, which was firmly and utterly silent on Indigenous rights questions. These were just not questions relevant for urban planning, I discovered. I was met with particularly blank looks from urban planners based in local government, even in municipal areas where there were active relationships between the council and local Indigenous leaders. The total lack of engagement between everyday urban planning processes in Melbourne and Indigenous people was deeply striking.

My purpose in this chapter, then, is to take this rather worrying, yet perhaps hardly surprising, field experience and interrogate why Indigenous interests and rights remain much less visible in urban planning and policy practice (and I will argue also in scholarship) than in the fields of natural resource management and environmental planning. I am not setting out to critique the literature on this subject, a scholarship which is robust and growing from many diverse and insightful perspectives.

Instead, I want to explore two related arguments that seem increasingly important for our field. First, the urban context appears to present planning with both conceptual and practical challenges for the idea of coexistence between Indigenous and Western systems, a notion articulated by Peters and Walker (2005). Second, this challenge arises at least in part because we have not yet taken a sufficiently deconstructive stance to planning as a cultural practice itself. The "long shadow" of colonial processes, violence, and dispossession (see Porter 2010) remains a vivid presence for Indigenous people in urban contexts.

In thinking through what Indigenous planning in cities might mean, I will use a broad conceptual framing of the notion of "coexistence." Such a framing draws attention to two things: First, the multiple, conflicting, and relational ways by which we collectively occupy and use space. Second, that it is perfectly possible that different claims about space and place (values, activities, use rights, and political jurisdictions) by different groups can be "held together" in at least a rough and temporary sense, albeit sometimes loose, always changing, and highly contested. Coexistence, then, suggests some possibilities of considerable potential for examining the position of Indigenous claims within cities. One further brief point concerning focus and scope in this chapter: my arguments relate particularly to British settler-states and so the literature from which I draw here and the kinds of reference points I draw on and the vocabulary I use come principally from those contexts. There is a particular emphasis on Australia and Canada as these are where my own research is currently being undertaken.

To begin sketching out these omissions and silences, I want to start with the story of Melbourne, and more precisely, my recent research experience in Melbourne, as it exemplifies the occlusions that concern me. Following from that, I turn to the notion of coexistence and give it some more conceptual definition and clarity. The chapter then offers a characterization of the literature on Indigenous planning in urban contexts and suggests what kinds of developments might now be important to more fully and justly recognize the "persistent footprint" (Howitt and Lunkapis 2010, 110) of Indigeneity in cities.

A BRIEF EXCURSION TO MELBOURNE

The city of Melbourne in what is now the state of Victoria in Southern Australia is built on the lands of three Koorie language clans: the Boon Wurrung, Woi Wurrung, and Watha Wurrung clans (Presland 2010;

Clark 1998). Boon Wurrung language speakers identify with areas which
now make up the southern and southeastern suburbs of Melbourne all
the way down the coast of what is now called Port Phillip Bay (Presland
2010). The Woi Wurrung–speaking clans identify with the northern
parts of what is now Melbourne in the area that was drained by what is
now called the Yarra River and its many tributaries. One particular Woi
Wurrung clan, the Wurundjeri people, were often seen around the early
Melbourne colonial settlement, and the Woi Wurrung language group
is now often simply referred to as "Wurundjeri," so I will use that terminology here. Speakers of the Watha Wurrung language are connected
to areas west of what is now the Werribee River in western Melbourne,
down the other coast of Port Phillip Bay beyond the other major Victorian city of Geelong (Presland 2010). Wurundjeri, Watha Wurrung, and
Boon Wurrung peoples continue to live in Melbourne, and are effecting
some change in planning systems in the city by continuing to assert their
title and aspirations for their traditional country.

The contemporary context in which those Indigenous nations operate,
however, is one that does not easily accommodate Indigenous planning.
Contemporary Melbourne is a massively sprawling, relatively wealthy,
lively city, with a rapidly growing population putting further pressure
on the peri-urban area. Planning debates in Melbourne circulate around
the difficulty of managing growth on the fringes, and the concomitant
difficulty of achieving increased density within the existing urban area.
Relatively unconstrained by natural topography at its fringes, and pres-
sured by recent population growth driven by migration, there is real
capacity for Melbourne to simply keep sprawling outward. Melbourne
is a city experiencing significant development pressure, particularly on
its fringes.

Up until 2006, urban land-use planning of this nature in Melbourne
was utterly disengaged and radically silent on Indigenous interests in
the space that Melbourne occupies. While one can find respectful and
nicely worded statements of recognition of an Indigenous past in some
planning documents, they are always written either in the preface or
on the inside cover, a token of recognition towards what is seen as an
anachronistic and backwards culture. For example, in 2002, the Victorian state government released its metropolitan strategic plan for Melbourne, entitled *Melbourne 2030*, which stated on the inside front cover:

> Since time immemorial, Aboriginal people have cared for this
> land and its natural and cultural resources. This long and unique

association continues today through the Aboriginal communities who live and work in metropolitan Melbourne. Accordingly, the Victorian Government is proud to acknowledge Aboriginal people as the original inhabitants of this land (Department of Infrastructure 2002, iii).

It is worth noting that the most recent update to that plan, *Melbourne@5million*, did not contain even that broad acknowledgement (Department of Planning and Community Development 2008). Such statements are an important gesture, but have little to do with what appears in the policy "nuts and bolts," which of course themselves profoundly affect Indigenous interests. The only reference to Indigenous people within the text of *Melbourne 2030* concerns protection of Indigenous cultural heritage sites.

Where "Indigenous planning" has been developing in Melbourne is through the social welfare model. There are significant efforts to address welfare and social issues such as poverty, homelessness, unemployment, and substance abuse among Melbourne's Indigenous residents, particularly in some inner city municipal authorities. Yarra City Council, for example, an inner city municipality just to the east of the central business district covers some of Melbourne's most rapidly gentrifying districts. Collingwood, one of those inner city neighbourhoods, is also home to a substantial Aboriginal and Torres Strait Islander population, made famous in local singer/songwriter Archie Roach's song *Charcoal Lane*. Yarra City Council appointed an Indigenous community planning officer on a permanent basis to prepare a community plan to address a range of social issues including the marginalization, vilification, and social problems faced by Indigenous people (City of Yarra 2009). Yet the city planning function of the same council has nothing to say about the interface between their jurisdiction and planning responsibility, and Indigenous people.

Where there is some movement in the Melbourne context around the recognition of Indigenous interests in planning and urban development is around cultural heritage protection. In 2006, the Victorian government passed new Aboriginal cultural heritage management legislation that provides considerably greater powers for Aboriginal people to be involved in urban development decision making where it might affect protection of cultural heritage. Under the Aboriginal Heritage Act 2006 (Vic), Indigenous organizations that represent the traditional owner group of an area can apply to become "Registered Aboriginal Parties" (or RAPS) over Aboriginal cultural heritage in that area. RAPS act a little like a planning authority – they are a statutory consultee on the cultural heritage implications of new developments in their recognized area, and have the power to substantially reshape or even limit urban development where they find that Indigenous cultural heritage values are threatened.

Indigenous organizations have to apply to gain RAP status through a government-driven process managed by Aboriginal Affairs Victoria. This involves vetting of governance structures and administrative procedures, as well as establishing that the organization is properly representative of those Indigenous families and individuals that are entitled, in traditional law terms, to control cultural heritage across the territory for which they are seeking recognition. Up until now, this inclusion of Indigenous inter-ests around cultural heritage within planning has been left until the last minute, when cultural heritage inspectors from the RAPS walk in front of bulldozers on development sites to check for archaeological remnants. The legislation assumes "recovery" of artefacts is always possible: when cultural heritage evidence is found the development halts until the arte-facts can be recovered from the site and moved somewhere else.

The new Victorian cultural heritage legislation is critical to ensuring protection, under massive urban development pressure, of archaeo-logical remnants. Yet such recognition is of an extremely limited type, as if Indigenous culture and interests are anachronistic: frozen in a pre-colonial time, and entirely unrelated to property rights, governance, and law. There is little scope for properly recognizing contemporary cultural associations, and no possibility for reconstituting a full recognition of the coexistence of an Indigenous domain about place and its govern-ance alongside the non-Indigenous planning system. A critical issue for Indigenous people is to gain control over resources and have a more significant influence over the institutional processes that shape territor-ial development (Rangan and Lane 2001, 148). A recognition and con-stitution of a legitimate Indigenous presence in planning solely around cultural heritage management falls a long way short of this aspiration. In the next section, I turn to look at this notion of coexistence to explore what conceptual and practical possibilities it might offer.

THE NOTION OF COEXISTENCE

Claims from different groups and a diversity of socio-cultural perspec-tives are nothing new to planning, and to that extent Indigenous plan-ning has often been situated as another "site" or expression of cultural difference for planning (see, for example, and utilizing slightly different contexts, Sandercock 2003; Jackson 1997; Rangan 1999; Porter 2006; Umemoto 2001). Such analyses can expose the impact that planning has on different identity groups, including Indigenous people, and can be insightful in exposing where silences around cultural identity are present within planning. This is important both in theoretical and practical terms not least because it opens up the urgency of creating practical openings and spaces for Indigenous voices to participate more fully in planning processes.

Yet two related challenges arise, both of which suggest that different kinds of conceptual and practical approaches might also be required. First, packaging Indigenous group-based difference and claims as one of many other sites of cultural difference, or interest in planning outcomes and processes, reduce Indigenous interests as merely another form of stakeholder, another "table" to be constituted within the existing pattern and order of decision making. Within planning, this translates into the incorporation of traditional Indigenous knowledge, or consultation and engagement in relatively mainstream ways with Indigenous groups and peoples. Calls for Indigenous self-determination fundamentally challenge this view and expose it as deeply insufficient (see Alfred 1999; Dodson 1994). This is because such approaches ignore the historical fact that Indigenous people never rescinded their own forms of governance to colonial powers. They serve to "tame" Indigenous claims by incorporating those claims into dominant cultural and legal frameworks. This is a very real problem in the politics of Indigenous recognition because, as Laclau and Mouffe (2001) show, every reconfiguration of social relations occurs with reference to "master signifiers." We can see this very simply in the way that Indigenous rights have found expression in national park planning through mechanisms of joint management. The essential foundation of protected area planning, the values of conservation and protection at its core, and the assumptions of appropriate use and development are the framework into which Indigenous joint management partners are often incorporated. This is not to belittle efforts at joint management, merely to indicate that they are always already constituted within a certain cultural framing.

Survival of Indigenous sovereignty in legal and territorial terms is critical here: the particular claims Indigenous people are often making challenge the premise on which Western planning systems assume their spatial legitimacy and authority. Far from being "another stakeholder" or indeed "another ethnicity" to be brought into a planning decision-making forum, Indigenous sovereignty challenges the very premise of that decision-making forum in the first place. This "claim-above-claims" – that Indigenous people constitute a particular kind of actor in relation to planning processes – is situated within, and arises from, historically constituted colonial power relations. We cannot, therefore, simply "add" Indigenous people to the list of stakeholders because the particular constellations and outcomes of colonial violence and power constitute the contemporary rights claims of Indigenous peoples in very different ways. Indigeneity, as Maaka and Fleras point out, is inherently a "politicisation of 'original occupancy' as a basis for entitlement and engagement" (2000, 89).

Second, and related to this, is that the "stakeholder" approach, as it is often applied in practice, tends towards the paternalistic. When Indigenous people are accommodated as another group within planning, their claims are reduced to a needs-based dimension where planning can "service" those needs by simply becoming a neutral provider. It locks the relationship into a paternalistic one of need and service-based outcomes. It also fails to recognize the much more substantive and fundamental challenge that Indigenous claims make to planning, which is the assertion of a substantively different form of property and use rights, knowledge forms, human-environment relationships, and mechanisms of law and governance in relation to space and place.

One of the reasons that Indigenous claims mount such a substantive challenge to planning theory and practice is that they call into question the foundations of Western planning: its conceptualizations of space and place, its understanding of human-environment relationships, and its assumptions about the correct forms of governance and management of both of these things. I have argued elsewhere that such claims also show how planning is itself a culturally constituted mode of being in space, with its own spatial rationalities and desires (see Porter 2010). The nature of Indigenous claims, then, is quite profound for planning: they are about the right to self-determine according to Indigenous cultures and human-environment relationships. In that sense, those rights claims are spatially or territorially substantive in that they are about discrete places. They are also politically substantive in the sense of addressing questions of power, legitimacy, and authority in decision making.

Coexistence as a notion is conceptually and practically helpful, as it potentially offers a way to break through these inherent dilemmas not by reconstituting the Indigenous "Other," but by reframing the relations between Indigenous title law and governance and Western title law and governance. Coexistence might most easily be defined as "sharing space" in more just, equitable, and sustainable ways (see Howitt and Lunkapis 2010) where Indigenous rights can be seen to coexist alongside other rights, both of which are constituted as two or more possible cultural expressions of claims in space and place. The existence of one does not render the existence of the other obsolete. It is in that sense a recognition of multiple and overlapping jurisdictions, as Fleras (2000) conceptualizes, or the "strange multiplicities" that Tully (1995) advocates. Coexistence requires some kind of "rough equality" (Fraser 1995) and a recognition of the other as an equally viable and legitimate party to conflicts about place.

Here we come to the crux of a very thorny post-colonial dilemma: in recognizing the limitations of the "incorporation" approach, or what Tully (2004) would call the "monological mode" of recognition, we see how those "master signifiers" cannot be transcended. And yet simultaneously we see the impossibility of a "return" to a pre-colonial existence. "We are all here to stay" is what the province of British Columbia's *New Relationship* document states, following Chief Justice Lamer's evocative statement in the *Delgamuukw* ruling. How then can we break through oppressive practices even as we recognize the pervasiveness of the "master signifiers" from which they arise and the continued injustice embedded in the very structures of our different ways of "staying"? Coexistence as a notion that embodies the possibility of different modes of being existing right alongside each other offers real possibilities for this difficult dilemma. Like Bill Reid's *Spirit of Haida Gwaii* sculpture (see Tully 1995; Barry and Porter 2012), the notion of coexistence is not one of consensus, but rather one that is comfortable with conflict and the possibility of incommensurability. It does not seek to resolve away the tensions inherent in any post-colonial relationship, but sees that as constitutive of this particular social domain. But perhaps more importantly, it sees the possibility for uneasy points of consensus to be reached and then reconstituted. This is precisely what Mouffe is arguing with her rejection of "post-political" liberalism and her call for renewed recognition that the social field is appropriately conflictual and political (Mouffe 2005).

The language of coexistence is particularly important in the legislative and policy frameworks of Indigenous recognition in many settler-states. It deserves some scrutiny here to see precisely how it works against the more normative ideal I have just set out. In Australia, coexistence was tested in the *Wik* case where the High Court agreed that the Wik peoples' Native title could coexist alongside leaseholder rights (*The Wik Peoples v State of Queensland* [1996] 187 CLR 1). In Canada, the language is one of "accommodation." In the *Haida* decision in 2004, the Canadian Supreme Court held the government responsible for a "duty to consult" and accommodate Aboriginal rights when those might be impacted by a decision (*Haida Nation v British Columbia [Ministry of Forests]* 2004 SCC 73). Coexistence as a legal notion rather shook the establishment, certainly in Australia around the Wik case, yet it is hardly a revolutionary idea. Coexisting rights have long been a feature of the law in places such as Britain where, for example, public rights-of-way express a coexisting right for members of the public to walk across privately owned land. Coexistence in legal and practical terms, then, allows for the recognition and realization of different claims to space, and indeed what might appear to be incommensurable claims.

One of the key problems in these legal frameworks is their tendency to incorporate Indigenous interests into the dominant, culturally hegemonic legal framing of Western property rights. Under Australia's Native title regime, coexisting use and ownership rights are constituted as another form of title recognized through Western legal principles over a defined territory. For planning, they determine the specific bounded areas where Indigenous rights are recognizable to non-Indigenous law, and fix the nature of those rights and the people with whom they are vested. Most importantly, they are often the outcome of negotiation processes that exert significant pressure on Indigenous claimants to give up large swathes of their territory or significant components of their rights in order to achieve a minimal recognition. This is also a charge levelled at the Canadian treaty negotiation process where First Nations often must "trade away" rights and title more generally to secure their interests over much smaller, circumscribed pockets of their territory.

The limitations of these monological modes can be further seen in the recording and legalization of rights and title. Formal expressions of the recognition of Indigenous interests is achieved by government-appointed officials drawing boundaries on maps and the names (people and organizations) who can speak for that area. Mapping and boundary-drawing verify, and hold for all time, the spatial and political extent of recognition. In Australia, for example, the formal process of recognizing Aboriginal and Torres Strait Islander pre-existing rights to their country is through the Native title regime. This landmark legislation, which arose out of the High Court's decision in *Mabo* (*Mabo v Queensland* [No. 2]

(1992) 175 CLR 1), establishes a framework for claims to country to be lodged, heard, and decided by a tribunal. Once a determination has been reached by the National Native Title Tribunal on that claim, and the process often involves a negotiation with other propertied interests in the claim area, the extent of the recognition of Indigenous rights and title in spatial terms is fixed on a map.

Boundary-drawing and mapping define and fix where Indigenous rights "exist" and where they do not. As Howitt and Lunkapis quite rightly point out, the High Court's rather "slippery" notion of coexistence has meant that "Native title could be corralled into spaces that were generally remote from the spaces of urban and regional development" (2010, 114). Yet we know that people-place relationships in Indigenous cultures are not structured in this way, and that customs and cultures pertaining to the rights to use, speak for, and trade within/across territory is not structured like Western legal title, but according to familial and kinship ties, cultural obligations, and the shifting seasonal nature of environmental resources. But the boundaries and the process of mapping them and their political affiliations create certainty that hallmark of a neo-liberal Western planning system. Mapping the spatial and political extent of recognized Indigeneity contains and subdues it, subjecting it to the regulation of other stakeholders within the land development system. It means that planners, land managers, and developers have certainty about where (or not) Indigenous interests reside.

Such forms of coexistence, then, are the very limited, monological modes that Tully (2004) problematizes. Indigenous rights have simply been accommodated into that system as another layer, another boundary, on the title map. Howitt and Lunkapis argue that they "simply render up Indigenous interests as a set of quaint, antiquated echoes of history to be extinguished and (in more generous regimes) compensated" (2010, 110–11). This monological mode of "incorporation," one that accommodates Indigenous interest within the dominant culturally hegemonic framework, works to tame the challenge that those interests gave rise to in the first place. What it means in practical terms is that for Indigenous people to achieve recognition of their land tenure and rights in material ways often results in a highly codified, constrained, and bounded conception of what those rights mean in practice. Monological modes of recognizing coexistence ascribe to Indigenous property rights the characteristics of Western property rights. The spatial extent of the rights are required to be established and made certain (drawing boundaries on the map), the scope and content of the rights are required to be established and certain (land use rights), and the governance of those rights are also required to be made certain (the ascription of particular rights to particular people or families).

Our current models, then, of attempting to "share space" with Indigenous peoples are deeply flawed. They have fallen foul of precisely the conditions that Tully diagnoses and cannot be fixed by tinkering with procedure. Instead, we need a profound rethink of what it actually means to "coexist," and part of this rethink must be a more analytical and deconstructive stance towards planning's own systems of thinking and rationalities about property, place, and governance (see Porter 2010). More importantly, for my task here, what does it all mean in cities? Can cities be places where "coexistence" is possible?

THE SILENCES OF INDIGENOUS URBAN PLANNING

Regardless of what Western legal convention might recognize, cities have a "persistent footprint" of Indigeneity (Howitt and Lunkapis 2010, 110). Cities exist on traditional territory, whether that be "claimable" under non-Indigenous legal regimes or not. Indigenous people whose traditional territory is now urban continue to exert a connection to their country in rich and diverse ways that represent the changing cultural expressions of that connection. Yet we rarely grapple with what it means to recognize coexistence in cities and the kinds of challenges – conceptual and practical – to which such recognition gives rise.

In this section, I want to look at the difference between what can be seen as two rather separate literatures about Indigenous planning in the urban and environmental domains. My purpose here is not to undertake a systematic analysis of these fields, but simply to sketch out some of the ways in which Indigeneity is framed within the scholarship in urban contexts. This is not constituted as a critique but as a set of questions in order to open out space for more debate and further effort around where planning research and practice might need to develop on the important question of Indigenous rights in urban planning contexts. More precisely, I am asking: Why does the urban literature appear to be so different from the environmental in its conceptual framing of the relationship between Indigenous people and planning? How might we interpret these framings, and how do they matter? Such questions are important for the two related arguments I want to advance in this chapter: first, that the urban context appears to present planning with both conceptual and practical challenges for the idea of coexistence; and second, that this arises at least in part because we have not yet taken a sufficiently deconstructive stance to planning as a cultural practice itself.

There is a very substantive literature addressing the relationship between Indigenous peoples and state-based planning around natural resources, protected areas, or other notionally non-urban spaces and places. This is because protected areas have become key sites in post-colonial contests about Indigenous land rights, and this has subsequently flowed through into the management and planning practices for those places. By way of a brief sketch, that literature includes a substantial deconstruction of the notion of wilderness (see, for example, Cronon 1995; Langton 1996; Palmer 2004, 2006; Lawrence 2002; Spence 1999; Porter 2007, 2010), and a reconstitution of Indigenous rights at the very heart of protected area management and planning (Stevens 1997; Beltran 2000; Jentoft, Minde and Nilsen 2003) as well as natural resource management (Howitt et al. 1996; O'Faircheallaigh 2008, Rangan and Lane 2001). There is also an important field of literature conceptualizing the governance relationships between Indigenous peoples and state-based environmental planning (see, for example, Barry 2011) and scholarship that takes issue in a very critical way with claims that community-based, collaborative initiatives are by definition more progressive and herald more just outcomes for Indigenous peoples (see, for example, Lane and Williams 2008; Lane 2003; Lane and Corbett 2005; Porter 2010). Collectively, these diverse areas of scholarship, all focusing on environmental planning, have progressed understandings of what coexistence means in national parks, forests, coastal management zones, mining areas, and water catchment systems. That work has, most importantly, moved beyond the basic recognition of Indigenous peoples as "another stakeholder" at the planning decision-making table, to a more full appreciation of the differently constituted rights and title that such recognition must also bring. Moreover, there has been a significant shift in practice, such that recognition of Indigenous rights in environmental planning is now, albeit with varying degrees of commitment and success, standard (see, for example, Beltran 2000; Dudley 2008).

There is also a considerable scholarship about Indigenous peoples and cities. Again, my purpose here is not to review this comprehensively, but merely to broadly characterize its various areas of focus. One focus of the literature is to analyze the city as a site of Empire, deconstructing the urban-Indigenous relationship as one characterized by uneven and violent colonial power relations (see, for example, Edmonds 2010; Jacobs 1996; Shaw 2007; Blomley 2004; Stanger-Ross 2008; Anderson and Jacobs 1997; Gale 1972; Anderson 1993; Morgan 2006; King 1990; Harris 2002) with an important planning dimension coming from a Middle Eastern context (Yiftachel 1996; Yiftachel and Fenster 1997; Yiftachel, Goldhaber and Nuriel 2009). A particularly rich seam of scholarship has focused on understanding Indigeneity as cultural difference, raising particular challenges for planners in urban settings (see, for example, Peters 1996, 2007; Wilson and Peters 2005; Jojola 2008; Umemoto 2001; Sandercock 2003). Related to this is a substantive focus on questions of sovereignty, self-governance, or Indigenous governance (Barcham 1998; Barron and Garcea 1999; Todd 2003; Peters 1992, 1995, 2005; contributions to Hylton 1999; Walker 2006a, 2006b). While it is widely recognized that sovereignty and self-government are at the heart of Indigenous politics, there is also a literature that looks at the moments of interface, when Indigenous people are engaged with non-Indigenous forms of governance in urban settings (see, for example, Walker 2008c; Belanger and Walker 2009). On substantive urban matters, there is a literature documenting the many and varied ways that Indigenous people are marginalized and impoverished either within urban settings or by urban processes (see, for example, Cardinal 2006; Graham and Peters 2002; Hanselmann 2001; Peters 2005, 2006; Walker 2003, 2005), and particularly around housing (contributions to Newhouse and Peters 2003; Walker and Barcham 2010; Walker 2008a,b; Peters and Robillard 2007).

This is by no means a comprehensive list; it is skewed towards the literature from those British settler-state contexts which are my focus here, and is only a schematic grouping of themes. As a brief sketch, however, it offers some insight into the scope of the field. It seems that the urban literature is much more constitutive of Indigenous people as an "urban policy problem" and less focused in relation to how contemporary Indigenous title, governance, and the expression of aspirations relating to economic and cultural development might be engaged in urban planning. We might perceive there to be, then, a substantive disjuncture between the rather separate literatures on environmental planning and urban planning. Why are we addressing quite different kinds of questions depending on whether we work in environmental or urban planning contexts? Why does the urban scholarship much less often address the persistence of title in cities? Why does urban planning practice not seem to have noticed the seismic shifts in Indigenous rights recognition, whereas environmental planning practice is now full of examples, guidance, and policy about Indigenous planning?

Clearly part of the answer is that Indigenous people face very different challenges in cities, such that questions of housing and social welfare provision, for example, have been front and centre of both policy and scholarship. Perhaps it is right and proper that these fields of scholarship and practice are evolving differently. Yet something seems to jar, and in doing so suggests it is worthy of further discussion. I do not mean that there is something "wrong" with the existing body of knowledge about urban Indigenous peoples. Instead, I am simply suggesting that some critical reflective thinking about the dominant discrepancy in the way we discuss Indigenous planning in different kinds of places (urban and non-urban) might be very fruitful. This disjuncture appears to disavow the possibility of reconstituting Indigenous land bases in cities and misrecognizes Indigenous peoples within cities as either another type of "urban stakeholder" or as the recipient of social welfare. While both participation in planning and the provision of vital urban services are clearly critically important material questions for urban Indigenous communities, neither do much justice for reparation of colonial histories of dispossession. That reparation must surely be at least a part of the field of Indigenous planning in urban settings.

Moreover, it is rather perverse that we live in a predominantly urban world and yet are only scraping the surface of the question of Indigenous peoples and their rights in cities. While Indigenous migration and mobility patterns are fluid and quite diverse, substantial proportions of national Indigenous populations live in urban areas. Recent statistics show just how urban various Indigenous populations within nation-states actually are: 84 per cent of Māori in Aotearoa-New Zealand live in cities (Statistics New Zealand 2006), 50 per cent of the combined First Nations, Metis, and Inuit population in Canada live in cities (Environics Institute 2010), and in Australia, 43 per cent of Aboriginal and Torres Strait Islander people reside in urban centres (Biddle 2009). Those urban populations tend to be very diverse in their makeup and represent the results of substantial rural-urban migration trends and policies of assimilation. They are complex and therefore the challenge that coexistence raises in cities demands further attention.

What might our attention, then, be drawn to? One conceptual approach I see as urgently important is to take a more critical deconstructive analytical stance to both cities themselves and to city planning to unlock different questions and possibilities for Indigenous planning in urban contexts. The foundations of such an approach are already in place. Many of the accounts of urban colonial development from the fields of geography, socio-legal studies, and critical history, for example, show cities to be far from "settled" and instead deeply riven by the continued presence of colonial power relations. They are themselves the "tools of conquest" (Stanger-Ross 2008, 543). Let us look at a few examples of such accounts.

Jacobs' (1996) account of the struggles over the Swan River Brewery site in Perth, Western Australia is an excellent example of this body of work. Urban Perth, in Jacobs' analysis, remains an Indigenous place, violently elided by the continuation of the dispossessory practices that planning becomes in such contexts. Blomley's (2004, 107) contribution has also charted how cities remain thoroughly "unsettled" through successive waves of dispossession. For Blomley, dispossession is a continuing phenomenon, and his analysis charts both the theft of swathes of property from Indigenous peoples in the early colonial periods, as well as the piece-by-piece removal of reserved land from within cities such as Victoria, Vancouver, and Melbourne in more recent times. Shaw's (2007) analysis of Aboriginal politics and struggle around The Block in Redfern, Sydney also "unsettles" the post-colonial imagination of Sydney as a cosmopolitan, fully modern city, fully evacuated of Aboriginal presence. She documents the process of racialization of spaces within Sydney as either spaces of "whiteness" or "blackness," and the divisive and oppressive urban practices that result.

More recently, Edmonds, in her examination of the early colonial period in both Melbourne (Australia), and Victoria (Canada), challenges the assumption that colonial frontiers were always in the non-urban spaces. Instead, she shows how cities and towns were "mosaic frontiers" (6) of often violent colonial contestation. Also discussing frontiers, but in a slightly different way, Yiftachel (1996) and Yiftachel and Fenster (1997) show how the "internal frontiers" within cities work to exert social control over Indigenous peoples. Yiftachel's more recent work serves to highlight processes of "gray spacing" in urban colonial relations (Yiftachel 2009). In both these contributions, planning and urban policy is analyzed as the key mechanism whereby that social control is structured and performed. Such a focus adds an important nuance to this field: it purposefully studies the mundane and everyday ways that colonial dispossession continues to be enacted.

Cities remain the places where colonialist mentalities of traditionalism and essentialism continue to exert considerable power. As Walker and Barcham state, "the place of authentic Indigeneity in the public perception has remained outside of urban areas" (2010, 314). From a historical perspective, Mawani's (2005) socio-legal work helps interrogate how Indigenous identity and the claims that flow from that, are constituted within mainstream legal and policy doctrine. Through analyzing court cases in British Columbia in the early 1920s when Indigenous people occupied Vancouver's Stanley Park, Mawani shows how questions of identity, authenticity, and spatiality are intricately bound together. Ultimately, the claimants in these cases had their identity as Aboriginal people quashed by the courts, who determined them to be in an "in-between" space (neither Native nor white) and therefore regarded them as squatters in the park. This intricate interplay of the authenticity of Indigenous identity and the location of its expression remains deeply embedded in legal and policy domains for city planning today.

All of these studies are examples of the areas of critical scholarship that re-place Indigenous peoples firmly into urban histories, from their early colonial foundings to the contemporary city. To this extent, we can see that "the founding of cities generated specifically urban colonial politics" (Stanger-Ross 2008, 546). Such a conceptualization may allow us to grapple with Indigenous planning in cities in a different register – one that more intentionally looks for how those urban colonial politics persist. Their critical deconstructive approach to both cities themselves (their spatiality, the urban processes that structure their development) and the legal-political domain that governs cities (within which we would have to include city planning) opens up the prospect of cities as contested post-colonial sites, hardly settled, and deeply implicated in ongoing colonial processes of dispossession and marginalization. They give rise to two insights that suggest answers to the questions I posed earlier about why Indigenous people and urban planning are placed so uneasily together in the literature.

First, the very existence of cities is seen as an ultimate material representation of imperial power, such that Indigenous rights and title cannot be readily conceived in urban areas. Cosmopolitan urbanism represents a dense, intense modernity, appearing as a final extinguishment, a complete erasure, of Indigenous title. "Traditional" connections of Indigenous people to lands now urbanized are seen as simply impossible, swept away by modern urban life. The persistence of this deeply racist spatiality of Indigenous identity and rights comes partly from the dominance of liberalized private property rights, and partly from a persistent racialized positioning of Indigenous people as not fully modern and therefore "other" to the urban. For Indigenous people whose territory is now urban, the threshold for recognition of title is virtually unattainable.

None of that is "real," but is instead the construct of persistent and oppressive colonial processes of dispossession. Such processes have been exposed in their colonial historical context, such as through Cole Harris's critically important work in the British Columbian context (Harris 2002, 2004). Harris exposes the precise use of reservations to "clear" urban settlements of Indigenous peoples and their title: "The allocation of reserves in British Columbia defined two primal spaces, one for Native people and the other for virtually everyone else" (2002, 265). In a more precisely urban context, Stanger-Ross's study supports this finding, showing how the Vancouver city plan of 1929 "embraced the notion that the removal of Aboriginal residents from the area had eliminated any Aboriginal claim to the reserve" (2008, 555). It is clear that analyses of contemporary city plans in settler states would reveal precisely the same assumptions and processes. Where Indigenous people are not apparently "present," their rights and title are conveniently seen to no longer exist.

Related to this is the blatant disregard and forceful opposition of powerful urban lobby groups when Indigenous rights are asserted, even in limited ways, within urban contexts. Cities are seen as the engine of growth, and in the neo-liberal urban policy world that dominates the contexts I address in this chapter, an assertion of Indigenous rights and title constitutes a direct threat to private property rights and thereby the development potential of a city. This is why in the Australian context, so much effort was put into providing legal "certainty" for freehold and some leasehold titles. The High Court in its original *Mabo* judgement specified that freehold title extinguished Native title, as did the Commonwealth and most state governments in their legislative responses to that decision. In the state of Victoria, where Melbourne is the capital city, the Conservative government at the time, led by Premier Jeff Kennett, passed a particularly regressive statute called the Land Titles Validation Act (1994) (Vic) which made land claims in Victoria virtually unwinnable. Alongside these legal arguments about "certainty" and private property rights was a veritable torrent of racist media around the challenge that Indigenous rights recognition might pose for "settled" Australia. Kennett joined other Australian state premiers claiming that suburban backyards, that sacred icon of the Australian urban "way of life," were under threat from Aboriginal land claims. This demonstrates how plainly apparent it is that cities are viewed as places where Indigenous people do not belong. This notion must be urgently challenged.

A second part of the answer to my earlier questions is that Aboriginal people who have moved to cities in what might be seen as a general demographic shift in the post-war period of rural-urban migration (see Graham and Peters 2002; Barcham 1998; contributions to Taylor and Bell 2004) are seen as inauthentic in their Indigenous identity. A political and identity division occurs between those who claim pre-settlement rights to urban spaces, and those who have moved in more recent times. Barcham (1998), and Wilson and Peters (2005) chart the importance of rural-urban migration trends in Māori (Aotearoa-New Zealand) and First Nation (Canada) populations over recent years. Both studies find that the significant demographic and social restructuring that is a result of this trend is leading to new forms of cultural expression and politics, Indigenous institutions, and self-identity. Yet these contemporary and urban forms of Indigeneity are being deliberately and systematically excluded from what remain highly essentialized forms of recognition of "authentic" Aboriginal identity. Barcham (1998) describes this as the "re-*iwi*-ization" (*iwi* is the Māori word for tribe) of Māori politics in Aotearoa-New Zealand, particularly through the recent revival of the Treaty of Waitangi. Legal opinions, court rulings, and policy doctrine that freezes Indigenous traditions and institutions into "tribal" modes excludes contemporary expressions of Indigeneity and its institutional forms. Moreover, it becomes a difficult challenge for Indigenous politics more generally, as it appears to undermine all of the careful work of identity construction and claim differentiation that Indigenous people have made to nation-states to achieve the minimal rights recognition made to date. When Aboriginal people move to cities they "lose" (and choose to do so) their connection to traditional authentic identity and the possibility of claims that might flow from that. This is a popular stereotype and assumption that Walker and Barcham (2010) have helped expose. Quoting from an Indian-Eskimo Association of Canada 1962 policy, Wilson and Peters (2005) clearly establish the evidence that when Indigenous people migrated to cities they were then assumed to take on mainstream, urban cultural values and automatically rescind their Native values (see Wilson and Peters 2005, 399).

It is this conceptual and racially constituted myopia that has enabled planning to fail to see Indigenous rights as legitimate for planning, and more easily recognize and accommodate Indigenous interests outside of urban environments. Indigenous interests are simply easier to notice in places that are not built up or radically modified by the processes of industrialization. This is not a factual blindness, it cannot be rationalized away by population figures or the extent of land claims. It is a racially constructed structural silence. Indigenous people are only "more present" in environmental planning domains because non-Indigenous society consistently fails to recognize the "persistent footprint" (Howitt and Lunkapis 2010) of Indigeneity within urban areas. It is a persistently colonial worldview that just does not see an authenticity and legitimacy for Indigenous rights claims in cities because cities are not places where authentic Indigeneity is seen to survive. Urban processes are assumed to have entirely expunged Indigenous interests from the spaces produced by urbanization. But it is only an appearance built on persistent racialized assumptions of appropriate Indigenous ways of being and cultural expressions.

The discrepancy within the field of Indigenous planning, then, is just as surely bound up in this racialized blindness. This does not amount to charging the literature with racialized blindness – this is not at all my point. The scholarship and practice that attends to the very important and material questions of effective, just, and culturally appropriate service delivery is very important, as is the literature that critically exposes how planning procedures continue to exclude, marginalize, and silence Indigenous voices. Necessary, yes, but not sufficient for addressing this myopia. It is the disjuncture (between how Indigenous planning relationships are conceived of in cities and how they are conceived of outside of cities) that must become an area of focus, to conceive more insightfully the very nature of the field "Indigenous planning." For this field to fully "emerge" following Jojola's (2008) suggestion, it must grapple with planning and the urban condition as sites that remain pervaded by historically constituted colonial power relations. My argument is that this disjuncture is at least in part produced by an insufficient deconstruction of planning as itself a culturally situated practice. A particularly crucial consequence of this is that we have missed the essential point that planning has a particular formulation for producing place ("forest," "city," "suburb") and this profoundly shapes our ability to either see or ignore Indigenous interests. If planning were conceived as merely one of many sites of cultural expressions of human-environment relationships, it would become urgently obvious that planning must recognize Indigenous rights in urban areas just as fully and conspicuously as in any other place. A conceptual framework of coexistence, alongside a more critical deconstructive stance towards cities as entities and the city planning processes that shape them, offers the foundations for those activities.

This is where I see an important role for our scholarship: towards a deeper decolonization of planning (see Porter 2010). While it is important that we are able to recognize the different world view of Indigenous peoples from that of planning, we remain unable to recognize that planning itself has a culturally situated worldview. This would require a more critical genealogical inquiry into planning processes and procedures. Without that recognition, it is very difficult to proceed to a more just and meaningful recognition of urban coexistence.

CONCLUSION: URBAN INDIGENOUS PLANNING?

Indigenous planning is most fruitfully seen as Jojola (2008, 42) describes: "The formulation of a theory of action ... [as] a radical re-examination of contemporary planning practice through long-term learning, the empowerment of community voice, and the advocacy of culture and tradition." At its heart must surely be principles of stewardship, cultural identity, collective rights, and the political requirement of land and governance restitution for Indigenous peoples in the contemporary cultural forms Indigenous people express. It must be a meaningful and just recognition of coexistence that rejects a simple "incorporation" of Indigenous knowledge, values, or land tenure into mainstream planning. This must include attention to all of the sites of planning in the post-colonial, both environmental and urban.

How can our scholarship support these important political and cultural projects? One of the ways we must work is in a much more deconstructive mode that highlights and analyzes planning's own cultural identity, principles, and assumptions. Indigenous planning can only begin to transcend the dilemmas of incorporation and inclusion if there is a mutual recognition of multiple life-worlds, multiple cultural expressions of human-environment relationships and their management. We have not yet called that worldview of planning to account for itself as a "culture among other cultures," to paraphrase Latour (1991). Planning as a system, a set of linked processes, a suite of knowledge and related practices, and a profession, takes on a universality that becomes ideological and oppressive in post-colonial contexts. We have not sufficiently called planning to account for its assumed dominance and universality in its preconceptions about space and place, the entrenched assumptions about appropriate human-environment relationships, and about the narrow conception of liberal property rights and interests. I am not suggesting we should do away with planning; indeed, quite the opposite. Can we bring ourselves to a point of meaningful recognition of Indigenous coexistence in cities? If we are to do so, cities must be seen as unsettled places where Indigenous title, connection, and contemporary culture rightfully belong.

REFERENCES

Alfred, T. 1999. *Peace, Power, Righteousness: An Indigenous Manifesto.* Oxford: Oxford University Press.

Anderson, K. 1993. "Race, Place and the Origins of Sydney's Aboriginal Settlement 1972–3." *Journal of Historical Geography* 19(3):314–35.

Anderson, K., and J.M. Jacobs. 1997. "From Urban Aborigines to Aboriginality and the City: One Path Through the History of Australian Cultural Geography." *Australian Geographical Studies* 35(1):12–22.

Baker, R., J. Davies, and E. Young, eds. 2001. *Working on Country: Contemporary Indigenous Management of Australia's Lands and Coastal Regions.* Melbourne: Oxford University Press.

Barcham, M. 1998. "The Challenge of Urban Māori: Reconciling Conceptions of Indigeneity and Social Change." *Asia Pacific Viewpoint* 39(3):303–14.

Barron, F.L., and J. Garcea, eds. 1999. *Urban Indian Reserves: Forging New Relationships in Saskatchewan.* Saskatoon: Purich Publishing.

Barry, J. 2011. "Building Collaborative Institutions for Government-to-Government Planning." Unpublished PHD thesis, School of Community and Regional Planning, University of British Columbia.

Barry, J., and L. Porter. 2012. "Indigenous Recognition in State-Based Planning Systems: Understanding Textual Mediation in the Contact Zone." *Planning Theory* 11(2):170–87.

Belanger Y., and R. Walker. 2009. "Interest Convergence and Co-production of Plans: An Examination of Winnipeg's 'Aboriginal Pathways'." *Canadian Journal of Urban Research* 18 (1) Supplement:118–39.

Beltran, J. 2000. *Indigenous and Traditional Peoples and Protected Areas: Principles, Guidelines and Case Studies.* Gland, Switzerland and Cambridge, UK: IUCN and WWF.

Biddle, N. 2009. "Location and Segregation: The Distribution of the Indigenous Population Across Australia's Urban Centres." CAEPR working paper 53/2009. Canberra: Centre for Aboriginal Economic Policy Research, Australian National University, online http://caepr.anu.edu.au/Publications/WP/2009WP53.php. Accessed 19 December 2011.

Birckhead, J., T.D. Lacy, and L. Smith, eds. 1992. *Aboriginal Involvement in Parks and Protected Areas*. Canberra: Aboriginal Studies Press.

Blomley, N. 2004. *Unsettling the City: Urban Land and the Politics of Property*. New York: Routledge.

Cardinal, N. 2006. "The Exclusive City: Identifying, Measuring, and Drawing Attention to Aboriginal and Indigenous Experiences in an Urban Context." *Cities* 23 (3):217–28.

City of Yarra. 2009. *Smith Street Community Plan*. Richmond: City of Yarra Council.

Clark, I.D. 1998. *Place Names and Land Tenure – Windows into Aboriginal Landscapes: Essays in Victorian Aboriginal History*. Clarendon, Victoria: Heritage Matters.

Cronon, W. 1995. "The Trouble with Wilderness; or Getting Back to the Wrong Nature." In *Uncommon Ground: Toward Reinventing Nature*, edited by W. Cronon. New York: ww Norton & Co.

Department of Planning and Community Development. 2008. *Melbourne@5million*. Melbourne: State of Victoria.

Department of Infrastructure. 2002. *Melbourne 2030: Planning for Sustainable Growth*. Melbourne: State of Victoria.

Dodson, M. 1994. "Towards the Existence of Indigenous Rights: Policy, Power and Self-Determination." *Race and Class* 35 (4):65–76.

Dudley, N. 2008. *Guidelines for Applying Protected Area Management Categories*. Gland, Switzerland: IUCN.

Edmonds, P. 2010. *Urbanizing Frontiers: Indigenous Peoples and Settlers in 19th-Century Pacific Rim Cities*. Vancouver: UBC Press.

Environics Institute. 2010. *Urban Aboriginal Peoples Study: Background and Summary of Main Findings*. Toronto: Environics Institute, online at http://uaps.ca/. Accessed 19 December 2011.

Fleras, A. 2000. "The Politics of Jurisdiction: Pathway or Predicament?" In *Visions of the Heart: Canadian Aboriginal Issues*, second edition, edited by D. Long and O.P. Dickason. Toronto: Harcourt Canada.

Fraser, N. 1995. "From Redistribution to Recognition? Dilemmas of Justice in a 'Post-Socialist' Age." *New Left Review* I:212, 68–93.

Gale, F., with A. Brookman. 1972. *Urban Aborigines*. Canberra: Australian National University Press.

Graham, K.A.H., and E. Peters. 2002. "Aboriginal Communities and Urban Sustainability." CPRN discussion paper F/27. Ottawa: Canadian Policy Research Network Inc., online at http://www.cprn.org/doc.cfm?doc=163&l=en. Accessed 19 December 2011.

Hanselmann, C. 2001. *Urban Aboriginal People in Western Canada: Realities and Policies*. Calgary: Canada West Foundation, online at: http://cwf.ca/pdf-docs/publications/September2001-Urban-Aboriginal-People-in-Western-Canada-Realities-and-Policies.pdf. Accessed 19 December 2011.

Harris, C. 2002. *Making Native Space: Colonialism, Resistance, and Reserves in British Columbia*. Vancouver: UBC Press.

– 2004. "How Did Colonialism Dispossess? Comments from an Edge of Empire." *Annals of the Association of American Geographers* 94 (1):165–82.

Howitt, R., and G.J. Lunkapis. 2010. "Coexistence: Planning and the Challenge of Indigenous Rights." In *The Ashgate Research Companion to Planning Theory: Conceptual Challenges for Spatial Planning*, edited by J. Hillier and P. Healey. Farnham: Ashgate.

Howitt, R., J. Connell, and P. Hirsch, eds. 1996. *Resources, Nations and Indigenous Peoples: Case Studies from Australasia, Melanesia and Southeast Asia*. Melbourne: Oxford University Press.

Hylton, J.H. ed. 1999. *Aboriginal Self-Government in Canada: Current Trends and Issues*, second edition. Saskatoon: Purich Publishing.

Jaireth, H., and D. Smyth, eds. 2003. *Innovative Governance: Indigenous Peoples, Local Communities and Protected Areas*. New Delhi: Ane Books.

Jackson, S. 1997. "A Disturbing Story: The Fiction of Rationality in Land Use Planning in Aboriginal Australia." *Australian Planner* 34 (4):221–6.

Jacobs, J.M. 1996. *Edge of Empire: Postcolonialism and the City*. London: Routledge.

Jentoft, S., H. Minde, and R. Nilsen, eds. 2003. *Indigenous Peoples: Resource Management and Global Rights*. Delft: Eburon.

Jojola, T. 2008. "Indigenous Planning: An Emerging Context." *Canadian Journal of Urban Research* 17 (1):37–47.

King, A.D. 1990. *Urbanism, Colonialism and the World Economy: Cultural and Spatial Foundations of the World Urban System*. London: Routledge.

Laclau, E., and C. Mouffe. 2001. *Hegemony and Socialist Strategy: Towards a Radical Democratic Politics*. London: Verso.

Lane, M.B. 2003. "Participation, Decentralization, and Civil Society: Indigenous Rights and Democracy in Environmental Planning." *Journal of Planning Education and Research* 22:360–73.

Lane, M.B., and T. Corbett. 2005. "The Tyranny of Localism: Indigenous Participation in Community-Based Environmental Management." *Journal of Environmental Policy and Planning* 7 (2):141–59.

Lane, M.B., and G. McDonald. 2005. "Community-Based Environmental Planning: Operational Dilemmas, Planning Principles and Possible Remedies." *Journal of Environmental Planning and Management* 48(5):709–31.

Lane, M.B., and L.J. Williams. 2008. "Color Blind: Indigenous Peoples and Regional Environmental Management." *Journal of Planning Education and Research* 28:38–49.

Langton, M. 1996. "What Do We Mean by Wilderness? Wilderness and Terra Nullius in Australian Art." *The Sydney Papers,* 8 (1):11–31.

Latour, B. 1991. *We Have Never Been Modern.* Hemel Hempstead: Harvester Wheatsheaf.

Lawrence, D. 2002. *Kakadu: The Making of a National Park.* Carlton: Melbourne University Press.

Maaka, R., and A. Fleras. 2000. "Engaging with Indigeneity: Tino Ranga-tiratanga in Aotearoa." In *Political Theory and the Rights of Indigenous Peoples,* edited by D. Ivison, P. Patton, and W. Sanders. Cambridge: Cambridge University Press.

Mawani, R. 2005. "Genealogies of the Land: Aboriginality, Law, and Territory in Vancouver's Stanley Park." *Social and Legal Studies* 14 (3):315–39.

Morgan, G. 2006. *Unsettled Places: Aboriginal People and Urbanisation in New South Wales.* Adelaide: Wakefield Press.

Mouffe, C. 2005. *On the Political.* Abingdon: Routledge.

Newhouse, D. and E. Peters. 2003. *Not Strangers in These Parts: Urban Aboriginal Peoples.* Ottawa: Policy Research Initiative.

O'Faircheallaigh, C. 2008. "Negotiating Cultural Heritage? Aboriginal-Mining Company Agreements in Australia." *Development and Change* 39 (1):25–51.

Palmer, L. 2004. "Bushwalking in Kakadu: A Study of Cultural Borderlands." *Social and Cultural Geography* 5 (1):109–19.

– 2006. "'Nature,' Place and the Recognition of Indigenous Polities." *Australian Geographer* 37 (1):33–43.

Peters, E. 1992. "Self-Government for Aboriginal People in Urban Areas." *The Canadian Journal of Native Studies* 12 (1):51–74.

– 1995. *Aboriginal Self-Government in Urban Areas.* Queens University: Institute of Intergovernmental Relations.

– 1996. "'Urban' and 'Aboriginal': An Impossible Contradiction?" In *City Lives and City Forms: Critical Research and Canadian Urbanism,* edited by J. Caulfield, and L. Peake. Toronto: University of Toronto Press.

– 2005. "Indigeneity and Marginalisastion: Planning for and with Urban Aboriginal Communities in Canada." *Progress in Planning* 63:327–404.

– 2006. "'[W]e Do Not Lose our Treaty Rights Outside the … Reserve': Challenging the Scales of Social Service Provision for First Nations Women in Canadian Cities." *Geojournal* 65:315–27.

– 2007. "First Nations and Métis People and Diversity in Canadian cities." In *Belonging? Diversity, Recognition and Shared Citizenship in Canada*, edited by K. Banting, T.J. Courchene, and F.L. Seidle. Ottawa: Institute for Research on Public Policy.

Peters, E., and V. Robillard. 2007. "Urban Hidden Homelessness and Reserve Housing." In *Aboriginal Policy Research*, edited by J.P. White, P. Maxim, and D. Beavon. Toronto: Thompson Educational Publishing.

Peters, E., and R. Walker. 2005. "Indigeneity and Marginalisation: Planning for and with Urban Aboriginal Communities in Canada.: *Progress in Planning* 63:327–39.

Porter, L. 2006. "Planning in (post)Colonial Settings: Challenges for Theory and Practice." *Planning Theory and Practice* 7 (3):383–96.

– 2007. "Producing forests: A Colonial Genealogy of Environmental Planning in Victoria, Australia." *Journal of Planning Education and Research* 26 (4):466–77.

– 2010. *Unlearning the Colonial Cultures of Planning*. Aldershot: Ashgate.

Pratt, M.L. 1991. "The Arts of the Contact Zone." *Profession* 91: 33–40.

Presland, G. 2010. *First People: The Eastern Kulin of Melbourne, Port Phillip and Central Victoria*. Melbourne: Museum Victoria Publishing.

Province of British Columbia. no date. *New Relationship*, online at http://www.newrelationship.gov.bc.ca/shared/downloads/new_relationship.pdf. Accessed 9 October 2011.

Rangan, H. 1999. "Bitter-Sweet Liaisons in a Contentious Democracy: Radical Planning through State Agency in Postcolonial India," *Plurimondi* I:2:47–66.

Rangan, H., and M.B. Lane. 2001. "Indigenous Peoples and Forest Management: Comparative Analysis of Institutional Approaches in Australia and India." *Society and Natural Resources* 14:145–60.

Sandercock, L. 2003. *Cosmopolis II: Mongrel Cities in the 21st Century*. London: Continuum.

Shaw, W. 2007. *Cities of Whiteness*. Malden: Blackwell.

Spence, M. 1999. *Dispossessing the Wilderness: Indian Removal and the Making of the National Parks*. New York: Oxford University Press.

Stanger-Ross, J. 2008. "Municipal Colonialism in Vancouver: City Planning and the Conflict over Indian Reserves, 1928–1950s." *The Canadian Historical Review* 89 (4):541–80.

Statistics New Zealand. 2006. *QuickStats about Māori*, online at http://www.stats.govt.nz/Census/2006CensusHomePage/QuickStats/quickstats-about-a-subject/maori.aspx. Accessed 19 December 2011.

Stevens, S. ed. 1997. *Conservation through Cultural Survival: Indigenous Peoples and Protected Areas*. Washington DC: Island Press.

Taylor, J., and M. Bell, eds. 2004. *Population Mobility and Indigenous Peoples in Australasia and North America*. New York: Routledge.

Todd, R. 2003. "Urban Aboriginal Governance: Developments and Issues." In *Not Strangers in these Parts: Urban Aboriginal Peoples, Canada Policy Research Initiative*, edited by D. Newhouse and E. Peters, online at: http://www.horizons.gc.ca/doclib/AboriginalBook_e.pdf. Accessed 19 December 2011.

Tully, J. 1995. *Strange Multiplicity: Constitutionalism in an Age of Diversity*. Cambridge: Cambridge University Press.

– 2004. "Recognition and Dialogue: The Emergence of a New Field." *Critical Review of International Social and Political Philosophy* 7 (3):84–106.

Umemoto, K. 2001. "Walking in Another's Shoes: Epistemological Challenges in Participatory Planning." *Journal of Planning Education and Research* 21:17–31.

Walker, R. 2003. "Engaging the Urban Aboriginal Population in Low-Cost Housing Initiatives: Lessons from Winnipeg." *Canadian Journal of Urban Research* 12 (10):99–118.

– 2005. "Social Cohesion? A Critical Review of the Urban Aboriginal Strategy and its Application to Address Homelessness in Winnipeg." *Canadian Journal of Native Studies* 25 (2):395–416.

– 2006a. "Searching for Aboriginal/Indigenous Self-Determination: Urban Citizenship in the Winnipeg Low-Cost-Housing Sector, Canada." *Environment and Planning A*, 38:2345–63.

– 2006b. "Interweaving Aboriginal/Indigenous Rights with Urban Citizenship: A View from the Winnipeg Low-Cost Housing Sector." *Canada Citizenship Studies* 10 (4):391–411.

– 2008a. "Aboriginal Self-Determination and Social Housing in Urban Canada: A Story of Convergence and Divergence." *Urban Studies* 45 (1):185–205.

– 2008b. *Social Housing and the Role of Aboriginal Organisations in Canadian Cities*. Montreal: Institute for Research on Public Policy.

– 2008c. "Improving the Interface Between Urban Municipalities and Indigenous Communities." *Canadian Journal of Urban Research* 17 (1):118–39.

Walker, R., and M. Barcham. 2010. "Indigenous-Inclusive Citizenship: The City and Social Housing in Canada, New Zealand and Australia." *Environment and Planning A* 42:314–31.

Wilson, K., and E. Peters. 2005. "'You Can Make a Place for It': Remapping Urban First Nations Spaces of Identity." *Environment and Planning D: Society and Space* 23:395–413.

Yiftachel, O. 1996. "The Internal Frontier: Territorial Control and Ethnic Rela-
    tions in Israel." *Regional Studies* 30 (5):493–508.
–   2009. "Critical Theory and 'Gray Space': Mobilization of the Colonized."
    City 3(2–3):240–56.
Yiftachel, O., and T. Fenster, eds. 1997. "Frontier Development and Indigenous
    Peoples." *Progress in Planning*. London: Pergamon.
Yiftachel, O., R. Goldhaber, and R. Nuriel. 2009. "Urban Justice and Recogni-
    tion: Affirmation and Hostility in Beer-Sheva." In *Searching for the Just City:
    Debates in Urban Theory and Practice*, edited by P. Marcuse, J. Connolly,
    J. Novy, I. Olivo, and C. Potter. New York: Routledge.

Lands and Resources

13

Capacity Deficits at Cultural Interfaces of Land and Sea Governance[1]

RICHARD HOWITT, KIM DOOHAN, SANDIE
SUCHET-PEARSON, GAIM LUNKAPIS,
SAMANTHA MULLER, REBECCA LAWRENCE,
SARAH PROUT, SIRI VELAND, AND SHERRIE CROSS

Intercultural approaches to planning and governance in natural resource management (NRM) have become common in many jurisdictions. In various configurations such as co-management, Indigenous and community protected areas, place-based collaboration, and joint management agreements, these approaches bring together local, often Indigenous or customary landowners with state agencies and commercial interests in some sort of collaboration to plan, manage, and evaluate the use of places and resources, and provide services ranging from environmental protection to market supply. In many of these hybrid systems, technical experts, state agents, and academics contribute to capacity-building activities that aim to create, develop, and/or enhance the capacity of community participants to contribute to the management tasks – to "improve" the fit between resource management and communities.[2] It is widely assumed that capacity is absent only from the local, Indigenous, and community components of such systems and institutions. This chapter draws on mainly Australian experience to argue that it is often capacity deficits in government agencies, commercial interests, and non-Indigenous institutions that most dramatically affect collaborative governance of intercultural environmental systems. Significant capacity deficits include lack of knowledge, understanding, skills, and competence in basic issues of social science, cultural awareness, and locally contextualized knowledge.

This chapter canvasses conceptual and ethical issues facing scholarly research at these difficult intercultural interfaces. Our approach acknowledges and respects the primacy of Indigenous and customary governance systems in Indigenous domains and identifies several key notions, such as situatedness, scale, governance, sustainability, mobility, and hybridity as useful in reframing concerns about capacity deficits in land and sea governance systems to support nurturing more just and effective practices and relationships in intercultural governance.

Colonial and post-colonial constructions of property rights in natural resources within the territorial and political domains of Indigenous peoples are clearly a significant element of post-colonial states' political, jurisdictional, and economic claims against Indigenous rights to self-determination. Even if it is unintentional, these management systems easily erase, and at best constrain, the rights created by pre-existing and persistent Indigenous systems of law. They typically privilege management plans that restrict Indigenous peoples' access to, control over, and benefit from their traditional territories and resources. Even where they extend some recognition of Indigenous rights, the responsible institutions are defined by and accountable to the state whose claims and power to allocate resource rights to third parties is the foundation of Indigenous dispossession, marginalization, and exclusion.

Put simply, it has become commonplace for post-colonial NRM systems to assume an unassailable right to govern natural resources, Indigenous peoples, property systems, and the relationships between them without consideration for the issues that arise from the complex, contested, overlapping, and hybridized jurisdictions produced by colonial and post-colonial histories. Emphasis on scientific, economic, and political criteria in management decisions often eclipses questions of culture, context, and rights. Indeed, in many environmental settings, the apparent urgency of systemic vulnerabilities and failures sees social and cultural dimensions of NRM marginalized (at best), dismissed, or opposed.

The chapter advocates support for governance systems that prioritize decolonization, improvements in social and environmental justice, and more secure and sustainable livelihoods and improved health and well-being for Indigenous peoples. We invite scholarly, economic, and political discourse that focuses on those goals rather than solely in terms of the efficacy, efficiency, and sustainability of resource management systems for the needs of commercial markets. Following Howitt and Suchet-Pearson (2006) we aim to destabilize the assumption that terms such as "planning" and "management" can be assumed as benign technologies to secure good governance of environments, places, and resources in intercultural spaces of colonization. Such terms risk obscuring the ideological and ontological foundations when accepted unproblematically as appropriate goals for engagement across profound cultural differences.

INTERCULTURAL CAPACITY IN DOMINANT NRM INSTITUTIONS

For Indigenous groups in many areas, some form of division of power, some form of coexistence in governance over territories, lives, resources, and places has been rendered necessary by the imposition of political processes and property laws that deny persistent rights and responsibilities constructed in customary law, and by historical circumstances that have constrained the exercise of ancient jurisdictions of customary law. Legal or political resolution of contested sovereignty has generally been resolved by settlements that entrench the powerful legal and political institutions of the state, and provide limited recognition and autonomy to Indigenous institutions in ways that constrain the exercise of sovereignty and autonomy. It is, therefore, necessary for contemporary Indigenous governance institutions and processes to respond to those circumstances, and for scholarship on intercultural systems of NRM to address questions of power, governance, and process openly and thoughtfully. It would be naïve to assume that achieving political settlement of long-standing Indigenous claims and securing some form of "co-management" guarantees just and sustainable outcomes or viable self-determination for Indigenous parties. Indeed, there are many examples where participation in such settlements or the institutions that result risks becoming more a co-optation than an empowerment, and where the terms of engagement are more likely to foster conflict, disadvantage, and continuing exclusion and marginalization than equitable and sustainable coexistence, recognition, and security for Indigenous groups.

Part of the underlying problem is the belligerent and arrogant insistence of Eurocentric systems of thought, governance, and management on their inherent superiority. For the beneficiaries of the dominant culture it is self-evident that technical expertise accredited by the dominant culture is necessary to perform the complex technical tasks of NRM. Yet this approach dismisses local accreditation, understanding, authority, and self-determination framed within Indigenous accountability systems, and reduces the complex value-laden task of governance to the apparently technical task of management. A slippery double movement of delusion simultaneously renders Indigenous peoples' and institutions' intercultural competence and capacity to work the in-between spaces of cultural domination, irrelevant to the task of management, and transforms the ignorance, incompetence, and incapacity of the state, state-accredited technical experts, and resource corporations into a legitimate representation of a wider public interest.

In this context, critical scholarship on resource management and planning should challenge the dominant assumptions that immiserize Indigenous peoples and reinforce Indigenous exclusion and pauperization in resource and environmental management systems.[3] It should certainly identify and analyze the capacity deficits of dominant institutions and knowledge systems, and point clearly to the need for intercultural competencies and the development of new capacities and competencies in those institutions.

The emergence of so-called adaptive management systems offers an example of how failure to demand intercultural competence entrenches the low capacity of mainstream NRM thinking to respond to the challenges of ontological pluralism and coexisting rights, knowledges, and values in NRM systems. For example, in adaptive systems for river management, hydrologists, ecologists, engineers, and agronomists use advanced computational and engineering techniques to allocate and manage agricultural, potable, industrial, and environmental flows of water for competing needs. Fisheries managers adjust catch quotas and seasons. Foresters adjust cutting schedules. Mine managers monitor tailings storage and regeneration plans. Few of these sophisticated systems, however, prioritize adaptation to changing social dynamics (Rodgers 1998; Maretsky et al. 2002; Olssen et al. 2004; Allen and Curtis 2005), and even fewer prioritize adaptive responses to intercultural issues. Populated with technical experts pursuing more and more data, these systems have become more sophisticated and demanding at the same time as they have become even less inclusive and responsive to the wider challenges of coexistence.

Without seeking to dismiss the value of work across the society-natural resources interface, and the integration of fields such as sustainability science, community development, and development studies, at the real-world social and environmental interfaces between the dominant Eurocentric cultures and Indigenous rights there is a lot of ground to cover. At its best this work has shifted the focus of scholarship and policy towards capacity-building, using needs assessments, impact assessments, and community planning to encourage delivery of a wide range of skills and training to Indigenous participants in NRM systems to support their participation in expert systems (Carter 2008). Although generally well-intentioned, this work slips easily into deep colonizing modes of practice, assuming that the necessary skills, knowledge, and capacities for inclusion are absent from Indigenous communities. This approach risks reinforcing colonial and post-colonial assumptions that such systems are best framed in terms of co-management, in which the Indigenous other is invited to participate in and contribute to the improved efficacy of systems whose basic purpose, structure, and operations are consistent with Eurocentric understandings of human-nature relationships.

ENGAGING THE CONTEXTS OF COEXISTENCE

For critical scholars, the challenge is to contribute new tools to the conceptual toolkit and to frame practical contributions to reshaping and rethinking resource landscapes from within the (post)colonial institution of the modern university system. This cannot be achieved by pursuing naïve notions of returning to a pre-colonial idyll or trading the violence of colonial and neo-colonial state-and-corporate power for a neo-Indigenist plutocracy, or a localized kleptocracy. Contemporary scholarship needs to engage with people and issues, and become woven into processes of decolonization. It needs to operate in ways that are simultaneously local and accountable within customary governance systems, rigorous and credible in robust and disciplined academic debates, and coherent and responsive within wider scales of national governance and global economic, political and environmental processes. Our work needs to take local knowledge seriously, without becoming naively localized; it needs to challenge the local as robustly as it challenges the corporate and state interests in power structures. Suchet's idea of situated engagement (Suchet 1999) points to the serious intercultural, interpersonal, and cross-scale dimensions of this challenge, as well as a need to be locally responsive and engaged.

Our view is that the academy faces an important challenge to develop capacity to change how scholars engage with transdisciplinary knowledge within and between multiple cultures and how they respond to diverse ways of being-in-place at the diverse and changeable interfaces between human and non-human domains. For researchers working in these fields, this challenge involves extending opportunities for these new competencies and intercultural capacities to be built within the key institutions of scholarship, such as ethics committees, research granting

bodies, and tenure committees, as well as NRM institutions and government agencies for community development, environmental protection,
and economic advancement. Disciplinary cultures need to find ways to
support new forms of governance and collaboration in learning exchan-
ges, intercultural and transdisciplinary collaboration, and research-and-
learning that happens in new ways both within and beyond tertiary
classrooms, and within and beyond the structures of accredited degree
programs and research projects. The research community must acknowledge that no research with Indigenous communities is neutral or impar-
tial. Recognizing that complex social contexts, political agendas, and
cultural interpretations are all implicated in NRM research in Indigenous domains invites – indeed compels – researchers to reflect on the
ethical foundations and social impacts of their research and to make
considered and accountable choices about conceptual frameworks and
research methods. The following discussion considers some examples
before returning to focus on the challenge of addressing institutional
capacity deficits in NRM systems.

Scales of Governance: Erasure and Reconstruction

Because it focuses attention on persistent institutions, relationships, and
values that underpin Indigenous claims in NRM systems, Cross (2006)
advocates the idea of "contemporary Indigenous governances" as a
more appropriate entry point in Indigenous domains than more generic
ideas such as community. Cross's study on the consultation programs
employed with the Australian federal government's 1991–2000 reconciliation policy demonstrates the significance of building responsiveness
to Indigenous community agency and governance into the research process. Cross's initial focus was on the way that governments had scaled
the consultative processes, but her open-ended interview and analytical
methodologies encouraged the study participants to expand the study
parameters. This produced a new study focus on Indigenous governance
processes in the participants' communities, and the ways in which the
reconciliation policy and consultation processes reinforced colonial patterns of interaction.

Cross's idea of contemporary Indigenous governances is both a well-
supported empirical concept arising from her research, and a political
intervention that challenges the assumed privileged status of governments
in formulating Indigenous affairs policy. It is a conceptual tool that insists
the scholarly researcher engages with the presence of Indigenous govern-

ance, values, and institutions rather than reinforcing the ideological claims of absence, loss, and lack of capacity that dominate many discourses of Indigenous involvement in environmental governance and NRM.

Having acknowledged the need to recognize and engage with contemporary Indigenous governances, Cross explores the nature and consequences of historical and continuing erasure of the scales at which Indigenous governance is exercised. The hierarchically scaled structures and practices employed with the reconciliation consultative program gave an appearance of a democratic process for reflecting Indigenous community opinion on the documents. But in fact, these processes almost entirely excluded Indigenous community opinion – the dominant theme in this study being a pervasive, structured, and diversely expressed critique that the reconciliation policy and its (largely predetermined) consultative documents held no promise or capacity to change the structural framework of engagement between Indigenous communities and the Australian government. Her account of the reconciliation process, which operated as a scaled structure and discourse of exclusion, management, and marginalization, contrasts markedly with the construction of new scales of Indigenous governance in the Native title processes underway in South Australia and reported by Agius et al. (e.g., 2002, 2007). In that work, rather than imposing practices and structures of consultation and participation that suited the state and its agencies, the Aboriginal Legal Rights Movement facilitated and supported Indigenous processes, practices, and lines of authority by which a body of community opinion and priorities could be delivered to government. Indeed, the South Australian process has built various scales of intervention to produce Indigenous authority as the basis for local and regional agreements on land, sea, and resource use and access. Cross's examination of the reconciliation process and the South Australian experience in Native title negotiations suggest that erasure processes that characterize colonial (and contemporary deep colonizing) relationships[4] – including research relationships – can be reversed through negotiating changes within contemporary Indigenous governances to develop systems of decision making and accountability that link future challenges to important cultural and social values.

Security, Belonging, and Risk

At its core, the Australian colonial project has always rigorously attempted to order space and police the movement and behaviours of Indigenous peoples within it. The legislative, economic, and regulatory domains of resource and environmental planning and management have been central technologies in this process. Creating property rights in natural resources and the places that host them, colonial and contemporary governments have defined Indigenous Australians as "out of place." Policies intended to "open up" country for use and occupation, explicitly sought to "clear the way" for development. Settler discourses of emptiness, occupation, and possession characterize Indigenous Australians' relationships to their traditional lands, waters, territories, and resources in terms of absence, erasure, and denial. These dominant settler discourses deny, erase, and silence alternative pluralist and inclusive discourses based on the realities of presence, coexistence, and belonging of Indigenous landscapes (Howitt 2012). In doing so, they create images of insecurity and uncertainty that reinforce the idea that settler (and now national) security and certainty are to be built on assumptions of power, exclusion, and control – governance as a set of predetermined and imposed rather than negotiated outcomes.

Indigenous Australians face a number of disciplining public discourses, whatever their location or practice in space (Prout and Howitt 2009). If they live in the "wilderness" of remote Australia they may be judged authentically Indigenous, but unwilling to embrace modernity and the mainstream of Australian life characterized by settlement and productivity. If they live settled, rural, or urban existences, popular discourse may render them assimilated, without legitimate voice in land use or heritage negotiations, and perhaps, no longer truly Indigenous (Porter 2006; Prout 2006, 2008, 2009a, 2009b).

Indigenous Australians, however, have consistently engaged in spatial practices that subvert the hegemonic "cadastral grid" (Byrne 2003) and the settlement expectations of the state, in order to nurture their sociocultural and spiritual identities, and economic livelihoods. Countercolonial researchers have been increasingly drawn to exploring these connections and activities in ways that quietly disrupt unimaginative and constricting discourses about Indigenous relationships to kin and country. In his compelling account of Indigenous relationships to country in rural New South Wales, Byrne (2003) drew upon "geobiographies" as a methodological tool which provided local Indigenous peoples with a framework for telling their stories of relationship to country from which conventional scholarship had rendered them long since absent. The result was a rich narrative tapestry of how Indigenous peoples had adapted their relationships to place and renegotiated their sense of belonging in the midst of change. These narratives of "trespass" he described as

> a systematic refusal of the boundaries of the cadastral system, a
> refusal to acknowledge its legitimacy, a constant prodding and test-
> ing of its resolve. These experiences and the relating of them are
> a significant part of Aboriginal folklore ... but there also seems
> implicit in it a refusal to accept that the cadastral grid exists, a
> refusal that emulates the white settler failure to acknowledge the
> existence of the spatiality of the Dreaming or of any Aboriginal
> native title to country ... With a tactical, wilful blindness, they
> appear to answer negation with negation (Byrne 2003, 181).

Many Indigenous Australians continue to negotiate their sense of socio-cultural security and belonging through mobilities – the spatial acts of traversing the cadastral grid – that strategically connect them to kin and country (Prout 2008, 2009a, 2009b). These mobilities and the spatial and social networks they create provide a key foundation for Indigenous peoples' sense of security and belonging, and consequently for their capacity to understand and respond to the challenges of social, economic, and environmental change. The current discourses of vulnerability and resilience, like longer-standing discourses of service provision and access, privilege non-Indigenous notions of relationships to place and belonging. They create institutional and regulatory arrangements that by-pass and sideline contemporary Indigenous institutions, values and understandings (Veland et al. 2010). They prioritize scientific and government discourses of risk, purpose, and value, and seek to discipline Indigenous participation to compliance to the dominant discourses of order, purpose, and success.

In the setting of co-management and the new geographies of coexistence, questions of security, belonging, and risk have therefore become central to questions of governance of environment and resources. The dominant policy models assume that national security, resource security, and economic security are best constructed on the basis of the false certainties of dominant settler discourses. Yet those dominant models have proved spectacularly unsuccessful in understanding and responding to the security, service, and human rights needs of Indigenous citizens. There is a long history of Indigenous mobility being pathologized by governments and constructed as a threat to orderly development. Indeed, in the current context of environmental risks arising from climate change, and social risk arising from the social catastrophes experienced in many remote Indigenous communities in remote Australia, imposed spatial discipline through forced relocations, denial of infrastructure and resources to remote settlements, and constructing certain categories of places and citizens as "at risk" have re-emerged as acceptable policy parameters in government circles. Despite the recency of criticisms of the Howard Government's defence of the stolen generations policies in Australia as "well-intentioned," Commonwealth, state, and territory Labor Party governments have returned to well-intentioned imposition of policy solutions designed to discipline Indigenous mobilities and manage risks experienced by Indigenous people. Any efforts to secure resource and environmental governance solutions that are pluralist, inclusive, respectful, and sustainable in this context has once again become more difficult.

Sustainable Livelihoods and Renewable Resources

One of the key challenges for Indigenous peoples is the challenge of securing sustainable livelihoods in the context of the denial of access to rights, resources, and opportunity across multiple generations. The passage of the Declaration of the Rights of Indigenous Peoples through the General Assembly of the United Nations is cause to celebrate, but it is a long way from securing enforceable obligations on nation-states to recognize and support Indigenous autonomy and success. It is still common to see states assuming the right, ability, and capacity to determine Indigenous futures, and that this is done with the patronizing self-righteousness of do-gooder saviours whose rationale for intervention is often flimsy, self-interested, and hostile to both local and global values of justice and sustainability. For example, the Australian government's 2007 emergency intervention into Northern Territory Indigenous communities narrated a "crisis" involving child abuse, but enacted a program of governance, control, and coercion that mistook the urgent need to support local Indigenous governances for an excuse to further erase those Indigenous institutions and authorities in favour of external authority imposed and resourced by the state and accountable to state expectations, understandings and demands. This was not a negotiated coexistence but a politicized diminishing of Indigenous authority and autonomy. The resources were not directed towards sustainable livelihoods, but towards short-term and unsustainable movements in specific indicators for a political purpose. The change of government has produced little change in that orientation.

The task of securing sustainable livelihoods in many Indigenous domains is a difficult challenge. Remote from conventional markets, reliant on connections to mainstream economic opportunity through commodity markets in which states and corporations have alienated local resource rents and control, and lacking access to infrastructure and capacity to change things, many Indigenous communities face bleak prospects in moving beyond subsistence and hybrid welfare-market-subsistence economies. Efforts to move into post-carbon economies through carbon offset markets based on Aboriginal knowledge, traditions of "caring for country," labour, and governance, such as fire management systems in North Australia's savannahs (e.g., Lendrum 2007), will struggle with the failure of Australian governments to put in place predictable and effective responses to climate risk scenarios. The term "Caring for Country" entered Australian usage in environmental management from Aboriginal English, where it typically refers to the set of principles, relationships, actions, and responsibilities that simultaneously nurture landscapes, human and non-human presences in and elements of the landscape, and the knowledge on which those practices that are glossed as caring for country emerges (Young et al. 1991; Rose 1996). It is now commonly used in policy and environmental programs as a synonym for environmental management or eco-centric development principles.

Government investment in policies and programs that further entrench Eurocentric and science-only environmental management systems, and Eurocentric and market-only resource management systems continue to pre-empt the sorts of nation-building identified as foundational to Indigenous autonomy, security, and sustainability (e.g., Cornell 2006). The currently dominant approaches risk disciplining pro-Indigenous social, cultural, political, and environmental programs for change to narrowly defined economic development goals in remote and marginalized locations, and reducing local governance and accountability to technical reporting on efficacy and efficiency. Supporting and nurturing regional economies that service the needs and aspirations of local people is just as significant in pursuing just and sustainable regional economic development as identifying and supporting opportunities that rely on external, market-defined, or constrained linkages. For example, locally oriented programs within contemporary Indigenous governance structures and providing integrated environmental services such as fire management, quarantine control, feral animal and weed control, and threatened species support are at least as significant to Indigenous futures as large-scale resource-based development projects and other capital intensive strategies if the goal is building local capacity and strong locally sustainable institutions that deliver successful regional development within Indigenous frames of reference.

Integrating social, economic, political, and environmental strategies for change to secure sustainable ways of being together for remote Aboriginal communities is an urgent challenge of research and governance. It is common for government-led approaches to participatory or consultative programs casting environmental and community management priorities as needing to contribute to (even on occasion become subsidiary to) "real" (market-based) economic development opportunities. These approaches risk recasting natural resource managers as simply identifying and recommending management strategies for natural resources for economic exploitation. They do not see Country as a fundamental constituent of culture, economy, and society in Indigenous terms. They fragment human-to-human and human-to-nature relationships in ways that entrench exclusion and marginalization. Continued fragmentation, conflict, and poor integration across policy areas, service providers, and community members will guarantee continued but avoidable human and environmental cost. Generating Indigenous scholarship to tackle these concerns is an urgent imperative.

Hybridity and Corporate Engagement

Few corporations or government agencies have moved to acknowledge the need to develop their institutional capacities to work with Indigenous agency on Indigenous terms. In the Eurocentric frames, capacity is – virtually by definition – something that is lacking only on the side of the Indigenous other. Fragile discourses of corporate social responsibility have created some opportunities to challenge the assumption of capacity, but remain tightly contextualized in market judgments and regulatory environments (Lawrence 2009; Howitt and Lawrence 2008). An important element of the scholarly agenda must be consideration of the ways in which resource corporations engage with intercultural NRM systems.

One of the more iconic examples of troubled and inappropriate engagement between Indigenous people and corporate interests in Australia was that of the Argyle Diamond Mine located in the remote East Kimberley region of Western Australia. Dillon and Dixon (1990) offer a detailed account of the events leading up to the signing of the highly contentious Good Neighbour Agreement (also known as the Argyle Agreement) by four local Indigenous people. This action marked the beginning of a formal relationship between Aboriginal people and Argyle, albeit a relationship located within a fundamentally unequal and paternalistic context. Few commentators would identify Argyle as a site of intercultural engagement – yet recent work drawing on detailed corporate and community sources allows a somewhat surprising reframing of those assumed relationships. In essence, the emerging picture of what was happening at the mine site was something far more complex and challenging than the conventional narrative of an iconic representation of a simple binary of opposites within which Aborigines were seen as powerless local victims in the face of powerful large global corporations and that an operating diamond mine necessarily destroyed, in every way, Aboriginal sacred sites.

Doohan's (2007, 2008) careful and engaged consideration of the role of cultural performance and transformative practice on the part of Indigenous people, as well as corporate representations, allows a more nuanced appreciation of the power, symbolic or otherwise, that Indigenous people have exercised at Argyle. It shows that, in the face of conflict and disruption to their world, local Indigenous people have enlisted their symbolic representations of power and meaning – the Barramundi and her manifestations – to initiate processes of culturally appropriate resolution of unfinished business and the (re)integration of themselves and their country and the miners at Argyle. The miners, in an effort to ensure the uninterrupted continuation of the mine and an enhancement of their brand, have called upon their own performances and cultural practices by, for example, signing Memoranda of Understanding with Aboriginal traditional owners and other forms of agreements, incorporating Indigenous practice into their occupational health and safety procedures, and holding "ceremonies" of acknowledgement and completion.

That is, at Argyle we see the deployment of multiple strategies of engagement, including localized forms of cultural capital, as well as corporate policies with local and global application within the contemporary context of regional development and emerging Indigenous governance practices. By engaging in practices in order to achieve a balance and reformulation of relationships between the Aboriginal participants in particular and other forces in their worlds, including the Barramundi and the Argyle miners, the participants have transformed the existing relationships and the possibility of continuing process of transformation of ongoing relationships without the loss of their identity or that of the corporate participants or requiring the merging of two. Argyle's iconic status should perhaps be seen more as a hybrid space of industrial mining *and* a site for the contemporary expression of a continuing Aboriginal tradition.

The local Aboriginal people applied their own cultural foundations and normative principles over many years to (re)establish the most (culturally) appropriate way to "manage" their country and the resources in it – including sub-surface diamonds. They used their ceremonial practices and their country-based responsibilities to protect the workers at the mine, to extend the life of the mine, and to "update" the "legal/formal" basis of relations between themselves, Argyle as a corporate entity, and the wider Australian community by utilizing the recently enacted provisions of the Native Title Act 1993 to protect their right to be in a relationship with Argyle Diamonds.

At the same time they enlisted the assistance of their country and all that is embedded in it to commit ensuring the continuing life of the mine, their critical role and required presence at the mine, and as beneficiaries of the mine's continuing operation. It is beyond the scope of this chapter to detail the cultural practices that were enlisted, but suffice to say that they laid the basis for a range of ceremonial activities at the mine site as Aboriginal people turned increasingly to their own "technologies" in order to increase the supply of diamonds at Argyle and thus prevent the closure of the mine.

Doohan's work develops an alternative view of Argyle, which challenges the more typical iconic representation of Argyle as a site where Aboriginal people are the passive victims of a corporate global mining operation, and where the juxtaposition of sacred site and resource is represented as a zero sum game in which only one of these entities can exist at any time. She discusses ceremonial actions of Aboriginal people "to make more" at the mine site, as well as their explanations of those actions, all of which demonstrate that for local Aboriginal people "Argyle" continues to be a sacred site and is now also an operating diamond mine. This opens up the possibility that an operating mine site and an Aboriginal sacred site can coexist. However, such a conclusion does not suggest that governments and corporations can obviate their responsibilities to respect traditional owners' statements of concern and disagreement about mining their traditional country, nor can it ameliorate the continuing disadvantage experienced by Aboriginal people in East Kimberley on a daily basis, nor can such an understanding alone can be a satisfactory or "better outcome" for Indigenous people.

Nonetheless, in taking a multi-layered and intercontextual approach to the theatre of Argyle it has been possible to identify the enlivened space of "Argyle" that is both geographically grounded and intercultural. In this enlivened space of the Barramundi Dreaming, local cultural practices and formal agreement-making sustains the Aboriginal worldview in a way that the dominant society does not, and yet it is essentially a local hybrid space where Aborigines and miners have engaged in relationships that find expression in written documents, in oral accounts, and in ceremonial performances conducted at the mine (albeit constrained by events and economic realities played out at the global scale and by the dominant culture) and, importantly, in the everyday interactions between Aboriginal people and miners. The skills required to allow these culturally challenging opportunities to become practices demand not only a theoretical articulation but also an approach – a praxis from scholars who are experts in the fields of negotiation, management, and planning – that enables decolonizing relationship formation rather than entrenches the mostly unrecognized habits and expectations of the dominant society.

Land-Use Planning and Impact Assessment: Product or Process?

Intercultural skills are also needed in the domains of land-use planning where modernist state power shapes everyday practices that are commonly used as technologies to assert discipline over the messy spaces of coexistence and bring order (framed within the dominant approaches to governance and NRM) to the processes of spatial development and governance. These practices often erase, restrict, and transform Indigenous domains and intercultural spaces of coexistence and participation into domains of state regulation and dominance. Indeed, urban and regional land-use planning has not only enabled modernizing governments to transform Indigenous territories into managed landscapes subject to development controls and the practices of professional planning. Planning practices have also disciplined and controlled the ancient jurisdictions of Indigenous governance to create new spaces for development within existing natural and cultural landscapes, and managed the legal, social, political, discursive, and territorial spaces of pluralist coexistence.

Much of the construction of the state developmentalist agenda is constituted through project approvals and the assessment of development proposals on a project-by-project basis. Thus, in the regulatory context, impact assessment becomes a crucial management tool. In the Indigenous context, impact assessment becomes a crucial point of intervention, and the need for tools to reorient impact assessment towards the intercultural domain rather than the state's agenda is an important area of concern. For engaged scholarship, the field of practice involving impact assessment is a valuable moment for critical examination of the way the intercultural domain unfolds and operates.

In many jurisdictions, a rhetoric of democratic participation and consensus-based decision making is advocated by the state and corporate planning professionals who discount the historical processes that create the structures of exclusion, marginalization, and racism in modern pluralist societies. The tyranny of consensus creates enormous pressures on local Indigenous groups to comply with the developmentalist agenda. Indeed, regulatory systems often entrench the understanding that access to even basic resources, infrastructure, and opportunities is conditional upon such compliance. Thus NRM and land-use and development planning systems impose consensus as a top-down insistence on conformity to a formulation of the public interest that is hostile to local Indigenous values, and compliance is secured at the cost of cultural diversity, traditional and customary rights, and equitable participation in and access to benefits and opportunities of development processes. Such practices violate local customary practices. They bypass and in the process produce erasure of customary law and governance structures. They typically disrupt local social and economic relationships and alter existing local cultural and physical landscapes and their accessibility to and meaning for the Indigenous community.

Social impact assessment is a field of practice that integrates engaged social science scholarship into elements of state and corporate decision making, and the interface between Indigenous and dominant societies. It offers a range of tools to facilitate analysis, monitoring, and management of the social consequences of development and conservation (Cosslett et al. 2004, 3). One of those tools – community mapping – offers a means of harnessing new technology to translate Indigenous land-use and knowledge systems into language that is understood by a state government (Chapin et al. 2005; Peluso 1995). Lunkapis (2010; also Howitt and Lunkapis 2010) suggests combining these tools to challenge the dominant land-use and natural resource governance systems in a powerful critique based on his own experiences as an Indigenous citizen and state town planner. His investigation of Malaysian town planning systems considers how land-use planning techniques, such as community mapping and social impact assessment, can enhance Indigenous self-determination, self-governance, and public participation in the planning process (see also Loomis 2000; Ridder and Pahl-Wostl 2005; Xanthaki 2007).

Community mapping involves cartographic techniques that are capable of representing spatial realities with hidden meanings. Documenting, protecting, and advocating Indigenous land use through community mapping has been pursued in many countries (Lydon 2002; Parker 2006; Peluso 1998; Pollock and Whitelaw 2005; Warren 2005; Wood 2005) and used to support many different projects. They can carry a certain degree of authority but may also exacerbate community vulnerabilities by recording information in ways that disarticulate it from its customary owners and their authoritative use of it, creating excuses to bypass people in planning and development processes. Clearly, the presence of a community-generated map is no guarantee that members of a particular community have reached an agreed position on a particular project or opportunity. But the impact assessment process and mapping activities themselves can be pursued in ways that foster willingness to work together across difference and to advocate for a participatory and collaborative planning approach that engages in the process of challenge and transformation.

To meet this challenge, it is best that community mapping projects are assessed independently using the established conceptual framework of social impact assessment (see for example Barrow 2000, 33; Howitt 2001, 335). This process will be able to gauge the likely outcome and the degree of support for sustainable land-use initiatives. Integration of community mapping and social impact assessment encourages open communication between state regulators, resource developers, and disadvantaged and excluded groups, and supports equitable and collaborative learning processes to secure rather than erase Indigenous institutions and authority on the ground.

Embracing the Commotion of Co-motion

In Australia, Indigenous rangers – groups created under local Indigenous management for environmental activities, such as wildlife and site protections, research, control of invasive species, and so on (Muller 2008a, 2008b, 2008c) – are increasingly gaining recognition and being resourced for their contribution to mainstream NRM processes. However, the administration and documentation of Indigenous "Caring for Country" approaches are dominated by mainstream NRM frameworks which marginalize intangible elements of Caring for Country (Weir and Muller forthcoming). State powers are reinforced by the "objectivity" of "science" limiting Indigenous authority in the NRM domain (Palmer

2004). Consequently, those resource management activities that do not challenge dominant culture's views are more readily granted resources (Gibbs 2003). Governments have asserted "selective valuation" or sought to work with "legible" components of Caring for Country in seeking to engage with the Indigenous domain, assigning significance to familiar rather than alien priorities. The "incomprehensible" (O'Malley 1998), "illegible" (Christie 2007), or "invisible" (Howitt 2001) components of Caring for Country are thus ignored and accountability acts as a technology of erasure within formal administrative structures and processes.

Science and sustainability discourses position Indigenous knowledges as "lacking" answers and assume the need for an imposition of external, universally relevant knowledge. Indigenous knowledges are thus assessed for the "facts" they can contribute to the management process, for their objective components rather than their performance (Muller forthcoming). Through such a lens, Indigenous knowledges are seen to "lack" rather than be acknowledged as complete epistemologies. As such, the power of dominant society is protected through the camouflage of "objectivity" of science in protecting Eurocentric values and power structures, and justifying intervention by the state. Resources are tied to these "objective," "scientific," or "quantitative" outcomes at the expense of an Indigenous-determined framework. Therefore, whilst Indigenous ranger groups are able to achieve management actions, their own ontological frameworks are erased from the administrative structures (Muller 2008). Therefore recognition is only based on how Caring for Country can contribute to NRM outcomes and Indigenous priorities for Caring for Country then slip through the resourcing gaps. To only resource the overlap between the two disrespects the ontological foundations on which Caring for Country is built and the rights of Indigenous peoples to operate from that basis and therefore to self-determine their own futures.

Ranger groups must weave together resources from a variety of sources to create "spaces" in its operation for staff to attend funeral ceremonies, to visit sites of significance, and other Yolngu Caring for Country processes (see Muller 2008). This weaving must be almost invisible, such that the explicit and celebrated "achievements" of groups are framed in terms of NRM outcomes, with Indigenous processes occurring in the margins. Whilst groups are able to create space to get work done within the flexibility and margins of program management and goodwill of certain agencies, the overarching system does not recognize the foundations on which Indigenous approaches are based, therefore these foundations are not explicitly celebrated, acknowledged, or resourced in their own rights.

The legitimation of Eurocentric administrative and legislative systems has led to a co-optation of the Caring for Country agenda to be about NRM. Legislative and administrative procedures have erased Yolngu scales of governance and accountability. Therefore the only terms of reference for holding projects accountable are based on Eurocentric assumptions. Yet Eurocentric ontologies are inadequate for encompassing alternative ontological perspectives. Instead, discourses of science, management, and sustainability dominate and erase Yolngu constructions. The power manifest in these constructions is rendered invisible by the promotion of the idea of objective truths of universal assumptions (Muller 2012). The assumptions of absence, the assumption of the need to impose universal answers leaves no "space" or "place" for self-determined, locally contextualized development or management processes. This is where the exercise of power is most visible, for to provide space is to relinquish or share control, exactly what is necessary to create more equitable partnerships. The real challenge lies in resourcing Indigenous groups for holistic services provided in ways that make sense within the Indigenous framework based on their own aspirations for managing country. These arguments do not dismiss the need of partnerships, but instead aim to achieve ontologically equitable collaborations.

The unruly, intangible, illegible, and often invisible elements of Caring for Country are not easily subsumable within universal scientific or administrative processes. Indeed, their very presence is often assumed to be inappropriate and messy, some kind of chaos or commotion. Yet this perceived commotion is actually part of a prescribed system of law and regulation that has been the foundation of Indigenous worldviews and therefore is essential for self-determination. Esteva's (1987) idea of co-motion, of moving together, can be (re)framed within the context of Indigenous land and sea management. Rather than external agents working to pro-mote particular approaches or outcomes, the idea of co-motion is to co-mote, together, without imposition or pro-motion in predetermined ways. Inevitably such a co-motion will result in a perceived commotion as two worldviews may not be able to understand each other. However, embracing the commotion of co-motion is the only way to achieve truly equitable partnerships.

Self-determination that is only allowed to exist within predetermined frameworks and administered through Western accountability systems can never be truly determined by Indigenous groups themselves. The critical issue here is that resources are still necessary from the state, and the state is obliged to provide resources for its Indigenous citizens, but how can these resources be freed from the shackles of administrative and accountability procedures that are only framed on dominant ontological perspectives? Unless there is an explicit space for self-determined and self-managed accountability systems and processes, Caring for Country will always be limited to agency within the prescribed programs or on the fringes. The challenge of co-motion is to re-imagine institutions in which the state can provide resources to Indigenous groups even if governments do not understand the ontological underpinnings of Caring for Country. This re-imagining is a challenge to Indigenous ranger groups and to the state, and will necessitate focus on process and relationship, over outcome, intervention, and control.

CAPACITY DEFICITS IN DOMINANT NRM INSTITUTIONS

We have aimed here to outline an agenda for engaged and collaborative scholarship that challenges and rectifies the lack of intercultural capacity within dominant institutions of land-use planning, NRM, and environmental governance, and addresses the consequences of intercultural incompetence and incapacity for Indigenous rights and the sustainability of culturally diverse communities. Drawing on our experience within mostly Australian settings, we have identified and discussed a range of ideas on which we invite debate and disagreement. While advocating the urgency of that debate, we also acknowledge that it is the process of debate and practice, particularly debate and practice within the domains of intercultural NRM that will produce the opportunities to transform the existing shortcomings of thought and practice. As the other contributions to this volume demonstrate, the need to connect together parallel discourses across different disciplines, communities of practice, and jurisdictions has much to offer in this work.

In addressing Indigenous issues, the social inclusion agenda for the discipline and many higher education institutions has typically emphasized questions of exclusion and preparation. We support continued attention to these matters and encourage higher levels of recruitment and support for Indigenous practitioners in research, teaching, and professional roles (e.g., Frantz and Howitt 2012), but also advocate the development of a second dimension to this work. Addressing the capacity deficits of universities, government agencies, NRM institutions, and our own disciplines and professional communities to secure high levels of intercultural competence along with knowledge, skills, and understanding of pluralist settings and values that acknowledge, respect, and respond to cultural diversity must become a priority in professional education and development. We suggest that professional bodies and teaching disciplines need to nurture ideas firmly grounded in recognition that being human is fundamentally about being-together-in-places (Howitt 2011). The challenge to engaged scholarship presented by the realities of messy, conflicting, awkward, and fragile geographies of coexistence is a challenge to produce ideas that equip NRM institutions and their staff to see, think, and act more coherently, more responsibly, more generously, and more equitably towards just, sustainable, and inclusive futures.

NOTES

1   This chapter represents a synthesis of a long and dispersed dialogue amongst staff and graduate students studying human geography at Macquarie University and in a variety of field sites. We would particularly like to acknowledge contributions to our discursive community from others, particularly Parry Agius, Joh Bornman, Robyn Dowling, Bob Fagan, Leah Gibbs, Sue Jackson, Marcia Langton, Kate Lloyd, Deborah Rose, Tammy Russell, Tracker Tilmouth, Jan Turner, Jess Weir, and Deirdre Wilcock, along with the Indigenous people and organizations whom each of us has worked with.

2   See Li 2007 for discussion of "improvement."

3   See e.g., Porter (2004), Lane and Hibbard (2005), and Jojola (2008) for discussion of Indigenous planning scholarship.

4   The term "deep colonizing" is taken from Rose (1999) and refers to the ways in which well-intentioned interventions aimed at improving the lives of disadvantaged people often reinforces both the power of the colonizing system and the loss of agency of "the other." Li (2007) offers a detailed account of a similar process under the guise of the "will to improve" in a development studies context.

REFERENCES

Agius, P., J. Davies, R. Howitt, and L. Johns. 2002. "Negotiating Comprehensive Settlement of Native Title Issues: Building a New Scale of Justice in South Australia." *Land, Rights, Laws: Issues of Native Title* 2 (20):1–12.

Agius, P., and T. Jenkin. 2007. "(Re)asserting Indigenous Rights and Jurisdictions within a Politics of Place: Transformative Nature of Native Title Negotiations in South Australia." *Geographical Research* 45 (2):194–202.

Agius, P., T. Jenkin, S. Jarvis, and R. Howitt. 2007. "(Re)asserting Indigenous Rights and Jurisdictions within a Politics of Place: Transformative Nature of Native Title Negotiations in South Australia." *Geographical Research* 45 (2):194–202.

Alfred, T. 1999. *Peace, Power, Righteousness: An Indigenous Manifesto.* Toronto: Oxford University Press.

Allan, C., and A. Curtis. 2005. "Nipped in the Bud: Why Regional Scale Adaptive Management Is Not Blooming." *Environmental Management* 36 (3):414–25.

Barrow, C.J. 2000. *Social Impact Assessment: An Introduction.* London: Arnold.

Byrne, D.R. 2003. "Nervous Landscapes: Race and Space in Australia." *Journal of Social Archaeology* 3 (2):169–93.

Carter, J.L. 2008. "Thinking Outside the Framework: Equitable Research Partnerships for Environmental Research in Australia." *The Geographical Journal* 174 (1):63–75.

Chapin, M., Z. Lamb, and B. Threlkeld. 2005. "Mapping Indigenous Lands." *Annual Review of Anthropology* 34 (1):619–38.

Christie, M.J. 2006. "Transdisciplinary Research and Aboriginal Knowledge." *The Australian Journal of Indigenous Education* 35:78–89

Cornell, S. 2006. *Indigenous Peoples, Poverty and Self-Determination in Australia, New Zealand, Canada and the United States.* Joint Occasional Papers on Native Affairs. Tucson and Cambridge, Native Nations Institute, University of Arizona, and Harvard Project on American Indian Economic Development.

Cosslett, C., D. Buchan, and J. Smith. 2004. *Assessing the Social Effects of Conservation on Neighbouring Communities: Guidelines for Department of Conservation Staff.* Wellington: DOC Science Publishing.

Cross, S. 2006. *The Scale Politics of Reconciliation.* PhD thesis. Department of Human Geography, Macquarie University.

Dixon, R.A., and M.C. Dillon. 1990. *Aborigines and Diamond Mining: The Politics of Resource Development in the East Kimberley Western Australia.* Nedlands: University of Western Australia Press.

Doohan, K. 2007. *Making Things Come Good: Aborigines and Miners at Argyle.* PhD thesis. Department of Human Geography, Macquarie University.

– 2008. *Making Things Come Good: Relations Between Aborigines and Miners at Argyle*. Broome, WA: Backroom Books.

Esteva, G. 1987. "Regenerating People's Space." *Alternatives* 12 (1):125–52.

Frantz, K., and R. Howitt. 2012. "Geography for and with Indigenous Peoples: Indigenous Geographies as Challenge and Invitation." *GeoJournal* 77:727–31.

Gibbs, L. 2003. "Decolonising, Multiplicities and Mining in the Eastern Goldfields, Western Australia." *Australian Geographical Studies* 41 (1):17–28.

Howitt, R. 2001. *Rethinking Resource Management: Justice, Sustainability and Indigenous Peoples*. London and New York: Routledge.

– 2011. "Ethics as First Method: Research Issues in Intercultural Natural Resource Management." Keynote address. June 2011. International Symposium on Society and Natural Resources, Kota Kinabalu, Malaysia.

– 2012. "Sustainable Indigenous Futures in Remote Indigenous Areas: Relationships, Processes and Failed State Approaches." *GeoJournal* 77 (6): 817–28

Howitt, R., and R. Lawrence. 2008. "Indigenous Peoples, Corporate Social Responsibility and the Fragility of the Interpersonal Domain." In *Earth Matters: Indigenous Peoples, the Extractive Industries and Corporate Social Responsibility*, edited by C. O'Faircheallaigh and S. Ali. Sheffield, 83–103. Greenleaf Publishing.

Howitt, R., and G.J. Lunkapis. 2010. "Coexistence: Planning and the Challenge of Indigenous Rights" in *Ashgate Research Companion to Planning Theory*, edited by J. Hillier and P. Healey, 109–33. Farnham: Ashgate.

Howitt, R., and S. Suchet-Pearson. 2006. "Rethinking the Building Blocks: Ontological Pluralism and the Idea of 'Management'." *Geografiska Annaler: Ser B, Human Geography* 88 (3):323–35.

Jojola, T. 2008 "Indigenous Planning – An Emerging Context." *Canadian Journal of Urban Research* 17 (1) Supplement:37–47.

Lane, M., and M. Hibbard. 2005. "Doing It for Themselves: Transformative Planning by Indigenous Peoples." *Journal of Planning Education and Research* 25:172–84.

Lawrence, R. 2007. "Corporate Social Responsibility, Supply-chains and Saami Claims: Tracing the Political in the Finnish Forestry Industry." *Geographical Research* 45 (2):167–76.

– 2009. *Shifting Responsibilities and Shifting Terrains: State Responsibility, Corporate Social Responsibility and Indigenous Claims*. PhD thesis. Department of Sociology, Stockhom University, and Department of Environment and Geography, Macquarie University.

Lendrum, M. 2007. *Fire Management, Carbon Abatement and Sustainable Futures on Country for Indigenous Australians: The West Arnhem Land Experience*. Unpublished BEnvMgt (Honours) thesis. Department of Human Geography, Macquarie University.

Li, T.M. 2007. *The Will To Improve: Governmentality, Development and the Practice of Politics*. Durham and London: Duke University Press.

Loomis, T.M. 2000. "Indigenous Populations and Sustainable Development: Building on Indigenous Approaches to Holistic, Self-Determined Development." *World Development* 28 (5):893–910.

Lunkapis, G.J. 2010. *Understanding Land Use and Natural Resources (LUNaR) Governance: A Case Study of Sabah, Malaysia*. Department of Environment and Geography, Macquarie University.

Lydon, M.F. 2002. *(Re)presenting the Living Landscape: Exploring Community Mapping as a Tool for Transformative Learning and Planning*. Thesis submitted. School of Environmental Studies, Faculty of Law, University of British Columbia.

Meretsky, V.J., and D.L. Wegner et al. 2000. "Balancing Endangered Species and Ecosystems: A Case Study of Adaptive Management in Grand Canyon." *Environmental Management* 25 (6):579–86.

Muller, S. 2008a. *Making Space to Care for Country*. PhD thesis, 333. Department of Human Geography, Macquarie University.

Muller, S. 2008b. "Accountability Constructions, Contestations and Implications: Insights from Working in a Yolngu Cross-Cultural Institution, Australia." *Geography Compass* 2:1–19.

– 2008c. "Community-Based Management of Saltwater Country, Northern Australia." *Development* 51: 139–43.

– 2008d. "Indigenous Payment for Environmental Service (PES) Opportunities in the Northern Territory: Negotiating with Customs." *Australian Geographer* 39 (2):149–70.

– 2012. "'Two Ways': Bringing Indigenous and Non-Indigenous Knowledges Together." *Country, Native Title and Ecology*, edited by J. Weir, 59–79. Canberra: ANU ePress.

Olsson, P., and C. Folke et al. 2004. "Adaptive Comanagement for Building Resilience in Social–Ecological Systems." *Environmental Management* 34 (1):75–90.

O'Malley, P. 1996. "Indigenous Governance." *Economy and Society* 25 (3):310–26.

Palmer, L. 2004. "Fishing Lifestyles: 'Territorians,' Traditional Owners and the Management of Recreational Fishing in Kakadu National Park." *Australian Geographical Studies* 42 (1):60–76.

Parker, B. 2006 "Constructing Community Through Maps? Power and Praxis in Community Mapping." *Professional Geographer* 58 (4):470–84.

Peluso, N.L. 1995. "Whose Woods Are These? Counter-Mapping Forest Territories in Kalimantan, Indonesia." *Antipode* 27 (4):383–406.

Pollock, R.M., and G.S. Whitelaw. 2005. "Community-Based Monitoring in Support of Local Sustainability." *Local Environment* 10 (3):211–28.

Porter, L. 2004 "Unlearning One's Privilege: Reflections on Cross-Cultural Research with Indigenous Peoples in South-East Australia." *Planning Theory & Practice* 5 (1):104–9.

– 2006. "Rights or Containment? The Politics of Aboriginal Cultural Heritage in Victoria." *Australian Geographer* 37 (3):355–74.

Prout, S. 2006. *Security and Belonging: Aboriginal Spatial Mobility Practices and the Provision of Basic Government Services in Yamatji Country, Western Australia*. PhD thesis. Department of Human Geography, Macquarie University.

– 2008. "On the Move? Indigenous Temporary Mobility Practices in Australia." CAEPR working paper no. 48, Centre for Aboriginal Economic Policy Research. Canberra: ANU.

– 2009a. "Security and Belonging: Reconceptualising Aboriginal Mobilities in Yamatji Country, Western Australia." *Mobilities* 4 (2):177–202.

– 2009b. "Vacuums and Veils: Engaging with Statistically 'Invisible' Indigenous Population Dynamics." *Geographical Research* 47 (4):408–21.

Prout, S., and R. Howitt 2009. "Frontier Imaginings and Subversive Indigenous Spatialities." *Journal of Rural Studies* 25 (4):396–403.

Ridder, D., and C. Pahl-Wostl. 2005. "Participatory Integrated Assessment in Local Level Planning." *Regional Environmental Change* 5 (4):188–96.

Rose, D.B. 1996. *Nourishing Terrains: Australian Aboriginal Views of Landscape and Wilderness*. Canberra: Australian Heritage Commission.

– 1999. "Indigenous Ecologies and an Ethic of Connection." *Global Ethics and Environment*, edited by N. Low, 175–87. London: Routledge.

Rogers, K. 1998. "Managing Science/Management Partnerships: A Challenge of Adaptive Management." *Conservation Ecology* 2 (2). Accessed online at: http://www.consecol.org/vol2/iss2/resp1.

Suchet, S. 1999. *Situated Engagement: A Critique of Wildlife Management and Postcolonial Discourse*. PhD thesis. Department of Human Geography, Macquarie University.

– 2002. "'Totally Wild?' Colonising Discourses, Indigenous Knowledges and Managing Wildlife." *Australian Geographer* 33 (2):141–57.

Veland, S., R. Howitt, and D. Dominey-Howes. 2010. "Invisible Institutions in Emergencies: Evacuating the Remote Indigenous Community of Warruwi,

Northern Territory Australia, from Cyclone Monica." *Environmental Hazards: Human and Policy Dimensions* 9:197–214.

Warren, C. 2005 "Mapping Common Futures: Customary Communities, NGOs and the State in Indonesia's Reform Era." *Development and Change* 36 (1):49–73.

Weir, J., and Muller, S. Forthcoming. "Caring for Country Is Not Natural Resource Management." *Geographic Research*.

Wood, J. 2005. "'How Green Is my Valley?' Desktop Geographic Information Systems as a Community-Based Participatory Mapping Tool." *Area* 37 (2):159–70.

Xanthaki, A. 2007. *Indigenous Rights and United Nations Standards Self-Determination, Culture and Land*. Cambridge and New York: Cambridge University Press.

Young, E., H. Ross, J. Johnson, and J. Kesteven. 1991. *Caring for Country: Aborigines and Land Management*. Canberra: Australian National Parks and Wildlife Service.

Iwi Futures: Integrating Traditional Knowledge Systems and Cultural Values into Land-Use Planning

TANIRA KINGI, LIZ WEDDERBURN, AND
OSCAR MONTES DE OCA

Contemporary notions of planning within the New Zealand Māori context are underpinned by a world view that includes an intimate relationship between humans and the natural environment. The connection between Māori and their ancestral lands has evolved over many generations of continuous occupation. Underpinning this connection is an understanding that humans and the natural environment share a common ancestry. Knowledge of these genealogical connections, along with customary practices are key components of the Māori world. Traditional (pre-European) systems of land-use and environmental management were based on an entrenched understanding of these interrelationships, and while much of this knowledge has been lost over recent generations, the cultural concepts remain embedded in land-owning communities.

Land development under the current land tenure system, however, faces a number of constraints. The legislation has produced large numbers of registered owners, which slows decision making and increases administration costs. Effective planning processes need to account for these institutional and cultural contexts. This chapter describes the development of an Integrated Decision Support Framework (IDSF) – "Iwi Futures" – that draws on two case studies to illustrate its application. The framework utilizes a range of tools that provide information to landowners at varying scales – from a single property (i.e., farm) to multiple properties, and then up to the catchment level and beyond. The key problem that the Iwi Futures framework addresses is the ineffectiveness of current approaches to land and rural community planning in New

Zealand that do not incorporate local realities and cultural values and aspirations of the land-owning communities.

The chapter has four sections. Section one provides a brief overview of the institutional structures governing Māori land, including the tenure system and ownership structures. Section two outlines the Māori worldview towards land and the environment. Section three outlines the framework and introduces the two case studies. The final section makes some closing remarks and identifies areas of further research.

THE INSTITUTIONAL FRAMEWORK: *WHENUA*, MĀORI LAND TENURE, AND OWNERSHIP STRUCTURES

Māori refer to land as *whenua*. Māori land, or Māori freehold land as it is referred to under the Māori Land Act (Te Ture Whenua Māori) 1993, is around 1.5 million hectares or 5 per cent of the total area of New Zealand. The small area of land under the control of Māori is the legacy of New Zealand's colonial history which saw a rapid decline in landownership by the Indigenous population following the introduction of the Native Land Act in 1862, the Native Land Court three years later, and other legislation that confiscated land deemed to be "idle" in the interests of the newly established New Zealand colony. Māori own "general land" (land available on the open land market) while holding interests in their ancestral lands. This creates two parallel land tenure systems where Māori land is almost exclusively owned by the descendents of the original owners, handed down through successive generations to the current owners (Kingi 2009a, 2009b, 2008).

A somewhat unique characteristic of Māori land is the relative ease by which it was codified and registered in the nineteenth century. Specific knowledge of occupation and land use, and in particular the genealogical records of individuals going back many generations, was held by particular members of a tribe or clan. However, a general understanding of boundaries was common knowledge and very useful for nineteenth-century Native Land Court surveyors when registering land and allocating individuals' names against certificates of title. These names are the "original" owners and when these titles were amalgamated into larger blocks, the size of the individual interests in the final blocks depended on the area of titles. As successive generations have inherited their land interests these are increasingly fragmented (or fractionated). Title fractionation occurs where additional owners receive a diminished fraction or portion of the land represented by the title.

The average size of the current certificates of title is around sixty hectares, but they range from less than one hundred square metres to over five hundred hectares. The average number of registered owners is seventy per title, but again this figure ranges from one to over four hundred owners per title. Owners can have multiple interests in more than one block of land, which has resulted in owner-interests numbering more than two million, and they are increasing by 185,000 per year with successions (Te Puni Kokiri 2011). This statistic has an important implication for land-use and community planning. As the number of owners with every generation increases significantly, so, too, does the diversity of views on how the land should be used and the priorities for the communities that live on or close to the ancestral land.

An additional factor that impacts on planning is the ownership structure. The two main structures that control close to 60 per cent of all Māori land are Ahuwhenua trusts (approximately five thousand) that control around 750,000 hectares, and Māori incorporations (166 that control 210,000 hectares) (MAF 2011). The distribution of land administered by these structures is, however, skewed with a small number dominating. Te Puni Kokiri (2011) recently identified forty incorporations that control nearly 80 per cent of incorporation land, and one hundred trusts control over 60 per cent of trust lands. At the other end of the scale, almost two thousand trusts manage less than five hectares and an even greater number manage land between six and fifty hectares. The most startling statistic however, is that over 60 per cent of land titles representing approximately 20 per cent of Māori land (or over 280,00 hectares) has no formal structure.

Ownership structures are critical mechanisms for decision making and to carry out rudimentary administration functions. Land-use planning without a structure is extremely difficult, if not impossible. When there is a structure and the numbers are large (sometimes in the thousands), decision making is unfortunately not that much simpler. It is therefore important that effective planning incorporates tools, processes, and skill sets that are flexible and adaptable to a wide range of demands that are likely to emerge from the owners.

TE AO MĀORI – THE MĀORI WORLD (OR WORLDVIEW)

A worldview is a phrase that often inadequately tries to capture customs, values, attitudes, and beliefs of a particular group or individual. This section will attempt to outline a set of core belief systems, values, and attitudes that reflect Māori views, in general, about their relationship to their natural environment. Obviously this statement does not apply equally to all individuals or to any particular individual at any point in time. But the following knowledge sets (*mātauranga*) can often be heard in incantations, laments, proverbs, carvings, and other art forms, and in particular, genealogy (*whakapapa*) recited from memory.

Mātauranga

The Māori worldview is underpinned by traditional and cultural knowledge (*mātauranga*) and an in-depth understanding of the relationship between humans (*ira tangata*) and the natural world (*te ao*), or, more specifically, the world of life (*te ao tūroa*) and the world of light (*te ao mārama*). Marsden and Henare (1992), in their widely referenced monologue on environmental guardianship (*kaitiakitanga*), provided useful insights into key concepts of Māori cosmogony and philosophy, including genealogy (*whakapapa*).

According to Marsden (1975), Māori acknowledged three realms of reality: (1) *Te ao aro-nui* – the world of sense and perception (or the world as we perceive it); (2) *Te ao tua-uri* – the world behind the world of our perceptions; and (3) *Te ao tua-ātea* – the transcendental, eternal world of the spirit (Figure 14.1). Māori believe that although we cannot prove the existence of Te ao tua-uri or comprehend it directly, we can be trained to penetrate this realm. This was the primary purpose behind the careful selection and training of priests (*tohunga*). Te ao tua-uri comprises a complex series of "rhythmical patterns of energy" (Marsden 1975, 198) that underpin values and cultural practices (*tikanga*). The following definitions are primarily taken from Marsden.

Tikanga

There are a large number of values and cultural or customary practices that are routinely maintained by Māori communities. Core values link the spiritual and physical dimensions with geographical place through genealogical lineage and the balancing of energy between the realms. Examples of core values include *ūkaipōtanga*, *wairuatanga*, and *tau utuutu*.

Ukaipōtanga is the connection to a specific physical location linked to a person's birth place. Māori refer to their birth place as *tūrangawaewae*, or, place of standing, and they often refer to themselves as *te hau kāinga*

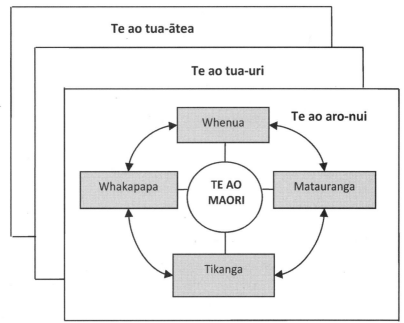

Figure 14.1   Te Ao Māori – a Māori worldview

(*hau* in this context refers to the vital essence of land; and *kāinga* is the residence, or home, literally meaning place where fire has burnt) in relation to their homeland. *Wairuatanga* derives from *wairua*, meaning literally twin waters, or the spiritual aspect of humans that accompanies the physical. Tau utuutu is the act of reciprocity, including giving and receiving, but also maintaining balance in the natural order. Acts such as felling trees, hunting animals, or fishing were never carried out lightly, nor without seeking and receiving prior permission by tohunga who would give the appropriate incantation (*karakia*) to maintain balance.

Complementary to core values were a set of related secondary values are aimed at guiding human behaviour. These include *whānaungatanga*, *manaakitanga*, *kotahitanga*, *kaitiakitanga*, and *rangatiratanga*. Whānaungatanga is the bond of kinship through common ancestry. Manaakitanga is reciprocal and unqualified acts of giving and support. Kotahitanga means maintaining a unity of purpose that acknowledges the interdependency between family and tribal groupings. Kaitiakitanga derives from *tiaki*, meaning to guard or keep watch, so kaitiakitanga is the responsibility to nurture and care for the natural environment.

Te Pū (root) → *Te More* (taproot) →*Te Weu* (rootlets) →*Te Aka* (vine) → *Te Rea* (growth) →

→ *Te Waonui* (primeval forest) → *Te Kune* (conception) → *Te Whē* (sound) →

→ *Te Kore* (non-existence) → *Te Pō* (darkness)

Figure 14.2   Cosmological origins of life

Source: Buck 1987, 435

Rangatiratanga, or *tino rangatiratanga*, is an expression of authority, sovereignty, and the legitimacy of a family grouping or tribe.

Whakapapa

Whakapapa, the final box in Figure 14.1 literally means to create inter-connected layers and that each of these layers depicts the complex inter-relationship between humans, the natural environment, and the realms. Central to Māori cosmogony is the creation of deities and the personi-fication of natural phenomena. Whakapapa therefore takes an intrinsic role in Māori thought processes. Shirres (1997) refers to it as the eternal present because of its capacity to ensure knowledge of genealogical con-nections to humans and the natural environment that provides a power-ful linkage across time and space.

Genealogies formed a taxonomic structure that provided a rationale and order to the Māori world. The study of traditional or folk taxono-mies by ethnobiologists has revealed complex taxonomic classifications where oral societies developed systems to describe existing patterns in nature (Attran 1993; Berlin 1992). A key function of taxonomies is the derivation of a classification system that explains function and order in the natural world. Whakapapa describes elements and relationships, but closely aligned with this is the use of narratives to explain the nature of the relationships.

Whakapapa allows the structuring of genealogical trees to explain the origin of the universe and the creation of life. Although the details vary from tribe to tribe, the general structure of the genealogical narratives remains fairly consistent. Genealogical descent from the divine forces or deities (*atua*) is preceded by sequential growth, depicted as the develop-ment of a forest that is followed by a void and darkness (Figure 14.2).

The progression starts with the root (*te Pū*) and ends with a void or non-existence (*te Kore*) and darkness (*te Pō*). The development of earth

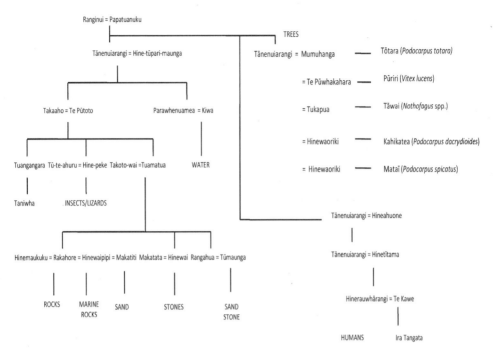

Figure 14.3   Common genealogy – humans and the natural environment

mother (*Papatūānuku*) and sky father (*Ranginui*) occurred during te Pō. Best (1982a, 1982b) and Smith (1913, 1915) give detailed descriptions, although other versions of the cosmogonic genealogy are much longer (see Best 1982a, 69). Cosmological narratives, or axioms, played an important role in explaining the complexities of the genealogical connections between the various components of the natural world. The creation story of the separation of Papatūānuku (a.k.a. Papa) and Ranginui (a.k.a. Rangi) is based on a number of varying narratives. The brief version below is one of a number and there are others which may conflict with this account. Six children took part in separating Rangi and Papa and each of their names was associated with dominion or authority over aspects of the physical world – wind, sea, forests, and so on (see Best 1982a, 1982b; Buck 1987; Marsden 1975, 2003; Smith 1913, 1915; Buck 1987, 439). The deity credited with the creation of humans is also the deity for the natural environment. Figure 14.3 illustrates the genealogical linkages.

The connection that Māori have with their natural environment is not only based on a deep seated appreciation for the environment, but also a profound knowledge of the genealogical relationships illustrated in Figure 14.3. While the exact genealogical records may vary across tribes, the level of influence that genealogical knowledge has on decision making with individuals and groups also varies. It would be an overgeneralization to claim that this knowledge has a consistent and predictable effect on landowners in relation to land use and community planning in contemporary Māori society. Its influence on landowner behaviour, nonetheless, is apparent when discussions on land and community development are held. Examples of these will be given in the next section.

IWI FUTURES – AN INTEGRATED DECISION SUPPORT FRAMEWORK (IDSF)

The aim of the Iwi Futures research program was to develop a nationally applicable Māori land and resource decision support framework specifically designed for Māori landowners (individuals, organizations, and groups) throughout New Zealand to facilitate the sustainable land and community development.[1] The problem that it addressed was that standard approaches did not reflect Māori social and cultural imperatives, nor did they build capability with the communities to implement change. We argued that landowners could apply a systematic and comprehensive process that evaluates resources, explores alternative systems, and analyzes future pathway options through an integrated framework that has mātauranga at its core. A clear advantage of the Iwi Futures approach is that it is underpinned by landowners identifying and defining the social, cultural, and environmental drivers/priorities, and then exploring and developing options that lead to improved resource utilization and economic development that is environmentally sustainable and acceptable by the community.

We also incorporated a functional integrity approach (Thompson 1997) that views agriculture as a complex system of production practices, social values, and ecological relations. Functional integrity is a dynamic concept that changes depending on the observer's worldview. The concurrence of the Māori worldview and the institutional framework that land-owning Māori communities function within introduces a further set of functions related to the aspirations of the landowners alongside social, economic (i.e., productivity and utilization gains), and environmental aspirations within a planning framework (Wedderburn et al. 2010). The framework will also increase capability to design, manage, and evaluate resilient and flexible production systems that are responsive to external environmental shocks (e.g., climate change) and market changes (e.g., access requirements and consumer preferences).

Figure 14.4 outlines the Iwi Futures IDSF. The framework provided a systematic decision-making process for users to follow starting with understanding the owners (people – *tangata whenua*), describing and assessing resources (including land and water – *whenua*), generating development options (strategies – *rautaki whenua*) and then deliberating on future pathways (choices – *te ara whakamua*). This was an attempt to integrate socio-cultural imperatives with comprehensive land-resource assessments, complex simulation modelling, and a deliberative process to allow future land-use options to be assessed against a range of functions identified by landowners. The dotted boxes give examples of key questions that informed and guided the framework's development and application.

Iwi Futures Cases

The Iwi Futures program was based on four organizations that varied in size (land area), scale of agricultural operations, number of owners, and ownership structures and each was located in different geographic locations in New Zealand. Two of these cases are included here. We worked collaboratively with representatives of the land-owning community and appointed decision makers and administrators of the land to develop and apply the IDSF (Figure 14.4). The two case study organizations are Waimarama Incorporation and Aohanga Incorporation. Waimarama Incorporation is one of three Māori incorporations located on ecologically fragile but highly sought after coastal land around Waimarama in the Hawkes Bay. The incorporation (approximately two thousand hectares in size) aims to expand its land base through leases with neighbouring blocks and has identified alternative land-use options that will diversify their production base away from the pastoral sector. Aohanga Incorporation is approximately 7,280 hectares with the majority of the land in sheep and beef production and forestry. Aohanga Inc. has around 1,500 owners. Both organizations are located on the east coast of the North Island of New Zealand where there is increased frequency of summer droughts. Building resilience into their land use to cope with this was a key driver for these properties.

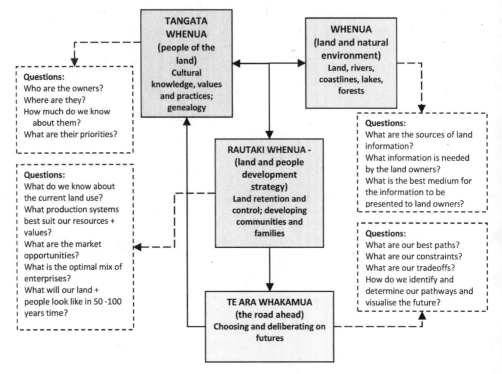

Figure 14.4   Iwi Futures – Integrated decision support framework

Methodology

A systems approach (Maani and Cavana 2007) was applied in the case studies to make transparent the relationships between people, natural resources, economics, and culture. Interviews were conducted with individual members of the case study organizations to document cultural values and knowledge about the land and its owners (Jahnke et al. 2010). Workshops using soft system methodologies were held with members of the farm committees to identify their aspirations for the land (Wedderburn et al. 2004a, b; Kingi et al. 2010).

A full description of the underlying soil, vegetation, water, and Indigenous cultural sites was developed for each of the properties using on-ground surveys, land manager experience, land-use databases, and historical data (Harmsworth and Mackay 2010). All the data was placed into a GIS database. An analysis of the current performance of the farm's productive and environmental pastoral outcomes was undertaken using

Farmax and Overseer models (King et al. 2010). Farmax is a computer simulation model that allows individual farms to be modelled and enables a wide range of "what if" scenarios to be explored. The program matches pasture growth data with a livestock system to optimize profit. Overseer models the nutrient balance of a farming system and produces outputs related to environmental emissions (e.g., N, P, methane, nitrous oxide, and carbon equivalents). The IDSF included additional tools for the two case studies. For Ahoanga, the IDSF included a whole farm risk optimization model used to assist Aohanga Incorporation evaluate land-use options involving maximizing farm income, minimizing environmental effects (nitrogen leached, GHG emitted), and maintaining the option to trade in carbon through forestry. For Waimarama, the IDSF included a spatially explicit agent-based model used to explore future scenarios of land-use change and illustrate trade-offs between community aspirations under each scenario.

The underlying principles from the work with these Māori organizations over the duration of the program included the need for: (1) tools and processes to be flexible in their capacity to incorporate cultural and social imperatives alongside bio-physical and economic objectives; (2) tools to be accessible, affordable, and user-friendly; (3) processes to be participatory in order to build capacity in their use and application, while also reducing the reliance on outside experts; and (4) processes to facilitate collaborative learning between participants and researchers.

Waimarama Incorporation

Using a systems approach and focus group interviews with the management committee, the following question was developed: "What are the factors and relationships that influence the future of Waimarama?" This process allowed the land-owner decision makers to view factors in greater depth and in a systemic manner to allow for greater insight to their processes and behaviours. It also offered the opportunity to identify in their system where they could target actions for major impact and then used this to identify strategic directions for the Waimarama Incorporation, including the exploration of potential joint opportunities with other Māori owners in the catchment.

Constructing and verifying the resulting Causal Loop Systems Map provoked discussion on the distinction between the farm operation and the wider Waimarama community. The map reflected their interrelationship and noted the importance of the linkage between farm profitability and the achievement of community outcomes. Three key leverage points were identified by the committee: (1) the role of leadership in the form of a well-informed best team comprising the management committee of the farm; (2) farm profitability and its links to economic viability and farm resource status; and (3) the willingness of the wider Waimarama community to participate in activities. Kaitiakitanga was added as an overarching principle.

The Causal Loop Systems Map was then used to identify aspirations that the committee would use as criteria for evaluating potential new land-use options in a deliberative process. The following criteria were identified: appropriate use of resources; favourable market opportunities, inclusive of the wider family community (*whanau*); grow Waimarama's catchment opportunities; diversify farm base; improve economic viability; protect and enhance heritage; and develop the best team for the farm. We then asked the committee to answer the question, "How do land-use options meet aspirations?" the committee used a numeric scale to rank the effects of different land uses to their aspirations.

We used GIS simulation and an agent-based model to provide the Waimarama committee with a mechanism to explore catchment-wide possibilities to engage with other Māori landowners to articulate common values and to discuss the possible trade-offs of scenarios on the land and people. A number of scenarios were developed using the GIS database developed for each case study (Harmsworth and Mackay 2010) to identify areas suitable for conservation initiatives, the outputs from Farmax and Overseer models (King et al. 2010) to identify joint farm improvement options and land valuation data to make assumptions about potential future land fragmentation (lifestyle blocks). The model allowed for assuming behaviour differences between Māori and non-Māori landowners in the catchment. Trade-offs between aspirations were illustrated using a radar plot using the committee's ranking.

The Waimarama committee organized a number of meetings in 2010 inviting all Māori landowners in the catchment and Iwi Futures researchers. The results from the IDSF were used to support discussion about joint development opportunities. One researcher was invited in March 2011 to continue supporting these conversations, illustrating the permanent nature of the relationships between the Māori owners and the Iwi Futures researchers. The concept of whanau was an integral part of the research enabling connections to be made with people and land, and gave an entry point into the community. The multiple ownership structure results in the potential for an individual to be connected to more than one property. This enables the transfer of information between farms and allows opportunity to physically network enterprises, as an individual may hold a decision-making role on the governing committee of more than one farm. As the case study with Waimarama demonstrated, there is a potential for land-use diversification to enable achievement of goals where strategic alliances need to be formed and institutional structures defined for viable business to occur.

Aohanga Incorporation

Aohanga Incorporation is a large property (approximately 7,280 hectares) with approximately 2,500 hectares used for sheep and beef production, and two thousand hectares in indigenous forestry. The remaining area is exotic forestry and significant areas of the farm reverting to scrub and gorse. The land block and community are located on the eastern coastline of the North Island with the majority of owners (around 1,500) living outside of the region, largely because of reduced employment opportunities. The property faces a number of challenges with the prospect of increasing climatic temperatures and reduced rainfall. Opportunities for diversification are of interest to the Committee of Management, particularly with areas of high-quality land around the two rivers and thirteen kilometres of coastline.

A systems approach was also applied using several focus group interviews over two years to develop Causal Loop Systems Maps and deliberation models. Key issues raised by the owners included diversification away from pastoral agriculture towards forestry, rural tourism, horticulture, and aquaculture. Information requirements are also high but there is uncertainty around access and capability to use and apply technologies.

The isolation of the station and the two rivers plus coastline provides opportunities for alternative revenue streams. However, the isolation also produces challenges with the lack of infrastructure, particularly communication and other services essential for tourism. Holistic people and land development that was consistent with tikanga and incorporated mātauranga was a key platform for the committee to retain the connection between the owners and the land. An important output for the committee and landowners was the transfer of historical and traditional knowledge in relation to the location of historical knowledge and cultural sites of significance into a digital format provided an initial starting point for deliberating on future pathway planning. Visualizing cultural and historical records has proven to be a key platform for effective planning.

The incorporation of cultural information into a format that can be used for planning is critical. This enabled questions relating to the biophysical characteristics of the land, and coastal and freshwater resources to be answered within a broader socio-economic and cultural context. Increased productivity of the farming and forestry components while balancing cultural requirements of protecting cultural sites and ensuring owner access was identified as a significant challenge for the committee of management to resolve. The team therefore developed a "land and resource evaluation" model that will allow users to assess alternative enterprises and development options within a tikanga and mātauranga context.

The Aohanga whole farm risk optimization model used the outputs from the land and resource evaluation model to identify areas suitable for all potential livestock and forestry opportunities for development. The financial and environmental performance of each of these potential opportunities were modelled using Farmax and Overseer and yield tables for regimes of pine, Douglas fir, and other tree species. The model then was used to generate different scenarios according to different criteria, such as maximizing farm income, minimizing environmental effects (nitrogen leached, GHG emitted), and maximizing carbon sequestration. Results from the model were used to assist the committee by proposing feasible development strategies. We are currently engaged with Aohanga Incorporation to further develop the Iwi Futures IDSF by including aquaculture and horticulture opportunities, and to develop a climate change mitigation/adaptation strategy.

CONCLUDING REMARKS

Planning frameworks that assist communities to move towards their objectives are often those that reflect the language, customs, and values of those communities. The IDSF demonstrates the application of a process and a set of tools that enables landowner representatives to define, determine, and deliberate on alternative future pathways. A combination of whakapapa, land-use modelling, and customary knowledge is seen as the key to improving the utilization and sustainable development of Māori land with multiple owners. The IDSF provides a framework that will organize multiple activities and coordinate different quantitative and qualitative data sets in a visual format that allows for discussion and deliberation within a collective decision-making environment.

A key lesson for the research team has been the importance of working with the community to look backwards to understand the historical, political, and cultural context that has shaped the community. Both case study communities described in this chapter placed a heavy emphasis on documenting historical and cultural knowledge as a key platform to moving forward. Underpinning this process, however, is the need for a high level of trust between researchers and the land-owning groups. A crucial point in the successful implementation of the IDSF is therefore the partnership that is formed between research, industry, and landowners, particularly as the analytical tools require expert knowledge to operate and interpret.

Engagement processes driven by Western science are often fragmented and most times prescriptive, denying participant researchers the opportunity for collaborative learning. The relationships researchers develop with Indigenous groups are also not often of a permanent nature, also denying the opportunity for both researchers and Indigenous groups to cross the boundaries between professional and personal relationships.

One of the main outcomes from Iwi Futures was to offer a positively enriching experience for both researchers and land-owning groups, overcoming traditional engagement process shortcomings. After the official project ended, there is continuing active interaction between both parties, looking for new opportunities (or excuses) to keep in touch. For researchers involved in Iwi Futures, this resulted in an increased sense of satisfaction and personal enrichment.

The IDSF has linked Indigenous knowledge with Western science and industry knowledge to form a holistic framework for framing questions, and evaluating and designing land-use options that have the potential to balance multiple outcomes and confer functional integrity. The processes and tools that populate the framework can be applied to a generic audience.

NOTE

1   The Iwi Futures research program was funded by the Foundation for Science and Technology, 2008 to 2010.

REFERENCES

Attran, S. 1993. Cognitive Foundations of Natural History: Towards an Anthropology of Science. Cambridge, UK: Cambridge University Press.

Berlin, B. 1992. *Ethnobiological Classification: Principles of Categorization of Plants and Animals in Traditional Societies.* Princeton, NJ: Princeton University Press.

Best, E. 1982a. *Māori Religion and Mythology (Part I).* First published 1924 as Dominion Museum Bulletin No. 10. Wellington, NZ: Government Printer NZ.

– 1982b. *Māori Religion and Mythology (Part II).* First published 1924 as Dominion Museum Bulletin No. 11. Wellington, NZ: Government Printer NZ.

Buck, P. 1987 [1949]. *The Coming of the Māori.* Wellington: Whitcoulls.

Chambers, R., and P. Richards. 1995. "Preface." In *The Cultural Dimension of Development: Indigenous Knowledge Systems*, edited by D.M. Warren, J. Slikkerveer, and D. Brokensha, xiii–xiv. London: Intermediate Technology Publications.

Haami, B., and M. Roberts. 2002. "Genealogy as Taxonomy." *International Social Science Journal* 54 (173): 403–12.

Harmsworth, G., and H. Heke. 2010. *Waimarama Inc. Technical Report: Resource Stocktake for Waimarama Catchment and Land Blocks.* Landcare Research Contract Report. Iwi Futures.

Harmsworth, G.R., and A. MacKay. 2010. "Land Resource Assessment and Evaluation on Māori land." Abstract for the Whenua Sustainable Futures with Māori Land Conference, Rotorua. 21–23 July.

Harmsworth, G., A. Sutherland, H. Heke, J. Procter. 2010. *Aohanga Inc. Technical Report: Resource Stocktake for Owahanga Land Block and Catchment.* Landcare Research Contract Report. Iwi Futures.

King, W., G. Lambert, C. Dake, and D. Smeaton. 2010. "Iwi Futures Assessment of Sheep and Beef Farm System Performance and Opportunities for Production Increases." Presentation at the Whenua Sustainable Futures with Māori land Conference, Rotorua. 21–23 July.

Kingi, T.T. 2008. "Māori Land Ownership and Management." *Making Land Work. Volume 2: Case Studies on Customary Land and Development in the Pacific*, 129–51. Canberra: Australian Agency for International Development (AusAID).

– 2009a. "The Future of the Māori Agricultural Sector." *Journal of the NZ Institute of Primary Industry Management* 13 (2):23–6.

– 2009b. "Māori Land Ownership and Economic Development." *The New Zealand Law Journal* November:396–400.

Kingi, T.T, M.E. Wedderburn, and O. Montes de Oca. 2010. "Balancing Cultural Imperatives into Agricultural Development and Environmental Management: A Decision-Making Framework for Māori Land Owners."

Presentation at the Whenua Sustainable Futures with Māori land Conference, Rotorua. 21–23 July.

Maani, K.E., and R.Y Cavana. 2007. *Systems Thinking, System Dynamics.* Wellington: Pearson Education.

Marsden, M. 1975. "God, Man and Universe: A Māori View". In *Te Ao Hurihuri: The World Moves On*, edited by M. King, 191–219. Wellington: Hicks Smith & Sons.

Marsden, M. 2003. *The Woven Universe.* Edited by Royal, C.T.A. Otaki: The Estate of Rev. Māori Marsden.

Marsden, M., and T.A. Henare. 1992. *Kaitiakitanga: A Definitive Introduction to the Holistic World View of the Māori.* Wellington, NZ: Ministry for the Environment.

MAF. 2011. *Māori Agribusiness in New Zealand: A Study of the Māori Freehold Land Resource.* Wellington: Ministry of Agriculture and Forestry.

Roberts, M., B. Haami, R. Benton, T. Satterfield, M. Finucane, M. Henare, et al. 2004. "Whakapapa as a Māori Mental Construct: Some Implications for the Debate Over Genetic Modified Organisms." *The Contemporary Pacific* 16 (1):1–28.

Salmond, A. 1991. *Two Worlds: First Meetings Between Māori and Europeans 1642–1772.* Auckland: Viking Press.

Shirres, M.P. 1997. *Te Tangata: The Human Person.* Auckland: Snedden & Cervin.

Shortland, E. 1998. *Māori Religion and Mythology.* Christchurch: Kiwi Publishers.

Smith, P.S. 1913. The Lore of the Whare Wananga or Teachings of Māori College. *Journal of the Polynesian Society* 3.

– 1915. The Lore of the Whare Wananga or Teachings of Māori College. *Journal of the Polynesian Society* 4.

Te Puni Kokiri. 2011. *Ko Nga Tumanako O Nga Tangata Whai Whenua Māori: Owner Aspirations Regarding the Utilisation of Māori Land.* Wellington: Te Puni Kokiri.

Thompson, P.B. 1997. "The Varieties of Sustainability in Livestock Farming." In *Livestock Farming Systems – More than Food Production*, edited by J.T. Sørensen. Proceedings of the Fourth International Symposium on Livestock Farming Systems. EAAP publication no. 89:5–15.

Wedderburn, M.E., T.T. Kingi, M. Paine, and O. Montes de Oca. 2011. "West Meets South: Livestock Farming a Means to Achieve Functional Integrity?" Proceedings of the IXth IRC LiFLoD Workshop, livestock farming embedded in local development: a functional perspective to alleviate vulnerability of farming communities. Rosario, Argentina.

Wedderburn, M.E., T.G. Parminter, R.W. Webby, M.B. O'Connor, I.A. Power. 2004a. "The Interconnections of Māori, Landscape and Business." Canberra: Agri-Food Research network, Landscape and Rurality.

Wedderburn, M.E., T.G Parminter, R.W. Webby, R. Pikia. 2004b. "Land Stewardship and Farming for Economic Social and Cultural Goals: A Māori Perspective." OECD expert meeting on farm management indicators and the environment, New Zealand.

Williams, H.W. 1975. *A Dictionary of the Māori Language*, seventh edition. Wellington: A.R. Shearer, Government Printer, NZ.

The Power and Peril of "Vulnerability": Lending a Cautious Eye to Community Labels

BETHANY HAALBOOM AND DAVID NATCHER

Over the past fifty years, the Arctic climate has undergone dramatic change. These changes have resulted in a myriad of interrelated effects within the Arctic's socio-ecological system. For example, between 1953 and 2003, winter surface air temperature in Alaska and northwestern Canada rose between 3 to 4°C (IASC 2010). The result has been a combination of impacts, including the thinning of sea ice (Belchansky et al. 2004), more rapid retreat of glaciers (Oerlemans 2005), and the thawing of permafrost (Couture et al. 2003). Together these changes are occurring at a rate faster than even the most pessimistic scenarios of climate change had projected (Warren et al. 2010).

More than simply isolated or ephemeral occurrences, the changes affecting the Arctic's physical environment are also affecting the marine and terrestrial systems in many new and unforeseen ways (Overland et al. 2004). For example, the reduction of Arctic sea ice is proving to have a considerable impact on the migration and residency patterns of ice-dependent marine mammals (SEARCH 2005), while changing weather patterns and increased snow accumulation have been attributed to the decline in caribou (*Rangifer tarandus granti*) populations across the Canadian North (Griffith et al. 2002).

Given their level of exposure to these environmental changes in the Arctic, northern communities are seen as being particularly vulnerable to the effects of climate change. As defined by the Intergovernmental Panel on Climate Change (IPCC 2007, 883), vulnerability is the degree to which a [community] is susceptible to, and unable to cope with, adverse effects of climate change, including climate variability and extremes. Vulnerability is a function of the character, magnitude, and rate of climate change and variation to which a community is exposed and its capacity to effectively adapt to change.

Vulnerability has also been defined as the degree to which a community is likely to experience harm due to exposure (Chapin et al. 2010). Based on these conditions, some have identified northern Indigenous communities as being at particular risk due to a progressive erosion of their adaptive capacity brought about by social, cultural, political and economic change, narrow economic bases, and a general diminution of local human resources (Duerden and Beasley 2006; Lemmen et al. 2008; Warren et al. 2010). Those communities considered most vulnerable to the effects of climate change are the more remote northern communities that continue to pursue subsistence-based ways of life (Prowse and Furgal 2009, 291).

While we acknowledge that northern communities are likely being challenged at a rate and scale never yet encountered (Abele et al. 2009), we are concerned about the very real, though perhaps unintended, consequences of characterizing northern Indigenous communities as vulnerable. Specifically, we are concerned that the vulnerability label can create powerful ways of viewing Indigenous peoples (and the regions they inhabit) that do not necessarily reflect emic realities. Our concerns, and our calls for caution with the use of the term "vulnerability," are not abstract remonstrations. Rather, this chapter will illustrate the potential consequences of the application of labels to particular peoples and regions, however unintentional they may be. We do this through a review of development critiques in the context of the Global South. We also examine the use and possible consequences of the vulnerability label in the context of community relocation policies and the formation of Indigenous identities.

Importantly, our purpose here is not to dissect the concept of vulnerability through an "expert" lens – we acknowledge the complexity of the term and the many areas in which it has been applied. Nor is our objective to offer an extensive review of how vulnerability has been defined and debated in the academic literature; this has been done quite effectively by others (see, for example, Watts and Bohle 1993; Kelly and Adger 2000; Eakin and Luers 2006; Manyena 2006). Rather, our objective is to take a step back and consider vulnerability as a power-laden concept whose application could hold very real consequences for the populations who are bestowed such a label. In this way this chapter serves as a cautionary tale, a consideration of what *could* transpire, and a type of informed speculation. Overall, we encourage more careful and critical attention to the power and potential peril of labels, as they may work against the interests and aims of those communities we hope to assist through our research.

THE CONCEPT OF VULNERABILITY

Arriving at a common definition for vulnerability remains elusive and somewhat ambiguous due in large part to the number of academic disciplines in which the term has been applied. With over two dozen different definitions (Manyena 2006), the concept of vulnerability has been criticized for lacking a unified theory or arriving at widely accepted indicators or measurements (Watts and Bohle 1993). While there may not be complete agreement on how vulnerability should be defined, some commonality can be found in its conceptual application. First, vulnerability has been understood as one's exposure to a physical hazard. The biophysical aspect of vulnerability focuses on the nature of the physical hazard to which humans are exposed. People are deemed more or less vulnerable based on their proximity to a hazardous location or activity (Dow 1992). Second, vulnerability can refer to human sensitivity to that hazard which is determined by pre-existing social, economic, and political conditions (Kelly and Adger 2000; Turner et al. 2003; Reid and Vogel 2006). Important consideration is given to the degree to which people are sensitized to a physical hazard, including social, political, and economic conditions that make exposure unsafe or threatening. Specific examples include levels of inequality, poverty, power dynamics, social networks, institutions, and food security (Adger and Kelly 1999; Kelly and Adger 2000; Ford and Smit 2004). Third, vulnerability can refer to a community's inability to address, plan for, and adapt to risks (Blaikie et al. 1994; Smit and Pilifosova 2003; Ford, Smit and Wandel 2006), and the adaptive capacity "of actors, both individuals and groups, to respond to, create, and shape variability and change in the state of the system" (Chapin et al. 2010, 23). Historically it has been the economically marginalized and the politically un-empowered who are considered most vulnerable due to deficiencies in their adaptive capacity (Turner II 2010, 572).

Increasingly, and particularly in the context of climate change research, all three of the above dimensions have been applied in combination to assess the vulnerability of northern Indigenous communities. For example, changes in the Arctic's bio-physical systems have had a direct impact on the health, range, and population distribution of many marine and terrestrial species that northern Indigenous peoples rely upon (e.g., seals, caribou, polar bears, and narwhal) (Ford et al. 2006; Ford et al. 2008; Pearce et al. 2010). Shifts in species distribution can also introduce new animal-transmitted diseases and redistribute existing diseases among animal populations, further affecting the health and well-being of northern communities (Prowse and Furgal 2009, 290). In addition, changing bio-physical conditions have resulted in reduced accessibility to traditional food sources such as walrus, seal, and caribou (Ford et al. 2006; Ford et al. 2009; Pearce et al. 2010), and increased travel risks for Indigenous hunters (Furgal and Seguin 2006; Pearce et al. 2010). If these conditions persist, as they are currently projected to (Furgal 2008), northern communities may be challenged to meet basic dietary needs through the harvest of wild foods. According to Prowse and Furgal (2009, 290), it will be those "environmentally exposed" communities that are high consumers of a limited number of traditional food species and have limited access to market foods who will be most affected. Within those specific communities it will be the Elders, those individuals already suffering from poor health, and those who regularly consume and prepare country foods by traditional means, including the consumption of raw or fermented foods, who will be most at risk. Youth in Indigenous communities have also been identified as "at risk" based on their lack of traditional ecological knowledge and limited ability to adapt to changing environmental conditions (Ford et al. 2006). Another dimension of vulnerability not linked to harvesting practices is damage to existing infrastructure such as heated buildings and transportation facilities through the thawing of permafrost (Hayley 2004; Instanes et al. 2005). In this context, vulnerability reflects the risks of inhabiting areas at risk from climate change and associated natural disasters (Alexander 1993).

While acknowledging the limits of generalizing climate vulnerability across all northern communities, a report published by the Government of Canada (Lemmen et al. 2008) notes that larger municipalities will be less vulnerable than smaller, more remote communities due to their capacity to adapt to change via economic diversification, enhanced technology, infrastructure, and more accessible health care services. To enhance their own adaptive capacity, it has been suggested that smaller, remote communities diversify their local economies and create more wage-earning opportunities. Although greater involvement in full-time jobs may hasten the "current trends of social and cultural erosion" (presumably through a transition away from traditional harvesting activities), enhanced economic opportunities may provide significant benefits to communities, thereby lessening the net impact on human vulnerability (Prowse and Furgal 2009, 292). Even while continuing to sustain traditional lifestyles, it has been suggested that smaller communities should seek funding support from government and other emerging institutional support systems in order to cope with changing environmental conditions (Ford et al. 2008). Though an expensive option, the relocation of those communities identified as being most vulnerable has also been put forth as a potential solution (US Arctic Research Commission Permafrost Task Force 2003). Therefore, to reverse the vulnerable status bestowed upon Indigenous communities, calls have been made for greater community integration into the larger market economy, as well as outside support and externally generated solutions.

Notwithstanding the best intentions of these recommendations, such responses seem reminiscent of well-criticized development policies applied to the Global South, and implemented, at least partially, as a reaction to the underdevelopment label. It also harkens back to colonial policies implemented in the Canadian North – a scenario perhaps being reinvented, albeit unintentionally, through the application of the vulnerability label to characterize Indigenous peoples in the North in the context of climate change.

UNDERSTANDING VULNERABILITY THROUGH THE LENS OF UNDERDEVELOPMENT

Based on critiques demonstrating the power and consequences of the underdevelopment label, we underscore the importance of lending a critical and cautious eye to the application of the vulnerability label in the context of climate change and northern Indigenous peoples. The parallels between vulnerability and development labels are not only directly relevant, but also exceedingly apparent in light of the unique socio-political and historical positioning of Indigenous peoples within Canada's Arctic.

The concept of underdevelopment became prominent in the English language lexicon following the Second World War, and has been implicated in the production of vulnerable subjects and regions (Bankoff 2001). Its deployment was rooted in Western concerns about the "abnormal" life-styles and socio-economic conditions in the Global South – regions such as Asia, Africa, and Latin America (Watts and Bohle 1993). Populations with lifestyles not mimicking those of Western nations were uniformly painted with the underdevelopment label. This label became internalized at the level of societies and nations, leading people of developed nations to imagine others "as underdeveloped, a state viewed as synonymous with poverty and backwardness, and one determined by assuming West-ern standards of attainment as the benchmark against which to measure this condition" (Bankoff 2001, 23).

While there were material conditions that justified attention to these regions, the underdeveloped label also lent credence, legitimacy, and a sense of urgency to the production of misguided solutions generated by powerful Western nations and international institutions. These solutions were aimed at generating economic growth by assimilating the Global South into larger market economies. The introduction of advanced tech-nologies, monetary and fiscal policies, industrialization, agricultural developments, increased trade, as well as education and Western Euro-pean values were geared towards advancing the interests and lifestyles of so-called vulnerable and destitute peoples in these regions.

The agents of label production were those situated well outside of the everyday experiences of people residing in these underdeveloped regions. These actors included governments, industry, academic researchers, financial institutions such as the World Bank and International Monet-ary Fund, and the United Nations. As Escobar (1999, 385) states, "Like the landing of the Allied forces in Normandy, the third world witnessed a massive landing of experts, each in charge of investigating, measuring, and theorizing about ... this or that little aspect of third world societies." At the same time, the concept of development became professionalized and depoliticized in order to facilitate its deployment through the more neutral and esteemed platform of scientific research.

The result of interventions arising from the introduction of under-development was the subjection of Third World populations to market fluctuations, often with a reduced capacity for providing basic needs (Weissling 1989). These conditions then gave rise to increased depend-ency on Western institutions and resources, and the loss of local control over their own resources, as well as the revenue produced from these resources (Pretes 1988). In other words, "Poor peoples' ability to define and take care of their own lives was eroded in a deeper manner than perhaps ever before" (Escobar 1999, 382).

The overlapping history of development and Indigenous peoples in the Canadian Arctic is apt reason for considering the parallels of this history and current-day legacies, to those of development discourses and the Global South. With the decline of the fur trade, Indigenous peoples, and specifically the Inuit, were induced by the Canadian government to relocate into permanent regional settlements during the 1950s and 1960s. This "inducement" and "coercion" was at least partially reflective of Indigenous peoples' feelings of intimidation, fear, and subservience towards government administrators (RCAP 1994). The locations of these new settlements were chosen by the Canadian government, not by the Inuit, and were rationalized on the belief that Inuit had outstripped the local availability of wildlife resources and could not afford commercially purchased foods without sustained income from wage earning opportunities, thereby rendering the Inuit both dependent upon the government and "vulnerable" to the changing social and ecological conditions of the North (RCAP 1994, 135). The Canadian government's efforts to support its claims to sovereignty in the High Arctic have also been cited as a justification for relocation initiatives (Dickason and MacNab 2009).

Relocation plans originated in the political centres of Canada's south, from agents and institutions most removed from the lived realities of Indigenous communities, but with the "expertise," power, and authority to define the problem(s) and enact solutions affecting the lives of northern Indigenous peoples. This displacement resulted in the production of what has been termed a "Fourth World" (Paine 1971). Rather than benefiting through relocation initiatives, many northern Indigenous communities experienced extreme hardships, including famine, disease, inadequate housing, and social disorder among others (Dickason and McNab 2009). They also continue to struggle with the consequences of externally controlled administrations that often undermine Indigenous autonomy and decision-making authority.

As with the development label that justified misplaced policy interventions in the Global South, misguided policies based on externally defined problems led to actions that actually produced less favourable outcomes for Indigenous peoples, in addition to ongoing relationships of dependency with commanding and remote institutions. In fact, the Inuit became "one of the most heavily assisted, administered, and studied groups on earth" (Zaslow 1971, 301). As in the context of development, it is those in relative positions of power, yet who remain unfamiliar with, and unmindful of local and regional contexts, who intervene to sometimes injurious consequences.

Despite this adverse historical legacy, dependence on outsiders to help Indigenous communities cope with the present-day climate change burden is often presented as seemingly inevitable as "the transfer of resources to vulnerable societies (in terms of financial means, technologies, or expertise) in order to help them to prepare for and cope with unavoidable impacts of climate change are ... necessary elements of a comprehensive climate policy" (Füssel and Klein 2006, 304). While it is true that the "practices and products of Arctic science are helping to catalyze and lend support to Indigenous peoples to publicize their important status in climate change processes" (Martello 2008, 372), these practices and products may also result in poor planning and unintended consequences for Indigenous peoples. Given this, we question whether the vulnerability label may actually produce more problems than it seeks to solve. We explore these issues in more detail with respect to a contemporary community relocation policy, wildlife management, and formation of Indigenous identities.

COMMUNITY RELOCATION PLANNING IN ALASKA

On the Alaskan coast, relocating Indigenous communities in response to climate change has been an ongoing, enduring process for many years. The enhanced vulnerability of coastal communities has been attributed to increased temperatures of 2 to 3.5°C over the last thirty-five years, reduction in sea ice and sea-level rise, concomitant storm surges and flooding, and the erosion of coastlines on which communities are located (IPCC 2007). Increased awareness and knowledge about climate change processes has resulted in intensified scientific and policy attention towards these communities as climate change is thought to be accelerating their vulnerable status. In response, a number of government-supported relocation and infrastructure enhancement projects have been proposed. For example, Marino (2009) has examined the case of Shishmaref, Alaska, where, after years of shoreline stabilization efforts, state and federal governments approved tentative plans for community relocation that was supported by community members, though funding remains elusive. While there have been a number of government departments involved in the planning process, including housing, transportation, education, and health, Shishmaref residents have, to their frustration, been relegated to the periphery of the planning process, though they have made efforts to counter this. The frustration of community members has been further compounded by plans that would have them relocated to urban centres, plans which community members were concerned could result in social, linguistic, and cultural disintegration. Despite this, the relocation option continues to be championed by some policy-makers. As Marino (2009, 46) states, "real local power within the state's planning is relatively absent, despite the good intentions by all to include local voices."

We highlight this case in particular because it illustrates a problematic policy response that generates even greater dependency on government and further marginalizes Indigenous peoples from the decisions that affect them most. First, this case illustrates a reinvention of dependency (on top of those that may already exist) through the need for funding and government administrative activities to move Shishmaref residents to relative safety, yet to places that remain objectionable to local residents. Second, there is limited Indigenous agency and voice in decision making because outsiders maintain control of the planning process, though Shishmaref residents are trying to change this. While perhaps unintended, this case reflects and reinforces Indigenous peoples as vulnerable subjects of climate change policy efforts. We raise the possibility that such treatments may be (at least partially) reactions to broader and pervasive characterizations of Indigenous peoples as "vulnerable" populations who have been victimized by climate change and are in need of external assistance and expertise to determine their futures and aid in their rescue. Such characterizations may result not only in planning responses that alienate and subjugate Indigenous peoples in the planning process, but also ill-fated outcomes, which can further harm rather than help Indigenous communities.

IDENTITY AND AGENCY

The ardent uptake and application of the vulnerability has been used not only by scientists and policy-makers, but has been adopted by some Indigenous peoples themselves. At one level this strategy has aided Indigenous peoples in their efforts to generate support for their valued way of life, traditional knowledge, and the environments where they live. As Martello (2008) observes, there are strong links between global change science and Indigenous identity and activism. This includes struggles for rights, empowerment, and preservation of traditional lifestyles and culture.

We raise concerns, however, that such efforts may actually be hampered, rather than helped, by the uptake of the vulnerability label.

This label, and what it implies, can be internalized by those targeted to receive them. The Oxford Thesaurus (2000) includes synonyms for the term "vulnerable" that include damaged, helpless, powerless, and weak. Uptake of the "vulnerability" label may therefore mean adopting an identity of victimization, disempowerment, and dependency; identities that can be linked to legacies and experiences that Canada's Indigenous peoples are actively seeking to counter and rectify. As shown in the development literature, it was not long after being labelled "underdeveloped" that those in the newly created "Third World" began to view themselves as "inferior, underdeveloped, and ignorant" (Escobar 1999, 386).

In the case of the Canadian Arctic, the introduction and uptake of the vulnerability label by Indigenous peoples could serve to reinvent historically adverse experiences linked to colonial rule both socially and psychologically through label internalization. It could also limit or hinder effective coping mechanisms by assuming and predetermining the capacity (or lack thereof) of Indigenous peoples to deal with environmental change. This possibility should be of concern to Indigenous peoples given that "ideas about how people are likely to cope in an emergency or a disaster are shaped by prior experience but also by a cultural narrative that creates a set of expectations and sensitizes people to some problems more than others; it provides a frame through which people understand and make sense of their experience" (Furedi 2007, 485).

DISCUSSION

Alexander (1993) and others (Watts and Bohles 1993; Blaikie et al. 1994) have raised the important question as to whether individuals who reside in regions prone to physical hazards consider themselves vulnerable or are even familiar with the concept (as one that has been introduced by outsiders). Research has shown individuals may experience hazardous conditions, and/or the onslaught of these conditions, as part of their everyday existence to which they have grown accustomed, but which do not necessarily deem them "vulnerable" (along with what it denotes). For example, Lahiri-Dutt and Samanta (2007, 327) documented the attitudes and responses of community members living in the lower reaches of the Damodar River in India, an area prone to frequent floods, shifting river channels, and river bank erosion. The experiences and understandings of local residents of their own situation was considerably different to those of development agents and government representatives who characterized community members as vulnerable to seasonal flooding and in need of relocation. As Bankoff (2001, 29) states, the limited observation by external agents demonstrates that the "discourse of vulnerability ... belongs to a knowledge system formed from within a dominant Western liberal consciousness and so inevitably reflects the values and principles of that culture."

While we recognize that vulnerability and climate change studies have also sought to demonstrate the adaptive capacity of Indigenous peoples to changing environmental conditions (e.g., Newton 1995; Berkes and Jolly 2001; Ford et al. 2008; Ford and Furgal 2009), the vulnerability label nonetheless endures. The persistence of the label and what it denotes detracts from the positive and existing capacities of Indigenous peoples to cope with environmental change, as well as longer histories that demonstrate this ability. Arguably, it has been periods of change that have motivated the adaptation of northern Indigenous people for centuries. Challenge-and-response theory has been used to show how times of environmental change can lead to adaptive human responses. Such times of change include the Medieval Warming Period (AD 1000 to 1300) when climate change and subsequent shifts in species distribution served as stimulus for more intensive Inuit adaptations in the eastern Arctic (Fagan 2008). Studies in other global regions have similarly documented innovative responses to environmental change by Indigenous peoples. In Solway's (1994) examination of the effects of the 1979 and 1987 drought in Botswana, she found that rather than resulting in crisis and conflict, climate-induced drought brought about innovation with respect to local production techniques; a form of "revelatory crisis" (Sahlins 1972) that helps explain how climate change can lead to innovative human responses. Similarly, Juul (2005, 112) has argued that climatic shocks, seen often as detrimental to the survival of northern Senegal pastoralists, have actually triggered important social and political changes. Rather than pastoralists being vulnerable to change, climate change facilitated social, technological, and strategic innovations that have most often gone unnoticed by intermittent observers.

That the vulnerability label persists is at least partly based on a "concern that future changes in conditions may exceed conventional coping capacities" (Ford and Smit 2004, 296). We would argue, however, that history speaks to these coping abilities as being anything but conventional. Rather, adaptive mechanisms should be interpreted as dynamic, versatile, and well-tailored to environmental change. Wenzel (2009) documents that there is both remote and more recent historical evidence of Inuit coping in response to climate change that includes changing the animals that they hunt in response to certain species becoming less abundant and others more so. "With respect to climate change and the accompanying ecological changes that may affect Inuit subsistence, it is worth remembering that they [Inuit] have an experiential baseline that spans a millennium of adaptation" (Wenzel 2009, 97). Newton (1995, 119) similarly speaks to the competence of Indigenous communities who have survived in changing environments for millennia.

CONCLUSION

In this chapter we have addressed potential issues with the imposition of the vulnerability label ascribed to Arctic Indigenous communities. First, we have argued that the vulnerability label with its accompanying set of assumptions is most often generated by those who may be more or less unfamiliar with the complexities of local culture, economies, and capabilities. Second, we raise concerns that such labels can generate actions and responses built upon how peoples and places come to be seen and understood. This includes the potential for ill-informed and misguided policy interventions that may be at odds with the values and priorities of communities themselves. It may also result in greater dependencies on external forms of support and interventions – situations that Indigenous peoples have long sought to reverse. Last, we raise the possibility that the vulnerability label has the potential to shape how northern Indigenous peoples come to see themselves as they construct their own identities – identities that, once conveyed, may ultimately work to their disadvantage in gaining greater autonomy over their own affairs.

Admittedly, Indigenous communities in the Arctic are being challenged in profound ways, whether from climate-induced changes in the biophysical environment or by other globalizing processes. However, we caution against the uncritical use of vulnerability to characterize Indigenous communities who are now confronting these challenges and urge those involved in social dimensions of climate change research to (re)consider and interrogate how such a label might reinforce historically uneven relationships of power and dependency. It is important to note that we are not calling for a complete abandonment of the term. However, we do encourage greater consideration of the subjective and individualized understandings of what "vulnerability" may or may not entail (Dutt and Samanta 2007). This includes considering whether the populations who are bestowed this label consider themselves to be "vulnerable," or whether such a term even exists in their cultural repertoire. A fuller understanding of local perceptions concerning risk and environmental change is therefore required rather than assuming a priori that such changes are necessarily problematic (Forsyth 2003, 174). We believe that the attainment of this level of understanding demands research that is committed to prolonged engagement and persistent observation that results in "thick description" of local contexts (Schwandt 2007). We also feel this requires continuous solicitation of local reaction in order to construct more meaningful and equitable "emic-etic elaboration" (Guba and Lincoln 1986, 19). This approach is in staunch contrast to rapid appraisal methodologies that at best achieve shallow interpretations of local peoples and the conditions they deal with on a daily basis.

It must be emphasized that the concept of vulnerability did not emerge from the experience of communities, nor is it an ontological "given" (Furedi 2007). Rather vulnerability is being employed as a diagnostic tool for gauging the inherent limitations and dependencies of communities experiencing change. Far from being value neutral, such practices are bound by social constructions and infused with political and ethical power. As Forsyth (2003, 182) explains, "the very definition of who is allowed to be 'expert' in framing, measuring, and addressing risks is crucial in determining which knowledge or alternative conceptualizations of problems are accessed." Given this, we believe that the practice of labelling communities as vulnerable risks undermining Indigenous agency and their efforts to achieve greater autonomy.

As researchers become more engaged in the human dimensions of climate change research, we must be prepared to question and continually re-examine the conceptual underpinning of our research. Such a commitment will no doubt require a willingness to step outside of our own cultural and scientific frame of reference and consider both the power and potential peril of such engagement. This is particularly important given that it will likely be Indigenous communities who stand to reap the unintended consequences of our research.

ACKNOWLEDGMENTS

We gratefully acknowledge the journal *Arctic* for their permission to include work in this chapter that was originally published in 2012 as "The Power and Peril of 'Vulnerablity': Approaching Community Labels with Caution in Climate Change Research." *Arctic* 65 (3): 319–27.

REFERENCES

Abele, F., T.J. Courchene, F.L. Seidle, and F. St-Hilaire, eds. 2009. *Northern Exposure: Peoples, Powers and Prospects in Canada's North.* Ottawa, ON: Institute for Research on Public Policy.

Adger, W.N., and P.M. Kelly, 1999. "Social Vulnerability to Climate Change and the Architecture of Entitlements: Mitigation Adaptation Strategies." *Global Change* 4:253–6.

Alexander, D. 1993. *Natural Disasters.* New York: Chapman and Hall.

Amstrup, S.C., E.T. DeWeaver, D.C. Douglas, B.G. Marcot, G.M. Durner, C.M. Bitz, and D.A. Bailey, 2010. "Greenhouse Gas Mitigation Can Reduce Sea-Ice Loss and Increase Polar Bear Persistence." *Nature* 468:955–8.

Bankoff, G. 2001. "Rendering the World Unsafe: 'Vulnerability' as Western Discourse." *Disasters* 25 (1):19–35.

Belchansky, G.I., D.C. Douglas, and N.G. Platonov. 2004. "Duration of the Arctic Sea Ice Melt Season: Regional and Interannual Variability." *Journal of Climate* 17 (1):67–80.

Berkes, F., and D. Jolly. 2001. "Adapting to Climate Change: Social-Ecological Resilience in a Canadian Western Arctic Community." *Conservation Ecology* 5 (2):18. Accessed online at: http://www.consecol.org/vol5/iss2/art18.

Blaikie, P., T. Cannon, I. Davis, and B. Wisner. 1994. *At Risk: Natural Hazards, People's Vulnerability and Disasters.* London: Routledge.

Brosius, J.P. 1997. "Prior Transcripts, Divergent Paths: Resistance and Acquiescence to Logging in Sarawak, East Malaysia." *Comparative Studies in Society and History* 39: 468–510.

Chapin III, F.S., G.P. Kofinas, and C. Folke, eds. 2010. *Principles of Ecosystem Stewardship: Resilience-Based Natural Resource Management in a Changing World.* New York: Springer.

Clark, D.A., D.S. Lee, M.M.R. Freeman, and S.G. Clark. 2008. "Polar Bear Conservation in Canada: Defining the Policy Problems." *Arctic* 61 (4):347–60.

Couture, R., S. Smith, S.D. Robinson, M.M. Burgess, and S. Solomon. 2003. "On the Hazards to Infrastructure in the Canadian North Associated with Thawing of Permafrost." Proceedings of Geohazards 3rd Canadian Conference on Geotechnique and Natural Hazards. Edmonton, Alberta: The Canadian Geotechnical Society: 97–104.

Derocher, A.E. 2010. "The Prospects for Polar Bears." *Nature* 468:905–6.

Dickason, O.P., and D.T. MacNab. 2009. *Canada's First Nations: A History of Founding Peoples from Earliest Time, Fourth Edition.* Toronto, ON: Oxford University Press.

Dow, K., 1992. "Exploring Differences in Our Common Future(s) – the Meaning of Vulnerability to Global Environmental Change." *Geoforum* 23 (3):417–36.

Dowsley, M., and G. Wenzel 2008. "The Time of the Most Polar Bears: A Co-management Conflict in Nunavut." *Arctic* 61 (2):177–89.

Duerden, F., and E. Beasley. 2006. "Assessing Community Vulnerabilities to Environmental Change in the Inuvialuit Region, NWT." In *Climate Change: Linking Traditional and Scientific Knowledge,* edited by J. Oakes and R. Riewe, 123–41. Winnipeg: University of Manitoba Indigenous Issues Press.

Eakin, H., and A.L. Luers. 2006. "Assessing the Vulnerability of Social-Environmental Systems." *Annual Review of Environment and Resources* 31:365–94.

Escobar, A. 1992. "Imagining a Post-Development Era? Critical Thought, Development and Social Movements." *Social Text* 31/32:20–56.

– 1999. "The Invention of Development." *Current History* 98 (631):382–6.

Fagan, Brian. 2008. *The Great Warming: Climate Change and the Rise and Fall of Civilizations.* New York: Bloomsburg Press.

Ford, J.D., and C. Furgal 2009. "Foreword to the Special Issue: Climate Change Impacts, Adaptation and Vulnerability in the Arctic." *Polar Research* 28:1–9.

Ford, J.D., W.A. Gough, G.J. Laidler, J. MacDonald, C. Irngaut, and K. Qrunnut 2009. "Sea Ice, Climate Change, and Community Vulnerability in Northern Foxe Basin, Canada." *Climate Research* 38:137–54.

Ford, J.D., and B. Smit 2004. "A Framework for Assessing the Vulnerability of Communities in the Canadian Arctic to Risks Associated with Climate Change." *Arctic* 57 (4):389–400.

Ford, J.D., B. Smit, and J. Wandel. 2006. "Vulnerability to Climate Change in the Arctic: A Case Study from Arctic Bay, Canada." *Global Environmental Change* 16:145–160.

Ford, J.D., B. Smit, J. Wandel, M. Allurut, K. Shapa, H. Ittusarjuat§, and K. Qrunnut§. 2008. "Climate Change in the Arctic: Current and Future Vulnerability in Two Inuit Communities in Canada." *The Geographical Journal* 174 (1):45–62.

Forsyth, T. 2003. *Critical Political Ecology: The Politics of Environmental Science.* London: Routledge.

Freeman, M.M.R., R.J. Hudson, and L. Foote, eds. 2005. *Conservation Hunting: People and Wildlife in Canada's North.* Edmonton, Alberta: Canadian Circumpolar Institute Press.

Freeman, M.M.R., and G.W. Wenzel 2006. "The Nature and Significance of Polar Bear Conservation Hunting in the Canadian Arctic." *Arctic* 59 (1):21–30.

Furedi, F. 2007. "The Changing Meaning of Disaster." Area 39 (4):482–9.

Furgal, C. 2008. "Climate Change Health Vulnerabilities in the North." In *Human Health in a Changing Climate: A Canadian Assessment of Vulnerabilities and Adaptive Capacity*, edited by J. Seguin, 63. Ottawa, ON: Health Canada.

Furgal, C., and J. Seguin 2006. "Climate Change, Health, and Vulnerability in Canadian Northern Indigenous Communities." *Environmental Health Perspectives* 114 (12):1964–70.

Füssel, H., and R.J.T. Klein. 2006. "Climate Change Vulnerability Assessments: An Evolution of Conceptual Thinking." *Climatic Change* 75:301–29.

Griffith, B., D.C. Douglas, N.E. Walsh, D.D. Young, T.R. McCabe, D.E. Russell, R.G. White, R.D. Cameron, and K.R. Whitten. 2002. "The Porcupine Caribou Herd." In *Arctic Refuge Coastal Plain Terrestrial Wildlife Research Summaries*, edited by D.C. Douglas, P.E. Reynolds, and E.B. Rhode, 29. US Geological Survey, Biological Resources Division, Biological Science Report USGS/BRD/BSR 2002–0001.

Guba, E.G., and Y.S. Lincoln. 1986. "But Is It Rigorous? Trustworthiness and Authenticity in Naturalistic Evaluation." In *Naturalistic Evaluation. New Directions for Evaluation*, No. 30, edited by D. Williams. San Francisco: Jossey-Bass.

Hayley, D.W. 2004. *Climate Change: An Adaptation Challenge for Northern Engineers*. Association of Professional Engineers, Geologists and Geophysicists of Alberta, Alberta. Accessed online at: http://www.apegga.org/members/publications/peggs/web01-04/expert.htm.

Instanes, A., O. Anisimov, L. Brigham, D. Goering, B. Ladanyi, J.O. Larsen, and L.N. Khrustalev. 2005. "Infrastructure: Buildings, Support Systems, and Industrial Facilities." In *Arctic Climate Impact Assessment, acia*, edited by C. Symon, L. Arris, and B. Heal, 907–44. Cambridge: Cambridge University Press.

Intergovernmental Panel on Climate Change (IPCC). 2007. Climate Change 2007 – The Physical Science Basis. Working Group I to the Fourth Assessment Report, 996. Cambridge: Cambridge University Press.

International Arctic Science Committee (IASC), Peter Saundry (lead author). 2010. "Changes in Air Temperature and Infrastructure in the Arctic." In *Encyclopedia of Earth*, edited by Cutler J. Cleveland. Washington, DC: Environmental Information Coalition, National Council for Science and the Environment. [First published in the Encyclopedia of Earth 9 February 2010; last revised date 9 February 2010]. http://www.eoearth.org/article/Changes_in_air_temperature_and_infrastrucuureiin_the_Arctic. Accessed 20 December 2010).

Juul, K. 2005. "Transhumance, Tubes, and Telephones: Drought Related Migration as a Process of Innovation." In *Beyond Territory and Scarcity: Exploring Conflicts over Natural Resource Management*, edited by Q. Gausset, M.A. Whyte, and T. Birch-Thomson, 112–34. Stockholm: Elanders Gotab.

Kelly, P.M., and W.N. Adger. 2000. "Theory and Practice in Assessing Vulnerability to Climate Change and Facilitating Adaptation." *Climatic Change* 47:325–52.

Lahiri-Dutt, K., and G. Samanta. 2007. "'Like the Drifting Grains of Sand': Vulnerability, Security and Adjustment by Communities in the Charlands of the Damodar River, India." *South Asia: Journal of South Asian Studies* XXX (2):328–49.

Learmonth J.A., C.D. Macleod, M.B. Santos, G.J. Pierce, H.Q.P Crick, and R.A. Robinson. 2006. "Potential Effects of Climate Change on Marine Mammals." *Oceanogr. Mar. Biol.* 44:429–56.

Lemmen, D.S., F.J. Warren, J. Lacroix, and E. Bush, eds. 2008. *From Impacts to Adaptation: Canada in a Changing Climate*, 448. Ottawa, ON: Government of Canada.

Li, T.M. 2002. "Engaging Simplifications: Community-Based Resource Management, Market Processes and State Agendas in Upland Southeast Asia." *World Development* 30 (2):265–83.

Manyena, S.B. 2006. "The Concept of Resilience Revisited." *Disasters* 30 (4):433–450.

Marino, E. 2009. "Immanent Threats, Impossible Moves, and Unlikely Prestige: Understanding the Struggle for Local Control as Means towards Sustainability." In *Linking Environmental Change, Migration, and Social Vulnerability*, edited by A. Oliver-Smith and X. Shen, 42–50. Bonn, Germany: United Nations University Institute for Environment and Human Security Publication Series No. 12.

Martello, M.L. 2004. "Global Change Science and the Arctic Citizen." *Science and Public Policy* 31 (2):107–15.

– 2008. "Arctic Indigenous Peoples as Representations and Representatives of Climate Change." *Social Studies of Science* 38:351–75.

Newton, J. 1995. "An Assessment of Coping with Environmental Hazards in Northern Indigenous Communities." *The Canadian Geographer* 39 (2):112–20.

Oerlemans, J. 2005. "Extracting a Climate Signal from 169 Glacier Records." *Science* 308:675–777. DOI: 10.1126/science.1107046

Overland, J.E., M. Spillane, and N.N. Soreide. 2004. "Integrated Analysis of Physical and Biological Pan-Arctic Change." *Climate Change* 63 (3):291–322.

Oxford Paperback Thesaurus. 2000. Compiled by B. Kirkpatrick. Oxford: Oxford University Press.

Paine, Robert, ed. 1971. *Patrons and Brokers in the Eastern Arctic*. Institute of Social and Economic Research, Memorial University of Newfoundland. Newfoundland Social and Economic Papers No. 2.

Pearse, T., B. Smit, F. Duerden, J. Ford, A. Goose, and F. Kataoyak. 2010. "Inuit Vulnerability and Adaptive Capacity to Climate Change in Ulukhaktok, Northwest Territories, Canada." *Polar Record* 46 (237):157–77.

Pretes, M. 1988. "Underdevelopment in Two Norths: The Brazilian Amazon and the Canadian Arctic." *Arctic* 41 (2):109–16.

Prowse, T.D., and C. Furgal 2009. "Northern Canada in a Changing Climate: Major Findings and Conclusions." *Ambio* 38 (5):290–92.

Regehr, E.V., N.J. Lunn, S.C. Amstrup, and I. Stirling. 2007. "Effects of Earlier Sea Ice Breakup on Survival and Population Size of Polar Bears in Western Hudson Bay." *Journal of Wildlife Management* 71 (8):2673–83.

Royal Commission on Aboriginal Peoples (RCAP). 1994. *The High Arctic Relocation: A Report on the 1953–1955 Relocation*, 190. Ottawa, ON: Minister of Supply and Services.

Sahlins, M. 1972. *Stone Age Economics*. Chicago: Aldine/Atherton Inc.

Smit, B., and O. Pilifosova. 2003. "From Adaptation to Adaptive Capacity and Vulnerability Reduction." In *Climate Change, Adaptive Capacity, and Development*, edited by J. Smith, R.T.J. Kelin, and S. Hug, 9–28. London: Imperial College Press.

Schwandt, T.A., 2007. "Judging Interpretations." *New Directions For Evaluation* 4:11–14.

Solway, J.S. 1994. "Drought as a Revelatory Crisis: An Exploration of Shifting Entitlements and Hierarchies in the Kalahari, Botswana." *Development and Change* 25:471–95.

Stirling, I. 2002. "Polar Bears and Seals in the Eastern Beaufort Sea and Amundsen Gulf: A Synthesis of Population Trends and Ecological Relationships over Three Decades." *Arctic* 55 (5):59–76.

Stirling, I., and A.E. Derocher. 2007. "Melting Under Pressure: The Real Scoop on Climate Warming and Polar Bears." *The Wildlife Professional* Fall:24–43.

Stirling, I., A.E. Derocher, W.A. Gough, and K. Rode. 2008. Response to Dyck et al. (2007) on "Polar Bears and Climate Change in Western Hudson Bay." *Ecological Complexity* 5 (3):193–201.

Stirling, I., and C.L. Parkinson. 2006. "Possible Effects of Climate Warming on Selected Populations of Polar Bears (Ursus Maritimus) in the Canadian Arctic." *Arctic* 59 (3):261–75.

Study of Environmental Change (SEARCH). 2005. *Plans for Implementing the International Polar Year and Beyond*, 104. Fairbanks, Alaska: Arctic Research Consortium of the United States (ARCUS).

Turner, T. 1992. "Defiant Images: The Kayapo Appropriation of Video." *Anthropology Today* 8 (6):5–16.

Turner II, B.L. 2010. "Vulnerability and Resilience: Coalescing or Paralleling Approaches for Sustainability Science?" *Global Environmental Change* 20:570–76.

US Arctic Research Commission Permafrost Task Force. 2003. *Permafrost, and Impacts on Civil Infrastructure* 62. Arlington, Virginia: 01–03 Arctic Research Commission.

Warren, F.J., T. Kulkarni, and D.S. Lemmen, eds. 2010. *Canada in a Changing Climate*. Ottawa, ON: Government of Canada.

Watts, M.J., and H.G. Bohle 1993. "Hunger, Famine and the Space of Vulnerability." *GeoJournal* 30 (2):117–25.

Weissling, L.E. 1989. "Arctic Canada and Zambia: A Comparison of Development Processes in the Fourth and Third Worlds." *Arctic* 42 (3):208–16.

Wenzel, G.W. 2009. "Canadian Inuit Subsistence and Ecological Instability – If the Climate Changes, Must the Inuit?" *Polar Research* 28:89–99.

Zaslow, M. 1988. *The Northward Expansion of Canada 1914–1967*. Toronto: McClelland & Stewart.

Indigenous Source Water Protection: Lessons for Watershed Planning in Canada

ROBERT PATRICK

Forces of colonization that began in the early 1800s continue to produce a geography of poor drinking water for First Nations in Canada. In this chapter, the concept of source water protection is expanded to include traditional knowledge. Extending the dominant source water protection concept nested in and constrained by Western science to embrace traditional knowledge offers potential for a more inclusive and holistic perspective on water generally, and watershed protection specifically. Such a model offers opportunity for broader community engagement, incorporation of Elder's knowledge, local empowerment, and renewed hope for improved access to safe drinking water for First Nations in Canada.

As of July 2010, 116 First Nation communities in Canada (roughly one in five communities) were under a drinking water advisory (Health Canada 2010). A drinking water advisory is a preventative measure to protect public health from confirmed or suspected microbial or chemical contamination (Health Canada 2009). Many First Nation communities have lived under these conditions for extended periods of time, including the 282 residents of Neskantanga First Nation in northern Ontario who have remained under a boil water advisory since it was first issued in 1995 (Polaris Institute 2008; Eggertson 2008). In Saskatchewan, Yellow Quill First Nation near Saskatoon was put on a boil water advisory also in 1995 and remained under advisory until 2004 (Polaris Institute 2008). These are not isolated cases, nor are they uncommon conditions for First Nations in Canada. A boil water advisory is issued after there is confirmation of water supply contamination with fecal pollution indicator organisms (Health Canada 2009). As an indicator of compromised drinking water quality, boil water advisories issued by federal or provincial health authorities for First Nation community water systems are two-and-a-half times more frequent than for non-First Nation communities. Community water systems are defined here as any water system with two or more water connections. Approximately 30 per cent of First Nation community water systems in Canada are classified as high-risk systems, and the number of water-borne infections in First Nation communities is an alarming twenty-six times higher than the Canadian national average (Eggerton 2006). It is recognized that non-First Nation communities also have boil water advisories; however, these advisories tend to be for shorter duration while receiving much greater public profile. For example, a "boil water advisory" issued for the Greater Vancouver area (now Metro Vancouver) in November 2006, the result of winter rains causing landslides and high raw water turbidity, received front page mainstream media attention before the advisory was cancelled after just three days. By comparison, many First Nation communities experience prolonged periods of boil water advisories lasting many years. Health Canada (2009) reported that the average duration of all drinking water advisories reported between 1995 and 2007 (n=654 advisories) was 343 days, with the maximum duration lasting 4,716 days, almost thirteen years.

The response from the federal authority responsible for First Nations water in Canada, Aboriginal Affairs and Northern Development Canada (AANDC), was the instalment of water treatment facilities in certain First Nation communities. This response has had only limited success for several reasons. First, the high capital cost of water treatment is often prohibitive for most small water system operators. Second, high operation and maintenance costs of water treatment further limit the viability of such technology in rural regions already experiencing limited financial resources. Third, operator retention in First Nation communities has been problematic across Canada. Trained water operators continue to be drawn away from First Nation communities because of higher paying water operator jobs in nearby urban centres. Fourth, in many cases across Canada, inappropriate or wrongly sized advanced water treatment technology has been ineffective at treating local raw water conditions. Collectively these problems limit the potential benefit of water treatment technology to address water quality issues faced by First Nation communities in Canada.

What other water management options are available to First Nations to help improve access to safe drinking water? Recent attention in the water resources literature is given to the importance of the multi-barrier approach to safe drinking water.

MULTI-BARRIER APPROACH

The Canadian Council of Ministers of the Environment (2004) define the multi-barrier approach as "an integrated system of procedures, processes and tools that collectively prevent or reduce the contamination of drinking water from source to tap in order to reduce risks to public health." The goal of the multi-barrier approach in drinking water management is to reduce the risk of drinking-water contamination through system redundancies, or barriers, built into the water system. The water resources literature identifies five main barriers that make up the multi-barrier approach. From source (watershed or aquifer) to tap (end user), the five barriers are:

1 source water protection;
2 water treatment (including chlorination, filtration, ultra-violet light, etc.);
3 water distribution system (including water system design, repair, maintenance);
4 water testing and monitoring; and,
5 emergency response plan.

These five barriers are intended to serve as a linear system of redundancies. Should any single barrier fail, a combination of the remaining barriers will provide adequate safety to public health. The focus in this chapter will be on the first barrier in the multi-barrier approach to safe drinking water: source water protection.

SOURCE WATER PROTECTION

Source water protection (SWP) is broadly defined as watershed and aquifer planning for the protection of drinking-water supplies. SWP is practiced largely through land-use planning practices aimed at the protection of drinking water supplies. SWP aims to reduce the risk of water-borne contamination at the water source (Davies and Mazumder 2003). SWP makes economic sense for at least three principal reasons. First, it is many times less expensive to protect a water source from contamination than it is to remediate after contamination (Job 1996). Second, it is more cost effective to invest in natural capital, such as purchasing development rights or to restrict land-use activities within a watershed, rather than to invest in physical capital, such as water treatment technologies (National Research Council 2000; Chichilnsky and Heal 1998). Third, attention to SWP helps maintain source water conditions, a practice that reduces water treatment plant challenges and costs (Gullick 2003). Moreover, Kundell and DeMeo (2000) identify additional rational for SWP, including preservation of environmental quality and citizen engagement and awareness. In the absence of watershed or groundwater management for the protection of drinking water sources, unwanted contaminants may freely, and unknowingly, enter the water supply creating a public health concern.

The concept of SWP gained widespread attention in Canada soon after the May 2000 water contamination event at Walkerton, Ontario. The deaths of seven people and water-borne illnesses of over 2,300 people initiated a two-year public inquiry led by Justice Dennis O'Connor of the Ontario Appeals Court. How is it that people in Ontario, arguably one of Canada's wealthiest provinces, could die from consuming municipal drinking water? The public inquiry noted that the causes of this tragedy were many, but the necessary action to prevent a similar tragedy was simple: source water protection.

Source water protection recognizes that effective water resources planning demands close attention to land-use practices and activities within source water areas. SWP is, therefore, a land and water-planning process encompassing numerous initiatives and programs. The components of any SWP planning process include:

· delineation of watershed or groundwater recharge area;
· inventory of potential sources of contamination;
· assessment of vulnerability of water supply to contamination; and,
· implementation of a source protection management plan.

In the aftermath of the water contamination event at Walkerton, most provincial and territorial governments in Canada responded with the introduction of new drinking water governance structures, policies, or legislative frameworks in support of source protection planning and management. In Saskatchewan, the provincial government established the Saskatchewan Watershed Authority (SWA) under the Ministry of Environment. One of the key activities of the SWA is the creation of SWP plans in the more populated southern watershed areas of the province. Other provincial and territorial governments in Canada are at various stages of SWP plan development. For example, in 2010 the Government of the Northwest Territories adopted a Water Stewardship Strategy prioritizing a broad range of action statements, including the development of community SWP plans.

Given the frequency and duration of water advisories in First Nation communities, is there a role to be played by source water protection? Is there a need for greater attention to SWP on First Nation lands? Perhaps more importantly, how might the practice of SWP differ for First Nations?

ORIGINS OF SOURCE WATER PROTECTION

The use of the term "source water protection" is exclusive to the non-Indigenous Western water science literature. The concept itself a manifestation of colonial land and water management practices. Tracing the origins of SWP as a concept in the water resources literature brings us to seventeenth-century England. Kundell and DeMeo (2000) reference a statement of Lord Delaware made in 1610 regarding the importance of "not washing any unclean linen within twenty feet of the old well or new pump nor dare to do the necessities of nature within less than a quarter mile of the fort." Further, the consequence of not protecting sources of drinking water was made evident when public health pioneer John Snow (1813–58) meticulously mapped the pattern of cholera outbreak in London, England in 1854. Snow's mapping exercise revealed that cholera occurred much more frequently in customers purchasing water from one specific water company. The East London Company drew its water from the lower Thames River in London, a source long contaminated with London's sewage. Identifying the link between source water and disease in the mid-1800s initiated significant changes in water supply management directed at improving water quality many years before the isolation of the actual water-borne organisms responsible for cholera and typhus (Aramini et al. 2000).

The formal use of the term "source water protection" has been traced to language of the European Union's *Water Framework Directive*. In the United States, Gullick (2003) reports a resurgence in SWP after the Safe Drinking Water Act Amendments of 1996 were passed. One of the most cited, and celebrated, examples of SWP in North America is the case of New York City where, in the early 1990s, upstate watershed areas were protected in the interest of avoiding expensive water treatment (National Research Council 2000). In Canada, it was the events at

Walkerton in May 2000 that sparked interest in SWP. The term "source water protection" finds origin in Western science, a term nested in colonial water management policy.

SOURCE PROTECTION IN SASKATCHEWAN

In response to the events of both Walkerton, ON, and more specifically, North Battleford, SK, the province of Saskatchewan established the Saskatchewan Watershed Authority (SWA), a Crown Corporation to administer numerous water-related Acts, including the Saskatchewan Watershed Authority Act, 2005. The stated mandate of the SWA is to lead "management of the province's water resources to ensure safe drinking water sources and reliable water supplies for economic, environmental and social benefits for Saskatchewan people" (Saskatchewan Watershed Authority). The mandate does not discern between different groups of people within Saskatchewan, and it is therefore presumed that this mandate extends to all First Nations people in Saskatchewan. Of the major activities listed by the SWA is a call to "develop and implement watershed protection plans through public consultation and in cooperation with local communities." Again, it is presumed that this major activity would include all communities, both First Nations and non-First Nations. The development of watershed protection plans was identified in the Saskatchewan Safe Drinking Water Strategy (October 2002) as a priority of government. By 2011, significant progress has been made on the development of these plans with approximately nine SWP plans either completed or nearing completion. Of interest is that all these SWP plans are in the southern portion of the province and not specific to First Nation communities. To date, the entire northern half of Saskatchewan (north of Prince Albert) has not received SWP planning. In addition, while summary reference is made to First Nations in the existing SWP plans, there is no specific mention of policies applicable to First Nations lands. Presumably, the jurisdictional gap between the federal and provincial governments respecting First Nations' access to water is a constraining factor facing First Nations' inclusion into the existing SWP plans of the Saskatchewan Watershed Authority.

It is in the interest of good watershed planning to be inclusive of all watershed residents in the planning processes, particularly for defining roles and responsibilities for the implementation of the plan itself. In Saskatchewan, these planning processes are coordinated and resourced by the provincial SWA in consultation with local non-government organizations and community stakeholders. Though some Aboriginal communities are represented in watershed planning, not all First Nations have a voice in these processes. There is space for participation by First Nations in the planning process but for many First Nations it means accepting an extra task on a voluntarily basis and without certainty that such effort will be of any benefit to the First Nation community. As noted by Duncan and Bowden (2010), linkages between the Saskatchewan Watershed Authority and First Nations are, for the most part, informal with various levels of co-operation on groundwater assessments, for example. To date, just four SWP plans have been developed in First Nation communities in Saskatchewan by a private consultant. These four plans have not followed the planning model set out by the SWA that has been practiced in other parts of the province.

TREATY RIGHTS AND WATER

In Canada, the Indian Act (1876) created, among other things, "Indian reserves," or institutional "islands" of forced settlement. Such forced settlement had two major impacts on access to safe water. The first is that these relatively small and isolated reserves have limited access to surface water supplies. The size of a reserve was determined based on the size of the population to be assigned to a given reserve. The preferred locations of reserves were based in part on the separation of Indigenous groups, and less on the availability of reliable water (Stonechild and Waiser 2010). The second major impact forced settlement has had on access to safe drinking water is that the lands surrounding these Indian reserves have become used for urban development, recreation, agriculture, forestry, mining, and other land uses administered by non-First Nation agencies. While directly affected by these land-use activities, Indigenous peoples in Canada have no control over these land uses (Patrick 2010). Access to and control over lands and resources adjacent to Indian reserves is at the discretion of state interests of the provincial and federal government. This jurisdictional conundrum is further complicated for Indigenous peoples in Canada as the federal government has authority over lands and waters "reserved for Indians." Arguably, the impact of development from outside reserve lands on water quality and quantity within reserve lands – and other traditional lands – contradicts the promise made between Indian peoples and the British Crown during treaty signing that took place in the late 1800s. Today, statements increasingly suggest that the promise made during treaty-making, "that

Indian people would continue to have access to healthy water," has not been upheld (TATC 2011). Consistently we are reminded that water, and more specifically the right to healthy water, was never surrendered at the time of treaty-making (Keepers of the Water V; TATC 2011). The connection between treaty and water rights is captured best by a Saddle Lake Elder who, citing actual wording from the original treaty, stated: "So long as the grass grows and the water flows ... First Nations never surrendered their right to water"; and further, that "treaty is water and water is treaty" (TATC 2011).

Today, Indigenous communities continue to fall under a weak legal framework with respect to drinking water on reserves (von der Porten and de Loë 2010). A new legal framework is being considered by the federal government (the proposed First Nations Safe Drinking Water Act), but at this time there are no laws or regulations in Canada that govern the provision of drinking water in First Nation communities (Duncan and Bowden 2010). The basic water and waste-water management systems (such as tanker-trucked water and septic systems) are managed locally, with no overarching federal regulatory framework. Unlike the United States and the European Union, Canada does not have national, legally binding standards for drinking water, but merely voluntary drinking water guidelines. The result is a patchwork of drinking water laws which create disparity not only between provinces, but also leave Indigenous peoples disproportionately vulnerable to water-borne diseases, drinking water advisories, and the health effects of poor water quality (Duncan and Bowden 2010). This situation clearly violates the fiduciary responsibility of the Canadian government in light of treaty agreements made between Indian peoples and the British Crown prior to creation of Canada. The long delay in action to remedy this condition speaks to the patience and resolve of Indigenous leadership and the procrastination of the Canadian federal state.

The federal government has provided no regulatory framework for water management on reserves. The current water management and planning regime in First Nation communities is managed through the federal government in a semi-regulatory framework based on capital agreements. These capital agreements are determined and administered by AANDC. Access to federal funding for First Nations is conditional upon terms set out in a capital agreement. The terms of the capital agreement are determined by the federal government and may include conditions to be met by the First Nation that are wholly unrelated to the immediate needs of that First Nation.

FIRST NATIONS SOURCE WATER PROTECTION IN
SASKATCHEWAN

The first examples of First Nations SWP plans in Saskatchewan were completed in 2008 in the North Saskatchewan watershed. The North Saskatchewan River Basin Council (NSRBC) initiated work towards these SWP plans as early as 2007. Together with the former First Nations Agricultural Council of Saskatchewan and Aboriginal communities in the watershed, the NSRBC has worked to develop source water protection plans for four First Nations in Saskatchewan. In order of completion, these First Nations are: Muskeg Lake Cree Nation, Sweetgrass First Nation, Witchekan First Nation, and Thunderchild First Nation. These plans are separate from the North Saskatchewan Source Water Protection Plan and other similar plans of the Saskatchewan Watershed Authority. These First Nation SWP plans were developed with financial support from various agencies, such as Agriculture and Agri-Food Canada, Environment Canada, Indian and Northern Affairs Canada, and the Federation of Saskatchewan Indian Nations. As a result of these efforts, these First Nation communities have their own source water protection plans, as well as background reports on the condition of water quality in their communities.

One of the important aspects of these community-based source water protection plans is that they contain community values and key actions associated with community priorities; however, since the First Nation source water protection plans are created independently from the broader watershed source water protection plan, the scale of assessment is smaller. In other words, the boundaries of the First Nation define the SWP boundary and not the watershed boundary of the First Nation. Policies and key actions do not, and legally cannot, address water quality vulnerabilities that may exist outside the First Nation boundary. Land-use activities on Crown-owned land, private lands, or federal lands cannot be controlled by adjacent First Nations. In this sense, SWP is of limited value to First Nations in that any best management practices to mitigate land-use impacts on water quality would normally prescribe a watershed boundary for source protection, and not an imposed political boundary such as an Indian reserve boundary.

In spite of this condition, the AANDC Protocol for Safe Drinking Water in First Nations recommends source water protection standards and steps for planning source water protection. AANDC currently have no resources for funding, monitoring, or aiding in the implementation of source water protection planning. In recent years, AANDC has contracted with Environment Canada to develop source water protection tools for use in Aboriginal communities. Some of these tools were passed on to the First Nations Agricultural Council of Saskatchewan when they were conducting a source water protection pilot project in the North Saskatchewan River Watershed with Muskeg Lake Cree Nation, Sweetgrass First Nation, and Witchekan First Nation. Aboriginal Affairs and Northern Development Canada is the only source of funding for water-related management yet it has no clear mandate to support source water protection. Thus, the financing of source water protection is the responsibility of the chief and council of the individual First Nation. The political will in Indigenous communities for practicing source water protection may be present but with no means of accessing dollars to develop source water protection plans, progress will be slow. In Saskatchewan, First Nation partnerships with Saskatchewan Watershed Authority and local watershed stewardship groups such as the North Saskatchewan River Basin Council (NSRBC) has become a first step towards watershed-scale collaboration and communication.

To date, four SWP plans are within the North Saskatchewan River Basin, and the plans themselves facilitated through the efforts of the NSRBC. The development of these plans was undertaken by a consultant with only limited input from the broader community and other stakeholders. On the surface, these plans look similar to any other SWP plan. These plans define source water protection and provide rationale for their development and use. Introductory topics contained in these plans include community background, land and water-use issues and concerns, water conservation, water quality and quantity, and natural habitat conditions. In each section are recommendations for specific action in each of these key areas. For example, under the heading of "Natural Habitat," the recommendation reads: "That the community members undertake a clean-up of the entire reserve to remove all hazards, waste materials and debris." The remainder of the plan highlights specific "Key Actions" to implement the plan. One key action suggests: "[to] conduct a survey of the abandoned cisterns in the community" (Key Action 1); or "[to] develop an action plan to decommission cisterns" (Key Action 2).

The strength of these plans is that they are locally produced, involved some level of local participation in their development and were supported through the Saskatchewan Watershed Authority and the North Saskatchewan River Basin Council. The plans include prioritized key actions to be addressed by each community. From well decommissioning to landfill remediation, prioritized key actions are listed within the SWP plan.

The content of these early First Nation SWP plans in Saskatchewan captures the core components expected of any SWP plan. In this sense the plans very much resemble any other rational planning document drafted in the context of Western science. Reference to Indigenous traditional knowledge, alternative belief systems, and the spiritual connection of Indigenous peoples to water is largely absent in these early First Nations SWP plans. One exception found in the Sweetgrass First Nation SWP plan is reference to a Dene Elder, Prophet Ayah, who "told of a coming time when there would be no more water in the world, except for water in Great Bear Lake," a condition that would "attract people from around the world to fight over the last global waters in Dene country." The Sweetgrass SWP plan also concludes by making summary reference to the Sweetgrass First Nation as "Keepers of the Earth," acknowledging that the First Nation holds an "understanding of the ancient origins of the North Saskatchewan River," as well as "the far-reaching impacts the SWP plan would have on future generations." Beyond these summary comments, the SWP plan provides only limited reference to Indigenous knowledge briefs. One might expect a First Nation source water protection plan to be inclusive of Indigenous traditional knowledge and belief systems along with rational planning and Western science.

So how might Indigenous traditional knowledge influence and inform SWP plans? At a time when government and non-government organizations are looking for ways to protect source waters this question may well be worth investigation (Keepers of the Water IV, V). Suggested here is an attempt at Indigenizing source water protection as a means of recognizing the Indigenous water perspective, but also to examine how such a perspective may enrich SWP more broadly for all communities and regions.

INDIGENOUS WATER PERSPECTIVE

As part of Indigenous source water protection planning it is important to understand the "water perspective" held by First Nations in Canada. In Lavalley (2006) it is revealed that the Indigenous perspective on water is significantly different than that held by Western science. For example, where the Western view interprets water as a "resource," to be used by and for humans, the Indigenous perspective views water as a "spiritual, living entity." As any living entity, water assumes human characteristics, capable of displaying calmness when unimpeded, or anger when not respected. Lavalley (2006) reports First Nations' connection to water, indeed all creation, including plant life, the sky world, animals, earth, all things. By viewing water as a living entity the thought of harming water through pollution becomes ever more difficult to imagine. This interconnected, holistic view of water reveals that it is not possible to affect water quality without affecting the human condition. At present, this holistic perspective is not captured in existing SWP plans.

First Nations often express dissatisfaction with the taste of tap water (TATC 2011). The modern practice of adding chlorine to drinking water in order to kill all "living things" directly conflicts with Indigenous views of "living water." Killing all life in water renders water dead. The Western science approach of "manufacturing" safe drinking water directly conflicts with the Indigenous understanding of "water as life" (Keepers of the Water V). It is here that the Western view of safe drinking water is in conflict with Indigenous traditional knowledge. Based on this perspective it would be expected that any First Nation SWP plan would strongly support proactive source protection measures over chemical treatment.

Additionally, Indigenous culture often refers to the nurturing, life-giving properties of water, pointing to the human experience of our first water environment: our mother's womb (Keepers of the Water IV, V; TATC 2011). Moreover, the link between women and water is strongly represented in many Indigenous cultures. Women are the "Water Keepers," the protectors of water, and as such are expected to take a lead role in conducting water ceremonies in their respective communities (Keepers of the Water IV). Additionally, water is commonly associated with grandmother Moon, an association that links the moon with women. In this way, women as life givers maintain a special connection to and understanding of water. The practice of moon ceremonies, for example, honours the important linkages between women, water, and the moon (Lavalley 2006). At present, this perspective is not captured in First Nation or non-First Nation SWP plans in Saskatchewan.

Indigenous culture recognizes water as the medium through which plant medicines will grow. In this context, water is the "pharmacy" of Indigenous medicines (Lavalley 2006). By extension, the natural environment, including all water, is the "supermarket," providing food for human sustenance (Lavalley 2006). From an Indigenous perspective, the rationale for protecting source water goes far beyond the reach of protecting drinking water alone. Rationale for SWP planning in the

Indigenous context will include the protection of medicinal plants and healthy food supplies for all living entities.

Additionally, Indigenous teachings identify humans as "custodians of the land and water." This custodian role required that the condition of the land and water be maintained in the condition we received it from our ancestors to be passed on to future generations. This perspective is consistent with the modern, Western concept of intergenerational equity found in sustainable development discourse. The concept of "custodian," or steward, has not been explicitly captured to date in mainstream SWP plan documents which tend to address more pragmatically the needs of the present, that is, to protect drinking water sources from immediate risk of contamination. The intergenerational, or custodial, rationale for SWP has similarly not been integrated into SWP plans to date.

The important role of Elders in respect of water–related knowledge cannot be overstated. According to some Elders, water never rests (TATC 2011). Today, water is fatigued and can't keep up with waste inputs, a condition emulated in humans and all other living creatures connected to water (Lavalley 2006). As a result, human health continues to decline along with the diminished state of water (Keepers of the Water V). Elders warn of the negative impacts of taking water for granted. For example, when waste water is sent down a drain we do not see the impacts of this modern convenience. Disconnected from water gathering and appropriate waste water disposal, our relationship to water has increasingly been diminished (TATC 2011). Elders have stated that this diminished relationship with water will only lead to further disrespect for water. Elders have professed that this condition may lead to the need for humans to purchase water as a result of poor "natural" water quality (Lavalley 2006). This prophecy seems to have come to reality; today, the annual sale of bottled water is in the millions of dollars just in Canada alone. The modern practice of bottling water and its associated commodification, according to Indigenous traditional knowledge, is tied to the loss of our human relationship with water. It would seem that Indigenous traditional knowledge has accurately predicted this reality.

For generations, traditional teachings of water have been practiced through ceremony (von der Porten and de Loë 2010). As foundational elements of knowledge, ceremonies are central to Indigenous culture whereby individuals find expression in all life forms, including water (Keepers of the Water 2010, 2011). Ceremonies provide a means of giving thanks for water. In contrast, water ceremonies or celebrations are not common in Western culture. When water is celebrated in non-

Indigenous culture it has tended to occur at the national or global scale, such as the United Nations World Water Day, an event drawing media attention at the national and international level yet facilitating little opportunity for individual or community engagement. Again, SWP planning that has been nested in Western science has given little attention to local and community-scale celebration of water. First Nation SWP plans have the opportunity to acknowledge the significance of water celebration and find ways to embrace such practice in First Nation communities (Keepers of the Water V). The immediate benefits of water celebration will assist communities in the promotion of intergenerational engagement, water awareness, and traditional teachings. Traditional ceremony is one means by which young people can be introduced to and show respect for, water. Elders have a role to play in this resurgence of water ceremony and therefore should be consulted for their views on how to protect water (Lavalley 2006). Western science has the opportunity to learn from this more traditional teaching and give greater attention to water as "a life giving spirit" as opposed to "a resource for consumption." In the words of Elder Marie Adam, Athabasca Chipewyan First Nation (Alberta): "Right from the time you're conceived, you're in water, then you're floating in water for the next nine months. That's why we say that water is so sacred, because it is life" (Keepers of the Water IV).

Indigenous SWP planning will differ from other SWP plans by drawing attention to water as living spirit, as medicinal, as life giving, and as a "life form" worthy of celebration in a way that restores human respect for water. Indeed, an Indigenized SWP planning program has potential for offering much more than a rational planning process aimed solely at water resource protection through Western science's "best management practices." An Indigenized SWP planning process could positively inform all SWP plans by extending the reach of science to incorporate, or at least be respectful of, Indigenous traditional knowledge and other ways of knowing water.

According to Lavalley (2006), present-day decision making in water management both on and off-reserve, involves little input from Elders and women. Instead, Western technical advice has been sought from the "expert, water science elite," often representing state interests and funded through state resource revenues. Those practicing SWP planning in Canada to date continue to place exclusive reliance on technical information. As such, little, if any, value is placed on Indigenous traditional knowledge respecting water. More than ever, government regulations often stand as the sole condition regulating source water protection.

Table 16.1   Perspectives on water

Western science	Indigenous knowledge
Reactive management	Proactive planning
Water as resource	Water as medicinal, spiritual, living entity
Decision by government, trained managers	Decisions from Elders, women
State control and licensing of water	Community celebration of water, gifting to water
Water as global scale discourse	Water celebrated at local scale
Expert elite, scientist, government managers	Elder, youth, women empowerment

In the meantime, Indigenous peoples are increasingly calling for the uptake of Elder knowledge from their communities, particularly when a development activity off-reserve has potential to impact on-reserve water conditions (Keepers of the Water IV). Elders provide lessons for today based on their experiences of yesterday. Legacy mining of uranium is one example from northern Saskatchewan. Elders from Wollaston Lake, SK reveal stories of radioactive waste ore in the 1950s being dumped into rivers and lakes of the north. Similar stories are told by Elders in the Northwest Territories that handled uranium "yellowcake" from Radium City, Great Bear Lake.

An Indigenized SWP plan will seek participation from Elders, youths, and women. First Nation community members, and especially Elders, need to be included as core participants in SWP planning. Only through the participation of Elders, women, children, and all community groups will SWP planning reach its potential. Such inclusion of community will also help ensure SWP plan implementation. Table 16.1 provides a brief synopsis of perspectives on water from both a Western science world view and an Indigenous traditional knowledge world view.

CONCLUSION

The colonial system of state-imposed Indian reserves helped to create a geography of poor water for First Nations in what became Canada. State-enforced reserve boundaries restricted human movement to safer water and traditional food sources with consequent negative impacts on human health. This colonial practice restricted water and food security among Indigenous peoples while creating dependency relationships with agencies of the state. The legacy of this dependency relationship is expressed today in expensive and often wrongly sized water treatment plants, coupled with long-term debt repayment programs.

The extraction of minerals, timber, and other resources, combined with land-use change, has impacted source waters adjacent to reserve lands, as well as other traditional lands. Only now, in the post-Walkerton era, is Western science turning to source water protection as a means of watershed-scale planning. While the practice of swp is deemed "pro-active," the timing of Western science swp is rather late. As we have seen, Indigenous traditional knowledge has, for a long time, respected water in a very different way.

Land-use activities operating outside reserve boundaries that have no restrictions imposed from within the reserve boundaries have potential to impact First Nation water quality. Chemical sprays on forests and crops, not to mention urban point source discharge and industrial mining extractions, continue to put on-reserve populations at various levels of risk (Hanrahan 2003). The result has produced not only a geography of poor water and colonial dependencies, but also a condition of power-lessness in land-use decisions respecting land and water (Patrick 2011; Windsor and McVey 2005). While the intention of such colonial practice was forced assimilation, the result has been quite the opposite. The promises made during treaty ensured even access to water "for as long as the rivers flow and grasses grow" (TATC 2011). The surrendering of Indigenous rights to water was something unimaginable to First Nations at treaty signing (TATC 2011; Keepers of the Water V). Access to safe water was not something traded away at treaty (TATC 2011). Indigenous peoples respect for water provides an important lesson to non-Indigenous peoples.

Through the Canadian Constitution Act 1867, and other more recent legal arrangements, the federal government controls, regulates, and manages water on First Nation lands. Yet, many Elders express concern that their own people no longer "know" the water on their own lands (Keepers of the Water V). The creation of Indian reserves presents a difficult challenge to all Indigenous peoples intent on developing swp plans. At a minimum, First Nations will need the co-operation and partnership of adjacent landowners during the swp plan-making process. Next, it will be necessary for First Nations to hold veto power over any development activity that poses a risk to their source water. Duty to consult requires that any development activity with potential to contaminate a water source must be vetted to the affected Indigenous population for their approval. Without approval, such activity must not proceed. This is consistent with federal fiduciary responsibility respecting Indigenous rights to healthy water recognized by treaty. Above all, First Nations must not be seen as mere stakeholders, but as rightful and legal users of the land and water recognized by treaty.

In many ways, swp planning is consistent, at least in principle, with Indigenous traditional knowledge. The concept of proactive planning for source water protection aligns well with First Nations' perspective about water – that is, respect for water and caretakers of water. And yet, Indigenous traditional knowledge adds considerably more to the human relationship with water. Not captured in current swp discourse is any notion of "living water" offering "medicinal, healing powers," or water as a "spiritual entity, a gift from the stars." Because of this, swp planning in First Nation communities has potential to facilitate Elders' teaching on water in First Nation communities. First Nations swp planning has further potential to inform Western science swp planning to recognize water as something more than a "resource" for human use and management. Indigenous swp planning should acknowledge the perspectives of Elders, youths, and women by incorporating Indigenous traditional knowledge where appropriate. Second, in an administrative sense, First Nation swp plans will be challenged to affect change in land-use practices outside First Nation boundaries.

Communication with "outside" stakeholders affecting First Nation water quality will be critical to the success of First Nation swp planning. Next, in a political sense, and where treaties exist, such as the Canadian Prairie region, First Nation swp plans should contain language reminding the reader of Indigenous rights to healthy water as well as the state's fiduciary responsibility in this regard. Finally, in a technical sense, First Nation swp will also need to address the Western science technical issues and concerns at both the watershed and community scale.

Any discussion of First Nation swp planning needs to be done in a sensitive, respectful manner. Presenting swp planning to First Nations as the "Western science solution" to First Nation water woes is inappropriate on two levels. First, it is inappropriate because many First Nations hold a long spiritual relationship with water and to suggest that swp will suddenly bring an awareness of water to First Nations is disrespectful. Second, it would be inappropriate to tell First Nations to "fix" their water quality problems. In most cases, First Nation source water has become compromised not from the activities of the First Nation, but rather from activities originating from off-reserve industrial activity. The suggestion that swp is necessary to correct First Nation water quality problems could be taken as a suggestion that First Nations are the sole cause of their water problems.

Indigenizing SWP opens new opportunities for incorporating Indigenous traditional knowledge into what has been a Western science-driven agenda. SWP planning by and for First Nations has potential to offer much more than technical recommendations for water safety and security. Suggested here is that Indigenous SWP plans should reflect local First Nation values and perspectives about water. The outcome of such a process may help empower Elders and women as decision makers around water and embrace traditional teachings to youth, while reminding the federal state of its fiduciary and treaty responsibilities.

REFERENCES

Aramini J., J. Wilson, B. Allen, J. Holt, W. Sears, M. McLean, and R. Copes. 2000. *Drinking Water Quality and Health Care Utilization for Gastrointestinal Illness in Greater Vancouver.* Population and Public Health Branch. Guelph, ON: Health Canada.

Canadian Council of Ministers of the Environment. 2004. *Source to Tap. The Multi-Barrier Approach to Safe Drinking Water.* Prepared by the Federal-Provincial-Territorial Committee on Drinking Water.

Chichilnisky, G., and G. Heal. 1998. "Economic Returns from the Biosphere." *Nature* 391 (February):629.

Constitution Act, 1867 (British North America Act, 1867) 30 & 31 Victoria, c. 3.

Davies, J-M., and A. Mazumder. 2003. "Health and Environmental Policy Issues in Canada: The Role of Watershed Management in Sustaining Clean Drinking Water Quality at Surface Sources." *Journal of Environmental Management* 68:273–86.

Duncan, L., and M.A. Bowden. 2010. *A Legal Guide to Aboriginal Drinking Water: A Prairie Provinces Perspective,* 131. Alberta: Tomorrow Foundation; Alberta Law Foundation; Walter & Duncan Gordon Foundation.

Eggerton, L. 2006. "Safe Drinking Water Standards for First Nations Communities." *Canadian Medical Association Journal* 174 (9):1248.

– 2008. "Despite Federal Promises, First Nations' Water Problems Persist." *Canadian Medical Association Journal* 178 (8):985.

Government of Saskatchewan. *Saskatchewan's Safe Drinking Water Strategy.* http://www.saskh2o.ca/PDF/LTSDWS_report2003.pdf. Accessed 12 October 2011.

Gullick, R.W. 2003. "AWWA's Source Water Protection Committee Outlines How to Maintain the Highest Quality Source Water." *Journal of American Water Works Association* 95 (11):36–42.

Hanrahan, M. 2003. "Water Rights and Wrongs." *Alternatives Journal* 29 (1):31–4.

Health Canada. 2009. *Drinking Water Advisories in First Nations Communities in Canada. A National Overview 1995–2007.* http://www.hc-sc.gc.ca/fniah-spnia/pubs/promotion/_environ/2009_water-qualit-eau-canada/index-eng.php. Last accessed 26 August 2010.

– 2010. *How many First Nations communities are under a Drinking Water Advisory?* http://www.hc-sc.gc.ca/fniah-spnia/promotion/public-publique/water-eau-eng.php#how_many. Last accessed 25 August 2010.

Indian Act, R.S.C.1985, c. 1–5.

Job, C.A. 1996. "Benefits and Costs of Wellhead Protection." *Ground Water Monitoring and Remediation* 16 (2):65–8.

Keepers of the Water IV. 2010. Hatchet Lake First Nation. Wollaston Lake, SK. 19–23 August.

Keepers of the Water V. 2011. Northlands Denesuline Nation. Lac Brochet, MB. 10–14 August.

Kundell, J.E., and T.A. DeMeo. 2000. *Source Water Protection: A Guidebook for Local Governments.* Georgia Water Management Campaign. The University of Georgia.

Lavalley, G. 2006. *Aboriginal Traditional Knowledge and Source Water Protection: First Nations' Views on Taking Care of Water.* Chiefs of Ontario and Environment Canada.

National Research Council. 2000. "Watershed Management for Source Water Protection." In *Watershed Management for Potable Water Supply: Assessing the New York City Strategy*, 130–57. Washington, DC: National Academy Press.

Patrick, R.J. 2011. "Uneven Access to Safe Drinking Water for First Nations in Canada: Connecting Health and Place Through Source Water Protection." *Health and Place* 17:386–9.

Polaris Institute. 2008. *Boiling Point! Six Community Profiles of the Water Crisis Facing First Nations within Canada.* Ottawa, ON.

Safe Drinking Water Foundation. 2009. Position Paper: A Review of the Engagement Sessions for the Federal Action Plan on Safe Drinking Water for First Nations.

Saskatchewan Watershed Authority. *What We Do.* http://www.swa.ca/AboutUs/WhatWeDo.asp. Accessed 12 October 2011.

Stonechild, B., and B. Waiser. 2010. *Loyal Till Death*. Markham, ON: Fifth House Publishers.

Sweetgrass First Nation. 2009. *Source Water Protection Plan*. North Saskatchewan River Basin Council.

Touchwood Agency Tribal Council (TATC). 2011. Moving Towards Safer Drinking Water For First Nations Conference. 7–9 September. Saskatoon, SK.

von der Porten, S., and R.C. de Loë. 2010. *Water Challenges and Solutions in First Nations Communities*. Waterloo, ON: Water Policy and Governance Group

Windsor, J.E., and J.A. McVey. 2005. "Annihilation of Both Place and Sense of Place: The Experience of the Cheslatta T'En Canadian First Nation within the Context of Large-Scale Environmental Projects." *The Geographical Journal* 171 (2):146–65.

17

Boundary-Riding: Indigenous Knowledge Contributions for Natural Resource Decision Making in Northern Australian Regions

CATHY ROBINSON AND MARCUS LANE

Over the past few decades, key legal and political developments in Australia, and specifically in Northern Australia, have provided new prospects for Indigenous peoples to gain recognition of their rights and responsibilities, and to play a greater role in natural resource use and management (NRM) decisions (Hill and Williams 2009). For Indigenous people, the kinds of opportunities being pursued and claims made reflect not only the centrality of their territories to their culture and identity, but also their aspirations to economic opportunities, and political representation and independence (Hibbard et al. 2008; Langton and Palmer 2003; Sutton 2003). In turn, these claims reflect the unique and diverse laws, religious attachments, and knowledge systems that govern the way in which Indigenous people use, trade, and manage natural environments and resources across terrestrial, and water domains (Baker et al. 2001; Lane and Hibbard 2005).

Political and legal recognition of the role of Indigenous Australians in managing Australia's environment has matured from imported European perceptions of Australia as an empty Indigenous "wilderness" to recognition of Native title and Indigenous land management systems (Langton and Palmer 2003). Yet government-driven policy in Australia continues to frustrate Indigenous people's efforts to develop and exercise their capacities to participate in natural resource planning decisions and to influence policy development (Lane and Williams 2008; Ross et al. 2009). "Top-down" regulatory policies have often been locally inappropriate and contested, have failed to deliver their objectives, and have often delivered multiple unanticipated and negative social and environmental impacts. Dillon and Westbury's (2007) analysis of the impact of Australia's recent policies in Northern Australia suggests that there are still insufficient government resources to respond to the needs of Indigenous Australians and that much of Northern Australia has attributes of a "failed" state. As a result, many parts of remote Australia have suffered due to the poor performance of successive governments, in terms of both providing the basic necessities for human development and assisting in efforts to "close the gap" of disadvantage between Indigenous and non-Indigenous Australians (Australian Institute of Health and Welfare 2010; Australian Government 2011).

Poor Indigenous participation in Australia's social and environmental policies has sparked considerable debate about Indigenous rights and involvement in policy-making in Australia (Hill and Williams 2009; Ross et al. 2009). This debate has centred on issues surrounding the relationship between Indigenous people and the state, the design of appropriate planning styles for Indigenous affairs, the capacity constraints affecting Indigenous participation in policy decisions, and the impacts of government programs on Indigenous lands and lives (ATSISJC 2009). Effective Indigenous input into the design of policy objectives and the delivery of programs has been identified as fundamental to the success of policy initiatives (Altman and Whitehead 2003; Baker et al. 2001; Hill et al. 2012). Even so, some Indigenous leaders choose not to engage in particular policies for fear that their participation would suborn rather than enable Indigenous objectives in policies cloaked in the rhetoric of empowerment (cf. Scott 1985).

This chapter focuses on one thread in this complex fabric of environmental policy: heritage assessment and development. It is concerned with examining the ways in which Indigenous knowledge has been integrated into NRM targets and programs in Northern Australian regions. Environmental governance has been regionalized across Australia, with the federal government devolving considerable resources and decision-making responsibilities to communities and non-government institutions. This new national program has received significant funds from The National Heritage Trust program and allows communities and non-government institutions to manage the design and implementation of sustainable development policies and programs (Lane et al. 2004), and it marks a significant and long-term policy commitment to the re-scaling of NRM governance to the regional level (Lane et al. 2009). At the core of this national experiment has been a shift away from government-driven planning and management towards a greater reliance on regional NRM bodies to coordinate the preparation, implementation, monitoring, and evaluation of NRM plans and investment strategies (Australian Government 2003). As a result, central governments now act through non-government actors and institutions to develop and deliver NRM policies at regional and local scales (Lane et al. 2004; cf. Rhodes 1997).

Sustainable NRM relies on an effective system of governance that is capable of linking scientific and experience-based knowledge to collective decision making and management action. In Australia, Indigenous knowledge is an essential component of designing NRM programs because of its importance in enabling Indigenous people to participate in the delivery of those programs (Hill et al. 2010; Smyth et al. 2004). While the ideal of utilizing Indigenous knowledge in this way is widely advocated (Berkes 2009), the integration and translation of Indigenous, scientific, and other types of knowledge to inform regional NRM programs has received less critical and empirical attention.

Our analytical focus is on Indigenous NRM facilitators, funded by the Australian government to act as a "practical two-way link" to increase Indigenous access to Trust program funds and to provide a "communication link" between Indigenous land managers and Commonwealth and state governments (Australian Government 2005). Our research shows that the efforts of these Indigenous facilitators were frustrated by a range of factors, including: (1) ignoring the geographies of Indigenous organizations' NRM activities when establishing regions as a focal scale of NRM planning; (2) poor funding opportunities for Indigenous people to participate in regional NRM programs; and (3) using a narrow definition of Indigenous knowledge contributions to inform NRM planning decisions. We conclude that this new model of NRM governance requires knowledge-brokering practices that are more sensitive to the respective roles of expert and experiential knowledge in planning and policy, and, in particular, to the distinctiveness and importance of Indigenous knowledge in Indigenous domains.

BOUNDARY-RIDING AND KNOWLEDGE BROKER "WORK"

To situate our analysis, we build on Friedmann's (1987) theory of planning as the transfer of knowledge to action for the purpose of moving towards a vision of a "good" society, and his conceptualization of planning as a continuum that ranges from social guidance to social transformation. As Friedmann (1987, 38) describes: "Whereas the former is articulated through the state, and is concerned chiefly with systematic change, the latter focuses on the political practices of system transformation." Friedmann's work opened up the field of planning to look beyond the conventions of the "expert" professional planner and to consider involving citizens in policy development. This has led to considerable interest and utilization of decentralized planning approaches that can appropriately consider local knowledge contributions through decentralized (or "bottom-up") planning approaches (e.g., Connick and Innes 2003; Healey 1999).

In the small but growing field of "Indigenous planning," many scholars have used the theoretical foundations discussed above to examine how planning can enhance (or frustrate) the social transformation that recognizing Indigenous claims for self-determination and resource sovereignty requires (e.g., Lane and Hibbard 2005). The term "Indigenous planning" also includes an interest in the "radical planning" strategies of Indigenous communities that seek to transform planning to achieve Indigenous community goals (Jojola 2008; Lane 2003; Sandercock 1999).

Our interest in Friedmann's (1987) work is his consideration of the planners and planning institutions that work at the interface of societal guidance and social transformation planning paradigms. Friedmann (1987, 38–9) highlights that planners engaged in mediating between these two models of planning are "necessarily in conflict" due to the competing interests "of a bureaucratic state and the interests of the political community," as well as competing visions of what constitutes a "good society" and how this goal should be achieved. The ability of organizations and individuals to ensure decision making is technically and socially "robust" has been the subject of intense academic interest and critique (Jasanoff 2004).

Institutional capacity to translate available knowledge into strategic policy decisions has also been the subject of interest in the field of sustainability science, and the link between knowledge and action is central to identifying mechanisms to "bridge the gap" (Clark 2007, 1737). Described as "boundary work," these mechanisms are critical to facilitating the transfer of useable knowledge into policy domains for sustainable development (e.g., Cash et al. 2009; Jacobs et al. 2011). Boundary agents or "brokers" act as "bridges" between formal and informal institutions and networks, and play an important role in this social process of knowledge interaction and co-production (Jasanoff 2004; Michaels 2011). A broker's ability to build trust between individuals and institutions and to enable a process of collaborative learning, has been identified as critical to enabling two-way communication between both sides of the boundary (Robinson and Wallington 2012).

Effective and equitable cross-cultural knowledge integration and translation can be derailed by both brokering individuals and supporting organizations, and planning scholars have highlighted the agency of planners and planning organizations in either blocking or building the co-operation required for robust knowledge integration and shared decision making (e.g., Forester 1989; Lane and McDonald 2005). Brokers cannot be thought of as a "neutral" bridge between social, knowledge, and institutional networks and worlds. Instead, they must be acknowledged as active agents in the production and reproduction of the social working relations involved in making planning decisions (Forester 1989). Planners and planning institutions are now required to take knowledge management strategies seriously in their efforts to manage available information in a manner that best fits the decision-making context or purpose (Clark 2007; Flyvberg 2002).

The role and impact of brokers' "boundary work" practices are particularly relevant to efforts to utilize Indigenous knowledge contributions to inform planning policies (Agrawal 2002; Robinson and Mununngguritj 2001). While technical forms of knowledge can provide quantitative information that is legitimized through scientific methodologies, local knowledge can offer personal and practical information that provides crucial insights into local contexts and customary practices (cf. Fischer 2000). The particular spiritual, moral, and experimental attributes of Indigenous knowledge systems add complexity to the knowledge "blending" task (Berkes 2009; Natcher et al. 2005; Wohling 2009). As Rose (1994, 2) argues from her involvement with the land claim process in Australia, Indigenous people's knowledge is contextualized by their relationship to each other and country, which in turn directs responsibilities to guide how this knowledge might be translated into Indigenous and broader planning goals:

> Knowledge is graded by age, some of it is demarcated by gender, and almost all of it is identified with country. Most knowledge itself identifies country: songs name country; designs indicate Dreamings in particular places. Knowledge has a powerful dielectric element:

it points to country and to relationships between the possessor of knowledge and the country to which it refers. Performance of knowledge (through song, dance, story, history, use of country) is a performance of ownership: it identifies the person as one with rights and responsibilities to that country. Countrymen share rights. Non-countrymen do not have the same rights.

Recent contributions from sustainability science and planning have started to focus on an action-orientated view of knowledge integration and utilization (e.g., Jasanoff 2004; Roux et al. 2006). This perspective focuses on the quality of collaborative relations established between partners who are engaged in linking knowledge for a particular management purpose or action. Robinson and Wallington (2012) have shown that the most successful boundary work practices with Indigenous people are collaborative and adaptive, involving iterative and ongoing communication and knowledge testing between actors on both sides of the boundary. We now turn to examine if these same relations of cooperation can create the institutional conditions required to appropriately manage Indigenous interests and knowledge claims.

RESEARCH CONTEXT AND METHODS

For over a decade, a significant national NRM policy reform agenda has required Australian governments and Australian citizens to consider how regional approaches to natural resource governance can best "Care for Our Country."[1] Fifty-six contiguous regions have now been mapped across Australia to structure the delivery of $1.25 (AUD) billion worth of Trust funding nationwide that has been rolled out over the past decade. Regional-scaled NRM programs have been supported and implemented based on an ecological premise that "the common biophysical characteristic of Australian regions endows ... [a programme of delivery] with a high potential for achieving good landscape-scale outcomes" (Keogh et al. 2006, 16). Federally sanctioned program objectives have been reinterpreted into regional NRM targets based on "best available science" and local community contributions, mediated by regionally organized boards and statutory committees (Lane et al. 2009).

A constant commitment throughout this regional NRM experiment has been an emphasis on maximizing community responsibility for environmental problems and solutions, and this, in turn, has prompted a need for community capacity-building (Wallington and Lawrence 2008). As the taskforce responsible for formulating the rationale behind this program outlined: "Industry, landholders, individuals and communities – including Indigenous and urban communities – all derive benefit from the use and management of natural resources and share responsibility for managing these resources sustainably" (NNRMTF 1999, 16).

National efforts to instigate "shared responsibility" for the sustainable management of Australia's environments has occurred in parallel with a widespread advocacy to support Indigenous people in their efforts to secure rights and responsibilities to their lands and natural resources (Sutton 2003). Altman et al. (2007) estimate that Indigenous lands now comprise some 20 per cent of the Australian land mass and contain areas of high conservation value, and the importance of Indigenous land management to social and environmental outcomes is now recognized (Garnett and Sithole 2007; Putnis et al. 2007). Indigenous involvement in environmental management also addresses some of the key issues identified as underpinning Indigenous socio-economic disadvantage (HREOC 2008) with research showing many positive outcomes for Indigenous social well-being, such as increased levels of school attendance and healthier individuals and families (Putnis et al. 2007; ATSISJC 2009).

Facilitators funded under the Trust program to broker Indigenous participation in natural resource planning are critical to facilitating the "two-way" knowledge exchange that is needed to build the capacity of Indigenous organizations to make strategic NRM decisions for their traditional lands. Specific guidelines govern regional NRM negotiations between government agencies and regional communities, and these guidelines require regional NRM organizations to include Indigenous knowledge contributions in NRM program design and to ensure that resources were provided to engage and build the capacity of Indigenous groups (Australian Government 2003).

The boundary work practices and perspectives of these facilitators form the analytical lens for our analysis that is based on research conducted by both authors. This analysis draws on a longitudinal investigation of regional natural resource arrangements across Northern Australia that was conducted over a three-year time frame using a mix of qualitative and quantitative methods (McDonald et al. 2005; Taylor et al. 2006; Robinson et al. 2009). A critical examination of facilitators' activities was also conducted in inland Australia as part of a critical examination of the institutional ingredients that enabled or disabled Indigenous participation in NRM programs established by the Trust (e.g.,

Lane and Corbett 2005; Lane and Williams 2008; Lane and Williams 2009; Robinson et al. 2008).

A key part of the methodological approach applied in each of these studies was to examine the perspectives of government and community planners involved in regional NRM practice. Questions regarding the utilization of Indigenous knowledge were asked in interviews with regional body personnel across Northern Australia in 2005 (n=20), a web-based survey conducted in 2004 (n=45), and interviews with Indigenous facilitators conducted in 2007 and 2008 (total n=57). Perspectives were also captured from workshops with regional body staff (including Indigenous facilitators) in Northern Queensland in 2007 and 2008, and a workshop with Indigenous facilitators working in northeastern South Australia, Northern Territory, and Queensland in 2008.

BROKERING THE GAP BETWEEN INDIGENOUS KNOWLEDGE AND REGIONAL NRM PROGRAMS OF ACTION

Indigenous facilitators reported that there is still much to learn in order to address the void between the policy and practice of environmental governance in regional Australia. While there was specific provision in the Trust program guidelines to support Indigenous people in accessing resources and participating in decision making, the institutional capacity to utilize available Indigenous knowledge and support Indigenous participation in NRM decision making was identified as a key challenge.

The need to find an ecologically appropriate scale for management or community participation has been the subject of considerable critique (Lane et al. 2004). In Australia, new regions have been mapped across the continent and have been used as a means of focusing decentralized arrangement and funds, but this strategy has produced troublesome outcomes for some Indigenous communities. For some communities, these new regions have cut through networks of Indigenous governance systems that were established to care for particular and neighbouring Indigenous lands, while other Indigenous communities have been incoherently lumped together under the one planning regime. The region negotiated by Girringun Aboriginal Corporation in Northern Queensland, for example, has now been cut into two NRM regions that require Indigenous traditional owners to engage in two regional planning arrangements and processes. Brokers interviewed reported on the enormous transaction costs that Indigenous organizations, such as Girringun, must bear in order to respond to variable institutional capacity to engage with Indigenous people's NRM planning agendas and support requirements.

Resourcing arrangements under the Trust have also frustrated Indigenous people and their capacity to access sufficient funds needed to undertake NRM programs. Although several policy measures were introduced to address the lack of Indigenous participation in NRM programs (Smyth et al. 2004), Lane and Williams (2008) report that only around 2 per cent of Trust funds available have been allocated to Indigenous organizations across the continent. Several factors have been identified that contribute to poor Indigenous access to Trust funds. Brokers, for example, cited the bureaucratic knowledge required to apply for and receive Trust funds (Lane and Williams 2009). This problem was compounded by the fact that many Indigenous communities were necessarily prioritizing other concerns such as basic welfare, health, and social issues over complicated funding applications (cf. Lane and Corbett 2005). In other cases, regional NRM bodies remained either frustrated or unmotivated in their efforts to engage Indigenous communities in NRM program objectives and investment opportunities (Lane and Williams 2008; Robinson et al. 2008).

In addition to these structural and resourcing challenges, cultural barriers prevented the development of effective knowledge systems that could support Indigenous people's efforts to contribute to planning activities in northern regions. Brokers reported that Indigenous knowledge contributions were dismissed when Indigenous input into planning processes became highly dynamic or contested, or when knowledge contributions were difficult to integrate into technical information required by Trust program guidelines (Robinson et al. 2009; cf. Agrawal 2002).

Indigenous groups willing or able to impart knowledge that could easily relate to priority NRM programs (such as the absence/presence of endangered species, use of fire, and location of waterholes) were rewarded with more program support for Indigenous NRM activities (e.g., Robinson et al. 2008). These narrowly defined avenues of Indigenous knowledge contributions led to a patchwork of different levels of Indigenous participation and capacity-building support across NRM regions (McDonald et al. 2005). As a result, some Indigenous communities remain unengaged or disengaged from NRM decisions or funding opportunities, despite being faced with pressing land degradation and species decline issues (Robinson et al. 2008, 237). More fundamentally, this narrow translation of Indigenous knowledge to inform NRM programs of action undermined an essential dimension of Indigenous epistemology which connects people and landscapes to the environment. The result was a brokering practice that privileged knowledge compartmentalization thus ensuring that the very power or point of incorporating Indigenous knowledge is elided (cf. Scott 1998).

Some of the regional planners and Indigenous facilitators interviewed also commented on the isolation they experienced in their brokering work efforts, describing their working environment as an "island" of activity that was "fragmented" by the problem definitions and possible solutions offered by available science, Indigenous community perspectives, or government authorities (Robinson et al. 2008). One informant's remarks about building relationships across the boundaries of wombat knowledge and management in South Australia capture this deficit: "The [state agency] wants to protect them, the Indigenous people want to eat them, and the NRM group wants to eliminate them as pests." A critical issue was that brokers lacked the institutional support they needed in order to access and blend Indigenous and other knowledge contributions (Northern Queensland Workshop 2008). Interviewees reported that this lack of support impacted on their ability to build the capacity for Indigenous people to have the knowledge to make good NRM decisions and to contribute to complex and contemporary NRM issues such as feral animals and weeds, that affected Indigenous livelihoods and lands (cf. ATSISJC 2009).

An ambivalence regarding the role and contribution of Indigenous landholders and Indigenous knowledge was also reported, and regional NRM organizations faced ongoing pressure to simply develop Indigenous-led NRM projects to – as one planner from the Gulf of Queensland described – "get runs on the board with a sector that is both a high priority to judge our performance and a high risk to get engaged" (Northern Queensland Workshop 2008). In addition, tight program deadlines and significant limitations in available information led to limited individual, Indigenous, or regional NRM organizational capacity to set regional targets or evaluate program performance based on a credible or legitimate knowledge base (e.g., Australian Government 2005; Robinson et al. 2009).

Regional NRM planners and Indigenous facilitators also reported on the careful, complex, and adaptive brokering strategies that were required to "ride" the boundary of interaction between government-led and Indigenous community-driven knowledge-action systems. As one broker from the Northern Territory explained, these efforts relied on an endless translation and conflict resolution task to "package [Indigenous knowledge contributions to] sell ... in a grant, to report on our performance ... and then allow [Indigenous knowledge and Indigenous planners agendas] to be [re-translated] ... back to support Indigenous-driven projects." In some cases, these brokering efforts failed to "close the gap" needed to ensure that boundary work was accountable to both sides of the boundary.

In many cases the void between the rhetoric and reality of incorporating Indigenous knowledge resulted in broker fatigue, as regional NRM planners embarked on endless efforts to ensure Indigenous people within the region were informed, support NRM directions that the Trust was willing to fund, and comply with a program aspiration to institutionalize a regional approach to NRM governance. The result was a weak planning system that often failed to involve Indigenous people in practical deliberations about the purpose and practice of NRM activities occurring on their lands and in NRM regions. Many of the planners and Indigenous facilitators interviewed also noted a persistent practice of "watering down" discussion about NRM issues with Indigenous people in many regions, meaning that Indigenous NRM focused primarily on "easy issues and projects" where Trust and Indigenous community agendas could be easily satisfied without confronting more complex and long-term issues.

CONCLUSIONS

Ongoing debate about how planning can respond appropriately to Indigenous interests and agendas highlights the need for a more sophisticated understanding of the role of knowledge in planning and policy (Fischer 2000; Friedmann 1987). Our understanding of policy formation has been enriched by theories emphasizing its cognitive and discursive aspects and highlights that knowledge exchange and translation is not an apolitical or one-way process (Agrawal 2002; Forester 1989; Roux et al. 2006). This perspective exposes the epistemological legacy underpinning policy decisions in modern nation-states such as Australia that "fixes its gaze so firmly on the West that it can only catch glimpses of other human beings through a glass, darkly" (Gregory 1994, 177). Slowly these stubborn, imported planning rationalities are being decoded, recalled, and renegotiated on the ground, including the consideration of how Indigenous people's interpretations of their relationships to country might be utilized to inform environmental management goals and programs.

A regional approach to natural resource planning is now entrenched in Australian policy, and this approach seeks to reduce the limitations of "societal guidance" planning tradition and to build local citizen capacity to embark on transformative planning and share the responsibility of sustainability with the nation-state (Lane et al. 2004; Wallington and Lawrence 2008). Reports of the frustrations of regional NRM planner and facilitator efforts to "ride the boundary" of interactions between Indigenous, local, and scientific knowledge and regional NRM programs highlight the problems involved in mediating "top-down" and "bottom-up" planning agendas that Friedmann (1987) observed in planning environments where both planning traditions are evident.

If Indigenous people are to engage in sharing and developing the knowledge that underpins NRM decisions for regional Australia, brokering efforts need to be able to manage the different ways in which causal relationships are generated and legitimized between these different knowledge contributions and claims. Indigenous leaders are calling for structural reform to achieve this goal across all policies and programs that govern the development policy agendas affecting Indigenous Australians. If Australia's regional approach to NRM governance is to take Indigenous calls for policy reform seriously, critical attention needs to be paid to the extent to which Indigenous Australians can gain access to shaping public policy goals and outcomes, and the degree to which they are given control over resources needed to deliver these planning objectives.

Indigenous-led NRM partnerships and initiatives that have emerged across Northern Australia highlight that Indigenous Australians are eager to actively participate in identifying the kind of institutional support needed to integrate Indigenous knowledge with other available knowledge, and to link this with programs of action (Hill et al. 2012). Our research and analysis of how Indigenous knowledge contributions are being managed by Australia's regional resource planning institutions and planners suggests that this reform is going to require more flexible and inclusive approaches than can be provided through fixed scales of NRM decision making or tokenistic access to Trust funds.

Evidence from inquiries into the environmental, social, and cultural health of Northern Australia warns that sustainability thresholds are being crossed and that equitable outcomes for Indigenous lands and peoples are real and urgent (HREOC 2008; Sutton 2009; Woinarski et al. 2007). Structural reform of NRM governance might need to focus on fostering the kind of co-operative relations that are required to build the knowledge-action systems necessary for sustainably using and managing Northern Australia's regions. The capacity of Indigenous organizations and communities to translate available knowledge and engage in regional NRM planning decisions is a critical requirement of effective NRM governance systems which does not always exist in many NRM regions. It remains to be seen if regional NRM planners and organizations can build the support that Indigenous people need to engage as planners and to bring other forms of knowledge and modes of reasoning to the policy table.

The boundary between Western rationality and Indigenous knowledge has come to mark not only the barrier between two competing epistemologies but, more profoundly, a crisis in the way we seek to develop policies to steward the common good. As the limits of scientific rationality have been identified (e.g., Scott 1998), a chorus of calls for the application (and indeed, integration) of Indigenous knowledge have been heard (e.g., Berkes 2009). The problems encountered by the "boundary riders" interviewed in this study suggest that this impasse is not yet resolved. The path ahead surely lies in the development of more sophisticated approaches to policy-making and knowledge brokering. Navigating this path just as surely requires recognition that epistemological borders also mark deeper ideological and cultural cleavages. These are borders less easily crossed.

NOTE

1   "Caring for our Country" program reflects the latest iteration of the regional NRM policy and funding program, see http://www.nrm.gov.au/publications for more details about the regional NRM policy initiative. Refer to Lane et al. (2009) for a critical examination of the assumptions, ideologies, and impacts of the regional NRM policy and associated programs.

REFERENCES

Agrawal, A., 2002. "Indigenous Knowledge and the Politics of Classification." *International Social Science Journal* 54: 287–97.

Altman J.C., G.J. Buchanan, and L. Larsen. 2007. *The Environmental Significance of the Indigenous Estate: Natural Resource Management as Economic Development in Remote Australia.* CAEPR discussion paper, Canberra.

ATSISJC. 2009. *Social Justice Report*. Australian Human Rights Commission and the Aboriginal and Torres Strait Islander Social Justice Commissioner. Sydney, Australia.

Australian Government. 2003. *National Framework for Natural Resource Management Standards and Targets*. Canberra: Natural Resource Management Ministerial Council.

– 2005. *Intergovernmental Agreement on a National Action Plan for Salinity and Water Quality*. http://www.napswq.gov.au/publications/iga.html.

– 2011. *Closing the Gap. The Indigenous Reform Agenda*. http://www.fahcsia. gov.au/sa/indigenous/progserv/ctg/Pages/default.aspx.

Australian Institute of Health and Welfare. 2010. *Australia's Health 2010*. Australia's Health Series no. 12. Canberra, Australia.

Baker, R., J. Davies, and E. Young, eds. 2001. *Working on Country: Indigenous Environmental Management in Australia*. Melbourne: Oxford University Press.

Berkes, F. 2009. "Evolution of Co-management: Role of Knowledge Generation, Bridging Organizations and Social Learning." *Journal of Environmental Management* 90 (5):1692–1702.

Cash, D.W., W.C. Clark, F. Alcock, N. Dickson, N. Eckley, D. H. Guston, J. Jager, and R.B. Mitchell. 2003. *Knowledge Systems for Sustainable Development*. Proceedings of the National Academy of Science 100 (14):8086–91.

Clark, W.C. 2007. *Sustainability Science: A Room of Its Own*. Proceedings of the National Academy of Science 104:1737–8

Connick, S., and J.E. Innes. 2003. "Outcomes of Collaborative Water Policy Making: Applying Complexity Thinking to Evaluation." *Journal of Environmental Planning and Management* 46:177–97.

Dillon, M., and N. Westbury. 2007. *Beyond Humbug: Transforming Government Engagement with Indigenous Australia*. South Australia: Seaview Press.

Fischer, F. 2000. *Citizens, Experts, and the Environment*. Durham and London: Duke University Press.

Flyvberg, B. 2002. "Bringing Power to Planning Research. One Researcher's Praxis Story." *Journal of Planning Education and Research* 21:353–66.

Forester, J. 1989. *Planning in the Face of Power*. Berkeley: University of California Press.

Friedmann, J. 1987. *Planning in the Public Domain: From Knowledge to Action*. Princeton: Princeton University Press.

Garnett, S., and B. Sithole. 2007. *Sustainable Northern Landscapes and the Nexus with Indigenous Health*. Canberra: Land and Water Australia Report.

Gregory, D. 1994. *Geographical imaginations*. Oxford: Blackwell Publishers.

Healey, P. 1999. "Institutionalist Analysis, Communicative Planning and Shaping Places." *Journal of Planning Education and Research* 19 (2):111–21.

Hibbard, M., M.B. Lane, and K. Rasmussen. 2008. "The Split Personality of Planning. Indigenous Peoples and Planning for Land and Resource Management." *Journal of Planning Literature* 23 (2):136–51.

Hill, R., and L. Williams. 2009. "Indigenous Natural Resource Management: Overcoming Marginalisation Produced in Australia's Current NRM Model." In *Contested Country: Local and Regional Natural Resource Management in Australia*, edited by M.B. Lane, C.J. Robinson, and B. Taylor. Collingwood: CSIRO Publishing.

Hill, R., C. Grant, M. George, C.J. Robinson, S. Jackson, and N. Abel. 2012. "A Typology of Indigenous Engagement in Australian Environmental Management: Implications for Knowledge Integration and Social-Ecological System Sustainability." *Ecology and Society* 17(1):23. http://www.ecologyandsociety.org/vol17/iss1/art23/.

Hill, R., J. Kristen, K.J. Williams, P. Pert, C.J. Robinson, A.P. Dale, D.A. Westcott, R. Grace, and T. O'Malley. 2010. "Effective Community-Based Natural Resource Management for Biodiversity Conservation in Australia's Tropical Rainforests." *Environmental Conservation* 37 (1):73–82.

HREOC. 2008. "Human Rights and Equal Opportunity Commission." *Native Title Report.* http://www.hreoc.gov.au/social_justice/nt_report/ntreport08/index.html.

Jacobs, K., L. Lebel, J. Buizer, L. Adams, P. Matson, E. McCullough, P. Garden, G. Saliba, and T. Finan. 2011. *Linking Knowledge with Action in the Pursuit of Sustainable Water-Resource Management.* Proceedings of the National Academy of Science, [online] DOI:10.1073.

Jasanoff, S. 2004. "Ordering Knowledge, Ordering Society." In *States of Knowledge. The Co-production of Science and Social Order*, edited by S. Jasanoff, 13–45. London and New York: Routledge.

Jojola, T.A. 2008. "Indigenous Planning – An Emerging Context." *Canadian Journal of Urban Research* 17 (1):37–47.

Keogh, K., D. Chant, and B. Frazer. 2006. *Review of Arrangements for Regional Delivery of Natural Resource Management Programmes.* Final report. Canberra: Ministerial Reference Group for future NRM programme delivery.

Kroon, F.J., C.J. Robinson, and A.P. Dale. 2009. "Integrating Knowledge to Inform Water Quality Planning in the Tully-Murray Basin, Australia." *Marine and Freshwater Research* 60:1183–8.

Lane, M.B. 2003. "Participation, Decentralization, and Civil Society: Indigenous Rights and Democracy in Environmental Planning." *Journal of Planning Education and Research* 22 (4):360–73.

Lane, M.B., and T. Corbett. 2005. "The Tyranny of Localism: Indigenous Participation in Community Based Environmental Management." *Journal of Environmental Planning & Policy* 7 (2):142–9.

Lane, M.B., and M. Hibbard. 2005. "Doing It for Themselves. Transformative Planning by Indigenous People." *Journal of Planning Education and Research* 25:172–84.

Lane, M.B., and G. McDonald. 2005. "Community-Based Environmental Planning: Operational Dilemmas, Planning Principles and Possible Remedies." *Journal of Environmental Planning and Management* 48 (5):709–31.

Lane, M.B., G.T. McDonald, and T.H. Morrison. 2004. "Decentralisation and Environmental Management in Australia: A Comment on the Prescriptions of The Wentworth Group." *Australian Geographical Studies* 42 (1):103–15.

Lane, M.B., C.J. Robinson, and B. Taylor, eds. 2009. *Contested Country: Local and Regional Environmental Management in Australia.* Melbourne: CSIRO Publishing.

Lane, M.B., and L.J. Williams. 2008. "Colour Blind. Indigenous Peoples and Regional Environmental Management." *Journal of Environmental Planning and Management* 48:709–31.

– 2009. "The Natural Heritage Trust and Indigenous Lands. The Trials and Tribulations of 'New Technologies of Governance'." *Australian Geographer* 40 (1):85–107.

Langton, M., and L. Palmer. 2003. "Modern Agreement Making and Aboriginal People in Australia: Issues and Trends." *Australian Aboriginal Law Reporter* 8:1–31.

Lejano, R.P., and H. Ingram. In press. "Collaborative Networks and New Ways of Knowing." *Environmental Science and Policy.* DOI:10.1016/envsci.09.005.

McDonald, G., B. Taylor, J. Bellamy, S. Hoverman, C. McAlpine, T. Smith, C.J. Robinson, and S. Heyenga. 2005. *Case Studies in Regional Natural Resource Management in Northern Australia.* Healthy Savanna Planning Systems Project Benchmark Report I. Tropical Savannas Management CRC.

Measham, T.G., C. Richards, C.J. Robinson, S. Larson, and L. Brake. 2011. "Genuine Community Engagement in Remote Dryland Regions: Natural Resource Management in Lake Eyre Basin." *Geographical Research* 49 (2):115–235.

Michaels, S. 2011. "Matching Knowledge Brokering Strategies to Environmental Policy Problem and Settings." *Environmental Science and Policy* 12 (7):994–1011.

Morrison, T.H. 2006. "Pursuing Rural Sustainability at the Regional Level. Key Lessons from the Literature on Institutions, Integration and the Environment." *Journal of Planning Literature* 21:143–54.

Natcher, D.C., S. Davis, C.G. Hickey. 2005. "Co-management: Managing Relationships, not Resources." *Human Organization* 64:240–50.

NNRMTF (National Natural Resource Management Task Force). 1999. *Managing Natural Resources in Rural Australia for a Sustainable Future: A Discussion Paper for Developing a National Policy.*" Canberra: Standing Committee for Agriculture and resource Management.

Putnis, A., P. Josif, and E. Woodward. 2007. *Healthy Country Healthy People. Supporting Indigenous Engagement in the Sustainable Management of Northern Territory Land and seas. A strategic framework.* Darwin: CSIRO.

Rhodes, R.A.W. 1997. *Understanding Governance: Policy Networks, Governance, Reflexivity and Accountability.* Buckingham: Open University Press.

Rose, D.R. 1994. "Whose Confidentiality? Whose Intellectual Property?" In *Claims to Knowledge, Claims to Country. Native Title, Native Title Claims and the Role of the Anthropologist,* edited by M. Edmunds. Proceedings of a conference session on Native title at the annual conference of the Australian Anthropological Society, University of Sydney, September, Australian Institute of Aboriginal Torres Strait Islander Studies, Canberra.

Robinson C.J., and N. Munungguritj. 2001. "Sustainable Balance: A Yolngu Framework for Cross-Cultural Collaborative Management." In *Working on Country: Indigenous Environmental Management in Australia,* edited by R. Baker, J. Davies, and E. Young, 92–107. Melbourne: Oxford University Press.

Robinson, C.J., B. Taylor, and R. Margerum. 2009. "On a Learning Journey to Nowhere? Evaluating Outcomes of Natural Resource Planning in Northern Queensland Regions." In *Contested Country: Local and Regional Environmental Management in Australia,* edited by M.B. Lane, C.J. Robinson, and B. Taylor, 201–14. Melbourne: CSIRO Publishing.

Robinson, C.J., and T.J. Wallington. 2012. "Boundary Work: Engaging Knowledge Systems in Co-management of Feral Animals on Indigenous Lands." *Ecology and Society* 17 (2):16. http://dx.doi.org/10.5751/ES-04836-170216.

Robinson, C.J., L. Williams, and M.B. Lane. 2008. "A Broker Diagnostic for Improving Indigenous Governance of Dryland Environments." In *People, Communities and Economies of the Lake Eyre Basin* (compiled reports), edited by T.G. Measham and L. Brake, 76–90. DKCRC Research Report 45. Alice Springs: Desert Knowledge Cooperative Research Centre.

Ross, H., C. Grant, C.J. Robinson, A. Izurieta, D. Smyth, and P. Rist. 2009. "Co-management and Indigenous Protected Areas in Australia: Achievements and Ways Forward." *Australasian Journal of Environmental Management* 16 (4):242–52.

Roux, D.J., K.H. Rogers, H.C. Biggs, P.J. Ashton, and A. Sergeant. 2006. "Bridging the Science Management Divide: Moving from Unidirectional Knowledge Transfer to Knowledge Interfacing and Sharing." *Ecology and Society* 11 (1):4. http//www.ecologyandsociety.org/vol11/iss1/art4/.

Sandercock, L. 1999. "Knowledge Practices. Towards an Epistemology of Multiplicity of Insurgent Planning." *Plurimondi* 1 (2):169–79.

Scott, J.C. 1985. *Weapons of the Weak: Everyday Forms of Peasant Resistance.* Yale: Yale University Press.

Scott, J.C. 1998. *Seeing Like a State: How Certain Schemes to Improve the Human Condition Have Failed.* Yale: Yale University Press.

Smyth D., S. Szabo, and M. George. 2004. *Case Studies in Indigenous Engagement in Natural Resource Management.* Report prepared for The Australian Government Department of Environment and Heritage. http://www.nrm.gov.au/publications/case-studies/indigenous-engagement.html.

Sutton, P. 2003. *Native title in Australia: An Ethnographic Perspective.* Cambridge: Cambridge University Press.

Taylor, B., G. McDonald, S. Heyenga, S. Hoverman, T. Smith, and C.J. Robinson. 2006. *Evaluation of Regional Planning Arrangements for Natural Resource Management 2005–2006: Benchmark Report II. Healthy Savanna Planning Systems Project.* Tropical Savannas Management CRC, Australia.

Wallington, T., and P. Lawrence. 2008. "Making Democracy Matter: Responsibility and Effective Environmental Governance in Regional Australia." *Journal of Rural Studies* 24:277–90.

Wohling, M. 2009. "The Problem of Scale in Indigenous Knowledge: A Perspective from Northern Australia." *Ecology and Society* 14 (1):1 [online]. URL: http://www.ecologyandsociety.org/vol14/iss1/art1/.

Woinarksi, J., B. Mackey, H. Nix, and B. Trail. 2007. *The Nature of Northern Australia. Its Natural Values, Ecological Processes and Future Prospects.* Canberra: ANU Press.

18

Representing and Mapping Traditional Knowledge in Ontario Forest Management Planning

The knowledge that Indigenous peoples have in relation to the environment has come to be referred to variously as "traditional ecological knowledge," "Indigenous knowledge," or "traditional knowledge," among other terms. For the purposes of this chapter, the term "traditional knowledge" (TK) will be used, in keeping with the *United Nations Declaration on the Rights of Indigenous Peoples*. In Canada, the past two decades have seen substantial interest in this knowledge, and its investigation is now emerging as an independent field of study, complete with theory, research approaches, models, and potential applications (Berkes 2008; Houde 2007; Shackeroff et al. 2007).

The *United Nations Declaration on the Rights of Indigenous Peoples* asserts that Indigenous peoples have rights and distinct responsibilities pertaining to their own territories and to future generations. Included in this is the right to protect and control TK (UNGA 2007). In recent years, Indigenous peoples have increasingly called for the incorporation of TK into decision-making processes that impact their lives, lands, and waters (Menzies and Butler 2006). Following the release of the Brundtland Report in 1987 and the findings of the United Nations Conference on Environment and Development in 1992, official recognition of TK in environmental and resource management (ERM) has been formalized in various nation-states. In Canada, support for the consideration of TK in ERM has been gaining momentum for over two decades (Manseau et al. 2005; McGregor 2010).

This increased interest in TK in ERM is regarded as a significant step forward by Indigenous peoples. A variety of new opportunities have been generated whereby Aboriginal peoples in Canada are able to offer input into various ERM undertakings. At the same time, however, there is an increasing understanding of a real need to "protect" TK from the very people who "seek" it. This chapter will explore this tension more fully within the context of forest management planning (FMP) in Ontario. Specifically, it will look at Ontario Ministry of Natural Resources' (MNR) efforts over the past fifteen years to formalize Aboriginal involvement in FMP through a process it calls "Aboriginal values mapping" (AVM), which remains one of the main mechanisms for representing TK in FMP in Ontario.

This chapter is informed by doctoral research conducted on the topic of Aboriginal participation in FMP and AVM in Ontario. The original research was undertaken a decade ago (McGregor 2000), yet more recent work has drawn remarkably similar conclusions (LaRose 2009; Sapic et al. 2009), suggesting that the challenges originally described are institutional and systemic in nature, and will take some time yet to resolve.

The research on this topic to date has been primarily concerned with comparing and contrasting experiences and viewpoints of TK in FMP between Aboriginal people (community representatives of First Nations) and their non-Aboriginal counterparts (managers/planners in government and industry). In the original research on this topic, perspectives were sought from the three major groups most involved in the AVM process: Aboriginal peoples, industry representatives, and government officials. This chapter compares and contrasts views of TK and AVM from these three main groups and also identifies similarities where they exist. This analytical approach is central to this chapter as the tension is explored between those who seek TK and those who wish to protect it. By comparing and contrasting viewpoints, however, I am not suggesting that Aboriginal and non-Aboriginal peoples are homogenous groups; understandings of TK, AVM, and FMP can and do vary within each group. Nonetheless, common themes and patterns are identified, explored, and discussed in this chapter based on the experiences members of each group described.

ABORIGINAL AND NON-ABORIGINAL PERCEPTIONS OF TRADITIONAL KNOWLEDGE: A LACK OF SHARED MEANING

TK is increasingly recognized, not only within the Ontario forest sector but also nationally and internationally, as a vital component in the move towards increased forest sustainability (Cheveau et al. 2008; Houde 2007; McGregor 2006). However, understandings of its precise meaning, role, and application remain elusive at both the policy and operational levels.

There have been attempts to gain an appreciation of TK application in Canadian FMP, but for the most part (despite the strong statements made in the National Forest Strategy in 1992 and 1998, and later in 2003), little has actually been achieved and it remains relatively unexplored on the ground (Cheveau et al. 2008; Stevenson 2005). In terms of theory, there has been a limited amount of rethinking of the underlying assumptions regarding the incorporation of TK into FMP, due largely to a growing dissatisfaction of the actual practice (or lack thereof) of TK in forest management regimes (Cheveau et al. 2008; McGregor 2010; Stevenson 2005).

The recognition of Aboriginal contributions to sustainability can be said to be generally well-intentioned (Berkes 2008; Stevenson 2006). It is the practice and application (and indeed the general lack thereof) of TK in FMP that has come under scrutiny. There are a number of explanations offered as to why TK application has not yet been adequately realized in FMP (see Tables 18.1 and 18.2 for lists of apparent reasons). Overall, however, it must be understood that as a concept, TK originates external to Aboriginal communities; it is a term coined by non-Aboriginal academics to describe something such academics thought they knew about Aboriginal people. As such, TK has not been uncritically accepted by Aboriginal peoples (Houde 2007; McGregor 2000).

Thus, despite the interest in TK by forest managers, planners, policymakers, academics, consultants, and even Aboriginal communities themselves, the meaning of TK (as well as a widely accepted method for its appropriate application) remains both elusive and controversial. There is no commonly accepted view of the term.

An in-depth analysis of the issues around defining TK is beyond the scope of this chapter, and has been examined in other texts (e.g., Houde 2007; Menzies 2006). The current literature on TK does reveal, however, that Aboriginal and non-Aboriginal people tend to hold different ideas of what TK means (McGregor 2009). In particular, Aboriginal peoples tend to conceptualize TK as a way of life (LaDuke 1999; McGregor 2004), while non-Aboriginal environmental professionals tend to see it as a body of knowledge (Berkes 2008; Johnson 1992). As well, Aboriginal people often view the people, the knowledge, and the land as a single, integrated whole; they are regarded as inseparable (McGregor 2004). As Roberts (1996) points out:

> Capturing a single aspect of traditional knowledge is difficult. Traditional knowledge is holistic and cannot be separated from the people. It cannot be compartmentalized like scientific knowledge, which often ignores aspects of life to make a point. However, traditional knowledge parallels scientific knowledge.

Despite the differences, both Aboriginal and non-Aboriginal peoples do share some common understandings of TK, including: the idea that TK is grounded in experience and observation over time in particular ecosystems; the realization that TK is generally passed on orally from Elders to the younger generations; and the recognition that TK does indeed take the form of knowledge (Crowshoe 2005). It is therefore more accurate to express the fundamental difference in Aboriginal/non-Aboriginal understandings of TK as follows: from an Aboriginal viewpoint, non-Aboriginal definitions of TK represent only a part of Aboriginal definitions. The Aboriginal definitions include non-Aboriginal viewpoints; however, as noted above, Aboriginal people understand TK to represent a way of life, which is far broader, holistic, and all-encompassing (spiritual) than a "knowledge system."

BARRIERS TO APPLYING TK IN ERM

Aboriginal and non-Aboriginal people agree that the application of TK in ERM is fraught with challenges, and both groups identify similar barriers to this process. Discussed below are some of these barriers, as expressed by both groups.

Non-Aboriginal Perceptions

Barriers to the incorporation of TK into ERM in Canada have been explored by a number of scholars. Many of the barriers are long-standing and have not been adequately addressed. Many are systemic and will require substantive restructuring of existing relations between Aboriginal and non-Aboriginal society in Canada in order to be resolved. Table 18.1 presents examples of barriers expressed by non-Aboriginal researchers.

Table 18.1   Barriers to TK use as perceived by non-Aboriginal researchers

- Western scientists' skepticism of TK, and inability to accept TK as valid
- Ethnocentrism
- Erosion of TK through assimilation of Aboriginal people into Western culture
- Holders of knowledge are not considered "traditional" by external interests
- TK is viewed as disappearing rather than changing or evolving
- Lack of resources to document TK and difficulties in trying to reconcile two worldviews
- Lack of appropriate methods for documenting and utilizing TK
- TK is usually subordinate to Western science due to political power imbalance
- Utilization of Western methods to collect, verify, and validate TK
- Language and translation issues: Western or scientific terminology may not reflect the meaning of the information shared
- Disciplinary and methodological barriers between natural and social scientists attempting to work together on TK issues
- Aboriginal people are expected to conform and adapt to Western scientific methods but not vice versa
- Lack of will and capacity to accept TK on the part of state managers, scientists, etc.
- TK is decontextualized, commodified, and sanitized into forms that conform to the dominant agenda

Source: Berkes, 2008; Bocking 2005; Chapeskie 1995; Johnson 1992; Nadasday 1999, 2003; Stevenson 2005; and Wolfe et al. 1992.

Aboriginal Perceptions

Aboriginal views of barriers to applying TK in environmental or resource management regimes have been documented by both non-Aboriginal and Aboriginal people. Table 18.2 presents some key examples.

The literature reveals many similarities between Aboriginal and non-Aboriginal views of barriers to the incorporation of TK in resource management. Some concerns are unique to Aboriginal people because they are the people from whom TK is sought. This situation is complicated by the unequal distribution of power which characterizes Aboriginal/non-Aboriginal relations in Canada and in FMP (Stevenson 2005). Brubacher and McGregor (1998) discuss this power imbalance in relation to forest management in Canada:

> Further compounding the distance between these understandings is the fact that dialogue around [TK] takes place on the basis of a largely dis-empowered Aboriginal minority talking to the dominant culture, in the language of the dominant culture and within the existing institutional frameworks that govern forest management.

This unequal power relationship and its impact on the utilization of TK in resource management, including forestry, is recognized by others,

Table 18.2   Barriers to TK use as perceived by Aboriginal researchers

- Aboriginal and non-Aboriginal definitions of TK differ (external definitions are imposed)
- Discomfort with the Western scientific requirement to control and interfere with nature
- Cross-cultural barriers and misunderstandings
- Difficulty trying to communicate TK to people and systems focused on Western scientific method, and who do not share Aboriginal traditions, experience, or values
- TK and scientific knowledge are not regarded as equal in state systems; TK is trivialized
- Lack of involvement of Aboriginal people in research and decision making
- Not enough time or money to conduct studies properly
- "Outsiders" only interested in certain aspects of TK; do not include "laws" or "taboos" in their considerations
- "Ownership" of TK (studies, maps, etc.) should remain with the people
- Abuse of TK has made many Aboriginal people reluctant to share it
- Outsiders often don't contact or work with the right people
- Outsiders do not ask the right questions or don't record information properly
- Outsiders don't seem to have the time or patience to listen carefully and understand what is being shared
- Aboriginal people feel they are "forced" to conform to dominant culture
- TK is used to "legitimize" unsustainable outside interests (a requirement)
- TK is not accepted or regarded as valid because it is not expressed in written form
- During TK research processes, Aboriginal people are treated as objects of study rather than as partners
- Western resource-use paradigms are a poor fit for Aboriginal resource-use paradigms
- Loss of passing on TK to younger generations within Aboriginal communities, due to colonization
- Cannot practice TK due to alienation from or destruction of much of their traditional territory
- Rejection of spirituality as a core element of TK

Source: AFN 1995; AFN and Inuit Circumpolar Conference 1991; Battiste and Henderson 2000; Bombay 1996; Brubacher and McGregor 1998; McGregor 2004, 2010; Roberts 1996

such as Chapeskie (1995), Nadasday (2003), Stevenson (2005), Wyatt (2008). Despite the well-documented challenges for considering TK in FMP, some Aboriginal groups continue to participate in such processes. Marc Stevenson (2005, 2006) observes that Aboriginal peoples continue to participate so they can advance their goals and rights in such forums. With the odds stacked against them, "it is no small gesture" for Aboriginal peoples to participate in FMP (2005).

ABORIGINAL VALUES AND FOREST MANAGEMENT PLANNING

In a national review of various "mechanisms" that are utilized to incorporate TK in forestry, the province of Ontario identified a Native values mapping process (now called Aboriginal values mapping) as an example of an application of TK in FMP (Brubaker and McGregor 1998). Ontario's FMP process aims to protect a range of forest values, including the values of Aboriginal peoples, as part of a concerted move towards sustainability. Accounting for a full range of forest values is a defining feature of sustainable forest management (CCFM 1992, 1998; NFSC 2003). The overall approach for including values in FMP involves geographically identifying them and then designing protection measures for them (Sapic et al. 2009). Although mapping "values" of the forest has been associated with sustainable forest management, it has its origins in identifying non-timber values that act as constraints for timber harvesting (Sapic et al. 2009). An enduring characteristic of "accepted" forest values (or non-timber values) is that they must be geographically definable; this remains true in current forest management practices in Ontario.

The forest sector recognizes that Aboriginal peoples have unique values associated with the forest, although commonalities exist with broader society (CFS 1998; LaRose 2009; MNR 2007). Despite this recognition, however, the Aboriginal values of interest to forest management planners are those which are geographically specific. Aboriginal values are thus conceptualized in FMP in the same way forest values are in broader society. Sapic et al. (2009) note that "this type of definition narrows Aboriginal values to geographic places rather than considering the full range of values of Aboriginal peoples." Nonetheless, Ontario forest management planning remains focused on mapping as the primary process for the acquisition of Aboriginal values.

The relationship between "Aboriginal values" (as required by FMP process) and TK is of relevance to the FMP process. TK does not equal Aboriginal values. It is more appropriate to describe the relationship as follows: TK informs the identification and protection of Aboriginal values in the FMP process. A notable commonality between the two concepts is that both terms and their definitions originate from outside Aboriginal people and their communities. This has occurred in spite of the fact that Aboriginal people are regarded as the "holders" of this coveted knowledge. Aboriginal people find themselves forced to react to these concepts in order to retain some influence over matters that concern them.

ABORIGINAL VALUES: PREDETERMINED AND PRE-DEFINED

Despite the directive to include Aboriginal values in FMP, identifying Aboriginal values remains an ambiguous undertaking. In order to identify Aboriginal values and thereby protect them, an understanding of their nature is required. It becomes important for resource planners and managers charged with the responsibility of protecting these values to try and define what Aboriginal values are, as well as to identify their location. Different values, such as wildlife and cultural values, have different prescriptions for protection. There is a need to know what kinds of values exist if appropriate guidelines are to be applied or protection is to be negotiated during the various planning stages (MNR 2007).

In Ontario's process, however, forest management planners have been preoccupied largely with the location only of Aboriginal values, having had pre-defined notions of what these values are. This has led to situations where, if an Aboriginal community does not participate in Aboriginal values mapping, a map is completed without their input (McGregor 2000). Pre-defined "Aboriginal values" already institutionalized in the FMP process are used to guide AVM. In such cases, Aboriginal values are defined as "cultural/heritage" values (the definition most familiar to forest management professionals), and are included as part of the non-timber forest values which must be considered in forest management planning. In this way, Aboriginal values can (from the perspective of forest managers) be relatively easily addressed because there are existing guidelines in forestry for these types of concerns. The *Timber Management Guidelines for the Protection of Cultural Heritage Resources* (1991) has recently been replaced by the *Forest Management Guide for Cultural Heritage Values* (2007) as the technical framework for defining, identifying, and protecting cultural heritage values from forest management operations. The guide recognizes five classes of cultural heritage values: archaeological sites, archaeological potential areas, cultural heritage landscapes, historical Aboriginal values, and cemeteries. These guidelines influence greatly the perception among forest planners and managers about what Aboriginal values are supposed to be and how these values are to be protected.

The Aboriginal values mapping process therefore already exists within the institutional framework before Aboriginal people are even approached to identify their values for protection. Forest management planning teams hold preconceived ideas about the nature of Aboriginal values. Research conducted to date reveals a definite bias as to the perceptions of Aboriginal values held by forestry professionals involved in FMP in Ontario (LaRose 2009; McGregor 2000; Sapic 2008). The view forest managers tend to hold is that Aboriginal values are location and site-specific. Aboriginal values are thought to be physical in nature. Where this is clearly not the case, as in identified spiritual and cultural values, they are thought to be representable in physical terms (i.e., able to be located in a physical space).

Aboriginal people, by contrast, view values as being very broad, holistic, and flexible in nature (LaRose 2009; McGregor 2000; Sapic et al. 2009). Aboriginal values, as First Nations people understand them, take on a range of meaning consisting of whatever is important to the community or individual members. Some values are collective, such as ceremonial sites; others are family or clan-oriented (e.g., totems, burial sites, or berry patches); and some are individual (e.g., favourite fishing spots) (McGregor 2000).

Most First Nations raise the issue of how difficult it is to define Aboriginal values. The earlier research has noted how awkward it is for Elders to be asked to draw imaginary lines around values, such as burial or ceremonial sites, that are important to identify during the Aboriginal values mapping exercise (McGregor 2000). Elders are often not comfortable with this exercise, although they do participate in some cases in order to try and protect the values important to them. The values associated with these belief systems are not necessarily limited to "where" an event occurs (a specific location). This is not to say that Aboriginal peoples are not spatially or geographically inclined. For the First Nation respondents in the original research (McGregor 2000), it was shown how a particular value may have properties or aspects which are also found in other value types. For example, a communal burial or ceremonial site may be described as having physical properties (location), but also encompasses cultural and spiritual aspects. It other words, the Aboriginal value can be physically located, but location alone is not sufficient in defining (or protecting) that value. The values are experienced as holistic; a value may be labelled for the sake of brevity by one individual as cultural, but may be described by another as spiritual or physical. It is difficult to distinguish between spiritual and cultural values and then to identify their physical locations to be mapped. Sapic et al. reveal that we are currently no further ahead in terms of reconciling what is meant by Aboriginal values: "The concept of Aboriginal values in FMP is not completely clear and individuals' values are not sufficiently defined" (2009). Sapic et al. continue, stating that according to Aboriginal peoples in northwestern Ontario, the forest is interdependent and holistic in nature: "Everything is pretty well intertwined, it's not just one value stuck over there, that space, and there is nothing in between" (Sapic et al. 2009, 793). Aboriginal peoples thus identified significant difficulties in spatially defining values.

Larose (2009) in her northwestern Ontario research found similarities as well as differences in the values that Aboriginal and non-Aboriginal peoples hold with respect to the forest. She found that both groups "indicated the forest as a 'home' and a place where important aspects of their lives takes place." However, she found the differences between the values of the two groups striking, noting that "the important characteristics of the forest most emphasized by First Nation participants were in relation the spiritual, sacred and cultural aspects of the forest as they relate to traditional activities … it was the connection or relationship with the land that was characterized as spiritual."

Attempting to map TK through the AVM process or even broad based land-use and occupancy mapping has serious limitations. O'Flaherty et al. (2008), in their work with Pikangikum First Nation, identified mapping as a way to "combine both indigenous and science based knowledge" in ways that would facilitate communication between the First Nation community and provincial-level managers and planners. O'Flaherty et al. nevertheless found that "as much as maps can present information provided by Pikangikum Elders, maps cannot properly express the content of Pikangikum's knowledge system that is largely transmitted through oral and non-verbal means." Johnson et al. (2006), in a review of the value of Indigenous mapping projects, noted that "while Indigenous communities generally recognize fluid and flexible boundaries over land and resource use, once these boundaries become fixed within a Western cartographic representation, the fluid and flexible nature of Indigenous thinking is lost." Johnson et al. add that land and occupancy mapping "can force Indigenous knowledge to fit within the fixed boundaries of the Western map and can provide valuable representation in legal proceedings, but in the end, it is a technique that further perpetuates the loss of Indigenous geographic knowledge."

When a value has many dimensions it poses great difficulty for forest management when it comes to ensuring that all of these dimensions are accounted for as part of Aboriginal values protection. It is challenging to ascertain specifically what the "value" is in the given Aboriginal value. First Nations people are required to decide what aspect of the Aboriginal value is worth protecting (e.g., to choose to protect its physical location through mapping it in the forest management process but to violate its spiritual integrity in doing so). This practice is regarded as culturally inappropriate in light of the holistic nature of Aboriginal values.

Aboriginal peoples thus understand and express Aboriginal values quite differently, clearly challenging the location-specific bias that

forestry professionals and heritage planners bring to the planning process (LaRose 2009; McGregor 2000; Sapic et al. 2009). Recognizing this
issue, input from Aboriginal people was sought in the development of
the new *Forest Management Guide for Cultural Heritage Values*. There
is now specific mention of Aboriginal values in the document, unlike in
its predecessor, yet little change has occurred in practice. Despite over
fifteen years of experience in the FMP process in Ontario and a new
guide to protect forest values, Aboriginal values are not finding adequate
expression in the AVM process.

THE POTENTIAL FOR ABORIGINAL-DIRECTED MAPPING

More indigenous territory has been claimed by maps than by guns. This
assertion has its corollary: more indigenous territory can be reclaimed and
defended by maps than by guns.

                                                          Nietschmann 1995

Indigenous experts often view outsiders's efforts to define or map Indigenous
knowledge as a self-defeating exercise. The formalities and style of
conventional topographic maps define the terms under which Indigenous
knowledge is to be represented, it is often an uncomfortable fit.

                                                                AFN 1995

Cultural Survival in 1994 devoted an entire issue to the benefits and perils
of mapping Indigenous territories. Bernard Nietschmann, an activist and
advocate of Indigenous mapping, observed that, until recently, "almost
all maps were made by invading and occupying powers." To the extent
that maps represent such power, they are neither neutral nor unprob-
lematic (Harris and Hazen 2005). Indigenous peoples are conscious of
the role cartography has played in the dispossession of Indigenous communities of land and resources and thus approach such endeavours with
caution. Despite this, Indigenous peoples in Canada have been involved
in mapping for political purposes for over four decades.

   With the increased interest in TK in ERM across Canada, and in
response to cautions offered by Aboriginal peoples participating in
resultant processes, the Assembly of First Nations (AFN) in 1995 conducted an extensive review of the feasibility of representing Indigenous
knowledge in cartographic, pictorial, or textual forms. The AFN (1995b)
reported that:

Indigenous People may also have a skeptical attitude towards maps, which are often associated with external power sources. Maps have had instrumental value for colonial authorities, for administrative purposes, or are useful for people to find their way through strange territories. But they have generally been redundant to Indigenous Peoples. It is as though an architect's drawing is needed for living in one's own house.

However, under certain circumstances, this antipathy towards maps now appears to be contradicting itself; some Indigenous communities and representative associations have taken to mapping certain elements of their traditional knowledge and practice. This reversal signifies that mapping is now acquiring instrumental value for Indigenous peoples, as part of their strategy for dealing with external interests.

The decision by Aboriginal people to document, at least in some cases, TK in textual formats such as maps is relatively recent. Traditional "land-use and occupancy" studies, ongoing in Canada since the 1970s, still represent this country's most common form of expressing TK in cartographic or geomatic form. However, "Indigenous communities have their own cartographic traditions … and since these cartographies are often stored in songs, stories or rituals, they are generally performative and process in nature and frequently fail to be recognized as cartographic representations" (Johnson et al. 2006).

Aboriginal peoples have been "mapping" for thousands of years, and prior to the arrival of Europeans, "had developed a vast geographic knowledge of their homeland and had their own cartographic conception of where they lived" (Nantel 1999). Like TK, spatial knowledge was shared through oral tradition. As well, Aboriginal maps could be made in snow, campfire ash, or sand; they could be drawn on skin, textiles, birch bark, or rock; or could be built three-dimensionally out of available materials (Nantel 1999). Oral methods, Poole (1998) writes, could result in "topography transformed into poetry and songs, stellar reconstructions for celestial marine navigation." Raffan (1993) continues, recalling that "everyone in Lutselk's, it seemed had stories to tell about the Thelon area, and many of the stories were maps in their own right – about how to navigate safely, both physically and spiritually, through an abundant but harsh land." Indigenous maps were thus also created and stored mentally. "Inuit knowledge was of stories and places, lives and experiences all wrapped in a living landscape of the mind." Raffan

(1993) refers to Elders as "spiritual geographers." Aboriginal maps were, and still are, created within a cultural, spiritual, and social context.

Clearly, despite the pitfalls, there are links between TK and mapping. TK is one of the primary sources of knowledge for mapping. Maps represent a certain aspect of this knowledge (AFN 1995; Johnson et al. 2006; Tobias 2000). Many projects are initiated by Aboriginal peoples in Canada in recognition of this. Undertakings which seek to conserve traditions, document knowledge, manage or conserve the environment, or aid in the assertion of rights, involve mapping as a key component (see, for example, O'Flaherty et al. 2008). Hrenchuk (1993) stresses the critical link between TK and mapping:

> Land use and occupancy studies also demonstrate both specific and comprehensive aspects of traditional knowledge. Specifically, traditional ecological knowledge is reflected in the data collected concerning particular resources, for example, where and when to find specific game. This information relates both to the relationship of animals and the environment, and to the cultural utilization and transmission of this knowledge. Comprehensively, traditional ecological knowledge is reflected in the delineation of the intimate and extensive knowledge of the topography in which the specific ecological information is held. This is not solely route-finding knowledge, but an expression of the concrete ways in which the animals, land, and community are linked. The notion of occupancy rests on the premise of traditional and continuing knowledge of the land and its resources.

Despite the scepticism of mapping held by many Aboriginal people, maps are also viewed as at least one of the tools that can be used to assist in the assertion or establishment of rights and in the protection of lands (AFN 1995; Bryan 2009; Gonzalez et al. 1995; Johnson et al. 2006; Poole 1995a; Walsh 1998). Although maps have been used to colonize and claim Aboriginal territories (AFN 1995; Bryan 2008; Nietschmann 1995), Indigenous people all over the world are now using available technology to create their own maps which are rooted in TK and are "far more accurate and detailed" than many maps produced in other ways (Gonzalez et al. 1995).

Indigenous people possess knowledge of the land upon which they have lived for thousands of years. The source of information for maps is thus long-standing and reliable. As noted above, many Aboriginal groups in Canada initiate cultural revival projects or assert rights which include mapping as a core feature (McDonald et al. 1997; Poole 1995c; Tobias 2000). Maps, then, can be tools for Aboriginal community empowerment if generated and utilized appropriately. If misused, they can also serve as a tool for oppression and alienation.

AVM currently remains preoccupied with meeting the pre-defined requirements of an externally initiated and perpetuated process. This process has been inspired, conducted, and directed by non-Aboriginal people in Ontario forest management planning. It seeks to capture, in map form, Aboriginal peoples' knowledge. The fact that it is an externally driven process with very specific purposes in mind remains true even if a First Nation chooses to conduct the exercise within their own community, utilizing their own knowledge and resources. The values data eventually have to be shared in suitable form to be utilized in the dominant external framework of FMP. The community is coerced into defining their knowledge and values for a state management regime which already holds preconceived notions of what their responses should look like (Sapic 2009). Aboriginal peoples are often in a position of identifying values in a process which may or may not recognize their values as valid or credible, as well as attempting to map certain values which may not be appropriately mapped. This is perceived as a loss of control of traditional knowledge in the form of "values" to a dominating regime. The whole process of AVM is therefore troublesome and thus, in numerous cases, Aboriginal people continue to resist it.

As soon as traditional knowledge is shared with outsiders in the form of text or a map it becomes vulnerable. It has been separated from both its holder and the traditional controls that govern its appropriate use. It is absolutely critical that Aboriginal people maintain control over their own knowledge, although it can by all means be shared with others. Compounding this problem is the power imbalance that characterizes most current relationships between the seekers of the knowledge and the holders of the knowledge. Clearly, these are some of the fundamental issues that need to be addressed further in Ontario's forest management planning process.

TO MAP OR NOT TO MAP: WHEN SHOULD ABORIGINAL PEOPLES PARTICIPATE IN FMP?

The broader context for the consideration of TK in FMP is thus one characterized by conflicts over land, authority, and jurisdiction. Such processes, including values mapping, arguably occur within a broader context of continued colonialism (Bryan 2009; Johnson 2006; McGregor 2006), a reality explicitly recognized by First Nations decades ago. The relationship between Aboriginal and non-Aboriginal peoples is defined by its inherent imbalance of power (RCAP 1996). Thus, it is unlikely that the debate on the merits and perils of Indigenous mapping will be resolved in the near future.

Despite the criticisms of AVM, it is also noted as an important activity by some Aboriginal peoples (Larose 2008; McGregor 2000; Sapic et al. 2009). Aboriginal peoples want to protect their knowledge and resources. It is not just important to protect the value from forest operations; it becomes crucial to be able to access and regain management of the value to assist with the recovery of nationhood that Aboriginal peoples seek.

There has been a long history of sustained attempts to colonize and assimilate Aboriginal people by dominant society. Despite this, there is a movement to try and learn from Aboriginal people the knowledge they have managed to maintain throughout. It becomes, then, crucial and more productive to support Aboriginal people in their recovery and their attempts to realize their rightful place in Canada. In light of this, the AVM process takes on a new importance: it can either be a help or a hindrance to Aboriginal people.

Yet both Aboriginal peoples and Canadian governments have reasons for holding back. Aboriginal peoples are reluctant to fully engage in such processes as prior experiences have demonstrated the need to protect their knowledge from inappropriate use (AFN 1995). For their part, Canadian governments are reluctant to fully engage with Aboriginal peoples on Aboriginal terms due to the need to adhere to existing government bureaucratic and political processes (Nadasdy 2006; White 2006).

Mapping, particularly mapping elements of TK, has taken on "instrumental" value for Aboriginal peoples "as part of their strategy for dealing with external interests" (AFN 1995). The Assembly of First Nations speculates on how First Nations are navigating this land mine of difficulties. Just as Indigenous knowledge has changed over time to meet challenges and ensure survival of the community, mapping projects have also evolved to meet the changing requirements for survival. Maps have acquired new survival value, a value which, though they weren't necessarily written down, they had for thousands of years prior to contact with Europeans. "To the degree that Indigenous knowledge is about survival, it evolves in response to pressures that threaten survival. In this respect, as a means of dealing with pressures upon Indigenous lands, geomatics has acquired an instrumental value" (AFN 1995). The AFN continues, stating that "the principle objective is not to comprehensively represent Indigenous knowledge but to defend Indigenous rights to lands and resources." Mapping then, is part of an overall strategy, a long-term vision, but not the end in itself.

Indigenous peoples in Ontario (as in other places in Canada and in the world) have established respectful and reciprocal relationships with their territories since time immemorial. Indigenous legal scholar John Borrows writes that

> Aboriginal peoples have a pre-occupation. It is *of* land. They occupied land in North America prior to others arrivals on its shores. Over the past 250 years Aboriginal peoples have been largely dispossessed of their lands and resources in Canada. This dispossession has led to another Aboriginal pre-occupation. It is *with* land. It is crucial to their survival as peoples. It loss haunts their dreams. Its continuing occupation and/or reoccupation inspires their vision.
>
> Aboriginal people regard their land as sacred; it is integral to their culture and identity. They want to continue living on territories that has sustained them for thousands of years. Yet the Crown now claims occupation of traditional Aboriginal lands (2005).

Quite simply, Aboriginal peoples in Canada are involved in FMP because of this preoccupation with land and the need to maintain and re-establish connection with their territories in order to survive as people. As Borrows (2005) establishes, there are a number of strategies and tactics utilized by Aboriginal people to re-establish connections to territories now controlled by the Crown.

One such strategy involves Aboriginal people participating in FMP processes that will move them a step closer to having a say over their traditional territories. This type of participation helps to establish Aboriginal "interest" in traditional territories under the Crown's control (Borrows 2005). Another facet of Aboriginal participation in FMP concerns Indigenous peoples' sense of responsibility to try to ensure sustainability. There is a strong ethic of responsibility felt by many Indigenous people that compels them to assist in addressing these challenges (Arquette et al. 2004; Clarkson et al. 1992).

Aboriginal peoples most certainly recognize the pitfalls of participating in state-led environmental and resource management processes, and the high risks of perpetuating inequalities that currently exist. On the other hand, Aboriginal peoples are not going to idly watch the continued destruction of their territories. Navigating a way through this difficult situation remains a characteristic of Aboriginal involvement in ERM in Canada. Many communities choose to actively resist such processes; others participate with an eye on realizing the goal of re-establishing or maintaining relationships with their territories, while still others actively engage in negotiating a space for Indigenous ERM in Canada.

Within a framework in which Aboriginal peoples can use maps as tools for meeting some of their goals, maps can be a powerful and positive force. It seems, therefore, reasonable to suggest that under the proper circumstances, Aboriginal values mapping should potentially be able to assist Aboriginal people in achieving goals in forest management planning. The Aboriginal values mapping process can be viewed as a potential mechanism for influencing forest management activities on traditional territories. It can be part of a larger, longer-term Aboriginal strategy for regaining control over traditional territories (Borrows 2005).

CONCLUSION

There are no easy answers to the dilemma: "map," or be "mapped." In the final analysis it is a decision that Aboriginal peoples themselves must make while being open to the full risks involved in such endeavours. Some scholars call for a complete overhaul (read: "decolonizing") of the political and institutional frameworks that support the status quo (McGregor 2010; Stevenson 2005). Such processes are not likely to occur quickly enough for most Aboriginal peoples, however. Aboriginal peoples cannot continue to wait, as ever-increasing environmental challenges are faced on a daily basis. Though progress on this front must continue to be made, a variety of incremental steps can also be taken every day to challenge, deconstruct, and decolonize unequal relationships with the broader Canadian state and its institutions. Piece by piece, many Indigenous and non-Indigenous scholars and activists are calling for the affirmation and enactment of various Indigenous traditions (political, legal, economic, environmental, etc.) as a central strategy for challenging colonial systems. Others are promoting the negotiation of an FMP process that can "truly balance the needs, rights and interests of all forest users" (Stevenson 2005). Perhaps in this way, Aboriginal values mapping can be applied as one piece of the puzzle in moving towards the reclamation of Indigenous nationhood.

REFERENCES

Arquette, M., and M. Cole. 2004. "Restoring Our Relationship for the Future." In *In the Way of Development: Indigenous Peoples, Life Projects and Globalization*, edited by M. Blaser, H. Feit, and G. McRae, 332–49. New York, NY: Zed Books; Ottawa, ON: International Development Research Centre.

Battiste, M. and J. Henderson. 2000. *Protecting Indigenous Knowledge and Heritage: A Global Challenge*. Saskatoon, SK: Purich Publishing.

Berkes, F. 2008. *Sacred Ecology*, second edition, 336. Philadelphia, PA: Taylor and Francis.

Bombay, H. 1996a. *Aboriginal Forest-Based Ecological Knowledge in Canada*. Ottawa, ON: National Aboriginal Forestry Association.

Bocking, S. 2005. "Scientists and Evolving Perceptions of Indigenous Knowledge in Northern Canada." In *Walking a Tightrope: Aboriginal Peoples and Their Representation*, edited by U. Lischke and D. McNab. Waterloo: Wilfred Laurier University Press.

Borrows, J. 2005. *Crown Occupations of Land: A History & Comparison*. Prepared by the Ipperwash Inquiry. Office of the Attorney General, Government of Ontario. http://www.attorneygeneral.jus.gov.on.ca/inquiries/ipperwash/policy_part/research/index.html.

Bryan. J. 2009. "Where Would We Be Without Them? Knowledge, Space and Power in Indigenous Politics." *Futures* 41:24–32

Brubacher, D., and D. McGregor. 1998. *Aboriginal Forest-Related Traditional Ecological Knowledge in Canada*. Contribution for the 19th Session of the North American Forest Commission, Villahermosa, Mexico. 16–20 November. Ottawa, ON: National Aboriginal Forestry Association for the Canadian Forest Service.

Canadian Council of Forest Ministers (CCFM). 1992. *Sustainable Forests: A Canadian Commitment*. Hull, QC: National Forest Strategy, Canadian Council of Forest Ministers.

– 1998. *National Forest Strategy 1998–2003: Sustainable Forests, A Canadian Commitment*. Ottawa, ON: National Forest Strategy, Canadian Council of Forest Ministers.

– 2003. *National Forest Strategy 2003–2008: Sustainable Forests, A Canadian Commitment*. Ottawa, ON: National Forest Strategy, Canadian Council of Forest Ministers. http://nfsc.forest.ca/strategies/strategy5.html. Accessed 31 January 2006.

Canadian Forest Service (CFS). 1999. *Traditional Ecological Knowledge within the Government of Canada's First Nation Forestry Program: A Case Study*. Canadian Forest Service. Natural Resources Canada.

Chapeskie, A. 1995. *Land, Landscape, Culturescape: Aboriginal Relationships to Land and The Co-management of Natural Resources. A Report for the Royal Commission on Aboriginal Peoples.* Ottawa, ON: Land, Resource and Environmental Regimes Project.

Cheveau, M., L. Imbeau, P. Drapeau, and L. Belanger. 2008. "Current Status and Future Directions of Traditional Ecological Knowledge in Forest Management: A Review." *The Forestry Chronicle.* 84 (2):231–43.

Clarkson, L., V. Morrrissette, and G. Regallet. 1992. *Our Responsibility to the Seventh Generation: Indigenous Peoples and Sustainable Development.* Winnipeg, MB: International Institute for Sustainable Development.

Crowshoe, C. 2005. *Sacred Ways of Life: Traditional Knowledge.* Prepared for the National Aboriginal Health Association. Ottawa, ON. http://www.naho.ca/firstnations/english/documents/FNC-TraditionalknowledgeToolkit-Eng.pdf.

Gonzalez, N., F. Herrera, and M. Chapin. 1995. "Ethnocartography in the Darien." *Cultural Survival Quarterly* 18 (4):31–3.

Higgins, C. 1998. "The Role of Traditional Ecological Knowledge in Managing for Biodiversity." *Forestry Chronicle* 74 (3):323–6.

Houde. N. 2007. "The Six Faces of Traditional Ecological Knowledge: Challenges and Opportunities for Canadian Co-Management Arrangements." *Ecology and Society* 12 (2).

Harris & Hazen. 2005. "Power of Maps: (Counter) Mapping for Conservation." *ACME: An International E-Journal for Critical Geographies,* 99–130.

Hrenchuk, C. 1993. "Native Land Use and Common Property: Whose Common?" In Traditional Ecological Knowledge: Concepts and Cases, edited by J. Inglis, 69–86. International Program on Traditional Ecological Knowledge and International Development Research Centre, Ottawa, ON.

Johnson, J., R. Louis, and A. Pramano. 2006. "Facing the Future: Encouraging Critical Literacies in Indigenous Communities." ACME: *An International E-Journal for Critical Geographies,* 81–98.

Johnson, M., ed. 1992. *Lore: Capturing Traditional Environmental Knowledge.* Ottawa, ON: Dene Cultural Institute and the International Development Research Centre.

LaDuke, W. 1999. *All Our Relations: Native Struggles for Land and Life.* Cambridge, MA: South End Press.

LaRose, D. 2009. *Adapting to Change and the Perceptions and Knowledge in the Involvement of Aboriginal Peoples in Forest Management: A Case Study with Lac Seul First Nation.* Unpublished manuscript. Masters of Science in Forestry. Faculty of Forestry. Lakehead University.

Manseau, M., B. Parlee, and G. Ayles. 2005. "A Place for Traditional Ecological Knowledge in Resource Management." In *Breaking Ice: Renewable Resource and Ocean Management in the Canadian North*, edited by
F. Berkes, R. Huebert, H. Fast, M. Manseau, and A. Diduck. Calgary, AB:
University of Calgary Press.

McDonald, M., L. Arragutainaq, and Z. Novalinga, compilers. 1997. *Voices
from the Bay: Traditional Ecological Knowledge of Inuit and Cree in the
Hudson Bay Bioregion*. Canadian Arctic Resources Committee, Ottawa, ON.

McGregor, D. 2000. *From Exclusion to Co-Existence: Aboriginal Participation in Ontario's Forest Management Planning*. PhD thesis. University of
Toronto.

– 2000. "The State of Traditional Ecological Knowledge Research in Canada:
A Critique of Current Theory and Practice." In *Expressions in Canadian
Native Studies*, edited by R. Laliberte, P. Settee, J. Waldram, R. Innes, B.
Macdougall, L. McBain, and F. Barron, 436–58. Saskatoon, SK: University of
Saskatchewan Extension Press.

– 2004. "Coming Full Circle: Indigenous Knowledge, Environment and Our
Future." *American Indian Quarterly* 28 (3/4):385–410.

– 2005. "Traditional Ecological Knowledge: An Anishinabe-Kwe Perspective."
Atlantis Women's Studies Journal 29 (2):103–9.

– 2006. "Aboriginal Involvement in Ontario Sustainable Forest Management:
Moving Toward Collaboration." *Recherches Amerindiennes au Quebec*
XXXVI, No-2-3:61–70.

– 2008b. "Linking Traditional Ecological Knowledge and Western Science:
Aboriginal Perspectives on SOLEC." *Canadian Journal of Native Studies* 28
(1):139–58.

– 2010. "The Earth Keepers Solid Waste Management Planning Program: a
Collaborative Approach to Utilizing Aboriginal Traditional Knowledge and
Western Science in Ontario" *The International Journal of Canadian Studies.
Les représentations des Premières nations et des Métis/Representations of
First Nations and Métis* (2010.1) 41:69–98.

Menzies, C., ed. 2006. *Traditional Ecological Knowledge and Natural
Resource Management*. Lincoln, NE: University of Nebraska Press.

Nadasdy. P. 2003. *Hunters and Bureaucrats: Power, Knowledge, and Aboriginal-State Relations in the Yukon*. Vancouver, BC: University of British
Columbia Press.

– 2006. "The Case of the Missing Sheep: Time, Space, and the Politics of
'Trust' in Co-management Practice." In *Traditional Ecological Knowledge
and Natural Resource Management*, edited by C. Menzies, 127–52. Lincoln,
NE: University of Nebraska Press.

Nantel, M. 1999. *So as to Hold Many Sheep: Towards Culturally Appropriate GIS.* Unpublished major paper. Faculty of Environmental Studies, York University.

National Forest Strategy Coalition (NFSC). 2003. *National Forest Strategy (2003–2008). A Sustainable Forest: The Canadian Commitment.* Ottawa, ON: NFSC. http://nfsc.forest.ca

Nietschmann, B. 1995. "Defending the Miskito Reefs with Maps and GIS: Mapping in Sail, Scuba and Satellite." *Cultural Survival Quarterly* 18 (4):34–7.

O'Flaherty, R., I. Davidson-Hunt, and M. Manseau. 2008. "Indigenous Knowledge and Values in Planning for Sustainable Forestry: Pikangikum First Nation and the Whitefeather Forest Initiative." *Ecology and Society* 13 (1):6–16.

Ontario Ministry of Natural Resources (MNR). 2004. *Forest Management Planning Manual for Ontario's Crown Forests.* Toronto, ON: Queen's Printer for Ontario.

– 2007. Forest Management Guide for Cultural Values. Toronto, ON: Queen's Printer Press for Ontario.

Ontario Ministry of Natural Resources (MNR), and Ministry of Culture and Communications (MCC). 1991. *Timber Management Guidelines for the Protection of Cultural Heritage Resources.* Ministry of Natural Resources, Toronto, ON.

Pearce, M., and R. Louis. 2008. "Mapping Indigenous Depth of Place." *American Indian Culture and Research Journal* 23 (3):107–26.

Poole, P. 1998. "Indigenous Lands and Power Mapping in the Americas: Merging Technologies." *Native Americas, Akwe:kon's Journal of Indigenous Issues* 15 (6):34–43

Poole, P. 1995a. "Geomatics: Who Needs it?" *Cultural Survival Quarterly* 18 (4):1.

– 1995b. "Land-Based Communities, Geomatics and Biodiversity Conservation: A Survey of Current Activities." *Cultural Survival Quarterly* 18 (4):74–6.

– 1995c. *Indigenous Peoples, Mapping & Biodiversity Conservation: An Analysis of Current Activities and Opportunities for Applying Geomatics Technologies.* Biodiversity Support Program Peoples and Forest Program Discussion Paper. Landover, MD: Corporate Press.

Pikangikum First Nation and Ontario Ministry of Natural Resources (PFN and MNR). 2006. *Keeping the Land: A Land Use Strategy for the Whitefeather Forest and Adjacent Areas.* Pikangikum, ON: PFN, with MNR (Red Lake).

Raffan, J. 1993. "Where God Began." *Equinox* 71 (September/October):44–57.

Roberts, K. 1996. *Circumpolar Aboriginal People and Co-Management Practice: Current Issues in Co-Management and Environmental Assessment.* Calgary, AB: Arctic Institute of North America with Joint Secretariat – Inuvialuit Renewable Resources Committee.

Royal Commission on Aboriginal Peoples (RCAP). 1996. "Lands and Resources." In *Report of The Royal Commission on Aboriginal Peoples Volume 2: Restructuring the Relationship,* 421–685. Ottawa, ON: Canada Communication Group – Publishing.

Sapic, T., U. Runesson, and P. Smith. 2009. "Views of Aboriginal People in Northern Ontario on Ontario's Approach to Aboriginal Values in Forest Management Planning." *The Forestry Chronicle* 95 (5):789–801.

Shackerof, J., and L. Campbell. 2007. "Traditional Ecological Knowledge in Conservation Research: Problems and Prospects for their Constructive Engagement." *Conservation and Society* 5 (3):343–60.

Spak, S. 2005. "The Position of Indigenous Knowledge in Canadian Co-management Organizations." *Anthropologica* 47 (2):233–46.

Stevenson, M. 2005. *Traditional Knowledge in Sustainable Forest Management.* Edmonton, AB: Sustainable Forest Management Network.

– 2006. "The Possibility of Difference: Rethinking Co-management." *Human Organization* 65 (2):167–80.

Tobias, T. 2000. *Chief Kerry's Moose: A Guidebook to Land Use and Occupancy Mapping, Research Design.* Vancouver, BC: Union of BC Indian Chiefs and Eco-Trust Canada.

United Nations General Assembly. 2007. *United Nations Declaration on the Rights of Indigenous Peoples.* www.un.org.

Walsh, P. 1998. "The Power of Maps." *Winds of Change* 13 (3):28–33.

White, G. 2006. *Cultures in Collision: Traditional Knowledge and Euro-Canadian Governance Processes in Northern Land-Claim Boards* vol. 59. no. 4:401–14.

Wolfe, J., C. Bechard, P. Cizek, and D. Cole. 1992. *Indigenous and Western Knowledge and Resource Management Systems.* University School of Rural Planning and Development, University of Guelph, ON.

World Commission on Environment and Development (WCED). 1987. *Our Common Future.* Oxford, UK: Oxford University Press.

Wyatt, S. 2008. "First Nations, Forest Lands, and 'Aboriginal' Forestry in Canada; From Exclusion to Co-management and Beyond." *Canadian Journal of Forest Research* 38:171–80.

19

Our Beautiful Land: The Challenge of Nunatsiavut Land-Use Planning

ANDREA PROCTER AND KEITH CHAULK

In 2005, the Inuit of northern Labrador, Canada, signed a land claims agreement with the federal and provincial governments to share the governance of the region of Nunatsiavut ("our beautiful land" in Inuttitut) (INAC 2005). After almost thirty years of negotiations, hope is high that, finally, the Inuit will regain control over their homeland and will be able to govern themselves based on their own values and priorities. One opportunity for this resurgence in Inuit governance is land-use planning.

Chapter 10 of the final agreement requires that the Nunatsiavut government and the provincial government of Newfoundland and Labrador jointly develop and approve "a single, comprehensive Land Use Plan" for Nunatsiavut, not including federal lands and waters (INAC 2005, 10.3.8). Nunatsiavut is 72,520 square kilometres and encompasses Inuit ancestral homes and harvesting areas, rich mineral resources, abundant char and salmon rivers, and caribou habitat. A co-management body was created in 2008 to develop this plan over a three-year period (2008–11). The Regional Planning Authority (RPA) consists of two Nunatsiavut-appointed representatives and two provincially appointed representatives, and is assisted by a certified planner.[1] At the time of writing (July 2011), the RPA is finalizing a draft plan for Nunatsiavut.

This chapter explores the practical and structural challenges of planning in an Inuit territory, but it also examines the larger political context of land-use planning and Aboriginal-state relations in Labrador, which we argue has significant bearing on the success of the planning process.

As we see it, the ability of Labrador Inuit to achieve their goals through land-use planning is related to a number of issues, including:

1 the ability of the RPA and the planner to understand the diverse goals and perspectives of Inuit through widespread Inuit participation in planning;

2 the structural limitations of planning to accommodate alternative or innovative options;

3 the strength of the co-management process in obtaining approval of the RPA's draft plan from both the provincial and the Nunatsiavut governments; and

4 the ability of both governments to adhere to the plan and to continue to keep Inuit interests foremost in the future.

Each of these issues is relevant during various stages of land-use planning, but all four will ultimately influence the success of planning in Nunatsiavut.

PLANNING IN NUNATSIAVUT

The Labrador Inuit Land Claims Agreement divides the jurisdiction of lands and resources of Nunatsiavut among four different government bodies. In general terms, the Nunatsiavut government owns the surface rights of Labrador Inuit Lands (LIL) (15,799 km²), and the provincial government owns Labrador Inuit Settlement Area lands outside LIL (43,071 km²). In addition, the federal government has jurisdiction over Torngat Mountains National Park (where land-use planning is controlled by a separate park co-management board), as well as all tidal waters, a region referred to in the final agreement as the Marine Zone. Finally, the Inuit community governments control land-use planning for the Inuit Community Lands (Table 19.1). Subsurface rights and royalty regimes vary with each land category.

The land use plan for Nunatsiavut (or the "Labrador Inuit Settlement Area" – LISA – as it is officially called by the provincial government) relates only to lands under the jurisdiction of the Nunatsiavut and provincial governments. The plan will "guide the future conservation, development, and utilization of the land, waters, and other resources within LISA" for a ten-year planning period taking into account a number of factors outlined in the land claim agreement, including natural resources and existing patterns of natural resource use, health and quality of life, economic needs and opportunities, cultural factors and priorities, and the rights of Inuit (Draft Regional Land Use Plan Dec 2009, 7; INAC 2005, 10.4.3). The RPA and the planner established principles and

Table 19.1   Major land and water categories in Nunatsiavut

Land or water category	Jurisdiction	Area
Labrador Inuit Lands (LIL)	Nunatsiavut Government	15,799 km²
Torngat Mountains National Park	Federal Government	9,700 km²
Specified Material Lands (all are within LIL)	Nunatsiavut Government	3,950 km²
Inuit Communities	Inuit Community Governments (with NG on LIL)	Includes 4.58 km² of LIL
LISA outside of the above	Provincial Government	43,071 km²
Total area of land in LISA		72,520 km²
Tidal waters (the "Zone")	Federal Government	48,690 km²

objectives based on these factors, and developed a draft plan in consultation with Inuit, the general public, and the two governments in 2012. As of the end of 2012, both governments are deciding how or if to amend and approve it. The Executive Council of the Nunatsiavut Government has given its approval of the draft, but neither government has officially approved the plan. Once both governments have approved it, the plan will be legally binding.

COMMUNICATION AND CONSULTATION

The Regional Planning Authority envisions that the land use plan for Nunatsiavut will respond, first and foremost, to Inuit environmental, social, cultural, and economic interests. Given the diversity of the Labrador Inuit, however, the task of defining these Inuit interests is a challenge.

Of the approximately seven thousand beneficiaries of the Labrador Inuit land claim, 37.2 per cent live within Nunatsiavut, in one of the five communities of Nain, Hopedale, Makkovik, Postville, and Rigolet (Draft Regional Land Use Plan January 2010, 12). Each of these communities has its own distinct social history, economy, and land-use patterns. The families from northern communities that were relocated in the 1950s form sub-populations in some communities that still experience high levels of social trauma (Brice-Bennett 1994). Historical distinctions in land use between village-based families and homestead-based families also remain important in how people currently use the land and sea. Economic strategies, ties with other parts of Labrador, Quebec, and Newfoundland, and immigration patterns all differ widely, both between and within each community (Brice-Bennett 1977a; Williamson 1996).

The other 62.8 per cent of Inuit beneficiaries live either in the Upper Lake Melville communities of Happy Valley-Goose Bay/Mud Lake (28.7 per cent) and North West River (4.3 per cent), or elsewhere in Canada (29.8 per cent) (Draft Regional Land Use Plan January 2010). In similar fashion, Inuit in these communities have varied historical and current land-use patterns, economic behaviours, social ties, and immigration patterns. Despite the relatively low number of beneficiaries, the diversity of social, cultural, and economic aspects is remarkable.

The geographical expanse of Nunatsiavut provides another layer of complexity onto the task of determining how the land should be used in accordance with Inuit priorities. Roughly the size of New Brunswick, Nunatsiavut extends from fjords and islands of the northern coast to inland caribou highlands to the southern forests around Lake Melville, with vast ecological and geographic diversity in between.

In attempting to understand all of this diversity, the planner obtained as much map data (including text documents and databases) as was available, although the extent of this material was limited (RPA notes, September 2009). Much of the detailed knowledge about the region has not been catalogued, but instead remains with Inuit who know the land intimately. The limitations of the three-year timeframe for developing the plan and the money allocated for it prevented the RPA from undertaking any of its own research on understanding Inuit priorities, but it is the hope of the RPA and the planner that people will share this information with them during community consultations (RPA notes, September 2009).

Although the initial plan was that the planner would spend much of his time in Nunatsiavut, this has not occurred. Instead, the RPA agreed that the planner should be based in the provincial government offices in St John's (a distance of approximately one thousand kilometres from central Nunatsiavut and culturally very different) in order to be near the provincial planning division, but putting the process at an immediate disadvantage in understanding current Nunatsiavut realities. Given these obstacles, the RPA members and the planner have relied heavily on the two Inuit representatives on the RPA to provide them with a sense of current Inuit perspectives, despite the well-acknowledged fact that it is impossible to assume that these two people alone would be able to thoroughly understand and articulate all perspectives of this diverse constituency (see also Lane 1997). The Nunatsiavut beneficiaries appointed by the Nunatsiavut government to the RPA, Isabella Pain and Wilfred Pilgrim (and before him, Keith Chaulk), all have extensive expertise in governmental processes and environmental management. Isabella Pain, who was born and lives in Nain, is a former land claims negotiator for the Labrador Inuit Association, and has years of experience in Inuit politics and in the mining industry. Dr Keith Chaulk, from North West River, is a wildlife biologist and has worked for the Canadian Wildlife Service, the Labrador Inuit Association, and currently, Memorial University of Newfoundland. Wilfred Pilgrim, who replaced Keith on the RPA in 2009, was born and raised in Postville and is an environmental scientist with almost forty years of experience in working in the health science and resource management field. The combined expertise of these appointees is very impressive, and their views hold great authority within the RPA. Nonetheless, they are only two (or three) voices.

A number of meetings and trips took place early in the process (2006–09), but the first formal RPA consultation with Inuit about the draft plan took place in January 2010. Some Inuit expressed their frustration during these consultations about what they perceived as their late involvement in the process. They felt that it was very difficult for them to adequately learn about planning and then offer some incisive comments in the time allowed for consultations. Some felt that consultations about the plan occurred too far along in the process, as the structure of the draft plan had already been determined. Some said that they would have preferred to be involved earlier when the concepts were more nebulous (RPA notes, February 2010). The RPA and the planner recognized that consultations and ongoing communications with Inuit have not been as extensive as they might have been, but most members felt that the general public would not have been able to provide input without a draft plan and, especially, without maps (RPA notes, September 2009).

The consultations occurred in semi-formal settings in meeting rooms in each community and consisted of a PowerPoint presentation by the planner, followed by general discussion. Some Inuit voiced their concern and sense of discomfort about this formality: "I've never seen these people in my life," commented one man, pointing at the planner and the provincial appointees. "And they tell me that they're making a plan for Nunatsiavut? Have they even been there?" (RPA notes, February 2010). A number of planning scholars have argued that communication with Aboriginal participants in the planning process needs to accommodate local forms of interaction, social complexities, and decision making (Cosgrove and Kliger 1997; Lane 1997). The RPA and the planner are well aware that these meetings were not ideal, but again, they organized them as such because of the pressure to develop a plan in three years as required by the land claim agreement (RPA notes, February 2010).

Smaller and more frequent meetings that would have developed the relationships of trust and better mutual understanding would have been difficult to arrange because of pressures on the RPA related to available finances, timeframe, human resources, and information. Because of these pressures, participants in the planning process often decided not to seize opportunities for adapting the planning process to Inuit involvement, but instead worked towards finalizing the plan in the most expedient manner. Although Inuit now have a seat at the decision-making table, this participation is not automatically resulting in planning that can accommodate the different realities of Nunatsiavut.

STRUCTURAL LIMITATIONS OF PLANNING

The level and quality of participation in the planning process is fundamental to the incorporation of Inuit goals and perspectives into the plan. The structural foundations of land-use planning and the act of incorporation itself also have a significant impact on the ability of Labrador Inuit to address their governance goals. A growing number of studies criticize the colonial and ontological foundations of planning as being foreign to and suppressing Aboriginal perspectives (Howitt and Suchet-Pearson 2006; Porter 2007; Nadasdy 2003). These studies have documented a number of cases in which the planning process has either rendered Aboriginal peoples or their interests invisible through various methods of statecraft (Scott 1998), or has incorporated Aboriginal perspectives in a way that does not challenge or modify the existing governmental structure and thus reproduces colonial relationships.

A striking example of the imposition of state structures on Inuit governance is the incongruity between established jurisdictional boundaries and Inuit perspectives. As elsewhere in Canada, the ocean and its resources are under the jurisdiction of the federal Fisheries and Oceans Canada, while land usually falls under provincial jurisdiction. However, this conceptual division of the environment is not a model shared by Labrador Inuit, who consider the sea ice to be an extension of the land (Williamson 1997; Brice-Bennett 1977b; Mulrennan and Scott 2001).

From late autumn to early summer, land-fast sea ice forms along the Labrador coast and provides many important travelling routes and harvesting opportunities. Sea ice was specifically included in the original land claim proposal as an area of importance to the Inuit, but the other governments failed to recognize this interest during the land claims negotiations. In the Labrador Inuit Land Claim Agreement, Inuit negotiated the right to travel and harvest on the sea ice, but the federal government refused to concede any rights to ownership or governance beyond an advisory role (Mulrennan and Scott 2001).[2] The land use plan, as a creation of the final agreement, is required to follow these jurisdictions, and has no power to control activities on sea ice. The plan therefore officially includes coastal regions and islands, but, incongruously, not the water or sea ice that surround them. RPA discussions have led to the inclusion of references in the plan about the importance of traditional land uses on sea ice and the need to consider these uses when considering potential developments and transportation links, but the plan has no real authority to control sea ice issues.

One of the initial goals of the Nunatsiavut planning process was adapting planning to Inuit realities. All RPA members strongly support the vision that the Nunatsiavut plan will be based specifically on Inuit goals and concerns. The translation of these goals into the planning framework, however, often requires modifications that illustrate planning's structural foundations and shortcomings.

One Inuit member of the RPA stated in 2008, "I want a plan that recognizes the significance of resources and the Inuit reliance on the land to maintain our culture. I want to develop a plan that allows Inuit to live as Inuit" (RPA notes, April 2008). The RPA and the planner restated this in a way to make it more amenable to their planning process: "Inuit have a strong desire to retain Inuttitut, traditional knowledge, cultural, spiritual, and historical ties to the land. To accomplish this, they require a sustainable supply of country food which in turn requires protection of land in the all-inclusive Inuit understanding of the word" (Draft Regional Land Use Plan, December 2009, 12, emphasis in original).

The RPA therefore identified three main concerns that would guide the plan's designations:

1 the Inuit desire to have a sustainable supply of country food;
2 the potential for tourism; and
3 the potential for mineral development.

So as to attend to the first concern, the RPA proposed the concept of the Traditional Use Designation (TUD). This designation prohibits mining and destructive land uses, and the RPA has applied it to the primary area where "Inuit continue to live, gather, hunt and trap for country food." This area consists of a linear strip along the coast, as well as coastal islands, caribou habitat, and waterfowl nesting areas. Under the land claims agreement, Inuit have the right to pursue their traditional activities throughout Nunatsiavut. The TUD, therefore, is not the only area where harvesting can occur, but it establishes protected habitats where land use can be controlled.

On the one hand, the TUD acknowledges the cultural and economic value that many Inuit place in harvesting, and which has historically been overlooked and undermined by government authorities (Procter 2012; Ames 1977; Usher 1982). The possibility that the province might agree to favour Aboriginal harvesting practices over development would be an important breakthrough for Aboriginal peoples in Labrador.

On the other hand, the limitations that are made explicit in a TUD reflect more upon the structural limitations of a planning framework than the translation of Inuit values. Whereas the Inuit aspire to "retain Inuttitut, traditional knowledge, cultural, spiritual, and historical ties to the land," and to "allow Inuit to live as Inuit," the TUD aims to narrow its usage to the protection of habitat in a manner that maintains "a sustainable supply of country food." This interpretation reflects the bias of planning to translate holistic cultural values into a measurable economic outcome.

Perhaps planners find that incorporating definable economic activities in delineated spaces fits their methodologies better than the incorporation of larger and non-quantifiable cultural relationships with the environment. Harvesting activities are but one facet of a broader cultural framework that includes sharing, kinship, spirituality, intergenerational learning, shared values, and a relationship with the land (Usher et al. 1995; Nuttall et al. 2005).

Equating Inuit interests to "harvesting" alone disavows the depth and breadth of the cultural values that are associated with this activity. The TUD is a static approach that does not adjust to the variability of factors related to the continued vitality of harvesting, such as wildlife population fluctuations and movements, global markets, seasonal and climatic variability, and changing harvesting patterns. A less prescriptive and more flexible approach that relates to other factors might better address broader issues involved with the vitality of harvesting and the range of issues related to it, such as political support for the harvesting economy, ensuring Inuit access to the land, and maintaining widespread ecological integrity.

On the other hand, a less prescriptive approach may also result in future governments making planning decisions that may not have Inuit interests in mind. The RPA is directed to develop a comprehensive land use plan for the entire region, but the division in jurisdictions between

LIL (NG jurisdiction) and LISA outside LIL (provincial jurisdiction) may overshadow the comprehensiveness of the plan if the certainty of the TUD is not used. As we will discuss in the next section, the political decision-making process for the development of the Nunatsiavut plan therefore also plays an important role in fostering or restraining the ability of groups to discuss, build consensus, and adopt broader or alternative options.

In early 2010, the draft plan was made public. The RPA held consultations in Nunatsiavut communities and in Upper Lake Melville and St John's, where large numbers of Nunatsiavut Inuit live. The focus of public concerns centred on the RPA's large area designation of the TUDs. There was further dissatisfaction voiced on the fact that Inuit communities were not directly involved in developing these TUDs. Because the communities could only respond to a draft, the discussions were less about whether a TUD was even appropriate and more on where the designations should be applied.

In consultations about the draft plan, beneficiaries and stakeholders were divided on whether the level of environmental protection afforded by the application of the TUD was necessary or too broad. Many Inuit beneficiaries and others felt that the level of protection was adequate, and some had suggestions for other areas to be protected, such as salmon and char rivers, migratory bird areas, and headwaters. Mining interests and some at the provincial Department of Mines and Energy felt that this use of the designation was too restrictive. Some Nunatsiavut government officials also felt that it was too restrictive, as the designation of many of the coastline Labrador Inuit lands as TUD would restrict the Inuit share of royalties from mining. Under the land claims agreement, the Nunatsiavut government gets a 25 per cent share of royalties from mines on Labrador Inuit lands, whereas it gets only 5 per cent of royalties on other settlement lands. The structure of the land claims agreement therefore pressures the Nunatsiavut government to subsidize itself by developing Inuit-owned lands. The RPA compiled the range of comments, and revised the draft plan.

As specified in the land claim agreement (INAC 2005, chapter 10), community residents and the Nunatsiavut and provincial governments will review and comment on the plan at various stages of the drafting process. The first formal consultation about the draft plan occurred in early 2010, and the RPA has compiled and incorporated many of the comments into the plan. It then sent the revised draft to both governments for their review. At this stage, the two governments have the authority to suggest changes to sections of the plan that pertain to lands under their own jurisdiction. A newly revised draft plan will then undergo a second round of community consultations under the guidance of a Commissioner, who will write a report for the RPA on recommended changes. After further revision, the two governments will have another opportunity to modify the plan as it relates to their jurisdictions before approving it. Once the plan has been finalized and approved by Nunatsiavut and the province, it is legally binding on both governments.

THE STRENGTH OF THE CO-MANAGEMENT PROCESS

In order to judge the effectiveness of Nunatsiavut land-use planning in promoting Inuit concerns and goals, it is important to understand planning within the larger context of Inuit-government relations in Labrador. Inuit were historically excluded from state land governance, but Aboriginal land claims negotiations and the global movement towards increased local participation have altered the situation considerably. Despite all drawbacks of the planning process, some Inuit feel that they have consented to a legitimate compromise: they have assumed a degree of authority over the expanse of their homeland and the hard-fought agreement of the provincial government that it will co-operate with them to manage this land.

The political dynamics between the Nunatsiavut and provincial governments and the RPA co-management body play an important role in determining whether Inuit goals and concerns will be addressed through planning. The RPA is attempting to develop a plan that prioritizes Inuit interests and is not guided by jurisdictional distinctions. All four members of the RPA (the two provincial appointees and the two Nunatsiavut appointees) are relatively independent of both governments (as they are not government employees), so they are not tied to policy restrictions or other governmental considerations. Their attempts to ignore jurisdictional boundaries will help to ensure that Inuit priorities are applied throughout the region, and not simply to the relatively small area covered by Labrador Inuit Lands. However, this goal may run into some problems later in the process because as the draft plan makes its way through the two governments for approval, both governments have the authority to suggest and implement changes to sections of the plan that pertain to lands under their own jurisdiction.

Despite all the limitations of the planning process in embracing and adapting itself to Inuit values, if the governments refuse to accept parts of the RPA's draft plan, then even the remnants or partial aspects of Inuit perspectives within the plan may be abandoned.

The prospect of the provincial government overruling the RPA is a real concern, and the RPA has discussed the issue on a number of occasions (RPA notes, May 2009). The province has a long history of ignoring Aboriginal rights and of promoting the exploitation of Labrador. However, it is also partly because of this history that many Labrador Inuit feel that land-use planning within the framework of a land claims agreement may be their best option to reclaim governance of Nunatsiavut. The contentious history of Inuit-state relations in Labrador will help to put that sentiment in context.

Inuit have experienced many years of outside interests laying claim to their lands and resources, often at the encouragement of the provincial government. In the late 1700s, the Newfoundland government supported Moravian missionaries in their efforts to contain Inuit on mission lands in northern Labrador because Inuit were threatening British commercial fishing interests to the south. The Crown agreed to give land grants of one hundred thousand acres to the Moravians around their missions in northern Labrador. These grants provided the Moravians with almost complete control of trade and other economic and social aspects of the north coast, a situation that lasted until the early 1900s.

Newfoundland interests have always viewed Labrador as a valuable fishing resource, but it was only in the early 1900s that this interest was turned inland towards the abundant mineral and hydroelectric resources. When the Newfoundland government began to realize the land's potential, it started more rigorously to assert its jurisdiction over Labrador, including the northern coastal region of the Labrador Inuit. Governmental authority gradually subsumed many Inuit customary laws and governance bodies, such as the Village Elders committees, through resource harvesting regulations and permitting requirements (Ames 1977; Usher 1982). Inuit were able to exert less and less control over their own land use and the land use of others, such as mineral exploration companies. In the 1950s, the provincial government granted vast swaths of land in Labrador to industrial companies for minimal returns, and maintained an open access policy for mineral exploration throughout the region.

On the north coast, Inuit felt the impact of this open access in the 1970s and again in the 1990s when exploration companies buzzed with excitement about uranium and then nickel and copper. Local people were startled by the ability of these companies to draw boundaries around land that families had used for generations, and to control access and activities on this land, despite a long history of Inuit use and assumed ownership of the land (Williamson 1996). This sense of apprehension was apparent in Labrador Inuit Association's (LIA) pamphlet, *Mineral Development in Northern Labrador*, published in 1996 during the midst of a claim staking rush. Inuit frustration about their obvious lack of power to influence decisions about land and resources fuelled their sense of urgency about finalizing a land claims settlement and establishing Inuit rights to management, use, and ownership (Andersen and Rowell 1993).

Many Inuit saw the land claims process as the only potential avenue for redress of the colonization of their lands and lives. The provincial government has staunchly denied any kind of special recognition for Aboriginal peoples in Newfoundland and Labrador. When the province joined Canada in 1949, all mention of governmental obligation towards Aboriginal peoples was omitted from the Terms of Union (Tanner et al. 1994). The federal and provincial governments were both very reluctant to assume any responsibility for Aboriginal issues, and the Labrador Inuit were for a long time denied the same legal status as other Inuit in Canada. When the federal government announced in 1973 that it would now negotiate outstanding comprehensive claims, many Inuit felt that this option was their best hope of gaining an adequate degree of reparation.

The provincial government, however, expressed very little interest in making many concessions during land claim negotiations with the Inuit until the Voisey's Bay nickel discovery in the mid-1990s created the political pressure to do so. Until this point, the government had refused to agree to Inuit ownership of any sizable land quantum, and was very reluctant to negotiate either the sharing of potential benefits with Inuit from future developments or the sharing of management roles with Inuit (Haysom 1992). However, unresolved Inuit claims to land and resources in the region impeded the proposed mine, which promised a much-needed economic boost for the province, and so the government finally agreed to fast-track land claims negotiations and to settle the issue of Inuit land rights. The ensuing land claim agreement removed the uncertainty caused by the existence of potentially extensive Inuit rights to the entire area by limiting and defining these rights to smaller and more specific regions and jurisdictions.[3]

From the first, land-use planning in Nunatsiavut was the result of compromise. Negotiations between the LIA and the provincial government over questions of land rights and ownership were difficult until both sides agreed that co-managing the land claims area might solve many of their outstanding concerns. Both sides conceded something of their position — the Labrador Inuit agreed to reduce their land quantum of Inuit-owned lands, and the province agreed to co-manage land-use planning for the entire region (Toby Andersen, personal communication 2008; B. Warren, personal communication 2008). The Inuit would therefore be able to influence the type and extent of human activities permitted in most of Nunatsiavut, but the province would retain ownership over the majority of the co-managed region. This compromise was difficult to sell internally within both the provincial government and the LIA. Provincial government officials at the administrative level had not historically supported land-use planning because politicians wished to maintain their discretionary control over land issues (B. Warren, personal communication 2008). Many Inuit were very unhappy with the small amount offered as Inuit-owned lands (15,799 square kilometres), and the LIA had to work hard to convince its Inuit members that the compromise was worthwhile.

One rationale for the compromise was that co-managed land-use planning could prove to be a useful tool in protecting the habitat of species that are of fundamental importance to Labrador Inuit, such as caribou. As LIA negotiators explained in 1993, the Inuit wanted a land claim agreement that allowed them "to maintain a way of life that respects the importance of hunting, trapping, fishing, and gathering in the modern world" (Andersen and Rowell 1993). Co-managed control over land-use activities for an entire region allows Inuit to address the issue of habitat protection more extensively than if they only managed their own portion. Wide-ranging species such as caribou, polar bear, and migratory birds occupy much larger territories than the current Labrador Inuit lands. In addition, land ownership under Canadian law does not, by itself, provide protection against incursions by the state or by mining companies who are guaranteed free entry for exploration under provincial mining laws. Co-managed land-use planning therefore offers Inuit much greater influence over habitat protection and other aspects of land management related to harvesting concerns (Andersen and Rowell 1993; Usher 1982). The combination of land ownership and land-use planning co-management in the final land claims agreement thus provided the Nunatsiavut government with multiple means to achieve their goals.[4]

The once-strained relationship between the Labrador Inuit and the provincial government has improved over recent years, although the co-management arrangement of the Nunatsiavut land-use planning process will help to illustrate the actual strength of this relationship. The first example of co-management between the Inuit and the provincial government – the Voisey's Bay Environmental Management Board – encountered many difficulties, due in large part to the negative attitude of provincial (and federal) bureaucrats towards Aboriginal rights.[5] Building on this experience, the RPA seems to be a vast improvement on this first body, and the future land-use planning decisions of the provincial and Nunatsiavut governments will reveal the degree to which co-management can work to promote Inuit interests in Labrador.

If the provincial government respects the co-management process and agrees to the full extent of the TUD in the RPA's draft plan, the planning process could be seen as a success for the incorporation of Inuit perspectives and interests (however partial) into land-use planning. If the Nunatsiavut and provincial governments instead assert that they each will separately manage lands under their own jurisdictions – LIL for Nunatsiavut, and LISA outside LIL for the province – then the goal of co-operative and comprehensive land-use planning for the entire region of Nunatsiavut will not have been met. Given the political pressure on both governments to fulfill their obligations as laid out in the Labrador Inuit Land Claims Agreement, it is doubtful that the land-use planning process would fail to produce some form of comprehensive plan. But, as one member of the RPA commented, the provincial government's general encouragement of "free-for-all" development has conflicted with the RPA's comprehensive planning approach during consultations, and threatens to derail the co-operative nature of the planning process for Nunatsiavut.

FUTURE PROSPECTS

The future success of land-use planning in maintaining Inuit priorities depends equally on political will as it does on the flexibility of the planning process. Although the approved plan will be legally binding on both governments, the ability of officials to enforce the plan and to follow its principles in making decisions will also determine the plan's success. Other mechanisms, such as the five-year review, the amendment process, and the development of future ten-year plans will offer further opportunities for improvement in the process, as this one plan will obviously not be the final planning product. The relationships developed through this drafting process will continue to evolve. The Inuit constituency's level of engagement with planning may increase, provincial bureaucrats' degree of understanding of Nunatsiavut issues (and of planning!) may improve, and more creative forms of planning may develop in the future.

Nonetheless, the potential drawbacks are many. The current and future politics involved in co-management can limit the potential for new and creative Inuit governance, and the structural biases of planning can constrain the possibilities of promoting Inuit perspectives. Levels of Inuit participation and involvement in Nunatsiavut governance, including the planning process, must be high if the Nunatsiavut government is to fully respond to the diverse Inuit constituency, as well as to hold the provincial government accountable for its land claims agreement obligations.

The new role in governance is also not without its complexities. Labrador Inuit are now involved as participants in the decision-making process, as beneficiaries of Inuit Impact and Benefit Agreements, and as constituents of a regional government that has fiscal obligations to support itself. The compromise involved in agreeing to co-managed land-use planning allows Labrador Inuit much more political power than they were afforded in the recent past, but it also draws them into assuming roles that, in the end, may pressure them into producing the same procedures and decisions of the provincial government.

The effectiveness of Nunatsiavut land-use planning in promoting Inuit goals is yet to be determined, and it will change as the planning context develops with time in Labrador. The fact that Inuit have a seat at the decision-making table means that they will be able to influence this process and to remodel the forms of land governance to better suit their lives. Through and beyond this process, Inuit have the opportunity to determine their own methods of Indigenous planning, designed and directed by Inuit, Inuit interests, and changing Inuit needs. Although this initial involvement in state land-use planning illustrates the reliance on the inherent structural and political limitations of the process, future Inuit participation may well encompass vastly different methods and techniques if it increasingly reflects the growing movement of Indigenous planning. Nunatsiavut land-use planning is an ongoing project in which Inuit have a central voice, and it holds the potential for innovative approaches.

ACKNOWLEDGEMENTS

The authors wish to express much appreciation to the RPA for allowing Andrea Procter access to their meetings, and to the RPA members, Robert Griffiths, Toby Andersen, Carl McLean, Doug Blake, Stan Oliver, Bob

Warren, Adrian Tanner, David Natcher, Jamie Skidmore, and Ted Jojola for their helpful comments and suggestions on earlier drafts of this chapter.

NOTES

1 The planner is required to be "a fellow or full member of the Canadian Institute of Planners" (INAC 2005, 10.4.2).
2 The Labrador Inuit agreement is similar in this respect to other land claims agreements, with one significant difference: although the federal government did not recognize Inuit ownership rights to marine areas, it did agree to define Inuit rights to commercial marine harvesting.
3 The provincial government also removed the Voisey's Bay area from the land selection process of the land claims negotiations altogether during this time. In exchange for Inuit rights and benefits as outlined in chapter 8 of the final agreement, the Voisey's Bay area was excluded from both LISA and LIL (B. Warren, personal communication 2009).
4 Other instruments under the final agreement that influence land governance include conditions established for specified material lands (see INAC 2005, chapter 4), nuclear substances (chapter 4), NG exploration standards requirements for LIL, NG environmental assessment legislation (chapter 11), water and ocean management (chapters 5 and 6), wildlife and plant management (chapter 12), fisheries management (chapter 12), access to LIL (chapter 4), archaeology (chapter 15), and self-government provisions (chapter 17), as well as the land-use planning regime in chapter 10.
5 Keith Chaulk sat on the Voisey's Bay Environmental Management Board on behalf of the Labrador Inuit Association from 2003–05.

REFERENCES

Ames, R. 1977. *Social, Economic, and Legal Problems of Hunting in Northern Labrador*. Prepared for the Labrador Inuit Association, Nain, Labrador.
Andersen, Toby. 2008. Personal communication. Happy Valley-Goose Bay, Labrador.
Andersen, Toby, and Judy Rowell. 1993. "Environmental Impacts for the Labrador Inuit of Canada's and Newfoundland's Land Claims Policies". In *Common Ground: Northern Peoples and the Environment*, edited by J. Jacobs and W. Montevecchi. Proceedings of a symposium held at Memorial University of Newfoundland, St John's, 25 October 1991. St John's: ISER.

Brice-Bennett, C., ed. 1977a. *Our Footprints Are Everywhere: Inuit Land Use and Occupancy in Labrador*. Nain: Labrador Inuit Association.
– 1977b. "Land Use in the Nain and Hopedale Regions." In *Our Footprints Are Everywhere: Inuit Land Use and Occupancy in Labrador*, edited by C. Brice-Bennett. Nain: Labrador Inuit Association.
– 1994. "The Redistribution of the Northern Labrador Inuit Population: A Strategy for Integration and Formula for Conflict." *Zeitschrift fur Kanada-Studien*. N .2, Band 26:95–106.
Cosgrove, Laurie, and Beverley Kliger. 1997. "Planning with a Difference: A Reflection on Planning and Decision Making with Indigenous People in Broome, Western Australia." *Urban Policy and Research* 15 (3):211–17.
Haysom, V. 1992. "The Struggle for Recognition: Labrador Inuit Negotiations for Land Rights and Self-Government." *Études Inuit Studies* 16 (1–2):179–97.
Howitt, Richard, and Sandra Suchet-Pearson. 2006. "Rethinking the Building Blocks: Ontological Pluralism and the Idea of 'Management'." *Geografiska Annaler* 88B (3):323–35.
INAC (Indian and Northern Affairs Canada). 2005. *Labrador Inuit Land Claims Agreement*. Ottawa: INAC.
Labrador Inuit Association (LIA). 1996. *Mineral Development in Northern Labrador*. Pamphlet. Nain: LIA.
Lane, Marcus. 1997. "Aboriginal Participation in Environmental Planning." *Australian Geographical Studies* 35 (3):308–23.
Mulrennan, M., and C. Scott. 2001. "Aboriginal Rights and Interests in Canadian Northern Seas." In *Aboriginal Autonomy and Development in Northern Quebec and Labrador*, edited by C. Scott, 78–97. Vancouver: University of British Columbia Press.
Nadasdy, P. 2003. *Hunters and Bureaucrats: Power, Knowledge, and Aboriginal-State Relations in Southwest Yukon*. Vancouver: UBC Press.
Nuttall, M., F. Berkes, B. Forbes, G. Kofinas, T. Vlassova, and G. Wenzel. 2005. "Hunting, Herding, Fishing, and Gathering: Indigenous Peoples and Renewable Resource Use in the Arctic." In *Arctic Climate Impact Assessment*, 649–90. Cambridge: University of Cambridge Press.
Porter, L. 2007. "Producing Forests: A Colonial Geneaology of Environmental Planning in Victoria, Australia." *Journal of Planning Education and Research* 26:466–77.
Procter, Andrea. 2012. "Nunatsiavut Land Claims and the Politics of Inuit Wildlife Harvesting." In *Settlement, Subsistence, and Change among the Nunatsiavummiut (Labrador Inuit)*, edited by D. Natcher, L. Felt, and A. Procter, 253–80. Winnipeg: University of Manitoba Press.

Regional Planning Authority. 2009. Draft Regional Land Use Plan for the Labrador Inuit Settlement Area. December. St John's and Happy Valley-Goose Bay: RPA.

– 2010. Draft Regional Land Use Plan for the Labrador Inuit Settlement Area. January. St John's and Happy Valley-Goose Bay: RPA.

Regional Planning Authority notes. 2008. A. Procter, meeting observer. April.

– 2009. A. Procter, meeting observer. May.

– 2009. A. Procter, meeting observer. September.

– 2010. Public consultation in St John's. A. Procter, meeting observer. 24 February.

Scott, J.C. 1998. *Seeing Like a State: How Certain Schemes to Improve the Human Condition Have Failed*. New Haven: Yale University Press.

Tanner, Adrian, John C. Kennedy, Susan McCorquodale, and Gordon Inglis. 1994. *Aboriginal Peoples and Governance in Newfoundland and Labrador*. A Report for the Governance Project, Royal Commission on Aboriginal Peoples. St John's.

Usher, P. 1982. *Renewable Resources in the Future of Northern Labrador*. A report to the Labrador Inuit Association. Nain, Labrador.

Usher, P., M. Baikie, D. Demmer, D. Nakashima, M. Stevenson, and M. Stiles. 1995. *Communicating about Contaminants in Country Food: The Experience in Aboriginal Communities*. Ottawa: Inuit Tapirisat Kanatami.

Warren, B. 2008; 2009. Personal communication. Happy Valley-Goose Bay, Labrador.

Williamson, T. 1996. *Seeing the Land is Seeing Ourselves: Labrador Inuit Association Issues Scoping Report*. Prepared for the Labrador Inuit Association. Nain, Labrador.

– 1997. *Sina to Sikujâluk: Our Footprint. Mapping Inuit Environmental Knowledge in the Nain District of Northern Labrador*. Prepared for the Labrador Inuit Association. Nain, Labrador.

PART FOUR

Conclusion

20

Indigenous Planning: Towards A Seven Generations Model

TED JOJOLA

There is very little written about the ethical, methodological, and epistemological approaches to community design and planning by Indigenous communities. Historically, the mainstream professions have overlooked these in favour of Euro-Western practices. This concluding chapter will explore the manner in which Indigenous populations have used a seven generations model to plan for meaningful community development.

A SEVEN GENERATIONS MODEL

Within an individual's lifetime, it is not unusual that an extended family consists not only of oneself, but those that are three generations before and three generations after. This is the intergenerational family — great-grandparents, grandparents, parents, "you", children, grandchildren, and great-grandchildren. Fundamentally, the middle generation – you – represents the centre point of a bridge that spans the past and the future. The knowledge of the past informs the present and, together, it builds a vision towards the future. This is known as the seven generations model.

Among Indigenous communities, the life experience of getting to know someone in every generation is not unusual. Rather, it is a given. As lives play out, these intergenerational relationships give credence to the collective notion that those yet unborn will inherit that which has already been gained and valued. This right of inheritance is invested in land and culture.

There existed a time when Indigenous communities were intact and whole. They had a distinct and profound sense of being and a philosophy that articulated the relationships of the physical and spiritual world (Ortiz 1969). As generations of people have successively lived over time in the same place, they have evolved unique worldviews.

The worldview is an embodiment of a balanced relationship between humankind and the natural world. Over time, each succeeding generation assumes the values and practices that are necessary to sustain them. Values, such as the right-of-inheritance and collective responsibility, serve to lay the foundation for the transfer of meanings and cultural practices. It is everybody's responsibility to make sure that those generations that preceded or follow him or her continue to maintain the community's worldview. This process is at the heart of sustainability.

Civilizations from the great American Southwest are a testament to how sustained collective human interaction moulded a landscape. The approaches embodied natural science and philosophy. The famous settlement of Pueblo Bonito in north-central New Mexico is an example. The Anasazi who initiated its construction never expected to live through its completion. Rather, their expectation was that each succeeding generation would continue and complete the design in accordance to a set of founding beliefs. The major phases of its construction were from AD 1120–1250 (Fagan 2005). Assuming that the average generation was around nineteen years, this period roughly corresponds to 130 years, or seven generations.

It was the first generation that set the blueprint in motion. The successive generations continued to refine its design. Its architecture embodies the spiritual and cultural meanings of their worldview. These were replete with a collective vision that was more profound than any individual's design. The geometry, technology, and symbolism represented the principal elements of a cultural toolbox. It represented a high order of science whose understandings are still being uncovered (Sofaer 1997).

The beauty of the process is that the seven phases of its construction endured time and place. Despite the fact that the individuals who initiated it did not live to see its completion, the ensuing generations never strayed from the vision. Over time, later generations modified the technologies and building methods leading to its completion. Despite the fact that it took seven generations to construct, it did not become a place that resembled a body of disparate parts and pieces. In the end it became a unified and coherent whole.

Such an understanding was the foundation for the planning and development of Indigenous communities before colonialism. At the time of contact, Europeans found vibrant Indigenous societies that sustained complex, if not transformative, civilizations. Their societies included philosophers, priests, ecologists, scientists, engineers, builders, artisans, architects, and planners. The worst aspect of colonialism was that Indigenous knowledge was devalued or destroyed in the name of conquest and domination.

An example of this history resides in the prefecture of Puebla, a National Heritage site and Mexico's third largest city. On its outskirts are the remnants of a remarkable Aztec community called Cholula. Today, it is the site of an unstated sacred cultural landscape. Originally a centre of spiritualism, it was second in importance to Tenochtitlan, the Aztec capital of Mexico City. Cholula's historic centre is a twenty-block area (approximately five square kilometres). Today, this area contains 156 Catholic churches!

Why are there so many churches? It was Spanish conquistador Hernán Cortés who was the first European to traverse upon this sacred place. It was the second largest Aztec city in the region and was reported to have 365 temples, each one built in homage to a deity associated with each day of the year. In 1519, Cortés's army massacred the people there and took control. Unfettered, under orders from Cortés, the Spanish colonialists systematically began replacing each Aztec temple with a Catholic church. The most famous of these is the Catholic cathedral of Iglesia de Nuestra Señora de los Remedios (Church of Our Lady of Remedies). Completed in 1592, it sits atop the largest pyramid by volume ever constructed in the world. Its name in the Nahuatl language, *Tlachihualtepetl,* means "artificial mountain" (McCafferty 2001).

Cholula is only one of numerous instances where Indigenous civilizations have been lost. Today, we can imagine only what knowledge was lost and forever erased. As for others, like those southwestern Pueblo communities of Walpi, Taos, and Acoma, they have endured in the same places for millennia. They survived the colonial onslaught and have retained a large share of their cultures and traditions. Today, they continue to be challenged by outside imposition and modernization. If they are to survive, society needs to reconsider the value of their cultural knowledge. It is a lesson that should not be lost to others.

WESTERNIZATION

By and large, Westernization undermined and undercut the seven generations model. The linkages that bonded the generations were disrupted though Euro-Western practices intended to forcibly remove Indigenous communities from their territories, culture, and children.

The most prevalent feature of US federal Indian policy was taking over the ownership and control of traditional Indigenous homelands. During America's founding, Indian policy was predicated on securing hegemony over "unsettled" lands and, as a corollary, the so-called "primitive" people that inhabited them. In the US, Jeffersonian idealism, the General Allotment Act (Dawes Act), and the Public Land Survey System represented strategies aimed at parceling lands and dispossessing Native people from their homelands (Jojola and Imeokparia n.d.).

American society has always exhibited the unbridled tenacity to appropriate and harness everything and anything in the pursuit of growth, oftentimes for its own sake. This has too often been done without consideration to the impacts of the land and the people. In the context of Western expansion, Indian people were considered "impediments" to this goal. As a result, many were exterminated (or nearly so), or removed elsewhere and confined to areas that were so foreign to them that they could barely eke out their subsistence.

This is despite the fact that tribal communities at the turn of the nineteenth century were already situated in the so-called American frontier. That frontier was not a barren wilderness. On the contrary, tribes had already built much of the infrastructure which explorers and settlers appropriated to develop their roadways, farmsteads, and townships.

As an example, the southeastern Cherokee had already built extensive Overhill towns at the time of Western contact. These were organized around a main central township plaza that was bounded by council houses — one octagonal for winter and one rectangular for summer. This town was considered the "mother town," or capital of the territory. Other towns formed a radial pattern and interconnected their territories into an economic, political, social, and cultural region. As contact with outsiders ensued, the Cherokees enlisted groups like the Protestant Moravians to educate their youth so as to compete with the advancing white culture (Champagne 1992).

Perhaps because of such success, the Cherokee posed a major threat to the unmitigated advance of Western civilization. The Indian Removal Act of 1830 was the capstone of the Manifest Destiny policy intended to remove tribes inhabiting lands east of the Mississippi to so-called unsettled Indian territories in Oklahoma. In 1829, a Cherokee writer lamented, "We are abused people," as their townships, located along the Appalachians, bore the full brunt of thousands of gold miners intent on occupying their territories.[1] Despite the fact that the Cherokee people had modelled themselves after American democratic ideals and established a high standing as a literate, civilized society, they were removed by military force during the infamous 1838 Trail of Tears.

This onslaught was repeated in other regions, including the upper-Midwest, Western Pacific, and Alaska. In effect, through removal or acts of genocide, any semblance of traditional habitations were erased. Their plight became a case of arrested development. That is to say, these tribes lost the ability to develop and improve their plight. As a last desperate attempt to save their civilizations, many were forced to take their culture underground. In this manner, their cultures were unable to advance their civilizations further.

Mainstream society has attempted to temper such egregious acts through the "melting pot" theory. This is an attempt to paint the American settlement experience as a necessary extension of progress and urbanization (Turner 1962). Under this theory, the movement of populations from rural areas to urban areas resulted in the blending of cultures, with each one adding their own distinctive flavour or color to the brew. The unspoken aspect of that process, however, is that such mixing eventually ends up as an undistinguishable muddle. This type of mixing is antithetical for Indigenous people. Rather, the goal of the seven generations model is to maintain and build upon their cultural distinctions. This is the basis of its strength, not weakness.

It was seen as necessary, therefore, to undermine cultural identity. The notion of "Indian" was equated to a primitive mode of existence. Anthropological theories made little of how Native people successfully adapted and integrated new ideas and concepts into their culture so as to adapt and survive. Rather, they promulgated the concept that tribes could be differentiated into two categories — those that were "traditional" and those that were "modern." Those that ostensibly held onto cultural traditions and resisted attempts to assimilate them were considered backwards and subjected to punitive policies. Those who accepted Westernization were considered progressive and enticed with rewards. Such distinctions influenced Indian policies.

A classic case is found in the Hopi Tribal Nation of Arizona. In 1904, two opposing factions broke away from the historic village of Oraibi and established two newer settlements. Bacavi became the domain of the "Friendlies," or progressives, and Hotevilla became the domain of the "Hostiles," or traditional faction (Whiteley 1988). Bacavi was characterized as supporting the education of their children and "civilized ways."

Hotevilla, on the other hand, was characterized as opposed to education and the "white men's ways." A state highway separates the villages and the only "neutral" ground lay midway between them. This is the Hotevilla-Bacavi school (Titiev 1992).

As a consequence of this split, individuals were given a clear choice as to which ideology to pursue. Over time, the respective habitations became a reflection of these choices with individuals subsuming a lifestyle adapted to one or the other. Bacavi residents became more integrated into the larger surrounding economy. Their leaders accepted land allotments that the Indian Superintendent assigned to them. In time, their community began to embrace all aspects of modernization, including indoor plumbing, phone lines, and electricity. It became known as a "commoner village," shedding many traditional religious practices.

In contrast, Hotevilla residents became more place-centred and resisted the wage-economy lifestyle. They revived traditional agricultural practices by making land assignments according to traditional clanships. Being traditional, however, did not necessarily mean that Hotevilla did not embrace some facets of modern amenities. Although they prohibited the construction of electric lines and pipes for a domestic water system, they did adapt newer self-reliant technologies like solar panels. These were deployed for refrigeration and powering up small appliances. This adaptation was already in evidence in the early 80s, long before they "caught fire" among green conservationists.

Among traditionalists like the Hotevilla, individuality becomes subsumed by the embodiment of the collective. The bases of these values are invested in land, but not as an individual property right. Instead, valuation is seen in the longer-term with the operative principle being that of land tenure. As families occupy and sustain the land over successive generations, the notion of property becomes one of inheritance. By being born in a context, individuals see this inheritance as a birthright. The community is mobilized so as to make certain that the collective upholds individual activities. And unlike the mainstream society, the acquisition and retention of an inheritance becomes a necessary aspect of sustaining community.

Of course, such practices overlay even deeper divisions that entail governance. How leadership manages land and distributes it for the good of the people is how they control growth. Such actions, over a long and sustained period, translate into distinctive patterns of settlement and development. This aspect has eluded academics in their discussions of power relationships. Concepts such as "Indigeneity" have become a beleaguered post-colonial battleground of identity politics in the face to transnationalism (Roach and Egan 2008). The manifestation of place as an outcome of local power and control is not acknowledged.

Identity politics is another important aspect of maintaining a sense of place. Too often, however, identity politics pits membership against birthright. The use of racial criterion, such as blood quantum, is used to determine tribal membership. Because of the infusion of new sources of wealth and prosperity, notably from Indian gaming, the concept of blood quantum has become even more divisive. Given the historic propensity of Native people to marry outside of their tribe, either among other tribes or non-Indians, it will probably only be a matter of time before few, if any, people can claim "full-blood" lineage.[2]

Along with tribal blood quantum, Native language proficiency and participation in "traditions" is no longer being used as a measure of "belonging." Children who meet the membership criteria of blood, but are detached from their traditional culture, are accepted. On the other hand, mixed-blood children whose parents grow up traditionally are denied tribal membership because of their lack of blood quantum. That situation undermines their right of inheritance.

In order to sustain community, it is necessary to maintain continuity throughout the seven generations. And although language and participation in traditional activities may serve as a surrogate in measuring tribal identity, it fails to account for how their feeling of belonging contributes to meaningful participation. The role of parenting is fundamental to that process. The key is preparing children to assume their positions as productive and knowledgeable adults, irrespective of blood quantum.

The earliest purveyors of assimilation understood these connections and developed practices to destroy them. Allotment land policies implemented blood quantum as a way to assign lands in a manner that would eventually discriminate against mixed-blood unions. They also used education to disempower tribal communities through the practice to removing children from their parents; "kill the Indian, and save the child" became the unequivocal battle cry of the Indian boarding school system.

Construction of Indian boarding schools began as early as the 1860s and continued well into the 1930s. They purposely removed school-age children to distant places where they were boarded for the duration of their education. They were seldom permitted to return for fear that they would escape and revert to their "uneducated" ways. When the Bureau of Indian Affairs changed its policies in the thirties to allow Indian day schools to be built alongside villages and townships, it was for the purpose of mitigating the effects of dislocation. Unfortunately, these day schools rarely went beyond the fourth or sixth grade, again requiring children to seek schooling away from their communities.

In the 1950s, Indian children were subjected to Indian relocation and many were forced to move with their parents to urban centres. Those that remained behind were subjected to the public school system and bussed to adjacent schools outside of their reservations. President Johnson's War on Poverty created Head Start programs on Indian lands. It was not until the onset of the Indian Self Determination Act in the seventies, though, that tribal governments were given the opportunity to contract their own educational programs and schools. Additionally, there were private and parochial schools. Most recently, charter schools have been instituted under the institutional reform agendas of No Child Left Behind.

In an editorial about one typical Pueblo Indian family's experience, the cumulative effect of such policies over the generations was detailed. It began with the grandparents, both of whom had no formal education. Their children all completed their schooling at the Indian boarding school. After one of them became a parent, the eldest grandson went to parochial school and the youngest grandson went to public school. Eventually, a great-grandson ended up attending a private school (Jojola 1993). The lack of continuity has not afforded them a way to build consensus on the value of education.

The value of education affects more than cultural identity. It also contributes in significant ways to the evolution of physical form. For example, the construction of boarding schools planted the physical seeds that led to the emergence of modern proto-towns within reservations. Its physical plant might have been the first place to get electrification and water for sanitation. Quarters of the teachers and administrators became sited along grid pattern roadways. Other complexes, like Indian health clinics, were constructed nearby. As Native people relocated adjacent to such facilities they created new settlements influenced along these same patterns.

With the advent of Indian self determination, tribal governments were able to contract services and construct their own buildings and housing. New sources of funds, like casino gaming, allowed them to design new schools and plan new settlements. Some communities were successful in using these new initiatives to integrate their own cultural and traditional designs. Schools that were done in this manner became particularly meaningful for them. There was further evidence that the incorporation of cultural elements and spaces became important factors in Native student success (Claflen n.d.).

By and large, however, most schools are still not readily accessible to the communities they serve. This has created social distance between the institution and the community (Jojola and Lee 2011). The role and impact of schooling in supporting the intergenerational family continues to be downplayed. Instead, measures of success continue to be based on Western measures of attainment, not on community values.

PLANNING FOR SEVEN GENERATIONS – RECLAIMING THE PARADIGM

Today many Indigenous communities are no longer whole, but are instead comprised of fragments made from pieces and parts of their worldview. They have been sliced and diced, so to speak, due to the external imposition of changes, whether originating from cultural genocide or benevolence.

Instead, communities are faced with pieces – snippets of understanding as they have survived in the language and meaning retained by Elders, women, clan leaders, and medicine people. In short, Indigenous communities have lost, or are losing, their ability to use elements of their philosophies and operationalize them in a manner that affirms their holistic practices. They need to become clear about the meaning and significance of what they do and why they do it – the worldview. This leads to an important tenet of Indigenous planning: *Process must be informed by the Indigenous worldview.* The fact of the matter is that community and culture are intrinsic. In the words of a student, "Culture is not a fad, it is a way of life!"[3]

An Elder from an Alaskan earth lodge tradition related it in another way. He said, "You know, I would never have guessed that in my lifetime I would see our culture turned upside-down." "What do you mean?" I prodded. "Well, when I was a young child, our people used to live below the ground. We had earth lodges. We used to bury our people above ground on the top of scaffolds. Today, it's the exact opposite. We build our new houses on scaffolds above ground and now we bury our people below."[4]

This is a narrative about how the community's worldview has been radically altered. Due to Euro-Western incursions, many essential connections have been regulated out of existence. Cultural scholarship is predicated upon experiential learning, social engagement, and adherence to traditional customs. Such knowledge is passed onto other generations. It is how cultural relationships have solidified over time.

This leads to the second tenet of Indigenous planning: *Indigenous voices need no translation*. Such cultural lessons can only be understood from the experiential perspective. And, too often, unwitting outsiders – which many planners are – make the wrong judgments by imposing their own cultural values on others.

A conversation with a young Inupiat (Alaskan) child over the topic for a science class project serves to illuminate this dilemma.[5] As I struggled to tie a relevant topic for a science fair project into his culture, I suggested, "Why don't you count the number of people in your village?" "Naw," he said, "that's boring." "Ok," I prompted, "what else can you count? [Silence] ... what about dogs?" "Dogs?" he said. "Yeah, dogs," I mused. "Well," he said, "did you know we can shoot and kill any dog that is running around loose?" He immediately fixated on the look of astonishment on my face. "You're kidding me, right?" I exclaimed, "because where I come from dogs are pets." "Here, dogs earn their keep," he retorted. "They're working animals. They're aggressive and they can chew you up if they're on the loose. So we shoot them."

The goal of any planning conversation must be the transfer of knowledge. As seen in the above dialogue, it is the only way to expose misassumptions about a community. Yet is appears that very few meaningful dialogues occur that bridge needs and service integration. Sharing information and building collaborative ways of engagement are central to a seven generations model.

Today, many have forgotten how to talk to one another and build consensus – not the simple-majority type, but an all-or-nothing style of consensus. Such consensus is based on cultural protocol and elocution. Oratory as practice among leaders required time in order to synthesize a resolution. It once dominated the governance process (Jojola 1998). The lack of meaningful dialogue has hampered the ability of tribal governance to think past their immediate deadlines. Due to the imposition of countless federal programs and projects, Indigenous communities have been in a reactive mode rather than a proactive one.

This state of affairs has been described as "attemptive planning."[6] This is characterized by development within tribal lands that is both discontinuous and disconnected. It is the result of community development that reflects incremental and reactive planning, which, over time, creates a settlement where the parts of the community are disparate from one another. They neither add up to a meaningful whole nor create a sense of place.

An example of this disconnect is housing. How many generations of dealing with US federal Housing and Urban Development (HUD) will it take to get it right (Jojola 1976)? Traditionally, no one in a community was homeless. Indeed, vernacular solutions were infinitely more adapted to the environment and the provision of housing was often borne by the collective with little or no cost for the individual.

A planner in the Oneida Nation of Wisconsin learned this in an unexpected way. As housing manager, she met with Elders individually to prepare them for a replacement program intended to provide new housing. In the meeting, she explained at length the benefits of living in a modern house. An Elder responded, "Well, it certainly sounds wonderful and all … but, you know what? If I move into that new house I will die!" Dumfounded, she replied, "I don't understand, this house is supposed to make your life easier." "But that's the point," the Elder retorted. "Every morning, I look forward to waking up in a chilly house. I go outside to chop wood for the stove, bring water into the house and warm it up. When these chores are done, I know I have done something. My blood is circulating and this keeps me alive. What am I going to do when I move into this modern house? I won't have anything to look forward to!"[7]

The lesson implied in this encounter is that Indigenous communities are not a blank slate. Individuals already carry the weight of their own education as lived through experience. That revelation underscores a fundamental tenet of Indigenous planning: *The essence of Indigenous scholarship is Native self.*

By giving voice, people are poised to take their rightful role as enablers of their own community. It challenged her to rethink the solution. The Elder passed a valuable lesson about a purposeful life onto the planner. It challenged a basic assumption that simply because something was "new," it was better.

A Seneca scholar, born on the Cattaraugus reservation in New York, expressed the same situation in another way.[8] She was an adolescent in 1964, the year that the Kinzua Dam inundated two-thirds of their bottomland residences. The places that many Senecas intimately knew were erased and their traditional homes razed. They were relocated into suburban-style HUD housing developments. In a short period, these new places erupted in social pathologies where families were dislocated, Elders and children became isolated from one another, and new economic pressures forced the households to seek a more dependent lifestyle.

In her words, "We never knew what it was to be poor until people were moved into these houses."

This event transformed them. It undercut their culture by taking them away from a subsistence-based economy towards dependency. This new housing made them strangers in their own lands. In such instances, societies begin to lose their way. The sum of its parts does not add up to the whole. It is the worst outcome for community.

That revelation hit one young single mother of three especially hard. After doing some critical analysis on community development for her tribe, in a moment of exasperation she exclaimed, "I suddenly realized that my community is a living hell."[9] And what she described was a tribe that was barely holding onto the thread of its culture, language, and traditions. Perhaps they were successful at venture capitalism but she was, first and foremost, lamenting the loss of community.

THE CHALLENGE

Indigenous design and planning is informed by an emerging paradigm that uses a culturally responsive and value-based approach to community development. Adherence to values such as stewardship and land tenure have tempered the immediacy of exploitative practices and reactionary planning. Leadership balances the immediacy of action (short-term) with a comprehensive vision of the future (long-term).

As tribal nations began to evolve their own civil authority after nationhood, the imposition of land-use planning, zoning control, and the engagement of rational planning approaches has replaced traditional ways of managing land. The role of collective governance over land, its ecological principles, and the cultural meaning of its landscape are diminished.

One major challenge is to reclaim practices that are more suited to cultural practices and sustainability. This sentiment was expressed in a quote from a Northwest tribal planner. In a moment of exasperation he proclaimed, "What we need is a value-based approach to comprehensive planning" (Jojola forthcoming). With this, he began to discuss how tribal governments were eroding their sovereign rights for short-term economic gain. This included a practice in the tribe's business management that penalized community members for participating in cultural practices during the work week.

Another challenge is to make certain that education is not simply a ticket to economic mobility. The goal of education is to advance an individual towards an occupation that will provide the economic means for them to move and work elsewhere. In mainstream American society, identity is principally attuned to property and ownership. An individual becomes the sum embodiment of saleable goods. When an individual grows discontent, he or she is ready to move elsewhere. In a manner of speaking, they become "economic nomads." Unfortunately, for many Indigenous communities it is beginning to work exactly the same way.

As a consequence, many communities are bleeding their children to urban centres. Demographics show conclusively that young populations between the ages of eighteen to twenty-four migrate away from their homes to nondescript urban centres for employment and education. They leave behind the homelands that once provided for what social scientists describe as a life-to-death existence (Redfield 1969). Others simply succumb to the pathologies of urban life (Carpio 2011; Robbins 2011).

Sadly, such social pathologies bring additional costs to the community. Young people are faced with becoming strangers in their own community. Because the community is ill prepared to develop and support them, they force young people to choose between facing a dismal life at home or leaving for better educational or economic opportunities. Once they leave, it is difficult to reintegrate them back into the cultural fold.

Another challenge attends to leadership styles. Although assimilative policies may no longer be overt, leaders still continue to force decisions that do not have the benefit of a collective understanding. The lack of attendance to the past in favour of only the present results in a planning future that is short sighted.

A way to break this cycle is to revalue education. Although learning comes to the individual, it is tempered within the collective. Indigenous communities draw on the seven generations model to assure that the transfer of knowledge is sustained over successive generations. They become shared moments over time. They are purposeful.

Indigenous communities continue to face other challenges in reconstructing their sense of completeness. Many generations have ensued since colonial practices began to infringe upon Indigenous practices, culture, and identity. Among many Indigenous communities, the traditional worldviews that they once held have become lost, in others fragmented, and in others secularized.

Indigenous people have tenaciously held onto one basic responsibility – that it is their collective right to assert themselves as stewards of their territories. For as long as they are able to sustain themselves, it will allow them to pursue a seven generations planning model. The ability of the collective society to bring clarity and cohesion to its planning process can only be attained through the timeless interactions of its succeeding generations.

The stakes are high. A Pueblo parent best summed it up:

> The day might come when everything is so contaminated with the air, the water, the land, that they'll come to the Pueblo and tell us, "You know what? You guys – sorry to tell you this – but your land is condemned ..."
>
> And so my question is, where do we all go – a group of three thousand of us – to go live where we can still live, and we know who our neighbour is, and we know who lives behind us, in front of us, or in back of us? ... We'll have no idea about language, songs, dances, culture, nothing. It's just erased.
>
> I want our children to be totally reaching their potential but also hanging onto who they are because I think that's important; not only for our survival but I think that it's the survival of the whole world.[10]

The only antidote for dysfunctional community development is inter-generational participation. It represents the biggest challenge that faces Indigenous communities today. And like all living organisms that inhabit Mother Earth, these are both the same and, in the same breath, different. Thus, each community is invested in determining what it values and what it is worth to its community — and there is no one single solution for all.

The seven generations model must dominate.

NOTES

1 Excerpt from the *Cherokee Phoenix*, the first Native American newspaper in the US.
2 These patterns have been particularly evident beginning with findings on American Indians and Alaska Natives (AI/AN) in the 2000 and 2010 US Census. The trends indicate a reduction in fertility, an increase in individuals identifying their race as "AI/AN in combination," and a larger percentage of AI/ANs residing outside Indian reservation lands.

3 The point was highlighted during the Master of Community & Regional Planning thesis defence of Rebecca Rae, Jicarilla Apache, University of New Mexico, 2009.

4 This conversation occurred in 1989 during a visit to Unalakleet, Alaska.

5 Ibid.

6 A planning student, Cheyenne Ringlero, who used it to describe the type of development that was found in Indian reservations surrounding the Phoenix, Arizona region, coined this term.

7 This excerpt is taken from a report on the findings from eight tribal regional summits, done by the author for the National Congress of American Indians (forthcoming).

8 Conversation with Tassy Parker, RN, PHD, Associate Professor of Family & Community Medicine and Nursing, University of New Mexico.

9 Identity is withheld. The individual was a graduate student at Arizona State University in 2010 when this comment was made.

10 This quote is excerpted from a study on Indian Education. See Jojola and Lee 2011.

REFERENCES

Carpio, Myla Vicenti. 2011. *Indigenous Albuquerque*. Texas Tech University Press.

Champaign, Duane. 1992. *Constitutional Governments Among the Cherokee, the Choctaw, the Chickasaw, and the Creek*. Stanford: Stanford University Press.

Claflen, G.L.J. (n.d.). *The Navajos as a Developing Nation: Seeking an Authentic Architecture for Rural Cultural Landscape*. Unpublished manuscript.

Jojola, Theodore. 1976. *Memoirs of an American Indian House: The Impact of a Cross-National Housing Program on Two Reservations*. Masters Thesis in city planning. Massachusetts Institute of Technology. Limited book publication funded by the Laboratory for Architecture & Planning, MIT, and the Atherton Trust.

– 1993. "Indian Elders Mix Signals on Education." *Albuquerque Journal*, Editorial.

– 1998. "Indigenous Planning: Clans, Intertribal Confederations and the History of the All Indian Pueblo Council" in *Making the Invisible: Insurgent Planning Histories*, edited by Leonie Sandercock. University of California Press.

– Forthcoming. *Planning in Indian Country: Regional Conversations: Report of Findings for 8 Regional Tribal Summits*, 2007–09. National Congress of American Indians.

Jojola, Theodore, and Tiffany Lee. 2011. *Indian Education in New Mexico, 2025*. NM Public Education Department, Indian Education Division, Report of Findings.

Jojola, Theodore, and Timothy Imeokparia. Forthcoming. "Fitting a Square Peg in a Round Hole: The History of Tribal Land-Use Planning in the United States" in *World of Indigenous North America*, edited by Robert Warrior. New York: Routledge.

Fagan, Brian. 2005. *Chaco Canyon*. New York: New York University Press.

McCafferty, Geoffrey G. 2001. "Mountain of Heaven, Mountain of Earth: The Great Pyramid of Cholula as Sacred Landscape" in *Landscape and Power in Ancient Mesoamerica*, by R. Koontz, K. Reese-Taylor, and A. Headrick, 244–70. Boulder: Westview Press.

Ortiz, Alfonso. 1969. *The Tewa World : Space, Time, Being, and Becoming in a Pueblo Society*. University of Chicago Press.

Redfield, Robert. 1956. *The Little Community, and Peasant Society and Culture*. University of Chicago Press.

Roach, David, and Andrea Egan. 2008. "The Equivocal Definition of Indigeniety and Ambivalent Government Policy toward Self-Determination in New Zealand's Health and Foreign Policy Apparatus." *Junctures* 11 (December):21–41.

Robbins, Catherine. 2011. *All Indians Do Not Live in Teepees (or Casinos)*. Winnipeg: Bison Books.

Sofaer, Anna, 1997. "The Primary Architecture of the Chacoan Culture: A Cosmological Expression" in *Anasazi Architecture and American Design*, 88–132. Albuquerque: University of New Mexico Press.

Turner, Frederick Jackson, c. 1962. *The Frontier in American History*. New York: Holt, Rinehart & Winston.

Titiev, Mischa. 1992. *Old Oraibi : A Study Of The Hopi Indians Of Third Mesa*. Albuquerque: University of New Mexico Press.

Whitely, Peter. 1988. *Bacavi: Journey to Reed Springs*. Northland Press: Flagstaff.

Contributors

ROBERT ADKINS has worked as a community and economic development consultant for ten years. He spent twenty-five years in the Pacific Northwest wood products industry, including ten years operating his own company. He has MAS in community and regional planning, and public administration from the University of Oregon.

CHRIS ANDERSEN, a Métis from Prince Albert, Saskatchewan, holds a PhD in sociology from the University of Alberta. He is an associate professor in the Faculty of Native Studies, and is currently director of the Rupertsland Centre for Métis Research at the University of Alberta.

GIOVANNI ATTILI is a researcher at the University of Rome La Sapienza. He is the 2005 recipient of the G. Ferraro Award for best urban planning PhD thesis in Italy. His research attention is focused on the use of images and multimedia as catalyst of social interaction in urban planning processes (www.mongrel-stories.com).

SHAUN AWATERE (Ngāti Porou) is a resource economist for Landcare Research in Hamilton, New Zealand. He has been working to improve the incorporation of Mātauranga Māori (Māori knowledge) into local government planning by developing the systems and processes that will enable Māori values to be integrated into urban design and development.

YALE BELANGER is an associate professor of Native American studies at the University of Lethbridge. He is affiliated with the Alberta Homelessness Research Consortium and the Canadian Homelessness Research

Network. He is an editorial board member for the Australian Housing and Urban Research Institute.

KEITH CHAULK is Inuit from Nunatsiavut, Labrador. He received his BSc in biology from Dalhousie University, MSc in biology from Acadia University, and PhD in cognitive and behavioural ecology from Memorial University. He is director of the Labrador Institute of Memorial University. Keith has also worked for the Canadian Wildlife Service and Nunatsiavut government.

STEPHEN CORNELL is a professor of sociology, director of Udall Center for Studies in Public Policy, and faculty associate of Native Nations Institute, all at the University of Arizona. Co-founder of the Harvard Project on American Indian Economic Development, he writes widely on Indigenous self-determination, governance, and economic development.

SHERRIE CROSS is an honorary associate in human geography at Macquarie University. Her PhD thesis explored the erasure of Indigenous scales of governance throughout the history of Australian Indigenous affairs policies, focusing in particular on reconciliation (1991–2000).

KIM DOOHAN is an honorary associate at Macquarie University, where she completed her PhD in human geography. She has worked for more than twenty-five years as an independent consultant with Australian Aboriginal people in remote regions of northern Australia and adheres to a highly ethical and collaborative form of community engagement.

KERRI JO FORTIER is a member of the Simpcw First Nation. She was the Nation's community planner from 2007 until 2011 and continues to assist with planning as the natural resource manager of Simpcw First Nation. Kerri Jo's work has also focused on youths, health, and sustainable economic development partnerships.

BETHANY HAALBOOM is an environmental geographer with an interest in human-environment relationships and the socio-political processes that underlie those relationships. Much of her research focuses on Indigenous peoples' responses to protected areas and mining projects. Bethany is a lecturer in environmental studies at Victoria University, New Zealand.

LISA HARDESS is a sustainability and community planner and educator with Hardess Planning Inc. Lisa's expertise includes sustainability, education and training, evaluation, participatory engagement, planning for climate change, mentorship, and project management. Lisa was manager of building sustainable communities at the Centre for Indigenous Environmental Resources from 2005 until 2010.

GARTH HARMSWORTH (Te Arawa, Ngati Tuwharetoa, Ngati Raukawa, Tuhourangi) is a senior environmental scientist based in Palmerston North, New Zealand, and has worked for Landcare Research since 1992. His career spans over twenty-six years in resource management, land resource assessment, national environmental databases, GIS applications, and Indigenous research.

SHARON HAUSAM is tribal planner for Pueblo of Laguna and lecturer in the University of New Mexico's community and regional planning program. She has worked with tribes on land use, water, forest, economic development, and transportation planning. Sharon has a PhD in urban and regional planning from the University of Wisconsin-Madison.

MICHAEL HIBBARD is professor emeritus in the Department of Planning, Pubic Policy and Management at the University of Oregon. Prior to becoming an academic he worked as a reservation planner and has consulted and published widely on planning with Indigenous communities.

RICHARD HOWITT is a professor of human geography at Macquarie University, and teaches planning, environmental studies, and geography. His research deals with social impacts of mining on Indigenous peoples and local communities, and is concerned with the interplay across scales of social and environmental justice, particularly in relation to Indigenous rights.

THEODORE (TED) JOJOLA is distinguished professor and regents' professor of community and regional planning at the University of New Mexico. He is the founder of the university's Indigenous Design and Planning Institute and co-founder of the Indigenous Planning Division of the American Planning Association. He is an enrolled tribal member of the Pueblo of Isleta.

TANIRA KINGI is a science advisor in the land and environment group with AgResearch in New Zealand. His research interests focus on the development of land-use change and farm systems optimization frameworks that incorporate socio-cultural components. Tanira is affiliated to Ngati Whakaue and Ngati Rangitihi (Te Arawa).

MARCUS LANE is professor and dean (academic) of arts, education, and law at Griffith University, Brisbane, Australia. He has long-standing research interests in natural resource management and governance, Indigenous lands management, and regional planning. He holds an honorary professorial position at the University of Queensland.

REBECCA LAWRENCE is a post-doctoral fellow at Umeå University. Since 2006 she has worked part-time as advisor to the Human Rights Unit of Saami Council, an umbrella organization representing Saami organizations in Norway, Sweden, Finland, and the Kola Peninsula of Russia.

GAIM LUNKAPIS has a PhD from Macquarie University, and is currently in the geography unit at the Universiti Malaysia Sabah. He began his career as state town planner and later assumed the role of project manager and research officer for DANCED-Malaysian sponsored projects, the integrated coastal zone management, and environmental local plan.

LAURA MANNELL is a professional planner. She has had the opportunity to work in a variety of contexts including government, academia, and the private sector. Much of her work and research has focused on community-based planning with Aboriginal communities across Canada.

HIRINI MATUNGA is assistant vice-chancellor, communities, and professor of Indigenous planning at Lincoln University, and past-director of the Centre for Māori and Indigenous Planning and Development. He is of Ngai Tahu, Ngati Porou, Ngati Kahungunu and Rongowhakaata (Māori), and Ngati Paerangi (Atiu, Cook Islands) descent.

DEBORAH MCGREGOR is associate professor of geography and Aboriginal studies at the University of Toronto. She is Anishnaabe from Whitefish River First Nation, Birch Island, Ontario. Her research focus is on Indigenous knowledge in relation to the environment, centred on environmental management, forestry, sustainable development, and water governance.

OSCAR MONTES DE OCA is science impact leader for resilient communities at AgResearch in New Zealand. He has a background in behavioural modelling, quantitative complexity, and systems science. He has been involved in the development and implementation of research frameworks for effectively conducting multicultural research, integrating Western and Indigenous knowledge.

SAMANTHA MULLER is adjunct fellow at Flinders University, Australia. Since 2001 she has been undertaking research with and working for independent Aboriginal and Torres Strait Islander organizations in northeast Arnhem Land, Torres Strait, and South Australia. She completed her PhD at Macquarie University in 2009.

DAVID NATCHER is an applied cultural anthropologist. His research generally explores the human dimensions of environmental management with a focus on Indigenous land tenure systems. David is a professor in bioresource policy, business, and economics, and research director for the Indigenous Land Management Institute at University of Saskatchewan.

FRANK PALERMO is director of the Cities and Environment Unit and professor of planning at Dalhousie University. A fellow of the Canadian Institute of Planners and Royal Architectural Institute of Canada, he created the international award-winning First Nations Community Planning Model, applied with over thirty First Nations across Canada.

ROBERT PATRICK is associate professor and chair of the Regional and Urban Planning program at the University of Saskatchewan. He worked for twelve years as a regional planner in British Columbia. Robert often works with Indigenous communities to help improve source water quality through collaborative planning and integrated water resource management.

CRAIG PAULING (Ngāi Tahu, Kati Mamoe, Waitaha, Ngāti Mutunga) has worked for his iwi over the last ten years on projects focused on strengthening the role and place of Mātauranga Māori in the contemporary landscape. He is currently employed by the Canterbury Earthquake Recovery Authority as a strategic analyst.

KURT PETERS (Blackfeet/Powhatan) earned his doctorate at University of California, Berkeley, and taught at California State University Sacramento and UC Berkeley. He is emeritus professor of Native American and comparative ethnic studies at Oregon State University, and the founder and director of the Native American Collaborative Institute.

LIBBY PORTER teaches human geography at Monash University. Her expertise includes the relationship between planning and Indigenous peoples in the contexts of Australia and Canada. Libby worked in planning practice in Australia before joining the academy. She is assistant editor of *Planning Theory and Practice*, and founding member of Planners Network UK.

ANDREA PROCTER holds a PhD in anthropology from Memorial University. Her research focused on resource management and Indigenous rights, especially in Nunatsiavut, Labrador, and Nunavut. Andrea's dissertation explored cultural differentiation and resource management in the creation and current governance of Nunatsiavut.

SARAH PROUT specializes in Indigenous population mobility and public policy in Australia and other settler-states. Her interests include the development of relevant, reliable, and representative indicators of Indigenous well-being, urban-based Indigenous populations, and Indigenous housing. She is associate professor at Combined Universities Centre for Rural Health in Western Australia.

CATHY ROBINSON is senior scientist and leads the geography, human ecology, and sustainability research group in the Commonwealth Scientific and Industrial Research Organization, Division of Ecosystem Sciences in Australia. Her research examines knowledge and governance systems for collaborative decision making in environmental planning contexts, including watershed management, Indigenous lands management, and natural resource management programs.

SHADRACH ROLLESTON (Ngāi Te Rangi) has research interests in urban design, and Indigenous knowledge and environmental perspectives. His background is in town planning, Māori resource management, and policy advice. He has worked as an adviser and planner for central and local governments, the private sector, and his tribal group.

LEONIE SANDERCOCK is professor of community and regional planning at the University of British Columbia and chairs its Indigenous community planning curriculum initiative. She is the award-winning author of a dozen books and has produced and co-directed two documentary films.

CRISPIN SMITH is a planner and engineer from Montreal. His work has focused on community planning, urban design, public engagement, civil engineering, and international development. He has worked with government, NGOs, the United Nations, and consulting firms across Canada, West Africa, the Caribbean, Southeast Asia, and the Middle East.

SANDIE SUCHET-PEARSON is senior lecturer in human geography at Macquarie University. She has examined community development in the context of mining operations on Cape York Peninsula, strategies used by Indigenous peoples in wildlife management in Canada and Africa, and Indigenous self-determination and cultural tourism in northeast Arnhem Land, Australia.

SIRI VELAND has a PhD in human geography from Macquarie University. Her thesis, *Indigenous Contexts of Climate and Change: Narrating Local Realities within Global Discourses*, explores social and environmental change in a remote Indigenous Australian community. She is post-doctoral research associate at Brown University and honorary associate at Macquarie University.

RYAN WALKER is associate professor and past-chair of the Regional and Urban Planning program, University of Saskatchewan. He has expertise in urban planning with Indigenous communities and administers the Canadian Pacific Partnership Program in Aboriginal Community Planning. He was previously a lecturer in planning at Massey University.

LIZ WEDDERBURN is principal scientist and portfolio leader for agriculture policy and Māori agribusiness with AgResearch in New Zealand. She uses her skills in applied ecology and social process to integrate knowledge held by farmers, industry, policy, communities, iwi, and science to address risk and uncertainty associated with land and water.

Index

Not all cited authors are listed in the index; readers requiring a complete list of cited authors and works should refer to the reference lists at ends of chapters. For works with multiple authors only the first named author is listed.